Introduction to International Political Economy

Sixth Edition

David N. Balaam

University of Puget Sound

University of Washington, Tacoma

Bradford Dillman

University of Puget Sound

PEARSON

Boston   Columbus   Indianapolis   New York   San Francisco   Upper Saddle River
Amsterdam   Cape Town   Dubai   London   Madrid   Milan   Munich   Paris   Montréal   Toronto
Delhi   Mexico City   São Paulo   Sydney   Hong Kong   Seoul   Singapore   Taipei   Tokyo

Editor in Chief: Ashley Dodge
Senior Acquisitions Editor: Melissa Mashburn
Editorial Assistant: Megan Hermida
Director of Marketing: Brandy Dawson
Executive Marketing Manager: Kelly May
Marketing Coordinator: Theresa Rotondo
Managing Editor: Denise Forlow
Program Manager: Maggie Brobeck
Manager, Central Design: Jayne Conte

Cover Designer: Karen Noferi
Cover Art: G Brad Lewis/Getty Images
Media Director: Brian Hyland
Digital Media Project Manager: Tina Gagliostro
Full-Service Project Management and Composition Service:
    Sudip Sinha/PreMediaGlobal
Printer/Binder: RR Donnelley/Harrisonburg
Cover Printer: RR Donnelley/Harrisonburg
Text Font: 10/12, Sabon Lt Std Roman

Library of Congress Cataloging-in-Publication Data
Balaam, David N.
Introduction to international political economy / David N. Balaam, Bradford Dillman.—6th ed.
    pages   cm
  Includes index.
  ISBN-13: 978-0-13-340239-1
  ISBN-10: 0-13-340239-8
 1. International economic relations.   I. Title.
  HF1359.B33 2014
  337—dc23   2013008405

10 9 8 7 6 5 4 3 2 1

ISBN-10: 0-13-340239-8
ISBN-13: 978-0-13-340239-1

BRIEF CONTENTS

CONTENTS

PART II   Structures of International Political Economy

CHAPTER 6
The Production and Trade Structure   125

CHAPTER 7
The International Monetary and Finance Structure   151

PART IV   Transnational Problems and Dilemmas

CHAPTER 20

The Environment: Steering Away from Climate Change and Global Disaster   511

PREFACE

As we started working on this edition of the text, most of us felt as if the dark cloud of the global financial crisis was still over us. Reading the international and business sections of major newspapers, we witnessed the European Union plunge deeper into economic trouble as members such as Greece and Spain fell into debt traps and most of the countries using the euro as a currency lapsed into recession. Unemployment and austerity continued to inflict severe social and even psychological damage on people the world over. The November 2012 Doha meeting on climate change failed to produce an agreement to limit carbon dioxide emissions, signaling that large countries still consider economic growth to be a higher priority than addressing major environmental dilemmas. As a result, we may be in for another global tragedy—one that will not be reversible.

Despite the reelection of President Barack Obama, political gridlock in Washington, DC prevents the United States from addressing its most important problems or leading the world toward reforms of global governance. The dominant economic liberal ideology and policies associated with globalization have come under serious intellectual and political challenges. So far nothing has emerged to replace this popular ideology.

The war in Afghanistan continues, while the U.S. drone campaign has ratcheted up in Afghanistan, Pakistan, and other Muslim nations. Ethnic and religious conflicts persist in parts of the Middle East, Somalia, Sudan, and the Democratic Republic of the Congo. Syria has been in the midst of a terrible civil war that has left more than 70,000 dead.

Fortunately, there are rays of hope. The Arab Spring brought down dictators in Egypt, Tunisia, Libya, and Yemen, opening up the possibility that the Arab world will finally join the community of democratic nations. The Occupy Wall Street movement and anti-austerity protests in Europe and elsewhere gave a new voice to citizens and social groups, re-focusing attention on inequality, poverty, and the seeming dominance of corporations in the political systems of developed nations. China, Africa, and South America have continued to grow economically, bringing more of their citizens into the middle class.

How are we to understand this current historical juncture that appears to be both on the verge of an abyss and on the cusp of a more promising era for some countries? Do we see a new global political and economic order beginning to take shape with China, India, and Brazil poised to claim greater influence in international institutions? Can states, international organizations, nongovernmental organizations, and global social movements effectively deal with the effects of hypermobile capital, bring more economic growth without overtaxing the environment, and satisfy political demands peacefully? These are a few of the many questions we raise in this sixth edition of the text.

Our major goal is to provide students with the tools necessary to delve deeper into issues, develop their critical thinking skills, and understand many of the theoretical and policy dynamics of the global political economy. Rather than profess just one set of beliefs and explanations, we offer a variety of different perspectives so that our readers will be able to form their own opinions about controversial issues. In this edition, each chapter begins and concludes with some thought-provoking theses; we hope that students will use them as a springboard from which to independently reflect on global problems and patterns.

NEW TO THIS EDITION

This sixth edition of the text has significant revisions and updates. Many of the chapters contain extensive coverage of the global financial crisis and the European debt crisis, connecting them to social protests in the United States, Europe, and the Middle East. We focus more closely on how IPE theories and structures help us explain and interpret many North–South disputes that are changing the contours of global governance. There is greater attention to why national and international institutions have not been successful in addressing serious global energy, food, and environmental problems. Five chapters have been extensively rewritten, and there are ten new text boxes.

The revisions to look for in the text are in

- Chapter 1, "What Is International Political Economy?" is a revised introductory chapter that shows students how IPE can help them understand key ramifications of the financial crisis, especially the Arab Spring, the Occupy Wall Street movement, and the Euro zone debacle. It updates and clarifies how globalization ties into many themes in the text.
- Chapter 3, "Wealth and Power: The Mercantilist Perspective," provides more examples of neomercantilist policies and a new call-out box on the struggle over rare earth minerals.
- Chapter 4, "Economic Determinism and Exploitation: The Structuralist Perspective," has a new call-out box on the ideas of Noam Chomsky.
- Chapter 6, "The Production and Trade Structure," includes more analysis of updated trade and production data and has a new discussion of outsourcing.
- Chapter 8, "International Debt and Financial Crises," is thoroughly revised, with new theses, new sections on different kinds of debt, and more concise explanations of debt crises in the 1980s and 1990s. New sections explain the reactions of Keynesians and the Occupy Wall Street movement to the financial crisis. There are also new sections on the unfolding Euro zone crisis, the effects of austerity, and potential reforms to the global finance structure.
- Chapter 9, "The Global Security Structure," is extensively rewritten, with a strong focus on realist perspectives and a broad history of changes in the security structure since the beginning of the Cold War. The chapter provides an overview of the Obama administration's security policies, including greater reliance on drones, and a new focus on non-traditional security threats. New call-out boxes deal with drone operators and the International Criminal Tribunal for the former Yugoslavia.
- Chapter 10, "The Knowledge and Technology Structure," offers a new section on global struggles over control of information and a new call-out box on WikiLeaks.

- Chapter 12, "Toward a More Perfect (European) Union," is thoroughly revised, with a broad history of the political economy of European integration and a new second half explaining the unfolding crisis in the Euro zone—including the bailout programs, EU institutional problems, and the role of the troika in dealing with the debt crisis.
- Chapter 13, "Moving into Position: The Rising Powers," has a new section on Brazil that contrasts recent economic successes with growing environmental problems. Updates on India focus on corruption and inequality. There is extensive discussion of China's rising middle class and the debate over whether China is adapting to global norms or undermining international cooperation. It is now a complete BRICs chapter.
- Chapter 14, "The Middle East: The Quest for Development and Democracy," examines the Arab Spring and its potential for generating democratic political systems. The implications for changes in regional geopolitics are also discussed. We also analyze the Israeli—Palestinian conflict in more depth.
- Chapter 15, "The Illicit Global Economy," has a new call-out box on Gibson Guitar company and the Lacey Act. Several new examples of timber, antiquities, and animal trafficking are given.
- Chapter 18, "Food and Hunger: Market Failure and Injustice," includes a new call-out box on biofuels.
- Chapter 19, "The IPE of Energy Resources: Stuck in Transition," is thoroughly revised, with new sections on fracking, the clash of fossil fuel production versus environmental protection, and the role of major oil companies in shaping global energy policies and slowing the shift to renewables. Two new call-out boxes discuss fracking and Nigeria's "resource curse."
- Chapter 20, "The Environment: Steering Away from Climate Change and Global Disaster," places a new emphasis on the urgency of addressing problems of global warming and climate change. New sections examine debates at the recent Durban and Doha climate talks.

FEATURES

While covering the "nuts and bolts" of IPE theories and issues, many of the chapters provide students with a historical context in which to understand the subject matter. More importantly, in contrast to other introductory texts, we challenge students to think critically when it comes to applying these theories to different issues and policy problems.

As in previous editions, the book begins with five chapters that to set out some basic tools for studying IPE. Chapter 1 introduces the fundamental elements of the subject and some recent developments in what has become a very popular field of study. We begin with relatively simple tools and concepts that deal with the nature of IPE—its subject boundaries, the three dominant IPE theories, four global structures, and the levels of analysis. Chapters 2, 3, and 4 explore the three dominant analytical approaches to studying IPE that remain influential today: mercantilism, economic liberalism, and structuralism. Chapter 5 introduces two alternative perspectives (constructivism and feminism) that have grown in importance in recent years.

Part II of the text examines the web of relationships and structures that tie together a variety of international actors including nations, international organizations, nongovernmental organizations, and multinational corporations. Chapter 6 focuses on the production and international trade structure. Chapter 7 provides an outline of the international monetary and finance structure and problems, which in Chapter 8 are applied to Third World debt, the global financial crisis, and the European financial debt crisis. Chapter 9 focuses on changes in the international security structure, including shifts from national to individual security concerns and the possibility of a transition from a unipolar to a multipolar balance of power. Chapter 10 examines struggles among international actors over knowledge and technology, with significant attention to intellectual property rights.

In Part III, Chapter 11 examines the problem of development and some of the different strategies that less developed countries have used to "grow" their economies and modernize their political institutions. Chapter 12 traces the integration process that has created the European Union and the serious economic challenges for Euro zone states. Chapter 13 covers the political-economic changes in the "emerging" countries of Brazil, Russia, India, and China. Chapter 14 addresses the Middle East and North Africa, a region fraught with conflicts and engulfed in sweeping political changes since 2011.

Finally, in Part IV, as part of an effort to understand a number of important global problems and issues, Chapter 15 covers illicit activities involving trafficking of people, drugs, and other items. Chapter 16 examines the dynamic and problematic issue of the movement of people around the world—in this case through tourism and migration. Chapter 17 examines the important role of transnational corporations in the international political economy. Chapters 18, 19, and 20 discuss the interconnections between global food, energy, and environmental problems, employing many of the analytical tools developed earlier in the book.

All the chapters end with a list of key terms that are in bold print in the chapter, discussion questions, and suggested readings. Recommended websites related to each chapter can be found at the text website at **www.upugetsoundintroipe.com**. The website also includes a list of recommended videos and documentaries faculty and students can use to gain more detailed background and ideas about different topics.

ANCILLARY MATERIALS

MySearchLab. Need help with a paper? MySearchLab saves time and improves results by offering start-to-finish guidance on the research/writing process and full-text access to academic journals and periodicals. To learn more, please visit www.mysearchlab.com.

Goode's World Atlas (0-321-65200-2). First published by Rand McNally in 1923, Goode's World Atlas has set the standard for college reference atlases. It features hundreds of physical, political, and thematic maps as well as graphs, tables, and a pronouncing index.

This text is available in a variety of formats—digital and print. To learn more about our programs, pricing options, and customization, visit www.pearsonhighered.com.

ACKNOWLEDGMENTS

This textbook is truly a cooperative effort. We would like to thank all of the people at Pearson Education who have helped us, including Carly Czech, Melissa Mashburn, Megan Hermida, Maggie Brobeck, and Beverly Fong, for their suggestions and most of all for their patience throughout this process. Thanks also to Sudip Sinha at PreMediaGlobal for his work in overseeing copyediting and other aspects of the book's production. Professor Pierre Ly provided valuable suggestions for this edition of the text. We would like to thank and recognize the following colleagues for their contributions: Richard Anderson-Connolly (authored and updated Chapter 4); Monica DeHart and Nick Kontogeorgopoulos (co-authored Chapter 16); Leon Grunberg (revised Chapter 17); Cynthia Howson (wrote the section on feminist contributions to IPE in Chapter 5); Sunil Kukreja (authored Chapter 11); and Emelie Peine (wrote the Brazil section in Chapter 13 and contributed to Chapter 18). In the fifth edition, Hendrik Hansen (Professor of Politics and Government at Andrássy University Budapest, Hungary) contributed to portions of Chapter 12; Ryan Cunningham and Rahul Madhavan wrote sections of Chapter 13, and Ross Singleton contributed to Chapters 2, 7, and 10.

We would also like to thank Dean Kris Bartanen and Associate Academic Dean Sarah Moore at the University of Puget Sound for providing funds to hire a student research assistant. Ardea Smith was an invaluable assistant, doing background research for several chapters and updating all of the tables and other data in the text. We thank Kirsten Schlewitz, Jess Martin, Jordan Anton, Ryan Cunningham, Rahul Madhavan, Matthew Pedro, and Georgina Allen for writing or co-writing some of the call-out boxes that appear in this edition. They also did research and/or provided editorial assistance on various chapters of the text. A number of people in our local communities supported us every day through provocative discussions and introspection along the way: Ed Jones, Oscar Velasco-Schmitz, Bill Hochberg, Curtis Brooks, Melissa Bavlnka, Brendan Balaam, Brandon Green, Dee Sontag, Debbie Brindley at Repast Cafe, Paul Hill, Eleanor Goodall, Paula Wilcox; Dave's Peps group comprised of Jason Hahn, Jason Mulvihill-Kuntz, Jason Bavuso, and Michal Bryc; Roberta Torgerson and Elisabetta Valentini of PercorsoItaliano; and in Italy, Bruno Porcellana and Roberta Melcore. And we could not have written this book without the many ideas, critiques, and feedback from our IPE students at the University of Puget Sound and the University of Washington, Tacoma.

Finally, Dave would like to thank his sons David Erin and Brendan, along with his daughter Amelie and wife Kristi Hendrickson, for their patience and loving support throughout the project. Brad would like to thank Joanne, Harry, and Noelle for their encouragement, inspiration, and love.

Our thanks, also, to the reviewers: Jason Enia, Sam Houston State University; Nader Entessar, University of South Alabama; Felix E. Martin, Florida International University; and Dwayne Woods, Purdue University.

We dedicate this edition of the text to all those people everywhere who have remained resilient in the face of the financial crisis and who continue to fight to change our world for the better after political and economic elites let them down.

DAVID N. BALAAM AND BRADFORD L. DILLMAN
SEATTLE AND TACOMA, WASHINGTON

ABOUT THE AUTHORS

Richard Anderson-Connolly is Professor of Sociology at the University of Puget Sound and teaches courses in methodology, social stratification, and urban sociology.

David Balaam is Professor Emeritus of International Political Economy at the University of Puget Sound. His publications include articles on agricultural trade policy and various food and hunger issues. He is currently a lecturer at the University of Washington, Tacoma.

Monica DeHart is Associate Professor of Anthropology at the University of Puget Sound and teaches courses on the cultural politics of global development and transnational migration in and from Latin America. She is the author of *Ethnic Entrepreneurs: Identity and Development Politics in Latin America* (Stanford University Press, 2010).

Bradford Dillman is Professor and Chair of the International Political Economy Program at the University of Puget Sound. He teaches courses on IPE, the Middle East, the illicit global economy, and intellectual property rights. He authored *State and Private Sector in Algeria* (Westview Press, 2000) and has written numerous articles and book chapters on the Middle East and North Africa.

Leon Grunberg is Professor of Sociology at the University of Puget Sound and teaches courses on social stratification and sociology through literature. His research interests focus on globalization, the changing world of work and organizations, and patterns of cross-national stratification. He is co-author of *Turbulence: Boeing and the State of American Workers and Managers* (Yale University Press, 2010).

Cynthia Howson is Lecturer in Politics, Philosophy, and Economics at the University of Washington, Tacoma. She teaches courses on economic development, gender, political economy, and globalization.

Nick Kontogeorgopoulos is Professor of International Political Economy at the University of Puget Sound and teaches courses on IPE, development, and tourism. His publications focus on ecotourism and wildlife tourism in Southeast Asia.

Sunil Kukreja is an Associate Academic Dean and Professor of Sociology at the University of Puget Sound. His teaching and research interests include the sociology of development, the political economy of Southeast Asia, and race relations. He is editor-in-chief of the *International Review of Modern Sociology*.

Emelie Peine is Assistant Professor of International Political Economy at the University of Puget Sound. She teaches courses on IPE and food and hunger. Her research focuses on relations between Brazil and China and the role of multinational agribusiness in the global food regime.

Perspectives on International Political Economy

The first chapter of the text deals with the fundamental nature of international political economy (IPE) and some analytical issues related to its multidimensional character. Chapters 2 through 4 are the core chapters of the text that explore the history and policies associated with the three dominant IPE perspectives, namely economic liberalism, mercantilism, and structuralism. These theoretical tools are useful in understanding many political, economic, and social issues in the global economy of the past as well as the present. Chapter 5 develops two alternative IPE perspectives—constructivism and feminism—that derive, in part, from the three main outlooks under study.

What Is International Political Economy?

We Are the 99%: A Haitian hillside.

Georgina Allen

When a philosopher has once laid hold of a favorite principle, which perhaps accounts for many natural effects, he extends the same principle over the whole creation, and reduces to it every phenomenon, though by the most violent and absurd reasoning. Our own mind being narrow and contracted, we cannot extend our conception to the variety and extent of nature . . .

David Hume, "The Sceptic"

THE DARKNESS ON THE EDGE OF TOWN

What are the chances you will find a good paying job—or any job for that matter—when you graduate from college in the next few years? Have your parents or people you know lost their jobs, the family home, or a big chunk of their retirement savings? How are *you* adjusting to the financial crisis? Maybe things haven't been that bad for you, yet! Reading the headlines of any major newspaper, you might sometimes worry that the world is on the brink of a global economic catastrophe, if not a second Great Depression. The effects of the global economic crisis have made many people feel tense, fearful, and depressed.

The collapse of the U.S. housing market in 2007 morphed into a credit crisis that threatened some of the biggest banks and financial institutions in the United States and Europe. Government leaders responded with a variety of bank rescue measures and so-called stimulus packages to restart their economies. These interventions angered many ordinary folks who felt that the bailouts rewarded bankers and CEOs who had caused the crisis in the first place. Meanwhile, many people around the world were forced out of their homes and became unemployed. They suffered cuts in social services, health care benefits, and education spending when governments were forced to trim budgets.

As we write in late 2012, the hoped-for recovery has proved elusive. Unemployment in the United States is stuck at 7.9 percent; in the European Union (EU), it has risen to 11.6 percent (23.4 percent for young people). Home foreclosures and stagnant incomes continue to place enormous strain on many families' finances. The EU has fallen into another recession, with countries like Greece, Italy, Spain, and Portugal so deep in debt that they might slide into national bankruptcy, causing the EU's monetary system to collapse. People seem to have lost confidence in national and international political institutions that underpin capitalism and democracy. Is this what the Great Transformation from industrial to post-industrial society was supposed to look like? Are globalization and the so-called "creative destruction" of new technologies shrinking the middle classes in Western countries and permanently shifting economic dynamism to Asia and Latin America?

Adding to the sense of gloom are events around the world in the last few years. High oil prices have benefitted giant oil companies while hurting consumers. The giant British Petroleum (BP) oil spill precipitated an environmental catastrophe in the Gulf of Mexico. Japan's Fukushima earthquake and tsunami damaged several nuclear power plants, causing release of dangerous radioactive material across a large swath of territory. High agriculture commodity prices have raised the cost of food and increased levels of world hunger. Because there has been little progress in reducing reliance on fossil fuels, capping carbon emissions, or investing in alternative energy resources, the threat of catastrophic climate change looms larger. And wars in Syria, Afghanistan, Somalia, and the Congo are destroying the livelihoods of millions of people.

Hope on the Horizon?

Is there only gloom and doom around the globe? Surely, no! As we discuss in Chapter 13, emerging powers such as China, India, Brazil, and Russia have dramatically reduced poverty in the last fifteen years and made it possible for hundreds of millions of people to join the middle class. Fortunately, they continued to grow at a fairly robust pace after 2007; more jobs, investment, and consumption in these countries helped keep the rest of the world from falling into a deeper recession. For most of the last decade, sub-Saharan Africa has also grown surprisingly fast, thanks in part to high prices for oil and commodities exports. And the European Union won the 2012 Nobel Peace Prize, a reminder that—despite its serious economic and social problems today—the community has advanced the causes of "peace and reconciliation, democracy, and human rights" for more than sixty years.

Along with these rays of hope are three interrelated global developments that merit discussion at the beginning of this textbook because they are profoundly shaping the international political economy: the Arab Spring, the European sovereign debt crisis, and the Occupy Wall Street (OWS) movement. Taking place on three different continents since 2011, they have shaken political institutions and spurred waves of political protests in response to a variety of social and economic ills. None of us knows how these momentous developments will play out, but we can be sure that they will affect our daily lives and pocketbooks for many years. Each is a double-edged sword: a potential harbinger of positive change and a potential foreshadowing of worse yet to come. In other words, each development can either help lead to a more stable, prosperous world in which human security is better guaranteed or render divisions within and between societies wider than before so that cooperative relations and a fairer distribution of resources remain ever more elusive goals.

The Arab Spring took the world by surprise—a reminder that social scientists still do not have good tools to predict when and why large-scale changes will occur in complex socio-political systems. On December 17, 2010, a Tunisian street vendor named Mohamed Bouazizi set himself on fire in reaction to harassment by police officers. His death sparked street demonstrations that brought down the Tunisian government one month later. Protests spread like wildfires to other countries in the Middle East and North Africa. After eighteen days of mass demonstrations, Egypt's authoritarian president Hosni Mubarak resigned on February 11, 2011, replaced by a military council. On February 15, residents of Benghazi, Libya, rose up against the regime of Muammar Qaddafi. Following months of NATO bombing and rebel fighting, Qaddafi was killed on October 20, 2011, and a National Transitional Council took power. The dramatic political protests—which captivated television viewers and Twitter-feed followers around the world—created an opportunity for a number of Arab countries to join the community of democratic nations. Yet the crackdown in Syria showed the world how determined some authoritarian leaders in the Middle East are to remain in power—even at the expense of killing tens of thousands of their own citizens. With the genie of Arab political opposition out of the bottle, countries in the Middle East and North Africa are rapidly changing. Fortunately, high oil prices and a return to relative stability in many places could improve conditions in 2013.

Along with the Arab Spring came President Barack Obama's withdrawal of all U.S. troops from Iraq at the end of 2011. An ignominious end to an imperial endeavor, the withdrawal seemed to signal that the U.S. public was no longer willing to pay for wars that drain the public treasury. President Obama refocused

U.S. policy on fighting against the Taliban in Afghanistan and ratcheting up pressure on Iran to abandon its effort to develop nuclear weapons. Many analysts believe that Obama's decisions reveal a significant weakening of U.S. influence in the Middle East. Perhaps to counteract this decline, Obama decided to bolster the American military presence in the Pacific by cultivating ties with countries afraid of China's rise and stationing 2,500 troops permanently in northern Australia beginning in November 2011.

A second development—the European sovereign debt crisis—relentlessly gathered steam after 2010 in the face of a prolonged recession that made it hard for some countries to pay back huge loans to domestic and foreign banks. European Union leaders had hoped to contain the debt problems in Greece and Ireland, but governments in Spain and Portugal also began to have trouble raising new money by issuing new government bonds. All four countries in 2012 had to get financial bailouts in exchange for adopting painful government spending cuts that contributed to high unemployment. Even with help from the European Central Bank, these countries have dire conditions that threaten the stability of the European financial system.

Europe's responses to its debt crisis have stimulated widespread social unrest. Severe austerity measures have spawned street protests throughout the continent and brought changes of government in Greece, Italy, and Spain. Some EU leaders and analysts believe that the crisis will spur European countries to form closer ties, while others foresee the death of the euro and the prospect of national bankruptcies as some countries refuse to pay back onerous loans. If problems worsen in France and Italy, the EU could unravel economically, causing another deep global recession. The crisis is forcing Germany to decide if it is willing to share the costs of making the EU stronger, or if it will pursue its purely national interests. The outcomes will likely cause changes in Europe's traditionally generous social programs and in Europe's influence in the world.

A third development started as an anti-Wall Street protest in New York City's Zuccotti Park on September 17, 2011. Two weeks later, the Occupy Wall Street movement had quickly spread to many major U.S. cities, with encampments and "general assemblies" in public spaces. Similar "occupations" occurred in Europe, Israel, Chile, and Australia. Although the majority of participants in the OWS social movement have been students, union workers, progressive activists, and the unemployed, their ideas seemed to resonate with a significant number of the middle class. Calling themselves the "99%" (in contrast to the wealthiest 1 percent of Americans), OWS protestors criticized financial institutions, condemned Wall Street greed, and called for a reduction of corporate control over the democratic process. Although OWS encampments disappeared, the movement took up new campaigns in 2012, including efforts to stop home foreclosures and reduce student debt.

What do these three developments have in common? While each has its own causes, the protestors collectively represent a reaction to corrupt government and growing inequality. In three large regions—the Middle East, Europe, and North America—movements sought protection from financial and cultural globalization that left people feeling at the mercy of market forces. In many cases, protestors felt that they were unfairly forced to bail out the wealthy but denied a chance to share many of the benefits of previous growth. Austerity policies that many governments had adopted since 2008—and even earlier in the Arab countries—cut into a host of public social programs such as education and relief for the poor. Many disgruntled citizens disagreed with their leaders, who argued that such reductions were necessary to reduce the size of government, balance national budgets, and stimulate economic recovery.

While Arabs claimed a political voice that had been squashed by decades of dictatorial rule, Americans and Europeans seemed to demand a new kind of politics freed from the grip of special interests and big money. In all three cases, elites who were supposed to be the experts on political and financial affairs suddenly were at a loss to explain why things had gotten so bad under their watch. With a loss of faith in Arab regimes, EU leaders, and U.S. bankers came a certain "denaturalization" of ruling ideologies such as economic liberalism. A new emphasis was placed on democratic participation and economic fairness.

Despite a new *zeitgeist* in the air in three continents, old political and economic institutions were still resilient. Many regimes held firm in the Middle East. American banks grew even bigger after government bailouts, and more money than ever poured into the campaign war chests of Democratic and Republican political candidates. EU political elites continued to make deals that seemed designed to save big investors and banks rather than ordinary citizens. The alternatives to the old did not always promise a better future, either. In the aftermath of the Arab Spring, Islamists like Egypt's new president Mohamed Morsi made their own undemocratic power grabs, seeking to impose religiously conservative policies and weaken women's rights. Reactions against austerity in Europe strengthened extreme right-wing parties in Greece and France while fueling anti-EU or secessionist sentiments in the United Kingdom and Catalonia. And by refusing to organize and engage in "normal" politics, the OWS forces dissipated—leaving normal two-party gridlock in Washington after the November 2012 elections.

The Road Ahead

By discussing above the three big developments, as well as the problems and promises in the global economy, we have hopefully given you a sense of some of the important phenomena we seek to understand in international political economy. Not unsurprisingly, there are fierce debates about the causes of current crises and the best solutions to them. One of the arguments we make in this text is that to adequately describe and explain the current global financial crisis—or any of the other issues covered in the different chapters—we must use an analytical approach that synthesizes methods and insights derived from economics, political science, and sociology as conditioned by an understanding of history and philosophy. As you delve deeper into the material, you will learn a variety of theories and analytical tools that help us interpret the interrelationships of the state, market, and society in different nations.

The IPE method bridges different academic disciplines to better explain complex, real-world problems that span physical and intellectual boundaries. While this statement might sound a bit formal and confusing at this point, keep in mind that we do not think you need to be an economics major, a specialist in finance, or a Middle East expert to understand the basic parameters of the global financial crisis or the Arab Spring. This book is written for students who have limited background in political science, economics, or sociology, as well as for those who want to review an assortment of topics in preparation for graduate school.

In the next section, we look at how to study IPE—its three distinct analytical perspectives and a number of methodological issues with which IPE students should become acquainted. All the chapters in the book cover important theoretical and policy issues that have connections to the three developments we have mentioned—and to many more. In this way, we hope students might better understand different dimensions of the problems and then make some reasoned judgments about how to solve them.

Later in this chapter, we discuss the popular phenomenon of globalization as a way to introduce students to many of the political-economic conditions that led up to the global financial crisis. Many IPE experts have asserted that the economic liberal ideas behind globalization may have contributed to the crisis. Opinions differ, however, on whether or not the crisis signals the end of laissez-faire economic policies, or even the end of capitalism itself.

THE WHAT, WHY, AND HOW OF INTERNATIONAL POLITICAL ECONOMY

Our discussion of the financial crisis and its consequences makes clear that today's complex issues can no longer be easily analyzed and understood by using any *single* set of disciplinary methods and concepts. Those who study IPE are, in essence, breaking down the analytical and conceptual boundaries between politics, economics, and sociology to produce a unique explanatory framework. Following are several examples of questions that traditional academic disciplines might ask as they seek to explain the global financial crisis. Each discipline focuses on different actors and interests:

- *International Relations:* How much has the financial crisis detracted from the ability of states to pay for military defense? How has the crisis affected the conditions of war or terrorism in poor states? As Europe, Japan, and the United States struggle, will emerging countries like China, India, and Brazil gain more political influence in international institutions?
- *International Economics:* How has the crisis impacted foreign investment, international trade, and the values of different currencies?
- *Comparative Politics:* What is the capability of political institutions within different nations to respond to the needs of the unemployed? What new political forces are emerging and with what effects on political coalitions?
- *Sociology:* How has the crisis affected consumption trends for different groups such as the upper, middle, and lower classes? How do the effects of inequality vary on the basis of ethnicity and gender?
- *Anthropology:* How have different societies in history dealt with crises related to how they allocate scarce resources? And how have these crises impacted their cultures, values, and societal norms?

Focusing on a narrow range of methods and issues enhances intellectual specialization and analytical efficiency. But any single discipline offers an *incomplete* explanation of global events. Specialization promotes a sort of scholarly blindness or distorted view that comes from using only one set of analytical methods and concepts to explain what most decidedly is a complex problem that could benefit from a multidisciplinary perspective.

What Is International Political Economy?

When defining IPE, we make a distinction between the term "international political economy" and the acronym IPE. The former refers to what we study—commonly referred to as a *subject area* or field of inquiry that involves tensions among states, markets, and societal actors. In this text, we tend to focus on a variety of actors and issues that are either "international" (between nation-states) or "transnational" (across the national borders of two or more states). Increasingly today, many analysts use the term "global political economy" instead of "international political economy" to explain problems such as climate change, hunger, and illicit markets that have spread over the entire world, and not just a few nations. In this book, we often use these two terms interchangeably.

The acronym IPE also connotes a *method of inquiry* that is multidisciplinary. IPE fashions the tools of analysis of its antecedent disciplines so as to more accurately describe and explain the ever-changing relationships between governments, businesses, and social forces across history and in different geographical areas. What are some of the central elements of the antecedent fields of study that contribute to IPE?

First, IPE includes a *political* dimension that accounts for the use of power by a variety of actors, including individuals, domestic groups, states (acting as single units), international organizations, nongovernmental organizations (NGOs), and transnational corporations (TNCs). All these actors make decisions about the distribution of tangible things such as money and products or intangible things such as security and innovation. In almost all cases, politics involves the making of *rules* pertaining to *how* states and societies achieve their goals. Another aspect of politics is the kind of public and private *institutions* that have the authority to pursue different goals.

Second, IPE involves an *economic* dimension that deals with how scarce resources are distributed among individuals, groups, and nation-states. A variety of public and private institutions allocate resources on a day-to-day basis in local markets where we shop. Today, a market is not just a place where people go to buy or exchange something face to face with the product's maker. The market can also be thought of as a *driving force* that shapes human behavior. When consumers buy things, when investors purchase stocks, and when banks lend money, their depersonalized transactions constitute a vast, sophisticated web of relationships that coordinate economic activities all over the world. Political scientist Charles Lindblom makes an interesting case that the economy is actually nothing more than a system for coordinating social behavior! What people eat, their occupation, and even what they do when not working are all organized around different agricultural, labor, and relaxation markets. In effect, markets often perform a social function of "coordination without a coordinator."[1]

Third, the works of such notables as Charles Lindblom and economists Robert Heilbroner and Lester Thurow help us realize that IPE does *not* reflect enough the *societal* dimension of different international problems.[2] A growing number of IPE scholars argue that states and markets do not exist in a social vacuum. There are usually many different social groups *within* a state that share identities, norms, and associations based on tribal ties, ethnicity, religion, or gender. Likewise, a variety of transnational groups (referred to as **global civil society**) have interests that cut *across* national boundaries. A host of NGOs have attempted to pressure national and international organizations on issues such as climate change, refugees, migrant workers, and gender-based exploitation. All of these groups are purveyors of ideas that potentially generate tensions between them and other groups but play a major role in shaping global behavior.

How to Study IPE: Contrasting Perspectives and Methodologies

The three dominant perspectives of IPE are economic liberalism, mercantilism, and structuralism. Each focuses on the relationships between a variety of actors and institutions. A strict distinction between these perspectives is quite arbitrary and has been imposed by disciplinary tradition, at times making it difficult to appreciate their connections to one another. Each perspective emphasizes different values, actors, and solutions to policy problems but also overlooks some important elements highlighted by the other two perspectives.

Economic liberalism (particularly *neoliberalism*—see Chapter 2) is most closely associated with the study of markets. Later we will explain why there is an increasing gap between **orthodox economic liberals (OELs)**, who champion free markets and free trade, and **heterodox interventionist liberals (HILs)**, who support more state regulation and trade protection to sustain markets. Increasingly, HILs have stressed that markets work best when they are embedded in (connected to) society and when the state intervenes to resolve problems that markets alone cannot handle. In fact, many HILs acknowledge that markets are the *source* of many of these problems.

Many liberal values and ideas are the ideological foundation of the globalization campaign. They are derived from notable thinkers such as Adam Smith, David Ricardo, John Maynard Keynes, Friedrich Hayek, and Milton Friedman. The laissez-faire principle, that the state should leave the economy alone, is attributed to Adam Smith.[3] More recently, economic liberal ideas have been associated with former president Ronald Reagan and his acolytes, who contended that economic growth is best achieved when the government severely limits its involvement (interference) in the economy.

Under pure market conditions (i.e., the absence of state intervention or social influences), people are assumed to behave "rationally" (see Chapter 2).

That is, they will naturally seek to maximize their gains and limit their losses when producing and selling things. They have strong desires to exchange and to generate wealth by competing with others for sales in local and international markets. According to OELs, people *should* strongly value *economic efficiency*—the ability to use and distribute resources effectively and with little waste. Why is efficiency so important? When an economy is inefficient, scarce resources go unused or could be used in other ways that would be more beneficial to society. This idea has been applied to the new global economy and is one of the basic principles behind globalization.

Mercantilism (also called economic nationalism) is most closely associated with the political philosophy of **realism,** which focuses on state efforts to accumulate wealth and power to protect society from physical harm or the influence of other states (see Chapters 3 and 9). In theory, the **state** is a legal entity and an autonomous system of institutions that governs a specific geographic territory and a "**nation.**" Since the mid-seventeenth century, the state has been the dominant actor in the international community based on the principle that it has the authority to exercise **sovereignty** (final authority) over its own affairs.

States use two types of power to protect themselves. **Hard power** refers to tangible military and economic assets employed to compel, coerce, influence, fend off, or defeat enemies and competitors. **Soft power** comprises selective tools that reflect and project a country's cultural values, beliefs, and ideals. Through the use of movies, cultural exports and exchanges, information, and diplomacy, a state can convince others that the ideas it sponsors are legitimate and should be adopted. Soft power can in many ways be more effective than hard power because it rests on persuasion and mutual exchange.[4] For example, Nobel Peace Prize recipient Barack Obama partly regained some of the world's support for the United States through a discourse emphasizing multilateral cooperation.

Structuralism is rooted in Marxist analysis but not limited to it (see Chapter 4). It looks at IPE issues mainly in terms of how different social classes are shaped by the dominant *economic* structure. It is most closely associated with the methods of analysis many sociologists employ. Structuralists emphasize that markets have never existed in a social vacuum. Some combination of social, economic, and political forces establishes, regulates, and preserves them. As we will see in the case of the financial crisis, even the standards used to judge the effectiveness of market systems reflect the dominant values and beliefs of those forces.

The Benefits of IPE

Each perspective in IPE sheds light on some aspects of a problem particularly well, but casts a shadow on other important aspects. By using a *combination* of the three dominant IPE methods and concepts (outlined in Table 1-1), we can move to the big picture—the most comprehensive and compelling explanation of global processes.

Not surprisingly, mixing together the disciplines of economics, political science, and sociology gives rise to an analytical problem: It is difficult to establish a *single* explanation to any IPE issue because each discipline has its own set of analytical concepts, core beliefs, and methodologies. Does this weaken the utility of IPE? Not at all. We must recognize that IPE is not a "hard science"; it may never

TABLE 1-1

Conflicting Political Economic Perspectives about State–Market Relations in Capitalist Societies

	Monetarism (Orthodox Economic Liberals)	Keynesian (Heterodox Interventionist Economic Liberals)	Developmental State Model (Mercantilism)	Socialism (Structuralism)	Social Democracy (Structuralism)
Main Ideas about Capitalism	"Laissez-faire"; minimal state intervention and regulation of the economy	The state primes (injects money—liquidity) into the economy to restore confidence in it and to stabilize it	The state plays a proactive role in the economy to guide and protect its major industries	The state controls the economy. Prices set by state officials. Emphasis on state planning and agenda setting	The government cooperates with businesses to promote economic growth and distribution
Values	Economic efficiency, technology, open and integrated international markets, globalization	Efficiency mixed with a variety of state political and social objectives	National security, state-managed economy, relative equality	Equality	Equity and relative equality
Thinkers	Adam Smith, David Ricardo, Friedrich Hayek, Milton Friedman, "the Chicago School"	John Stuart Mills, John Maynard Keynes, Robert Reich, Joseph Stiglitz, Dani Rodrik, Jeff Sachs	Friedrich List, Alexander Hamilton, Ha-Joon Chang	Karl Marx, Vladimir Lenin, Mao Zedong, Fidel Castro	James Galbraith, Robert Kuttner
Policy Tools	Preferably few. Monetary and fiscal policies necessary at times to help market function well. Free trade	States use monetary and fiscal policies. Promote "fair trade" policies that include some protectionist measures	Protectionist industrial and trade policies oftentimes necessary to make markets work and enhance national wealth and welfare	Monetary, fiscal, and fair trade policies that redistribute income to everyone in society	States use monetary and fiscal policies to redistribute income
Trade Policy Experts State Examples	Doug Irwin, Martin Wolf Hong Kong, U.S., Great Britain	Deepak Lal, Jagdish Bhagwati Germany, India, Mexico	Ha-Joon Chang Japan, South Korea	Walden Bello, Benjamin Barber Former East Germany, China before 1982	Amartya Sen Sweden

establish a comprehensive theory with easily testable propositions about cause and effect. The world is a messy laboratory. Social science has always reflected this in explanations of human behavior. IPE today represents an effort to *return* to the kind of analysis done by political theorists and philosophers *before* the study of human social behavior became fragmented into the discrete fields of social science. Both Adam Smith and Karl Marx, for example, considered themselves to be political-economists in the broadest sense of the term. One of our goals is to point out ways in which by mixing the elements of different disciplines we are better able to explain the global political economy.

One of the ways of doing this is to think of the antecedent disciplines of IPE as varieties of plants. Just as new plant varieties are produced by splicing parts of them together, since the early 1970s the mixing of disciplinary approaches has gradually helped an appreciation of the traditional idea of international political economy re-emerge, resulting in a productive and powerful hybrid field of study called IPE.

So what does the new mixture look like? To help answer this question, Susan Strange suggests that we focus on a number of common analytical and conceptual issues that cut across disciplinary boundaries. For her, the starting point for studying the connections and relationships between states, markets, and society is to focus on the question of *cui bono?* Who benefits from complex interactions in the international political economy?[5] One good example is Pietra Rivoli's book *The Travels of a T-Shirt in the Global Economy* that examines a "commodity chain."[6] Rivoli traces a T-shirt from the time the cotton in it is grown in West Texas, to textile manufacturing in China, to sales in the United States, and then on to Africa, where many donated T-shirts end up being sold in local markets. Her work examines the *process* by which a T-shirt is made, transported, marketed, and then resold. She raises many questions about politics (the power of special interest groups to affect trade rules), markets (for T-shirts in the United States and all over the world), and different societies (how T-shirt manufacturing has changed the lives of factory workers in China and small African businessmen). Rivoli documents her work with plenty of hard evidence and raises a variety of ethical and human rights questions.

We believe that Strange and Rivoli offer two excellent ways for students to start to think about the nature and different dimensions of IPE. It is not sufficient to just examine something from several different angles or perspectives. We must also key in on who benefits or loses from the processes we observe, how actors acquire and use their political power and economic resources, and the relationships between different groups in different societies.

IPE gives students the freedom to select an analytical approach or combination of approaches they feel best suits a particular issue. It is important to note that most of the time the way one explains a problem depends on the questions asked about it, the data available, and the theoretical outlook of the analyst herself. Benjamin J. Cohen, for example, sheds light on this issue in his discussion of the *transatlantic divide* between IPE scholars in the United States and Great Britain.[7] U.S. universities tend to prefer IPE theories organized around issues of causation. Emphasis is placed on asking questions about which there is "hard" data. The goal is to test theories with statistical techniques and empirical evidence to determine what causes a particular "pattern of relations." However, many British universities tend to think of IPE in terms of problems that are not as easy to quantify or for which statistical tests are not very useful. Their methods are rooted more in historical and philosophical understanding and centered on normative issues such as ethics and social justice.

Thus, we can say that IPE blends together distinct perspectives to produce a more holistic explanation. It is more flexible than most disciplines because it asks the analyst to choose how something should be studied and with what tools. Hopefully, with a multidimensional outlook we can conduct better analysis that may result in more effective solutions to global problems.

The Four Levels of Analysis

IPE theorists commonly use different **levels of analysis** in their research. In his famous book *Man, the State, and War*, Kenneth Waltz argues that explanations for causes of international conflict are located in different stages of an *analytical scale of increasing complexity,* ranging from individual behavior and choices (the individual level), to factors within states (the state/societal level), to something stemming from the interconnection of states (the interstate level).[8] More recently, many have argued that there is also a fourth global level that can be identified as causing specific problems.

The characteristics of the different levels of analysis are as follows:

The Global Level. This is the broadest, most comprehensive level of analysis. Explanations focus on how important global factors like changes in technology, commodity prices, and climate create constraints on and opportunities for *all* governments and societies. For example, as oil prices fluctuate dramatically, they force countries to adapt in ways that can contribute to recession, conflict, and energy-source innovations.

The Interstate Level. This level emphasizes how the relative balance of political, military, and economic power *between* states affects the probability of war, prospects for cooperation, and rules related to transnational corporations. The relative power of a state determines the ways in which it will associate with or exercise leverage over its allies and states with dissimilar interests. For example, as China grows stronger, it is forcing some of its Asian neighbors like Japan, the Philippines, and Vietnam to forge closer relations with the United States as a form of insurance against China's potentially aggressive behavior.

The State/Societal Level. Paradoxically, because the focus *narrows* to factors within states, explanations contain *more* causal factors. At this level, we emphasize how lobbying by socio-economic groups, electoral pressures, and culture influence the foreign policies of countries. In addition, we focus on how different types of governments and decision-making processes *within* a state shape the way that it interacts with others. For example, these factors help explain why democracies almost never go to war against other democracies or why politicians will adopt high tariffs on imports to try to help a domestic industry.

The Individual Level. This is the *narrowest* level and yet it contains the *biggest* number of factors that explain why individuals (usually state leaders) choose certain policies or behave in particular ways. This level emphasizes the *psychology*, personality, and beliefs that shape *choices* made by specific policy makers. For example, we might speculate that German chancellor Angela Merkel is reluctant to bail out spendthrifty Greece and Spain because of her deep-seated belief that countries—just like households—should live within their means. She is nicknamed the "Swabian housewife" because she supposedly behaves like a stereotypical wife in southern Germany, who is frugal, not ostentatious, and keeps a balanced budget.[9] Or, Merkel may not want to expand the euro money supply to help Greece because of her fears that it could cause the kind of crippling hyperinflation Germany experienced after World War I.

The four levels of analysis help us *organize* our thoughts about the different causes of, explanations for, and solutions to a particular problem. Like the three IPE perspectives, *each* level pinpoints a distinct but *limited* explanation for why something occurred. For example, global warming can be linked as much to U.S. resistance to the Kyoto Protocol's carbon-emissions caps as to the ineluctably rising demand for energy due to a rising global population. And the OWS movement can be linked as much to the effects of the global financial crisis as to specific elements in the U.S. constitution that produce political gridlock and an inability to lessen inequality. And the Arab Spring may have been caused as much by the region's economic decline in the face of competitive globalization as the human rights violations of leaders in Tunisia and Egypt. Thus, one of the paradoxes of the level of analysis problem is that to get a *bigger and more complex picture* of a problem, one is tempted to look at all the levels for possible answers. However, mixing the levels usually produces no *single* satisfactory answer to a problem. What to do? The level of analysis problem teaches us to be very conscientious about how we frame questions, what data we look at, and what we *expect* to find.

Figure 1-1 highlights the four levels of analysis and their connection to another conceptual organizing device we introduce next.

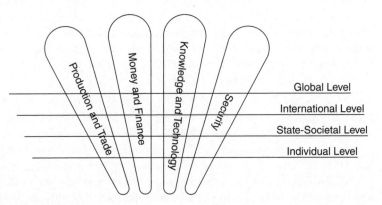

FIGURE 1-1
The Levels of Analysis and Four Structures.

Susan Strange's Four IPE Structures

In the text, we will often refer to Susan Strange's four *structures*: production and trade; money and finance; security; and knowledge and technology. For Strange, these "webs" are complex arrangements that function as the *underlying foundations* of the international political economy. Each contains a number of state and nonstate institutions, organizations, and other actors who determine the rules and processes that govern access to trade, finance, security, and knowledge. In Chapters 6 through 10, we examine what the rules and norms are in each structure, how they were created, who benefits from them, and who is contesting them.

The "rules of the game" in each structure take the form of signed conventions, informal and formal agreements, and "bargains." They act as girders and trusses that hold together each of these four major structures. As one might expect, each IPE structure is often filled with tension because different actors are constantly trying to preserve or change the rules of the structure to better reflect their own interests and values. For example, actors may sometimes pursue free trade policies and at other times erect protectionist trade barriers.

Finally, issues in one structure often impact issues in another, generating a good deal of tension and even conflict between actors. According to Strange, many disputes arise when states try to "shape and determine the structures of the global political economy within which other states, their political institutions, their economic enterprises . . . [and] people have to operate."[10] In our discussion of the four structures below, you can see examples of how they connect to the levels of analysis discussed earlier. We have pinpointed in brackets the causal factors and forces at different levels.

The four **IPE structures** are as follows:

> *The Production and Trade Structure.* The issue of who produces what, for whom, and on what terms lies at the heart of the international political economy. Making things and then selling them in world markets [*a global-level process*] earns countries and their industries huge sums of money, which ultimately can quite easily shift the global distribution of wealth and power. As we will see in Chapter 6, in recent decades there have been dramatic changes in international trade rules [*an interstate level factor*] that have shifted the manufacture of consumer goods such as electronics, household appliances, and clothing away from the United States and Western Europe. Many corporations that make these items have moved to newly emerging economies such as South Korea, Mexico, Brazil, China, Turkey, Poland, and Vietnam. Since the 1990s, governments of these emerging economies have sought to attract foreign investors to promote the production of a range of goods for export. At the same time, many unions and manufacturers in Western countries have lobbied their government for protectionist barriers against cheap imports from China in order to preserve jobs and profits [*a state/societal level factor*]. As emerging economies have earned more income but also had to deal with the effects of the current financial crisis, some have been reluctant to agree to new free-market trade policies in negotiations among members of

the World Trade Organization (WTO) because of pressure from vested interest groups [*a state/societal level factor*].

The Finance and Monetary Structure. With perhaps the most abstract set of linkages between nations, this structure determines who has access to money and on what terms, and thus how certain resources are distributed between nations. In this respect, money is often viewed as a means, not an end in itself. Money generates an obligation between people or states. International money flows [*a global level factor*] pay for trade and serve as the means of financial investment in a factory or a farm in another country. Financial bargains also reflect rules and obligations, as money moves from one nation to another in the form of loans that must be repaid.

Recently, the global financial and monetary structure has been marked by the movement of "hot money" chasing quick profits from one country to another, in part because many political elites hold ideological beliefs [*individual level factors*] opposed to strong international regulation of banks and corporations. Many believe that underregulated financial markets were in part responsible for financial crises in the 1990s in Mexico, parts of Asia and Latin America, and Russia, as well as for the current financial crisis. Some critics also charge that underregulated globalization may be partly responsible for breeding poverty and conflict in some of the depressed areas of the world.

The Security Structure. Feeling safe from the threats and actions of other states and nonstate actors is perhaps the most basic human need. At the global level, the security structure comprises those persons, states, international organizations, and NGOs that provide safety for all people everywhere. In Chapter 9 we will see why many experts claim that the demise of the Soviet Union and the end of the Cold War [*interstate level changes*] led to an *increase* in the number of small conventional wars *between* states and insurgencies *within* developing nations. The 9/11 attacks on the New York Trade Center also profoundly changed the informal rules of the security structure when George W. Bush's administration, dominated by neoconservatives with strong beliefs [*individual level characteristics*], shifted away from multilateralism and tried to impose its own version of hegemonic-unilateral leadership on the rest of world. Some scholars assert that the rising economic and military power of China [*an interstate level factor*] will lead Beijing to provoke conflict by making more strident territorial claims against India and countries around the South China Sea.

The Knowledge and Technology Structure. Knowledge and technology are sources of wealth and power for those who use them effectively. The spread of information and communications technology [*a global level factor*] has fueled industrialization in emerging countries and empowered citizens living under authoritarian regimes, as seen during the Arab Spring. Nations with poor access to industrial technology related to scientific discoveries, medical procedures, and new green energy, for example, find themselves at a disadvantage relative to others [*an interstate level phenomenon*]. Increasingly in the world today, the bargains made in the security, trade, and finance structures depend on access to knowledge in its several forms. The knowledge structure includes rules and patterns affecting intellectual property, technology transfers, and migration opportunities for skilled workers.

The connection between technology and conflict tightens by the day. Newspapers are full of stories about weapons of mass destruction (WMD), drones, and gun violence. New technologies [*global level factors*] have revolutionized the size of weapons and the effects they have when put to use. Many weapons can easily be transported in a backpack or small trucks. The ultimate miniature weapon may no longer be an atomic bomb or a chemical mixture, but a few grams of anthrax on a letter. In the hands of terrorists or state leaders with repugnant beliefs [*individual level factors*], technologically advanced weapons can endanger many lives.

PUTTING THE PIECES TOGETHER: GLOBALIZATION, THE FINANCIAL CRISIS, AND STATE–MARKET–SOCIETAL RELATIONS

One of the terms students will encounter throughout the book is **globalization.** In this section, we introduce you to this concept and briefly explain who it benefits and its relationship to a variety of issues, including the current financial crisis. Globalization is important because it has framed the four structures of the international political economy outlined above. Many of the rules and processes related to trade, money, technology, and security reflect this popular concept. Globalization has brought about a significant change in the way many experts and officials think about the international political economy. It has both strengthened and weakened the power of many institutions and actors along the way.

The term "globalization" began appearing in the IPE lexicon in the mid-1980s to describe the growing **interdependence** (interconnections) among people and states all over the world that resulted from the digital revolution and the spread of Western (U.S.) culture. Globalization also accounted for more trade and financial exchanges with other countries relative to a nation's gross domestic product (GDP). Beginning in the 1990s, the world seemed to be going through a major transformation that involved intense connections between states and their societies. Many IPE analysts suggested that a shift had occurred from a predominately Cold War, military-oriented world order (1947–1990), where states were preoccupied with territorial security and war, to something more akin to a pluralistic world order in which economic issues dominated the global agenda. Many academics, journalists, and public officials labeled this nearly twenty-five-year period of history since the collapse of the Berlin Wall as the "era of globalization."

The roots of globalization can be found in the early 1980s when U.S. President Ronald Reagan and British Prime Minister Margaret Thatcher popularized the ideas and policies associated with economic liberalism and free trade. In the later part of the 1980s and throughout most of the 1990s, many of the newly industrializing states in East and Southeast Asia grew quickly and steadily, turning their trade policies outward by adopting export-led growth strategies and integrating themselves into the new "global economy." During this period, the United States, Great Britain, and other industrialized nations engaged in a campaign to promote globalization with the explicit and implicit promise that, together with capitalism, it would increase economic growth while laying the groundwork for democracy the world over.

In the 1990s and much of the 2000s, many government officials, businesspeople, and academics in the industrialized nations remained enthusiastic about the potential economic benefits from interconnecting people in new, different, and profound ways. Columnist Thomas Friedman, for one, made globalization out to have an appeal that could not be denied. Globalization is usually characterized as

- an *economic process* that reflects dense interconnections based on new technologies and the mobility of trade and capital;
- the *integration* of national markets into a single global market;
- a *political process* that weakens state authority and replaces it with the power of deregulated markets;
- a *cultural process* that reflects a growing network of complex cultural interconnections and interdependencies in modern society.

Some analysts further claim that globalization

- is an *inevitable* occurrence that has produced a new form of capitalism—hypercapitalism;
- is a process for which *nobody is in charge;*
- *benefits* everyone, especially economically;
- furthers the spread of *democracy* in the world.[11]

Globalization connects people by reaching around the world faster, deeper, and more cheaply through an array of new digital technologies that include the Internet, fiber optics, and smart phones. Globalization emphasizes increased production and the free flow of huge amounts of capital in search of investment opportunities and new markets around the world. *Speed* and the *death of distance* are the necessary major features of twenty-first-century communications, commerce, travel, and innovation. Along with economic growth and personal wealth comes the demand for Western (read U.S.) mass consumer products.

For Friedman and free-market state officials, globalization manifested the power of unregulated and integrated markets to trump politics and greatly benefit society. It became synonymous with production efficiency, the free flow of currency (capital mobility), free trade, and individual empowerment. In his popular book *The Lexus and the Olive Tree,* Friedman asserted that globalization often required a "golden straightjacket"—a set of political restrictions and policies that must be implemented if states want to realize globalization's benefits.[12] The payoff would be a "triumph of the market" that produced economic prosperity and democracy everywhere in the world.

Friedman has gone on to argue that an intensely competitive new phase of capitalism—hyperglobalization—drives individuals, states, and TNCs to continually produce new and better products. In his book *The World Is Flat,* he argues that new technological developments are *in the process of* leveling the relationship of individuals to their states and to one another.[13] Leveling generates new opportunities for individuals to compete with people in their own society and with those in other countries. In short, despite a few shortcomings, globalization is here to stay and should be embraced.

Not surprisingly, globalization shaped the strategies of developing countries and has remained quite popular with elites and many citizens in the developed nations. It led to increased emphasis on a set of common rules and policies that all countries were expected to follow—implemented and overseen by international institutions such as the International Monetary Fund, the World Trade Organization, and many United Nations agencies. It was supposed to help create more peaceful relations between states that traded with one another, especially if U.S. hegemony (leadership) promoted it as an attractive option for the world's poor and downtrodden. Globalization was also expected to increase flows of people across borders, which might eventually lead to a better understanding between different groups. As globalization grew in popularity, so did traditional and national resistance (what political scientist Benjamin Barber called *jihad*) to many of its effects.[14] In the 1990s, the antiglobalization movement gained momentum. Many NGOs and other public-interest groups pitched their causes in newspaper articles and on their websites. Much of their focus was on negative consequences of globalization, such as sweatshop conditions in poor countries, damage to the environment, and maldistribution of income.[15] Many of these groups formed coalitions with labor, environmental, and peace activists and held massive demonstrations that often turned violent in cities such as Seattle, Washington, DC, Salzburg, Genoa, and Prague. Protesters denounced WTO, IMF, and World Bank policies that supposedly reflected an ideological obsession with the spread of global capitalism and minimization of controls on transnational corporations. Even the 1989 pro-democracy protests in Beijing's Tiananmen Square and the 2012 Arab Spring can in some ways be interpreted as reactions to the imposition of globalization-oriented policies by authoritarian regimes. Issues surrounding globalization have decisively affected local, regional, and even national elections. Others even argue that antiglobalization was a motive behind the 9/11 terrorist attacks on the United States.[16]

Critics saw globalization as merely a shibboleth of free-market champions—a wildcat version of capitalism that promised higher standards of living but increased the misery or marginalization of many people. Political scientists Leo Panitch and Sam Gindin have portrayed globalization (driven in part by the U.S. Treasury and the Federal Reserve) as a process of spreading U.S. economic practices and institutions to foreign countries: "It was the immense strength of US capitalism which made globalization possible, and what continued to make the American state distinctive was its vital role in management and superintending capitalism on a worldwide plane."[17] When such a process allows markets to trump politics, predictably the outcome often is devastating for society. According to Ignacio Ramonet, the former editor-in-chief of *Le Monde diplomatique,* society had become a slave to the market, which operates like clockwork, driven by economic and Social Darwinism, leading to excessive competition and consumption and the necessity of people to adapt to market conditions, at the risk of becoming social misfits and slowing the global economy.[18]

Friedman acknowledged that globalization alone would not automatically achieve success for everyone. In fact, he suggested that if it increased the rich–poor gap or left too many behind, it would likely generate opposition. Moreover, many scholars—and even Thomas Friedman himself—became concerned about the extent to which globalization was having a homogenizing effect on cultures around the world. Was it desirable to encourage the spread of U.S. business practices and consumption of U.S. products and symbols such as Big Macs, iMacs, and Mickey Mouse? Was globalization just a process of spreading the ideals and cultural patterns of the U.S. empire?

By the turn of the twenty-first century, it had become clear that most developing nations were not growing out of poverty as expected. A few newly industrializing countries (NICs)—China, Singapore, Taiwan, South Korea, Malaysia, and Thailand—did experience tremendous national and per-capita growth. And yet some of these newly emerging economies in Asia and other parts of the world experienced financial crises in the late 1990s that called into question whether fast growth was sustainable. Even though more unfettered (unchained) markets tended to help the well off in these societies, the gap between rich and poor expanded.

In a tacit admission that globalization was not delivering on its promises, the United Nations in 2000 established the Millennium Development Goals (MDGs) directed at increasing foreign aid for poorer nations, halving global hunger, reducing debt, and fighting diseases like AIDS. Contrary to predictions that globalization would lessen armed conflicts around the world, the former Yugoslavia plunged into civil wars throughout the 1990s, Rwanda suffered a genocide in 1994, and the Democratic Republic of the Congo experienced a terrible civil war between 1998 and 2003 in which more than two million people died. Also left behind by globalization were a number of "failed states" such as Sudan, Somalia, and Afghanistan, where civil wars destroyed societies. Then came 9/11 and the wars on terrorism and Iraq, which intensified tensions between the Western industrialized nations and many Islamic countries, even though the two groups of countries were more culturally and economically interconnected than ever before.

As explained in Chapters 19 and 20, many IPE scholars became concerned that pro-globalization policies were responsible for many of the global environmental problems that we face today. The emphasis on profitable, short-term economic choices has led to ecological catastrophes that already may not be reversible. Many would like to reform capitalism and redesign globalization so that people curtail the excessive use of the earth's resources. We can expect major problems in adjusting to a sustainable level of resource use in the industrialized nations—at the same time that China, India, and other developing nations make increasing demands on the raw materials of "Spaceship Earth."

Finally, the current global financial crisis and the distress of Europe have generated still more (intense) criticism of globalization and the economic liberal values and institutions that prop it up. As we write in late 2012, some pundits and economic prognosticators point to signs that "green shoots" are beginning to appear in the United States, China, and Brazil that herald economic recovery in 2013 and 2014.[19] Others believe that recuperation is not likely for some time. For example, economist Nouriel Roubini suggests the possibility of a "perfect storm"—an economic train wreck in the European countries using the euro, another U.S. recession, stalled growth in China and India, and a U.S.-Israeli war against Iran that raises oil prices 50 percent.[20] Whatever the case, until the financial crisis is adequately dealt with, many anti-austerity protestors, academics, and officials will continue to assert that more *managed* globalization would better serve everyone.

PRELUDE AND CONCLUSION

Having read about globalization—which underlies a number of the issues discussed in this text—we hope that you now have a flavor of how scholars of IPE examine the complex interrelationships in the world today. As you plunge into the chapters, the terminology, concepts, and countries that still seem unfamiliar will become clearer, and you will become much more fluent in the specific language of IPE. There are many more theoretical and policy issues that you will encounter, so as a prelude we introduce here some main questions that are highlighted in the text:

- How have states tried to manage *globalization's* negative externalities and impacts on the environment, resources, and society? (discussed throughout the text)
- What are the tensions between *market fundamentalism and protectionism*? In what ways are markets re-embedded into society and its cultural institutions? (especially Chapters 2–4)
- With the rise of global *production*, how have the gains from trade and growth been *distributed* between different social groups and countries? (especially Chapters 4, 6, 10, and 11)
- How do states balance their *domestic political needs* with their *international obligations*? (throughout the text)
- Can *national security and freedom* be reconciled? (especially Chapter 9)
- How do *social groups and ideas* influence markets and states? (especially Chapters 5 and 16)
- Are *relations between people* fundamentally cooperative or conflictual? (especially Chapters 2, 14, 16)
- What are the causes and consequences of *inequality* between and within countries? (especially Chapters 8, 11, and 14)
- How is the rise of *China, India, Russia, and Brazil* fundamentally reshaping the global economy? (Chapter 13)
- What do *financial crises* reveal about the *nature of capitalism* and challenges of market *regulation*? (especially Chapters 4, 8, and 12)
- Are *states losing power* relative to illicit markets and transnational corporations? (Chapters 16–19)

- How do *technological changes* affect political and economic processes? (throughout the text)
- To what extent can *hegemons* and international institutions provide *global governance* and systemic order in the face of social and political resistance? (throughout the text)
- What are the *analytical and policy linkages* between food, energy, and the environment? (especially Chapters 18–20).

Standing on the Precipice

Since the Cold War, a minority of states have employed a mixture of state-directed and free-market policies to achieve tremendous economic development, while much of the world has been unable to attain anything near that objective. What seems clearer to us all the time is that development—as we have commonly conceived it—may not be realized for many societies, especially in the face of pressures on the earth's resources. Furthermore, development is not something that ends once a nation becomes modern and industrialized. Instead, it is an ongoing process of political, economic, and social transformation in all societies.

At the same time, two major global processes are impacting states and societies in ways unimagined even thirty years ago. The first is a shift in the distribution of global wealth and power. Public officials have had to come to grips with the idea that the war on terrorism may not be "winnable" in any real sense of the term. For a variety of reasons related to the availability of dangerous technologies, porous state borders, and economic frustrations, national and personal insecurities may in fact be increasing.

Although the Cold War seems *passé*, the major powers—especially the United States, Russia, China, France, the United Kingdom, and Japan—have tended to fall back into viewing the global political economy with a familiar realist outlook that emphasizes power and conflict. Interestingly, the rise of India and China suggests that the international balance of power is shifting even faster than expected and in ways that could very well increase North–South tensions. This process has already weakened the global cooperation that will be necessary to solve problems such as terrorism, hunger, and climate change. The intransigent national interests of developed nations may soften through long-term negotiations with China, Brazil, and the Middle Eastern countries, or they may lead to more threats to world peace.

A second major shift in the global political economy relates to the benefits and costs associated with globalization. Clearly, the global financial crisis generated more skepticism about free markets and renewed support for more government intervention to save national economies. But we do not know if societies are willing to accept the insecurity and efficiency that globalization brings without a more democratic role in shaping its rules and rewards. It would seem obvious that because of the interconnectedness of states and markets, international institutions *must* play some role in solving international problems. Paradoxically, precisely at a time when more collaboration is necessary to solve an assortment of global ills, the compulsion of actors to cooperate for the sake of providing **global governance** remains weak. Dealing with the global financial crisis is just one such case.

We end this chapter with two hopes that we have for you. We hope that you will help humanity find a way to raise standards of living without destroying the earth's environment, climate, and biodiversity. We also hope that as you devise solutions to contentious economic and political problems, you show compassion for the most vulnerable people in the world.

KEY TERMS

international political
   economy 8
global civil society 9
economic liberalism 9
orthodox economic
   liberals 9

heterodox interventionist
   liberals 9
mercantilism 10
realism 10
sovereignty 10
hard power 10

soft power 10
structuralism 10
the level of analysis 13
IPE structures 15
globalization 17
global governance 22

DISCUSSION QUESTIONS

1. Pick a recent news article that focuses on some international or global problem, and give examples of how and where states, markets, and societies interact and at times conflict with one another. How hard is it to determine the analytical boundaries between the state, market, and society in this case?
2. Review the basic elements and features of the IPE approach: the three main theoretical perspectives, the four structures, the levels of analysis, and the types of power. Which ones do you feel you understand well and which ones need more work? Discuss the connection between each of the three theoretical perspectives and your own values related to IPE.
3. Define and outline the major features of globalization. Explain the connection between economic liberal ideas and globalization. Which of the three IPE perspectives (or combination of perspectives) about globalization do you agree with most? Explain why.
4. Based on what you have learned so far in this chapter and from reading newspapers, outline a few things you know about the connection between globalization, the financial crisis, and capitalism. Do you agree with those who suggest that the financial crisis raises serious concerns about the viability of capitalism? Explain.

SUGGESTED READINGS

Thomas L. Friedman. *The World Is Flat: A Brief History of the Twenty-First Century*. New York: Farrar, Straus and Giroux, 2005.

Robert Gilpin. Especially Chapter 1 in *The Political Economy of International Relations*. Princeton, NJ: Princeton University Press, 1987.

William Greider. *One World, Ready or Not: The Manic Logic of Global Capitalism*. New York: Simon & Schuster, 1997.

Pietra Rivoli. *The Travels of a T-Shirt in the Global Economy: An Economist Examines the Markets,* *Power, and Politics of World Trade*, 2nd ed. Hoboken, NJ: John Wiley, 2009.

Joseph Stiglitz. *Globalization and Its Discontents*. New York: W. W. Norton, 2004.

Susan Strange. *States and Markets*, 2nd ed. New York: Continuum, 1994.

Kenneth N. Waltz. *Man, the State, and War: A Theoretical Analysis*. New York: Columbia University Press, 1959.

NOTES

1. See Charles Lindblom, *The Market System: What It Is, How It Works, and What To Make of It* (New Haven, CT: Yale University Press, 2001), p. 23.
2. See Robert Heilbroner and Lester Thurow, "Capitalism: Where Do We Come From?" in their *Economics Explained: Everything You Need to Know about How the Economy Works and Where It's Going* (New York: Simon & Schuster, 1994).
3. See Adam Smith, *The Wealth of Nations* (London: Methuen & Co. Ltd., 1904).
4. For a detailed discussion of soft power and its utility in the international political economy, see Joseph Nye, *Soft Power: The Means of Success in World Politics* (New York: Public Affairs, 2006).
5. See Susan Strange, *States and Markets*, 2nd ed. (New York: Continuum, 1994), pp. 121, 136, and 234.

6. See Pietra Rivoli, *The Travels of a T-Shirt in the Global Economy: An Economist Examines the Markets, Power, and Politics of World Trade*, 2nd ed. (Hoboken, NJ: John Wiley & Sons, 2009).

7. See Benjamin J. Cohen, "The Transatlantic Divide: Why Are American and British IPE so Different?" *Review of International Political Economy,* 14 (May 2007), pp. 197–219.

8. Kenneth N. Waltz, *Man, the State, and War: A Theoretical Analysis* (New York: Columbia University Press, 1959). Waltz wrote about three "images" rather than three "levels," and both terms are used in discussions of this concept. The recent focus on globalization has generated a good deal of attention to the global level of analysis.

9. Julia Kollewe, "Angela Merkel's Austerity Poster-girl, the Thrifty Swabian Housewife," *Guardian*, September 17, 2012.

10. See Susan Strange, *States and Markets: An Introduction to International Political Economy* (New York: Basil Blackwell, 1988), pp. 24–25.

11. For a more detailed overview and discussion of globalization and globalism, see Manfred Steger, *Globalisms: The Great Ideological Struggle of the Twenty-First Century*, 3rd ed. (Lanham, MD: Rowman & Littlefield, 2009).

12. See Thomas Friedman, *The Lexus and the Olive Tree: Understanding Globalization* (New York: Farrar, Straus & Giroux, 1999).

13. Thomas Friedman, *The World Is Flat: A Brief History of the Twenty-First Century* (New York: Farrar, Straus & Giroux, 2005).

14. The term is used in this broad manner by Benjamin Barber, *McWorld vs. Jihad: How Globalism and Tribalism are Reshaping the World* (New York: Ballantine Books, 1996).

15. See, for example, many of the articles in Robin Broad, ed., *Global Backlash: Citizen Initiatives for a Just World Economy* (Lanham, MD: Rowman & Littlefield, 2002).

16. It should be noted that many historians point out that by some measures globalization was actually greater before, during, and after World War I. Also, some academics and experts warn us not to think of globalization as some big, deterministic process that controls everything going on in the world. Instead, they emphasize that it is a complex, messy set of processes of economic and social change, often grounded in history and local conditions, that cannot easily be reduced to a few generalizations or rhetorical arguments. See, for example, Michael Veseth's aptly titled *Globaloney 2.0: The Crash of 2008 and the Future of Globalization* (Lanham, MD: Rowman & Littlefield, 2010).

17. Leo Panitch and Sam Gindin, *The Making of Global Capitalism: The Political Economy of American Empire* (New York: Verso, 2012), p. 1.

18. See Thomas Friedman and Ignacio Ramonet, "Dueling Globalization: A Debate between Thomas Friedman and Ignacio Ramonet," *Foreign Policy* 116 (Fall 1999), pp. 110–127.

19. For example, see Simon Kennedy, "Economy Has Green Shoots from China to U.S. as Data Surprise," *Bloomberg*, November 15, 2012, at http://www.bloomberg.com/news/2012-11-14/economy-shows-green-shoots-from-china-to-u-s-with-data-surprise.html.

20. Peter Coy, "Nouriel Roubini on Threats to the Global Economy," *Bloomberg Businessweek*, August 9, 2012, at http://www.businessweek.com/articles/2012-08-09/nouriel-roubini-on-threats-to-the-global-economy.

Laissez-Faire: The Economic Liberal Perspective

Someone has to clean up the mess.

Mario Tama/Getty Images

Like many other terms in international political economy (IPE), the generic term "liberal-ism" suffers from something of a personality disorder. The term means different things in different contexts. In the United States today, for example, a liberal is generally regarded as one who believes in an *active* role for the state in society, such as helping the poor and funding programs to address social problems. Since the mid-1980s, someone who has been thought of more narrowly as an *economic liberal* believes *almost* (but not exactly) the opposite. For economic liberals (also referred to as neoliberals),[1] the state should play a *limited*, if not *constricted*, role in the economy and society. In other words, today's economic liberals have much in common with people who are usually referred to as "conservatives" in the United States, Europe, Canada, and Australia.

This chapter traces the historical rise of **economic liberalism** in eighteenth- and nineteenth-century England and in the United States and Europe in the twentieth century. We outline some of the basic tenets of capitalism, a focal point of liberal thought. Throughout the chapter, we also discuss the views about state–market–society relations of some of the most famous liberal political economists: Adam Smith, David Ricardo, John Maynard Keynes, Friedrich Hayek, Milton Friedman, and recent supporters of globalization.

The chapter ends with an explanation of the popularity of globalization, which helped divide **orthodox economic liberals (OELs)** from **heterodox interventionist liberals (HILs)** (see Chapter 1). Finally, we contrast the views of OELs and HILs on the recent financial crisis, focusing on the extent to which the crisis has weakened the precepts and policies associated with economic liberalism.

The appendix "The Market Model, Market-Based Resource Allocation, Economic Efficiency, Efficiency Versus Equity," appears in our website http://www.upugetsoundintroipe.com. It lays out the characteristics of a formal market model, develops the notion of efficiency, and then contrasts efficiency with equity. Students are encouraged to review the model in some detail to understand the basic assumptions many economists make about the role of the market in a liberal society.

There are four main theses in this chapter. First, economic liberal ideas continue to evolve as a reflection of changes in the economy and the power and influence of actors and institutions. Second, economic liberalism gained renewed popularity due to its association with the laissez-faire Reagan and Thatcher administrations, culminating in the globalization campaign of the 1990s. Third, since then orthodox economic liberalism has increasingly come under attack for its failure to predict or sufficiently deal with such things as the financial crisis and poverty in less developed countries (LDCs). Fourth and finally, we end with the suggestion that although weakened, laissez-faire ideas and policies are likely to remain popular in the United States and many other nations.

ROOTS OF THE ECONOMIC LIBERAL PERSPECTIVE

The liberal perspective today reveals many insights about political economy that mercantilists miss or do not address. Essentially, the broad term "liberalism" means "liberty under the law."[2] Liberalism focuses on the side of human nature that is competitive in a constructive way and is guided by reason, not emotions. Although liberals believe that people are fundamentally self-interested, they do not see this as a disadvantage because competing interests in society can engage one another constructively. This contrasts with the mercantilist view, which, as we will see in Chapter 3, dwells on the side of human nature that is more aggressive, combative, and suspicious.

Classical economic liberalism is rooted in reactions to important trends in Europe in the seventeenth and eighteenth centuries. François Quesnay (1694–1774) led a group of French philosophers called the Physiocrats or *les Économistes*.

Quesnay condemned government interference in the market, holding that, with few exceptions, it brought harm to society. The Physiocrats' motto was *laissez-faire, laissez-passer,* meaning "let be, let pass," but said in the spirit of telling the state, "Hands off! Leave us alone!" This became the theme of Adam Smith (1723–1790), a Scottish contemporary of Quesnay who is generally regarded as the father of modern economics. Smith and many since him, including David Ricardo, Friedrich Hayek, and Milton Friedman, display respect, admiration, and almost affection for the market, juxtaposed with different degrees of distaste for the state, or at least for its abusive potential.

In his famous book *The Wealth of Nations*, Smith opposed the mercantilist state of the eighteenth century, established on the principle that the nation is best served when state power is used to create wealth, which produces more power and national security (see Chapter 3). For classical economic liberals, individual freedom in the marketplace represents the best alternative to potentially abusive state power when it comes to the allocation of resources or organizing economic activity. However, for Smith the term "state" meant Britain's Parliament, which represented the interests of the landed gentry, not those of the entrepreneurs and citizens of the growing industrial centers. Not until the 1830s was Parliament reformed enough to redistribute political power more widely. As a Scot without land, who therefore could not vote, Smith had some reason to question the power structure of his time.

Smith also believed in the cooperative, constructive side of human nature. For him, the best interest of all of society is served by (rational) individual choices, which when observed from afar appear as an *invisible hand* that guides the economy and promotes the common good. He wrote:

> He [the typical citizen] generally, indeed, neither intends to promote the public interest, nor knows how much he is promoting it. By preferring the support of domestic to that of foreign industry, he intends only his own security; and by directing that industry in such a manner as its own produce may be of the greatest value, he intends only his own gain, and he is in this, as in many other cases, directed by an invisible hand to promote an end which was no part of his intention.[3]

Smith was writing at a time when the production system known as capitalism was replacing feudalism. He was the first to develop a comprehensive portrait of capitalism in *The Wealth of Nations*, originally published in 1776. What follows is a brief overview of some of the ideals and tenets of capitalism based in large part on Smith's work—or at least the way many economic liberals (both OELs and HILs) today interpret his work.

The Dominant Features of Capitalism

The five main elements of capitalism are as follows:

- Markets *coordinate* society's economic activities.
- Extensive markets exist for the exchange of land, labor, commodities, and money.

- Competition *regulates* economic activity; consumer self-interests motivate economic activity.
- Freedom of enterprise; individuals are free to start up any new business enterprise without state permission.
- Private property; the owner of a resource is legally entitled to the income that flows from the resource.

The first three tenets address the nature and behavior of markets. In the modern market, products and services are commodified—that is, a market price is established for goods and services as a result of producers setting prices for their goods and buyers paying for them. The political scientist Charles Lindblom makes an elaborate case for how markets *organize* and *coordinate* society today in ways quite different from the past.[4] Whereas before capitalism the economy was organized to serve society, today markets organize most of our lives in ways we are not aware of. Markets not only determine our jobs but also shape our choices about travel, entertainment, and food.

Another feature of capitalism is the existence of markets for land, labor, and money. The economic historian and anthropologist Karl Polanyi wrote extensively about how modern capitalism gradually came about in seventeenth-century Great Britain when land was privatized, people moved off the countryside and into small factories, and capital (money) was generated by trade. Land, labor, and capital were all commodified, which provided the financial foundation and labor for the industrial revolution and the society that today we recognize as capitalist.[5]

When economists say that competition *regulates* economic activity, they are referring to the ways in which markets convert the pursuit of consumer self-interests into an outcome that inevitably benefits all of society. According to Smith, the pursuit of individual self-interest does not lead to civil disorder or even anarchy; rather, *self-interest serves society's interests*. Smith famously said, "It is not from the benevolence of the butcher, the brewer, or the baker that we expect our dinner, but from their regard to their own interest. We address ourselves, not to their humanity but to their self-love, and never talk to them of our necessities but of their advantages."[6]

In a capitalist economy, self-interest drives individuals to make rational choices that best serve their own needs and desires. However, it is competition that *constrains* and *disciplines* self-interest and prevents it from becoming destructive to the interests of others. Under ideal circumstances, producers must compete with others, which forces them to charge reasonable prices and provide quality goods to their customers, or lose their business. Consumers also face competition from other consumers who may be willing to pay more for a product. Even if producers might want to push prices high to satisfy their narrow economic interests, and buyers might want to push prices low for the same reason, the force of competition keeps the pursuit of self-interest from going to the extreme.

Capitalism assumes that price competition also results in the *efficient* allocation of resources among competing uses. When economists say that markets coordinate society's economic activity, they generally mean that no one (especially the state) should be in charge of how resources are allocated. Market coordination entails a decentralized (spread out) resource allocation process guided by the tastes and preferences of individual consumers.

For capitalists, government intervention in the market generally distorts resource reallocation and frustrates the coordination function we have described. Competition also requires firms to be production efficient, in the sense that it pays to adopt cost-saving innovations in the production of goods and to remain on the cutting edge of product and process innovation, the delivery of services, and the management of resources. The leaders of even the most powerful firms such as Microsoft, Ericsson, or Petrobas must keep one step ahead of technologically audacious newcomers if they wish to retain their share of the market.

The last two tenets of capitalism deal with the role of the state in establishing freedom of enterprise and private property. Freedom of enterprise means that businesses can easily channel resources to the production of goods and services that are in high demand while simultaneously intensifying competitive pressures in these industries. When individuals are free to make their own career choices, they naturally prepare for and seek out careers or lines of employment in which they are likely to be most productive. Likewise, as economic circumstances change, labor resources will be rapidly redeployed to growing sectors of the economy as individuals take advantage of new opportunities.

Capitalists are adamant that the income of those who own capital is usually in the form of profits (as opposed to wages). Capital goods—plants, equipment, and tools that workers need—are the important subset of all commodities that are required to produce other commodities. In a capitalist economy, the owners pay for the costs of production—the wages of the workers, the raw materials, and all intermediate goods used in production—and then sell the finished commodities on the market. Whatever is left over, the difference between the revenue and the costs, belongs to the capitalist owners. This is a legal right of ownership, referred to as capitalist property rights. A capitalist may completely own a business, a local bar, or a high-tech start-up, for example. In contrast, the owners of a corporation are those who own its stocks, which can be bought and sold on a stock market.

When property rights are less clear, the incentive to use resources efficiently diminishes. Private property—clear title to land, for example—also encourages the owner to make investments in improving the land and provides the owner the collateral with which to obtain the credit necessary to do so. Consequently, the resource owner makes every effort to ensure that the resource is used efficiently (i.e., profitably).

Freedom of enterprise allows entrepreneurs to test new ideas in the marketplace. In a dynamic world of changing tastes and preferences, the availability of resources and new technologies foments product and production process innovation. In such an environment, entrepreneurs must rapidly redeploy their resources to changing circumstances when new opportunities arise. Freedom of enterprise also allows firms to increase or reduce their labor force as necessary. Because firms can easily expand and contract, the associated risk of changes is minimized, and competition is consequently enhanced.

What Smith is most known for, then, is the view that ideally a capitalist economy is self-motivating, self-coordinating, and self-regulating. Consumers determine how resources will be allocated; self-interest motivates entrepreneurs to develop and firms and their workers to produce the goods and services consumers desire; the market coordinates economic activity by communicating the ever-changing tastes and preferences of consumers to producers; and competition ensures that the pursuit of self-interest serves social (consumer) interests.

Smith, the Cynic and Moralist

Yet many historians and philosophers have come to view Smith as a more complex, nuanced philosopher, rather than associating him with only the invisible hand of the market, a phrase used only once in *The Wealth of Nations*. In fact, many of the ideas in his other major work, *The Theory of Moral Sentiments*, appear to contradict the more orthodox economic liberal ideas with which he is most often associated. We group Smith's caveats about the tenets of capitalism into three interrelated categories: the role of the state, the motives and behavior of capitalists related to preservation of the market, and a variety of moral issues.

Smith is clear that indeed the state has some necessary and legitimate functions in society, especially with regard to defending the country, policing, building public works, preventing the spread of diseases, enforcing contracts, keeping the market functioning, and helping to achieve individual rights. Smith is also quite adamant in his distrust of businesspeople and capitalists. Another of his famous quotes is that "people of the same trade seldom meet together, even for merriment and diversion, but the conversation ends in a conspiracy against the public, or in some contrivance to raise prices."[7] The pursuit of self-interest by a monopoly producer, for example, often leads to restricted output, higher prices for goods, and a consequent loss of social welfare. Smith also distrusted bankers and noted that employers always sought to keep wages low: "When the regulation . . . is in favor of the workmen, it is always just and equitable; but it is sometimes otherwise when in favor of the masters."[8]

How do businesspeople get these advantages? Smith believed that merchants often had a disproportionate influence over the Parliament and could press their "private interests." These special interests often solicited the power of the state to allow them to disregard competitive pressures and to convince those in power that "what they wanted was identical to the general interest."[9] Manufacturers often easily influenced the legislature such that they acquired the exclusive use of licenses, franchises, tariffs, and quotas. Often, their trading companies gained the sole right to sell products, keeping market prices above the natural price.

An example today is in the area of intellectual property rights, where companies like IBM, Samsung, and Pfizer have convinced governments to strongly protect patents, which are legal, temporary monopolies on inventions allowing a manufacturer to prevent others from using the invention without the manufacturer's permission. In 2007 alone, IBM and Samsung together won more than 5,800 patents. During the period 1996 to 2010 when Pfizer had a patent on Lipitor, one of the world's most popular drugs, cumulative sales of this cholesterol-fighting statin reached an astonishing $118 billion. Large-scale firms attempt to marshal the necessary resources and the power to control the markets for their new products with patents and copyrights. The risks of introducing new products, given the huge investments and time lags involved, are mitigated if these firms are *guaranteed* captive markets and consumer acceptance. Thus, many successful firms invest heavily in shaping consumer tastes and preferences via expensive, sophisticated, and sometimes subtle marketing campaigns. At the same time, corporations hire major lobbying firms to press the U.S. Congress or English Parliament for legislation that would help preserve their competitive advantage over other industries.

A comprehensive understanding of Smith's concerns about the role of the state in the economy and his unease about the integrity of capitalists elicits something more subtle than the dictum of laissez-faire universally associated with him. On the one hand, he *opposed* having the state try to direct investments because it might be counterproductive and unnecessary. And yet he *supported* the state exercising vigilance and enforcing competition policies to preserve competition and help the market work properly. Today we would say that in capitalist economies Smith feared **rent-seeking** (the manipulation of the state to rig the market in such a way as to reward powerful business interests with high prices and high profits). For Smith, absent competition, the invisible hand can no longer make competition work for the benefit of all society. While Smith leaves open the question of more specific issues about the how, when, and why of state regulation (an issue explored in more detail in Chapter 3), it is clear that he viewed the state (the *visible* hand?) as necessary if there was to be competition, lest capitalists themselves or powerful political interests represented by the state destroyed the market.

Unlike *The Wealth of Nations*, Smith's book *The Theory of Moral Sentiments* has been largely overlooked until recently. His views in it reflect his ambition to proactively structure the market in such a way that commercial activity would produce righteous and prudent people. As the labor force grew in size, he argued that the welfare of "servants, laborers, and workmen of different kinds" should be the prime concern of economic policy. Sounding a bit like Marx (see Chapter 4), Smith argued that "no society can surely be flourishing and happy, of which the far greater part of the members are poor and miserable."[10]

For Smith, the passion to pursue self-interest leads mercantilists to cut-throat competition in which winners create losers. On the other hand, economic liberals also pursue their self-interests, but their passions are *restrained* by competition that prevents anyone from gaining too much power that could lead to coercion. Serving one's own interests in a competitive society means competing to best serve *the interests of others*, to behave honestly, and to gain a reputation for *fairness*. In a world of intense competition, commercial society was a way to channel self-interest into a less morally corrupt society than during feudalism.

THE TRANSFORMATION OF LIBERAL IDEAS AND POLICIES

Adam Smith's writings were part of a broader intellectual movement that engendered intense economic and political change in society. Classical liberals, in general, at the time are represented by the writings of John Locke (1632–1704) in England and Thomas Jefferson (1743–1826) in the United States.

Economic theorists tend to think of laissez-faire in terms of markets. However, this philosophy also implies that citizens need to possess certain negative rights (freedoms *from* state authority, such as freedom from unlawful arrest), positive rights (which include unalienable rights and freedoms *to* take certain actions, such as freedom of speech or freedom of the press), and the right of democratic participation in government, without which positive and negative freedom cannot be guaranteed.[11] These classical liberal political ideas are embedded firmly in the U.S. Declaration of Independence and the Bill of Rights, which were becoming well known about the same time as Adam Smith's notion of consumer freedom.

Economic liberals tend to focus on the domain in which nation-states show their cooperative, peaceful, constructive natures through harmonious competition. As we will see in Chapter 6, international trade is seen as being mutually advantageous, not merely cutthroat competition for wealth and power. What is true about individuals is also true about states. As Smith wrote, "What is prudence in the conduct of every family can scarce be folly in that of a great kingdom. If a foreign country can supply us with a commodity cheaper than we ourselves can make it, better buy it of them with some part of the produce of our industry, employed in a way in which we have some advantage."[12] Smith generally opposed most state restrictions on free international markets. He condemned the tariffs that mercantilists used to concentrate wealth and power. "Such taxes, when they have grown up to a certain height, are a curse equal to the barrenness of the earth and the inclemency of the heavens."[13] However, Smith *did* support the mercantilist Navigation Acts that protected British industries by requiring their goods be shipped to British colonies in British vessels, an act of mercantilism (see Chapter 3).

David Ricardo (1772–1823) followed Smith in adopting the classical economic liberal view of international affairs. He pursued successful careers in business, economics, and as a Member of Parliament. Ricardo was a particular champion of free trade, which made him part of the minority in Britain's Parliament in his day. He opposed the **Corn Laws** (see the box "Britain's Corn Laws"), which restricted agricultural trade. About trade, Ricardo was one of the first to explore some of the precepts of a natural (scientific) law about trade. He argued:

> Under a system of perfectly free commerce, each country naturally devotes its capital and labour to such employments as are most beneficial to each. The pursuit of individual advantage is admirably connected with the universal good of the whole. By stimulating industry, by rewarding ingenuity, and by using most efficaciously the peculiar powers bestowed by nature, it distributes labour most effectively and most economically: while, by increasing the general mass of productions, it diffuses general benefit, and binds together, by one common tie of interest and intercourse, the universal society of nations throughout the civilized world.[14]

For Ricardo, free commerce makes nations efficient, and efficiency is a quality that liberals value almost as highly as liberty. Individual success is "admirably connected" with "universal good"—like Smith, no conflict among

▶ BRITAIN'S CORN LAWS

Britain's Parliament enacted the Corn Laws in 1815, soon after the defeat of Napoleon ended twelve long years of war. The Corn Laws were a system of tariffs and regulations that restricted food imports into Great Britain. The battle over the Corn Laws, which lasted from their inception until they were finally repealed in 1846, is a classic IPE case study in the conflict between liberalism and mercantilism, market and state.

Why would Britain seek to limit imports of food from the United States and other countries? The "official" argument was that Britain needed to be self-sufficient in food, and the Corn Laws were a way to ensure that it did not become dependent on uncertain foreign supplies. This sort of argument carried some weight at the time, given Britain's wartime experiences (although Napoleon never attempted to cut off food supplies to Great Britain).

There were other reasons for Parliament's support of the Corn Laws, however. The right to vote in Parliament was not universal, and members were chosen based on rural landholdings, not on the distribution of population. The result was that Parliament represented the largely agricultural interests of the landed estates, which were an important source of both power and wealth in the seventeenth and eighteenth centuries. The growing industrial cities and towns, which were increasingly the engine of wealth in the nineteenth century, were not represented in Parliament to a proportional degree.

Seen in this light, it is clear that the Corn Laws were in the economic interests of the members of Parliament and their allies. They were detrimental, however, to the rising industrial interests in two ways. First, by forcing food prices up, the Corn Laws indirectly forced employers to increase the wages they paid to their workers. This increased production costs and squeezed profits. Second, by reducing Britain's imports from other countries, the Corn Laws indirectly limited Britain's manufactured exports to these markets. The United States, for example, counted on sales of agricultural goods to Britain to generate the cash to pay for imported manufactured goods. Without agricultural exports, the United States could not afford as many British imports.

Clearly, the industrialists favored repeal of the Corn Laws, but they lacked the political power to achieve their goal. However, the Parliamentary Reform Act of 1832 revised the system of parliamentary representation but also reduced the power of the landed elites who had previously dominated the government, and increased the power of emerging industrial center representatives. The 1832 Reform Act began the political process that eventually abolished the Corn Laws by weakening their political base of support.

In an act of high political drama, the Corn Laws were repealed in 1846, which changed the course of British trade policy for a generation. Although this act is often seen as the triumph of liberal views over old-fashioned mercantilism, it is perhaps better seen as the victory of the masses over the agricultural oligarchy. Britain's population had grown quickly during the first half of the nineteenth century, and agricultural self-sufficiency was increasingly difficult, even with rising farm productivity. Crop failures in Ireland (the potato famine) in the 1840s left Parliament with little choice: either repeal the Corn Laws or face famine, death, and food riots.

The repeal of the Corn Laws was accompanied by a boom in the Victorian economy. Cheaper food and bigger export markets fueled a rapid short-term expansion of the British economy. Britain embraced a liberal view of trade for the rest of the century. Given its place in the global political economy as the *workshop of the world*, liberal policies were the most effective way to build national wealth and power. Other nations, however, felt exploited or threatened by Britain's power and adopted mercantilist policies in self-defense.

The Corn Laws illustrate the dynamic interaction between state and market. Changes in the wealth-producing structure of the economy (from farm to industry, from country to city) led eventually to a change in the distribution of state power. The transition was not smooth, however, and took a long time—important points to remember as we consider countries that have tried to open their economies and societies today. The case also illustrates that the market can be dominated by particular groups and is not apolitical or asocial, but reflects important social and cultural power.

people or nations is envisioned here. The free international market stimulates industry, encourages innovation, and creates a "general benefit" by raising production. In IPE jargon, economic liberals view the outcomes of state, market, and society relations as a **positive-sum game**, in which everyone can potentially get more by making bargains with others as opposed to not trading with them. Market exchanges of goods and services are mutually advantageous to both parties. Mercantilists, on the other hand, tend to view life as a **zero-sum game**, in which gains by one person or group necessarily come at the expense of others (see Chapter 3).

Sounding more like a social scientist than a philosopher, Ricardo argued that these positive-sum payoffs of trade bind together the nations of the world by a common thread of interest and intercourse. As is often argued by those who support globalization today, free individual actions in the production, finance, and knowledge structures create such strong ties of mutual advantage among nations that the need for a tie of security is irrelevant, or nearly so. Through open markets, the nations of the world are becoming part of a "universal society" united, not separated, by their national interests, weakening or entirely eliminating reasons for war.

JOHN STUART MILL AND THE EVOLUTION OF THE LIBERAL PERSPECTIVE

Political economy is a dynamic field, and the liberal view has evolved over the years as the nature of state–market–societal interaction has changed to reflect changing cultural values and ideas. A critical person in the intellectual development of liberalism was John Stuart Mill (1806–1873), who inherited the liberalism of Smith and Ricardo. His textbook, *Principles of Political Economy with Some of Their Applications to Social Philosophy* (1848) (published the same year as Marx's *The Communist Manifesto*), helped define liberalism for half a century.

Mill held that liberal ideas behind what had emerged as full-blown capitalism in Europe had been an important *destructive* force in the eighteenth century—even if they were also the intellectual foundation of the revolutions and reforms that weakened central authority and strengthened individual liberty in the United States and Europe. He developed a philosophy of social progress based on "moral and spiritual progress rather than the mere accumulation of wealth."[15] Mill doubted the extent to which the competitive process and economic freedom inherent in capitalism would turn the most powerful human motive—the pursuit of self-interest—into the service of society's welfare. At the time, many people were working in factories but living in much more wretched conditions than those that existed in Smith's and Ricardo's times. Whole families worked six days a week for more than eight hours a day. Many were routinely laid off with little notice.

Mill acknowledged the problems created by the market's inherent inequality of outcomes. He proposed that to achieve social progress, the state *should take* definitive action to supplement the market, correcting for its failures or weaknesses. He advocated *selective* state action in some areas, such as educating children and assisting the poor, when individual initiative might be inadequate in promoting social welfare. In general, Mill supported as much decentralization as was consistent with reasonable efficiency; the slogan was "centralize information, decentralize power." He believed parents had a duty to educate their children, and might be legally compelled to do so, but it was obviously intolerable to make them pay for this education if they were already poor. It was also dangerous for the state to take over education as a centralized activity. Thus, some state action—grants for people to pay for private school and the operation of "model schools," for example—was the suggested remedy.[16]

Mill's views on education and other social issues reflect the evolution of liberalism in his time. The guiding principle was still laissez-faire: When in doubt, state interference was to be avoided. However, within a political economy based on the connection of markets to individuals and society, some limited government actions were desirable. The questions for Mill, as for liberal thinkers since his time, are: when, how, and how far is government's *visible* hand justified as an assistant to or replacement for the invisible hand of the market? How far can the state go before its interference with individual rights and liberties is abusive?

JOHN MAYNARD KEYNES AND THE GREAT DEPRESSION

One of the most influential political economists of the twentieth century was John Maynard Keynes (1883–1946)—pronounced "canes," or "keinz" if you are British—who stands out in the evolution of liberalism for developing a subtle and compelling strain of liberalism called the Keynesian theory of economics, or sometimes referred to as **Keynesianism**. Much like Mill who was concerned with the negative impact of markets on society, Keynes's ideas were increasingly popular in the 1930s up through the Great Depression and World War II until the early 1970s. As was the case in the 1930s, in the face of the current financial crisis many experts have become critical of the popular laissez-faire outlook and look back to ideas of Keynes to explain the crisis and provide a variety of solutions to it.

A civil servant, writer, farmer, lecturer, and Director of the Bank of England, Keynes is known for refuting some of the basic principles of economic liberalism. He believed that the Great Depression was evidence that the invisible hand of the market sometimes errs in catastrophic ways. As early as 1926, he wrote:

> Let us clear from the ground the metaphysical or general principles upon which, from time to time, laissez-faire has been founded. It is *not* true that individuals possess a prescriptive "Natural liberty" in their economic activities. There is *no* "compact" conferring perpetual rights on those who Have or on those who Acquire. The world is *not* so governed from above that private and social interest always coincide. . . . Nor is it true that self-interest generally *is* enlightened; more often individuals acting separately to promote their own ends are too ignorant or too weak to attain even these. Experience does *not* show that individuals, when they make up a social unit, are always less clear-sighted than when they act separately.[17]

Keynes suggested that the laissez-faire version of classical liberalism can hardly offer an explanation of booms and busts because according to that model, such disruptions should not even occur. Remember that for OELs the market translates the rational and selfish behavior of individual actors (consumers, workers, firms, etc.) into an outcome that is socially optimal. The market is also seen as a self-correcting institution so that deviations from full employment—something that resulted from an outside "shock" to the system—should set in motion changes in prices, including wages and interest rates, that will quickly restore full employment.

In Keynes's view, the cause of recessions and depressions is that individuals tend to make decisions that are particularly unwise when faced with situations in which the future is *uncertain* and there is no effective way to share risks or coordinate otherwise chaotic actions. Keynes emphasizes that it *is* possible for individuals to behave rationally and in their individual self-interest and yet for the *collective result* to be both irrational and destructive—a clear failure of the invisible hand. The stock market crash of 1929, the Asian crisis of 1997, and the current global financial crisis demonstrate what can happen when investors are spooked and stampede out of the market (see Chapter 8).

In these conditions, people often predict a very bleak future or at least find it difficult to "think rationally" about the future, leading to what Keynes calls a **paradox of thrift**. What is the rational thing to do when one is threatened by unemployment? One rational response to uncertainty about your future income is to spend less and save more, to build up a cushion of funds in case you need them later (just as many people are doing today in the financial crisis). But if everyone spends less, then less is purchased, less is produced, fewer workers are needed, and income declines. Furthermore, the recession and unemployment that everyone feared *will* come to pass is in fact *sustained* by the very actions that individuals took to protect themselves from this eventuality. Keynes also worried about speculation in the international economy and the damage it could do if it was not regulated in some fashion. These conditions, then, make financial markets fragile and prone to economic disaster.

For Keynes, the solution is to combine state and market influences in a way that, in the spirit of Adam Smith, still relies on the invisible hand but supports a *larger but still limited* sphere of constructive state action. For Keynes, to offset its collective irrationality, society should direct "intelligence through some appropriate organ of action over many of the inner intricacies of private business, yet it would leave private initiative and enterprise unhindered."[18] That appropriate organ is the state. According to Keynes, the problem was to "work out a social organization which shall be as efficient as possible without offending our notions of a satisfactory way of life."[19]

During the Great Depression, many states used a combination of monetary and fiscal policy to sustain wages for labor and to stimulate economic growth. Because businesses were afraid to invest, instead of worrying about inflation, states temporarily ran a deficit so as to encourage production and consumption. In the United States, President Franklin Roosevelt adopted many other Keynesian policy suggestions including public works projects to stimulate employment, unemployment insurance, bank deposit insurance to improve investor confidence in banks, and social security.

Keynes also made clear that the state should use its power to improve the market, but *not* along the aggressive, nationalistic lines of mercantilism. He worried that under the strain of the Great Depression people could easily turn toward an ideology like Fascism or Nazism for solutions to their problems. He found communism and the Soviet regime repressive and their disregard for individual freedom intolerable. In contrast to his archrival Hayek, Keynes argued that a liberal system is one that respects individual freedom, not one that limits it for the sake of security. Much like Adam Smith, he argued that economics is a tool *not* to be divorced from issues related to how it can serve society. Beyond all else, Keynes was a moral humanist who wanted to get beyond the problem of accumulating wealth, which he viewed as "a somewhat disgusting morbidity," to a society where most people could instead spend their leisure time contemplating and living a good life.

The Keynesian Compromise: Reconciling State and International Interests

Keynes is also noted for the role he played in helping to reconstruct Western Europe after World War II and establishing the new international economic order. At a meeting of the Allied nations at Bretton Woods, New Hampshire, in 1944 two new institutions were created to manage the postwar economy: the IMF and the World Bank. Three years later, the General Agreement on Tariffs and Trade (GATT) was created to manage international trade. Keynes headed the British delegation, and the institutional result, though not his plan, certainly reflected many of his ideas.

One of the problems that arose from the meeting was how to square two objectives the Allies agreed were necessary to restore stability and economic growth to the international economy while helping states recover from the war. On the one hand, Keynes believed that on the domestic front positive government action was both useful and necessary to deal with problems the invisible hand did not solve. At the same time, he himself envisioned a liberal or open international system in which market forces and free-trade policies would play major roles in each state's foreign economic policy objectives. The **Keynesian compromise** was the idea that management of the international economy would be conducted through peaceful cooperation of states represented in the three Bretton Woods institutions based on embedded (entrenched) Keynesian ideas about the international political economy. States would work to *gradually* reduce their state regulatory policies so as to open their national economies as they recovered and became more competitive. The result was that domestic trade protection and capital controls became accepted exceptions to economic liberal polices in international negotiations.

The Keynesian flavor of **embedded liberalism**—strong international markets subject to social and political restraints and regulations reflecting domestic priorities—became the mainstream IPE view in the industrialized world from the 1930s into the 1970s, as many industrialized nations used state power to supplement, strengthen, and stabilize the market economy within the liberal Bretton Woods system of international institutions. In the early days of the Cold War, the international economy opened slowly generating a tremendous amount of economic productivity and growth. The mid-1960s were regarded as a "golden age" of steady economic growth in both the United States and Western Europe. In places such as Great Britain, France, West Germany, Sweden, and other nations, the role of the state was emphasized to a greater degree, creating something akin to a democratic-socialist system. In the United States, state policy became much more activist than in previous decades. The U.S. federal government played a very active role in the economy at home and abroad through such varied areas as space exploration, promoting civil rights, implementing the Great Society antipoverty programs, helping the elderly with Medicare medical insurance, and regulating business.

Many political economists argue that this post–World War II system worked well because the United States covered many of the expenses associated with maintaining the global monetary system and providing for the defense that each of the allies would have had to pay for alone. As a result, Japan and Western Europe could spend more for their recovery while benefiting from a system of open trade, sound money, and peace and security that stimulated the growth of markets everywhere. More generally, **hegemonic stability theory** is the idea that international markets work best when a **hegemon** (a single dominant state) accepts the costs associated with keeping them open for the benefit of both itself and its allies by providing them with certain international **public goods** at its own expense.[20]

But as time went on, U.S., West European, and Japanese interests changed, and as they did, hegemony gradually became more expensive for all involved to sustain (or put up with depending on one's perspective). By the late 1960s, states were driven by their domestic agendas to either sustain or increase the protection of their industries and growing economies. Economic growth gradually shifted wealth and power away from the United States and toward Western Europe and Japan, changing the fundamental (cooperative) relationship of the United States to its allies. At the same time, the United States felt strongly that the costs of fighting the war in Vietnam were becoming prohibitive without more allied financial and political support. It became more difficult to keep the international trade, monetary, and financial systems open.

THE RESURGENCE OF CLASSICAL LIBERALISM

In the late 1960s, President Nixon and others attacked Keynesianism and the cost of President Johnson's Great Society program, seeking to put more emphasis on economic growth instead of stability. As discussed in Chapter 7, in 1973 the United States replaced its fixed exchange rate system with a flexible exchange rate system, which led to increased speculation on currencies and more money circulating in the international economy. That same year Organization of the Petroleum Exporting Countries (OPEC) oil price hikes led to an economic recession in the industrialized nations, but also massive amounts of OPEC's earnings recycled back into Western banks. Meanwhile, many Western European states, Japan, Brazil, Taiwan, and South Korea were competing with the United States for new trade markets. Keynesian policies to deal with the recession generated stagflation—the coexistence of low growth and high inflation, which were not supposed to occur together.

In this environment of low economic growth and increasing competitiveness, Keynes's ideas were gradually replaced by those of the Austrian Friedrich Hayek

(1899–1992) and Milton Friedman (1912–2006). Their more orthodox economic liberal policy ideals and values featured "minimally fettered" capitalism—or a *limited* state role in the economy. These increasingly popular ideas laid the intellectual groundwork for what became a distinct variation of liberalism, otherwise known as economic liberalism or **neoliberalism.**

Hayek's most influential work, *The Road to Serfdom*, explored growing state influence that he felt represented a fundamental threat to individual liberty. In his view, the growing role of government to provide greater economic security was nothing more than the first step on a slippery slope to socialism or fascism. He warned against reliance on "national planners" who promised to create economic utopias by supplanting competition with a government-directed system of production, pricing, and redistribution. Drawing on older theories of economic liberalism, Hayek argued that the only way to have security *and* freedom was to limit the role of government and draw security from the opportunity the market provides to free individuals.

Contrasting the "collectivist" ideas of socialism with the virtues of an economy with real freedom, he wrote:

> The virtues which are held less and less in esteem . . . are precisely those on which Anglo-Saxons justly prided themselves and in which they were generally recognized to excel. These virtues were independence and self-reliance, individual initiative and local responsibility, the successful reliance on voluntary activity, noninterference with one's neighbor and tolerance of the different, and a healthy suspicion of power and authority. Almost all the traditions and institutions which . . . have molded the national character and the whole moral climate of England and America are those which the progress of collectivism and its centralistic tendencies are progressively destroying.[21]

Known for his support of monetarism, Hayek warned that when a state overspends or prints too much money, it can easily destroy an economy.[22] He chided social democrats for being unwilling to recognize that the price of a large welfare system is more government debt. A healthy economy requires that the state not interfere in private economic decisions. Instead of worrying about employment, the state should balance its budget, manage the money supply to control inflation, and encourage people to save. To do so requires taking control of the money supply out of the hands of politicians—lest liberty be lost when the majority pressures the government to spend more than it has.

Echoing Hayek's foundation, Milton Friedman wrestled with the problem of keeping government from becoming a "Frankenstein that would destroy the very freedom we establish it to protect." According to Friedman, government "is an instrument through which we can exercise our freedom; yet by concentrating power in political hands, it is also a threat to *freedom*."[23] In his book *Capitalism and Freedom*, he consciously returns to the classical liberalism of Adam Smith. Friedman stresses the classical liberal view that the market preserves and protects liberty. A state that takes its citizens' freedom through anything more than absolutely necessary action is no better than one that seizes their freedom guided by mercantilist, socialist, or fascist notions of security. Capitalism, with its free competitive market, naturally diffuses power and so preserves freedom.

Many of Hayek's and Friedman's ideas are echoed in the views of contemporary economic liberals like Paul Ryan, the 2012 Republican vice-presidential candidate in the United States. Writing in the conservative *Wall Street Journal*, Ryan argues that high-taxing, high-spending, highly indebted European states should not serve as models for good government. Rather, he believes that American freedom could best be ensured by, among other things, limiting the size of the state and relying on "families, communities, churches and local institutions—and [on] the government only as a last resort."[24] "Paternalistic government," Ryan asserts, "will stand in the way of the pursuit of happiness and the good life."

REAGAN, THATCHER, AND THE NEOLIBERALS

In the early 1980s, the classical economic liberal view of IPE reasserted itself even more forcefully through a movement called neoliberalism. Prime Minister Margaret Thatcher of Great Britain and U.S. President Ronald Reagan were the chief practitioners of policies that owed much more to Smith, Hayek, and Friedman than to Mill or Keynes. Thatcher's motto was TINA—"There Is No Alternative" to economic liberal policies.

Neoliberalism emphasizes economic growth over stability. President Reagan promoted "supply-side economics," which is the idea that lower taxes instead of increased spending by government would increase the money supply and generate its own demand, unleashing capital to businesses and consumers. The top income tax rate in the United States was cut in stages from 70 percent in 1980 to 33 percent in 1986.

Other features of **Reaganomics** (as it was popularly known then) were *deregulation* of banking, energy, investment, and trade markets (i.e., promoting free trade). Many national telecommunications, airline, and trucking industries were *privatized* (sold off to wealthy individuals or corporations) to allow for greater competition and freedom to set prices. Some public housing in Britain was privatized, and welfare programs in both the United States and Great Britain were "rolled back" (shrunk). Many neoliberals argued that the state was too big and not to be trusted. Echoing Smith, they maintained that its interests reflected powerful special interests, whereas the market was a neutral tool that redistributes income to those who are most efficient, innovative, and hard working. Although these policies might lead to greater income inequality, economic growth at the top of society would gradually "trickle down" to benefit labor and society's masses. Finally, the rule of thumb for both popular leaders was that the state was to minimally interfere in all areas of public policy except security, where both advocated a strong anticommunist stance.

As we discussed in Chapter 1, in the mid-1980s the United States began promoting globalization—the extension of economic liberal principles the world over—as a process that would expand economic growth and bring democracy to those nations integrated into this capitalist structure. Emphasizing the role of *unfettered* markets (unchained by the state), globalization promised to enhance production efficiency, spread new technologies and communication systems, and generate jobs in response to increased demand.

An integrated global economy was also expected to benefit millions of people trapped in poverty in developing nations. In the late 1980s, the "Washington Consensus" about the benefits of economic liberal policies and their connection to democracy was promoted in the policies of the General Agreement on Tariffs and Trade (GATT), the International Monetary Fund (IMF), and the World Bank. The success of these laissez-faire policies in the United States and Great Britain, combined with the collapse of communism in Eastern Europe in 1990, led some leaders in the faster-growing developing economies in Southeast Asia and Latin America to support more market-friendly policies. Most of the ex-communist regimes of Eastern Europe replaced centralized, inefficient state planning with more market-oriented development strategies.

THE 1990s AND 2000s: NEOLIBERALISM AND GLOBALIZATION UNDER ATTACK

Many attribute the global economic recovery after 1992 to deregulation and privatization, which became widespread policies in most parts of the world. It became commonplace to read that neoliberalism was practically and theoretically "triumphant." The Clinton administration continued to emphasize neoliberal ideas, negotiating a plethora of free-trade deals such as North American Free Trade Agreement (NAFTA) and helping create the WTO (see Chapter 6). Neoliberal-style capitalism and open markets continued to be directly linked to U.S. economic and military interests. Some Central and Eastern Europe states became members of the European Union's single market. Mexico, India, and China all adopted pro-market "reforms," encouraged foreign investment, and massively boosted trade with the United States.

However, in the mid-1990s, neoliberalism encountered increasing criticism, especially by anti-globalization protestors who accused it of causing violations of human rights, damaging the environment, depriving poorer countries of effective representation in international economic organizations, and fostering sweatshops in developing countries. Mass anti-globalization protests in major cities—capped by the "Battle of Seattle" in the spring of 1999—demonstrated that many civil society groups had lost faith in laissez-faire capitalism. Major recessions in Mexico in 1994, Russia in 1996, and throughout much of Southeast and East Asia in 1997 and 1998 led many officials in developing countries to question the merits of weakening regulations and encouraging massive capital flows across borders. Critics also noted that globalization had failed to deliver a more peaceful world, as evidenced by violent conflicts in and around the former Soviet Union and the spread of unconventional wars in "failed states" like Somalia and the Democratic Republic of the Congo. And yet overall support for globalization among Western policy makers, business elites, and economists remained strong.

By the mid-2000s, some public officials and intellectual *supporters* of globalization began to address potential problems with rapid, unregulated globalization. A good number of these critics were *not* inherently opposed to economic liberal ideas, but merely wanted today's IPE to be *managed better*. For example, Joseph Stiglitz, the former chief economist of the World Bank and Nobel Prize winner in Economics, has criticized IMF policies for making it difficult for many developing nations to get out of debt and benefit from globalization.[25] Economist Dani Rodrik has pointed out that too much economic integration, free trade, and unfettered capital flows pose a threat to democratic politics. Markets, he argues, have to be "embedded in non-market institutions in order to work well."[26] They will not be viewed as legitimate unless they reflect individual countries' national values, social understandings, and political realities such as voters' unwillingness to accept rampant inequality and limits on sovereignty.

Thomas Friedman, whose influential 2005 book *The World Is Flat* was something of a paean to globalization, also began to address some problems with neoliberalism—especially environmental damage. While acknowledging that open markets and technological change are bringing unprecedented opportunities for the rise of new middle classes in China and India, in his 2008 book *Flat, Hot and Crowded* Friedman deals with the costs due to loss of biodiversity, climate change, and energy shortages. Sounding more like a mercantilist, he suggests that governments need to create incentives for technological innovation leading to widespread renewable energy.[27] In fact, in a chapter called "China for a Day (But Not for Two)," he muses that the United States should have a day of authoritarian government to force the country to adopt good energy policies and energy efficiency standards—and then revert back to democracy and free-market capitalism!

Another scholar who recognizes unsustainable consequences of global neoliberalism is David Colander, an economist at Middlebury College. He argues that in a global economy, the operation of what economists call the "law of one price" means that wages and prices in the world *in the long run* would become more equalized as technology and capital spread more production and outsourcing to other countries. As a result, the United States would gain less and less from trade, wages would inevitably go down, and growth would decline as the United States loses its comparative advantage in most industries. Moreover, Colander believes that trade and outsourcing—which have benefited the majority *in the short run*—will soon cause the United States "to enter into a period of long-run relative structural decline, which will be marked by economic malaise and a continued loss of good jobs."[28]

And even liberal development economists by the mid-2000s were starting to acknowledge the problems that neoliberalism either caused or seemed to be incapable of solving in developing countries. Former World Bank economist William Easterly criticizes Western institutions for promoting policies and doling out foreign aid that utterly failed to help the poorest countries get out of poverty. The UN, the World Bank, the IMF, and others were imposing market-based policies on countries that lacked the social and political institutions like good government, accountable leaders, and uncorrupt courts to actually make markets work properly.[29] Easterly argues that poor countries need to be allowed to develop their own institutions to support a market system, even using protectionism and relying on innovative NGOs.

From a different angle, former World Bank director of research Paul Collier defends globalization for creating huge opportunities for about four billion people in developing countries. Yet, at the same time he criticizes it for leaving a billion people stuck in a poverty trap. This bottom billion is stymied by political, economic, and geographical problems that markets alone cannot overcome: civil war, natural resource abundance that undermines democracy, and being landlocked.

Instead of more globalization as the way out, Collier advocates some decidedly state interventionist help: military intervention in some failed states to restore order, allowing temporary trade protection, and setting up new international charters to promote norms and standards (through international pressure) that help reformers in the poorest countries.[30]

Thus, by the mid-2000s, a unique confluence of economic liberal scholars and anti-globalization activists pointed to the mounting problems and unintended consequences of neoliberal-inspired globalization. They proposed different solutions but shared the idea that the global economy needed some kind of better regulation and governance. Without always explicitly saying so, they recognized the idea that markets need to be embedded in social and political institutions in order to have legitimacy and to resolve fundamental human problems. In the short run, unfettered global markets failed to help the world's poorest and were destroying the environment. In the long run, through outsourcing and environmental degradation, they might even undermine the prosperity of those developed countries that uncritically worshipped them. It would take the global financial crisis that started in 2007 to convince policy makers that neither more globalization nor incremental, piecemeal reforms to globalization were enough to save economies from the tsunami of contradictions that neoliberalism had created.

The Financial Crisis: A Stake in the Heart or Just a Scratch?

This section focuses on the ideological debate between OELs and HILs, and not the specifics of the financial crisis itself. Before reading this section, instructors and students may want to read the more detailed coverage of the crisis in Chapter 8.

While there had been many grumblings about neoliberal globalization, no single event in recent history has seemingly undermined economic liberalism as much as has the recent financial crisis, which produced the most severe economic collapse since the Great Depression. At one particular moment in time the public could hear the hammer drive the stake further into the gap between laissez-faire and market interventionist supporters when the shaken former Chairman of the Federal Reserve Alan Greenspan gave testimony before the U.S. Congress in October 2008. He admitted that his faith in the self-regulating nature of financial markets had been misplaced—that "those of us who have looked to the self-interest of lending institutions to protect shareholders' equity, myself included, are in a state of shocked disbelief."[31] Greenspan also admitted that he made a "big mistake" and blamed his state of incredulity on a "flaw in the (economic) model" that defines how the world works.

The deep global recession seemed to shake the faith of even some of the most ardent proponents of free market capitalism. Before the crisis, Greenspan himself regularly assured Congress that financial markets and new complex financial instruments (derivatives) were self-regulating, and that rational, profit-maximizing financial actors would take all necessary precautions to ensure that excessive risk-taking and insufficient due diligence (regarding mortgage lending) would not be tolerated (although in 1996 he had famously cautioned about "irrational exuberance" in the stock market).

In retrospect, it appears that many banks and investment firms in capital deficit countries such as the United States and in parts of the European Union were more than willing to *incur excessive economic risk*, and that many institutions, state officials, and individuals egged them on. In fact, in an environment of free-wheeling "wildcat" capitalism, the beauty of high-yielding types of investments was that the original investors *profited* handsomely from the original deals they made, while the *risks* associated with these types of instruments were spread out to new investors and mortgage holders.[32] These schemes actually worked and made purchasing an expensive asset seem reasonable and reinforcing, virtually institutionalizing excessive risk-taking.

Until the financial crisis, many U.S. and British officials felt that the state should have a laissez-faire outlook of limited regulation and essentially let the banks police themselves. Today, many state officials and experts the world over have suggested that they had no recourse but to bail out their banks and other financial institutions. Certainly, Presidents Bush and Obama have believed it; neither felt he could afford the possibility of being wrong because the political and economic stakes were so high. Their drastic measures were not so much to save greedy and unethical bank officials whose improprieties generated huge profits for their institutions, but to stabilize the financial system and correct the policies that threatened to destroy it. For the most part the debate about state regulation of major banks and other financial institutions remains centered on who should do the bailing out and how much money should be spent on it.

So how did this happen? Why did banks take on so much risk? How could the ideas associated with neoliberalism that had proved to be scientifically correct and so popular seem to go down in flames? Or have they? In this section, we examine some of the connections between neoliberal theories, globalization, and the financial crisis.

An Outdated Economic Theory and Ideology

As noted earlier, Keynes was adamant that markets are prone to failure, with the Great Depression being a prime example of that reality. Since his time, many governments became better at dealing with smaller recessions that were considered a normal part of the business cycle. Using a variety of fiscal and monetary tools, they could tinker with supply and demand to right the economy through choppy waters. Milton Friedman and other monetarists associated with the so-called Chicago School emphasized that the nation's money supply was the key to inflation and that the market is a self-correcting mechanism. A companion theory, the "Efficient Market Hypothesis," claimed that "at every moment, *shares price themselves* in the market through attracting the input of all information relevant to their value."[33]

Policies based on these outlooks about the validity of free markets complemented by weak state deregulation seemed to work for some time in the developed countries. Fed chairman Greenspan criticized excessive state regulation of banks, and together with investors seemed to view recessions in the United States as a thing of the past. Furthermore, he and many banking institutions also seemed to regard investments by other nations in the United States—which helped finance

U.S. spending and trade deficits—as evidence of the correctness of an ideology that had spread throughout the international economy.

In the crisis aftermath, the economic liberal news journal *The Economist* uncharacteristically accused the "dismal science" of economics of being "seduced by their models" that are, however, full of holes, especially when it comes to quantifying fundamentals such as preferences, technology, and resources that do not fit the real world. Essentially, these models assume an equilibrium in markets when in fact (as Keynes maintained) many markets exhibit uncertainties (or disequilibrium). The result has been a focus on mathematical and deductive methods that encourage the belief that risk can be carefully managed. While these ideas have sounded simplistic, they have also been confusing—and "policymakers often fall back on highest order principles and broadest presumptions."[34] According to *The Economist*, macroeconomists in academia and within central banks have been too preoccupied with fighting inflation and too cavalier about recurring asset bubbles in markets.

In effect, some argue that free market theorists have underestimated distortions in markets, overestimated markets' ability to self-adjust, and failed to account for the long-term problems resulting from markets' short-term incentives. They have also suggested that the financial crises could shake up the discipline of economics and force it to rethink some of its basic scientific assumptions. However, indications are that it has not done very much yet. A recent study of economic curricula points to the entrenchment of rational-choice assumptions and a bias toward teaching the benefits of free markets.[35] Of course, many OEL-oriented faculty defend their discipline and offer alternative interpretations of market theory.[36]

In the face of such a major meltdown in the global financial system, why have laissez-faire ideas remained popular outside academia? Scholars have offered several possible answers to this question, as noted below.

First, behavioral economist Robert Schiller suggests that politicians and officials in the finance and business sectors—as in other professions—suffer from "group think." They tend to think alike, which is part of the reason for the entrenchment of theories that are slow to change. Second, laissez-faire policies have been much easier to understand as opposed to the "messy" role of politics, social values, and civil society in determining the appropriate distribution of resources both inside and between countries. Many believe that "letting the market decide" public policy is a correct and simple recommendation based on an "objective" study of the market.

Third, free market models have focused on economic growth instead of social stability and relative equality of income distribution. Ironically, the *promise* of greater wealth, faster growth, better jobs, and cheaper prices has been easier for the public (i.e., the masses) to buy into than the alternatives of higher taxes for more social programs, slower growth for environmental sustainability, and collective sacrifice today to benefit future generations.

Fourth, laissez-faire policies are heavily promoted by the wealthy, who dominate the media and fund political parties throughout the industrialized democracies. Simon Johnson, a former Chief Economist for the IMF, labels the private firms and actors who call the shots in Washington a "financial oligarchy"—an interconnected group of politically powerful people who move back and forth between Wall Street and Washington (and some university offices), "amassing a kind of cultural capital—a belief" that "large financial institutions and free-flow-ing capital markets were crucial to America's position in the world."[37] Chrystia Freeland, a global editor at Reuters, describes the same group and its global coun-terparts as a "plutocracy"—a class of super-rich oligarchs benefitting from tax breaks, government subsidies, and taxpayer-financed bailouts.[38] As portrayed by *Rolling Stone* blogger-reporter Matt Taibbi and by Charles Ferguson, director of the Academy Award-winning documentary *Inside Job*, the finance executives and lobbyists that make up part of this class have orchestrated a culture of corruption both on Wall Street and in Washington that serves their interests at the expense of the public.[39]

We Are All Keynesians Now (Again! At Least for a While?)

The financial crisis has brought to the fore a division between economic liberals. In this section, we contrast some of their arguments to demonstrate the rich-ness of the debate, the different views about the role of the state and globaliza-tion, and the re-emergence of Keynesian thought among HILs. For most HILs, Keynes has been a key figure because he explained uncertainty—exclusive of rational expectations—and justified efforts to manage the economy in such a way as to serve the broader interest of society instead of the wealthy. The crisis has led HILs to assert that states must act to save the financial system and even capitalism itself. Interestingly, some OELs agree. For example, in a *Financial Times* piece titled "The Seeds of Its Own Destruction," the OEL Martin Wolf acknowledges that "the era of financial liberalization has ended and that the state can be expected to play a bigger role in rescuing banks and adopting other interventionist measures."[40]

A few of the most often discussed HIL proposals (discussed in more detail in Chapter 8) are as follows:

- Spend more to grow the economy, without worrying too much about infla-tion. It is more important to create jobs.
- Invest more in new technology for energy and transportation, infrastructure, education, and health care.
- Impose tougher regulations on banks related to derivatives, deposit require-ments, pay, and bonuses.
- Break up big banks to increase competition.
- Better manage globalization, but without stopping it.

Most HILs agree on the need to increase government spending and expand the powers of existing regulatory institutions at the national and international levels. As Keynes would suggest, the financial system requires a sophisticated and effec-tive regulatory and legal framework that only the state can provide—a state strong enough to enforce those laws but without stifling the profit motive, economic free-dom, and individual liberty.

Most HILs are *not* opposed to globalization per se, but would like to see policies and programs that redistribute more wealth to the masses in industrialized nations and poorer people in developing nations. They recognize the need to reform institutions like the World Bank, the IMF, and the WTO to get away from a "one-size-fits-all mentality" of how economies should be run and of what rules countries have to follow. Related to this is a new emphasis on creating "policy space" for developing countries (at least in the short run) to be more protectionist, restrict capital flows somewhat, and have more lax rules on intellectual property rights. Presumably, this will allow them to grow faster and buffer them somewhat from global instabilities in currencies, investment flows, and commodity prices. HILs note that China and India have fared much better during the financial crisis precisely because these two have *not* fully adopted neoliberalism.

HILs also believe that the developed countries must actively help developing countries in ways they have not before. They emphasize that developed countries need to drop their remaining protectionist barriers to key LDC exports like textiles and agricultural goods and stop subsidizing their own industries. They need to allow more immigration from poorer countries. It would also be in their interest to forgive excessive debt held by poorer countries and increase foreign aid massively. HILs favor inducing countries to adopt more free market reform and democracy by offering them assistance rather than pressuring them.

Many HILs are open to the possibility of creating a different economy and social system, something that shifts the state–market formula to the left—akin to social democracies in Western Europe (see the "Ordoliberalism" box). A number of HIL scholars have found that Nordic countries and other nations that have some of the highest openness to the international economy (measured by the ratio of trade to GDP) also have some of the highest public expenditures on social programs (measured by the ratio of spending to GDP). This suggests, contrary to OELs, that high government spending is compatible with being open to and benefiting from global market participation. HILs also tend to accept—and even justify—the maintenance of different models of national capitalism within a broader global free market economy. Coordination between these different national systems of capitalism is more important than harmonizing all of their institutions and policies. In other words, when it comes to designing global institutions and rules, Dani Rodrik stresses the need for maintaining "escape clauses" and "opt-outs" so that individual countries can benefit from globalization in a way that is most consistent with their political realities, cultural needs, and resource constraints.[41]

As HILs have adopted a more nuanced set of assumptions about global state–market relations, OELs have been less accepting of this foray back into Keynesianism. The Obama administration sided more with HILs than OELs by adopting regulations so that the system could not "go back to the way it was." Why? It may be that the president feared a backlash in the 2012 election if he did nothing to reform Wall Street. And a number of Democratic lawmakers share his interventionist views. However, many powerful Congresspeople and members of the financial sector remain OEL-oriented. Alex Berenson goes even deeper to suggest that Americans are by nature "basically conservative people" who distrust the state, but who also have an "appetite for risk."[42] While Europeans might prefer social democracy, wealthy elites in the United States prefer a wilder version of capitalism.[43] Also distasteful to most Americans are the

ORDOLIBERALISM AND THE SOCIAL MARKET ECONOMY[a]

Economic liberalism had been largely discredited in Europe by the 1920s. Economic liberalism, particularly in Germany's post–World War I Weimar Republic, had come to be associated with economic chaos, political corruption, and the exploitation of the working class.[b] In response to this perception and to Hitler's consequent rise to power, a small group of academics at Freiburg University developed a new conception of liberalism they called *ordoliberalism*. Walter Eucken (1891–1950), Franz Böhm (1895–1977), and Hans Grossman-Doerth (1894–1944) founded this school of thought. Ordoliberals believe that the failings of liberalism resulted from the failure of nineteenth- and twentieth-century *laissez-faire* policy makers to appreciate Adam Smith's insight that the market is embedded in legal and political systems.

Ordoliberal thought reflects the humanist values of classical liberalism, including the protection of human dignity and personal freedom. Ordoliberals espouse the classical liberal notions that private decision making should guide resource allocation, that competition is the source of economic well-being, and that economic and political freedom are inextricable. Like classical liberals, they also believe that individuals must be protected from excessive state power and that political power should be dispersed through democratic processes that maximize participation in public decision making. Ordoliberals also emphasize that individual freedoms must be protected from private power in the form of monopoly control of markets and influence used to create special privileges that rig markets in favor of those dominant firms.

Ordoliberals believe that the market process will support and promote liberal values only if appropriate rules governing the market process (property law, contract law, trade law, competition policy, etc.) are established by the state. *Ordo*, from the Latin, means "order." The rules governing the market process should be "constitutional" rules immune from political manipulation that reflect the shared liberal values of society. With such a

framework in place, the market process will reinforce the economic and political freedoms so central to the liberal conception of the good society. With such a framework in place, the efforts of powerful firms to subvert the market process (via price controls, import restrictions, subsidies, restrictive licenses, etc.) will be deemed "unconstitutional." Politicians will be in a strong position to resist the special pleadings of powerful interest groups, and the power of the state in general to influence market outcomes will be severely restricted. A privilege-free economy will be the highly desirable result.

Ordoliberal thought has had a profound influence on economic and political policy in the European Union. Current European competition policy clearly incorporates ordoliberal principles. It severely restricts the behavior of dominant firms—particularly, any practices that might inhibit the entry of small- or medium-sized rivals. By maintaining open markets, European competition authorities hope to foster economic freedom in the form of freedom of entry, thereby enhancing economic opportunity, promoting competition, and diffusing economic and political power. Microsoft's antitrust problems in Europe can be better understood in this light.[c]

Ordoliberalism does have an inherent ethical stance. Market outcomes generated within an appropriate legal and political framework are nondiscriminating, privilege-free outcomes and are likely to be just outcomes.[d] Ordoliberals recognize, however, that some income redistribution will likely be called for, given the limited productivity of some individuals—often due to circumstances beyond their control.

Other German intellectuals, principally Alfred Müller-Armack (1901–1978), accepted key ordoliberal principles but challenged the ordoliberal notion that market outcomes are just outcomes. Müller-Armack argued that supplemental "social" policies are necessary to ensure that market outcomes will indeed be consistent with a "good" society. Further, these supplementary rules might indeed affect specific market outcomes so as to privilege certain segments of society. Müller-Armack is credited with developing the basis of the "social" market economy that characterizes many modern European states.[e]

References

[a]Ross Singleton is the author of this text box.
[b]The discussion of ordoliberalism in this and the following paragraphs is based largely on David J. Gerber, "Constitutionalizing the Economy: German Neo-Liberalism, Competition Policy and the 'New' Europe," *The American Journal of Comparative Law*, 42 (1994), pp. 25–88.
[c]"Microsoft on Trial," *The Economist*, April 28, 2006, www.economist.com/agenda/displaystory.cfm?story_id=E1_GRSDSRP.
[d]Victor J. Vanberg, "The Freiburg School: Walter Eucken and Ordoliberalism," Walter Eucken Institute, Freiburg Discussion Papers on Constitutional Economics, November 2004, p. 2.
[e]Ibid.

populist-socialist regimes in Venezuela, Bolivia, Chile, and Ecuador that have made a wider distribution of goods and services to the masses one of their key political objectives.

In light of these factors and others, OELs prefer to keep the main laissez-faire characteristics of the free market, subject to a few, more passive reforms. They propose to

- limit government support for banks, infrastructure projects, and social welfare programs;
- decrease regulation of many parts of the economy;
- cut taxes of the wealthy and middle class to stimulate economic growth;
- foster *more* globalization, which is good for the United States and the world.

When it comes to the financial crisis, many OELs argue that it was the fault of government, not banks. The Federal Reserve created the housing bubble beginning in 2001 by dropping interest rates that decreased the cost of borrowing. This put more money into the hands of homebuyers who could not afford payments in the long run. OELs also argue that the crisis was an exceptional event in the history of capitalism, one that occurs very infrequently—due more to flaws in human nature than flaws in capitalism itself.

Globalization has also proved to be a good thing, given the growth it produced in the industrialized states and the number of people it has lifted out of poverty in developing nations. OELs would like to see the United States push for a resumption of the Doha Round trade negotiations to lower more trade barriers in agriculture, services, and government procurement. They also believe that the United States needs to cut its budget deficit, with the goal of reducing the trade deficit and increasing national savings. They fear that big stimulus spending by world governments will generate inflation and more debt that future generations will have to pay off (by consuming less). In addition, OELs want governments to deleverage the commitments they have made to banks and industries, returning bailed out companies and assets to full private control.

Although the economic liberal foundations of capitalism will continue to be intellectually and politically challenged, nothing has so far emerged to replace them, as many fear that the alternatives are potentially worse.

CONCLUSION

This chapter has explained how the ideas and values associated with the economic liberal version of liberalism have changed in recent history to reflect major historical, political, economic, and social developments. Political economists Smith, Ricardo, Mill, Keynes, Hayek, Friedman, and others have debated the relationship of the state to society as capitalism has spread over large parts of the world, profoundly shaping global production and distribution.

During the Great Depression, a split emerged between those HILs who supported a positive role for the state in the economy and those OELs who saw the state's role in the economy and society as decidedly negative. In the 1980s, the chasm widened even more. The Reagan and Thatcher administrations implemented decidedly more OEL-oriented policies, emphasizing economic growth alongside cuts in domestic welfare programs. Globalization and the current financial crisis have led to serious criticisms of neoliberal ideals and neoliberal faith in markets. Many HILs

maintain that some state intervention serves the public interest, especially when it protects social groups and countries from the negative effects of the seemingly Darwinian global economy. OELs believe that austerity will lay a foundation for sustainable recovery.

Both orthodox and heterodox liberals ultimately believe that capitalism is a desirable system to maintain, despite the differences in how they propose to reform globalization and tackle the problems of debt and inequality. In that sense, they both place their faith in the ability of markets to promote the values and interests of most people in the world.

In Chapters 3 and 4, we turn to two other IPE perspectives—mercantilism and structuralism—and present some of the many explanations they offer for these same sorts of theoretical issues and practical dilemmas. As you will see, they believe that painful, periodic crises in capitalism are unavoidable and that unfettered markets will ultimately destroy the earth's ecology.

KEY TERMS

economic liberalism   26
heterodox interventionist
   liberals (HILs)   26
orthodox economic liberals
   (OELs)   26
rent-seeking   31

Corn Laws   32
positive-sum game   34
zero-sum game   34
Keynesianism   35
paradox of thrift   36
Keynesian compromise   37

embedded liberalism   37
hegemonic stability theory   38
hegemon   38
public goods   38
neoliberalism   39
Reaganomics   40

DISCUSSION QUESTIONS

1. What roles do self-interest, competition, and the state play in Adam Smith's views of the market?
2. Is Adam Smith the economic liberal many people assume he is? Explain your answer in a five-sentence paragraph.
3. Explain how the Corn Laws debate in nineteenth-century Britain illustrates the conflict between mercantilist and economic liberal views of international trade. Which side of the debate do you favor? Explain.

4. John Stuart Mill and John Maynard Keynes thought that government could play a positive role in correcting problems in the market. Discuss the specific types of "market failures" that Mill and Keynes perceived and the types of government actions they advocated.
5. Ronald Reagan and Margaret Thatcher are often cited for their support of neoliberalism. Summarize their policies and discuss how they differ from those of their economic liberal predecessors.

Finally, explain why you think they are still popular today. Or are they?

6. Compare and contrast OELs and HILs in terms of values, ideas, and policies. Which do you favor? Explain.

7. Based on what you know about the current financial crisis, do you agree with the suggestion that the crisis has seriously undermined economic liberal ideas and policies? Explain.

SUGGESTED READINGS

Jagdish Bhagwati. *In Defense of Globalization*. Oxford: Oxford University Press, 2005.

Thomas L. Friedman. *The World Is Flat: A Brief History of the Twenty-First Century*. New York: Farrar, Straus and Giroux, 2005.

Robert Skidelsky. *Keynes: The Return of the Master*. New York: Public Affairs, 2009.

Manfred B. Steger. *Globalization: A Brief Insight*. New York, NY: Sterling Publishing, 2010.

Joseph Stiglitz. *Freefall: America, Free Markets, and the Sinking of the World Economy*. New York: W. W. Norton, 2010.

NOTES

1. In this book we use the term "neoconservatives" or "neocons" to refer to members of the George W. Bush administration (and its supporters) who had a decidedly unilateral outlook about the world and U.S. power and capabilities to manage it (see Chapter 9).

2. Ralf Dahrendorf, "Liberalism," in John Eatwell, Murray Milgate, and Peter Newman, eds., *The Invisible Hand: The New Palgrave* (New York: W. W. Norton, 1989), p. 183.

3. Adam Smith, *The Wealth of Nations* (New York: The Modern Library, 1937), p. 400.

4. See Charles Lindblom, *The Market System* (New Haven, CT: Yale University Press, 2001).

5. Karl Polanyi, *The Great Transformation: The Political and Economic Origins of Our Time* (Boston, MA: Beacon Press, 1944).

6. See Smith, *The Wealth of Nations*, p. 114.

7. Ibid., p. 117.

8. Cited in David Leonhardt, "Theory and Morality in the New Economy," *The New York Times Book Review*, August 23, 2009.

9. See Jerry Mueller, *The Mind and the Market: Capitalism in Western Thought* (New York: Anchor Books, 2002), p. 69.

10. Cited in ibid., p 64.

11. Michael W. Doyle, *The Ways of War and Peace* (New York: W. W. Norton, 1997), p. 207.

12. Smith, *The Wealth of Nations,* p. 401.

13. Ibid., p. 410.

14. David Ricardo, *The Principles of Political Economy and Taxation* (London: Dent, 1973), p. 81.

15. Alan Ryan, "John Stuart Mill," in Eatwell et al., eds., *The Invisible Hand*, p. 201.

16. Ibid., p. 208.

17. John Maynard Keynes, "The End of Laissez-Faire," in *Essays in Persuasion* (New York: W.W. Norton, 1963), p. 312.

18. Ibid., pp. 317–318.

19. Ibid., p. 321.

20. U.S. economist Charles Kindleberger is generally credited as the originator of the hegemonic stability theory. See his *Money and Power: The Economics of International Politics and the Politics of International Economics* (New York: Basic Books, 1970).

21. Friedrich Hayek, *The Road to Serfdom* (Chicago, IL: University of Chicago Press, 1944), pp. 127–128.

22. Robert Lekachman and Borin Van Loon, *Capitalism for Beginners* (New York: Pantheon Books, 1981).

23. Milton Friedman, *Capitalism and Freedom* (Chicago, IL: University of Chicago Press, 1962), p. 2.

24. Paul Ryan "America's Enduring Ideal," *Wall Street Journal*, October 1, 2011.

25. See Joseph Stiglitz, *Globalization and Its Discontents* (New York: W. W. Norton, 2002).

26. Dani Rodrik, "Feasible Globalizations," in Michael Weinstein, ed., *Globalization: What's New?* (New York: Columbia University Press, 2005), p. 197.

27. Thomas L. Friedman, *Hot, Flat, and Crowded: Why We Need a Green Revolution—And How It Can Renew America* (New York: Farrar, Straus and Giroux, 2008).

28. David Colander, "The Long Run Consequences of Outsourcing," *Challenge, 48:1* (January/February 2005), p. 94.

29. William Easterly, *The White Man's Burden: Why the West's Efforts to Aid the Rest Have Done So Much Ill and So Little Good* (New York: Penguin Press, 2006).

30. Paul Collier, *The Bottom Billion: Why the Poorest Countries Are Failing and What Can Be Done about It* (Oxford: Oxford University Press, 2007).

31. "Greenspan Concedes Error on Regulation," *New York Times*, B1, October 24, 2008.

32. Robert J. Shiller, *The Subprime Solution: How Today's Global Financial Crisis Happened, and What to Do about It* (Princeton, NJ: Princeton University Press, 2008).

33. See Kevin Phillips, *Bad Money: Reckless Finance, Failed Politics, and the Global Crisis of American Capitalism* (New York: Viking, 2008), p. 74.

34. See "The Other-Worldly Philosophers," *Economist*, July 18, 2009, p. 66.

35. See Patricia Cohen, "Ivory Tower Unswayed by Crashing Economy," *New York Times*, March 4, 2009.

36. See Robert Lucas, "In Defense of the Dismal Science," *Economist*, August 28, 2009.

37. Simon Johnson, "The Quiet Coup," *Atlantic*, May 2008.

38. Chrystia Freeland, *Plutocrats: The Rise of the New Global Rich and the Fall of Everyone Else* (New York: Penguin Press, 2012).

39. See Matt Taibbi's blog at http://www.rollingstone.com/politics/blogs/taibblog; *Inside Job*, directed by Charles Ferguson, Sony Pictures Classics, 2010.

40. Martin Wolf, "Seeds of Its Own Destruction," *Financial Times*, March 8, 2009.

41. Dani Rodrik, *One Economics, Many Recipes: Globalization, Institutions, and Economic Growth* (Princeton, NJ: Princeton University Press, 2007).

42. See Alex Berenson, "How Free Should a Free Market Be?" *New York Times*, October 5, 2008.

43. See Robert Wade, "The Global Slump: Deeper Causes and Harder Lessons," *Challenge, 52:5* (September–October 2009), pp. 5–24.

Wealth and Power: The Mercantilist Perspective

The State Über Alles: Egyptians in front of the Mugamma, a huge government building in Tahrir Square, Cairo, Egypt.

ZUMA Press, Inc./Alamy

Our economic rights are leaking away. . . . If we want to recover these rights . . . we must quickly employ state power to promote industry, use machinery in production, give employment to the workers of the nation. . . .[1]

Sun Yat-sen, 1920

In Chapter 2, we noted how the financial crisis has generated a shift in outlook by many economic liberals toward the view that the state *must* play a bigger role in regulating banks, speculators, and financial markets in general. Governments worry that in the highly integrated global economy, the financial crisis threatens their state's national security by undermining their ability to secure themselves physically and psychologically against a variety of political and economic threats. They are also concerned about their capacity to deal with many of the unacceptable political and social costs of the crisis such as unemployment, the loss of health care, and damage to the environment.

Mercantilism is the oldest and psychologically most deeply embedded of the three IPE perspectives. It accounts for one of the basic compulsions of all people and nation-states: to create and sustain wealth and power in order to preserve and protect the nation's security and independence from any number of real and imagined threats. Historically, **classical mercantilism** connoted efforts by states to promote exports and limit imports, thereby generating trade surpluses that would strengthen the nation while protecting certain groups within society.

Realism is closely related to mercantilism in that it also emphasizes state efforts to achieve security (which are explored in more detail in Chapter 9). While mercantilists usually focus on economic threats to a country, realists emphasize a wider variety of physical threats—and encourage the use of both military and economic instruments to deter attacks on it. Of course, in a globalized political economy, it gets harder all the time to separate economic from military threats to nation-states. Today, **neomercantilism** accounts for a more complex world marked by intensive interdependence where states use a wider variety of instruments—especially economic ones—to protect their societies.

In this chapter, we explore many of the political-philosophical ideas associated with classical mercantilism, realism, and neomercantilism. The chapter follows a chronology that covers how and why mercantilist ideas evolved from the sixteenth century until today. We then discuss a number of neomercantilist policies related to the debate about how much the state should or should not interfere in markets in the face of globalization and the recent financial crisis.

We stress five theses in this chapter. First, historically, mercantilism is rooted in individuals' and states' desire for protection. Second, the history of mercantilism demonstrates that states have always been compelled to regulate markets, and that there are no beneficial effects of markets without the state's willingness to allow, sustain, and manage them. Third, states that pursue economic liberal objectives that include opening markets and promoting free trade do so when those objectives coincide with national interests. Fourth, paradoxically, globalization has *not* reduced the compulsion of states to protect themselves as economic liberals suggested it would. Rather, globalization has actually further *entrenched* national insecurities due to the increased tensions and conflicts it generates. Finally, mercantilists argue that states are finding it hard to cooperate with one another and with other global actors to solve problems such as the recent financial crisis.

MERCANTILISM AS HISTORY AND PHILOSOPHY

The history of mercantilism varies a good deal from that of economic liberal history (see Chapter 2). The classical mercantilist period of history is inextricably linked to the rise of the modern nation-state in Europe during the sixteenth through nineteenth centuries. During this period in Western Europe, the idea of state building and intervention in the economy for the sake of making the nation-state secure dominated political-economic thought. A nation is a collection of people who, on the basis of ethnic background, language, and history, or some other set of factors, define themselves as members of an extended political community.[2] The state is viewed as a legal entity, theoretically free from interference by other nations, which monopolizes the means of physical force in its society and exercises sovereignty (final political authority) over the people of a well-defined territory.[3] The political philosophy of mercantilism suggested why and how nation-states could generate the wealth and power needed to protect their societies and evolving economies from external threats.

The economic historian Charles Tilly emphasizes that war was the primary factor that motivated monarchs and other officials to organize their societies and adopt measures that would help secure the nation. Around the fifteenth century, small fiefdoms were compelled to form larger state units in order to be better able to protect themselves against other states.[4] Warrior-kings created bureaucratic agencies that performed a variety of functions related to keeping a budget, using money, and collecting taxes.[5] To control the nobles who often performed these functions in different locales, kings declared themselves the manifestation of state authority (what Louis XIV meant when he said, *L'État, c'est moi*—I am the state). Many kings conceded absolute property rights and limits on their power to nobles in return for their support in staffing the king's armies and assessing and collecting taxes. Some historians suggest that these agreements eventually led to the creation of "people parliaments," which were the genesis of modern democracy and constitutionalism when they secured more rights for peasants.

Over the next century, what we commonly recognize as nation-states emerged, albeit in a very uneven fashion. France, for instance, was already a "nation-state" in the fifteenth century, soon to be followed by England, Holland, Spain, and Sweden. (Germany and Italy would not be consolidated into national entities until later in the nineteenth century.) Cambridge economist Ha-Joon Chang explores some of the many ways that the Tudor monarchs Henry VII and Elizabeth I pursued what we would call today an **industrial policy** (a state-planned strategy to promote certain businesses).[6] These measures include the land enclosure acts (1760–1820), monopoly rights for certain businesses, and industrial espionage. Henry VII used tariffs and export subsidies in support of Britain's effort to capture control of the woolen industry from Holland. He sent royal missions to locate suitable places in England to manufacture woolen goods. For the next 100 years, England employed an import substitution policy (i.e., it allowed no woolen imports in order to promote local production) to compete with and intentionally ruin woolen manufacturing in the Low Countries (Belgium and the Netherlands).[7]

The practice of mercantilism gained a full head of steam after the Thirty Years' War ended in 1648. While gradually states came to be regarded as sovereign over the people within their territories, political authority became centralized in (national) state officials. Increased demands for security led to more efforts to extract income and resources from towns and cities. While agriculture had constituted the dominant source of income a century earlier, it was no longer enough. Monarchs and state officials increasingly looked to merchants and their trade as a much larger source of income for state treasuries. To promote economic growth, larger state bureaucracies set about connecting local and regional markets, establishing common currencies and weights, keeping records, and promoting infrastructural development. As a consequence, merchants acquired more property rights and rose to a higher social position, while increasing their investment in the economy.

Most accounts of the period suggest that the threat of war and violence marked the history of European states at the time. In the nascent European state system, no state could be counted on to guarantee the security of others; therefore, each state could look only to itself and its own wealth and power to protect its domain. These situations often resulted in a **security dilemma** whereby other states were easily threatened by the first state's efforts to increase its war-making capabilities. State officials tended to have a **zero-sum** outlook about state power whereby *absolute gains by one state meant absolute losses by another*. Territorial defense was always considered the state's first priority because prosperity and peace were useless if the nation was not protected from foreign invaders or internal groups who might overthrow the state. But because it was expensive to raise, equip, and maintain armies and navies, wealth also came to be regarded as one of the essential ingredients for achieving and preserving national security.

To many historians, mercantilism is also synonymous with the first wave of exploration and imperialism from 1648 to the end of the Napoleonic Wars in 1815. The search for gold and silver bullion by a variety of adventurers and conquerors helped fill state coffers. Colonialism, the occupation of another territory or state, backed by military power, was another important instrument states used to control trade and generate wealth and power. Colonies served as exclusive markets for the goods of the mother country and as sources of raw materials and cheap labor. The growing merchant class also supported a strong state that would protect its interests, and in return the state sanctioned monopolistic merchant control over certain industries that profited both merchants and the state via commercial trade. Many states employed subsidies to generate exports and promote the development of their colonial empires. The Dutch were quite successful, followed by the British who also created charter companies and supported commerce in urban centers where new technologies were employed to produce items to market and trade.

Economic historians Kenneth Pomeranz and Steven Topik have studied how the colonial powers beginning in the 1400s used these mercantilist policies to move up the global hierarchy.[8] They argue that the dominant powers regularly used violence and occupation to harness advantages for their own traders and government-chartered companies in the global market. Slavery was integral to their strategies of building cheap labor forces to extract raw materials like cotton, sugar, and tobacco from the New World. Britain forced China to open itself to opium exports from India so that Britain could balance its trade deficit with India. European powers competed with each other to control access to raw materials like cocoa, rubber, tea, and coffee, and they deliberately spread production of these commodities to areas under their control and ability to tax. For commercial gain and control of territory, they essentially committed genocide against indigenous peoples in the Americas and the Belgian Congo. In a rebuke of classical liberals who predicted that international commerce would lead to peace and prosperity, Pomeranz and Topik state, "This rosy picture of the healthy effects of the spread of the market economy unfortunately hides the historic foundation of violence upon which it was built and the continuing use of force that persistently underlay it, particularly in the non-European world."[9] In other words, during the historical accumulation and redistribution of wealth, "bloody hands and the invisible hand often worked in concert; in fact, they were often attached to the same body."[10]

Rather than emphasizing economic growth only through trade and colonialism, Prime Minister Walpole (1721–1742) continued his efforts to promote England's woolen industry as another source of revenue. The British sheep and textile industries increased the profitability of land and generated jobs along with the consumption of taxable goods. To protect British manufacturing, the government raised tariffs on competitive goods and subsidized exports. Competitive imports into Great Britain from its colonies were banned, including cloth from India that was superior to that of the British, which destroyed Irish mills and delayed the emergence of the U.S. textile industry. All of these efforts were directed at enhancing state wealth and power in an increasingly economically competitive and politically hostile environment. Without these state protectionist measures, Great Britain would not have been able to support its growing economic wealth and imperial power.

The Economic Liberal Challenge to Mercantilism

Between the 1840s and 1870s, economic liberal ideas attributed to Adam Smith and David Ricardo grew in popularity in Great Britain and gradually replaced mercantilism as the cornerstone of its political-economic outlook. Even then, many policy makers accepted the idea that markets were self-adjusting and that the role of the state should be *laissez-faire*—to stay out of the market. What accounts for the rise of these economic liberal ideas that challenged mercantilism?

Adam Smith's *The Wealth of Nations* was published in 1776, and it attacked mercantilism for restricting economic competition, which led to production inefficiencies. Yet, it wasn't until the end of the Napoleonic Wars in 1815, when Great Britain became the most efficient producer of manufactured goods, that officials began to press for free trade. England finally adopted a free-trade policy in 1840 but did not completely eliminate its trade tariffs until 1860. A variety of accounts suggest that Great Britain adopted a free-trade policy only as more officials and thinkers made the case that free trade was better for Great Britain than mercantilism (see Britain's Corn Laws in Chapter 2). Following on the heels of Smith, the famous businessman and Member of Parliament David Ricardo helped popularize the idea of **comparative advantage**—that even when a country can produce a variety of goods more efficiently than other countries, it should specialize in producing only a select number of items and trade with other countries for the other goods it needs.

Despite his reputation, Smith was not the doctrinaire defender of free enterprise as most of his followers presume. He did champion individual (consumer) liberty and worried that the state could mess up an economy, but he also had a bit of a protectionist side. He supported taxes on luxury carriages, alcohol, sugar, and tobacco. As many historians note, he favored the Navigation Acts that required that only English ships could transport goods between Great Britain and its colonial possessions. Both Smith and Ricardo also viewed free trade as a policy that would help manufacturers market woolen and other British products throughout the world. Ricardo himself accepted exceptions to free trade "within narrow limits" until they were no longer necessary.

Clearly, free trade was *not* an ideological end in itself. The noted economic historian Karl Polanyi argues that there is strong historical evidence that, contrary to the precepts of economic liberalism, economically liberal states *themselves* merely used free-trade policy as another tool to protect and support their own industries, while seeking to gain a competitive advantage over other states.[11] Theories of comparative advantage and free trade would have others specialize in growing and selling wheat to Great Britain, while buying expensive British manufactured goods. Britain also did not oppose the use of trade tariffs to help British companies acquire and sustain technological leads over others, especially in the case of textile manufacturing.[12] Interestingly, in the face of rising European and American competition by the late 1870s, wealthy British financiers and manufacturers joined working class groups in a growing countermovement *against* open market policies and in favor of market regulation and trade protection. A mercantilist historical outlook also emphasizes that as universal suffrage (the right to vote) spread in the late nineteenth century, the state came under pressure to provide more benefits to society.

Most historians note that with renewed emphasis on mercantilism after 1870, **economic nationalism** (people's strong sense of identification with and loyalty to their nation-state) became even more entrenched in interstate relations and helped generate a second wave of imperialism at the end of the century. Germany, Japan, and Italy arrived on the scene and began acquiring their own colonies. According to Polanyi, the retreat from economic liberalism in Great Britain significantly weakened the European balance of power system, which would be replaced by a bipolar structure that led to World War I in 1914.

Meanwhile on the Other Side of the Atlantic: Overlooked Protectionism in U.S. History

In the nineteenth century, emerging powers such as the United States and the German principalities protected themselves from what they perceived as Britain's aggressive economic liberal policies. Two important examples of contributions to mercantilist thought at the time came from the American Alexander Hamilton (1755–1804) and the German Friedrich List (1789–1846). In his *Report on the Subject of Manufactures* to the first Congress, Hamilton argued—in opposition to the ideas of Thomas Jefferson—that specialization in agricultural production was not in the best interest of the United States. Specializing in farming would not make the United States either economically or militarily powerful enough to compete with potential enemies, let alone compete with Britain's ability to manufacture a variety of industrial goods and services the new nation needed. In terms that are familiar even today, Hamilton argued for the protection of the U.S. **infant industries** and a strong role for the state in promoting its own domestic industries.[13] He also favored export subsidies to make U.S. goods more competitive abroad and to offset subsidies granted by foreign states. Hamilton wrote:

> It is well known . . . that certain nations grant bounties [subsidies] on the exportation of particular commodities, to enable their own workmen to undersell and supplant all competitors in the countries to which those commodities are sent. Hence the undertakers of a new manufacture have to contend not only with the

natural disadvantages of a new undertaking, but with the gratuities and remunerations which other governments bestow. To be enabled to contend with success, it is evident that the interference and aid of government are indispensable.[14]

The nineteenth-century German political-economist Friedrich List was an even more vigorous proponent of mercantilist policies. Exiled from his home—ironically for his radical free-trade views—List came to the United States in 1825 and witnessed firsthand the results of Hamilton's economic nationalist policies. The United States was building itself up and achieving independence and security. In his essay "The Theory of the Powers of Production and the Theory of Values," he argued that *the power of producing* [is] *infinitely more important than wealth itself.*[15] In other words, it is more important to invest in the future ability to produce more than to consume the fruits of today's prosperity.

For List, the manufacturing of industrial goods along with investment in education and the development of new technology was more important than investment in agriculture alone. The production of a wide variety of goods and services was the most desirable basis for national wealth and power. List wrote that manufacturing and other occupations "develop and bring into action an incomparably greater variety and higher type of mental qualities and abilities than agriculture" and that "manufactures are at once the offspring, and at the same time the supporters and the nurses, of science and the arts."[16]

The writings of Hamilton and List incorporated a spirit of patriotic economic nationalism that was very much a reaction to Great Britain's economic liberal ideas and free-trade policies. List argued that these policies did not equally benefit exporters and importers; because British technology was more advanced and its labor more efficient than European labor, its goods were more attractive to the Europeans than those produced locally. List argued that in a "cosmopolitan" world there could be no free trade until states could compete with one another on an *equal footing*. To the extent that Great Britain opposed mercantilist policies, it was "kicking away the ladder" for other countries, preventing them from climbing the ladder of development with the same policies Great Britain itself had used to achieve its wealth and power. He recommended that until the United States and Europe had "caught up" with Great Britain, they had to protect their infant industries as a way to level the playing field with the British. He also suggested that Prussian and German city-states would benefit by forming a union (which they did some forty years later), whose combined economic and military might would be able to withstand Britain's power. Ironically, one of the motives of countries that formed the European Economic Community after World War II was to be able to better compete with the United States and Japan.

During the nineteenth century, the U.S. government encouraged people to go west, work hard, and establish property rights. Ideas of Manifest Destiny and divinely sanctioned economic expansion left a big impression on the emerging national psyche. During the War of 1812, the U.S. Congress doubled tariffs, which became part of a U.S. economic development plan until World War II. Between 1800 and 1848, a series of land treaties, wars, and negotiations expanded the territory of the United States to incorporate the Louisiana Territory, Florida, Oregon, Texas, and the Mexican concession. President Lincoln developed a canal system and raised tariffs to 50 percent, where they remained until World War I. Signed into law during the Civil War, the Homestead Act of 1862 granted 160 acres to anyone who claimed and farmed it for five years. The army cleared (ethnically cleansed) the west of native Indian tribes. Congress subsidized railroads along with manufacturing, coal, iron, steel, banking, and real estate. While the Army Corps of Engineers helped build the country's infrastructure, a lenient immigration policy encouraged and rewarded mainly white settlers. All of these government-funded developments contributed to economic prosperity and helped the United States arrive on the world scene as a major economic power by the 1880s.[17]

In the area of trade policy, Congress reduced trade tariffs in 1913, but it raised them back up to 37 percent by 1925 for manufactured goods, helping the United States become the fastest growing country in the world. Other countries were also growing behind tariff walls: Germany, Austria, Sweden, and France. At the onset of the Great Depression, the Smoot–Hawley Tariff Act raised average U.S. tariff rates to a record high of 48 percent. As many nations adopted similar policies to protect and promote their industries, it was inevitable that national interests would clash with "beggar-thy-neighbor" behavior. Many blame the Smoot–Hawley tariffs for contributing to the Great Depression and then World War II. However, according to Ha-Joon Chang, trade tariffs were not a radical departure from history. In the United States and many other countries, markets were never more than partially open, and trade was really not all that free.[18]

Keynes, the Great Depression, and the Postwar Order

Just as many today blame unregulated market forces, greed, and stupidity for causing the 2007 global financial crisis, many people in 1929 blamed banks and speculators for the stock market crash, which subsequently increased unemployment and poverty in many parts of the world. Many lost faith and confidence in market capitalism, which led to increasing support for Fascism and Nazism. Germany experienced rampant unemployment, which increased economic nationalism and the tendency of officials to see others as evil.[19] Many revolutionary movements emerged in Europe, Latin America, and Asia.

Recall from Chapter 2 that in the 1930s the ideas of John Maynard Keynes gained in popularity because of pressure on the state to respond to more voters and higher expectations, rendering the laissez-faire ideology no longer politically acceptable. Keynes offered more positive ideas about how the industrialized nations could restart their economies and deal with the social effects of the depression. He believed not only that markets sometimes fail but also that recessions and depressions can last a long time. To diffuse the tendency of people to support authoritarian leaders, states needed to step in and prime the pump of the national economy to stimulate employment, deal with the negative social effects of the depression, and restore confidence in the capitalist system.

After World War II, Keynes's ideas also substantially shaped the design and role of the three Bretton Woods institutions—the GATT, the IMF, and the World Bank. Economic liberals tend to argue that after the war, the United States and its World War II allies (minus the Soviet Union and China) promoted a new international political-economic order with a variety of economic liberal objectives. The GATT brought down trade barriers. (Interestingly, Keynes himself supported

Great Britain continuing to use high trade tariffs to help its recovery and the recovery of its former colonies). The IMF helped eliminate currency discrimination. The World Bank helped European nations recover from the war, and later helped least developed countries (LDCs) develop. U.S. officials proposed that under the leadership of the United States a *gradual* opening of international markets would also prevent the sort of mercantilist conflicts that had plagued states before World War II.

On the other hand, mercantilists (and their realist cousins) focus on political-economic objectives that these same institutions served: *sustaining* capitalism within the pro-Western industrialized nations and *defending* these capitalist countries by "containing" Soviet and international communism (see Chapter 9). Furthermore, there would be no economic liberal order without military power to back it up. The United States benefited from the use of the U.S. dollar as the world's key currency and from the U.S. hegemonic role as provider of liquidity, finance, aid, and military protection to the Atlantic Alliance. Other collective goods that the United States provided its allies to earn their Cold War support included trade concessions (e.g., reduced import tariffs) and food aid.

Most mercantilists and realists would agree that the United States made a *political bargain* (the visible hand) with its Atlantic partners (plus Japan and later South Korea) whereby the United States let them be somewhat protectionist economically if they did what they could to contain communism. U.S. trade concessions involved sacrifices or costs that took the form of gradual gravitation of some jobs to lower-paid workers in Europe and Japan as they recovered after the war. For many allied policy makers at the time, a big concern was whether opening the international economy too quickly could hurt the recovery of Europe and Japan, making it possible for communism to gain a foothold there. This consideration was yet another reason to allow Europe and Japan to continue using a variety of international trade and domestic protectionist measures and to gradually open their markets until they were better able to compete with the United States.

THE ENTRENCHMENT OF NEOMERCANTILISM

In 1973, the **Organization of Petroleum Exporting Countries (OPEC)** oil cartel changed the face of the international political economy when it suddenly raised the price of oil by four times overnight, embargoed oil shipments to the United States and the Netherlands, and reduced oil shipments to the rest of the world by 25 percent (see Chapter 19). The resulting increase in the price of oil—followed by another price hike in 1979—and the transfer of massive amounts of currency to oil-rich countries were thought to have economically weakened the West and made OPEC a political and an economic power. Most industrialized nations and many developing nations incurred major economic recessions. The dependence of the West on OPEC oil helped push the issue of *economic security* higher on the policy agenda of oil-importing nations everywhere in the world. Control over oil and its production suddenly became as important as solidarity among NATO alliance members (who split over how to manage the oil crisis).

Aside from the issue of oil dependency, at least two other factors produced a significant shift in the international political-economic structure in the early 1970s. One was a change in the power structure of the world from bipolarity to multipolarity (see Chapter 9). After the United States withdrew from Vietnam in 1973, the Nixon administration implemented a pentagonal balance of power configuration, in part based on increasing **interdependence** between national markets. At the same time, many of the industrialized economies shifted away from Keynesian ideas about economic stability to more market-led economic growth strategies.

In response to the oil crisis and recession, the United States and many of its allies pushed for more emphasis on opening international markets through GATT negotiations and on a bilateral basis. As U.S. debt increased, trade was often looked to as a way to increase exports and generate jobs. States such as Japan and South Korea would take advantage of a more open international economy with bigger markets by adjusting their national growth strategies to focus on export-led growth.

Before World War II, many states had erected high tariff barriers, boycotted other states' exports, or even gone to war in response to other states' mercantilist policies. But by the 1970s, these measures were less politically useful and acceptable because their costs to society were too high. Increasing (complex) interdependence between the military and economic interests of many states made it harder to be overtly protectionist or isolationist. In order to protect local producers and defend a variety of national interests, states turned to neomercantilism—a set of more subtle and craftily designed policies that had the effect of reducing their vulnerability to international competition without undermining their overall commitment to freer trade under the GATT. Many of the neomercantilist techniques were not explicitly prohibited by international trade agreements.

States used a variety of neomercantilist policies to generate economic growth, control the business cycle, and eliminate unemployment. These measures included government spending for various programs, regulation of industries, capital controls, and interest rates changes. Also, a variety of state industrial policies included subsidies for research and development, state-owned corporations, and state-distributed banking credits. Some states employed export subsidies to lower the price of goods, making them more attractive to importers. The United States and the European Community routinely subsidized their farmers and used export subsidies to reduce their commodity surpluses and grab larger shares of export markets (see Chapter 6). By the 1980s, neomercantilist measures played an increasingly greater role in the arsenal of state measures to defend their societies and protect their interests.

An important example of neomercantilism in the 1970s was the U.S.-led campaign to decrease dependence on OPEC countries in order to enhance industrialized states' economic security. The United States sponsored the development of a "strategic petroleum reserve" and promoted development of the North Slope oil fields in Alaska. Other national policies included tax breaks for people who adopted measures to cut home energy use, a 55-mile-per-hour automobile speed limit, daylight savings time, and state funds for the development of alternative energy resources. Congress imposed fuel mileage requirements on automobile manufacturers to push them to design more fuel-efficient cars. Even today, many states continue to wrestle with the issue of dependency on foreign oil by providing incentives to insulate homes, funding public transportation, and supporting the manufacture of vehicles that run on biofuels, natural gas, or electricity.

Another example of neomercantilism in the 1970s was the increasing use of **nontariff barriers (NTBs)** (see Chapter 6) such as complex government regulations pertaining to health and safety standards, licensing and labeling requirements, and domestic content requirements that blocked certain imported goods. Similarly, countries imposed **import quotas** that specified the quantity of a particular product that could be imported. The United States and the European Union still apply import quotas to many agricultural items such as sugar to help their domestic producers compete with foreign producers. Another way to limit imports was through a Voluntary Export Agreement (VEA)—a negotiated quota or "gentlemen's agreement" between an exporter and an importer whereby the exporter "voluntarily" complies with the importer's "request" to limit exports, for fear that the importer may resort to imposing a more costly form of protection on the exporter's goods.

Japan was particularly successful at using neomercantilist policies to achieve its *economic miracle*. By the late 1970s, many development experts concluded that Japan's success in export-led growth was partly due to heavy state involvement in the economy. The government—especially the Ministry of International Trade and Industry (MITI)—cooperated with industry officials and Liberal Democratic Party (LDP) members to carefully guide the development of industries.[20] Certain companies were selected to receive state and bank subsidies to make them more competitive with U.S. and European firms.

Japan complemented its protectionist trade measures with overseas investments and ownership of homeland businesses and industries. Clyde Prestowitz argues that Japan did more than support its most competitive industries; it also intentionally adopted an aggressive strategic trade policy. Because it lacked a natural comparative advantage in the production of certain products, it used a combination of state assistance and industry efforts to *purposefully* create such an advantage in favor of its industries.[21] Japan's success would later be emulated by the successful emerging economies, especially the Asian Tigers (South Korea, Hong Kong, Singapore, and Taiwan) and China.

Neomercantilism and the Globalization Campaign

As noted in Chapters 1 and 2, the 1980s and 1990s marked a period of greater interdependence and increasing popularity of economic liberal ideas. This set the stage for the launching of the globalization campaign that included efforts to integrate states into a global economic capitalist-oriented systemic structure. While Reagan and Thatcher focused on market-oriented policies and chipped away at the role of the state in the domestic economy, they simultaneously used political and military powers to advance their countries' interests in the global economy. All states faced a delicate balancing act of adapting to globalization but also moderating its negative effects on jobs and some national industries.

With globalization came greater political sensitivity to trade, which accounted for a bigger proportion of GDP and affected more sectors of the economy. The policies that states adopted in response to this sensitivity often provoked disputes with trading partners. As the noted political-economist Robert Gilpin argued, it was difficult for states to select the appropriate counter-responses without knowing what those states' intentions were. Gilpin made a useful distinction between **malevolent** and **benign mercantilist** intimidations. The former is a more hostile version of economic warfare and the expansionary policies nations employed to expand their territorial base and/or political and economic influence at the expense of other nations beyond what is regarded as reasonable to protect themselves.

In contrast, benign mercantilism is more defensive in nature, as "it attempts to protect the economy against untoward economic and political forces."[22] Of course, the problem is how to discriminate between the two in an environment where the difference seems to be a matter of degree rather than of kind.

Reagan is famous for redirecting the Nixon–Kissinger multipolar system of the distribution of power of the 1970s back into a bipolar order of yesteryear that featured the Soviet Union as the "evil empire." In conjunction with this security goal, the Reagan Doctrine encouraged (some would say coerced) many LDCs to adopt not only the anticommunist cause but also the economic liberal policies of the IMF, the World Bank, and the GATT (see Chapters 6–8). The Reagan administration and many academics expected that as developing nations integrated into the international economy, they would grow faster and become more democratic.

President Reagan also mixed economic liberal and mercantilist objectives at the start of the Uruguay Round of multilateral trade negotiations in 1985. One goal of these negotiations was to "level the playing field" by cutting NTBs and other trade restrictions so that states could compete economically with one another following the same set of rules and policies. In the 1980s and 1990s, Japan had acrimonious relations at times with the other countries because it kept running a huge trade surplus. The United States and Europe blamed their trade deficits on Japan's aggressive export-led growth strategy and import restrictions. Japan maintained that it sought only to strengthen its own national security through the use of benign neomercantilist industrial policies.

President Reagan often threatened to use Super 301 legislation (see Chapter 6) to *punish* Japan and Brazil for dumping their products on the market or using export subsidies to unfairly compete with the United States. He also threatened NATO allies with trade sanctions if they continued to import natural gas from the Soviet Union. The United States gradually put more pressure on Japan and newly emerging countries to lower their trade barriers and open their markets to more foreign (especially the United States) investment and competition. As we will see in the chapters to follow, U.S. efforts were not always successful as many of these countries continue to run huge balance-of-trade surpluses compared to long-term U.S. trade deficits.

The United States often found itself limited in the amount of pressure it could put on its most important allies. At the time—as is the case with China and Saudi Arabia today (see Chapter 7)—the United States was dependent on Japan to buy its exports and invest in U.S. Treasury bonds and securities. And pressuring NATO allies about their dependence on the Soviet Union merely strengthened criticism of U.S. foreign policy in Europe.

The United States and Japan repeatedly confronted one another in a series of trade disputes over items such as automobiles, rice, beef, and semiconductors. What one state regards as benign, another might interpret as malevolent behavior, especially when the policies of the first state inflict a good deal of stress and anxiety on the society of the second.

Neomercantilism and the Financial Crisis

Since the early 1990s, the neomercantilist policies of some states have raised the stakes for others that must grapple with lost jobs and broken families, the loss of electoral support for legislators, and ultimately the real or imagined loss of national wealth and power. The benefits of globalization and complex interdependence did not trump societies' vulnerability and sensitivity to competitors. People found it increasingly harder to adjust to globalization's dislocations and the instability of markets. In these situations, state officials were often pressured to respond with countermeasures of their own—to "strike while the iron is hot"—for fear of otherwise sending a message of weakness or disinterest to foreign competitors.

Political and economic competition *between* states has not ended; in fact, it has intensified in a more globalized world. In many cases, businesses have felt compelled to go abroad in search of resources, markets, and cheaper labor. Outsourcing labor has become the economically efficient and rational thing to do. Many neomercantilists go a step further and argue that globalization tends to *undermine* itself.[23] As wealth and power are diffused around the world, states are compelled to (re)invigorate their own power and authority in order to either protect themselves from globalization's negative effects or take advantage of its positive effects.[24]

For mercantilists, the recent global financial crisis is a good example of how laissez-faire ideas and globalization have undermined themselves. The crisis has increased tensions between states, uprooted many political and social institutions, and sparked renewed interest in protectionist and national security-oriented perspectives everywhere in the world. It has fueled illegal economies and increased U.S. dependence on China. Many countries have used it as an excuse to postpone dealing with potentially catastrophic environmental trends. It has tended to shift order away from U.S. hegemony to a more multilateral system.[25] And the financial crisis has undermined the idea that the U.S. economy is a model for the world.

LDC NEOMERCANTILIST POLICIES

As we will see in other chapters of this book, developing nations—just like developed countries—have been searching for a more pragmatic and subtle mix of policies that accounts for not only the interests of the market but also those of society and the state. They have continued to adopt neomercantilist measures in response to international economic competition and what some officials regard as malevolent threats.

In his influential book *Governing the Market*, political-economist Robert Wade argues that industrial policies had a decisive role in the development "miracles" in Japan, South Korea, and Taiwan.[26] The political elites and heads of bureaucracies in these East Asian countries steered domestic investment into sectors of the economy like shipbuilding and hard disc drives that the government considered key to economic transformation. They encouraged high rates of saving and manipulated prices in the economy to support infant industries. They also used a lot of public investment to complement private investment. They allowed the formation of large conglomerates. Moreover, they nudged firms to improve the quality of products and to export a high percentage of their finished products. All of these neomercantilist policies—characteristic of what Wade calls a "**developmental state**"—have been imitated by countries like Brazil, Mexico, and Argentina, but not always with the same positive results.

Similarly, Joshua Kurlantzick characterizes these policies as constituting a form of **state capitalism**—an economic system in which the state owns many enterprises or at least "plays a major role in supporting or directing them."[27] The state is not trying to weaken capitalism; rather, it is trying to channel markets to better serve the nation's long-term interests. He argues that state capitalism can foster entrepreneurship and innovation. He points out that thirty years ago, the Brazilian government gave the small aircraft maker Embraer subsidies, loans, and contracts when private investors would not extend capital to it. Now Embraer is the world's largest manufacturer of regional jets. The Singapore government has played the same role, providing "angel investments" to small startups and incentivizing them to invest in emerging technologies.

Cambridge University economist Ha-Joon Chang goes so far as to argue that governments can be rather successful in "picking winners" among industries—especially if they work closely with private companies. Governments can spare struggling businesses from having to worry about short-term profitability and instead allow them to be "patient capital"—focused on gaining market share and profits over the long term. For example, the Korean company LG in the 1960s wanted to be a textile producer, but the government forced it to build electric cables, which later laid a foundation for it to become a global electronics manufacturer.[28]

Chang also explains some of the important reasons why developing nations like Malaysia, Brazil, and China have continued to adopt neomercantilist trade policies as part of their development campaigns. According to Chang, developing countries have wanted to "catch up" with the richer and more technologically advanced countries. However, many have found that if while trying to "climb up the ladder" they accept the same rules as the leading countries, they may never get to the top of the ladder. As we outlined in Chapter 2, many IOs that reflect the interests of the major powers have worked to do away with a variety of protectionist measures. Making a case similar to Friedrich List's, Chang believes that developing nations need a (temporary) handicap of sorts.

He uses an analogy in sports to make the point. When players or conditions for opposing teams are unequal, we often object that the competition is unfair and that there needs to be a "level playing field." Just as we separate athletes by age and weight, we should allow developing countries to use some tools to compete more "fairly" with developed states that have many economic advantages and who originally made the rules in favor of their interests.

For many developing nations, trade protection not only plays a vital role in generating income but also helps protect local producers from foreign competition. And yet, as noted in Chapter 6, developing nations played almost no role in multilateral negotiations after World War II that produced the General Agreement on Tariffs and Trade (GATT). It is important to note that early GATT agreements reflected the interests of the developed nations in trade rules—which included preserving some trade protection while only gradually curtailing the use of import tariffs on industrial products. In the early 1990s, a number of developing nations did play a role in converting the GATT into the WTO in the Uruguay Round from 1986 to 1994. However, by then the basic principles of the international trade regime were set and difficult to change.

While most developing countries signed on to the new WTO agreement in 1994 that introduced new liberal norms for agricultural trade subsidies, trade in services, NTBs, and intellectual property rights (IPRs), they did not benefit as much from the final agreement as they had hoped they would. This laid the foundation for their unwillingness later on to reach a new deal in the Doha Round (see Chapter 6). They also redoubled efforts to form a number of their own negotiating coalitions to overcome what they feel are unfair trade rules.

Similarly, in the 1990s, the poorer developing countries complained that IMF and World Bank **structural adjustment policies (SAPs)** imposed on them felt like malevolent mercantilism. Many mercantilists charged that LDC growth rates actually *declined* over the same period when markets in many developing countries were supposedly opening up. SAPs amounted to nothing more than a "mission creep" (at least for the working class and poor) and the imposition of neoliberal policies. As List might argue today, IMF and World Bank SAPs were merely another example of state power being used to increase U.S., European, and Japanese wealth and power—and not noble, let alone useful, development tools as so often claimed.

The problem of *intentions* behind trade and structural adjustment policies tends to generate conflicts in multilayer trade negotiations such as those in the Doha Round. Many LDCs charge that a new agreement would make it difficult for developing countries to protect some of their "infant industries." They also suspect that by trying to require high labor or environmental standards in all countries, industrialized powers are masking protectionist support for their own inefficient industries. Despite their formal commitment to the international goals of opening up international trade and reducing trade barriers, members of the WTO remain quite protective of their own economic security and national independence.

NEOMERCANTILIST POLICIES TODAY

The kinds of contemporary neomercantilist policies that states frequently adopt depend on each state's level of development and its relative power in the international system. Poorer countries, as we have noted earlier, have a particular interest in "catching up" to the industrialized countries, but they must work within ideological and political constraints imposed on them by major powers and neoliberal institutions like the WTO, the World Bank, and the IMF. Advanced industrialized nations face the double challenge of competing with one another in high technology- and knowledge-based industries while stemming the loss of blue-collar manufacturing industries to emerging economies with abundant, low-cost labor. As globalization and international agreements have wedded all countries to a complex set of economic liberal principles, states have looked for new forms of benign mercantilist policies and carved out realms where they can still use tried-and-true mercantilist policies like quotas, tariffs, and plain old arm-twisting.

In this section, we survey two common types of neomercantilist policies found today: industrial and infrastructural policies and strategic resources policies. Although we focus on the developed countries' use of these policies, keep in mind that many developing countries resort to them as well. In fact, LDCs often point out that today's advanced industrialized nations used a variety of these policies throughout their *early history*, and thus, it is somewhat hypocritical of them to try to stop LDCs from using some of the very same policies today. What many emerging economies want are weak protection of IPRs; a mix of protectionism with some free trade; and time to improve institutions without undue pressure by Western countries to quickly become democratic and get rid of corruption. But the developed countries seem to be saying to emerging economies: "Do as we say, not as we did (and sometimes still do)!"

Industrial and Infrastructural Policies

Many states limit foreign investments in their country in a variety of subtle and not so subtle ways—often in an attempt to reduce threats to independence or national sovereignty. They can limit the percentage of shares in a domestic company (like an oil company) that foreigners can own or they can ban foreign investments in strategic industries like natural resource extraction, power generation, banking, and media (see the box China vs. Unocal). It is also common to make it difficult for foreigners to buy land or real estate on which to build factories, set up services, or accumulate office space. The intent of these policies is often to give domestically owned companies an advantage or to prevent foreigners from gaining too much control of a sector of the economy by forcing them to cooperate with local companies.

▌CHINA VS. UNOCAL[a]

In April 2005, Chevron Corporation, the largest U.S.-based oil conglomerate, made a $16.5 billion bid comprised of cash and stock offerings to acquire a controlling stake in its smaller domestic rival, Unocal. While financial analysts and key players on all sides considered the offer, another multinational energy giant stepped into the game with an unsolicited counter bid. The Chinese National Offshore Oil Corporation (CNOOC), a firm in which the Chinese government holds a 70 percent stake, leveraged its strong fiscal reserves to make what was at first glance a significantly more compelling proposal: $18.5 billion for Unocal, paid entirely in cash.

For Unocal's shareholders, however, choosing the better option quickly became more complicated than a simple analysis of balance sheets. As word of the CNOOC bid spread, concern arose in the United States over the prospect of a foreign government taking control of critical resource production. The deal quickly became a national security issue. On June 27, 2005, key Republicans and Democrats on Congressional energy committees wrote a letter to President George W. Bush warning that China's "aggressive tactics to lock up energy supplies" threatened domestic interests.[b] More than forty members of Congress signed a similar letter to the Treasury Department, urging a review of the deal for security reasons, and former CIA Director James Woolsey publicly referred to the CNOOC offer as part

of a "conscious long-term effort" to take control of U.S. energy resources.[c] Days later, the House of Representatives overwhelmingly (398 to 15) passed a resolution urging the president to block the deal as a threat to national security.[d]

Shortly after the Congressional resolution passed the House, the Chinese Foreign Ministry issued a harsh statement condemning the United States for erecting barriers in the face of business. The statement demanded that Congress "correct its mistaken ways of politicizing economic and trade issues and stop interfering in normal commercial exchanges between enterprises of the two countries."[e] Despite this tough rhetoric, CNOOC ended up dropping its bid. The U.S. government never directly blocked the deal as the House resolution was nonbinding and never cleared the Senate. Ultimately, the political barriers created by the controversy discouraged hopes for the efficacy of a CNOOC-operated Unocal. Fiscal advisors from top Wall Street firms came to a consensus that the extra $2 billion in cash was not worth the hassle that CNOOC's bid incited.[f]

Both China and the United States operated under fundamental mercantilist principles in approaching the China/Unocal incident, but neither addressed these reasons directly in public discourse. The United States framed the issue under the guise of realism as a security concern, and China retaliated with classic economic liberal language about interfering in the market. Ultimately, these political factors became part of the economic equation that favored Chevron's offer.

Though Unocal was a small player in the global oil industry—producing less than 200,000 barrels daily worldwide—its most lucrative holdings were based largely in and around Asia, and it claimed to be the largest producer of geothermal energy on that continent. According to its last quarterly Securities and Exchange Commission (SEC) filing as an independent firm, 57 percent of its revenue came from its Asian operations in Thailand, Indonesia, Myanmar, and Bangladesh.[g] China's incentive to control these regional energy resources is clear: for the first time in its history, the budding industrial nation has come to rely on foreign energy imports to meet its growing demand for oil. Acting through its controlling interest in CNOOC, the Chinese government was attempting to secure an oil supply line for its rapidly growing economy—a perfect example of neomercantilism at work.

The United States acted with equally mercantilist motivation in moving to block the deal. As the debate unfolded in the United States, many energy experts remained skeptical of the national security concerns ostensibly behind the controversy. They criticized the logic that the Unocal bid was part of a larger Chinese military supply strategy antagonistic to the United States, pointing out instead that the industrial growth inciting China's oil demand in the first place is dependent largely on the United States as a primary importer of Chinese industrial goods. Indeed, it is this

trade situation that provided a much more genuine cause for U.S. concern: By the time CNOOC submitted its bid, the United States already had a $160 billion trade deficit with China.[h] Moving to correct this rapidly expanding trade imbalance and block China from acquiring a strategic commercial asset, congressional leaders were clearly leveraging their political power in the name of national commercial interests.

References

[a]Ryan Cunningham conducted the research and produced a draft for this topic. Our thanks to him.
[b]Paul Blustein, "Many Oil Experts Unconcerned over China Unocal Bid," *The Washington Post,* July 1, 2005, p. D1.
[c]John Tamney, "Unocal Hysteria," *The National Review,* June 30, 2005.
[d]Peter S. Goodman, "China Tells Congress to Back Off Business," *The Washington Post*, July 5, 2005, p. A1.
[e]Ibid.
[f]"Why China's Unocal Bid Ran Out of Gas," *Business Week Online,* August 4, 2005, www.businessweek.com/bwdaily/dnflush/Aug 2005/nf20058084_5032_db0lb.htm?chan-search (accessed March 19, 2007).
[g]Unocal Corporation Form 10-Q, filed August 4, 2006, p. 29.
[h]Goodman, "China Tells Congress to Back off Business," p. A1.

Chang points out that the United States and European countries had many such restrictions until well into the twentieth century. Similarly, countries like Japan, Korea, and Finland had many formal and informal restrictions on foreign direct investment until well into the 1980s, but they still managed to grow rapidly.[29] For example, post–World War II European countries regulated foreign companies by controlling their access to foreign exchange and requiring them to buy some supplies from local producers. Japan prohibited foreign direct investment (FDI) in vital industries and limited foreign ownership at 50 percent in many industries. Instead of favoring foreign takeovers of local companies, it pressured foreign companies to license technology to local companies so that they could learn to manufacture products themselves. The legacy of these restrictions is very clear today. In 2011, the stock of FDI as a percentage of GDP in Japan was a paltry 3.8 percent, compared to 19.4 percent in the United States, 25.2 percent in Germany, and 34.3 percent in

France.[30] And Finland had draconian restrictions on FDI until the 1980s: among other things, foreigners could not own more than 20 percent of a company, and foreign banks were completely prohibited. Clearly, Japanese and Finnish models of economic success owed almost nothing to FDI, a finding that conflicts with economic liberal insistence on unfettered capital inflows.

Other significant government interventions in today's markets that many industrialized nations have adopted are designed to increase a country's competitiveness without being malevolently protectionist. Massive investments in public infrastructure and research are vital to business success, and they are effectively subsidized. When a state builds roads, power plants, and transportation systems, the benefits of its spending usually accrue to domestic workers and capitalists who become more efficient and productive as a result. One could argue that California has been a large, successful agricultural producer and exporter because of massive public investments for many decades in irrigation systems that bring water to the state from hundreds of miles away.

Former investment banker Felix Rohatyn argues in a recent book that massive American *public* investments in infrastructure and education had a key role in making the United States a powerful, innovative (and capitalist) country. These programs, parallels to which can be seen today in other countries, included the following: the Erie Canal, the Transcontinental Railroad, land-grant colleges, the Panama Canal, the GI Bill, and Eisenhower's interstate highway system.[31] Similarly, historian and economist Marc Levinson explains that before 1913, Americans living in rural areas who wanted to order goods from big-city stores could only get packages delivered by rail freight—and the private railroads charged a high rate. In 1913, Congress authorized the U.S. Post Office to deliver parcel posts up to 11 pounds—later raised to 50 pounds—at very competitive rates. The result, concludes Levinson, is that "thanks to the government's new role in handling packages, Americans everywhere, from big coastal cities to remote mountain ranches, could at last experience the joys of shopping by mail at far lower prices than they could find close to home." The government "revolutionized commerce," enabling the rapid growth of large retailers and a truly national market by driving down distribution costs.[32]

Likewise, public education and investments in higher education give widespread economic benefits to many nations. India and China have invested heavily in education and especially in research and development in health sciences, engineering, and the natural sciences, all of which have huge spillovers for domestic companies. Developed countries have done the same to spur innovation and the development of a "knowledge-based economy" (see Chapter 10).

Government procurement can also be a powerful neomercantilist mechanism to spread benefits to local businesses that are denied to foreigners. Most governments want their huge spending on goods and services to help domestic private companies and workers. For example, spillovers from U.S. defense spending have helped the aircraft manufacturer Boeing (see Chapter 17) become more competitive with Airbus in the commercial airliner industry. Australian political-economists Linda Weiss and Elizabeth Thurbon emphasize how the U.S. government uses procurement policies to create "national champions"—big, globally competitive companies like Lockheed, Motorola, IBM, and Microsoft—that rely on long-term government contracting. Even as the United States implements its own "buy national" procurement policies—most recently in the 2009 stimulus bill—it tries to get other countries to open up their public works projects to American companies. Weiss and Thurbon conclude that "although subject to multilateral discipline, government procurement offers a powerful tool for national economic promotion in an era of economic openness."[33]

More broadly, many scholars argue that government procurement has to be wedded to other public policies in order to nurture a national innovation system that can lead to large-scale domestic production of cutting-edge products. In a recent—and strongly mercantilist—report, the U.S. National Research Council argues that the federal government and state governments have to proactively assist U.S. private industries if they are to successfully compete against foreign companies receiving low-cost loans, subsidies, and tax breaks.[34] It wants the United States to do as governments in Germany, Taiwan, Korea, and Finland have: fund applied research institutions that help private companies translate technological breakthroughs into large-scale domestic manufacturing capacity. The council also pinpoints some traditional ways that the United States can regain global competitiveness: spend more on R&D and decrease the cost of tuition for college students. More importantly, it advocates for direct U.S. government support for strategic emerging industries such as semiconductors, solar power, advanced batteries, and pharmaceuticals. All of these measures reflect the contemporary mercantilist viewpoint that a country will lose power and global market share unless its government spends generously on infrastructure and education while deliberately and massively incentivizing *domestic* manufacturing.

Finally, Canadian political-scientist Patricia Goff reminds us that the purpose of helping one's own companies and industries is not necessarily just to save jobs, boost exports, or hurt foreigners.[35] In fact, the purpose may be much more defensive and noneconomic. She has examined how Canada and the European Union have strongly protected their culture industries—music, television, radio, film, and magazine publishing—from an American onslaught over the last sixty years. They use public ownership of some culture industries (like public television), tax incentives for local private investment in movie production, public loans and grants for artists, minimum local content requirements (on TV and radio programming), and ownership rules to preserve and nurture domestic culture producers. They do so not so much to keep foreign cultural products out as to promote their own distinct national identity, cultural diversity, and social cohesion. Preserving "cultural sovereignty" in the face of globalization's homogenizing effects is an eminently political goal, vital for nurturing a democratic citizenry that is well informed about its *own* history and values.

Strategic Resources Policies

Neomercantilists also believe that interdependencies are not always symmetrical (felt equally) between states. The suppliers of **strategic resources** and commodities like oil tend to view their capacity and the resulting dependency of others as something positive that improves their power and security. In many cases, the relatively high cost of oil, coupled with supplier threats to cut it off to client states, makes the issue of dependence on any resource or vulnerability to a supplier of that resource synonymous with a national security threat. Ideally, only complete self-sufficiency in raw materials would make a nation-state politically and economically secure. In the real world, however, states are constantly trying to minimize their dependence on others while fostering conditions that make others dependent on them.

Examples of this are common. France deliberately and massively expanded its nuclear power industry after the 1973 oil crisis. China has signed long-term oil supply agreements with countries in Africa and Latin America and invested in exploration as a way of getting "first dibs" on these global commodities instead of buying them in open markets in the future. The U.S. government has built costly strategic stockpiles of oil, tantalum (a key ingredient in cell phones and electronic equipment), and dozens of other minerals and metals used in electronics and weaponry. Even the Centers for Disease Control and Prevention manages a Strategic National Stockpile, a repository of medicines for use in case of a national emergency such as a terrorist attack or epidemic.

The motivation for these kinds of benign neomercantilism is in large part derived from the legitimate fear that other countries will use malevolent mercantilist polices to hurt one's own country. These fears today are not unfounded. Major powers and the United Nations have at various times imposed economic sanctions on countries such as Serbia, Iran, Syria, and Iraq, threatening their security and political stability. Industrial espionage is still widely practiced, whereby one country tries to steal the advanced technology of another. Theft of intellectual property is increasingly widespread in the world, manifested in counterfeiting and patent infringement, which can severely damage a country's companies (see Chapter 10).

Access to and control over **strategic resources** has always been a top concern of industrialized nations who fear that being "cut off" from energy, minerals, and metals will cripple their economy and weaken their war-fighting ability (see the box The Struggle over Rare Earths). In the past, colonial powers took direct control of many territories with important resources, or they built powerful militaries to guard these sources and prevent rival empires from threatening them. Industrialized democracies today usually try to establish political and military alliances with governments of big resource-producers like Saudi Arabia (oil) and Morocco (phosphates)—despite those countries' undemocratic political regimes. At the same time, they may establish stockpiles of resources or encourage domestic exploration and extraction by offering subsidies to national producers or by leasing public lands to them cheaply.

◤ THE STRUGGLE OVER RARE EARTHS

When the Japanese coast guard seized a Chinese fishing trawler in September 2010 near disputed islands in the East China Sea, little did Tokyo know that it would lead to a global dispute over rare earth metals—more than a dozen minerals used in iPads, flat-screen TVs, hybrid cars, and weapons systems. Beijing responded by temporarily cutting off rare earth exports to Japan—which had relied on China for 90 percent of its imports—sending Japanese manufacturers into a panic and dramatically pushing up prices for rare earths in global markets. Beginning in 2011 the Chinese government established export quotas on the minerals, a violation of WTO trade rules. Japan and the United States scrambled to find new sources, reopen domestic mines, and institute recycling programs in order to reduce dependence on China, which produced 97 percent of the world's supply in 2010.

Many analysts interpreted China's moves as a classic form of malevolent mercantilism whereby a state uses control of strategic resources to punish its rivals and privilege its domestic producers. According to Jane Nakano, the dispute "severely reduced Japan's comfort with China as a trade partner . . . and transformed Sino-Japanese economic relations from a mutually prosperous rivalry to one with an undertone of mistrust."[a] By reserving more rare earths for its domestic market, Beijing seemed intent on forcing overseas manufacturers that needed the minerals to move some of their factories to China—thereby facilitating a transfer of technologies to China from these high-tech companies and boosting Chinese production of key components used in the electronics and clean energy industries.[b]

Japan and the United States interpreted China's manipulation of rare earth markets as a potential threat to national security and an early warning of how this rising power might defy trade norms in the future. They responded with their own defensive mercantilist countermeasures. The Japanese government funneled huge subsidies to corporations to help them develop new rare-earth recycling processes and signed new agreements with the likes of Vietnam, Australia, and Kazakhstan to jointly develop new mines. In the United States, mining company Molycorp reopened a huge rare-earth mine in Mountain Pass, California that had been closed in 2002 for environmental reasons. The Department of Defense funded private research into more efficient ways to use rare earths and into finding substitutes for them. Together with Japan and the European Union, the United States filed a formal complaint with the WTO in April 2012 accusing China of violating the GATT and its WTO Accession Protocol. Moreover, private market actors around the world are moving rapidly to develop diversified supplies of rare earths like neodymium and beryllium, on land and from the seabed, to destroy China's monopoly.[c]

The minerals dispute can be seen as part of a wider struggle among East Asian nations to control the East and South China Seas. In recent years, China has asserted ownership over numerous small islands and island groups in these waters that are also claimed by Japan, Taiwan, the Philippines, and Vietnam. Each of these states covets the territorial waters around these islands, where rich deposits of oil and gas are believed to exist. The trawler incident occurred near the Senkaku Islands, controlled by Japan since 1895. Chinese nationalists may have seized on rare earths as a way to try to weaken Tokyo's position on the islands. When the Japanese government bought the Senkaku Islands from their private Japanese owners in September 2012, street protests erupted in China, the Chinese Navy sent ships near the islands, and Japan sent many coast guard vessels to the waters to warn off the Chinese.[d] An informal Chinese boycott of Japanese goods in late 2012 caused sales of Nissan, Toyota, and Honda cars in China to plunge, and Panasonic estimated that the boycott would cause billions of dollars in profit losses—the second worst yearly losses in the Japanese company's history.[e] The rare earths story reminds us that even in an interdependent, globalized economy, states worry deeply about strategic resources and are willing to play risky little games of brinksmanship to advance their economic interests and security.

References

[a]Jane Nakano, "Rare Earth Trade Challenges and Sino-Japanese Relations: A Rise of Resource Nationalism?" *National Bureau of Asian Research Special Report* 31 (September 2011): 65.

[b]R. Colin Johnson, "Rare Earth Supply Chain: Industry's Common Cause," *EETimes,* October 24, 2010, at http://www.eetimes.com/electronics-news/4210064/Rare-earth-supply-chain--Industry-s-common-cause.

[c]Tim Worstall, "Why China Has Lost The Rare Earths War: The Power of Markets," June 24, 2012, at http://www.forbes.com/sites/timworstall/2012/06/24/why-china-has-lost-the-rare-earths-war-the-power-of-markets.

[d]Martin Fackler, "Chinese Patrol Ships Pressuring Japan over Islands," *New York Times,* November 3, 2012.

[e]Jonathan Soble, "Nissan Cuts Forecast after China Boycott," *Financial Times,* November 6, 2012; Bruce Einhorn, "Panasonic Feels Pain of Chinese Backlash," *Bloomberg Businessweek,* October 31, 2012, at http://www.businessweek.com/articles/2012-10-31/panasonic-feels-pain-of-chinese-backlash.

Industrialized nations and rapid industrializers like China also encourage their national companies to diversify suppliers overseas, buy foreign resource-extracting companies, and buy concessions (exploration and production rights) in other countries. In recent years, foreign oil companies have been scrambling to buy concessions to explore offshore West Africa, where many think vast oil deposits may exist. Japan has not been successful in diversifying and reducing energy imports. Although it has increased energy efficiency and invested in nuclear power (before the Fukushima disaster), 90 percent of all its oil imports are from the Middle East. In contrast, the United States has deliberately and successfully diversified its oil and gas supplies as a matter of national security. Its top five suppliers of imported oil, in order of significance, are Canada, Saudi Arabia, Mexico, Venezuela, and Nigeria—only one of which (Saudi Arabia) is in the conflict-prone Middle East. And as the Arctic ice cover disappears, countries with territory inside the Arctic Circle and who make up the Arctic Council—Canada, the United States, Russia, Sweden, Denmark, Norway, Iceland, and Finland—are eager to develop potentially lucrative offshore oil and natural gas fields.

There is an ongoing tension in the global political economy as commercial development and national security are increasingly wedded in the minds of policy makers and corporations. As nations such as China develop major industrialized economies, the battle for control of scarce energy resources will no doubt become more intense. The U.S. actions in responding to the attempt by a Chinese company to buy Unocal Corporation in 2005 (see box) may well have set a new paradigm for international trade that is far more guarded and complicated—and neomercantilist—than the economic liberal globalization of the past three decades.

CONCLUSION

Of the three ideological perspectives most often used to explain IPE, mercantilism is the oldest and arguably the most powerful because it is so deeply entrenched in the psyches of state officials and their societies. For many neomercantilists, as it was for classical mercantilists and colonial powers in the nineteenth century, economic liberalism is simply another tool that state officials employ to protect their industries so as to achieve more wealth and power. All nations in the past have employed mercantilist policies and measures, as Great Britain did in the nineteenth century during the height of the popularity of economic liberal ideas about free trade. Likewise, the United States did the same throughout the twentieth century, even when it advocated free trade and globalization.

Mercantilist ideas have evolved over the years and adapted to changing conditions in the international political economy. Classical mercantilism tended to view threats to a nation's security by foreign armies, foreign firms and their products, and even from foreign influence over international laws and institutions. Both mercantilists and their realist cousins would also note that by their very nature states *can* be expected to use the economy, either legally or illegally, as a means to generate more wealth and power.

Certainly, neomercantilist policies are still responsible for a good deal of international conflict. Efforts to increase state wealth and power have proliferated since World War II, as a result of the growing interdependence of nations and globalization of the international political economy. Managing the international economy remains a complicated task that befuddles politicians and academics alike. Many of these issues demonstrate that despite OELs' efforts to isolate economics and markets from politics and society, mercantilists and HILs do not believe it can be done.

With the onset of deep interdependence between states in the 1970s and the globalization campaign of the 1990s, academic experts became aware of the tightening connection between domestic and foreign policy issues. The end of the Cold War in 1990 also helped blur the line between economic and broader national security concerns for most states. However, as discussed in Chapter 1, since the mid-1980s the popular ideas of economic liberalism and globalization envision a limited role for the state in the economy resulting in less conflict between nation-states. Curiously, some OELs envision the withering away of the nation-state as the global economy integrates into a single economic unit.

As long as states exist, they can be expected to give first priority to their own national security and independence. Today, all states continue to use protectionist measures to assist some of their manufacturing, agricultural, and service sectors. To a great extent, the *success* of globalization has also helped undermine the openness of the international political economy. As national industries have become more dependent on external sources of revenue and markets, public officials have also felt more *vulnerable* to developments in the international political economy, leading to arguments that market forces have weakened state power and authority significantly. Yet, protectionist policies have periodically proliferated as governments have attempted to reassert themselves and better manage their economies.

If Hamilton and List were still around, they would likely argue that as long as states are the final source of political (sovereign) authority, markets cannot be separated from them. For mercantilists and realists today, the world has not been ready for the market to rule all for very long. Globalization and financial crises have exposed the inadequacy of markets—which are often not self-regulating or self-adjusting—to protect societies. But things are not that simple, either. State-guided policies often fail to accomplish their objectives and can sometimes cause great damage to a society. Nevertheless, politics forces states to re-embed society into the market. Voters and citizens want protection from the excesses of the market at the same time that they want competitive markets to work better. As suggested in Chapter 2, HILs would agree with mercantilists that there would be no market without the state, and the invisible hand must serve more than the interests of a select few.

KEY TERMS

mercantilism   54
classical mercantilism   54
realism   54
neomercantilism   54
industrial policy   55
security dilemma   56
zero-sum   56
comparative advantage   57

economic nationalism   58
infant industries   58
OPEC   61
interdependence   62
nontariff barriers   62
import quotas   63
malevolent mercantilist   63
benign mercantilist   63

developmental state   65
state capitalism   65
structural adjustment
   policies   67
strategic resources   71

DISCUSSION QUESTIONS

1. Each of the IPE perspectives has at its center a fundamental value or idea. What is the central idea of mercantilism? Explain how that central idea is illustrated by the mercantilist period of history, mercantilist philosophy, and recent neomercantilist policies.

2. What is the difference between benign mercantilism and malevolent mercantilism in theory? How could you tell the difference between them in practice? Find a newspaper article that demonstrates the tensions between these ideas, and explain how the issue is dealt with by the actors in the article.

3. How much is economic globalization a threat to nation-states? Make a brief list of the positive and negative potential effects of a more integrated global economic system, and explain the basis for your opinion.

4. Compare and contrast some features of the Great Depression with those of the global financial crisis today. If Keynes were alive, what do you suppose he would propose the state do about the current crisis?

5. What potential drawbacks are there with state capitalism, governments "picking winners," and governments providing loans and subsidies to strategic industries?

SUGGESTED READINGS

Ha-Joon Chang. *Bad Samaritans: The Myth of Free Trade and the Secret History of Capitalism.* New York: Bloomsbury Press, 2008.

Alexander Hamilton. "Report on Manufactures," in George T. Crane and Abla Amawi, eds., *The Theoretical Evolution of International Political Economy: A Reader.* New York: Oxford University Press, 1991, pp. 37–47.

Friedrich List. *The National System of Political Economy.* New York: Augustus M. Kelley, 1966.

Mark A. Martinez. *The Myth of the Free Market: The Role of the State in a Capitalist Economy.* Sterling, VA: Kumarian Press, 2009.

Felix Rohaytn. *Bold Endeavors: How Our Government Built America and Why It Must Rebuild It Now.* New York: Simon & Schuster, 2009.

NOTES

1. Sun Yat-sen (1920), cited in Robert Reich, *The Work of Nations* (New York: Knopf, 1991), p. 30.

2. The concepts of *nation* and *nationalism* are the focus of the classic work by Hans Kohn, *The Idea of Nationalism* (New York: Macmillan, 1944) and of Eric J. Hobsbawm's *Nations and Nationalism Since 1780,* 2nd ed. (Cambridge: Cambridge University Press, 1992).

3. The classic definition of the state is Max Weber's, which emphasizes its administrative and legal qualities. See Max Weber, *The Theory of Social and Economic Organization* (New York: The Free Press, 1947), p. 156.

4. See Mark A. Martinez, *The Myth of the Free Market: The Role of the State in a Capitalist Economy* (Sterling, VA: Kumarian Press, 2009), pp. 106–110.

5. The history discussed in this section draws on Ha-Joon Chang's *Bad Samaritans: The Myth of Free Trade and the Secret History of Capitalism* (New York: Bloomsbury Press, 2008), pp. 40–43.

6. Ibid.

7. Ibid., especially Chapter 2.

8. See Kenneth Pomeranz and Steven Topik, *The World That Trade Created: Society, Culture, and the World Economy*, 2nd ed. (Armonk, NY: M.E. Sharpe, 2006).

9. Ibid., p. 141.

10. Ibid., p. 149.

11. See Karl Polanyi, *The Great Transformation: The Political and Economic Origins of Our Time* (Boston, MA: Beacon Press, 1944).

12. See Pietra Rivoli, *The Travels of a T-Shirt in the Global Economy: An Economist Examines the Markets, Power, and Politics of World Trade*, 2nd ed. (Hoboken, NJ: John Wiley, 2009), pp. 207–211.

13. For a detailed account of Hamilton's works, see Henry Cabot Lodge, ed., *The Works of Alexander Hamilton* (Honolulu, HI: University Press of the Pacific, 2005).

14. Alexander Hamilton, "Report on Manufactures," in George T. Crane and Abla Amawi, eds., *The Theoretical Evolution of International Political Economy: A Reader* (New York: Oxford University Press, 1991), p. 42.

15. Friedrich List, *The National System of Political Economy* (New York: Augustus M. Kelley, 1966), p. 144. Italics added.

16. Ibid., pp. 199–200.

17. The history in this paragraph is drawn from Martinez, *The Myth of the Free Market*, Chapter 6.

18. See for example, Chang, *Bad Samaritans*.

19. Martinez, *The Myth of the Free Market*, p. 150.

20. See, for example, Chalmers Johnson, "Introduction: The Idea of Industrial Policy," in his *The Industrial Policy Debate* (San Francisco, CA: ICS Press, 1984), pp. 3–26.

21. See, for example, Clyde Prestowitz, *Trading Places: How We Allowed Japan to Take the Lead* (New York: Basic Books, 1988).

22. Robert Gilpin, *The Political Economy of International Relations* (Princeton, NJ: Princeton University Press, 1987), p. 33.

23. See, for example, Tina Rosenberg, "Globalization: The Free Trade Fix," *New York Times Magazine,* August 18, 2002.

24. See, for example, Linda Weiss, *The Myth of the Powerless State* (Ithaca, NY: Cornell University Press, 1998), and Robert Wade, "Globalization and Its Limits: Reports of the Death of the National Economy Are Greatly Exaggerated," in Suzanne Berger and Ronald Dore (eds.), *National Diversity and Global Capitalism* (Ithaca, NY: Cornell University Press, 1996), pp. 60–88.

25. See Parag Khanna, *The Second World: How Emerging Powers Are Redefining Global Competition in the Twenty-first Century* (New York: Random House, 2008).

26. Robert Wade, *Governing the Market: Economic Theory and the Role of Government in East Asian Industrialization,* 2nd paperback ed. (Princeton, NJ: Princeton University Press, 2004).

27. Joshua Kurlantzick, "The Rise of Innovative State Capitalism," *Business Week,* June 28, 2012.

28. Ha-Joon Chang, *23 Things They Don't Tell You about Capitalism* (New York: Bloomsbury Press, 2010), p. 129.

29. See Chang, *Bad Samaritans,* for many examples (especially Chapter 4 "The Finn and the Elephant").

30. These are the OECD's preliminary figures for 2011. See Organisation for Economic Co-operation and Development, "FDI in Figures," (October 2012), at http://www.oecd.org/daf/internationalinvestment /investmentstatisticsandanalysis/FDI%20in%20 figures.pdf.

31. Felix Rohatyn, *Bold Endeavors: How Our Government Built America and Why It Must Rebuild It Now* (New York: Simon & Schuster, 2009).

32. Marc Levinson, "How the Postal Service Revolutionized U.S. Retailing," *Bloomberg.com,* August 23, 2012, at http://www.marclevinson.net/ParcelPost 082312.pdf.

33. Linda Weiss and Elizabeth Thurbon, "The Business of Buying American: Public Procurement as Trade Strategy in the USA," *Review of International Political Economy,* 13, no. 5 (2006), p. 718.

34. National Research Council, *Rising to the Challenge: U.S. Innovation Policy for the Global Economy* (Washington, DC: The National Academies Press, 2012).

35. See Patricia Goff, *Limits to Liberalization: Local Culture in a Global Marketplace* (Ithaca, NY: Cornell University Press, 2007).

Economic Determinism and Exploitation: The Structuralist Perspective

The Face of Exploitation: A mentally handicapped worker in a building materials factory in Kumishi, China.

AP Images/ImagineChina

The headlines from the *New York Times* on a seemingly ordinary day—February 12, 2012—read: Greece Passes Austerity Plan as Riots Rage; Admiral Pushing for Freer Hand in Special Forces; Romney Runs as an Outsider but Makes Room for Lobbyists; and Sectarian War in Syria Draws Neighbors In. How are we to make sense of these events? The structuralist perspective, with a focus on economic power and class conflict, offers a way to recognize their underlying logic. **Structuralism** has its roots in the ideas of Karl Marx but today encompasses a much broader group of scholars and activists. While most structuralists do not share the commitment to a socialist system as envisioned by some Marxists, they do believe that the current global capitalist system is unfair and exploitative and can be changed into something that distributes economic output in a more just manner. Indeed, the structure in structuralism is the global economic system. The global capitalist economy acts as an underlying system or order that is the driving force in society. It shapes society's economic, political, and social institutions and imposes constraints on what is possible.

Many claim that the sudden demise of socialist economies in the former Soviet Union and Eastern Europe and the more gradual transformation of Chinese communism into something closer to capitalism means that "Marx is dead." They believe we should stop using a structuralist analysis and embrace free markets as the best political-economic system. But recent developments related to the global financial crisis highlight not only the failures of free market capitalism but also the political clout of the economic elite, who receive bailouts while ordinary taxpayers struggle. Outside the seats of official power, millions of citizens continue to protest against free-trade organizations and U.S. imperialism. Those who feel excluded from economic progress, who believe that their share of the economic pie is too small, or who reject the legitimacy of the global capitalist elite represent a force that cannot be overlooked.

The structuralist perspective has no single method of analysis or unified set of policy recommendations. Rather, it is the site of an active, exciting debate that forces us to ask important questions. What are the historical events that created the capitalist structure? How does the global capitalist system operate? How are resources allocated? Is the allocation fair? What comes next and how do we get there? Moreover, this perspective is, at its roots, a critical one that challenges the existing state of affairs.

The main theses of this chapter are as follows: First, many see in structuralism not only the tools to conduct a scientific analysis of existing capitalist arrangements but also the grounds for a moral critique of the inequality and exploitation that capitalism produces within and between countries. Second, this framework of analysis is the only one that allows us to view international political economy (IPE) "from below," that is, from the perspective of the oppressed classes, the poor, and the developing Third World nations. In contrast to mercantilism and liberalism, it gives a voice to the powerless. Third, this perspective raises issues about human freedom and the application of reason in shaping national and global institutions. Finally, structuralism focuses on what is dynamic in IPE. It views capitalism and other modes of production as driven by conflict and crisis and subject to change. What exists now is a system and set of structures that emerged at a particular time and may one day be replaced by a different system of political economy.

After outlining some of the major ideas, concepts, and policies associated with both Marx and Lenin, we explore some of the more recent theories of dependency, the modern world system, and neoimperialism. We also briefly discuss some structuralist arguments about the recent financial crisis and conclude with some of their views about reform of the global political economy.

FEUDALISM, CAPITALISM, SOCIALISM—MARX'S THEORY OF HISTORY

The first great scholar to pioneer a structural approach to political economy was Karl Marx (1818–1883). Born in Trier, Germany, Marx did his most significant work while living in England, spending hours on research at the British Museum in London. Many of his views reflect the conditions he and his collaborator Friedrich Engels observed in English mills and factories at the height of the Industrial Revolution. Adults and children often labored under dreadful working conditions and lived in abject poverty and squalor. Marx's theory of history, his notion of class conflict, and his critique of capitalism must all be understood in the context of nineteenth-century Europe's cultural, political, and economic climate.

Marx understood history to be a great, dynamic, evolving creature, determined fundamentally by economic and technological forces. Marx believed that through a process called **historical materialism** these forces can be objectively explained and understood just like any other natural law.[1] Historical materialism takes as its starting point the notion that the *forces of production*, defined as the sum total of knowledge and technology contained in society, set the parameters for the whole political-economic system. As Marx put it, "The hand mill gives you society with the feudal lord, the steam mill society with the industrial capitalist."[2] At very low levels of technology (primitive forces of production), society would be organized into a hunting-gathering system. At a higher level, we would see an agricultural system using steel ploughs and horses, oxen, or other beasts of burden. This technological advancement (although still considered primitive by modern standards) causes a change in the social relations in society, specifically the emergence of feudalism. Instead of hunters and gatherers banding together in small-scale tribes with a relatively equal division of the economic output, feudalism is characterized by a large strata of peasant-farmers and a smaller aristocracy. The key Marxist claim is that changes in technology *determine* changes in the social system. Thus, Marx has been considered a *technological determinist*, at least within his theory of history.

Marx sees the course of history as steadily evolving from one system of political economy (or "mode of production," in his words) to another due to the growing contradiction between the technical forces of production and the social class or property relations in which they develop. In each of these modes of production, there is a **dialectical process** whereby inherently unstable opposing economic forces and counterforces lead to crisis, to revolution, and to the next stage of history. Over long periods of human history, the forces of production will continually improve because technology is simply an aspect of human knowledge. Once a discovery is made, whether the smelting of copper and tin into bronze or the development of a faster computer processor, knowledge of it tends to be retained and can be used and improved upon by subsequent generations. Human knowledge and technology have a ratchet-like quality—they can go forward a bit at a time but will not go backward.

For Marx, the agents of change are human beings organized into conflicting social classes. Because class relations change more slowly than technological development, social change is impeded, fostering conflict between the classes that in a capitalist society gradually produces a face-off between the bourgeoisie and the proletariat. According to Marx, the **bourgeoisie** are wealthy elites who own the means of production—or what today would be big industries, banks, and financial institutions. In British society, the bourgeoisie also made up the Members of Parliament and thus controlled the government—or state, as Marx would refer to it. In Marx's day, the **proletariat** were the exploited workers (including their families) in Britain's woolen mills, who received very low wages and sometimes died on the job. Gradually, it was thought, workers would realize their common interests and would organize and press on the bourgeoisie for higher wages and better working conditions.

Marx identified three objective laws that would, at some point, destroy capitalism from within. First, *the law of the falling rate of profit* asserts that over time as investment causes machines to replace workers, profits must decline and ultimately disappear. Second, *the law of disproportionality* (also called the *problem of underconsumption*) suggests that capitalism, because of its anarchic, unplanned nature, is prone to instability such that workers cannot afford to buy what they make. Like other classical economists, Marx believed in the *labor theory of value*, which argues that the value of a commodity is related to the amount of labor required for its production. He tried to demonstrate that workers were paid less than the full value of what they produced. Because workers were abundant (as poorer people moved from the countryside and into cities looking for work), the bourgeoisie were able to pay them less and make more profit for themselves from the sale of the goods the workers produced. Third and finally, *the law of concentration* (or *accumulation of capital*) holds that capitalism tends to create increasing inequality in the distribution of income and wealth. As the bourgeoisie continue to exploit the proletariat and as weaker capitalists are swallowed by stronger, bigger ones, wealth and the ownership of capital become increasingly concentrated in fewer and fewer hands. Marx viewed these as objective, inescapable features of the capitalist mode of production, which he predicted will result in the ultimate collapse of the system.

For Marx, capitalism is more than an unhappy stop on the road to socialism. It is also a *necessary* stage in history, which builds wealth and raises material living standards. It is the dynamic nature of market capitalism that lies at the heart of political economy. According to Marx, capitalism plays two historic roles. First, it transforms the world and in so doing breaks down feudalism, its historical antecedent. Second, it creates the social and economic foundations for the eventual transition to a "higher" level of social development. Marx argued that when class conflict becomes so severe that it blocks the advance of human development, a social revolution will sweep away the existing legal and political arrangements and replace them with ones more compatible with continued social and technological progress. In this way, history has already evolved through distinct epochs or stages after primitive communism: slavery, feudalism, and capitalism. Marx's *Communist Manifesto,* published in 1848, called for a revolution that would usher in a new epoch of history—socialism—which would, after yet still another revolution, finally produce pure communism.

As we will discuss in the next section, neo-Marxists and structuralists still accept the notion of exploitation, although it has been separated from the labor theory of value. Also, most neo-Marxist scholars no longer accept the claim that capitalism will someday destroy itself. Rather, it is generally accepted that Marx's mathematical analysis that produced this prediction was simply erroneous.[3] When socialism was regarded as inevitable it made sense to plan for it, but now that capitalism is recognized as a viable economic system, the entire discussion about socialism has shifted. Socialism may be a possible future, but it would have to be a political choice, not something imposed on society by Marx's deterministic laws of historical epochs. Nonetheless, many other ideas from Marx or from the school of thought he established contribute to an explanation of phenomena we still observe today in the international political economy.

SOME SPECIFIC CONTRIBUTIONS OF MARX TO STRUCTURALISM

A word of caution is in order concerning the nature of Marxist thought and its relationship to contemporary structuralism. Marx wrote millions of words; in so vast a body of work, he necessarily treated the main themes repeatedly and not always consistently. What Marx "said" or "thought" about any interesting issue is therefore subject to dispute. At the same time, Marxist scholars have interpreted his writings in many ways. Here we explore four ideas that are found in varying degrees within Marx's work and that have been further developed by neo-Marxists, structuralists, and other varieties of radicals up to the present. Some ideas that Marx considered to be of great importance are no longer regarded as useful by most current scholars. And many ideas that he presented have been modified (and hopefully improved) by subsequent scholars, which can be seen as part of the normal development in any field of academic inquiry.

The following four Marxist ideas are central to contemporary structuralist analyses of the international political economy: the definition of class, class conflict and the exploitation of workers, capitalist control over the state, and ideological manipulation.

The Definition of Class

To understand the Marxist notion of class, we must first define *capital*. Capital, what Marx called the means of production, refers to the privately owned assets used to produce the commodities in an economy. Car factories are capital, as are all the machines and tools inside them. A computer, when owned by a company, is capital. So are the desks, filing cabinets, cranes, bulldozers, supertankers, and natural resources like land and oil. Almost all production requires both workers and physical assets, and in modern economies, production processes can indeed be very capital-intensive.

When we speak of "capital goods," we mean more than simply the existence of such productive assets. Humans have used tools for much longer than capitalism has existed and socialist societies have machines and factories just like capitalist ones. To call an asset capital also means that it is privately owned, that somebody has legal ownership and effective control over that asset. In many cases today that ownership is merely a piece of paper or a computerized account representing stock in a corporation. The property rights in a capitalist society dictate that the owners of capital will receive the profits from the sale of commodities produced by the capital they own and the labor they hire.

Class is determined by the ownership, or lack of ownership, of capital. A minority of people will own a disproportionate share of the productive assets of the society; they constitute the capitalist class, also referred to as the bourgeoisie. In the United States, for example, the wealthiest 1 percent of the population owns 53 percent of all stocks and the top 10 percent owns 88 percent, leaving 12 percent of this financial asset for the remaining 90 percent of society.[4] Real estate, excluding a household's principal residence, has a similarly unequal distribution. Bonds are even more concentrated, with the top 1 percent owning nearly two-thirds of the total. The majority of the population owns very little capital, and indeed, many people own no productive assets or any shares of stock; they constitute the working class, known as the proletariat. Note that workers may own assets—houses, cars, appliances, and so on—that are not productive assets but simply possessions. They cannot be mixed with labor to form a commodity that could be profitably sold on a market. Implicitly, if not explicitly, Marxists regard the original distribution of assets as unjust, noting that historically a small number of people confiscated large amounts of land and other resources by means of violence and coercion. Thus, the contemporary consequences of this distribution are criticized for moral reasons.

Class Conflict and the Exploitation of Workers

For households in the capitalist class, profits are the leading source of income. For example, if the average return in the stock market is 5 percent per year and a capitalist household owned $50 million worth of stock in various corporations, then the income produced by that ownership would be $2.5 million in one year ($50 million times 0.05). This leaves the original $50 million intact and it comes without any requirement that the capitalists actually perform any work.

Workers, on the other hand, have little or no capital and therefore must sell their ability to labor to capitalists if they are to receive an income. In other words, businesses hire workers and pay them a wage or salary. Workers must work to receive an income. For Marxists, this inevitably leads to the exploitation of workers because of their weak bargaining position. In a capitalist economy, there is always a certain level of unemployment; that is, some workers are denied access to capital and thus the ability to produce goods (remember that production requires the combination of physical assets and labor). By restricting access to their productive assets, capitalists, in effect, create an artificial scarcity of capital. Even when there is 10 percent unemployment, there is likely to be sufficient idle machinery that could put everybody to work if put into operation. But it is actually profitable for businesses to keep some capital out of use in order to maintain a certain amount of unemployment. The presence of unemployed workers functions to keep down the wages of the employed—if one worker does not accept the going rate, then he or she can be easily replaced. Thus, unemployment allows capitalists to dominate workers and serves as the foundation for their exploitation.

The exploitation of workers by capitalists is a specific instance of power relations more generally. To say that actor A has power over B (or can dominate B) is to say that A is able to get B to act in ways that promote the interests of A and are contrary to B's.[5] This does not necessarily mean that B has literally no choice but simply that the options are configured to benefit A. When the armed robber tells the hapless victim, "Your money or your life!" the victim could choose the latter. Nonetheless, it is the case that the robber, due to the presence of a gun, has power over the victim because in either scenario the robber will make off with the money. The victim is coerced into making the least bad choice.

Many workers are in a similar situation: Either accept low wages or starve! Capitalism depends on "the existence of workers who in the formal sense, voluntarily, but actually under the whip of hunger, offer themselves."[6] Joan Robinson, the famous socialist-leaning post-Keynesian economist, captured the position of workers by remarking that the only thing worse than being exploited under capitalism is not being exploited. In other words, the worst outcome for those in the working class is to be unemployed, and it is the fear of unemployment that forces workers to accept low wages. Workers technically do have a choice, but the game is structured such that the best choice is still a bad choice for them, yet a good one for the capitalists. In sum, exploitation means that capitalists, because they have greater labor market power, are able to expropriate a share of the economic output that should belong to workers. Essentially, the capitalist forces his workers to accept a bad deal because the alternative is even worse.

We should be clear that class conflict does not necessarily mean a state of warfare or even hostility of any sort. In fact, many individuals may not even recognize the conflicting nature of their relationship with the other class. Class conflict usually results in a gain for one side at the expense of the other. The degree to which individuals in different classes act upon this fact is hard to predict. Furthermore, even when the conflict is recognized, it is possible that a compromise between classes can be found. The welfare states of Western Europe may be considered instances of such compromise. In states such as France, Germany, and Sweden, organized labor renounces the goal of a socialist society and offers a relatively harmonious relationship with business in exchange for high wages, adequate unemployment compensation, universal health care, paid vacations, and generous pensions.

Because workers are exploited, they share an objective economic interest in changing the economic system, while capitalists will have an interest in maintaining the status quo. The presence of an "objective" interest does not necessarily mean that workers will actually form a socially and politically active group or movement. Workers (1) may not subjectively recognize their common objective interest, or (2) may recognize their interest but be unable to organize. The first is an instance of **false consciousness** (discussed in the section "Ideological Manipulation"). The second may be the result of class struggle in which an organized capitalist class prevents the successful organization of the working class, for example, into unions, or the result of collective action problems that impede the working class from organizing itself (and these two may be interrelated in complex ways). In Marxist language, workers are often a class *in itself* without becoming a class *for itself*.

The central idea, however, is that the relationship between capitalists and workers is built upon an objective division of the economic output of a society into wages and profits. The actions of individual workers and capitalists will depend on many concrete historical variables, leading to civil war or revolution, to class compromise, or to passivity due to subjective ignorance. But regardless of the way in which the conflict plays itself out, class conflict is a fundamental objective characteristic of capitalist societies.

Capitalist Control over the State

The *state* is defined as the organization in a society that governs, by force if necessary, a population within a particular territory. Despite globalization, the modern state is still usually the most powerful organization within any society, typically possessing the strongest tools of repression in the form of military and police forces. Based on its powers, the state also exercises tremendous influence in picking economic winners and losers through taxation, spending, and regulations. Some of its most important regulations involve workplace and labor issues such as setting the minimum wage, writing and enforcing child labor laws, and establishing the ease or difficulty in forming labor unions. While states and their leaders are not omnipotent, they do indeed have the ability to help their friends and punish their enemies. It is therefore reasonable that both capitalists and workers would seek to "capture" the state, to apply the capacities of the state to their particular interests.

In the struggle to control the state, capitalists and workers have very different resources. The capitalist class has greater financial resources, and this often translates easily into influence in the political system. Capitalists are typically able to donate more money to probusiness candidates. The think-tanks used by officials to craft policies, such as the Brookings Institution or the Heritage Foundation, are largely funded by corporations or individual members of the capitalist elite. Furthermore, the state depends upon the investments of businesses in order to generate tax revenue and employment for its citizens; a climate that is too antibusiness will cause capital to flee elsewhere or at least reduce investment. Thus, even without direct attempts by capitalists to influence the state, many policies will promote their interests regardless.

For workers to turn their greater numbers into political power, the state must allow for strong democratic institutions that give workers an opportunity to organize and play a substantial role in policy making. In Western European countries that have proportional representation voting, workers' parties (Social Democratic or Socialist Parties) often win majorities or significant pluralities. Whereas capitalists have the power to relocate or reduce investment, workers may also attempt to influence a political system through strikes and protests. Often a strike is the response of a single union to a particular grievance with a firm, but when a large segment of the population is involved in a general strike, the entire economy can be halted and governments can be forced to respond to the demands of the working class. The efficacy of this kind of action depends heavily on the degree of solidarity among workers; if they do not hang together, then the capitalists will find them easy to divide and conquer. It is no surprise to Marxists that general strikes, or even the more limited secondary or sympathy strikes, have been made illegal in the United States.

Structuralists recognize that the influence of the state does not necessarily end at the border. Like mercantilists, they agree that any state can be regarded as an actor in a global system made up of other states. The relative military and economic strengths of the states will generally determine the winners and losers in any conflict. There is little disagreement between structuralists and mercantilists regarding the importance of the powers that states wield. The difference between the two IPE outlooks concerns the motives behind the use of state power. Whereas mercantilists see the state as an actor with its own interests (that *can* reflect the interests of all its citizens), structuralists believe that a state will act to advance the narrower interests of the class that dominates it—typically the wealthy capitalists.

In their search for profits, capitalists in the rich states not only exploit domestic workers but workers in other countries as well. The international situation is complicated because capitalists in any country are not only in conflict with their own workers but also have a complex relationship with capitalists in other countries. Meanwhile, capitalist firms do compete with other firms both domestically and internationally, yet they also form alliances with those firms on issues that impact the functioning of the global capitalist system. Thus, depending on the issue, capitalists in New York or London often form alliances with the local capitalist elite in Mexico City or Riyadh in order to keep profits up, workers weak, and wages down.

Ideological Manipulation

Power derives from the control over hard resources, like capital or the military, and the ability to force others to act in certain ways by structuring the choices of the weaker to the benefit of the stronger (see Chapter 9). Yet structuralists also accept that power is exercised through the deployment of ideology. An important goal of capitalist ideology is to give *legitimacy* to the capitalist economic system by controlling people's hearts and minds. Once the working class believes that the system is legitimate, it will believe that it is appropriate and just.

Somewhat paradoxically, a dictatorship, which relies upon brute military and police strength, is often the least stable system of government because it requires consistently high levels of surveillance and repression to maintain its power. The uprisings known as the Arab Spring are good examples of the responses by citizens who perceive their leaders as having an illegitimate claim to power. While even democratic societies possess arsenals of surveillance and repression, they tend to be less intrusive than those found in authoritarian systems. In a democracy, because citizens participate in fair elections, the leaders typically earn the consent of the led, including even those who voted for a different candidate or party.

When individuals regard a democratic political system as legitimate, they are also likely to believe that the capitalist system itself is proper and just. A belief by workers in the legitimacy of capitalism ensures that (1) they will not seek to replace it with something else (e.g., socialism) and (2) they will work harder within the present system, thus increasing the income of the capitalists who generally do not have to use force in order to protect the wealth they have obtained through the exploitation of the laboring class. Marxists would say that in effect, workers consent to their own exploitation. Given the importance of legitimacy, the capitalist class will actively seek to create an ideology in society that gives legitimacy to procapitalist institutions (see the box Noam Chomsky and the Power of Ideology below).

NOAM CHOMSKY AND THE POWER OF IDEOLOGY

Noam Chomsky, born in Philadelphia in 1928, is not only the leading structuralist of our time but also, according to a survey of academics, the most recognized intellectual alive today in the world.[a] Remarkably, his intellectual training and professional appointment is not even in political economy; instead, Chomsky is a professor of linguistics at M.I.T. who is regarded by many in the field as the most important linguist of the twentieth century. His ideas have even influenced philosophy and computer science. Over his long career he has frequently lectured on college campuses and given many television interviews—even one with Ali G.

In the field of political economy much of Chomsky's work has been an indictment of militaristic foreign policy and pro-corporate capitalism. Indeed, his very first published writing—at the age of 10—was a piece warning about the dangers of fascism. He has been a political activist in the civil rights struggle, the movement against nuclear weapons, and protests against U.S. military involvement in Vietnam, Latin America, and the Middle East. Although raised in a Jewish home where only Hebrew was spoken, he has become one of the leading critics of Israel, both for its treatment of Palestinians and its aggression toward its neighbors. Now in his eighties, Chomsky has offered his support for the Occupy Wall Street movement.

Although Chomsky denies that his work in political economy and linguistics are related, he clearly emphasizes the use of language as an instrument of domination under liberal, capitalist regimes. The creation and marketing of ideas requires resources and, although opinions cannot literally be bought and sold, their production in many ways is similar to the production of ordinary commodities. The consent of the proletariat to their own exploitation must be "manufactured" by powerful interests in society, including the state and the corporate media. Chomsky writes, "One of the prerogatives of power is the ability to write history with the confidence that there will be little challenge."[b]

The term for the marketing and dissemination of these ideas is "propaganda." For example, the threat of foreign enemies has been used by those in power in the United States to draw attention away from internal, class-based conflicts. For much of the twentieth century, the Soviet Union and communism served that function. More recently, Iraq, Afghanistan, and (Islamic) terrorism in general have been the enemies. Writing on the George W. Bush administration, Chomsky observed, "Manufactured fear provided enough of a popular base for the invasion of Iraq, instituting the norm of aggressive war at will, and afforded the administration enough of a hold on political power so that it could proceed with a harsh and unpopular domestic agenda."[c] Almost nothing has changed under the Obama administration except that Iran has replaced Iraq as the target of propaganda. Chomsky and his colleague Edward Herman created a propaganda model to explain the ways in which the "free press" in liberal, capitalist societies—especially in the United States—reports on events in ways that ultimately serve the interests of large corporations and the state.[d]

References

[a]For biographical information, see Peggy J. Anderson, "Noam Chomsky," *Great Lives From History: The Twentieth Century*, (2008), p. 1, Biography Reference Center, EBSCO *host;* "Chomsky, Noam," *Britannica Biographies* (2011), p. 1, Biography Reference Center, EBSCO *host;* and *Democracy Now*, "The Life and Times of Noam Chomsky," Interview, November 26, 2004.

[b]Noam Chomsky, *Hegemony or Survival: America's Quest for Global Dominance* (New York: Owl Books, 2004), p. 167.

[c]Ibid., p. 121.

[d]Edward S. Herman and Noam Chomsky, *Manufacturing Consent* (New York: Pantheon Books, 1988).

The superior financial resources of the capitalists typically means that pro-capitalist messages—the benefits of free trade, the need for low taxes on the rich, the desirability of limited government, and the problems with unions—will be stronger than a competing set of beliefs favored by workers. Workers, of course, are not powerless and at certain times on certain issues may succeed in persuading the public. But the game is biased in favor of capitalists, whose ideology permeates society through education and communications media. Once the subordinate class accepts this worldview, whether intentionally or by osmosis, its thoughts and actions are brought into line with the interests of the dominant class.

It is a great tragedy, according to Marxists, that capitalists not only exploit workers but also manipulate their beliefs so that they become ignorant of, or apathetic about, their own exploitation. Workers' belief in the legitimacy and benefits of capitalism is *false consciousness*. Is it possible that people could be fooled about what their own self-interest is? We should recall that the rule by monarchs in the Middle Ages in Europe was at least partially legitimized by an ideology promoted by the Catholic Church asserting a Divine Right to govern: to challenge the rule of the aristocracy was to offend God. Even today in Thailand, it is a serious crime to insult the king.[7]

For many people, Marxism is equated with socialism or communism. Yet, we can now see that Marx envisioned those systems as epochs of history that would come after capitalism. Marx's four major contributions to IPE (discussed earlier) can be separated from his theory of history and its prediction regarding the inevitability of socialism and then communism.

LENIN AND INTERNATIONAL CAPITALISM

V. I. Lenin (1870–1924) is best known for his role in the Russian Revolution of 1917 and the founding of the Soviet Union. In many ways, he turned Marx on his head, placing politics over economics when he argued that Russia had gone through its capitalist stage of history and was ready for a second, socialist revolution. Lenin is also known for his views on imperialism based on Marx's theories of class struggle, conflict, and exploitation. In his famous book *Imperialism: The Highest Stage of Capitalism* (1917),[8] Lenin explains how, through imperialism, advanced capitalist core states expanded control over and exploited what his contemporaries called "backward" colonial regions of the world, leaving them unevenly developed, with some classes to prosper and others mired in poverty. By the end of the nineteenth century, new colonies were established mainly in Central and Southern Africa, and they became the main sources of cheap labor, scarce resources, and an outlet for industrial investment of the advanced capitalist nations. These colonies produced coffee, tea, sugar, and other food commodities not found in mother countries.

The critical element fueling imperialism, in Lenin's view, was the centralization of market power into the hands of a few "cartels, syndicates and trusts, and merging with them, the capital of a dozen or so banks manipulating thousands of millions."[9] Because capitalism led to monopolies that concentrated capital, it gradually undermined the ability of capitalists to find sufficient markets and investment opportunities in industrial regions of the world. Of course, profit-seeking capitalists were unwilling to use their surplus capital to improve the living standards of the proletariat so that they could purchase more goods and services. To prevent capitalism from imploding, Lenin and others argued that imperialism therefore was a necessary outlet for surplus finance and allowed capitalism to survive. Imperialism allowed rich capitalist nations to sustain their profit rates, while keeping the poorer nations underdeveloped, deep in debt, and dependent on the rich nations for manufactured goods, jobs, and financial resources.

For Lenin, imperialism also signified the monopoly phase of capitalism or "the transition from capitalism to a higher system," by which he meant that the presence of monopolies and imperialism that followed was yet *another* epoch of history between capitalism and socialism, unaccounted for by Marx.[10] Finally, imperialism helped convert the poorer colonial regions into the new "proletariat" of the *international capitalist system*. According to Lenin, "Monopolist capitalist combines—cartels, syndicates, trusts—divide among themselves, first of all, the whole internal market of a country, and impose their control, more or less completely, upon the industry of that country," generating a world market.[11]

It is not surprising that Lenin's theory of imperialism has been very influential, especially among intellectuals in the less developed countries, where his views have shaped policies and attitudes toward international trade and finance generally. Before and especially after World War I, cutthroat competition among capitalist nations contributed to international tensions and conflict. Elites in poorer nations competed for capital and investment, which made them easy targets for production monopolies. In these regions and countries, communist revolutionaries and leaders, like Mao Zedong in China, Ho Chi Minh in Vietnam, and Fidel Castro in Cuba, organized anticolonialism and anti-imperialism campaigns and fought "wars of national liberation" against capitalist imperial powers.

Today, most structuralists no longer believe that the falling rate of profit for capitalists will cause the collapse of the capitalist mode of production. However, Leninist arguments about imperialism still remain influential in China, Vietnam, Cuba, Venezuela, and even in some industrialized nations that have active socialist and communist parties. Leaders of these and other countries still view capitalists as profit-seeking imperialists who seek opportunities abroad where democratic political institutions and the working class are weak.

No attempt to consider the political economy of relations between developed and developing countries is complete without considering theories of imperialism. We include Lenin's theory of imperialism under the general heading of "structuralism," as we did Marx's theories, because its analysis is based on the assumption that it is in capitalism's nature for the finance and production structures among nations to be biased in favor of the owners of capital. In theory, the relationship between capital-abundant nations and capital-scarce nations *should be* one of *interdependence*, because each needs the other for maximum growth. But for many structuralists, the result in practice is *dependence*, exploitation, and uneven development.

IMPERIALISM AND GLOBAL WORLD ORDERS

In this section, we explore some of the more recent structuralist theories of dependency, the modern world system, and modern imperialism (or neoimperialism) that trace their analytical approaches and policy prescriptions to both Marx and Lenin.

Dependency Theory

A structuralist perspective that highlights the relationships between what are referred to as core and peripheral countries, while calling attention to the constraints put on countries in the latter group, is called **dependency theory**. A wide range of views can be grouped together under this heading. Their differences, however, are less important to us here than what they have in common, which is the view that the structure of the global political economy essentially enslaves the less developed countries of the South by making them reliant to the point of being vulnerable to the nations of the capitalist core of the North. Theotonio Dos Santos sees three eras of dependence in modern history: colonial dependence (during the eighteenth and nineteenth centuries), financial-industrial dependence (during the nineteenth and early twentieth centuries), and a structure of dependence today based on the postwar multinational corporations.

Andre Gunder Frank has focused a good deal of attention on dependency in Latin America and is noted for his "development of underdevelopment" thesis.[12] He argues that developing nations were never "underdeveloped" in the sense that one might think of them as "backward" or traditional societies. Instead, once great civilizations in their own right, the developing regions of the world *became* underdeveloped as a result of their colonization by the Western industrialized nations. Along with exploitation, imperialism produced underdevelopment. In order to escape this underdevelopment trap, a number of researchers, including Frank, have called for peripheral nations to withdraw from the global political economy. In the 1950s and 1960s, the leadership of many socialist movements in the Third World favored revolutionary tactics and ideological mass movements to change the fundamental dynamics of not only the political and economic order of their society but also the world capitalist system.

Recently, some dependency theorists have recommended a variety of other strategies by which developing nations could industrialize and develop. Raul Prebisch, an Argentinean economist, was instrumental in founding the United Nations Conference on Trade and Development (UNCTAD). The developing nations that have joined this body have made it their goal to monitor and recommend policies that would, in effect, help redistribute power and income between Northern developed and Southern developing countries. Many dependency theorists, however, have been more aggressive about reforming the international economy and have supported the calls for a "new international economic order" (NIEO), which gained momentum shortly after the OPEC oil price hike in 1973. The important point to make here is that dependency theories have served as part of a critique of the relationship of the core to peripheral nations. Whether that relationship can—or even should—be equalized is a matter usually played out in the political arena.

Modern World System Theory

One fascinating contemporary variant of the structuralist perspective focuses on the way in which the global system has developed since the middle of the fifteenth century. This is the **modern world system (MWS)** theory originated by Immanuel Wallerstein and developed by a number of scholars, including Christopher

Chase-Dunn. Capitalist in nature, the world system largely determines political and social relations, both within and between nations and other international entities.

For Immanuel Wallerstein, the world economy provides the sole means of organization in the international system. The modern world system exhibits the following characteristics: a single division of labor whereby nation-states are mutually dependent on economic exchange; the sale of products and goods for the sake of profit; and, finally, the division of the world into three functional areas or socioeconomic units that correspond to the roles that nations within these regions play in the international economy.[13] From the MWS perspective, the capitalist **core** states of northwest Europe in the sixteenth century moved beyond agricultural specialization to higher-skilled industries and modes of production by absorbing other regions into the capitalist world economy. Through this process, Eastern Europe became the agricultural **periphery** and exported grains, bullion, wood, cotton, and sugar to the core. Mediterranean Europe and its labor-intensive industries became the **semiperiphery** or intermediary between the core and periphery.

It would be easy to define the core, periphery, and semiperiphery in terms of the types of nations within each group (such as the United States, China, and South Korea, respectively), but the MWS is not based primarily on the nation-state. In this theory, the core represents a geographic region made up of nation-states that play a partial role in the MWS. The force of bourgeois interests actually exists, in varying degrees, in every country. Every nation has elements of core, periphery, and semiperiphery, although not equally. In common with Marx, then, the MWS theory looks at IPE in terms of class relations and patterns of exploitation.

According to Wallerstein, the core states dominate the peripheral states through unequal exchange for the purpose of extracting cheap raw materials instead of, as Lenin argued, merely using the periphery as a market for dumping surplus production. The core interacts with the semiperiphery and periphery through the global structure of capitalism, exploiting these regions and also transforming them. The semiperiphery serves more of a political than an economic role; it is both exploited and exploiter, diffusing opposition of the periphery to the core region.

Interestingly, on some issues Wallerstein attempts to bridge mercantilism (and political realism) with Marxist views about the relationship of politics to economics. For instance, as a mercantilist would, he accepts the notion that the world is politically arranged in an anarchical manner—that is, there is no *single* sovereign political authority to govern interstate relations. However, much like a Marxist-Leninist, he proposes that power politics and social differences are also conditioned by the capitalist structure of the world economy. According to Wallerstein, capitalists within core nation-states use state authority as an instrument to maximize individual profit. Historically, the state served economic interests to the extent that "state machineries of the core states were strengthened to meet the needs of capitalist landowners and their merchant allies."[14] Wallerstein also argues that, once created, state machineries have a certain amount of autonomy.[15] On the other hand, politics is constrained by the economic structure. He asserts, for instance, that strong (core) states dominate weak (peripheral) ones because placement of the nation-state in the world capitalist system affects the nation state's ability to influence its global role. As Wallerstein puts it, "The functioning then of a capitalist world economy requires that groups pursue their economic interests within a single world market while seeking to distort this market for their benefit by organizing to exert influence on states, some of which are far more powerful than others but none of which controls the world-market in its entirety."[16]

One problem with Wallerstein's theory is precisely what makes it so attractive: its comprehensive, yet almost simple way, of characterizing IPE. Many criticize his theory for being too deterministic, both economically and in terms of the constraining effects of the *global* capitalist system. Nation-states, according to Wallerstein, are not free to choose courses of action or policies. Instead, they are relegated to playing economically determined roles. Finally, Wallerstein is often faulted for viewing capitalism as the end product of current history. In this sense, he differs from many structuralists who feel that political-economic systems are still a choice people have and not something structurally determined.

Neoimperialism, Neocolonialism, and Empire-Building Redux

As we suggest in several chapters throughout this text, the term **neoimperialism** describes a newer, more subtle version of imperialism that structuralists claim the United States and other industrialized nations have been practicing since the end of the Vietnam War in 1975. Neoimperialism differs from classic imperialism in that states no longer need to occupy other countries in order to exploit or control them.

Harry Magdoff (1913–2006), who edited the socialist journal *Monthly Review*, provides a good example of the older, *orthodox* version of Marxist-Leninist ideas related to U.S. imperialism. In his 1969 book *The Age of Imperialism: The Economics of U.S. Foreign Policy*, Magdoff established some of the same themes adopted by dependency and MWS theorists—especially those that focused on capitalism's expansive nature. He argued that the motives behind U.S. efforts to promote the economic liberal policies of the GATT, the IMF, and the World Bank could not be separated from U.S. security interests. During the Cold War, U.S. intervention abroad was not the result of one leader's decision, but the result of underlying structural economic, political, and military forces governing U.S. foreign policy.

Contrary to realists who argued that the United States intervened in Vietnam and other developing nations to "contain communism," Magdoff claims that the United States was motivated by a breakdown of British hegemony, coupled with the growth of monopoly capitalism—domination of the international economy by large firms that concentrate and centralize production.[17] President Eisenhower had earlier linked maintaining access to the natural resources of Indochina (Vietnam, Laos, Cambodia, and Thailand) to U.S. security interests. But in his farewell address, Ike warned of the growing influence of the military–industrial complex and its tendency to exaggerate the strength of enemies in order to justify military spending.

When the Vietnam War ended in 1975, many believed that the "naked" version of classical imperialism was over. U.S. hegemony declined as U.S. economic growth slowed and the U.S. dollar weakened when the Bretton Woods system formally collapsed in 1971 (see Chapter 7). The 1973 OPEC oil crisis exposed the U.S. and other core countries' dependence on foreign oil. The U.S. public opposed military intervention in developing nations outside the U.S. "sphere of influence" in Europe, Japan, and Latin America.

However, by the late 1970s, a more classic type of imperialism resurfaced in the combined economic and military objectives President Carter established in his Carter Doctrine, proclaiming the U.S. willingness to intervene in the Persian Gulf to protect U.S. oil interests. In 1979, the Iranian Revolution overthrew the U.S.-backed Shah of Iran, threatening U.S. control over oil and U.S. influence in the Middle East. Soon after, the CIA supported efforts of the Mujahedeen in Afghanistan against the Soviet occupation.

In the 1980s, as part of the Reagan Doctrine, the United States renewed its efforts to intervene in developing nations that threatened U.S. economic and security interests. Reagan assisted Saddam Hussein in the Iran–Iraq war and unsuccessfully intervened in Lebanon in 1983 and 1984. To contain communism in the Western Hemisphere, Reagan backed the *contras* in Nicaragua. The United States also supported pro-Western authoritarian regimes in Guatemala, El Salvador, and other South American countries. All this time, he (and the presidents that followed him) never let up from seeking to control oil and assist Western oil corporations in the Middle East. One method of maintaining that influence was by giving military and other forms of aid to states like Saudi Arabia.

After the fall of the Soviet Union in 1991 and the Persian Gulf War in 1991, President Bush senior ushered in what many structuralists view as a "new age of imperialism." From the perspective of U.S. policy makers, because the Soviet threat was gone, the globalization campaign provided the United States with an opportunity not to intervene as much as it did during the Cold War. Core nations could penetrate peripheral states via trade, investment, and other policies that rendered them dependent on core states. The United States and other industrialized nations promoted globalization as a beneficial package of policies that would help all developing countries grow. The Washington Consensus, an understanding that economic liberal trade and investment best served this purpose, became the rationale for policies for the IMF, the World Bank, and the WTO.

Many structuralists viewed these financial institutions as mere "fronts" for a U.S. goal to exploit the periphery, especially in Southeast Asia and Central and Latin America. Throughout the 1990s, President Clinton promoted economic liberal policy objectives with *selective* military intervention abroad. His campaign of "engagement and enlargement" mixed hard and soft power to explicitly draw other countries into the global capitalist economy while expanding the scope of democracy. Based on some of the lessons learned in Vietnam, Clinton was not as overtly interventionist as Reagan. However, U.S. troops continued to be staged in many regions—for short periods of time. The U.S. military hit terrorist targets in Sudan and Afghanistan with cruise missiles launched from U.S. warships. In cases where U.S. interests were not as clear, such as Rwanda, the United States failed to intervene to save hundreds of thousands who died in a campaign of genocide. Clinton's preference for multilateral (relatively equal) relations with U.S. allies set the tone for joint NATO operations in the Balkans and for intervention in Kosovo in 1998.

As we discussed in Chapter 1, it was during the 1990s that many structuralists became quite critical of the latest phase of global capitalism—often referred to as hypercapitalism—that drives transnational corporations to produce new products in a supercompetitive global atmosphere in which individuals are made to feel better off but really are not. For many antiglobalization protestors, capitalism and globalization weaken local environmental laws, exploit labor, and are a major cause of poverty. And in many developing nations, they exacerbate class struggle between the world's richest fifth and nearly everyone else.

In the 1990s, the idea of imperialism once again appeared in U.S. policy-making circles but not in the *negative* context of military intervention abroad to protect economic interests. A growing number of neoconservatives (aka "neocons") such as Charles Krauthammer and Max Boot deplored the fact that when the Soviet Union fell, the United States missed an opportunity to capitalize on a "unipolar moment" by imposing its (benevolent) will on the rest of the world.[18] After 9/11, many policy officials and academics encouraged the new Bush administration to seize the moment and make maintaining U.S. hegemony—especially against "Islamo-fascism"—a central premise of U.S. foreign policy. Issuing a new Bush Doctrine that brazenly proclaimed that the United States "will not hesitate to act alone" or be restrained by conventions of international law, the Bush II administration invaded Afghanistan and Iraq.[19] In essence, when it came to security, the United States could do what it wanted, whenever it wanted, and with whatever instruments it chose.

A number of experts and academics also encouraged the administration to embrace the idea of *promoting* an American empire.[20] Although the administration never officially adopted the policy of empire-building, many argued that, in effect, many U.S. policies constituted behavior similar to that of the Roman and British empires. These policies included maintaining U.S. military installations and troops around the world and promoting the moralistic idea that the U.S. principles of liberty, equality, and individualism could not be questioned.[21]

Many structuralists argued that the Bush II administration's case for U.S. hegemony (and an empire) appeared to be more of the "naked" type of imperialism evident in earlier administrations. Professor of Geography and Anthropology Neil Smith argues that recent efforts to pacify Iraq and the Middle East have been part of a larger war and endgame to control not only oil but the global economic structure.[22] For some Bush administration neocons, the wars in Iraq and Afghanistan were indeed part of a conscious quest for empire, albeit not labeled as such. Once again, globalization and U.S. interests complemented one another.

Contrary to the expectations of many Americans, the election of Barack Obama has done little to change the global role of the United States. Despite his campaign promises in 2008, Obama continues to hold prisoners indefinitely in the detention facility in Guantanamo, Cuba, and continues to use military tribunals for those designated by the executive as "unlawful combatants."[23] Going beyond the militarism of the Bush administration, Obama has escalated the use of military drones to conduct extra-legal assassinations—even the illegal assassination of an American citizen.[24] Instead of repealing the PATRIOT Act, he reauthorized the law.[25] The United States has continued to give billions of dollars in aid to Israel—despite its illegal settlements in the occupied Palestinian territories.[26] And Obama has warned that "no options are off the table" with regard to preventing Iran from developing nuclear weapons—suggesting his willingness to order a military strike against the Islamic Republic.[27] Structuralism recognizes that militarism and empire-building are endemic to the American polity because the political structure operates on behalf of those with wealth and power. Empire serves the interest of capitalists. Despite the rhetoric, there is little real difference between Republicans or Democrats, Bush or Obama.

EQUALITY OR AUSTERITY? POLITICAL-ECONOMIC LESSONS FROM THE GREAT RECESSION

The world economy has hardly begun to recover from the recession triggered by the collapse of the housing market in the United States in 2007. Seen from a structuralist perspective, the crisis was an inevitable consequence of the increasing power of the capitalist class over the last forty years. Although some have pointed to an assortment of "bad behaviors" by bankers and elected officials—and fraud was certainly perpetrated by many on Wall Street during the "boom"—structuralists see the financial crisis and economic stagnation as the result of laissez-faire economic policies and not as an unfortunate consequence of a healthy system distorted by a few villains. A structuralist, of course, sees the problems as built into the *structure*.

Thus, many structuralists point to the massive increase in the inequality of income and wealth in the United States that began around 1970.[28] In 1968, the mean income adjusted for inflation of the richest 20 percent of Americans was approximately $102,000.[29] This had grown to $169,000 by 2010, a 66 percent increase. Over the same time, the mean income of the poorest 20 percent grew from $9,900 to $11,000, an increase of only 11 percent. The share of total national income going to the richest 20 percent of Americans grew from 43 percent to 50 percent, while the share going to the poorest 20 percent fell from 4.2 percent to 3.3 percent. Thus, the richest fifth of the population receive half the nation's income, while an equal number of people, the poorest fifth, receive about one-thirtieth. Adjusting for inflation, the median earnings of a full-time, year-round male worker were actually higher in 1973 than in 2008.[30] Over this 35-year period, the richest Americans claimed virtually all of the increase in new income produced by the economy, further increasing the power of capitalists and resulting in a higher degree of exploitation of the working class.

Debt played a key role in this story—as a source of purchasing power, as a means of redistribution, and as the trigger for the crisis. Ultimately, debt is a promise to make a stream of payments into the future for cash right now. As discussed in Chapters 1 and 8, from the 1990s to 2008, large numbers of middle class and poor people could more easily get credit cards and home mortgages. From 1989 to 2007, the mean level of mortgage debt for the middle class, defined as those between the 40th and 60th income percentiles, increased from $45,000 to $104,000.[31] This form of debt would not have been as troubling if housing prices had kept increasing. But when prices started coming down in 2006, many homeowners owed more on their mortgages than they could get by selling their houses. Credit card debt, on the other hand, is not backed up by any assets and is simply a promise to pay out of future income. Although the amounts are smaller, the mean credit card balances more than doubled, from $2,600 in 1989 to $5,600 in 2007, for those in the middle 20 percent of the income distribution. Overall, the degree of indebtedness grew for the middle class, leading the ratio of total debt to total assets to increase from 20.6 to 24.3 percent between 1998 and 2007.[32]

Initially, debt provides a boost to the economy because those who borrow the money are very likely to spend it on a car or other consumer goods, improvements to a house, or even a vacation. Of course, the loan plus interest must be repaid. When that happens, borrowers have less income to spend on consumer goods because they have to pay back the (wealthier) lenders. However, economic growth will suffer whenever households in the middle class must spend a large portion of their income to service their debt, which transfers a good deal of income to the wealthy instead of to purchasing goods and services. This leads to less production and lower employment in other firms, which generate ripple effects that decrease spending and production and increase unemployment in other parts of the economy. Structuralists also note that when lenders are repaid, they tend to consume a *smaller* share of their higher income. From a structuralist viewpoint, then, the U.S. economy has been operating on an unstable foundation of debt and inequality. Any trouble, such as an unexpected drop in housing prices or a setback in some other sector of the economy, could easily trigger a serious recession. While the bailout policies of many governments attempt to improve the balance sheets of banks and other financial institutions, the amount of debt held by the average household will remain at a very high level. Many households are now unable to borrow money for a renovation or car purchase that they would have funded through debt in the past.

Of course, the forces at work in the United States are also operating on a global level. In other words, class conflict is international. Since World War II, core nations of the industrial North have promoted the spread of neoliberal policies throughout developing regions of the world through the IMF, the World Bank, the WTO, and TNCs. Using international financial institutions, rich countries—just like rich individuals—have lent money to poor countries, setting into motion a stream of payments back to the rich. This dynamic does not simply apply to the poorest and weakest countries in the South but has moved since the recent economic crisis into Europe itself. Some of the smaller and less productive countries in the Eurozone have found themselves at risk of defaulting on their debt; they lack sufficient income to continue to make the stream of payments to their lenders, particularly to creditors outside their countries. For example, Iceland had borrowed heavily from foreign banks before the financial crisis; in the recession that followed, it was unable to make payments on the loans. Portugal and Greece ran into similar problems, and even larger countries like Spain and Italy are at risk.

The standard neoliberal response to economic crisis is known as "austerity," a curiously revealing word. Austerity shares a root with "austere," which means severely simple or without excess and luxury. In practice, **austerity measures** are changes to government policies so that spending is shifted away from social and welfare programs in order to find money to pay foreign creditors. If these measures prove insufficient—as in the case of Greece—taxes are increased. In order to remain in good standing with the dominant economic powers and international financial institutions, countries like Greece must squeeze their own citizens in order to pay foreign bankers. Not every country will accept this deal. It is possible, of course, to default on one's debts or to at least work out a deal with the creditors to restructure and reduce the payments. This is the path taken by Iceland, whose citizens rejected austerity and instead opted to pay back only part of the country's debt. Unlike Greece, Iceland is now experiencing a healthy economic recovery.

The responses from the masses to the economic crisis and the imposition of austerity measures are seen in the various "occupy" movements that began in Canada but gained the most fame on Wall Street. While the political left has a tendency to fragment into many single-issue campaigns, the Occupy Movement is largely unified around a class-based framing: the 99 percent versus the 1 percent (see Chapter 8). The movement and most structuralists call for substantial government regulation of global and national economies in order to transfer wealth and income from the upper class to those in the middle and working classes. The state must strengthen its capacity and willingness to regulate the shadow banking and financial system. Some support the idea of nationalizing banks and establishing more state institutions to compete with those in the private sector. Many would like to see stricter measures to regulate derivatives, executive salaries, and insider trading. If the masses are to regain confidence in the financial system, states must do more to assure their taxpayers that bank bailouts are not *rewarding* greedy officials with high salaries and bonuses.

On the global level, most structuralists support a variety of efforts to eradicate poverty, hunger, debt, and sickness in developing nations. Although IOs do not play a major role in Marxist theory, they have become increasingly important for any number of structuralist-oriented NGOs and activist groups. Many UN agencies have promoted programs that target women's issues, relief for refugees, human rights, and the preservation of indigenous societies. Many structuralists are also behind proposals to increase regulation of TNCs (see Chapter 17).

CONCLUSION

Structuralism in Perspective

Some people ask whether studying Marxism or structuralism in the post-communist era is worthwhile. But one does not need to support Soviet-style socialism in order to see the value in Marx's analysis of capitalism as a political economic system. In this chapter, we separated Marx's four main contributions to IPE—the definition of class, class conflict and the exploitation of workers, control of the state, and ideological manipulation—from his theory of history, which predicted the inevitable collapse of capitalism and its replacement with socialism (and ultimately communism). Structuralists, drawing upon core ideas from Marxism, emphasize the class-based nature of the contemporary international political economy. One cannot understand domestic economic policies or the international political economy without recognizing the conflict over the income derived from the division of the economic output into profits and wages.

Structuralists reject the optimistic liberal interpretation of free trade and deregulated markets, asserting instead that the inequalities in power between capitalists and workers, and the rich and poor countries, produce exploitation, inequality, unemployment, and poverty. The capitalist system tends to reproduce itself such that those who begin with more power and wealth are able to maintain that position at the expense of labor and the poor. Theories about imperialism, dependency, and modern world systems demonstrate that given states' vastly unequal starting places, it is naïve to believe that free markets operate on a level playing field that will somehow lead to the end of poverty. This is because the state itself is seen as largely responding to the pressure of the capitalist-elite class, a group that is increasingly global in their orientation, seeking profits wherever they can be found, and having almost no loyalty to the citizens of their home countries.

The structuralist version of anti-globalization calls for greater unity among workers from all countries and international trade and investment arrangements that no longer expose vulnerable developing countries to conditions that favor the core. This will require coordinated political action by those with fewer economic resources. Even Marx implied that not all decisions must be seen as beyond our collective control when he stated that "men make their own history, but . . . they do not make it under circumstances chosen by themselves, but under circumstances directly encountered, given and transmitted from the past."[33] Thus, for many structuralists today, a deep understanding of the economic structure *permits* the exercise of human freedom, understood as the application of human reason to the shaping of our world. Of course, not every change is possible; but some very substantial improvements almost certainly are. The precondition for such action will be the development of a new consciousness—one that sees the free market version of globalization as simply ideological manipulation by those in power with an economic interest in perpetuating the status quo.

KEY TERMS

structuralism   78
historical materialism   80
dialectical process   80
bourgeoisie   81
proletariat   81

false consciousness   84
dependency theory   90
modern world system
   (MWS)   90
core   91

periphery   91
semiperiphery   91
neoimperialism   92
austerity measures   96

DISCUSSION QUESTIONS

1. Summarize the four main contributions of Marxism to contemporary structuralism.
2. Compare and contrast Marx's and Lenin's views of capitalism. How and why did their views differ? Be specific and give examples from the chapter.
3. Outline the essential characteristics or features of neoimperialism, dependency theory, and the modern world system approach.

4. Outline the key elements of the structuralist explanation of the current financial crisis.
5. If you were to come up with a new ideology to replace the wildcat version of U.S. capitalism, what, if any, structuralist elements would it include?

SUGGESTED READINGS

Jeff Faux. *The Global Class War: How America's Bipartisan Elite Lost Our Future—And What It Will Take to Win It Back.* Hoboken, NJ: John Wiley, 2001.

John Bellamy Foster and Fred Magdoff. *The Great Financial Crisis: Causes and Consequences.* New York: Monthly Review Press, 2009.

Antonio Gramsci. *Selections from the Prison Notebooks,* Quintin Hoare and Geoffrey Nowell Smith., transl. and eds. London: Lawrence and Wishart, 1971.

William Greider. *One World, Ready or Not: The Manic Logic of Global Capitalism.* New York: Simon & Schuster, 1997.

V. I. Lenin. *Imperialism: The Highest Stage of Capitalism*. New York: International Publishers, 1939.

Karl Marx and Friedrich Engels. *The Communist Manifesto: A Modern Edition* (with an introduction by Eric Hobsbawm). New York: Verso, 1998.

Joseph Schumpeter. *Capitalism, Socialism, and Democracy*. New York: Harper & Brothers, 1942.

Immanuel Wallerstein. "The Rise and Future Demise of the World Capitalist System: Concepts for Comparative Analysis," *Comparative Studies in Society and History*, September 1974.

NOTES

1. For a discussion of Marx's methodology see Todd G. Buchholz, *New Ideas from Dead Economists* (New York: New American Library, 1989), pp. 113–120.

2. Karl Marx, *The Poverty of Philosophy* (New York: International Publishers, 1963), p. 122.

3. Ian Steedman, *Marx after Sraffa* (New York: Verso, 1977), pp. 170–175.

4. Arthur B. Kennickell, "A Rolling Tide: Changes in the Distribution of Wealth in the US, 1989-2001," in Edward Wolff, ed., *International Perspectives on Household Wealth* (Northampton, Mass: Edward Elgar, 2006), p. 50.

5. Steven Lukes, *Power: A Radical View* (London: MacMillan Education, 1991), p. 27.

6. Max Weber, *General Economic History* (New Brunswick, NJ: Transaction Books, 1981), p. 277.

7. A French novelist, Harry Nicolaides, was sentenced to three years in prison (reduced from the original six) for a passage in his work that was deemed unflattering to the crown prince. See "Thailand's Lèse-Majesté Law: The Trouble with Harry," *Economist*, January 24, 2009, p. 48.

8. V. I. Lenin, *Imperialism: The Highest Stage of Capitalism* (New York: International Publishers, 1993 [1939]).

9. Ibid., p. 88.

10. Ibid., p. 68.

11. Ibid.

12. See Andre Gunder Frank, "The Development of Underdevelopment," *Monthly Review* 18 (1966).

13. Immanuel Wallerstein, "The Rise and Future Demise of the World Capitalist System: Concepts for Comparative Analysis," *Comparative Studies in Society and History*, September 1974, pp. 387–415.

14. Ibid., p. 402.

15. Ibid.

16. Ibid., p. 406.

17. See John Foster Bellamy, *Naked Imperialism: The U.S. Pursuit of Global Dominance* (New York: Monthly Review Press, 2006), especially pp. 107–120.

18. See Charles Krauthammer, "The Unipolar Era," in Andrew Bacevich, ed., *The Imperial Tense* (Chicago, IL: Ivan R. Dee, 2003).

19. See "The National Security Strategy of the United States," The White House, September 17, 2002, at www.nytimes.com/2002/09/20/politics/20STEXT_FULL.html.

20. See, for example, Deepak Lal, "In Defense of Empires," in Andrew Bacevich, ed., *The Imperial Tense* (Chicago, IL: Ivan R. Dee, 2003).

21. See Chalmers Johnson, *The Sorrows of Empire: Militarism, Secrecy, and the End of the Republic* (New York: Metropolitan Books, 2004).

22. Neil Smith, *The Endgame of Globalization* (New York: Routledge, 2005).

23. Andy Worthington, "Guantanamo, Torture, and Obama's Surrenders," *CounterPunch*, 18:15 (September 1–15, 2011), p. 1.

24. Ibid.

25. Gail Russell Chaddock, "Patriot Act: Three Controversial Provisions That Congress Voted to Keep," *The Christian Science Monitor*, May 27, 2011.

26. United Nations Security Council Resolutions 242 and 465; Convention (IV) Relative to the Protection of Civilian Persons in Time of War. Geneva, August 12, 1949.

27. "Obama: All Options Remain on the Table to Prevent a Nuclear Iran," Haaretz.com, March 4, 2012.

28. See John Bellamy Foster and Fred Magdoff, "Financial Implosion and Stagnation: Back to the Real Economy," *Monthly Review*, December 2008, pp. 1–29.

29. Carmen DeNavas-Walt, Bernadette D. Proctor, and Jessica C. Smith, *U.S. Census Bureau, Current Population Reports, P60–239, Income, Poverty, and Health Insurance Coverage in the United States: 2010* (Washington D.C.: U.S. Government Printing Office, 2011), Table A3, Selected Measures of Household Income

Dispersion: 1967–2010. At http://www.census .gov/prod/2011pubs/p60-239.pdf.

30. Carmen DeNavas-Walt, Bernadette D. Proctor, and Jessica C. Smith, *U.S. Census Bureau, Current Population Reports, P60–236, Income, Poverty, and Health Insurance Coverage in the United States: 2008* (Washington D.C.: U.S. Government Printing Office, 2009), Table A-2, Real Median Earnings of Full-Time, Year-Round Workers by Sex and Female-to-Male Earnings Ratio: 1960 to 2008. At http://www.census.gov /prod/2009pubs/p60-236.pdf.

31. U.S. Federal Reserve, "2007 Survey of Consumer Finances Chartbook," www.federalreserve.gov /PUBS/oss/oss2/2007/scf2007home.html.

32. Brian K. Bucks, Arthur B. Kennickell, Traci L. Mach, and Kevin B. Moore, "Changes in U.S. Family Finances from 2004 to 2007: Evidence from the Survey of Consumer Finances," *Federal Reserve Bulletin*, February 2009, Table 12.

33. Karl Marx, *The 18th Brumaire of Louis Bonaparte* (New York: Mondial, 2005).

Alternative Perspectives on International Political Economy

Aung San Suu Kyi, Burma's pro-democracy opposition leader and Nobel Peace laureate.

Arthur Jones Dionio/Alamy

The international political economy manifests many boundaries and tensions due to conflicting interests, points of view, or value systems that come into contact with one another. The mainstream international political economy (IPE) theories of economic nationalism, liberalism, and structuralism frame issues in ways that capture some, but not all, of the most important elements of IPE today. One of the main intellectual projects of contemporary IPE is to expand its domain to include actors, frameworks, and ways of thinking that cannot easily be classified under the three main perspectives. One of the goals of this chapter is to highlight some of the ways in which IPE can be more inclusive—"without fences,"

101

as Susan Strange would say—by honestly confronting a broader range of important issues and theories in today's world without necessarily abandoning IPE's intellectual roots.

This chapter presents two alternatives or complements to the mainstream IPE theories: constructivism and feminist theory. Each asks us to think of IPE in a different and generally broader way. IPE in the next few decades, however it develops, will necessarily reflect and condition each of these views.

We begin with constructivism, a vibrant theory that focuses on the beliefs, ideas, and norms that shape the views of officials, states, and international organizations in the global system. It identifies an important role for global civil society in shaping the identity and interests of actors that wield enormous economic, military, and political power.

Feminist theory is concerned with the status of women and the role they play in relation to a variety of IPE issues, especially human rights and development. Along with constructivism, feminist theory focuses on the connections between gender and wealth, power, and authority. It identifies issues that are often ignored, such as the importance of family security, reproduction, and gendered beliefs in today's world. In the last twenty years a host of international organizations (IOs) and nongovernmental organizations (NGOs) have promoted women's rights, especially in developing nations. In many cases, IOs and NGOs have made end runs around states to accomplish this objective.

Before we begin, a word of caution is in order. Both of the IPE approaches described here are complex and controversial. As in the case of the three dominant IPE perspectives, many different viewpoints or variations exist within each critique. Our analysis is concise and therefore intentionally incomplete, and also therefore necessarily superficial. Our aim is to acquaint students with a variety of analytical tools and perspectives that may lead them to a deeper understanding of IPE issues.

CONSTRUCTIVISM

Many students find the constructivist perspective exciting because it focuses on issues and actors that are often overlooked in studies that are typically labeled "the IPE" of something or other. **Constructivism** is a relatively new perspective in IPE and international relations, and it focuses on the role of ideas, norms, and discourse in shaping outcomes. Constructivists reject the realist assertion that by simply observing the distribution of military forces and economic capabilities in the material world we can explain how states will interact. Institutions like the state, the market, or IOs are constructed in a social context that gives them meaning and patterns of behavior. How power is used, what goals states have, and how countries interact depend on the ideas that actors have about those things. As actors interact with each other, they create meanings about their own identity and purpose, and those meanings can change. In this section, we explore the ideas of constructivists and provide many examples of the tools they use to interpret important global issues. We look at constructivists' understanding of war and peace issues, the actors they assert are important shapers of the world, and some of the analytical tools they use.

Views of Conflict and Cooperation

Constructivism makes different fundamental assumptions than realism and economic liberalism. Whereas realists (see Chapters 3 and 9) argue that the balance of power conditions states' behavior, constructivists suggest that conflict or cooperation between two or more actors is a product of those actors' different values, beliefs, and interests. One of realism's central assumptions is that a potentially anarchic "self-help" world forces all actors to make security their first priority, lest they be attacked or overtaken by other states. Questions of identity and interest formation are considered to be analytically irrelevant. Social factors such as beliefs and values do not have causal power because they will always be overwhelmed by the structural realities of a self-help world.[1]

Economic liberals share the realist assumption of an anarchic world but hold that well-designed institutions can create the possibility for countries to share positive-sum gains. Like realists, they believe that institutions such as capitalism and conditions such as interdependence order the international political economy. Social factors have little direct effect on these institutional structures or processes.

On the other hand, constructivist Alexander Wendt argues that "structure has no existence or causal power apart from processes. Self-help and power politics are institutions, not essential features of anarchy. Anarchy is what states make of it."[2] In other words, the existence of potential anarchy alone is not sufficient to produce a self-help world. A combination of social processes associated with different actors' identities and subjective interests causes them to view anarchy in terms of a world of potential chaos and disorder. For Wendt, we do live in a self-help world, only because over time we have come to "believe" that self-help is a consequence of anarchy. The international system is quite orderly; most of the time, states act in accordance with formal and informal rules and norms.[3] The fact that some states are now regarded as "rogue states" is testimony to the idea that they have not behaved in a way acceptable to the community of nations.

Drawing more on the individual and state/societal levels of analysis (see Chapter 1), constructivists contend that states are not only political actors, they are also social actors to the extent that they adhere to norms (rules of behavior) and institutional constructs that reflect society's values and beliefs. Why do some people or states cooperate more than others? Is it because they are threatened by a more powerful state? Perhaps! More often than not, though, states cooperate because they are predisposed to work with other states. Their societies value cooperation and prefer cooperative tactics to more violent means of solving common problems. A good example of this is the states in the United Nations that tend to have reputations for "neutrality," that act assertively to promote peaceful settlements of disputes, or that volunteer troops for UN peacekeeping missions. Many of these states are also the first to sign on to arms control treaties or human rights conventions because of strong views in their nations about the nature of international relations and foreign policy.

Constructivists have found that sometimes seemingly implacable rivals cooperate with one another because they come to have a shared understanding that they are part of a "**security community**"—a group of people that is integrated with a sense of a shared moral purpose and a certain level of mutual trust. Israeli political scientist Emanuel Adler has looked at how the Organization for Security and Co-operation in Europe (OSCE), set up in the mid-1970s as a process by which the Cold War sides could cooperate on security matters in Europe, eventually became a transmission belt for liberal ideas about the importance of freedom of the press, arms control, and protection of human rights.[4] The process of interaction the OSCE instituted between states, NGOs, and experts has inexorably spread a new, shared idea among participants that how a country treats its citizens within its own borders is a legitimate concern of other states and that that treatment should be governed by shared principles emerging through diplomacy and discussion.

This idea conflicted with traditional notions of state sovereignty, opening up the way for cooperation on security issues and constraining states in the Warsaw Pact, perhaps even supporting their prodemocracy movements. Since the collapse of the Berlin Wall, the OSCE has played a vital role in convincing European states—especially in Eastern Europe—to adopt new commitments to government transparency, free elections, and protection of minority rights. Constructivists argue that the OSCE shapes state behavior by defining what a "normal" European country comes to believe are its obligations to other states and its own citizens, irrespective of the country's particular foreign policy goals, historical rivalries, or military power. As more states formally commit themselves to these obligations and discuss them, it becomes harder to accept the alternative of violating them—not so much because of the "costs" of doing so but because of the shock it would pose to a country's own identity.

In addition to explaining international conditions that do not simply reflect the material distribution of power, constructivists also observe how states behave in ways that do not seem to reflect a cost–benefit calculation or some other kind of rational self-interest. States sometimes constrain themselves even when they might gain more by shirking international rules and using military force. For example, powerful states often respect the sovereignty of other weaker states even when it would be much more expedient to "teach them a lesson." In the face of egregious piracy by Somalis in the Indian Ocean and the Gulf of Aden, no major military has launched raids on well-known pirate lairs along Somalia's coast. Even on the high seas, the navies of powerful countries have respected international rules about search and seizure of suspected Somali pirate boats, even when it would be easier to just "shoot and ask questions later."

Also, militarily powerful states have been extremely reluctant to accept changes in the borders of existing states, even when it would be in their interest to do so. Only grudgingly and after many years did NATO members who had been policing Kosovo since 1999 accept its independence from Serbia. In places like Somalia and Iraq, where central governments were severely weakened due to civil war, the United States and the European Union refuse to recognize the independence of pro-Western autonomous regions like Somaliland and Iraqi Kurdistan. The norms of sovereignty and border fixedness are so strong that powerful states will forego the opportunity to "solve" major headaches by violating those norms.

When it comes to WMDs like nuclear and chemical weapons, constructivists help us understand why powerful states have not used them since World War II, despite these weapons' obvious military utility. International relations scholar Nina Tannenwald has analyzed the **"nuclear taboo"**—the strongly held norm among the permanent members of the Security Council that first use of nuclear weapons is unthinkable.[5] Even Israel and India, which face implacable enemies in their regions, have apparently internalized the norm that the use of nuclear weapons would be morally unacceptable. Tannenwald argues that the acceptance of the taboo—generated by a grassroots antinuclear weapons movement around the world—is what constrains states from employing nuclear weapons more than the fear that an enemy would retaliate with devastating effects. Similarly, international relations theorist Richard Price looks at how use of chemical weapons has become almost unthinkable. The stigmatization of their use is at odds with their obvious effectiveness. Price explains how nonuse springs from a country's understanding of itself: "Abiding by or violating social norms is an important way by which we gauge 'who we are'—to be a certain kind of people means we just do not do certain things."[6]

Actors That Spread New Norms and "Socialize" States

Constructivists have made an important contribution to IPE by explaining how a variety of non-state actors influence the behavior of states and markets. These scholars assert that economic liberals and realists have overlooked and underestimated social forces that generate and spread values, norms, and ideas that change the way the world works. We will focus on three "actors" that feature prominently in constructivist literature: transnational advocacy networks, epistemic communities, and IOs. As they interact with these actors, states learn ideas and are socialized to behave in new ways.

Constructivists often focus on transformation of an idea or set of beliefs about something. Examples abound, such as the increasing importance of human rights, a variety of environmental issues (see Chapter 20), and debt relief (see Chapter 11). In these and other instances, constructivists see an important role for non-state actors like NGOs and social movements in propagating new norms that states eventually accept, internalize, and craft their policies upon.

Political scientists Margaret Keck and Kathryn Sikkink, for example, have written about **transnational advocacy networks (TANs)**, defined as "those actors working internationally on an issue, who are bound together by shared values, a common discourse, and dense exchanges of information and services."[7] These interconnected groups include NGOs, trade unions, the media, religious organizations, and social movements that spread ideas internationally, frame new issues, and try to get states to accept new norms and interests, often about "rights" claims. TANs' influence comes more from their ideas than their often meager economic resources. They act as "norm entrepreneurs," using testimonies, symbolism, and name-and-shame campaigns to create a shared belief among political elites and social actors that, for example, human rights protection is an obligation, that torture is never acceptable, that debt relief for poor countries is "the right thing," or that human trafficking is a new form of slavery. According to Keck and

Sikkink, TANs spread their ideas by rapidly communicating information, telling stories that make "sense" to audiences far away from a problem, and holding states accountable for the principles that they have already endorsed in their own laws and international treaties.

The International Campaign to Ban Landmines is an example of the role of TANs in using issue framing and information politics to initiate global change. As discussed in the box Landmines, the Mine Ban Treaty was signed and ratified faster than almost any other treaty in history. Among the factors that led to its quick ratification were the efforts of treaty supporters to change the beliefs of people everywhere, along with the views of the security establishments of different states, regarding the need for landmines. World public opinion was swayed dramatically by information and photos about the effects of landmines, which often included the loss of a leg or arm by civilian noncombatants, especially in developing nations. People's beliefs were also challenged by the background studies of many NGOs that were easily communicated via the Internet and by rock stars and famous dignitaries such as Princess Diana of England.

You can probably find many other examples of TANs—and you may even be a member of a TAN without knowing it. For example, Greenpeace, the Natural Resources Defense Council, university students, and a number of affiliated groups led a grassroots campaign beginning in 2004 to convince Kimberly-Clark, the world's largest tissue manufacturer, to stop using pulp from old-growth forests in its Kleenex, Scott paper towels, and Cottonelle toilet paper. In 2009, the company finally agreed with this TAN to switch to a new sourcing policy based on recycled fibers and to support sustainable forest management.

Another group of non-state actors who diffuse ideas in the global political economy are "**epistemic communities**," defined as "professionals with recognized expertise and competence in a particular domain and an authoritative claim to policy-relevant knowledge within that domain or issue-area."[8] These are global networks of experts—often scientists—who have detailed knowledge about complex issues and who share common understandings of the truth about these issues, based on the standards of their profession. Although these epistemic communities are not politically motivated actors, political elites rely upon them for advice, technical explanations, and policy options. Thus, these experts can have a very profound role in "educating" power holders about what problems exist, how important they are, and even what can be done about them. The epistemic communities have "power" through the ideas and values they collectively transmit to policy makers and IOs.

Constructivists have studied many examples of how epistemic communities' knowledge and ideas matter. Peter Haas has shown how atmospheric scientists around the world studying the ozone layer disseminated the consensus scientific evidence about the effects of chlorofluorocarbons (CFCs) on ozone depletion. In coordination with colleagues in the UN Environmental Programme and the U.S. Environmental Protection Agency, they generated knowledge that provided an impetus to international negotiations on the Montreal Protocol to ban CFCs. Similarly, Haas points out that many international regimes to regulate global environmental problems such as climate change and acid rain have come about through a process of "**social learning**," in which epistemic communities taught

The case of antipersonnel landmines (APLs) directly connects the issue of personal security to the growing role of NGOs in the new global security structure. Landmines have a long history of use in conventional wars and low-intensity conflict settings. APLs were particularly popular during the 1970s and 1980s, when insurgent groups took advantage of their low price and simple use. They are hockey-puck-size containers buried in the ground that explode when someone steps on them or drives over them, and they cost approximately $3 each to make.

After the Cold War, APLs were considered by many to be unreasonable weapons because they "do not distinguish between civilians and combatants; indeed, they probably kill more children than soldiers."[b] This new realization of the detriment of APLs motivated a worldwide effort in the early 1990s to eliminate them completely. With worldwide support of the issue, including publicity from such celebrities as Princess Diana and Linda McCartney, the International Campaign to Ban Landmines (ICBL) gained rapid popularity after its founding in 1992. Current estimates put the number of remaining APLs at around seventy million,[c] most of them in developing countries such as Angola, Afghanistan, Cambodia, and Mozambique. They injure an estimated 25,000 people (a third of them children) every year.

The ICBL is an umbrella organization pulling together a number of NGOs into an anti-landmine advocacy campaign cosponsored by the Vietnam Veterans of America Foundation and Medico International.[d] Beginning with six core organizations, the ICBL has since expanded to include about 1,400 groups. In a very short time, the ICBL produced a comprehensive treaty that completely bans the use of landmines. Created under the auspices of the UN, the treaty calls on signatories to "never under any circumstances" "use," "develop, produce, otherwise acquire, stockpile, retain or transfer to anyone" antipersonnel mines. Each party also undertakes the duty "to destroy or ensure destruction of all anti-personnel mines." In Canada in December 1997, some 122 nations signed the treaty, officially named the Convention on the Prohibition of the Use, Stockpiling, Production and Transfer of Anti-Personnel Mines and on Their Destruction, but known more commonly as the Mine Ban Treaty. As of September 1998, some 40 nations had ratified the treaty, bringing it into international law in March 1999.

An interesting feature of the campaign itself was the method the NGOs used to further their cause. The ICRC commissioned an analysis of the military utility of APLs by a retired British combat engineer, who found them to be unnecessary and not as useful as has often been assumed. A number of NGOs also conducted extensive education campaigns to inform the public and state officials of the horrible effects of APLs, all the while lobbying, and also, in some cases, shaming state and military officials who resisted their discontinuation.

The Clinton administration claimed to support the treaty, but the United States did not sign it, for reasons related to the use of APLs as a defense mechanism in South Korea near the Demilitarized Zone (DMZ). As of the end of 2012, Russia, China, India, and the United States had not become signatories to the treaty. Thus far the ICBL is credited with the destruction of millions of antipersonnel mines and has been awarded the Nobel Peace Prize for its efforts. Its work is done primarily through advocacy networking and NGOs. The Hazardous-Life Support Organization (HALO Trust), a British de-mining organization, has been at the forefront of this effort since the beginning.

Most urgent for the international community to address in the war against APLs is increasing cooperation between states and other IOs to help move the process along, particularly their willingness to share information and allow de-mining forces into their countries.

References

[a]Many thanks to our students Meredith Ginn and Lauren Whaley, who helped research this issue.
[b]Warren Christopher, "Hidden Killers: U.S. Policy on Anti-Personnel Landmines," *U.S. Department of State Dispatch* 6 (February 6, 1995), p. 71.
[c]www.minesawareness.org.
[d]For an excellent discussion of the politics of the ICBL see Richard Price, "Reversing the Gun Sights: Transnational Civil Society Targets Land Mines," *International Organization* 52 (Summer 1998): 613–644.

policy elites and international institutions the expert scientific consensus on environmental issues. In other words, epistemic communities provided political negotiators "usable knowledge"—defined as knowledge having credibility, legitimacy, and saliency—that persuaded them to adopt sustainability treaties even though the negotiators may have been politically reluctant to do so initially.[9]

There are many other epistemic communities in the world, ranging from arms-control experts to development experts. Economists are also a community that disseminates fundamental ideas about economics to policy makers. Networks of economists spread the ideas of John Maynard Keynes in the 1930s and 1940s, laying the foundation for trade and financial policies adopted at Bretton Woods after World War II (see the next section). Similarly, Latin American economists (sometimes called the "Chicago Boys") trained in the United States had an important role in shaping the policies of neoliberalism in their home countries in the 1980s. By understanding the ideas these economists were socialized to believe in during graduate school in the United States, political scientist Anil Hira shows how these economists formed "knowledge networks" that enabled and rationalized the adoption of structural adjustment policies in Chile and other Latin American countries.[10]

In addition to TANs and epistemic communities, international organizations are also norm entrepreneurs: They "teach" states the interests they should have, the norms they should adhere to, and the policies they should adopt. In other words, IOs have a role in shaping what a state *is* (its identity), *wants* (its interests), and *does* (its policies). Constructivists stress that IOs often perform these things through discourse and social interactions with political elites and civil society in a country, not necessarily through military force, sanctions, conditionality, or material rewards.

Several examples of IOs that have been studied carefully by constructivists include the International Committee of the Red Cross (ICRC), the World Bank, and the United Nations. Martha Finnemore finds that individuals in the ICRC over many years convinced states that they should abide by humanitarian limits during war.[11] These norms about how to behave during war have become internalized in a number of states that observe these norms even though they would gain by flouting them. The World Bank and the UN have spread norms of poverty alleviation and the Millennium Development Goals that most developed countries have accepted as obligations (see Chapter 11).

Although the general public often perceives the UN as weak and ineffectual, it has had a very important role in spreading norms of gender equality and women's empowerment throughout the world. Its panoply of conferences, commissions, and protocols has not changed gender policies overnight, but it has set the stage for states to engage in a dialogue about women's rights when they otherwise might have not. And the UN has convinced states to write periodic reports about gender policies and to subject themselves to periodic supervision of their policies toward women. As the belief has spread that a respectable, "modern" member of the international community must accept the goal of greater gender equality and women's empowerment, recalcitrant states find it ever more costly and isolating to resist the gender mainstreaming discourse.

While constructivists agree with realists and economic liberals that states, in pursuit of their own self-interests, create some of the norms and values enshrined in the charters of IOs, they point out that these same states often find themselves constrained by these same norms and values. Martha Finnemore points out that a "unipole" like the United States spreads and institutionalizes liberal values in an effort to legitimize its own behavior and goals and to reinforce its soft power.[12] It was very successful in doing so through the Bretton Woods institutions. However, the United States weakens its soft power when it violates the very principles it has convinced its own people and other countries it stands for. For example, the United States was viewed as hypocritical for proclaiming its values of humanitarianism but breaking them by enforcing sanctions on Iraq from 1991 to 2003 that caused enormous suffering and death of civilians. And while proclaiming the importance of international law, the Clinton administration launched military action against Serbia in 1999 without the formal sanction of the UN Security Council (repeated again in 2003 against Iraq). States are haunted by their own principles and are usually less likely to violate them when they lose legitimacy from doing so. Constructivists believe that states often hold other states accountable by withholding legitimacy or crying "hypocrisy" when those states ignore what they say they stand for.

Tools and Concepts of Analysis

The four basic assumptions of constructivism applied to IPE are as follows:

1. Ideas, values, norms, and identities of individuals, groups, and states are socially constructed.
2. Ideas and values are social forces that are as important as military or economic factors.
3. Conflict and cooperation are products of values and beliefs.
4. Some international political changes are driven by changes in the values and beliefs of actors over time.

Constructivists have developed a number of concepts to describe processes that involve the power of ideas. They also have a number of analytical tools to trace how ideas and norms are important to explaining outcomes in the global political economy. In this section, we look at several of these concepts and tools: framing, problematization, discourse analysis, and the life cycle of ideas.

Framing is the ability to define what the essence of a global problem is: what is causing it, who is involved, what are its consequences, and therefore the approach to mitigating or resolving it. All actors try to frame through language, reports, propaganda, and storytelling. Frames are always political constructs or lenses that focus on a particular story that may or may not be the "right way" to analyze a complex problem. Frames make us see a problem in a certain way as opposed to another, and therefore greatly influence how we understand how we should behave toward the problem. By exploring framing and framers, constructivists help explain who influences the global agenda and how our approach to problems changes over time.

For example, by framing deforestation and the loss of biodiversity as tied to the historic disempowerment of indigenous peoples and corruption in poor countries, we overlook an alternative understanding that global environmental destruction is rooted in consumption patterns in rich industrialized countries. The frame that we adopt will radically change the way we interpret our own behavior and what we must do to deal with the problem. Similarly, by framing the mounting U.S. military failure in Afghanistan as rooted in the inability to control warlords' profits from heroin trade that fund the Taliban, the U.S. government downgrades an alternative story that failure is the inevitable result of widespread resistance to foreign occupation and NATO forces' "crimes" against innocent civilians.

"Conflict resources" has been pitched as a new frame to understand some conflicts in Africa. TANs convinced some states that civil wars in places like Sierra Leone and Congo have been tied to struggles over access to natural resources like diamonds and other minerals. Combatants fight not only to control the sources of these resources but also to gain money from them to buy weapons, destabilize governments, and terrorize civilians. We are led to believe that conflict can be reduced by cutting off combatants' ability to profit from diamonds by denying them access to international markets. The Kimberley Process is one such approach to conflict reduction arising from the framing of "blood diamonds" (see Chapter 16). Critics argue that although "conflict resources" framing may have gotten countries and companies to "do something" about Africa, it obscured the more important reasons for conflict rooted in colonial history, ethnic rivalries, and bad governance.

A number of scholars point out that states and IOs have been redefining climate change as a security threat. While epistemic communities of scientists have defined climate change as an environmental problem through their definitive research since the 1980s, the recent "securitization" of the issue has changed the way we understand it and respond to it. Julia Trombetta shows that by tying climate to security, the European Union, the United States, and the UN Security Council emphasize that it could cause violent conflicts, threaten island nations, spark mass migration, and undermine food supplies. Thus framed, it propelled them to take more dramatic measures to mitigate climate change and cooperate at the interstate level by focusing on risk management, precautionary policies, and carbon emissions reductions.[13] Similarly, political scientist Denise Garcia argues that by reframing climate change as a security threat, states have come to recognize that they must work multilaterally to solve such a complex problem. In so doing, states have begun to understand security in a new way—less as safety from territorial aggression and more as ensuring global human security through mutual action and reciprocal responsibilities.[14]

Problematization is an important domestic and international process by which states and TANs construct a problem that requires some kind of coordinated, international response. Constructivists argue that problems exist because we talk them into existence. Of all the problems in the world, ask yourself, what are the ones on your radar screen? How do you know what you should care about in the world or be worried about in the world? Which are the problems your country cares about and which it does not? What we care about is a reflection of our social environment, our culture, and the beliefs we share with others in our society. The problems we care about are also "constructed" by political elites and powerful lobbying organizations. The problems form lenses or filtering devices for you; rarely do you choose them yourself.

Constructivists trace the process by which "problems" become defined as problems. It is our perception of the problem that determines what countermeasures we will adopt. Today, much of the international community defines the following as problems: global warming, drug trafficking, Islamic terrorism, offshore tax havens, and North Korean missiles. These "problems" are not just "out there"; they become what we make them to be. For example, German political scientist Rainer Hülsse finds that the OECD countries talked the money-laundering problem into existence in recent years, even though the common practice of laundering the proceeds of crime had never been perceived as a big issue before.[15] Similarly, Peter Andreas and Ethan Nadelmann note that until the twentieth century, drug trafficking and drug use were not considered crimes that required a global prohibition regime.

Similarly, constructivists suggest that states have choices in terms of who they identify with and against. Enemies have to be defined into existence. There are no laws that will tell us who our enemies and friends are: We make them through a discursive, deliberative process informed by our culture, history, prejudices, and beliefs. Why has Iran been problematized as a pariah in the world in the last three decades? Haggai Ram argues, for example, that Israel has constructed an anti-Iran phobia, viewing Iran as posing an existential threat, in part because of completely unrelated anxieties over ethnic and religious changes within Israeli society.[16] In a similar way, countries create enemies by projecting their own fears on others like Iran and by attributing the characteristics of monsters, devils, madmen, and new Hitlers to leaders of some countries.

Discourse analysis is a particularly powerful tool for understanding where important concepts and terms come from and how they shape state policies, sometimes in very undesirable ways. Some constructivists trace changes in language and rhetoric in the speeches and works of important officials or actors on the state or international level. This is part of understanding the role of ideas in foreign policy. Officials talk their state's interests into existence, sometimes by adopting a discourse that resonates with an important lobbying group or sector of public opinion. Foreign policy can be seen as a social construct springing from a country's culture. We look at three examples of foreign policy issues that constructivists have interpreted through discourse analysis: Islamic terrorism, torture, and the clash of civilizations.

International politics professor Richard Jackson shows us that the way in which academics and states talk about problems creates meaning and limits the range of possibilities for actions. Through discourse analysis, he claims, we can understand the "ways in which the discourse functions as a 'symbolic technology,' wielded by particular elites and institutions, to: structure . . . the accepted knowledge, commonsense and legitimate policy responses to the events and actors being described; exclude and de-legitimize alternative knowledge and practice; naturalize a particular political and social order; and construct and maintain a hegemonic regime of truth."[17] He finds that an academic and political discourse has developed about "Islamic terrorism" that draws upon and reinforces historical stereotypes about Muslims, obscures understanding of the workings of Islamist movements, and paints a threat to Western civilization as so great that only counterterrorism or eradication are seen as appropriate responses to the "Enemy."

Richard Jackson has also used discourse analysis to explain how political elites in the United States repeatedly used a "highly-charged set of labels, narratives and representations" in such a way that "the torture of terrorist suspects became thinkable to military personnel and the wider public."[18] In other words, official public discourse created the conditions for a "torture-sustaining reality" in the United States by using language that dehumanized suspected terrorists and made the public—despite minority opposition—willing to accept the necessity to abuse them. Without assessing the power of this discourse, it is hard to explain how the United States could adopt a set of practices so at odds with its moral values.

Similarly, constructivists have analyzed how political scientist Samuel Huntington's concept of the *clash of civilizations* became a popular way in the 1990s to explain the roots of global conflicts. The more this clash of civilizations rhetoric was used to describe relations between countries, the more it became a sort of self-fulfilling prophecy that constructed conflict itself. In effect, the clash exists because we believe it exists and we act on that belief. The clash discourse has become accepted as the truth—a causal explanation—even in the face of overwhelming social scientific studies that find no significant link between religious beliefs and terrorism and that point out the difficulty in even ascribing a common set of values to huge groups of people like the "Islamic world" or the "West."

The final constructivist method we describe is tracing the **life cycle of ideas**. The aim is to determine where ideas and norms originate, how they spread, the other ideas they come in conflict with, and how they become "naturalized," that is, accepted by states and IOs as the self-evident justification of policies. This may require going back in history to look at individuals or movements that promoted what at the time seemed like radical or even naïve ideas. Or it may mean studying the spread of ideas through negotiations over an international treaty or internal deliberations of a big organization like the World Bank. Of the many ideas floating out there in the world about what the nature of problems is and what states should do about them, only a few come to shape state interests and identities. Constructivists show us how those ideas become institutionalized and very resistant to change, especially when widely accepted in IOs, treaties, and the discourse of states. Sometimes it takes a traumatic event or crisis—a war, a depression, the collapse of the Berlin Wall, or massive, sustained street demonstrations—to shake organizations out of their routine thinking and accept alternative ways of viewing the world and defining their role within it. The first four chapters of this textbook have looked at the life cycle of many academic ideas—and particularly how the 2007 global financial crisis has given birth to new ideas about global financial markets.

International relations theorist Charlotte Epstein has traced the life cycle of ideas about preservation of the environment and natural resources. These ideas originated with American Romantic authors and environmental organizations like the Sierra Club in nineteenth-century America.[19] As these ideas were transmitted to the global level, they became focused on protection of endangered species, and industrialized states cooperated to preserve highly symbolic individual species like whales. Northern states and NGOs like Greenpeace "socialized" biodiverse Southern states and ex-colonies to believe that taking a "green turn" toward species preservation was what a "good" member of the international community should do. This way of looking at protection of individual organisms has, to some extent, crowded out a different—and more sustainable—way of thinking about environmentalism that is focused on preservation of *entire ecosystems*.

Others have traced how dominant economic ideas have changed over time within academic communities, states, and IOs. John Maynard Keynes's ideas spread rapidly after World War II and became the underpinning of the Bretton Woods institutions (see Chapter 2). But a new neoliberal discourse rose to challenge these ideas in the 1970s and 1980s, spread by American economists who constructed a different worldview about development, protectionism, and the role of the state in an economy. Individuals within the IMF in particular spread the notion that capital account liberalization—that is, unrestricted flows of capital across borders—was an inevitable force in the global economy and a necessary policy for every state that wanted to develop rapidly. As with many of the ideas of the Washington Consensus, the liberalization ideas lost some of their intellectual hold on governments only in the face of shocks such as the Asian financial crisis and development failures in Africa and Latin America.

Similarly, in the 1990s the World Bank began to change some of its neoliberal views (and thus policies) of development in the face of sustained efforts by TANs, which slowly convinced it through shaming and lobbying to believe that promoting environmental and social norms like sustainable development, poverty alleviation, and gender equality were part of its mission—indeed even critical to its own identity and purpose as an organization.[20] Political scientist Catherine Weaver has also studied the World Bank's role in spreading the idea of "good governance." She argues that, due to external and internal drivers, the Bank's thinking on what is necessary for development has shifted somewhat from neoliberal orthodoxy to ideas about proper government institutions. Externally, empirical evidence of the failure of structural adjustment programs along with the success of state-interventionist policies in East Asia created opportunities for a change of thinking. Internally, pressure from lower-level staff and the appointments of James Wolfensohn as President and Joseph Stiglitz as Chief Economist fostered ideological acceptance that issues like corruption, rule of law, and public administration problems needed to be incorporated into Bank development policies. Even as ideas changed, Weaver contends that the Bank's unwillingness to hire non-economists who understand the cultural and political aspects of development has limited the effectiveness of its good governance programs.[21]

Depending on the topics students study and the questions they ask, constructivism can provide enlightenment about some dimensions of an issue that are not captured in other perspectives. That alone makes it worth knowing something about.

FEMINIST CONTRIBUTIONS TO IPE

Feminism has contributed to IPE scholarship in a variety of ways, and its influence can be seen throughout the discipline. Feminists began to make significant inroads in the social sciences during the 1970s, when IPE first developed as a discipline and the need for more interdisciplinary approaches became apparent. Feminists argue that every area of IPE—from the structure of state power to the allocation of political and economic resources—is impacted by gendered processes. Feminist theories and constructivist theories are often complementary because both perspectives challenge the positivist idea that concepts in IPE are unbiased or "value-free."

This section explains what feminism is, why it is important, and what some of its areas of consensus and debate are. Although almost all feminists agree that women and men are equally valuable and that gender "matters," they disagree on many other issues. Not surprisingly, feminists who subscribe to economic liberal, mercantilist, or structuralist perspectives often advocate different policies and approach research in different ways.

Women Matter; Gender Matters

Gendered analysis takes into account not just sex (biological males and females) but *gender* as the *socially constructed norms* that determine what is masculine or feminine. *Women* matter simply because women are intrinsically valuable as human beings. *Gender* matters to IPE scholars because to understand many issues in IPE we need to understand the way our values and assumptions about gender affect institutions. Seems pretty simple, right? But it took a long time to convince mainstream scholars and policy makers of those two points. In the examples that follow, we will look at how some policies have ignored women, with unfortunate consequences. Furthermore, feminists argue that efforts to "add women" to existing frameworks have often failed to adequately explain the role of gendered social norms and to produce gender-equitable outcomes.

Believing that men and women are *equally* valuable is the defining feature of feminism. This means that if a policy hurts women, feminists would argue that the policy is bad—even if it does not hurt men or children. For example, overexploitation of forest resources is a problem that concerns many governments and international aid donors like the World Bank. One effective policy response is for international actors (like donors and environmental NGOs) to work with governments and include local communities in Joint Forestry Management (JFM). Communities promise to protect the forest from illegal timber harvesting, grazing, and even fire, in exchange for non-timber resources. This is a sustainable, participatory policy, so it should be great for everybody, right? The problem in some cases such as India, political anthropologist Andrea Cornwall points out, is that women, who are not well represented on village committees that take up JFM, are still responsible for cooking, which means they still need wood.[22] In this case, criminalizing deforestation without providing women an alternative fuel for cooking food just means that women have to break the law and sneak into the forest at night to gather wood in order to fulfill their *gendered obligations as women* (providing food). Good for the community, but not so good for women.

Policies like JFM have different impacts on men and women. In fact, gender is so important that we might say *most* major policies—from food stamps to timber tariffs—affect men and women differently. During the first debates in 2009 over President Obama's stimulus package, feminists pointed out that promoting jobs in construction (as was advocated by many) meant job creation primarily for men. If women matter as much as men, some said, then stimulus money should also be directed toward sectors where there is greater representation of women in the labor force, such as health and education. The same question applies to international trade policy. Bilateral trade agreements may benefit men in the most powerful industries more than women in less important sectors of the economy. For example, NGOs like Action Aid and Women in Development Europe (WIDE) have criticized Europe's negotiations with India over a free-trade agreement because it privileges large corporations and ignores potential effects on women and other vulnerable groups.[23] How will this kind of agreement affect small farmers and informal sector traders who cannot compete with large producers? Does it matter that women tend more to be in the former groups than the latter?

A nonfeminist might argue that large industry and infrastructure investments are important types of spending, and women will benefit from more jobs and an improved economy even if most new jobs go to men. Historically, when gender experts have not been included in policy design, gender has been ignored. Often, this has a negative impact on women, but it also frequently works to the detriment of the policy's overall objectives. In the case of JFM, failure to consider gender-differentiated outcomes failed to protect women, but in doing so, it also failed to find a solution to women's overexploitation of forest resources. That is one reason why gender matters.

So, feminists have convinced IPE scholars as well as policy makers that women matter and therefore, gender-differentiated policy impacts matter. But gender matters for another reason. The roles assigned to men and women, our gendered resources and obligations, the things we buy, where we work, how much money we make, and our room for maneuver in making decisions—these gender-influenced things shape markets and affect the distribution of power and resources in society. To understand how gender affects policies and other issues in IPE, we contrast some feminist ideas regarding economic liberal, mercantilist, and structuralist perspectives. Keep in mind that most people do not fit neatly into one IPE perspective, but support policies or viewpoints that are influenced by multiple schools of thought.

Liberal Feminisms

Even within liberal traditions, there are many debates among feminists. Classical liberal feminists (sometimes called libertarian feminists) are most concerned with individual freedoms, freedom from coercion, and "self-ownership" for men and women. Politically, they are concerned primarily with *de jure* inequality, meaning laws that proactively discriminate against women by barring their right to vote, to enter contracts, to transfer property in a free market, to use contraception, and to be protected by the state when their inalienable rights are threatened. Laws that condone marital rape, domestic violence, or men's control over women's property are all examples of discriminatory practices.

In defining freedom in terms of individual rights and seeking to limit the coercive power of the state, liberal feminists often do not support laws that promote women specifically, including those that would regulate equal pay with men or guarantee access to public office. Some liberal feminists argue that "just" laws will not necessarily lead to actual equality. This means they support only laws that protect individuals from direct coercion (e.g., threats against one's body or property). Justice, from this perspective, requires only that the state apply just means, not that the resulting society be equitable.

Other liberal feminists tend to support individual rights and free markets, but argue that men hold a disproportionate share of power in society. Because this *institutionalized patriarchy* is not confined to the state, liberal feminists advocate for both legal and social change. For example, they advocated that state universities in the United States be required to provide equal athletic opportunities to both men and women (known as Title IX rules). They also lobbied for the Violence against Women Act (VAWA), in response to the systematic difficulty in effectively prosecuting perpetrators of rape, domestic violence, and other gender-based crimes. These laws attempted to compensate for existing social discrimination rather than to curb inherently discriminatory laws. Until the 1980s, liberal feminist advocacy and research tended to pay only limited attention to the gendered implications of macroeconomic policies that IOs like the World Bank and the IMF began to impose on poor countries.[24]

Since then, liberal (and other) feminists have studied the many effects of global markets and development projects on women. Structural Adjustment Programs (SAPs), instituted in many developing countries during the 1980s and 1990s, have been criticized for (among other things) reducing governments' investment in health, education, and other social services so as to disproportionately hurt women and children. Similarly, development programs and government aid have been found to disproportionately benefit men, who have greater access to capital, land, salaried jobs, pensions, and political networks. Many women spend a disproportionate amount of time doing unremunerated labor such as housework, subsistence farming, fuel gathering, and caring for children, the sick, and the elderly. In the case of the JFM example, liberal feminists criticized the original projects because they were not designed to have gender equitable impacts by taking these particular roles of women into account.

In contrast, Pietra Rivoli argues that the advent of free trade has been a great benefit to women in many poorer countries.[25] As textile and apparel production has moved to countries like China, it has created relatively high-paying jobs in urban areas for hundreds of thousands of young women who otherwise would be stuck in rural poverty. Despite the sweatshop-type conditions and poor labor practices in many of these clothing factories, women employed in them have gained higher incomes, economic autonomy, and even social liberation. Women's economic empowerment comes from China's industrialization and openness to global markets and investment. Over time, as the "bottom" of society rises, women may even gain more employee, union, and political rights. Similarly, the World Bank asserted in its *World Development Report 2012* that, overall, globalization has helped promote more gender equality.[26] Trade openness, economic integration, and the spread of information technology have created more jobs for women and spread new ideas about gender norms. Countries with export-intensive industries employing many women tend to lose international competitiveness unless they reduce gender inequality.

Finally, liberal feminists stress that the level of political rights that women enjoy in a country, along with their overall treatment, have important impacts on a country's overall economic health. Countries with stronger women's rights, lower fertility rates, better education for girls, and more women in government tend to have higher economic growth rates and more prosperous societies.

Feminist Critiques of Mercantilist Perspectives

Feminist scholars have played an influential role in questioning the assumptions and approaches of IPE scholars in the mercantilist and realist traditions. They have sought to redefine our understanding of international power and national security. Traditionally, the study of IPE has privileged macrolevel issues: the actions of nation-states, peace and war, international diplomacy, and global security, to name a few. By focusing research questions on states rather than cities, transnational corporations rather than small producers or grassroots organizations, and countries rather than households, IPE scholars make implicit assumptions that macrolevel institutions are masculine. Certainly, women's influence in society has been most visible in smaller arenas. In this way, by privileging the state, IPE scholars have (perhaps unwittingly) rendered women's contributions all but invisible.

Some feminist scholars have had considerable influence simply by approaching research from different levels of analysis, often by beginning at the household or community level. They find that because men and women have different gendered obligations, they also play very different roles in global processes and are impacted differently by them. More importantly, ignoring certain levels of analysis can lead to false assumptions. For example, feminists point out that economists previously assumed that households pool resources: Whatever money and assets coming in are shared by the family members. In fact, there is often conflict or negotiation between individuals about access to household resources, and that conflict is very often gendered.

Similarly, feminist scholars point out that state-centric IPE scholars have overlooked the informal and non-wage-based economy in which many women work. This sector is a critical underpinning of the market system as a whole and of the ability of a state to compete in the global economy. Many sectors of national economies have become "feminized," including caregiving, domestic services, education, and sexual services, where women face low wages, marginalization, and exploitation. Other service industries including customer service, administration, and health care are dominated by women. Some of these services can be provided to Europe or the United States electronically from India at much lower labor costs.

Feminist scholars have redefined the concept of security, showing the ways in which international relations are gendered and making women's often invisible roles more apparent. At the same time, feminist activists have promoted women's ability to participate in spheres of international diplomacy and military security. Traditional theories of international relations and national security have tended to ignore gender as an analytical tool. Many feminists argue that this is not just because women are excluded from positions of power, but because women's roles are considered unimportant.

For example, a team of political scientists, a psychologist, and a geographer—Valerie Hudson, Mary Caprioli, Chad Emmett, and Bonnie Ballif-Spanvill—have found a significant correlation between the security of women and the security of states.[27] States that have high levels of physical security for women tend to be more peaceful and have better relations with their neighbors. Conversely, states with high level of violence against women (measured by the prevalence of various forms of microaggression such as femicide, rape, domestic violence, and unequal rights) tend to be involved in more civil wars and violent conflicts with other states. Similar studies have found that states with higher levels of gender equality tend to be involved in fewer violent interstate disputes and conflicts. All of this research suggests that the status of women in societies has an important impact on interstate relations.

In her influential book *Bananas, Beaches and Bases*, Cynthia Enloe shows how diplomats and soldiers depend on the often unpaid and devalued work that women do. By studying the role of diplomats' wives or the way military bases depend on cooks, laundresses, nurses, and sex workers, she shows how private and personal relationships influence the international political arena. International policy makers, she argues, "have tried to hide and deny their reliance on women as feminized workers, as respectable and loyal wives, as 'civilizing influences,' as sex objects, as obedient daughters, as unpaid farmers, as coffee-serving campaigners, as consumers and tourists."[28] It would be easy to argue that the practical functions of everyday military operations or lawmaking do not directly influence larger processes. But the practical dynamics of political negotiations and military engagements can have a tremendous influence on their outcomes.

Feminist security theory shows how the invisibility of gender in theories of war has masked important dynamics, including the myth that wars are fought to protect society's most vulnerable sections. For example, women form the bulk of refugees and civilian deaths in war, and mass rape has been an important form of gender violence. When soldiers are allowed to rape, their leaders are using rape to *construct a particular masculinity*. In Darfur (and elsewhere), rape has been used to humiliate populations, to destroy families, and to drive people out of villages in order to access land. The importance of femininity and protection of women in people's ideas of family makes gender violence an effective tool for achieving a strategic military objective. In this way, gender is crucial for understanding questions of international security.

Structuralist Feminism

Marxist feminists challenge the idea that capitalism benefits women in almost any instance. Many see gender not as the key factor in exploitation but as a source of oppression that is facilitated by the capitalist system. Evelyn Reed, a prominent Marxist feminist, wrote in 1970: "It is the capitalist system—the ultimate stage in the development of class society—which is the fundamental source of the degradation and oppression of women."[29]

Other structuralist or radical feminists—often influenced by Marx—argue that patriarchy is part of a system of exploitation that requires a complete overhaul (though not necessarily a violent one). They may or may not believe that the best way to end exploitation is to end capitalism, but many would agree with Reed that there is a link between the power mechanisms that determine international relations and those that determine race, class, and gender relations. Women and people of color make up a disproportionate number of the poor in most countries, and structuralists argue that this is a result of systematic exploitation within and between countries.

Where liberal feminists criticize neoliberal economic policies when they hurt women, structuralist feminists see those policies as emblematic of a greater problem. Meanwhile, they criticize microfinance because the loans given through its programs actively promote women's involvement in capitalist competition, often aggravating inequality between women by failing to benefit the most vulnerable.

By highlighting the need to consider sources of inequality other than gender, the influence of structuralism challenged feminists to move beyond domestic policy and household relations toward more systemic and globally relevant arguments.

State-centric IPE scholars have overlooked how globalization has direct, specific effects on women. Many newly industrializing countries have encouraged foreign direct investment in export-oriented manufacturing facilities that employ a large number of women. Melissa Wright has studied how these factories in northern Mexico (called **maquiladoras**) and southern China treat women as "disposable," paying them low wages in dead-end jobs. Even though these women are important to global capital accumulation, a mythical discourse portrays them as "industrial waste" that can be easily "discarded and replaced" when they have lost the "physical and mental faculties" for which they were hired: dexterity, patience, and sacrifice.[30] Wright and others point out that many women resist this marginalization and disposability.

Women also tend to be disproportionately hurt by the restructuring of the global economy and adjustments to crises within it. Cuts in social services and public goods cause male and female unemployment, but have tended to force more women into poverty, double shifts, and informal activities like prostitution, which damage their physical and mental health.

Feminist scholars have made significant contributions to—and criticisms of—the way IPE is studied. Cynthia Enloe may have summed up best the importance of having a "feminist curiosity": "One cannot explain why the international system works the way it does without taking women's lives seriously. 'Experts' may be knowledgeable about banking interest rates, about the oil industry, about HIV/AIDS; nevertheless, if those experts fail to think seriously about women's lives, they are certain to produce deeply flawed understanding—explanation—of today's international political economy."[31]

SMUGGLING IN SENEGAL: GENDER AND TRADE POLICY

Senegal is one of the highly indebted poor countries (HIPCs) in West Africa that has adopted a variety of economic liberalization measures advocated by the World Bank and the IMF. One exception is its sugar industry (actually one company, CSS), which has enough political power that the government protects it from international competition by setting sugar import tariffs so high as to effectively ban imports. The Gambia, the small country surrounded by Senegal, has much lower tariffs, and its government is only too happy to have traders buy its cheaper sugar imported from Denmark and Brazil. Here, we have a recipe for smuggling.

In West Africa, market women are very important because trade is one of the few occupations available to women and because villages need access to basic supplies (like sugar). Given Senegal's international trade policy and women's gendered role as traders, women have become the majority of sugar smugglers. Sugar manufactured in Denmark and Brazil is packed, transported, and shipped (mostly by men) to The Gambia where (mostly male) customs officers charge applicable tariffs or determine a combination of tariff and a bribe. The sugar is bought and stored by high-volume wholesalers, and it is eventually picked up by drivers and regional wholesalers, all of whom

(continued)

are men. Finally, it makes its way to rural markets where male and female traders buy 50-kg sacks.

A story will illustrate what happens from Senegal.[a] Fatou Cisse is a mid-level trader in a border town that hosts a market once a week. She makes about $100 during a good month. She pays a neighbor (a 20-year old man) to take her by horse-cart three times a week to The Gambia, where she buys a 50-kg sack of sugar on credit from her regular supplier, a male immigrant from Mauritania. Her driver knows the bumpy terrain well and tries to get back to the village using paths that are not easily reached by customs officers' cars. They are not in luck. A male ex-trader from a nearby village who knows their schedule works with the customs officers as a secret informant. An officer soon finds Fatou and they begin to negotiate. She apologizes for breaking the law, but explains that she is having a very difficult time and desperately needs money for her family. He agrees to seize only half of her sugar (25 kg). According to Senegalese social norms, a good man (reflecting gender) and a good customs officer (reflecting authority figures) must be flexible and generous occasionally. Upon return to the customs bureau, the officer, the informant, and the bureau chief each take 10 percent of the seized sugar (2.5 kg) and report a seizure of 12.5 kg that will be picked up by government officials and resold at auction. Having paid $28 for her sugar, Fatou will sell what she has left at her weekly village market for $17.50. Luckily, she has just enough left over from the previous week to pay her supplier and try again.

Stories like this one illustrate both the complexity and the gendered nature of the globalization of production. Governments make international trade policies they hope will benefit their economies. For Senegal, this means some protectionism in response to powerful sugar lobbies—negotiations that are dominated by men. Because men and women have different obligations and opportunities, the roles they play are gendered, and they will find different niches available to them. In the case of the sugar trade, both men and women make choices and establish norms that will allow them to benefit from the niche created by the trade policy. Although laws are broken, everyone in the story makes a profit, including the governments involved. On the other hand, the opportunities available to women are very different from those available to men.

If you were an IPE scholar hoping to study the impacts of Senegalese sugar policies, you might choose to study only the negotiations between governments and industry officials, but your conclusions would be much more limited than if you considered the role of gender and investigated multiple levels of analysis.

Reference

[a]A composite account from a survey of women smugglers in Cynthia Howson, "Trafficking in Daily Necessities: Female Cross-border Traders in Senegal." PhD Thesis, SOAS, University of London, 2011.

CONCLUSION

Ideas are very powerful and *should* be taken seriously. The constructivist and feminist theories both challenge us to think about IPE in new and different ways. As John Maynard Keynes noted famously in the closing pages of his *General Theory*,

> the ideas of economists and political philosophers, both when they are right and when they are wrong, are more powerful than is commonly understood. Indeed the world is ruled by little else.

> Practical men, who believe themselves to be quite exempt from any intellectual influences, are usually the slaves of some defunct economist. Madmen in authority, who hear voices in the air, are distilling their frenzy from some academic scribbler of a few years back.[32]

The alternative perspectives discussed in this chapter provide us tools to better understand many global issues. They direct our focus to actors and forces that have been overlooked in the liberal, mercantilist, and structuralist perspectives. In so doing, they suggest that states and markets are not the only shapers of the world; other actors like individuals, women, and social movements profoundly influence global policies and struggles. They also remind us that the study of IPE cannot be divorced from moral and ethical questions. Unless we grapple with the different ways that individuals perceive the world, we will find it hard to explain what motivates their behavior.

KEY TERMS

constructivism 102
security community 104
nuclear taboo 105
transnational advocacy
 networks (TANs) 105

epistemic communities 106
framing 109
problematization 110

discourse analysis 111
life cycle of ideas 112
maquiladoras 119

DISCUSSION QUESTIONS

1. Do you think constructivism should get more attention as a social science theory? Why? Why not?
2. What criticisms can be made of constructivism? Do constructivists underestimate the importance of material power in affecting global issues?
3. What tools do we have to measure whether norms actually influence an actor's outlook and actions?
4. How might structuralist feminists respond to companies that outsource labor to sweatshops in poor countries?
5. Why do feminists argue that debates about national security need to consider gender? Do you agree?

SUGGESTED READINGS

Barbara Ehrenreich and Arlie Russell Hochschild. *Global Woman: Nannies, Maids, and Sex Workers in the New Economy.* New York: Henry Holt, 2002.

Cynthia Enloe. *Globalization and Militarism: Feminists Make the Link.* Lanham, MD: Rowman and Littlefield, 2007.

Gender Action. http://www.genderaction.org/

Helen Schwenken and Anna Basten, "Bibliography—Gender in International Political Economy." http://www.garnet-eu.org/fileadmin/documents/news/Bib-GIPE-all_incl_3rd_update-hs-2-2009.pdf.

Margaret Keck and Kathryn Sikkink. *Activist without Borders: Norms and Identity in World Politics.* New York: Columbia University Press, 1998.

Nina Tannenwald. *The Nuclear Taboo: The United States and the Non-Use of Nuclear Weapons since 1945.* Cambridge: Cambridge University Press, 2007.

Jacqui True. *The Political Economy of Violence against Women.* New York: Oxford University Press, 2012.

Alexander Wendt. "Anarchy Is What States Make of It: The Social Construction of Power Politics," *International Organization,* 46 (Spring 1992), pp. 391–425.

NOTES

1. See Kenneth N. Waltz, *Theory of International Politics* (Reading, MA: Addison-Wesley, 1979).
2. See Alexander Wendt, "Anarchy Is What States Make of It: The Social Construction of Power Politics," *International Organization,* 46 (Spring 1992), pp. 391–425.
3. Steve Smith, Alexander Wendt, and Thomas Biersteker, *Social Theory in International Politics* (Cambridge: Cambridge University Press, 1999).
4. Emanuel Adler, *Communitarian International Relations: The Epistemic Foundations of International Relations* (London: Routledge, 2005).

5. Nina Tannenwald, *The Nuclear Taboo: The United States and the Non-Use of Nuclear Weapons since 1945* (Cambridge: Cambridge University Press, 2007).

6. Richard Price, *The Chemical Weapons Taboo* (Ithaca, NY: Cornell University Press, 1997).

7. Margaret Keck and Kathryn Sikkink, *Activist without Borders: Norms and Identity in World Politics* (New York: Columbia University Press, 1998).

8. Peter Haas, "Introduction: Epistemic Communities and International Policy Coordination," *International Organization,* 46, no. 1 (Winter 1992), p. 4.

9. Peter Haas, "When Does Power Listen to Truth? A Constructivist Approach to the Policy Process," *Journal of European Public Policy,* 11 (August 2004): 569–592.

10. Anil Hira, *Ideas and Economic Policy in Latin America* (Westport, CT: Greenwood, 1998).

11. Martha Finnemore, *National Interests in International Society* (Ithaca, NY: Cornell University Press, 1996).

12. Martha Finnemore, "Legitimacy, Hypocrisy, and the Social Structure of Unipolarity: Why Being a Unipole Isn't All It's Cracked Up to Be," *World Politics,* 61:1 (January 2009): 58–85.

13. Maria Julia Trombetta, "Environmental Security and Climate Change: Analysing the Discourse," *Cambridge Review of International Relations* 21 (2008): 585–602.

14. Denise Garcia, "Warming to a Redefinition of International Security: The Consolidation of a Norm Concerning Climate Change," *International Relations* 24:3 (2010): 271–292.

15. Rainer Hülsse, "Creating Demand for Global Governance: The Making of a Global Money-Laundering Problem," *Global Society,* 21 (April 2007): 155–178.

16. Haggai Ram, *Iranophobia: The Logic of an Israeli Obsession* (Stanford: Stanford University Press, 2009).

17. Richard Jackson, "Constructing Enemies: 'Islamic Terrorism' in Political and Academic Discourse," *Government and Opposition,* 42:3 (2007), p. 397.

18. Richard Jackson, "Language, Policy, and the Construction of a Torture Culture in the War on Terrorism," *Review of International Studies,* 33 (2007), p. 354.

19. Charlotte Epstein, "The Making of Global Environmental Norms: Endangered Species Protection," *Global Environmental Politics,* 6:2 (May 2006): 32–54.

20. Susan Park, "Norm Diffusion within International Organizations: A Case Study of the World Bank," *Journal of International Relations and Development,* 8 (2005): 111–141.

21. Catherine Weaver, "The Meaning of Development: Constructing the World Bank's Good Governance Agenda," in Rawi Abdelal, Mark Blyth, and Craig Parsons, eds., *Constructing the International Economy* (Ithaca: Cornell University Press, 2010): 47–67.

22. Andrea Cornwall, "Whose Voices? Whose Choices? Reflections on Gender and Participatory Development," *World Development,* 31:8 (2006): 1325–1342.

23. WIDE, "The EU-India Free Trade Agreement negotiations: Gender and Social Justice Concerns. A Memo for MEPs," (2009). Available at www.boell-india.org/downloads/MEP_Memo_final__892009.pdf.

24. Gita Sen, "Gender, Markets and States: A Selective Review and Research Agenda," *World Development,* 24:5 (1996), p. 823.

25. Pietra Rivoli, *The Travels of a T-Shirt in the Global Economy: An Economist Examines the Markets, Power, and Politics of World Trade,* 2nd ed. (Hoboken, NJ: John Wiley & Sons, 2009).

26. See Chapter 6 of World Bank, *World Development Report 2012: Gender Equality and Development* (Washington, D.C.: World Bank, 2011), at http://go.worldbank.org/6R2KGVEXP0.

27. Valerie Hudson, Bonnie Ballif-Spanvill, Mary Caprioli, and Chad F. Emmett, *Sex and World Peace* (New York: Columbia University Press, 2012).

28. Cynthia Enloe, *Bananas, Beaches and Bases: Making Feminist Sense of International Politics* (Berkeley, CA: University of California Press, 2000), p. 17.

29. Evelyn Reed, "Women: Caste, Class or Oppressed Sex," *International Socialist Review,* 31:3 (1970), p. 40.

30. Melissa Wright, *Disposable Women and Other Myths of Global Capitalism* (London: Routledge, 2006), p. 2.

31. Cynthia Enloe, *Globalization and Militarism: Feminists Make the Link* (Lanham, MD: Rowman and Littlefield, 2007), p. 18.

32. John Maynard Keynes, *The General Theory of Employment, Interest, and Money* (New York: Harcourt Brace Jovanovich, 1964), p. 383.

Structures of International Political Economy

The first five chapters of this book have provided an intellectual foundation on which to build a sophisticated understanding of international political economy. We addressed three principal IPE perspectives and two alternative perspectives that are most often used to analyze IPE problems such as the global financial crisis. The next five chapters examine *structures* that tie together nation-states and other actors and that link national and global markets. As we noted in Chapter 1, Professor Susan Strange, a leading IPE thinker, focuses our study of international political economy on four core structures: production and trade, money and finance, security, and knowledge and technology.

Each of the four structures consists of a set of relationships and distinct rules (including tacit understandings) between political, economic, and social actors. We study how the structures connect people and condition the behavior of states, markets, and society. In examining the characteristics of these four structures, Strange encourages us to ask the simple question, *Cui bono?* ("Who benefits?"). This question forces us to go beyond description to analyze how each structure works, what sources of power were used to create it, and what benefits it provides to those who manage it today. Strange also encourages us to ask questions about the relationship of one structure to another.

In Chapter 6, we explain changes in global production and what terms or conditions prevail in the exchange of goods and services between countries. Because production and trade are closely connected to development, currency exchange rates, finance, technology, and security, they are some of the most controversial issues in IPE.

Our study of the finance and monetary structure is covered in two chapters. Chapter 7 presents some of the history, vocabulary, and basic concepts everyone needs to know about finance and the workings of various international monetary systems. Chapter 8 discusses several international financial crises, including the global financial crisis and the European debt crisis. We focus on their causes and effects, and some of the measures put forth by the IMF, the United States, and the European Union to address them.

In Chapter 9, we examine relationships and rules of behavior that affect the security of states, groups, and individuals within the global political economy. Some parts of the security structure are easy to recognize, such as the role of the major powers in determining war and peace. Other aspects, such as the role of terrorists and non-traditional security problems, are less visible but of equally critical importance.

In Chapter 10, we explore who produces, owns, and has access to knowledge and technology, and on what terms. Knowledge and technology shape the ability "to make and do things" that dramatically affect the balance of power between actors in the finance, production, and security spheres. One particular issue is intellectual property rights (IPRs), which profoundly affect who derives benefits from legal claims of ownership of a number of products.

The Production and Trade Structure

In the absence of a world government, cross border trade is always subject to rules that must be politically negotiated among nations that are sovereign in their own realm but not outside their borders.[1]

Robert Kuttner

Since 2009, the Obama administration has imposed high tariffs on imports of Chinese tires and solar panels into the United States and challenged China at the World Trade Organization over its unfair subsidies to domestic car manufacturers and its tariffs on imported U.S. steel and cars. During the 2012 U.S. presidential campaign, Republican candidate Mitt Romney attacked China for engaging in unfair trade practices such as currency manipulation and theft of U.S. patents and technology. As columnist Robert Kuttner tells us, trade is *always* political. In fact, many IPE theorists believe that no topic is more quintessentially IPE than trade. Not only does it continue to be very important for national officials, but the number of political actors and institutions outside the nation-state that shape and manage trade has increased significantly since the end of the Cold War.

The international production and trade structure is composed of the set of rules and relationships between states, IOs, businesses, and NGOs that influence what is produced and sold, where, by whom, and at what price. It links nation-states and other actors, furthering their interdependence and mutual benefits but also generating tensions between them.

This chapter surveys a variety of changes that have occurred primarily in the post–World War II production and trade structure. Not since the Industrial Revolution have we seen so many new goods and services produced in such new ways. Concurrently, in conjunction with the popularity of economic liberal ideas, many trade experts and officials in the Northern industrialized nations (the North) have sought ways to reduce the level of protectionist barriers that limit or distort trade. The United States and its allies created the General Agreement on Tariffs and Trade (GATT) in 1947 to promote liberal trade values and bolster U.S. political and military objectives. In an effort to further liberalize world trade, in 1995, the World Trade Organization (WTO) replaced the GATT.

The chapter concludes with a survey of other important trade issues, namely, the growing number of regional trade blocs and North–South trade disputes. These issues make trade one of the most complex and politically contentious areas in the international political economy.

This chapter presents three major theses. First, controversies about production and international trade stem from the compulsion of businesses and nation-states (rich and poor alike) to capture the benefits of trade while limiting its negative effects on producers and society. Second, recent criticisms of neoliberalism and globalization, coupled with the global financial crisis, have exacerbated the resistance of many emerging economies to further trade liberalization, causing an impasse in international trade negotiations. Third and final, state officials and social groups in many of the industrialized nations are increasingly calling for better controls on production and globalization to serve their national interests.

GLOBAL PRODUCTION

Because of its direct connection to trade, international production is of increasing significance to IPE students. A recurring theme in Thomas Friedman's work is the transformation of production processes associated with globalization. In *The Lexus and the Olive Tree,* Friedman focuses on how people the world over—but especially in the developed industrialized nations—are using sophisticated, multifunctional, postindustrial-age products and services.[2] Since the Industrial Revolution, innovation has changed radically, occurring in quantum leaps and at an exponential rate. The production process has also shifted from one based largely on assembly lines to the use of robots to make a wide variety of high-valued merchandise. The quintessential technologies of globalization include "computerization, miniaturization, digitization, satellite communications, fiber optics and the Internet." They help connect people everywhere in ways previously unthought-of—both for good and for bad.

While all this has been happening, the production process has also become much more fragmented due to vertical **specialization** and **outsourcing**. For example, Boeing's new 787 Dreamliner commercial jet is assembled in Everett, Washington, but many of its component parts are manufactured in other parts of the country and outside the United States. Although many companies save money by outsourcing, Boeing went billions of dollars over budget on the Dreamliner and had to delay its unveiling by three years in part because many foreign suppliers could not produce components with the correct specifications fast enough.[3] In his book *The World Is Flat*, Friedman shows how the rapid spread of production processes throughout the world (most recently to India and China) has empowered individuals to collaborate and compete globally. As anyone who has waited on the phone while speaking to a company "representative" in India can appreciate, new satellite communications networks make it easier to outsource production and services—although not always seamlessly or satisfactorily.

According to Friedman, "Every new product—from software to widgets—goes through a cycle that begins with basic research, then applied research, incubation, development, testing, manufacturing, support, and finally continuation engineering in order to add improvements."[4] Friedman's *flat world* is one of giant video screens, call centers, and the outsourcing of tax returns and flight reservations to places like India where workers are eager to obtain good-paying jobs tied to participation in the global economy. The transformation and globalization of production processes is occurring not only in manufacturing—it is also taking place in food, agriculture, and sophisticated national security systems.

Changes in where production takes place are frequently tied to changes in patterns of **foreign direct investment (FDI)**. FDI consists mostly of investments by foreign companies in factories, mines, and land. As indicated in Table 6-1, between 1980 and 2011 the value of global FDI inflows increased from $54 billion to $1.5 trillion. Historically, most inward flows of FDI were concentrated among the developed nations; as late as 2000, developed countries received 81 percent of FDI. However, by 2011 they took in only 49 percent, as investment rapidly spread out to every continent, especially Asia and South America, causing these areas of the world to become much bigger producers of manufactured goods and commodities. Within the developed regions, most FDI has flowed to the United States and the EU, but after the onset of the financial crisis in 2008 these regions lost a lot of investment and some more of their manufacturing. Beginning in the 1990s, the share of total world FDI for developing nations like China, Hong Kong, Singapore, Brazil, and Chile jumped significantly. Until the mid-2000s, very little FDI flowed to India, the former Soviet Union, the Middle East, and sub-Saharan Africa. But by 2008, investors began pouring money into India's services

TABLE 6-1

Net Inflows of Foreign Direct Investment (in billions of US dollars)

Region/Classification	1980	1990	2000	2008	2011
East Asia (including China)	1	9	117	185	219
Central and South America	6	8	77	128	149
European Union	21	97	698	542	421
United States	17	48	314	306	227
Arab States	-3	1	6	96	41
Sub-Saharan Africa	0.3	2	7	37	37
Developed Countries	47	172	1,137	1,019	748
52 Least Developed Countries	0.5	0.6	4	18	15
World	54	207	1,401	1,791	1,524

Source: United Nations Conference on Trade and Development, UNCTADSTAT, "Inward and outward foreign direct investment, annual, 1970–2011," at http://unctadstat.unctad.org/ReportFolders/reportFolders.aspx.

sector and Russia's booming manufacturing and energy sectors. Africa has seen a bigger inflow in recent years, partly due to Chinese interest in commodities in the continent. However, the least developed, poorest countries of the world have since 1980 been unable to attract any significant amount of FDI, undermining their future prospects for economic development.

According to Eric Thun, these patterns of investment have contributed to the mobility of capital and to the tendency of industries to leave the industrialized nations in search of new markets, cheap labor, or other production advantages in developing parts of the world (see Chapter 17). While private FDI to emerging countries has increased for the last two decades, official development aid has flatlined. Also, developing countries between 2000 and 2007 dramatically reduced their reliance on loans from foreign governments, the IMF, and the World Bank, but with the onset of the global financial crisis many of them borrowed more from these sources to invest in new development projects. As expected, many mercantilists and structuralists note that these trends have important consequences for the distribution of the world's wealth and power through international trade as well as for labor conditions, the environment, and other issues that we will discuss in later chapters.

The changes in global production can be clearly seen in GDP trends. The World Bank reports that in 2011 the world's GDP totaled $70 trillion, with the seventy high-income countries accounting for $46.6 trillion or 67 percent of the total (down from 78 percent of the total in 2005).[5] The 108 middle-income countries accounted for $23 trillion or 33 percent of the total, while the thirty-six lowest-income countries accounted for only $474 billion or just 0.7 percent of the world's total output. Undoubtedly, middle-income countries like China, Russia, Brazil, and India are producing a rapidly growing share of the world's goods and services, while the United States, the European Union, and Japan—especially since the onset of the global financial crisis—are producing a smaller proportion of the world's output. Sadly, the world's poorest countries—nearly 20 percent of all countries—simply do not contribute any significant goods or services to the global economy.

INTERNATIONAL TRADE

International trade occurs when goods and services cross national boundaries in exchange for money or the goods and services of other nations. Although most locally produced goods and services are consumed in confined markets, international trade has grown dramatically as a reflection of increased global demand and the internationalization of production. During the period from 1983 to 2011, for example, world exports of goods increased from a total of $1.8 trillion to $17.8 trillion. Between 2000 and 2011, world exports of commercial services such as travel, transportation, and insurance increased by more than 8 percent a year to reach $4.2 trillion in 2011.[6]

Based on these trends, national economies have become much more reliant on—and sensitive to—trade. According to the World Bank, international trade as a percentage of GDP went up significantly between 1995 and 2009: 23 to 26 percent in the United States, 58 to 71 percent in the EU27, and 17 to 25 percent in Japan.[7] As Table 6-3 indicates, for the world as a whole, international trade as a percentage of GDP went up from 38 to 56 percent between 1990 and 2010. Trade, then, ties countries together, generating significant economic, political, and social interdependence. For most states, trade is an easy way of generating income and jobs. For many developing nations, it is often a critical component of development plans. Thus, in a highly integrated international political economy, states are compelled to regulate trade in order to maximize its benefits and limit its costs to their economies. As a result, one state's trade policies can easily impose costly socio-economic adjustment problems on other states. Without a set of international rules and procedures, nationalistic trade policies could easily undermine the entire production and trade structure.

The production and trade structure pulls national leaders, IO and NGO officials, and the public in several directions at once. On the whole, economic liberals tend to emphasize that the rational thing for states to do is to agree on a common set of international rules that will maximize the gains from trade in a competitive global economy. Without these rules, many states and domestic groups are likely to incur substantial economic losses. Mercantilists and structuralists agree that there are economic gains to be made from trade, but they insist that trade is a much more complex and controversial topic because of the way it contributes to national power and how it benefits some groups more than others.

What follows is a discussion of how the three perspectives view trade and a brief overview of trade history.

THE THREE PERSPECTIVES ON INTERNATIONAL TRADE

From the sixteenth through the eighteenth centuries, there were no international trade rules as we know them today. Early European states aggressively sought to generate trade surpluses as a source of wealth for local producers, for royalty, and later for the bureaucratic state. To help local industries get off the ground, leaders discouraged imports so that people would have to buy locally produced goods. Mercantilists used trade to enhance their wealth, power, and prestige in relation to other states. In their fabulous collection of vignettes about trade since the 1400s, historians Kenneth Pomeranz and Steven Topik point out that states often adopted a mix of mercantilist, imperialistic, and free-trade policies to advance their interests, depending on their level of economic development and changes in technology.[8] They argue that although in theory free trade should benefit all countries, "There are virtually no examples of successful industrialization with 'pure' free trade (or for that matter with pure self-sufficiency). Even in the heyday of free trade, the United States and Germany achieved their impressive late nineteenth- and early twentieth-century growth behind high tariff walls; many other countries also had some kind of protection."[9]

Economic Liberals

Many economic liberal ideas about trade are rooted in the late eighteenth- and early nineteenth-century views of Adam Smith and David Ricardo, who were reacting to what they viewed as mercantilist abuses at the time. They proposed a distinctly liberal theory of trade that dominated British policy for more than a hundred years and is still influential today. Smith, of course, generally advocated laissez-faire policies (see Chapter 2). Ricardo went one step further; his work on the **law of comparative advantage** demonstrated that free trade increased efficiency and had the potential to make everyone better off. It mattered little who produced the goods, where, or under what circumstances, as long as individuals were free to buy and sell them on open markets.

The law of comparative advantage suggests that when people and nations produce goods, they give up other things they could have produced but that would have been more expensive to make than the goods they actually created. This is what economists call opportunity cost. The law of comparative advantage invites us to compare the cost of producing an item ourselves with the availability and costs of buying it from others, and to make a logical and efficient choice between the two. In Ricardo's day, as we saw in Chapter 2, the law of comparative advantage specified that Great Britain should import food grains rather than produce so much of them at home, because the cost of imports was comparatively less than the cost of local production.

For many economic liberals in the late 1800s, the world was supposedly becoming a global workshop where everyone could benefit from **free trade,** guided by the invisible hand of the market. Today, lightly regulated trade is also an integral part of other policies associated with the **Washington Consensus** promoted by the United States and other members of the World Trade Organization (WTO). A large (but far from universal) consensus exists that the benefits of a liberal, open international trade system far outweigh its negative effects.[10]

Mercantilists

As we outlined in Chapter 3, Alexander Hamilton and Friedrich List challenged what became accepted economic liberal doctrine about trade. From their mercantilist perspective, free-trade policies were merely a rationale for England to maintain its dominant advantage over its trading partners on the Continent and in the New World. For Hamilton, supporting U.S. infant industries and achieving national independence and security required the use of protectionist trade measures. Likewise, List argued that in a climate of rising economic nationalism, protectionist trade policies such as import tariffs and export subsidies were necessary if Europe's infant industries were to compete on an equal footing with England's more efficient enterprises.[11] More importantly, List maintained that in order for free trade to work for all, it must be preceded by greater equality between states, or at least a willingness on their part to share the benefits and costs associated with it.

Many neomercantilists today challenge the assumption that comparative advantage unconditionally benefits both or all of the parties engaged in trade. People employed in different industries or sectors of any economy can be expected to resist being laid off or moving into other occupations as comparative advantages shift around to different nations. In many cases, states can intentionally *create* comparative advantages in the production of new goods and services simply by adopting **strategic trade policies** such as provision of cheap loans and export subsidies to domestic producers. New technologies and other resources such as cheap labor can easily help one state's new industries gain a comparative (competitive) advantage over the industries of another state. This has been the case for farming and auto, steel, and textile manufacturing.[12]

Moreover, it is a political reality in democratic nations with representative legislatures that the state is expected to protect society and its businesses from the negative effects of trade. When many domestic groups and industries appeal to the government for protection, they are likely to receive help because politicians fear the wrath of constituents who face layoffs or competition from cheaper imports. In many cases, protection is a built-in feature of many democratic systems. Those who benefit from a small savings on the price of an imported article of clothing or new car due to free trade, for instance, usually do not speak as loudly as displaced workers who seek protection from free trade.

Trade protectionism is also associated with a fear of becoming too dependent on other nations for certain goods, especially food and items related to national defense. For example, Japan and China have worried that too much dependency on other states for energy imports can lead to economic or political vulnerability. Finally, some neomercantilists are concerned that the protectionist trade policies of a regional trade alliance such as the North American Free Trade Agreement (NAFTA) or the EU (discussed below) which are designed to help local industries might intentionally or unintentionally disrupt another country. As many mercantilists see it, economic liberal theories about trade cannot account adequately for the real political world in which states constantly manipulate production and trade.

THE VOCABULARY OF INTERNATIONAL TRADE POLICY

Some of the more important protectionist measures include the following:

- *Tariffs:* Taxes placed on imported goods to raise the price of those goods, making them less attractive to consumers. These are used to raise government revenue (particularly in developing nations) or, more commonly, as a means to protect domestic industry from foreign competition.
- *Import quotas:* Limits on the quantity of an item imported into a nation. By limiting the quantity of imports, the quota tends to drive up the price of a good; at the same time it restricts competition.
- *Export quotas:* Measures that restrict the quantity of an item a nation can export, with the effect of limiting the number of goods imported by another country. Examples include Voluntary Export Restraints (VERs) and Voluntary Restraint Agreements (VRAs). For example, the Multifibre Agreement (MFA) established an international set of rules for textile export quotas for both developed and developing countries.
- *Export subsidies:* Measures that effectively reduce the price of an exported product, making it more attractive to potential foreign buyers.
- *Currency devaluations:* The effect of making a nation's currency worth less makes exports to other countries cheaper and imports from abroad more expensive. Currency depreciation thus tends to achieve the effects, temporarily at least, of both a tariff (raising import prices) and an export subsidy (lowering the costs of exports). However, currency changes affect the prices of all traded goods, whereas tariffs and subsidies generally apply to one good at a time (see Chapter 7).

- *Nontariff barriers (NTBs):* Other ways of limiting imports, including government health and safety standards, domestic content legislation, licensing requirements, and labeling requirements. Such measures make it difficult to market imported goods and significantly raise the price of imported goods.
- *Strategic trade practices:* Efforts on the part of the state to *create* comparative advantages in trade by methods such as subsidizing research and development of a product or providing subsidies to help an industry increase production to the point at which it can move up the "learning curve" to achieve greater production efficiency than foreign competitors. Strategic trade practices are often associated with *state industrial policies,* that is, intervention in the economy to promote specific patterns of industrial development.
- *Dumping:* The practice of selling an item for less abroad than at home. Dumping is generally regarded as an unfair trade practice when used to drive out competitors from an export market with the goal of generating monopoly power.
- *Countervailing trade practices:* State defensive measures taken to counter the advantage gained by another state when it adopts protectionist measures. Such practices include antidumping measures and the imposition of countervailing tariffs or quotas.
- *Safeguards:* Other defensive measures, used when, after tariffs are reduced, a product is imported in quantities that threaten serious injury to domestic producers of like or directly competitive products.

Structuralists

Structuralists label the early mercantilist period as one of classical imperialism. Economic problems in the major European powers drove them to colonize underdeveloped regions of the world. Mercantilist policies that emphasized exports became necessary when capitalist societies experienced economic depression. Manufacturers overproduced industrial products, and financiers had a surplus of capital to invest abroad. Colonies served at least two purposes: they were places to dump goods and places where investments could be made in industries that profited from cheap labor and access to plentiful (i.e., inexpensive) natural resources and mineral deposits. Trade helped imperial countries dominate and subjugate the people and economies of the colonized territories.

Lenin and other Marxist theorists argued that national trade policies mostly benefited the dominant class in society—the bourgeoisie (see Chapter 4). During the early colonial period, underdeveloped regions of the world remained on the periphery of the international trade system, providing European powers with primary goods and minerals. Toward the end of the nineteenth century, capitalist countries used trade to spread capitalism into their colonies. Lenin attempted to account for the necessity of states with excess finance to take colonies in order to postpone revolution at home. The "soft" power of finance as much as the "hard" power of military conquest helped to generate empires of dependency and exploitation.

Structuralists argue that industrializing core nations converted colonies' resources and minerals into finished and semifinished products, many of which were sold to other major powers and back to their colonies. Although particular sectors (enclaves) in core economies developed, peripheral nations and regions *became underdeveloped* after being linked with industrialized nations through trade.[13]

Immanuel Wallerstein stresses the linkages between core, peripheral, and semiperipheral regions of the world.[14] Today, patterns of international trade are determined largely by an international division of labor between states in these three regions that drives capitalism to expand globally. The integration of global markets and free-trade policies associated with globalization are extensions of the same economic motives of imperial powers of the nineteenth and twentieth centuries.

In sum, each of the three IPE perspectives on trade contains a different ideological outlook. Today, a majority of academics and policy officials still favor an international trade system that is supposed to be *progressively* liberalizing and opening up. And yet, as we will see, most nations tend to behave in a mercantilist fashion and adopt protectionist measures when their national interests are threatened. Some developing and industrialized nations are concerned that trade may be more exploitative than mutually advantageous.

GATT AND THE LIBERAL POSTWAR TRADE STRUCTURE

Before World War II, trade rules largely reflected the interests of the dominant states, especially Great Britain, France, and Germany. Despite a few decades in which economic liberal ideas prevailed, protectionism was the order of the day. Trade rules were enforced at the point of a gun, as when the United States forced Japan to open its doors to U.S. trade in the 1860s and the European powers forced open China and the Ottoman empire in the nineteenth century.

During the Great Depression of the 1930s, protectionism spiraled upward while international trade decreased significantly, by an estimated 54 percent between 1929 and 1933, strangled in part by the Smoot-Hawley tariffs in the United States and onerous trade barriers enacted elsewhere. According to some historians, the trade situation and the depressed international economy helped generate the bleak economic conditions to which ultranationalist leaders such as Mussolini and Hitler reacted. It is important to note that, in contrast to the common assumption that the United States has always supported free trade, it was not until 1934 that the United States officially adopted a free-trade policy.

The post–World War II structure of the capitalist world's political economy was established in 1944 at the Bretton Woods conference in Bretton Woods, New Hampshire. There, Allied leaders, led by the United States and Great Britain, created a new liberal economic order that they hoped would prevent many of the interwar economic conflicts and problems that had led to World War II. In conjunction with this effort, the United States promoted the establishment of an International Trade Organization (ITO) to oversee new trade rules that would gradually reduce tariffs, subsidies, and other protectionist measures, offsetting mercantilist tendencies. The ITO never got off the ground because a coalition of protectionist interests in the U.S. Congress forced the United States to withdraw from the agreement, effectively killing it. President Harry Truman advanced a temporary alternative structure for trade negotiations under the **General Agreement on Tariffs and Trade (GATT)**. In 1948, the GATT became the primary organization responsible for the liberalization of international trade.[15] Through a series of multilateral negotiations called *rounds,* the world's main trading nations agreed to reduce their own protectionist barriers in return for freer access to the markets of others.

Two basic principles of the GATT were **reciprocity** and **nondiscrimination**. Trade concessions were reciprocal—that is, all member nations agreed to lower their trade barriers together. This principle was conceived as a way to discourage nations from enacting unilateral trade barriers. The loss in protection for domestic industry was to be offset by freer access to foreign markets. To prevent bilateral trade wars and support nondiscrimination, the principles of **national treatment** and **most-favored-nation** (MFN) treatment required that imported goods be treated the same as equivalent domestically produced goods and that imports from one nation could not be given preference over those from another. Theoretically, the GATT's membership was open to any nation, but until the 1980s most communist countries refused to join it, viewing it as a tool of Western imperialism.

Reciprocity and nondiscrimination proved to be potent during the early rounds of GATT negotiations, as members slowly peeled away the protectionist barriers they had erected in the 1930s and international trade expanded dramatically. In many cases, however, it was not possible to divorce politics from trade. Some nations were not always willing to grant reciprocity to their trading partners automatically; they granted it selectively to those they favored politically and withheld it from other states. Later in the chapter, we will discuss the case wherein the United States advanced a variety of foreign policy objectives by withholding or threatening to withhold MFN status from China.

Keep in mind that as an organization the GATT could not enforce its own rules; rather, members were responsible for fulfilling mutual trade obligations based on trust and diplomacy. Policy decisions were made through consensus, and thus implementation of polices often reflected a combination of political and economic interests. Written into the GATT were a series of exceptions from generalized trade rules for regional trade agreements (RTAs) and products such as textiles and agricultural goods. At first, these exemptions allowed many of the war-ravaged nations to resolve balance-of-payments problems. In the case of agriculture, they also reflected food shortages in Europe and the need for financial assistance to farmers and other groups.

Mercantilism on the Rebound

During the 1960s and early 1970s, the pace at which the Western industrialized economies had grown after the war began to slow appreciably; then the OPEC oil crisis in 1973 caused economic recession. Throughout this period international trade continued to grow, but not at the rate at which it had earlier. Under pressure to stimulate economic growth, many nations reduced their tariff barriers. At the same time, however, they devised new and more sophisticated ways to bolster their exports and limit imports. By the time the Tokyo round of the GATT (1973–1979) got underway, the level of tariffs on industrial products had decreased to an average of 9 percent. The Tokyo round tried to deal with a growing number of **nontariff barriers (NTBs)** that many believed were stifling world trade. Rules and codes were established to limit a range of discriminatory trade practices including the use of export subsidies, countervailing duties, dumping, government purchasing practices, government-imposed product standards, and custom valuation and licensing requirements on importers. Some new rules were also devised that covered trade with developing nations.

Many liberal trade theorists at the time argued that the Tokyo round did not go far enough in dealing with NTBs or with enforcing GATT rules. In the 1970s and 1980s, the industrialized nations encountered a number of old and also new kinds of trade problems. Trade among the industrialized nations quadrupled from 1963 to 1973, but increased only two and one-half times in the next decade. Meanwhile, trade accounted for increasingly higher percentages of GDP in the industrialized nations in the 1980s: around 20 percent for the United States, 20 percent for Japan, and an average of 50 percent for members of the EU. To put it mildly, trade policy continued to be a serious source of tension and disagreement among the industrialized nations, reflecting their increasing dependence on trade to help generate economic growth.

Japan, the quintessential mercantilist nation during this period, benefited from the liberal international trade system while erecting domestic trade and other protectionist policies. By the 1970s, Japan's export-led growth trade strategy began to bear fruit. Its Ministry of International Trade and Industry (MITI) helped pick corporate winners that it and other government officials felt would prosper in the international economy from state assistance. Most of these industries were high-employment, high-technology firms whose future looked bright. Working closely with their national firms, the Japanese and the Newly Industrializing Countries

(NICs) began assisting their firms in ways that would put them in a strong competitive position.[16]

The term "strategic trade policy" became synonymous with state efforts to stimulate exports or block foreign access to domestic markets. Aside from export subsidies and the use of a variety of import-limiting measures, proactive strategic trade policy measures often involved extended support for "infant industries." It also included "the use of threats, promises, and other bargaining techniques in order to alter the trading regime in ways that improve the market position and increase the profits of national corporations."[17] In the United States, for instance, the Omnibus Trade and Competitiveness Act of 1988 produced **Super 301**, which required the U.S. Trade Representative to annually list "priority" countries that unfairly threatened U.S. exports. The legislation was designed to put unilateral pressure on countries to negotiate with the United States to change their offending trade policies. In another example, France in 1982 sought to protect its VCR manufacturers from Japanese competition by requiring all imported VCRs to go through a tiny inland customs office in Poitiers where officials deliberately stalled the clearing of imports.[18] Also, Europe and the United States in the 1980s negotiated voluntary export restraints (VERs) with Japan in order to limit its exports of automobiles to their markets.

With the acceptance of some amount of trade protection, a more liberal (open) GATT system seemed compromised. Free trade was slowly replaced as the central principle by the notion of **fair trade** or a "level playing field," where states enacted policies to counteract some policies of their trading partners. Trade policy moved from the multilateral arena of GATT to a series of bilateral discussions such as those between the United States and Japan and between the United States and the EU.

The Uruguay Round

Under conditions of increasing protectionism, the Reagan administration sought to reassert the liberal vision of free trade. In addition, realist-mercantilists point out that the administration wanted to spread economic liberal policies to counter the influence of the "evil empire" (the Soviet Union) in developing nations. Thus was born the eighth GATT round—the Uruguay round. It began in 1986 in Punta del Este, Uruguay, and ended in December 1993. Generally speaking, economic liberals tend to view this round as a success because it spurred an increase in the volume and value of international trade. Many import quotas were eliminated, and export subsidies were brought under control. FDI surged alongside growth in trade, further embedding national economies in an interdependent international trade network.

The Uruguay round established new rules and regulations to limit protectionist measures such as "dumping" (selling goods at below fair market prices) and the use of state subsidies. Going beyond previous trade rounds, it established fifteen working groups that dealt with such items as market access for textiles and agricultural goods; intellectual property rights; restrictions on foreign investments; and trade in services. Discussion of these issues reflected recognition that as production changed and spread to different parts of the world, it affected both the amount and kind of international trade.

For the first time GATT trade negotiations dealt in a comprehensive manner with the contentious issue of agriculture. All of the major producers and importers of agricultural products routinely employ subsidies and other measures that, according to economic liberal critics, distort agricultural markets. Agricultural issues had been intentionally absent from previous GATT rounds because they were politically too contentious and would have prevented progress in areas where agreements were possible. This time trade officials made the issue of agricultural assistance and reform one of the main objectives of the Uruguay round.[19] The United States and the Cairns Group (composed of Australia and seventeen other pro–free-trade countries) led a politically radical effort to phase out all agricultural subsidies. After resistance by some U.S. farm groups and government officials, the United States agreed to *gradually* eliminate its domestic farm programs and agricultural trade support measures. EU efforts to significantly reduce their agricultural subsidies were complicated by the EU's Common Agricultural Policy (CAP)—a community-wide farm program that reflected the combined interests of its fifteen member states, with France most critical of efforts to decrease agricultural support. Bringing the EU's farm program in line with GATT reform proposals would be a politically difficult and complicated process that took almost five years to complete.

Many U.S. exporters expected a new multilateral agreement to produce 20,000 jobs for every $1 billion increase in exports and access to overseas markets for U.S. semiconductors, computers, and agricultural commodities.[20] However, agricultural trade remained one of the major sticking points of the negotiations, shutting them down on several occasions. Eventually, at the eleventh hour in November 1993, a consensus on agriculture was reached that reflected numerous "deals" and compromises between nations or blocs of nations. Under the new agreement, all countries were to reduce their use of agricultural export subsidies and domestic assistance *gradually* over a period of years. States were allowed to convert nontariff import barriers into tariff equivalents, which were then to be reduced in stages. However, because of the strength of farm lobbies and the importance of agricultural exports in many of these countries, the method for calculating tariff equivalents in most cases actually set new tariff levels *higher* than they had been, effectively nullifying efforts to reduce farm support. Trade officials claimed that progress was made toward liberalizing agricultural trade in the Uruguay round, but in reality, protectionism remained a key feature of agricultural trade.

It is important to note that the Uruguay round produced some sixty or so agreements on a host of other issues, including safeguards, rules of origin, technical barriers to trade, and textiles and clothing. The Uruguay round also became famous for creating the WTO and for institutionalizing what would become a set of global trade rules and regulations. GATT rules and a number of procedures became a legal element of the WTO. A new **General Agreement on Trade in Services (GATS)** liberalized trade in such things as banking, insurance, transport, and telecommunications services by applying the principles of national treatment and most-favored-nation to them. And a new agreement on **Trade-Related Aspects of Intellectual Property Rights (TRIPS)** required countries to maintain minimum standards for protection of patents, copyrights, and trademarks—and to effectively enforce those standards. Many delegates intended that remaining disputes over agriculture, trade in services, and advantages that TRIPS gave to developed states would be dealt with more directly in a future round of trade negotiations.

The WTO

The final agreement of the Uruguay round launched the new World Trade Organization, which by 2012 had 157 members accounting for 97 percent of global trade. Headquartered in Geneva, Switzerland, its primary job is to implement the GATT, GATS, and TRIPS agreements. It also acts as a forum for negotiating new trade deals, helps resolve trade disputes, and provides technical assistance and training programs to developing countries. Theoretically, WTO decisions are still to be made by a consensus of the members. Its decision-making structure includes a secretariat (administrative body), a ministerial conference that meets at least once every two years, and a general council composed of ambassadors and delegation heads that meets several times a year in Geneva.

The WTO uses **Dispute Settlement Panels (DSP)** that rule on trade disputes, giving the WTO an enforcement mechanism that the GATT did not have. An impartial panel of experts oversees cases submitted to it for resolution, and members can appeal its findings. Countries that refuse to enforce the rulings of a DSP can be subject to trade sanctions by member states. Several cases have gained significant press attention over the years, including a judgment against the EU's attempt to limit imports of hormone-fed U.S. beef into the EU. Another case was the transatlantic conflict over the production and use of genetically modified foods and organisms (GMOs) (discussed in Chapter 18). More recently, a long-running dispute over subsidies to aircraft manufacturers was adjudicated by panels that found both Boeing and Airbus had improperly received massive subsidies from the United States and the European Union, respectively.

For the most part, since the founding of the WTO, trade disputes have become more complex and politicized. Some nations have even threatened to withdraw from the WTO when DSP decisions go against them. So far, however, most states have either accepted the findings of dispute resolution panels or arrived at satisfactory resolution of trade spats through negotiations.

The Doha "Development Round"

The next round of multilateral trade negotiations was to begin in 1999, but the WTO's ministerial talks in Seattle ended in deadlock, with riots in the streets and antiglobalization protestors blocking delegates from entering the negotiations. The "Battle of Seattle" became a rallying cry for many antiglobalization activists concerned about violations of human rights in sweatshops, agribusinesses in developing countries, effects of large capitalist enterprises on the environment, lack of transparency in WTO decision-making, and a host of ethical issues.[21] Critics of many ideological persuasions questioned the WTO's ability to deal with these problems and the WTO's effects on sovereignty and competition policy.

After the events of 9/11, trade officials pushed to restart multilateral trade talks. At the 2001 ministerial meeting in Doha, Qatar (far away from protestors), the next multilateral trade round began. From the beginning, many developing countries complained that agreements reached in the Uruguay round had not resulted in significant gains for them. They also argued that before new trade agreements could be reached, the developed nations would have to make a concerted effort to include developing nations in the negotiation process. In recognition of this goal the Doha round was nicknamed the "Development Round" to reflect the growing importance of developing nations in the international trade system.

At Cancun, Mexico, in November 2003, ministerial talks broke down once again. U.S. Special Trade Representative Robert Zoellick blamed developing nations and NGOs (especially those associated with the antiglobalization campaign) for resisting efforts to reach a new agreement. Some developing countries claimed to be suffering more poverty, along with environmental, social, and economic damage, after implementing the WTO's rules. There was growing resistance to efforts by the United States, the EU, and Japan to implement the "Washington Consensus"—a one-size-fits-all strategy of economic development that included trade liberalization. Headed by Brazil, India, South Africa, and China, the Group of 20 (G20) (not to be confused with the financial G20), focused on cutting farm subsidies in the rich countries. As a bloc, they dismissed 105 changes in WTO rules that would have provided developed countries more access to their markets.[22]

To restart the talks the United States offered to cut subsidies if others did the same. However, the U.S. commitment to trade liberalization seemed hollow, given that the 2002 U.S. farm bill passed by Congress had *increased* U.S. farm and agribusiness support by $70 billion. Critics pointed out that these kinds of policies caused more overproduction and the dumping of excess commodities onto world markets, thereby distorting world commodity prices, displacing local production in developing countries, and depressing prices local farmers received. Even President George W. Bush recognized that continued U.S. and EU farm subsidies hurt poorer farmers in developing nations.

Late in 2005, the G20 pushed the United States and the EU to cut domestic agricultural support significantly and reduce agricultural export subsidies. At the Group of 8 (G8) meeting in the summer of 2006 in St. Petersburg, Russia, the major powers made yet another failed attempt to come to an agreement that would complete the Doha round. The Doha round mostly came to a halt in 2008. The developed countries insisted on greater non-agricultural market access (NAMA)—meaning that developing countries would lower tariffs on industrial imports dramatically.

Other issues on the Doha agenda included TRIPS, which many developing countries argue limits their access to generic medicines by protecting patents held mainly by U.S. companies (see the box "Patent Rights vs. Patient Rights" in Chapter 10). The United States retorted that allowing developing nations to produce cheaper generic drugs with compulsory licenses would hurt (the profits of) major drug manufacturers. The WTO failed to reach consensus on specific measures regarding "cultural products" (such as movies), insurance companies, security firms, banking across national borders, and protectionist "local content" legislation.

Many trade officials fear that the Doha round will never be successfully concluded, possibly leading to the demise of the WTO altogether. Some believe that the inclusion of the developing nations in the WTO has created such a large agenda that it has become nearly impossible to find consensual positions. Finally, some heterodox interventionist liberals (HILs) and mercantilists claim that without an assertive hegemon, the globalization of trade has made it too difficult for states to reconcile trade liberalization with domestic pressures for protection from trade's dislocating effects. President Obama has not actively sought to push other states into signing off on Doha.

REGIONAL TRADE BLOCS

Critics of the Doha round suggest that, instead of multilateral talks, states ought to pursue bilateral and regional trade agreements. In fact, the United States has already agreed to more than 300 bilateral agreements with other countries, with more on the way. It also belongs to a number of **regional trade agreements (RTAs)** such as NAFTA and Asia-Pacific Economic Cooperation (APEC) (see later), where it is easier for the United States to dictate terms. RTAs also have less bureaucracy, fewer members, and more room to account for the idiosyncrasies of partner states or to reconcile conflicting interests on a geographically regional level.

Regional trade blocs are defined as formal intergovernmental collaboration between two or more states in a geographic area.[23] They promote a mix of economic liberal and mercantilist trade policies, reducing barriers within the trade bloc while retaining trade barriers with nonmember nations. RTAs have grown prodigiously since the end of the Cold War. They are estimated to have covered nearly 60 percent of world trade by 2010. The most well-known regional trade blocs are the EU and NAFTA. Others include the Central American Free Trade Association (CAFTA), Mercosur, the Association of Southeast Asian Nations (ASEAN), the Economic Community of West African States (ECOWAS). Asia-Pacific Economic Cooperation (APEC) is an **intraregional trade bloc** that attempts to integrate eighteen Pacific and Asian nations into a nonbinding arrangement that would gradually remove trade barriers among members by 2020. As a promoter of the agreement, the United States hopes to further liberalize trade among the members while accelerating economic growth in the Asia-Pacific region. In 2011, 71 percent of EU exports and nearly half of NAFTA members' exports were intraregional.[24] The EU and NAFTA accounted for 49 percent of all global trade (imports and exports) of merchandise and commercial services in 2011. The EU alone accounted for 35 percent of global trade, compared to NAFTA's 15 percent, ASEAN's 6 percent, and Mercosur's 1.9 percent.[25]

Why so many RTAs? Are they good for trade? Technically, RTAs violate the GATT and WTO principle of nondiscrimination, but they are nonetheless legal entities. Article XXIV of the GATT and Article V of the General Agreement on Trade in Services exempt them, as long as they make an effort to liberalize trade within the bloc. In some cases, RTAs generate more efficient production within the bloc, either while infant industries are maturing or in response to more competition from outside industries. In other cases they attract FDI when local regulations and investment rules are streamlined and simplified. For many economic liberals, regional trade blocs are stepping-stones toward the possibility of a global free-trade zone as they gradually spread and deepen economic integration. However, not all economic liberals support RTAs. The noted supporter of globalization Jagdish Bhagwati is concerned that bilateral and regional free-trade agreements are likely to generate a "spaghetti bowl effect" of multiple tariffs and preferences, making it harder to eventually reduce trade protection measures significantly.[26]

Mercantilists tend to focus on the political rationale behind RTAs as well as the way in which they serve a variety of political and economic objectives. For some nations they can be bargaining tools used to prevent transnational corporations from playing one state off against another. A classic case, for example, was one of the arguments President Clinton made in support of U.S. efforts to help organize NAFTA—that the United States should be able to penetrate and secure Mexican markets before the Japanese did.[27] If the United States did not quickly bring Mexico into its trade orbit in 1993, Japanese investments in Mexico would negate U.S. influence over Mexico's future trade policies. As discussed in Chapter 3, these sorts of cases will always exist as long as states are the dominant actors in the international political economy.

We can also see political motivations behind the Trans-Pacific Partnership (TPP), the most important RTA that the United States is currently negotiating. Originally started by Brunei, Chile, New Zealand, and Singapore, the TPP now includes the United States, Australia, Canada, Chile, Malaysia, Mexico, Peru, and Vietnam. It is designed to significantly liberalize trade in agriculture, manufactured goods, and services; strengthen intellectual property rights protections; open government procurement markets; allow foreign corporations to initiate legal actions against countries that violate the agreement; and weaken preferential treatment governments give to state-owned companies.[28] Free-trade critics like Lori Wallach have called the TPP a "stealthy, slow-motion corporate coup d'etat, formalizing and locking in corporate rule over most aspects of our lives."[29] Supporters see the TPP as a way for the United States to gain trade advantages over Japan and the EU in Asia. More importantly, it is a way to create a strategic counterweight to China, whose rising economic and military power the United States and most TPP countries are increasingly worried about.

North-South Trade Issues

Tensions between the Northern industrialized and Southern developing nations over trade issues are not new. However, resistance to some of the measures proposed in the Doha round does reflect the increasing importance and influence of emerging nations such as Brazil, China, and India in the international production and trade structure.

In 1973, when the OPEC nations dramatically raised the price of oil for the first time, a coalition of developing nations in the UN called the Group of 77 (G77) demanded an entirely new international economic order (NIEO).[30] Based on complaints about the terms of trade favoring the developed states, the G77 sought major changes in trade policies to permit more access for their primary commodities into the heavily protected markets of the Northern industrialized countries. The

G77 also demanded a TNC "Code of Conduct" to give developing nations control over their own resources along with a stronger voice in GATT decision making.

Consistent with the political environment at the time, these demands produced no fundamental changes in GATT, IMF, or World Bank policies. The United States and other states responded that, rather than trying to change system rules and procedures, developing nations should become more integrated into the international economy. Because trade is an "engine to growth" and an essential element of development, developing nations would benefit from trade efficiencies if they brought down tariff barriers and opened their economies to FDI.

In the 1980s, these same economic liberal ideas became the basis of Northern recommendations for how developing countries could help solve debt crises caused by their heavy borrowing from Western banks and international finance agencies. Again, instead of changing the fundamentals of the international production and trade structure, the Northern nations promoted a set of policies packaged as the "Washington Consensus." Developing nations should grow their way out of debt by liberalizing their trade policies and opening up their economies to FDI. Many of these ideas also served as justification for structural adjustment policies (SAPs)—conditions the IMF and the World Bank required developing nations to adhere to when they borrowed money from these institutions (see Chapter 8).

As the globalization campaign took off in the 1990s, the WTO and the World Bank supported the views of many trade experts who argued that countries that have experienced strong export growth have lower levels of import protection than countries with declining exports. They contend that much of the economic growth that has occurred in developing nations since the 1970s is due, for the most part, to an emphasis on manufacturing goods for export (see Table 6-2). Today, the WTO continues to suggest that if developing nations remain committed to free-trade rules, they will attract foreign and domestic investors.

Structuralist and Neomercantilist Versions of Trade and Globalization

Structuralists are critical of liberal ideas about trade and their effects on North–South relations. In the 1960s, 1970s, and even into the 1980s, many structuralists recommended that developing countries insulate themselves from and resist the inherently exploitative capitalist international trade system. At the end of the Cold War, however, many Marxists accepted the necessity of trade but shifted their attention to reforming the international trade system.

Today, many structuralists argue that the WTO has perpetuated the exploitative relationship between the North and South. Although trade and development policies have helped many countries grow, they have left behind a great number of poor people. Robert Hunter Wade, for example, has carefully calculated that while trade has raised per capita incomes in many states, especially China and India, it has also generated significant inequality between and especially within the developing nations.[31]

Other numbers give a more mixed picture of how changes in trade have affected developing nations. As Table 6-2 shows, China grew its share of world merchandise exports from just 1.2 percent in 1983 to 10.7 percent in 2011, a testament to its astonishingly rapid industrialization. Six other emerging East Asian countries

TABLE 6-2

World Merchandise Exports by Region

Region/Country	Value (Billions of $) 2011	Global Share (%) 1983	1993	2003	2011
World	17,816	100.0	100.0	100.0	100.0
United States	1,480	11.2	12.6	9.8	8.3
South and Central America	750	4.4	3.0	3.0	4.2
Europe	6,612	43.5	45.4	45.9	37.1
Commonwealth of Independent States (CIS)	789	–	1.5	2.6	4.4
Africa	594	4.5	2.5	2.4	3.3
Middle East	1,251	6.8	3.5	4.1	7.0
Asia	5,977	19.1	26.1	26.2	31.1
China	1,898	1.2	2.5	5.9	10.7
Japan	823	8.0	9.9	6.4	4.6
Six East Asian traders	2,184	5.8	9.7	9.6	9.8

Source: World Trade Organization, *International Trade Statistics 2012*, pp. 24, 26, 211–214, at http://www.wto.org/english/res_e/statis_e/its2012_e/its2012_e.pdf.

Note: The Six East Asian traders are Hong Kong, Malaysia, Singapore, South Korea, Taiwan, and Thailand.

nearly doubled their share of world merchandise exports during the same period. As a result, the developing nations' share increased from 25 percent in 1993 to 41 percent in 2011. However, Africa and Latin America have failed to gain a larger share of world merchandise exports, an indication that they are falling behind relatively in terms of industrialization and competitiveness. And the vast majority of developing nations still account for only about one-fifth of the world's trade in manufactured goods. Stated differently, 84 percent of all manufactured goods that are exported come from the EU, China, Japan, the United States, and South Korea. Most developing countries are simply marginal exporters of manufactured goods.

In contrast, if we look at the exports of the Middle East and Africa, we find that in 2011 two-thirds of all their exports were fuel and minerals. For South and Central America, two-thirds of their exports were fuel, minerals, and agricultural products.[32] Structuralists would point out that this heavy reliance on exports of commodities mimics the pattern seen during the colonial eras.

On the positive side, despite a sharp drop in prices of global commodities in 2008 and 2009 due to the financial crisis, the overall trend in prices for fuel, minerals, and agricultural products between 2000 and 2011 has been very beneficial for exporters: prices rose at an average annual rate of 12 percent.[33] On the downside, the Middle East, Africa, and Latin America are vulnerable to swings in prices and global demand for primary products. Because trade has accounted for as much as 75 percent of the foreign exchange earnings of many developing nations, volatile export prices have sometimes caused severe economic recession and triggered debt crises. As Table 6-3 indicates, poor developing countries are

TABLE 6-3

Trade as a Percent of Gross Domestic Product by Region

Region/Classification	1980	1990	2000	2010
East Asia and the Pacific*	34	43	67	71
Latin America and Caribbean	28	32	44	47
South Asia	21	20	29	48
Middle East and North Africa	60	57	64	84
Sub-Saharan Africa*	63	52	63	65
High Income	40	38	49	56
Highly Indebted Poor Countries	56	47	58	69
World	39	38	50	56

Note: Trade is exports and imports of goods and services. * Includes only the developing countries in these regions.

Source: World Bank, *World Development Indicators* database, November 2012.

much more dependent on trade than wealthy developed countries. By 2010, trade as a percentage of GDP in East Asia and the Middle East was 71 and 84 percent, respectively. Trade as a percentage of GDP in heavily indebted countries, especially in Africa, had reached more than 69 percent, compared to approximately 56 percent in high-income countries.

Aside from these numbers, some structuralists and mercantilists focus more on the effects that trade has on specific societies instead of on general trends that provide distorted pictures of consequences. As we discuss in more detail in Chapter 18, Walden Bello claims that in the area of agriculture, trade liberalization and globalization have served the interests of the U.S. agricultural "dumping lobby" and a "small elite of Asian agro-exporters."[34] Other experts argue that the effects of NAFTA on Mexican small farmers have been devastating: Between 1994 and 2010 two million jobs were lost in the agriculture sector, especially due to imports of cheap U.S. corn. According to economic liberals, this consequence flows naturally from the shift from an agricultural to a manufacturing-based economy. Yet, the problem for many structuralists is that the outcome is usually not what society would choose for itself but what is imposed on it by the Northern states.

Many structuralists—and some mercantilists—also warn against the terrible consequences weak Southern states face when powerful Northern states use trade as an instrument to achieve their political, social, and economic objectives. In the 1980s, the Reagan administration applied trade restrictions on nations it felt were either supporters of communist revolutionary movements (for example, Vietnam, Cambodia, and Nicaragua), sponsors of terrorism (Libya, Iran, Cuba, Syria, and Yemen), or enforcers of racial segregation (apartheid South Africa). After the first Persian Gulf War, the UN sponsored trade sanctions against Iraq to punish it for invading Kuwait and to compel it to stop producing weapons of mass destruction (WMD). In the fall of 2006, the UN Security Council imposed sanctions against North Korea for its failure to stop producing and testing nuclear weapons and other WMDs. These sanctions included inspections of goods coming into and out of North Korea by boat, plane, or train. In recent years, the United States, the European Union, and their allies—sometimes with UN backing—have also imposed stringent sanctions on Iran, Syria, the Gaza Strip, and Burma.

By the mid-1990s, many states came to view trade sanctions as morally repugnant because of the pain they inflict on ordinary people (see Chapter 14). Many critics of trade sanctions point out that they usually do not cause any real change in a targeted state's policies.[35] Businesses and governments often can get around them because goods produced in one country are hard to distinguish from those produced in another. It is also difficult to determine how the target state will react and adjust to an embargo or boycott. In cases such as Nicaragua in the 1980s, Iraq in the 1990s, North Korea since 2006, and most recently Iran, economic sanctions have unintentionally helped prop up authoritarian leaders who resist the sanctions-imposing "imperial aggressors." These cases demonstrate that there is more to the use of sanctions than simply using trade to punish or reward a state. When it comes to which trade sanctions to use in a given situation, tensions often reflect conflicting interests of different domestic businesses and foreign policy officials. For the most part, trade remains a tool states use to help discipline or send a distinct message to other states.

While a number of mercantilists support economic liberal policies and globalization to the extent that they serve state interests, most believe that the largest gains from trade have gone to the biggest industrialized and industrializing countries. Turkey and India, as well as many states in Africa and Latin America, have suffered chronic trade deficits and have large international debt. Some mercantilists note that the United States has favored free trade except when it might benefit producers in developing nations at the expense of U.S. producers. After World War II, the United States and its allies used the GATT and the WTO, along with other trade and finance organizations, to lower tariff barriers and thereby expose the infant industries of developing nations to competition with the more mature industries of the industrialized nations.

Economist Dani Rodrik, a supporter of managed globalization, points out that in the past, high-tariff countries grew *faster* than those without tariffs.[36] According to economist Ha-Joon Chang, the developed states now want to "kick away the ladder" (take away protection) from under the developing nations.[37] Rodrik and Chang would support Bello's argument that protection serves a variety of "socially worthy objectives such as promoting food security for society's low income people, protecting small farmers and biodiversity, guaranteeing food security, and promoting rural social development."[38]

Critics of Globalization and Outsourcing

Two other recent developments have influenced North–South relations: **outsourcing** and the rise of fair-trade NGOs. Since the 1990s, a growing number of NGOs, many with structuralist views and closely connected to the antiglobalization movement, have focused attention on the connection between trade and issues such as the environment, global labor conditions, poverty, and human rights. NGOs such as Oxfam, Global Trade Watch, and Global Exchange have acquired first-hand information about the effects of Northern trade policies on developing nations and publicized it in speeches, newspapers, journals, and on their websites. To some extent, constructivist theorists (see Chapter 5) posit that these civil society groups are responsible for changing the way the general population of developed countries thinks about globalization and "free trade." Production and trade affect the environment in ways that states and businesses never anticipated, as the demand for more energy resources increasingly makes the true cost of trade incalculable. NGOs have played a role in monitoring the effects of TNCs on various societies, casting light on many of the ethical and judicial dimensions of outsourcing and job displacement. In some cases, NGOs have been a source of information for WTO dispute hearings. A growing number of NGOs and university students have developed alternative trade strategies. One such effort is the "fair trade" movement that seeks to give workers in developing countries higher prices for certified goods such as coffee, chocolate, handicrafts, quinoa, and timber.[39]

Polls in the United States indicate that support for free trade has gradually decreased without a consensus about its benefit to the U.S. economy. According to a 2010 survey by the Pew Research Center, 44 percent of Americans say free trade agreements are bad for the United States and 55 percent believe they cause U.S. job losses.[40] Three factors have contributed to this shift. First, many experts accuse China and other countries of erecting a multitude of unfair trade barriers to block potential American exports of goods and services, thereby hurting U.S. employment and growth.[41] Second, a large number of jobs in industrialized states have been outsourced to countries such as China. Even though a good case can be made that outsourcing generates more jobs globally than it takes away, the specter of a middle-aged, hard-working U.S. citizen losing her job to a poorly paid Chinese worker is politically hard to swallow. Third, the global financial crisis has seen many states question trade liberalization and globalization in the face of the impact this disaster has had on their societies.

Outsourcing of production—when companies transfer manufacturing or certain business functions overseas—has become one of the most contentious trade and employment issues in the developed countries. Beginning in the 1980s, companies transferred factories to Asia and Latin America to take advantage of cheap, plentiful labor. Free-trade agreements and lower transportation costs made it more efficient to produce clothing, household goods, and electronics overseas and export the items back to the United States and Europe. Pushing U.S. manufacturers to outsource, rapidly expanding retail chains like Wal-Mart and Target then imported goods from China, increasing profit margins substantially. (In 2010, Wal-Mart and Target imported the equivalent of more than 1,150,000 cargo containers by ship!) Although liberal economists tout the greater global efficiency and cheaper prices for U.S. consumers, critics argue that it is destroying American manufacturing and driving down wages of blue collar workers. Today, many companies are also outsourcing services—everything from customer service, data processing, back-office work, tax preparation, and insurance claims processing.

Mercantilists and HILs worry about the long-term consequences of outsourcing-driven trade on the U.S. economy. Former Intel CEO Andy Grove warns that when factories move oversees, there is less innovation and fewer jobs in the United States. And because less "scaling"—that is, turning new ideas into mass production—occurs in the United States, the result is this: "As happened with batteries, abandoning today's 'commodity' manufacturing can lock you out of tomorrow's emerging industry."[42] Outsourcers are prone to having their intellectual property stolen (especially trade secrets and patents), thereby losing their future competitiveness to Chinese companies. Companies have also suffered quality-control problems and lost knowledge about production processes.

Business journalist Charles Fishman has examined a new countertrend: **insourcing**.[43] In recent years, U.S. companies such as General Electric, Apple, Whirlpool, and Sleek Audio have brought some of their manufacturing capacity back to the United States. Changes in the global economy, in addition to factors cited above, are driving the process. Higher oil prices have increased the cost of transporting goods from China, just as the explosion in natural-gas production in the United States has decreased the cost of operating plants. Just as wages of Chinese workers are rising quickly, the weakening of American labor unions and the increasing number of so-called right-to-work states has significantly lowered U.S. labor costs. Mechanization and higher efficiency in U.S. industries also make wages a less important cost in overall production. Although there is unlikely to be a boom in U.S. manufacturing, it is ironic that some of the same globalization forces that spurred outsourcing two decades ago are now—in reverse—spurring insourcing.

CONCLUSION

The International Production and Trade Structure in Repose

Many economic liberal objectives associated with the production and trade structure have been achieved since World War II, resulting in a dramatic shift in production both within developed states and into emerging countries. This has helped increase the volume and value of international trade. However, a number of countertrends coexist within this liberal trade order, demonstrating that its values are not necessarily widely shared by many developing nations and NGOs.

Through a series of multilateral negotiation rounds, the industrialized nations have pushed for the liberalization of international trade in manufactured goods and some services. Many trade experts still contend that liberal trade rules will further integrate the global economy and increase global consumption.

And yet, in the Doha round many countries have resisted these policies. What was supposed to have been a "sweetheart" deal for developing nations has become an issue of political sensitivity for the Northern industrialized states, who are reluctant to eliminate all protection for agriculture, some services, and government procurement. Negotiations have been drawn out over a variety of other issues including information products, pharmaceuticals, and TRIPS.

Difficulties in multilateral negotiations also reflect tensions between the North and the South. The WTO's trade regulations reflect predominantly the interests of the North. Emerging countries now have increasing influence in multilateral negotiations, based on their importance to developed states as markets, sources of labor for TNCs, and sources of energy. Antiglobalization groups and NGOs have challenged the assumed benefits of free trade. As a result, Northern states have shifted attention away from the multilateral trading system and the WTO toward more bilateral and regional trade agreements. RTAs simultaneously embrace both the principle of free trade and the practical need for protectionism, making them acceptable to both mercantilists and economic liberals.

As we will see in the next two chapters, the money and finance structure has been in crisis since 2008. For now, the production and trade structure appears to almost be waiting for recovery from the latest financial crisis and for new emerging country coalitions to find their position in a new global order. Thus, the WTO members' current mixture of economic liberal, mercantilist, and sometime structuralist trade practices is best described as a **managed trade system**.

In many cases the state is unwilling to prevent private interests from playing the role of gatekeepers between domestic and international interests. At the same time, many states are still strong enough in the face of international calamities to fend off many of the forces that would weaken their power. Unless the production and trade structure undergoes major reforms, it may paradoxically be undermined by economic forces that will only generate *more* demand for protectionism.

KEY TERMS

specialization   127
outsourcing   127
foreign direct investment (FDI)   127
law of comparative
   advantage   130
strategic trade policies   131
General Agreement on Tariffs
   and Trade (GATT)   134
reciprocity   134
nondiscrimination   134

national treatment   134
most favored nation
   (MFN)   134
nontariff barriers (NTBs)   135
Super 301   136
fair trade   136
General Agreement on Trade in
   Services (GATS)   137
Trade-Related Aspects of Intellectual
   Property Rights (TRIPs)   137

Dispute Settlement Panel
   (DSP)   138
regional trade agreements
   (RTAs)   140
intraregional trade bloc   140
Structural Adjustment Policies   142
insourcing   147
managed trade system   148

DISCUSSION QUESTIONS

1. Discuss and explain the roles of production and trade in the international production and trade structure. Why is trade so controversial?
2. Outline the basic ways that mercantilists, economic liberals, and structuralists view trade. (Think about the tension between the politics and economics of trade.)
3. What are some of the basic features of the GATT and the WTO? Why is the Doha round a failure?
4. Outline the basic features of RTAs. Do you see RTAs as being primarily liberal or mercantilist

   in nature? Why have they proliferated in recent years?
5. Which of the three IPE approaches best accounts for the relationship of the Northern industrialized nations to the Southern developing nations when it comes to trade? Explain and discuss.
6. How have the United States and other nations used trade as a tool to achieve foreign policy objectives? On balance, is outsourcing good for the United States?

SUGGESTED READINGS

John H. Barton, Judith L. Goldstein, Timothy E. Josling, and Richard H. Steinberg. *The Evolution of the Trade Regime: Politics, Law, and Economics of the GATT and the WTO.* Princeton, NJ: Princeton University Press, 2008.

Ha-Joon Chang. *Bad Samaritans: The Myth of Free Trade and the Secret History of Capitalism.* New York, NY: Bloomsbury Press, 2008.

Brian Hocking and Steven McGuire, eds. *Trade Politics: International, Domestic and Regional Perspectives,* 2nd ed., London: Routledge, 2004.

Douglas A. Irwin. *Free Trade Under Fire,* 3rd ed., Princeton, NJ: Princeton University Press, 2009.

Kenneth Pomeranz and Steven Topik. *The World That Trade Created: Society, Culture, and the World Economy, 1400 to the Present.* Armonk, NY: M.E. Sharpe, 2013.

Dani Rodrik. *The Globalization Paradox: Democracy and the Future of the World Economy.* New York: W.W. Norton, 2011.

Joseph Stiglitz. *Making Globalization Work.* New York: W. W. Norton, 2006.

NOTES

1. Robert Kuttner, *The End of Laissez-Faire: National Purpose and the Global Economy after the Cold War* (New York: Knopf, 1991).
2. Thomas Friedman, *The Lexus and the Olive Tree: Understanding Globalization* (New York: Anchor Books, 1999).
3. See Michael Hiltzik, "787 Dreamliner Teaches Boeing Costly Lesson on Outsourcing," *Los Angeles Times*, February 15, 2011; Kyle Peterson, "A Wing and a Prayer: Outsourcing at Boeing," Reuters, January 2011, at http://graphics.thomsonreuters.com/11/01/Boeing.pdf.
4. Thomas Friedman, *The World Is Flat* (New York: Farrar, Straus & Giroux, 2005), pp. 3–47.
5. From the World Bank's World Development Indicators database, September 18, 2012, at http://databank.worldbank.org/databank/download/GDP.pdf.
6. See World Trade Organization, *International Trade Statistics 2012* (Geneva, Switzerland: World Trade Organization, 2012), pp. 24, 146, at http://www.wto.org/english/res_e/statis_e/its2012_e/its2012_e.pdf.
7. These figures are based on the sum of imports and exports of both goods and services at current prices as a percent of GDP. See World Bank, *World Development Indicators* database, November 2012.
8. Kenneth Pomeranz and Steven Topik, *The World That Trade Created: Society, Culture, and the World Economy, 1400 to the Present* (Armonk, NY: M.E. Sharpe, 2013).
9. Ibid., p. 248.
10. A good summary of this argument is given by Douglas A. Irwin, *Free Trade under Fire*, 3rd ed. (Princeton, NJ: Princeton University Press, 2009).
11. See Friedrich List, "Political and Cosmopolitical Economy," in *The National System of Political Economy* (New York: Augustus M. Kelley, 1966).
12. See, for example, Pietra Rivoli, *The Travels of a T-Shirt in the Global Economy*, 2nd ed. (Hoboken, NJ: John Wiley, 2009).
13. Andre Gunder Frank, *Latin America: Underdevelopment or Revolution* (New York: Monthly Review Press, 1970).
14. Immanuel Wallerstein, "The Rise and Demise of the World Capitalist System: Concepts for Comparative Analysis," *Comparative Studies in Society and History*, 17 (September 1974), pp. 387–415.
15. Technically, the GATT was not an international organization but rather a "gentlemen's agreement" whereby member parties (nation-states) contracted trade agreements with one another.
16. The classic study of Japan's mercantilism is Chalmers Johnson, *MITI and the Japanese Miracle: The Growth of Industrial Policy, 1925–1975* (Palo Alto, CA: Stanford University Press, 1982). An examination of "managed trade" in South Korea and Taiwan is in Robert Wade, *Governing the Market: Economic Theory and the Role of Government in East Asian Industrialization*, 2nd paperback ed. (Princeton, NJ: Princeton University Press, 2004).
17. Robert Gilpin, *The Political Economy of International Relations* (Princeton, NJ: Princeton University Press, 1987), p. 215.
18. World Bank, *World Development Report 1987* (Washington, DC: World Bank, 1987), p. 141.
19. For a more detailed discussion of agriculture's role in the Uruguay round, see David N. Balaam, "Agricultural Trade Policy," in Brian Hocking and Steven McGuire, eds., *Trade Politics: International, Domestic, and Regional Perspectives* (London: Routledge, 1999), pp. 52–66.
20. "U.S. GATT Flap Reverberates Around the World," *The Christian Science Monitor*, November 23, 1994, p. 1.
21. See, for example, Janet Thomas, *The Battle in Seattle: The Story behind and beyond the WTO Demonstrations* (New York: Fulcrum, 2003).
22. Lori Wallach, "Trade Secrets," *Foreign Policy* 140 (January/February 2004), pp. 70–71.
23. For a detailed discussion of regionalism and Free Trade Agreements, see John Ravenhill, "Regional Trade Agreements," in John Ravenhill, ed., *Global Political Economy*, 3rd ed. (Oxford: Oxford University Press, 2011), pp. 173–211.
24. World Trade Organization, *International Trade Statistics 2012*, p. 13, http://www.wto.org/english/res_e/statis_e/its2012_e/its2012_e.pdf.
25. Calculated from World Trade Organization, *International Trade Statistics 2012*, pp. 209–210, http://www.wto.org/english/res_e/statis_e/its2012_e/its2012_e.pdf
26. Jagdish Bhagwati, *In Defense of Globalization* (Oxford: Oxford University Press, 2004).
27. See John Dillin, "Will Treaty Give U.S. Global Edge?" *The Christian Science Monitor*, November 17, 1993.

28. See Congressional Research Service, "The Trans-Pacific Partnership Negotiations and Issues for Congress," November 21, 2012, at http://www.fas.org/sgp/crs/row/R42694.pdf.

29. Lori Wallach, "Can a 'Dracula Strategy' Bring Trans-Pacific Partnership into the Sunlight?" *Yes! Magazine*, November 21, 2012.

30. For a detailed discussion of the NIEO, see Jagdish Bhagwati, ed., *The New International Economic Order: The North South Debate* (Cambridge, MA: MIT Press, 1977).

31. Robert Hunter Wade, "Is Globalization Reducing Poverty and Inequality?" *World Development*, 32 (2004), pp. 567–589.

32. World Trade Organization, *International Trade Statistics 2012*, p. 62, at http://www.wto.org/english/res_e/statis_e/its2012_e/its2012_e.pdf.

33. See World Trade Organization, *World Trade Report, 2012* (Geneva, Switzerland: WTO, 2012), Table 1.2, p. 21. At http://www.wto.org/english/res_e/booksp_e/anrep_e/world_trade_report12_e.pdf.

34. See Walden Bello, "Rethinking Asia: The WTO's Big Losers," *Far Eastern Economic Review,* June 24, 1999, p. 77.

35. Dani Rodrik, "Goodbye Washington Consensus, Hello Washington Confusion?" *Journal of Economic Literature,* XLIV (December 2006), pp. 973–987.

36. See Ha-Joon Chang, *Kicking Away the Ladder: Development Strategy in Historical Perspective* (London: Anthem, 2002).

37. See Bello, "Rethinking Asia," p. 78.

38. Pew Research Center, "Americans Are of Two Minds on Trade," November 9, 2010, at http://www.pewresearch.org/2010/11/09/americans-are-of-two-minds-on-trade.

39. See Ed Gerwin and Anne Kim, "Why We Need Fairer Trade: How Export Barriers Cost America Jobs" (July 2010), report at http://content.thirdway.org/publications/318/Third_Way_Report_-_Why_We_Need_Fairer_Trade-How_Export_Barriers_Cost_America_Jobs_.pdf.

40. For an overview of the fair trade movement, see April Linton, *Fair Trade from the Ground Up: New Markets for Social Justice* (Seattle: University of Washington Press, 2012).

41. Andy Grove, "How America Can Create Jobs," *Bloomberg Businessweek*, July 1, 2012.

42. Charles Fishman, "The Insourcing Boom," *The Atlantic Monthly* (December 2012), at http://www.theatlantic.com/magazine/archive/2012/12/the-insourcing-boom/309166.

43. For detailed discussions of this argument, see Meghan O'Sullivan, *Shrewd Sanctions: Statecraft and State Sponsors of Terrorism* (Washington, D.C.: Brookings Institution Press, 2003); Richard Haas, "Sanctioning Madness," *Foreign Affairs,* 76 (November/December 1997), pp. 74–85.

The International Monetary and Finance Structure

Fast Money: The leading international currencies.

ImageState/Alamy

Since the 1990s the globalization of the international political economy has enhanced the speed and extended the reach of cross-border flows of capital. Like the other three international structures, oftentimes the monetary and finance structure is embroiled with tensions that render it difficult to manage effectively. As one expert notes, "In all modern societies, control over the issuing and management of money and credit has been a key source of power, and the subject of intense political struggles."[1]

With globalization and deregulation of the global economy since the 1980s have come increased currency exchange and transnational financial flows that influence employment, trade, and foreign direct investment, but also state programs and their security. One of the themes that stands out in this chapter is that, although economic liberal ideas called for states to deregulate their economies and cooperate with other states and IOs to open the global economy, some negative effects of globalization—including the recent global financial crisis—have compelled many states to re-regulate their societies and the monetary and finance structure.

We make six interconnected arguments in this chapter. First, after World War II the United States and its allies constructed a fairly tightly controlled international monetary and finance system that complemented their mutual goals of containing communism and gradually deregulating currency and finance markets. These measures manifested a situation where the United States could pursue "hegemony on the cheap," work toward the stabilization of Western capitalist economies, and contain communism. Second, as some of the security and economic interests of the Western alliance changed and diverged, exchange rates and capital controls were gradually allowed to reflect market conditions. The 1970s and 1980s, however, were marked by OPEC oil price hikes, increasing interdependence among states, and later globalization, along with many efforts to open up international currency and finance markets. At the same time, many states made efforts to control direct economic growth in ways that gradually weakened the international monetary and finance structure.

Third, since the end of the Cold War and pursuant to its continued hegemonic role in the international political economy, the United States has continued to run huge deficits in the current account of its balance of payments. Recently emerging economies such as China and Saudi Arabia have been investing their surplus capital into the United States and other current account deficit nations, which has enabled the United States to cover its balance-of-payments deficits. Fourth, the current financial crisis jeopardizes this U.S. strategy and continues to weaken the U.S. dollar and U.S. leadership of the current monetary and finance structure.

Fifth, the financial crisis has also severely weakened efforts by IOs, others states, and many nongovernmental organizations (NGOs) to resolve problems in debtor countries as well as help the developing nations overcome poverty. Sixth and finally, the global monetary and finance structure remains vulnerable to fluctuating market conditions, which should lead to increased state cooperation to deal with a number of problems that, if not resolved, could result in a global financial meltdown.

This chapter describes a number of fundamental elements of the international monetary and finance structure, including its institutions and who manages them, who determines its rules, how and why these rules change, and who benefits from its operation. This topic has its own specialized vocabulary. Once a student understands and appreciates the role of the basic pieces of this puzzle, it is easier to grasp other important ideas related to international political economy.

We begin the chapter by explaining the role of exchange rates in the international political economy and then move on to discuss three distinct international monetary and finance systems that have existed since the nineteenth century. We have found this history to be especially useful to students because it makes the entire topic easier to understand. In each period, we inquire into the major actors, the interplay of market forces and social interests that shape policies, and what accounts for shifts from one system to another. Inter-spliced between the first and second historical periods, we explain the role of the IMF and why its primary functions have shifted over time. We also explain the balance-of-payment problem and its connection to management functions of the IMF.

The chapter moves to a discussion of the role of the U.S. dollar in the international political economy today. Some experts are concerned that confidence in the world's strongest currency has deteriorated, in part due to the financial crisis. The chapter concludes with an assessment of the management of the monetary and finance structure. This discussion is also a conduit to Chapter 8, in which we analyze in more detail short- and long-term international debt and two financial crises, including the recent global financial crisis. As is our practice throughout the book, we use parts of the three major IPE perspectives to help us understand some of the more controversial aspects of this structure.

A PRIMER ON FOREIGN EXCHANGE

Foreign or **currency exchange rates** affect the value of *everything* a nation buys or sells on international markets. It also impinges on the cost of credit and debt, and the value of foreign currencies held in national and private banks. A special vocabulary is used when discussing currency or foreign exchange. Just as people in different nations speak different languages (requiring translation to understand one another), they also do business in different currencies, requiring the exchange of money from one denomination to another. Travelers and investors are often exposed to currency exchanges when they decide how much of their national currency it will cost to buy or invest in another country. Travelers can go to a local bank, exchange kiosk, or automated teller machine (ATM); slip in their debit card; and withdraw the needed amount of local currency. The machine (representing the banks that sponsor them) automatically calculates an exchange rate. Table 7-1 is an example of foreign exchange rates at particular points in time for the amount of local currency in your possession.

No wonder exchange rates are more important to banks and investors than to travelers: Each day they are buying and selling millions of dollars, British pound sterling, yen, euros, and other currencies. A change in the value of one currency (contrast 2009 with 2012 in Table 7-1) can mean huge gains or losses depending on how much market prices for currencies have changed in the recent past or might change in the future. What concerns states the most are short- and long-term shifts in the values of certain currencies to one another (discussed in more detail later).

TABLE 7-1

Foreign Exchange Rates for Selected Countries, Various Dates

Country	Currency	November 2, 2009 Currency Rate Per US$[a]	November 2, 2012, Currency Rate Per US$[b]
Great Britain	Pound	.61	.62
EU	Euro	.68	.77
Sweden	Krona	7.07	6.66
Japan	Yen	90.00	80.02
Mexico	Mexican Peso	13.29	13.04
Canada	Canadian Dollar	1.07	1.00
China	Renminbi	6.83	6.30
South Korea	Won	1,182.50	1,090.60
Russia	Ruble	29.19	31.37
India	Indian Rupee	47.04	53.78
South Africa	Rand	7.91	8.68
Malaysia	Ringgit	3.43	3.05
Indonesia	Rupiah	9,610.00	9,628.00
Israel	Shekel	3.78	3.87
Brazil	Real	1.74	2.03

[a]IMF, "Representative Exchange Rates for Selected Currencies for November 2009" at http://www.imf.org/external/np/fin/data/rms_mth.aspx?SelectDate=2009-11-30&reportType=REP.
[b]IMF, "Representative Exchange Rates for Selected Currencies for November 2012" at http://www.imf.org/external/np/fin/data/rms_mth.aspx?SelectDate=2012-11-30&reportType=REP.

Before moving on let's look at how currency exchange rates work. While most people no longer pay much attention to the math behind these transactions, it is important to learn more about the connection between foreign exchange and the money in your own bank at home. Until the advent of ATMs, most travelers quickly became accustomed to exchange-rate math used to convert one currency into another and back again. If the exchange rate was around $1.50 per British pound sterling, as it often was in the 1990s, it follows that a £10 theater ticket in the West End of London really cost $15 in U.S. currency (£10 at $1.50 per £ = $15). In the same way, that ¥1,000 caffé latte at the airport in Tokyo really cost $10—if the yen–dollar exchange rate was ¥100 per U.S.$ (¥1,000 ÷ ¥100 per $ = $10). Before long, tourists found themselves able to perform complex mental gymnastics to convert from one money, especially the longer they visited another country.

Yet another important feature of foreign exchange is related to how hard or soft certain currencies are. **Hard currency** is money issued by large countries with reliable and predictably stable political economies. This legal tender is traded widely and has recognized value associated with the wealth and power of many industrialized developed nations, including the United States, Canada, Japan, Great Britain, Switzerland, and the Euro zone (European countries that use the euro—see Chapter 12). A hard-currency country can generally exchange its own currency directly for other hard currencies, and therefore for foreign goods and services—giving it a distinct advantage. Therefore, a hard currency like the U.S. dollar (USD), the euro, or the yen is easily accepted for international payments.

Soft currency is not as widely accepted, and is usually limited to its home country or region. Its value may be too uncertain or the volume of possible transactions insufficient based on an absence of trade with other countries or conditions that raise suspicions about the stability of its political economy. Many less developed countries (LDCs) have soft currencies, as their economies are relatively small and less stable than those of other countries. A soft-currency country must usually acquire hard currency (through exports or by borrowing) in order to purchase goods or services from other nations. Another problem with a soft currency is that international lenders are generally unwilling to accept payment in soft currencies. These countries need to earn hard currency to pay their debts, which tend to be denominated in hard currency. Because only hard currencies get much international use, we focus on hard currencies in this chapter.

An important point to remember is that the exchange rate is just a way of converting the value of one country's unit of measurement into another's. It does not really matter what units are used. What *does* matter is the *acceptability* of the measurement to the actors (banks, tourists, investors, and state officials in different countries) involved in a transaction at any given time, and how much values *change* over time. Shifts in exchange rates can vary over different periods of time, depending on a variety of circumstances that impact the demand for one currency or another. Many political and economic forces affect exchange rates. These include the following:

- currency appreciation and depreciation
- currency-rate manipulation
- whether one's currency is fixed to the value of another currency
- interest rates and inflation
- speculation

When a currency's exchange price rises—that is, when it becomes more valuable relative to other currencies—we say that it **appreciates**. When its exchange price falls and it becomes less valuable relative to other currencies, we say it **depreciates**. For example, the USD *depreciated* relative to the Japanese yen between 2009 and 2012. A USD cost ¥ 90 in November 2009, but only ¥ 80.02 in November 2012. The fact that the USD *depreciated* relative to the yen also means that the yen *appreciated* against the USD. Or simply put, in terms of the USD, the yen increased in price from about 1.11 cents to 1.24 cents during this period. In the case of trade, changes in the exchange rates tend to alter the competitive balance between nations, making one country's goods a better value than another.

Changes in currency values have profound political and social consequences. As currency values change, there are always winners and losers. As we saw in Chapter 6, for example, as a nation's currency appreciates, companies that export goods and services will be hurt as their products become less competitive internationally. However, importers in the same country (consumers of foreign goods and services and companies using foreign inputs in their production processes) will benefit as those imports become cheaper.

Often exchange rates are set by the market forces of supply and demand. Later in the chapter, however, we will see that there is also considerable temptation for nations to purposefully manipulate currency values so as to achieve a desirable outcome for that state. At times, states (secretly) intervene in currency markets, buying up their own currency or selling it in an attempt to alter its exchange value. A central bank will buy (demand) and sell (supply) enough of its own currency to alter the exchange rate. At other times when the demand for the country's currency declines, a central bank will use its foreign reserves to buy (demand) its own currency, pushing up the value of its currency again.

Regardless of market conditions, for many states an *undervalued currency* that discourages imports and increases exports can be politically and economically good for some domestic industries. This shifts production and international trade in that state's favor. The dark side of currency depreciation is that when goods such as food or oil must be imported, they will cost more if the currency is undervalued. Undervaluation can also reduce living standards and retard economic growth, as well as cause inflation. As we will see in the case of China (see the box The Tangled Web of China's Currency Manipulation), many feel the nation has benefited more than lost from keeping its currency undervalued.

Sometimes LDCs *overvalue* their currency to gain access to cheaper imported goods such as technology, arms, manufactured goods, food, and oil. This may benefit the wealthy and shift the terms of trade in their favor. Although their own exported goods would become less competitive abroad, these LDCs could at least enjoy some imported items at lower cost.

In practice, it is hard for LDCs to reap the benefits of overvaluation in any meaningful way because their currencies are usually soft and not used much in international business and finance. This does not stop them from trying, depending on political circumstances. In many cases, this invariably winds up choking domestic production and leaving the LDCs dependent on foreign sellers and lenders for help. Agriculture seems to be especially sensitive to this problem. In some cases, developing countries with overvalued currencies have unintentionally destroyed their agricultural sectors and become dependent on artificially cheap foodstuffs.

In the 1990s, until the end of the decade, the value of the USD steadily climbed relative to the value of the currencies of many developing nations. While this helped the exports of the emerging nations, their consumers paid higher prices for many technological imports and value-added products. To stabilize the relationship between the USD and other currencies, many countries decided to peg (fix) their currency to the dollar. China pegged the yuan at 8.28 per USD. Because the United States and the EU are major importers of Chinese goods, if the USD depreciated relative to the euro and most other world currencies, so did the yuan. While the weaker currencies gained some stability in their relationship to the USD, developments in the U.S. economy were easily transferred into the developing nations, depriving them of some flexibility in currency exchange rates.

Two other important issues are inflation and interest rates. *All else being equal*, a nation's currency tends to *depreciate* when that nation experiences a *higher inflation* rate than other countries. Inflation—a rise in overall prices—means that currency has less real purchasing power within its home country. This makes the currency less attractive to foreign buyers, and it tends to depreciate on foreign exchange markets to reflect its reduced real value at home.

Likewise, interest rates and investment returns in general influence the value and desirability of the investments that a particular currency can purchase. If *interest rates decline* in the United States, for example, as they did in the 1990s and throughout the 2000s, then the demand for dollars to purchase U.S. government bonds and other interest-earning investments decreases, pushing the dollar's exchange rate to a lower value. In the same way, higher interest rates lead to an increased demand for the dollar, as dollar-denominated investments become more attractive to foreigners.

Finally, one of the major currency and finance issues that concerned John Maynard Keynes a great deal (see Chapter 2) was **speculation,** that is, betting that the value of a currency or market price for a certain item or service will go up and earn the owner a profit when it is sold. A currency generally rises and falls in value according to the value of goods, services, and investments that it can buy in its home market. If those who invest in currencies (speculators) believe (based on their understanding of the foreign exchange market model and anticipated changes in the various determinants of demand and supply) that a currency like the peso will appreciate in the future, they will want to buy pesos now to capitalize on the exchange rate fluctuations.

However, the increase in demand for pesos can easily raise their price as a direct result of investors speculating—predicting the value of the peso will rise because the Mexican economy is steadily growing or that it has discovered a new oil field in Baja California. This sort of speculation, which occurred in U.S. real estate after 2001, can drive up the value of an item, generating a big gap (bubble) between the normal market value of the item and a new value that reflects what Alan Greenspan labeled "irrational exuberance." Most real estate agents would say that actually the higher market value is the real price, to the extent that someone is willing to buy the item at that price.

Yet, as we will see in the cases of the Asian and the current global financial crises (see Chapter 8), bubbles can form when **hot money** (foreign investment in stocks and bonds not regulated by the state) moves quickly into a country, and bubbles can burst when investors rapidly pull their money out in anticipation that market prices will fall. While bubbles in the past caused hardship for many people, the severity of the current global financial crisis has caused many to question whether states and the IMF should not do more to regulate global capital movements.

THREE FOREIGN EXCHANGE RATE SYSTEMS

Since the nineteenth century, there have been three structures and sets of rules related to foreign exchange rates.[2] The first was the **gold standard,** a tightly integrated international order that existed until the end of World War I. The second was the Bretton Woods **fixed-exchange-rate system** created by the United States and its allies before the end of World War II and managed by the IMF. The current system is the "flexible" or floating exchange-rate regime. As we explore some of the basic features of these systems, we will also highlight capital mobility across national borders, an issue directly related to currency exchange.

The Classic Gold Standard: Phase I

We tend to think of the related issues of interdependence, integration, and globalization as post–Cold War phenomena, but from the end of the nineteenth century until the end of World War I, the world was supposedly even more interconnected than it is today. Cross-border flows of money increased in response to, among other things, interest rates and inflation in other countries. The leading European powers also invested heavily in their colonies. The currencies of these nations were part of a fixed-exchange-rate system that linked currency values to the price of gold, thus the "gold standard." Similar to the European Union today, some countries in specific geographic regions created "monetary unions" in which their currencies would circulate.[3]

Under the prevailing liberal economic theory of the time, the system was a *self-regulating* international monetary order. Different currency values were pegged to the price of gold. If a country experienced a balance-of-payments deficit—that is, it spent more money for trade, investments, and other items than it earned—corrections occurred almost *automatically* via wage and price adjustments. A country's gold would be sold to earn money to pay for its deficit. This resulted in tighter monetary conditions that curtailed the printing of money, raised interest rates, and cut government spending in response to a deficit. In turn, higher interest rates were supposed to attract short-term capital that would help finance the deficit. Domestic monetary and fiscal policy was "geared to the external goal of maintaining the convertibility of the national currency into gold."[4] Before World War I Great Britain's pound sterling was the world's strongest currency. And as the world's largest creditor, Great Britain loaned money to other countries to encourage trade when economic growth slowed.

The gold standard had a stabilizing, equilibrating, and confidence-building effect on the system. But by the end of the war the gold standard had died, though it was temporarily resurrected again in the early 1930s during the Great Depression. After World War I, Britain became a debtor nation and the U.S. dollar took the place of the pound sterling as the world's strongest and most trusted currency. According to many hegemonic stability theorists, the gold standard folded because the United States acted more in its own interest and failed to meet the international responsibility commensurate with its economic and military power.

Another argument is that while elites were committed to economic liberal values, public policy often reflected the growing influence of labor unions, the poor, and foreign investors who often controlled monetary policy in the colonies. The extension of the electoral franchise produced more government intervention, pressuring governments to avoid the automatic policy adjustments the gold standard required in order to meet domestic needs. Some states preferred to depreciate their currencies to generate trade rather than slow the growth of their economies or cut state spending. In a move to further insulate their economies, many of them adopted **capital controls** (limits on how much money could move in and out of the country). Even Keynes supported these measures, saying, "Let finance be primarily national."[5]

An important point is that many states gradually found that the "embedded" economic liberal ideas of a self-regulating economy did not work. The structuralist economic historian and anthropologist Karl Polanyi wrote that, by the end of

World War I, 100 years of relative political and economic stability ended when economic liberal ideas no longer seemed appropriate given world events and conditions.[6] As the European and U.S. economies became more industrialized and interdependent (even more so than today), they had been willing to cooperate with one another in order to live under the rules of a fixed-exchange-rate system. However, the negative effects of capitalism led to increased demands for more and different types of protection in various states. Many societies sought relief from a brand of capitalism that periodically failed as evidenced during the Great Depression.

The Bretton Woods System: The Qualified Gold Standard and Fixed Exchange Rates: Phase II

During the Great Depression, the international monetary and finance structure was in a shambles. "Beggar thy neighbor" trade policies that put national interests ahead of international interests resulted in some of the highest trade tariffs in history. The nonconvertibility of currency was also blamed for increasing hostility among the European powers that ultimately resulted in World War II.

In July 1944, the United States and its allies met in Bretton Woods, New Hampshire, to devise a plan for European recovery and create a new postwar international monetary and trade system that would encourage growth and development. In an atmosphere of cooperation, most of the fifty-five participating countries wanted to overcome the high unemployment conditions of the Great Depression and the malevolent *competitive currency devaluations* of the 1930s. Keynes, Great Britain's representative, believed that unless states took coordinated action to benefit each other, their individual efforts to gain at the expense of their competitors would eventually hurt them all.

At Bretton Woods the Great Powers created the International Monetary Fund (IMF), the World Bank, and what would later become the General Agreement on Tariffs and Trade (GATT) (see Chapter 6). Many argue that these institutions were empty shells that represented only the values and policy preferences of the major powers, especially the United States.[7] The World Bank was to be concerned with economic recovery immediately after the war and then development issues. The IMF's primary role was to facilitate a stable and orderly international monetary system and investment policies. It is still the IMF's role to facilitate international trade, stabilize exchange rates, and help members with balance-of-payments difficulties on a short-term basis. However, today the IMF also attempts to prevent and resolve currency and financial crises that have recently occurred in developing countries (see Chapter 8).

Two distinct IPE perspectives give primary responsibility for the institutional design and mission of the IMF to different players. From the economic liberal perspective, John Maynard Keynes was instrumental in convincing the Allied powers to construct a new international economic order based on liberal ideas proposed at the time. Note though that the **"Keynesian Compromise"** allowed individual nation-states to *continue* regulating domestic economic activities within their own geographic borders. In the international arena, in order to avoid another Great Depression, the IMF would collectively manage financial policies with the goal of eventually freeing up financial markets and trade. Global financial crises and collapse were to be avoided by isolating each nation's financial system and then regulating it in consideration of international conditions and developments.

At the conference, Keynes himself worked on setting up the World Bank. He was committed to creating an institution that could provide generous aid to both the victors and the vanquished nations after World War II. He especially wanted to prevent a repeat of the brutal and ultimately destructive terms the winners imposed on the losers at the end of World War I. He was adamant that creditors *should* help debtors make adjustments in their economies. Meanwhile, U.S. Treasury official Harry Dexter White's plan for the bank was to put nearly *all* of the adjustment pressure on debtor countries, without any symmetric obligation for creditors to make sacrifices.

In the case of the IMF, White's suggestions reflected the best interests of the United States, which emerged from World War II as the world's biggest creditor nation, and with no plans to give up that role. The U.S. Congress would not have approved a treaty that forced the United States to sacrifice just because Britain or another debtor country could not pay its bills. (In fact, the United States was adamant that Great Britain honor its wartime debts once the war was over.) The IMF, then, was designed to provide *temporary* assistance to all debtor countries while they adjusted their economic structures to the emerging international economy. The burden of adjustment ultimately fell on the debtors, not on both debtors and creditors, as Keynes had intended.

Immediately after the war, many realists viewed the United States as an *emerging but reluctant* major power, unwilling to assume the hegemonic role that Great Britain had played in the nineteenth century. The United States, which had the most votes on policy decisions (based on holding 31 percent of the IMF reserves at the time), used the IMF as an indirect way to promote an orderly liberal financial system that would lead to nondiscrimination in the conversion of currencies, confidence in a new order, and eventually more liquidity. These goals complemented U.S. liberal values, beliefs, and policy preferences at little cost to the United States.

For both mercantilists and realists, the IMF's institutional structure and monetary rules also reflected the interests of the Great Powers (as they were called at the time). Under pressure from the United States, the IMF adopted a modified version of the former gold standard's *fixed-exchange-rate system* that was more open to market forces, but not divorced from politics. At the center of this modified gold standard was a fixed-exchange-rate mechanism that fixed the rate of an ounce of gold at $35. The values of other national currencies would fluctuate against the dollar as supply and demand for those currencies changed. Additionally, governments agreed to intervene in foreign exchange markets to keep the value of currencies within 1 percent above or below par value (the fixed exchange rate).

As supply and demand conditions for other currencies changed, the trading bands established by the IMF defined limits within which exchange rates could fluctuate. (See Figure 7-6 on the IPE web page at www.upugetsoundintroipe.com for a representation of this arrangement). If the value of any currency increased above or fell below the band limits, central banks behind those currencies were required to step in and buy up excess dollars or sell their own currency until the currency value moved back into the trading bands limits, reestablishing a supply–demand equilibrium (par value). As in the earlier system, central banks could also buy and sell gold to help settle their accounts, which the United States often did. What officials liked about this system was that its *quasi-self-adjusting mechanism* allowed for diverse levels of growth in different national economies.

Confidence in the system relied on the fact that dollars could be converted into gold at a set price. At the end of World War II, the United States started with the largest amount of gold backing its currency. This arrangement politically and economically stabilized the monetary system, which desperately needed the members' confidence and a source of liquidity if recovery in Europe was to be realized. Once the Cold War began in 1947, the United States consciously accepted its hegemonic role of providing the collective good of security for its allies. This arrangement boosted Western European and Japanese recovery from the war and preserved an environment for trade and foreign investment in Western Europe. These policies also helped tie together the allies into a liberal-capitalist, U.S.-dominated monetary and finance system that complemented U.S. efforts to *divide* the West from the Soviet-dominated Eastern Bloc. Capital movements into and out of the communist nations were severely limited.

In this monetary arrangement, the U.S. dollar became the hegemonic currency, or **top currency**, one in great demand often used in international trade and financial transactions. This position afforded the United States many privileges when it came to using the dollar as a tool of foreign policy, but also imposed on it many management responsibilities. The United States benefited both economically and politically from this arrangement because, as part of the postwar recovery process, dollars were in great demand in most of Western Europe and in other parts of the world. When it came to trade and investments, other states often had to convert their currencies into U.S. dollars, which saved the United States a good deal of money on foreign exchange transactions and helped maintain the strength of the U.S. dollar against other currencies. The dollar was also the **reserve currency** that, because its international market value was fixed to gold, was held in central banks as a store of value.

THE IMF AND THE BALANCE OF PAYMENTS

At Bretton Woods, the IMF was set up to create stable and responsive international financial relations, just as central banks seek to create a favorable financial climate within the borders of each country. As of August 2012, it had a membership of 188 countries, a staff of 2,475 from 156 countries, and reserves of $360 billion. As of October 2012, the IMF had outstanding loans of $63 billion to 46 countries (Greece, Portugal, and Ireland accounted for 53 percent of all lending). The IMF director heads a board made up of twenty-five members from different countries who meet twice a year. Although members try to reach consensus, major policy decisions are decided on a weighted voting basis. The weight of a state's vote is related to how much it contributes to the IMF's reserves. Currently the United States has the most votes, with 16.8 percent. Japan is a distant second at 6.2 percent, with Germany at 5.8 percent and Great Britain and France both at 4.3 percent.

The **balance of payments** registers an accounting of all the international monetary transactions between the residents of one nation and those of other nations in a given year. It reflects what a nation produces, consumes, and buys with its money. Much like a personal check register (see Table 7-2), the *current account* records "deposits" or money inflows. For each nation, these deposits are derived from sales of produced goods and services (exports), receipts of profits and interest from foreign investments, and unilateral transfers of money or income from other nations. These transfers include foreign aid a nation receives, private aid flows, and money migrants send home to friends and families. According to the IMF, these receipts *should equal* money outflows related to the purchase of goods and services from other countries (imports), payments of profits and interest to foreign investors, and unilateral transfers to other nations.

When a state has a *current account surplus*, its receipts or earnings are greater than its "withdrawals" (expenditures), so that on net these international transactions increase national income. However, when a nation has a *current account deficit*, outflows or withdrawals are greater than inflows or deposits in a particular year, and the net effect of these international transactions is to reduce the national income of the deficit country.

What is commonly referred to as the *balance of trade* is usually defined and analyzed *separately* from other items in the current account. It registers a nation's payments and receipts for the exchange of goods and services only (receipts for exports minus payments for imports). Therefore, the balance of trade only *partially* reflects a nation's current account and so provides only a glimpse of the changes in a nation's financial position. The trade balance is important because of its direct effect on employment, as a large number of jobs in most economies rely on trade.

The other account in the balance of payments—the *capital and financial account*—includes longer-term economic transactions related to net foreign investments, borrowing and lending, and sales and purchases of assets such as

---

TABLE 7-2

Elements of Balance-of-Payments Accounts

	Current Account	Capital and Financial Account
Current account surplus examples: Japan, China	Foreign receipts for exports, receipts of investment income (interest and profit), and unilateral transfers are greater than equivalent foreign payments.	Increase in domestic ownership of foreign assets: "creditor" nation. Technically termed a capital and financial account deficit to balance the current account surplus
Current account deficit examples: United States, Mexico	Foreign payments for imports, payments of investment income (interest and profit), and unilateral transfers are greater than equivalent receipts.	Increase in foreign ownership of domestic assets: "debtor" nation. Technically termed a capital and financial account surplus to balance the current account deficit.

stocks, real estate, and rights to natural resources. The capital account is an indicator of the effect of international transactions on changes in a nation's holdings of assets or wealth with respect to other countries. If there is an overage (surplus) or net inflow of money to the capital and financial account, foreigners are net purchasers of a country's assets. If there is a net outflow (deficit) of funds, the country has increased its net ownership of foreign assets.

Normally, a surplus in one account must be offset by a deficit in another—establishing an accounting balance of zero. However, it is important to note that because the technical language of the balance of payments is quite confusing, it is a common practice to say that a nation has a *"balance-of-payments deficit (or surplus)"* when what is actually meant is a *"current account deficit (or surplus),"* with payments for goods, services, and transfers exceeding the corresponding receipts. When determining whether a nation is going into debt, state officials tend to regard the current account as being more important than the capital account. A nation with a current account deficit must either borrow funds from abroad or sell assets to foreign buyers to pay its international bills and achieve an overall payments balance. A current account deficit also *requires* a capital account surplus in order to balance the two accounts. Likewise, a current account surplus generates excess funds that can purchase foreign assets. There are many political consequences of any nation's balance-of-payments status. If a state has a large foreign debt, for instance, it will need to increase output at home to generate more exports and/or decrease consumption of imports.

Economically, politically, and socially, these are not easy choices for states and their societies to make, given the consequences for those who benefit and lose from different situations. Increasing output, for instance, might mean asking workers to accept lower wages, giving tax incentives to business firms, or removing regulatory roadblocks to more efficient production. Decreasing consumption might also involve raising consumer taxes, reducing government subsidies, cutting government programs, or increasing interest rates to discourage consumption, attract savings, and encourage foreign investment in the home economy. In these circumstances, it is easy to see why currency devaluation is so attractive to states, as it can quickly generate more exports by making goods less expensive. However, as we noted earlier, such a move is also likely to invite retaliatory "defensive" moves by other states, negating the economic gains of the first state and generating tension between states, as was the case during the interwar years.

Mexico and the United States, for example, tend to have current account deficits. The current global financial crisis highlights the extent to which the United States pays out more for imports, investment income to foreigners, and unilateral transfers for the war in Afghanistan than it receives from exports, investment income, and international transfers. To pay such bills, Mexico and the United States are usually pressed to raise funds on the capital and financial account by increasing their foreign debt or attracting investment funds from abroad, which the United States has been doing as of late (see also Chapter 8).

Table 7-3 includes the current account surplus of different states along with the amounts of **sovereign wealth funds (SWFs)** of various economies. As we discuss later in the chapter, SWFs are income states generate from international transactions (especially oil exports) that can be used to purchase foreign assets

TABLE 7-3

Current Account Balances and Sovereign Wealth Funds

Current Account Balance in 2011[a]		Sovereign Wealth Funds[b]		
G20 Major Economies	$Billion	Country	Total $Billion	Number of Funds
Germany	204	UAE	1,623	7
China	202	China	1,147	4
Saudi Arabia	158	Norway	593	1
Japan	119	Saudi Arabia	538	2
Russia	99	Singapore	405	2
Republic of Korea	27	Kuwait	296	1
Indonesia	2	Hong Kong	293	1
Argentina	0	Russia	150	1
European Union	−6	Qatar	100	1
Mexico	−9	United States	86	6
South Africa	−14	Australia	80	1
Australia	−32 (2010)	Libya	65	1
United Kingdom	−46	Kazakhstan	58	1
Canada	−49	Algeria	57	1
India	−52 (2010)	South Korea	43	1
Brazil	−53	Malaysia	37	1
France	−54	Azerbaijan	30	1
Italy	−72	Ireland	30	1
Turkey	−77	Brunei	30	1
United States	−473	France	28	1

[a]International Monetary Fund, *Principal Global Indicators Dataset—IMF.Stat*, accessed July 25, 2012.
[b]Sovereign Wealth Fund Institute, July 2012.

or to pay off foreign debts incurred in the past. To finance its growing debt, the United States has looked primarily to countries like China, Japan, Germany, Saudi Arabia, and other exporters with huge capital reserves earned from trade, to purchase U.S. Treasuries, property, and industries.

Ideally, the IMF would like to see equilibrium in a state's balance of payments. Theoretically, nations should spend only as much as they take in. Yet, in order for businesses to expand and the economy to grow, banks lend out more than they have on deposit to back their loans. So the international economy needs a source of liquidity (assets that can be converted to cash) for new investments and production that comes when a country runs a current account deficit, which the United States did for all but two years under the Bretton Woods monetary and finance system. A country that performs this collective good for the rest of the system is usually a hegemon, and in these circumstances it is often referred to as a "locomotive." When the hegemon's economy heats up, it helps generate growth that benefits other members of the system. On the other hand, if the United States cut its deficit by buying fewer automobiles, then Japan would probably produce fewer autos and Saudi Arabia would probably produce less petroleum. In essence, one state's falling deficit would be another's decreased surplus. Likewise, our political and economic tensions become their tensions. And as we noted in Chapter 2, the economic and political roles and responsibilities of hegemons are difficult to separate from political costs and benefits.

The Bargain Comes Unstuck

On the whole, hegemony and the provision of collective goods to U.S. allies after World War II came cheaply to the United States. During these heyday years of the Bretton Woods system from 1956 to 1964, the rules of the monetary and finance structure gave the United States many benefits and advantages when it came to monetary and security relations between the United States and Western Europe. The United States could spend freely for a variety of domestic programs such as the Great Society and, at the same time, fund the Vietnam War, by merely printing more money. The costs of those programs could not weaken the dollar against the value of gold, because under the rules at that time, the value of the dollar was fixed—or could not depreciate in value against gold. However, the artificially over-valued dollar also resulted in less demand for U.S. exports, which benefited Japan and Western Europe. Given that the United States was relatively less dependent on trade than Western Europe and Japan, the loss of business for the United States was a politically acceptable exchange for successfully achieving other political and economic objectives.

Because the United States was free to continue spending and running a deficit in its balance of payments, it effectively exported inflation (an oversupply of dollars) through the monetary system to its allies. As part of the arrangement, Western European banks were committed to buying up surplus dollars to bring the value of their currencies back inside the trading bands (relative to par value). However, the more the United States invested in Europe and spent for the Vietnam War, the more others complained of the U.S. privilege, undermining political relations between the allies. Increasingly, the United States came under pressure to cut back on government spending or to sell its gold in order to repurchase surplus dollars. At one point, French President Charles DeGaulle complained that France was underwriting the Vietnam War by holding weak dollars in its banks instead of converting them to gold, which would have nearly emptied the U.S. gold reserve.

Furthermore, the Western European economies had recovered sufficiently that they no longer needed or wanted as many U.S. dollars. In the words of Benjamin Cohen, the result was that the "political bargain" made between the United States and its allies after World War II, whereby the United States managed the monetary and finance structure to the benefit of all, had become unstuck.[8] In effect, the fixed-exchange-rate system was restricting the economic growth of U.S. allies and limiting the choices of state officials in politically unacceptable ways. The *success* of the fixed-exchange-rate system was also undermining the value of the U.S. dollar, weakening many of the monetary structure's institutions and rules, and weakening U.S. leadership of the structure as well. The structure had become too rigid, making it difficult for states to grow at their own pace and to promote their own interests and values.

To prevent a recession at home, in August 1971, President Richard Nixon *unilaterally* (without consulting other states) decided to make dollars nonconvertible to gold. The United States devalued the dollar, and, to help correct its deficit in the balance of payments, it imposed a 10 percent surcharge on all Japanese imports coming into the United States. Some scholars have suggested that the United States purposefully abandoned its role as a benevolent hegemon for the sake of its own interests. Both the United States and Western Europe accused one another of not sacrificing enough to preserve the fixed-exchange-rate system. From the U.S. perspective, Western Europe should have purchased more goods from the United States to help correct the balance-of-trade and balance-of-payments problems. On the other hand, the Europeans argued that trade was not the primary problem; instead, the United States needed to reform its own economy by cutting spending, which meant getting out of Vietnam and/or reducing domestic spending—two things that were politically unacceptable to the U.S. administration at the time.

The Float- or Flexible-Exchange-Rate System: Phase III and the Changing Economic Structure

In 1973 a new system emerged that is commonly referred to as the float- or **flexible-exchange-rate system**, or **managed float** system. The major powers authorized the IMF to further widen the trading bands so that changes in currency values could more easily be determined by market forces. Some states independently floated their currencies, while many of the countries that joined the European Economic Community (EEC) promoted regional coordination of their policies. Many states still had to deal with balance-of-payments issues, but the framework of collective management was meant to be less constraining on their economies and societies.

Several other developments contributed to the end of the fixed-exchange-rate monetary system. In the early stages of the Bretton Woods system, investment funds could *not* move easily among countries to take advantage of possible higher returns on interest or investments. Capital controls (restrictions on money moving in and out of a nation) and fixed exchange rates were manipulated to allow states to respond to domestic political forces without causing exchange-rate instability. Policy makers intentionally limited the movement of finance and capital between countries for fear that financial crises like those in the 1920s and 1930s could easily spread from one country to many others. Widespread currency convertibility (achieved by 1958), the large numbers of U.S. dollars pumped into the international economy via U.S. current account deficits, and the expansion of U.S. transnational corporation investments in Western Europe all led to pressure on state officials to bring down capital controls and to allow money to move more freely in the international economy.

By the late 1960s, many officials and businesses were looking outward for new markets and investments, leading to increased private capital flows in the form of direct TNC investments, portfolio investments (such as purchases of foreign stocks by international mutual funds), commercial bank lending, and nonbank lending. Flexible-exchange rates complemented the relaxation of capital controls, which added yet another source of global liquidity to complement lending by states and loans by the IMF, the World Bank, and regional banks.

The adoption of and structure of the flexible-exchange-rate system reflected several other influential political and economic developments, including the growing influence of the Japanese and West European economies, the rise of the Organization of Petroleum Exporting Countries (OPEC), and the shift toward a multipolar security structure (see Chapter 9). By the early 1970s, Japan's rising living standards and high rates of economic growth had turned Japan into a major player in international monetary and finance issues. Robert Gilpin and other realists make a strong case for the connection between the diffusion of international economic growth and wealth at the time and the emergence of a new multipolar security structure.[9] The flexible-exchange-rate system helped entrench a multipolar international security structure that would be cooperatively managed by the United States, the EU, Japan, and (later) China.

The rise of OPEC and tremendous shifts in the pattern of international financial flows after oil price increases in 1973–1974 and 1978–1979 transformed the system into a *global* financial network. Almost overnight, billions of dollars moved through previously nonexistent financial channels as OPEC states demanded dollars as payment for oil. This increased the demand for U.S. dollars in the international economy, which helped maintain the dollar's status as the top currency. Many of the OPEC "petrodollars" deposited in Western banks were recycled in the form of loans to developing countries that were viewed as good investment risks because of the increasing demand for consumer goods and natural resources (especially oil). However, between 1973 and 1979, the debt of developing nations increased from $100 billion to $600 billion, generating a debt crisis that will be discussed in more detail in Chapter 8.[10]

In the early 1980s, trade imbalances in the developed countries contributed to stagflation, or slow economic growth accompanied by rising prices—two phenomena that do not usually occur together. As the oil crises subsided, the U.S. dollar weakened in value. U.S. officials focused on fighting domestic inflation by raising interest rates to tighten the money supply, which slowed down the economy and contributed to an international recession. At this time a change in political-economic philosophy occurred in Great Britain and the United States. The prevailing Keynesian orthodoxy was swept aside in favor of a return to the classical liberal ideas of Adam Smith and Milton Friedman discussed in Chapter 2.

The governments of British Prime Minister Margaret Thatcher and U.S. President Ronald Reagan privatized national industries, deregulated financial and currency exchange markets, cut taxes at home, and liberalized trade policy. Theoretically, these measures were supposed to produce increased savings and investments that would stimulate economic growth. In 1983, economic recovery did begin, especially in the United States, stimulated by higher rates of consumption, a less restrictive monetary policy, and attention to fighting inflation—all policies that mainly benefited wealthier people. However, many experts suggest that a drop in world oil prices—more than anything else—stimulated economic growth in the industrialized nations.

Despite the laissez-faire rhetoric, Reagan's defense budget was the biggest since World War II, aimed at renewing the West's effort to contain the Soviet Union and communist expansion. These expenditures and a strong dollar led to increased prices for U.S. exports and lower import prices, which resulted in record U.S. trade deficits, especially with Japan. In order to shrink the U.S. trade deficit, the Reagan and the first Bush administrations, rather than cutting back on government spending or raising taxes, pressured Japan and other states to adopt adjustment measures that included revaluing the yen. Many mercantilist-oriented trade officials also accused Japan, Brazil, and South Korea of not playing fair when they refused to lower their import barriers or reduce their export subsidies (see Chapter 6).

Paradoxically, much like the case of China today, this situation also *benefited* the United States to the extent that high U.S. interest rates attracted foreign investments in U.S. businesses and real estate. The Reagan version of "hegemony on the cheap" helped correct the U.S. current account deficit and sustain the value of the U.S. dollar. More importantly, a strong dollar helped sustain U.S. hegemonic power and the Reagan administration's struggle against the "evil empire" of the Soviet Union. As was the case in the past, many U.S. allies did not agree with this outlook and pursued monetary and finance policies contrary to those of the United States.

By 1985, the United States had become the world's largest debtor nation, with a balance-of-payments deficit of some $5 trillion.[11] Many countries and U.S. exporters complained that the dollar was overvalued. Rapid capital flows were now contributing to volatile exchange rates, which interfered with FDI and international trade. As it had done 20 years earlier, the United States resisted making hard choices about currency adjustments that could threaten its economic recovery or lead to cutbacks in defense spending. Instead, in 1985, the United States pressed the other G5 states (Great Britain, West Germany, France, and Japan) to meet in New York, where they agreed to *intervene* (contrary to the Reagan administration's preferred policy of nonintervention) in currency markets to *collectively manage* exchange rates. The Plaza Accord committed the G5 to work together to "realign" the dollar so that it would depreciate in value against other currencies, thereby raising interest rates in the other economies.

The Roaring Nineties: Globalization and the Weakening Dollar

As the Reagan administration's neoliberal ideas became even more popular, they continued to influence developments in the international finance and monetary structure in the 1990s and early 2000s. Economic liberal policies and development strategies served as the basis of the "Washington Consensus" and globalization campaign (see Chapter 3). By the end of the Cold War in 1990, many of the controls on capital flows had been removed. Private capital flows came to dwarf official flows. In 1997, for example, net private capital flows amounted to $285 billion, compared to net official flows of only $40 billion. This capital bolstered newly emerging economies in Southeast and East Asia that emphasized export sales, limited imports, promoted savings, and postponed consumer gratification.

In the 1980s and 1990s, revolutionary advances in electronics, computing, and satellite communications enhanced the integration of national economies and further globalized the monetary and finance structure. Increased public and private finance also helped generate tremendous increases in the volume and value of international trade.

In the early 1990s, the dollar continued to lose value, depreciating an average of 15 percent against the currencies of major U.S. trade partners. The U.S. Federal Reserve Board decreased interest rates to improve exports and expand growth. By the mid-1990s, the U.S. economy had recovered: inflation fell, consumers spent more, and foreign investors increased demand for dollar-denominated assets. The newly created European Central Bank (ECB) maintained price stability for its members and helped insulate European currencies from the U.S. dollar.

These policy changes and efforts to make exchange rates serve state interests caused contradictions. The **Mundell Trilemma** accounts for this muddled situation where typically states desire three things at once: (1) the ability to respond to domestic political forces (often referred to as monetary autonomy), (2) international capital mobility (necessary for efficient international finance), and (3) stable exchange rates (desirable for smooth international trade and investment). The problem is that only any *two* of these goals are possible at the same time as the third option always cancels out the effectiveness of the other two.

For example, the United States and Japan have traditionally had levels of international trade that are relatively small compared with the domestic economy. It is more important for them to have a free hand in domestic economic policy and to have access to international capital markets for financing, instead of stable exchange rates. But Argentina and Hong Kong, both more dependent on the international economy, pegged their currencies to the USD, which made their exchange rates more stable but limited their ability to respond to domestic economic and political problems. As the Mundell Trilemma demonstrates, states could not find a desirable outcome just by deregulating their monetary and financial institutions.

THE GLOBAL FINANCIAL CRISIS: THE U.S. DOLLAR GOES WOBBLY

In the late 1990s and early 2000s, criticisms of both globalization and wildcat capitalism intensified. After the dotcom technology bust in 2001, a speculative real estate bubble contributed to a financial crisis in 2007 that spread from the United States to Europe and Oceania. The United States had continued to run huge deficits in the balance of payments and relied on countries like China, Japan, Germany, and Saudi Arabia to offset its growing debt through purchases of property and government Treasuries in the United States. As we saw in Table 7-3, SWF and reserve surplus countries invested in U.S. businesses or purchased U.S. stocks, Treasury bonds, and other securities, helping the United States correct its balance-of-payments deficits.

The financial crisis has raised a number of issues related to a weakening in the value of the dollar relative to other currencies. Even before the crisis, many officials and experts felt confident that the euro would eventually overtake the hegemonic role of the U.S. dollar in the global political economy, given the size of the EU market and population. When the euro was officially rolled out in 2002, it was valued at almost one-for-one against the U.S. dollar. By 2007, the dollar had dropped in value to roughly $1.80 to the euro. In the early 2000s, OPEC was unhappy using weaker dollars in its transactions because it had to sell more oil to make the same amount of money. In 2007, some OPEC members—especially Venezuela and Iran—pushed for oil to be priced in euros denominated against a basket (average price) of currencies. Only Saudi Arabia's intervention on behalf of the United States prevented this.

Some experts assert that because the United States continues to run large deficits in its balance of payments and has high levels of national debt, the dollar is bound to be replaced by something else, which we will discuss later. Others are not so pessimistic.

There are a variety of explanations for a weak U.S. dollar, especially since the early 2000s. A few among them are as follows:

- Continued increases in the U.S. balance-of-payments deficits
- Continued U.S. trade deficits, especially with countries like China
- Excessive U.S. domestic spending, and
- Excessive U.S. military spending

As noted earlier, the United States does not usually make exports a major priority given its large domestic market, its desire to live beyond its means, and relatively weak demand overseas for many U.S. products. Trade becomes more of a concern during recessions when unemployment goes up, as it did in the early 1980s and since 2008. Foreign exchange and monetary policies often play a role in trade disputes between the United States and other countries. A small change in exchange rates can have large effects on levels of imports and exports.

This is exemplified by U.S. accusations that China has purposefully kept down the value of its currency in order to increase its exports, at the expense of U.S. workers. Pegging the value of the yuan (officially called the renminbi) to the U.S. dollar, the People's Bank of China (China's equivalent of the U.S. Federal Reserve) can "artificially" maintain this exchange rate by using yuan to buy up U.S. dollars (and the currencies of other states that are converted to dollars) that enter China in the form of investments and export earnings. More yuan in the economy results in cheaper Chinese exports. Between 1994 and 2010, the United States and other nations pressured Beijing to abandon the practice of pegging the yuan to the USD. On a few occasions, the Chinese did revalue the yuan, but not enough to make a significant dent in the U.S. trade deficit with China. When the global financial crisis came to a head in 2008, Chinese officials once again fixed the value of the yuan to the dollar to help in their economic recovery. Once again, foreign officials accused China of "not playing fair" by holding down the value of the yuan against the dollar—this time by as much as 40 percent. To counter what they believed was classic competitive devaluation, some U.S. congressmen threatened to introduce a bill imposing a tariff on all Chinese goods coming into the United States unless China stopped manipulating its currency.

In 2010, China again abandoned the peg, but U.S. officials again pressured the IMF and the U.S. Treasury to brand China a "currency manipulator," which would entitle those hurt by China's actions to initiate remedial countermeasures. President Obama brought up the issue with Chinese officials at the 2012 APEC meetings in Vladivostok, Russia. Likewise, candidate Mitt Romney promised to label China a currency manipulator if he were elected president in 2012.

However, the situation is much more complicated than economists and politi-cians suggest, especially when dealing with the issue of *"cui bono"* (who benefits) from the status quo and when rates are allowed to fluctuate. Neoliberals would suggest that the loss of U.S. jobs should be measured against cheaper prices for U.S. consumers of Chinese products. Likewise, many U.S. companies operating in China also benefit from the situation. Others suggest that U.S. officials tend to single out China because of its huge trade surplus with the United States and its unwilling-ness to cooperate on international economic affairs. Finally, some experts note that Israel, Switzerland, France, Taiwan, and Japan often devalue their currencies for the same reasons as China. In most cases, it is hard to separate defensive from mali-cious intentions behind exchange rate manipulation. The Obama administration appears reluctant to retaliate against China because of big potential drawbacks. (See the box The Tangled Web of China's Currency Manipulation).

Others have worried that government spending for the **Troubled Asset Recovery Program (TARP)**, three rounds of **Quantitative Easing (QE1, 2, and 3)**, high levels of U.S. domestic spending, and the costs of the wars in Afghanistan and Iraq will inevitably lead to excessive inflation, more debt, and a weakening in the value of the dollar. For now, rather than sharply cutting spending, the United States relies chiefly on external sources of finance to cover its budget deficits, something the neo-liberal Fred Bergsten argues is risky and unsustainable.[12] Structuralists believe that excessive spending in terms of an "economic overextension" or "overstretch" often accompanies imperial policies and gradually weakens an imperial power.

Nevertheless, during the financial crisis many investors have continued to view the U.S. economy as a good asset venture. The realist Gabor Steingart of Germany's *Der Spiegel* magazine argues that the United States is considered safe because "one can almost completely rule out the possibility of political unrest in the United States. . . ."[13] Many states and individuals view U.S. "T-Bills" as stable purchases, given that the U.S. government is quite unlikely to default on its debt. U.S. Treasuries also pay interest and are highly liquid—meaning they can be easily turned into cash—which ensures that, as reserves, they are flexible in composition and do not decrease in value over time. To repeat, one of the privileges of being a global hegemon and holding the world's reserve currency is that the U.S. Treasury can repay international debt by creating more national currency and national debt.

At the same time, Steingart notes that U.S. stimulus packages require more borrowing and debt, putting downward pressure on the dollar. He likens the U.S. economy to an "economic giant on steroids," dependent on investment shots from countries with surplus capital. However, as with the "grand bargain" between the United States and its allies during the Cold War, the United States still provides a collective good for the international community by combating terrorism. Others help pay for this service to the extent that they invest in the United States and pur-chase its goods and services. Counteracting the concern about excessive debt is the worry that if U.S. military capabilities were to significantly weaken, a tipping point could be reached that undermines confidence and investment in the United States. As Steingart so aptly put it, "As long as the trusting outnumber the mistrustful, all is well. . . . The problems begin on the day this relationship begins to shift."[14]

Others analysts such as Paul Krugman believe that overall things are not so bad! Despite the financial crisis and what seems like excessive debt, a weak dollar

THE TANGLED WEB OF CHINA'S CURRENCY MANIPULATION[a]

In April 2010, the Obama administration was trying to walk a fine line between looking and acting tough, and giving in to the Chinese over the currency manipulation issue.[b] There are many reasons why both the Obama administration and the IMF are not in a hurry to push China harder on the issue. In sum, many experts and policy officials worry that to do so would be quite risky for both the United States and China.

First, China has hinted that it may dump U.S. Treasury bills that it has in its central bank's $1.5 trillion reserve. This is a nightmare scenario that could put further downward pressure on the U.S. dollar (leading to its demise as the top currency), depreciate the value of China's holdings in the United States, and further disrupt global financial markets. The immediate impact of such a move would be that the United States would not be able to finance its balance- of-payments deficit and debts. Even if China chose not to dump the dollar, it still could retaliate with other measures of its own such as import tariffs and quotas on imported goods. Second, given U.S. dependency on Chinese imports, driving up the price of Chinese goods *could* trigger rapid inflation in the United States.[c] This might then pressure the Fed into increasing interest rates, which could also slow the recovery of the U.S. economy.

Third, some argue that China's responsibility for the trade deficit with the United States is overstated and that a big revaluation of the yuan would do little to shrink it. Point in fact: the appreciation of the yuan after 2005 did not help close the U.S.–China trade gap that much.

Finally, some experts note that China's central bank wants to let the yuan gradually appreciate against the dollar anyway, but its Commerce Ministry (which represents the interests of exporters and manufacturers) would rather the value of the yuan remain where it is. In effect, China's policies resemble those of the United States to the extent that they reflect powerful domestic corporate interests and public opinion that cannot easily be changed by threats or intimidations. Harvard Law School professor Mark Wu notes that in 2010 China did let the yuan increase in value 3.6 percent against the dollar. However, Beijing wants to go slowly in order to let exports adjust, limit job losses, and contain social unrest.[d] Libertarian writer Mike Whitney also makes the case that many U.S. multinationals do *not* want the value of the yuan to appreciate, given their investments in export-dependent Chinese corporations.[e]

Whether or not China is guilty of currency manipulation is not as important as the issue of who benefits—*cui bono?*—from the currency situation. The United States and China have a highly interdependent relationship, which means that this issue is likely to be resolved at high diplomatic levels. The United States will have to make trade-offs if it wants Chinese cooperation on North Korea, Iran, terrorism, carbon emissions, and other big issues. Because currency valuation is as inherently political as it is economic, the outcome will not be decided solely on the basis of what is rational, nor is one side likely to prevail over all the issues in this case.

References

[a]Our thanks to Josh Anderson for helping research and draft the first version of this material in the fourth edition of the text. Dave Balaam and Brad Dillman updated it for this edition.

[b]See Sewell Chan, "U.S. Will Delay Report on Chinese Currency, While Urging an End to Intervention," *New York Times*, April 4, 2010.

[c]The relationship between the U.S. budget deficit and U.S. consumption, as well as the danger posed by America's large trade deficit, is explored in: Menzie D. Chinn, "Getting Serious about the Twin Deficits," *Council on Foreign Relations*, September 2005.

[d]Mark Wu, "China's Currency Isn't Our Problem," *New York Times*, January 17, 2011.

[e]See Mike Whitney, "China's Flawed Economic Model," April 6, 2010, at www.counterpunch.org /whitney04062010.html.

is *not* a significant problem, at least *not yet*. Inflation is low, and in fact more inflation could help the situation somewhat.[15] Furthermore, the argument that when the Fed "prints money" it causes inflation misconstrues the Fed's role in expanding credit and keeping currency in circulation. In fact, because record low interest rates and Quantitative Easing have not significantly increased the amount of credit, the United States could face *deflation*, as has Japan since 1990.

For now, many investors continue to bank on the United States as one of the best places in the world to invest. Ironically, foreign investors might only hurt themselves if the U.S. dollar quickly *depreciated* as a result of their lack of confidence in it. As happened during the Great Depression, other states felt it necessary to continue lowering their currency values to compete for export sales, which started a trade war.[16] Many believe that the dollar is likely to remain the world's currency anchor. According to the IMF, in the middle of 2012, 62 percent of official foreign exchange holdings were in dollars—a relatively modest decline from 71 percent in 1999. Other global factors that work in the favor of the United States include China's slowing economy; the destruction of the nuclear facilities in Fukushima, Japan after a tsunami in March 2011; and the ongoing debt crisis in the Euro zone. The United States could very well be the new locomotive (albeit a slowing moving one) that also leads to economic recovery in Europe.

If Not the Dollar, Then What?

In October of 2009, China, France, Japan, Russia, and some Persian Gulf countries reportedly discussed moving away from the dollar and replacing it with a basket of currencies and gold. Political economist Barry Eichengreen pointed out that many states had been considering this and other alternatives.[17] Some of the most popular recommendations were as follows:

- The U.S. dollar remains the reserve currency.
- The euro or Chinese yuan replaces the U.S. dollar.
- A supranational currency such as Special Drawing Rights (SDRs) replaces the dollar.
- A reserve system with a basket of currencies emerges.

For Eichengreen and others, the Euro zone predicament currently precludes the euro from becoming anything more than a reserve currency in the EMU. In Chapter 12 we discuss why, to date, only Germany wants some of the responsibilities associated with system management.

In China, 54 percent of official reserves were stuck in U.S. dollars at the beginning of 2012. At one point, China's central bank governor did recommend that SDRs replace the dollar as the reserve currency. Currently, the Chinese yuan is still not convertible everywhere; instead, it is used for cross-border trade and purchasing goods from China. This deters other countries from using the yuan for foreign exchange, trade, and bank payments. To change this, China would have to open its markets even more, commercialize and supervise its banks, and alter its growth strategy away from bank lending and a pegged currency. The financial crisis did cause it to spend more for recovery and employment rather than investing in foreign banks and projects, which worried many U.S. officials and bankers all over the world. However, with a slowdown in the economy in 2012, China was in no hurry to push the yuan beyond its major role in the Asian region.

A UN commission headed by Joseph Stiglitz recommended that SDRs play the role of a supranational reserve currency. This would help eliminate the privilege of countries like the United States that borrow large amounts of capital and whose domestic policies can impose adjustment problems on other states. The problem for now, however, is that SDRs are not accepted as foreign exchange. They cannot be bought and sold, and they are not liquid enough for states, corporations, and banks. To use them would require high costs and market restructuring. The IMF could help build a market for them, but it must be empowered by states to do so. It would have to issue additional SDRs during period of shortages.

STRUCTURAL MANAGEMENT AND ALTERNATIVE RESERVE CURRENCIES

For now, management of the global monetary and finance structure remains weak and ambiguous. The IMF and the World Bank increasingly play less important roles in regulating currency exchange and lending funds. The IMF's role was weakened significantly due to its handling of the Asian crisis when it resisted recommendations from Japan and West European partners. During the recent financial crisis, the IMF has resisted seriously evaluating the United States, its main benefactor. However, it is now trying to help some of the developed Euro zone nations such as Greece, Ireland, and Spain

Since the 1970s, the G8 (the United States, the United Kingdom, Germany, France, Japan, Italy, Canada—and later Russia) have managed difficult negotiations between finance ministers and central bank presidents. There are other lesser-known IOs that also cooperate on international financial and banking issues. The Basil Committee on Bank Supervision includes twenty-seven member states that coordinate to ensure standards for capital adequacy and supervise banking practices. The International Organization of Securities Commissions (IOSCO) sets standards on securities. The Bank of International Settlements (BIS) is an invitation-only group comprised of the central banks of important countries and others the members choose to include.

The global financial crisis has since spurred the finance G20 (not the same as the WTO's G20), representing more emerging economies that increasingly want to play a bigger role in negotiations on monetary and finance structure rules. Brazil, Russia, India, and China (the BRICs) have gained attention for their intransigence in some negotiations, but also for their hesitation to support stricter economic liberal policies and development strategies. Likewise, a number of the more successful Southeast Asian economies such as Indonesia, Malaysia, Thailand, and the Philippines stand in support of tamer versions of capitalism and a wider variety of emerging countries' (and even poor nations') interests in international negotiations related to FDI and currency exchange.

At the meeting of G20 finance ministers in Mexico City in early November of 2012, most states were worried that another great recession could come about if the debt crisis in Europe was not soon resolved. Likewise, there was fear that a failure by U.S. politicians to reach a deal to prevent automatic tax hikes and spending cuts from going into effect at the beginning of 2013 (the so-called fiscal cliff) could also trigger another recession. These types of events could easily increase or decrease the value of the major hard currencies in the world, signaling an adjustment in the global distribution of wealth and power.

CONCLUSION

In the United States and Western Europe, post–World War II monetary and finance policies were heavily influenced by fresh memories of the Great Depression. By isolating each nation's financial system and then regulating it, policy makers wanted to avoid another global financial crisis and collapse. Under the Bretton Woods system (1947–1971), investment funds could not move easily among countries to take advantage of higher returns. To stabilize and generate confidence in the system, the value of the U.S. dollar was fixed to gold, and exchange-rate fluctuations were limited to narrow foreign exchange trading margins. As the Western economies recovered, the structure and rules of the international financial system restricted states that wanted to realize more economic growth. The Bretton Woods fixed-exchange-rate system gave way to a flexible-exchange-rate system and less control over exchange rates and capital transfers.

The 1970s marked both an era of increasing interdependence and two international recessions related to high oil prices. In the 1980s, neoliberal policies and the onset of the globalization campaign spurred deregulation of finance, currency exchanges, and trade. After the Cold War ended, laissez-faire domestic policies and globalization grew in popularity, resulting in record amounts of global capital transfers. Many emerging economies, including Brazil and China, acquired huge amounts of capital from exports to developed nations. By the mid-1990s, globalization and a wildcat version of capitalism were also gradually undermining the global monetary and finance structure, along with the U.S. leadership position. Currency and financial crises in Asia and the United States (see Chapter 8) have raised serious challenges to a structure that allowed U.S. hegemonic privileges to continue.

The United States continues to borrow from (or be dependent on) surplus capital states to finance its deficit and high levels of domestic consumption, which recently added to a real estate bubble and a near collapse of the global financial system in 2008.

Once again, U.S. hegemonic responsibilities have become very expensive, both financially and politically. Because currency fluctuations and capital mobility can dramatically affect domestic employment and investment, the United States continues to look to other states to help finance its deficits, which, paradoxically, could further undermine the stability of the global monetary and finance structure. Despite the popularity of economic liberal ideas, states still feel compelled to intervene in foreign exchange and finance markets to achieve their own national objectives.

While there is evidence that the financial crisis has weakened the U.S. dollar, at this time it would be hard to imagine another currency as strong or trusted as the U.S. dollar. Cooperation still exists between the United States and states that benefit from U.S.-dominated international policies. Consequently, the monetary and finance structure reflects a situation where in terms of the Keynesian Compromise, domestic considerations still weigh more heavily than international interests. Today's global political economy is much more integrated than it was twenty-five years ago. Interdependence and globalization have redistributed wealth and political power. This has made it exceptionally difficult to manage the finance and monetary structure in ways that reflect the interests of all but the strongest, most developed states.

Increasingly, emerging economies are no longer willing to cede management control of the monetary and finance control to the United States, nor should they be expected to, given their more influential economic role in the global economy. This has made management of the financial structure both cumbersome and difficult. For that reason alone, a more multipolar and multilateral system might yet compel states to cooperate in order to produce a new order that satisfies their interests, lest the unpredictable hand of history makes those choices for them.

In the next chapter, we use many elements of the monetary and finance structure covered in this chapter to discuss several different types of debt crises. We then examine the recent financial crises in the United States and the EMU, caused by many of the same conditions that precipitated earlier crises. We conclude with a brief overview of some popular proposals to solve debt and financial problems.

KEY TERMS

foreign exchange rates   153
currency exchange rates   153
hard currency   154
soft currency   155
appreciation   155
depreciation   155
speculation   157

hot money   157
gold standard   157
fixed-exchange-rate system   157
Keynesian Compromise   159
reserve currency   161
balance of payments   161
sovereign wealth funds (SWFs)   163

flexible-exchange-rate
   system   166
managed float   166
Mundell Trilemma   169
Troubled Asset Relief
   Program, TARP   171
Quantitative Easing   171

DISCUSSION QUESTIONS

1. Outline the political, economic, institutional, and procedural features of the gold standard, the fixed-exchange-rate, and the flexible-exchange-rate systems. What are some of the political and economic advantages and disadvantages of each system?
2. Outline the institutional features of the IMF and its role in settling current account deficits.
3. If the U.S. dollar depreciates dramatically relative to the Chinese yuan, what effect would this likely have on consumers and businesses in each country? When is a falling dollar good or bad for the United States? Explain.

4. How have globalization and economic liberal ideas shaped developments in the monetary and finance structure? Cite specific examples from the chapter and in news articles.
5. The United States has experienced huge current account deficits that have made it dependent on investments from other states. What specific political and economic factors contributed to this condition? Who has the United States relied on the most to invest in the United States? Is it rational for these countries to invest in the United States? What impact does this situation have on the value of the U.S. dollar?

SUGGESTED READINGS

Benjamin J. Cohen. *The Geography of Money.* Ithaca, NY: Cornell University Press, 1998.
Barry Eichengreen. *Globalizing Capital: A History of the International Monetary System.* Princeton, NJ: Princeton University Press, 1996.

Barry Eichengreen. "The Dollar Dilemma: The World's Top Currency Faces Competition" *Foreign Affairs* 88 (September/October 2009), pp. 53–68.
Robert Wade. "The First-World Debt Crisis of 2007–2010 in Global Perspective," *Challenge* 51 (July/August 2008), pp. 23–54.

NOTES

1. Eric Helleiner, "The Evolution of the International Monetary and Financial System," in John Ravenhill, ed., *Global Political Economy*, 3rd ed. (Oxford: Oxford University Press, 2011), p. 216.

2. For a more detailed discussion of the history of the monetary and finance structure, see Helleiner, "The Evolution of the International Monetary and Financial System," pp. 215–243.

3. Two examples of these unions were the Latin American Union, which in 1865 included France, Switzerland, Belgium, and Italy; and the Scandinavian Union, which in 1873 included Sweden, Denmark, and later Norway. See Helleiner, ibid., p. 153.

4. Ibid., p. 155.

5. Cited in ibid., p. 156.

6. See Karl Polanyi, *The Great Transformation: The Political and Economic Origins of Our Time* (Boston, MA: Beacon Press, 1944).

7. See, for example, Oswaldo De Rivero, *The Myth of Development: Non-viable Economies and the Crisis of Civilization*, 2nd ed. (New York: Zed Books, 2010), pp. 31–41.

8. See Benjamin J. Cohen, "The Revolution in Atlantic Relations: The Bargain Comes Unstuck," in Wolfram Hanrieder, ed., *The United States and Western Europe: Political, Economic, and Strategic Perspectives* (Cambridge, MA: Winthrop. 1974).

9. See Robert Gilpin, *The Challenge of Global Capitalism* (Princeton, NJ: Princeton University Press, 2000), p. 6.

10. Reported in Thomas Lairson and David Skidmore, *International Political Economy: The Struggle for Power and Wealth*, 3rd ed. (Belmont, CA: Wadsworth, 2003), p. 104.

11. Gilpin, *The Challenge of Global Capitalism*, p. 6.

12. C. Fred Bergsten, "The Dollar and Its Deficits," *Foreign Affairs*, 88, November/December 2009.

13. See Gabor Steingart, "Playing with Fire," Spiegel Online, www.spiegel.de/international/0,1518, druck-440054,00.html.

14. See Gabor Steingart, *The War for Wealth: The True Story of Globalization, or Why The Flat World Is Broken* (Emmeryville, CA: McGraw Hill, 2008), p. 87.

15. Paul Krugman, "Not Enough Inflation," *New York Times*, April 5, 2012.

16. James Rickards, *Currency Wars: The Making of the Next Global Crisis* (New York: Penguin, 2011).

17. See Barry Eichengreen, "The Dollar Dilemma: The World's Top Currency Faces Competition," *Foreign Affairs,* 88 (September/October 2009), pp. 53–68.

International Debt and Financial Crises

The Greeks Must Endure: Protestors demonstrate against austerity in front of the Greek Parliament in February 2012.

Alexandros Beltes/EPA/Newscom

Readers of national newspapers have grown used to front-page articles about national debt problems and the ongoing global financial crisis. The burst of the U.S. housing bubble in 2007 caused a global recession that damaged many people's standard of living. As we write at the end of 2012, there are new storm clouds looming on the financial horizon. The U.S. Congress is still trying to lower the annual federal budget deficit through a combination of spending cuts and tax increases so that the government does not add significantly more to the long-term national debt already worth $16 trillion. The festering Greek debt crisis has reached the point where many economists believe Greece would be better off pulling out of the European Monetary Union (EMU). Other members of the Euro zone like Italy, Spain, Portugal, and Ireland continue to have high levels of sovereign debt, leading them to impose more unpopular austerity policies on their societies while seeking more loans from the European Central Bank if they expect to stay in the Euro zone and avoid default. Meanwhile, the entire EMU economy has plunged back into another recession that is expected to last through at least 2013.

You and your family might also be caught up in your own consumer debt crisis. Many people who bought homes in the 2000s later found themselves under water (owing more than their house was worth) and facing foreclosure. Others lost their jobs, unable to find good-paying alternatives. By September 2012, the average U.S. household had $7,150 of credit card debt. According to the College Board, 57 percent of students who graduated from a U.S. public university in 2010–2011 had debt that averaged $23,800 per person. By the end of September 2011, 13.4 percent of students had defaulted on student loans within the first three years of required repayment. While some of us have dealt with our financial suffering in silent desperation, others joined the Occupy Wall Street demonstrations in late 2011 or staged strikes and anti-austerity protests in Europe throughout 2012 to demand relief from the government.

Finance and debt issues seem to be clouded in mystery and "dark shadows"— supposedly too complicated for ordinary people to understand. Until recently, it was easy to assume that the "experts" would make the right decisions to manage national and global finance with everyone's best interests at heart. We now know better. Alan Greenspan, the former Chairman of the U.S. Federal Reserve, admitted to a congressional committee investigating the financial crisis in October 2008, "Those of us who have looked to the self-interest of lending institutions to protect shareholder's equity (myself especially) are in a state of shocked disbelief."[1] Other central bankers and financial industry leaders have also revealed themselves to have made bad financial decisions based on misleading ideological assumptions and incomplete information.

How did we get into this mess? Why has it been so difficult to clean it up? How do we prevent it from happening again? We will try to answer these questions by examining some of the causes of debt and financial crises since the 1980s and the tradeoffs governments have faced when trying to resolve them. Financial crises always engender struggles over the redistribution of resources. The corrective measures states adopt can profoundly reward some social groups and destroy the dreams of others. Political responses can span the gamut from more protectionism to less protectionism, austerity to stimulus, more fiscal integration to more state sovereignty, and from political inclusion to state repression. Crises can also produce long-term changes in our *ideas* about state-market relations and what is socially fair and legitimate.

The single most important feature of the global financial system today is the *globalization* of capital. Twenty-four hours a day, states, banks, and corporations move money around the world, whether to pay for imports, make investments, lend money, or distribute foreign aid. For example, in September 2012, $5 trillion of foreign exchange was traded *per day* in global currency markets. Increases in capital mobility and more flexible exchange rates have made the global financial system more interconnected and volatile.

Drawing on some of the themes introduced in Chapter 7, we examine important financial crises—beginning with the Third World debt problems of the 1980s and ending with the European sovereign debt crisis. First, we provide an overview of the different sources of debt and different characteristics of financial crises. Individuals, businesses, and states accrue debt for a variety of reasons, including to stimulate consumption, to make investments, and to finance spending. Their inability to pay it back can contribute to balance-of-payments problems, debt traps, credit crunches, and even economic depression.

Second, we look at debt crises that engulfed developing countries—especially Mexico—in the 1980s and mid-1990s and the role of the IMF in imposing policy changes to dig economies out of trouble. Third, we examine the dynamics of the Asian financial crisis of 1997–1998, triggered in part by speculative attacks that led to a currency crisis in Thailand. An era of unfettered capital flows went on to pummel Russia in 1998 and Argentina in 2001 as both countries' stock markets and currencies collapsed, forcing them to default on their foreign debt.

Fourth, we review the global financial crisis triggered by the bursting of a home mortgage bubble in the United States in 2007. Banks that had made risky investments teetered on the brink of collapse, requiring government bailouts as the world plunged into a recession. Fifth, we explain how the sovereign debt crisis in Greece spread to other European countries, causing a wider financial and banking crisis which threatens to tear apart Europe's Economic and Monetary Union (EMU). Sixth and finally, we survey some proposals for how states and IOs should solve current problems and better regulate the global financial structure to prevent future crises.

The key theses woven throughout the chapter are as follows:

- Events of the past thirty years indicate that finance and debt crises are not "black swan" events; rather, they are endemic to market-driven globalization.
- Crises have become geographically broader-based and longer-lasting, posing ever more serious threats to economic and political stability in the United States and Europe.
- The complexity and interconnectedness of global finance have made it more difficult for states and international institutions to manage the financial structure. The polarization of political elites in the United States and Europe and the fragmentation of interests in the Euro zone engender policies of financial brinksmanship.
- There is a growing consensus that the solutions to debt crises proposed by economic liberals—grounded in austerity and the structural adjustments of the Washington Consensus—do not work well and may even delay economic recovery. A more effective system of global governance and national bank regulations is needed to promote stability and mitigate the impact of financial markets on the world's poorest people.
- From a structuralist perspective, capitalism seems to be laying the seeds of its own destruction. The traditional welfare state is imploding. Inequality and

class warfare are on the rise. As German journalist Cordt Schnibben argues, "Truths about the rationality of markets and the symbiosis of market and democracy have gone up in flames."[2]

■ In surprising contrast to their experiences in the 1980s and 1990s, the BRICs (Brazil, Russia, India, and China) and some other developing countries have emerged relatively unscathed from the 2007 financial crisis—due in part to their growing middle classes and robust global prices for oil, minerals, food staples, and other exported commodities.

DEBT AND ITS RAMIFICATIONS

Debt serves a vital function in capitalism—facilitating new investments that help an economy grow and increase productivity. It comes in many varieties. As individuals, we are most familiar with household debt incurred when we use a credit card, get an auto loan, or take out a mortgage on a home. We borrow in order to consume, and if we fail to repay our debts we might go bankrupt or have our assets seized.

Private businesses take on debt for a variety of reasons—most importantly to finance new investments in plants and equipment, acquire other companies, and cover short-term expenses. They raise capital by issuing stocks and bonds or by borrowing from financial institutions. They can face debt repayment problems for different reasons, including loss of competitiveness, lower revenues in the midst of an economic downturn, or changes in exchange rates. Some may become insolvent, meaning they are unlikely to ever repay creditors, while others face liquidity problems, meaning they face short-term cash flow issues but are otherwise still viable businesses. Similarly, state owned companies typically borrow from their government or from public development banks.

States also borrow money on a regular basis to finance new infrastructure, cover budget deficits, or finance a trade deficit. They typically raise money by selling government securities and bonds. Their national and international creditors (lenders) include foreign governments, corporations, banks, hedge funds, and pension funds—some of the same actors who lend to companies. Lenders base their decisions on how much to lend, at what rate, and for how long based on their assessment of the likelihood that a government will make good on its debt.

Governments can repay debts in their own currency by simply printing more money, but at the cost of devaluing their currency and causing inflation. Banks and investors are constantly looking around the world for places to lend money, and they usually search for the best rates of return given estimated risks that include potential exchange rate fluctuations, changes in global demand, and political instability. Governments and companies can usually roll over or refinance old debt by, printing money or borrowing, unless creditors think they are so indebted that it is too risky to extend them more money—except at a higher interest rate. At this point, debt can become a destructive force, catching borrowers in a "debt trap" of ever-increasing expenses or bankruptcy, which makes it difficult to borrow in the future.

International debt problems can often lead to a balance-of-payments crisis (see Chapter 7). For example, if a country is running a trade deficit, it must try to export more goods and services, or it has to depend on other states to offset that deficit with investments in its country. The *lack* of foreign investment often leads to a capital account deficit—or financial debt. If the country is also unable to borrow from overseas under favorable terms, its international trade will be disrupted because needed imports may be too expensive to obtain.

These conditions can result in capital flight, when investors lose confidence in an economy and transfer their bank accounts out of the country to "safe harbor" nations. In turn, this creates an extreme shortage of funds in the debtor nation's banks, which sends national interest rates shooting up. It also puts pressure on states to defend the value of their currency by providing stronger currencies to those who cash out of the local currency on their way out of the country. If they cannot, officials may have no choice but to devalue the currency, which can easily destabilize their economy and society.

Debt problems related to a balance-of-payments crisis brought on by speculation and capital flight can disrupt trade and international financial relationships. A crisis in one nation can spawn additional crises elsewhere, as it did during the Great Depression of the 1930s. Resulting economic problems become political problems because it usually falls on the state and its leaders to implement the harsh policies necessary to get some relief from a "lender of last resort" like the IMF to bring international payments back into balance.

THE DEBT CRISES OF THE 1980s AND EARLY 1990s

Mexico kicked off the LDC debt crises in 1982 by announcing that it would default on its bank debt, stoking fears that other debtor countries like Brazil would follow its lead.[3] This crisis had its roots in the 1970s, when OPEC oil exporters recycled their petrodollars into Western banks and financial institutions, who in turn sought new investment possibilities and higher returns in LDCs. Western officials, who were giving out less Official Development Assistance (ODA), encouraged developing countries to borrow, especially because inflation rates were running ahead of interest rates on loans—creating negative *real* rates, which traditionally favor borrowers.[4] Instead of these loans resulting in rapid economic growth, the uncoordinated actions of financial markets generated a debt trap for both debtor states and their creditors.[5] In retrospect, too much was loaned to too many.

International banks headquartered in places like London and New York continued to throw good money after bad, just so that governments could sustain interest payments on earlier loans. Eventually, with so much debt outstanding, the banks were in as much trouble as the debtor nations—a typical Keynesian concern. The IMF—in coordination with the World Bank—stepped in to extend new loans to debtors in exchange for their adoption of trade liberalization and cutbacks in state spending. Once an IMF package was put together, commercial banks rescheduled debts, and Western governments and banks extended new loans. In essence, debtor states only refinanced their loans and stretched out the time period for repayment. While a few countries like South Korea and Turkey recovered and generated new income from exports, others went deeper into the red.

Facing these problems in 1985, U.S. Treasury Secretary James Baker came up with the so-called Baker Plan, whereby commercial banks and Western governments would extend larger, longer-term loans to fifteen big debtors in exchange for their implementation of market-oriented structural changes that would help them "grow" their way out of the debt. However, the plan did not work, in part because new sources of credit from banks and the World Bank were ill-timed and slow in coming. Moreover, while countries tried to expand their exports all at once, commodity and oil prices collapsed, leaving some nations even worse off. Compounding this problem was a recession in industrialized countries that shrunk the market for LDC exports. In some cases, loan money was used in unprofitable projects or was siphoned off by corrupt leaders.[6]

By the late 1980s, debtor states faced acute social and political tensions stemming from dissatisfaction with international debt management. A number of Latin American states threatened to unilaterally suspend all or part of their debt-service payments. The Reagan administration promoted some gimmicky forms of financial relief such as *debt swaps*, whereby some amount of debt could be swapped with a bank for land or valuable properties in debtor countries. Although it would have been in the collective interest of banks to clear their books of bad loans so as to reduce the risks that debtors would completely default, the banks were caught in a situation referred to as the "prisoner's dilemma." Each wanted others to forgive some of the debt but was unwilling to do so itself, for fear that it would bear a cost that would not be shared by those who paid nothing to solve the problem.

In 1989, President George H. W. Bush initiated another program—the Brady Plan—whereby banks gave debt relief to debtors in exchange for low-risk bonds issued by the debtor countries that were backed up by U.S. Treasuries as collateral. Thanks to Washington's intervention, countries like Mexico benefited from some debt relief (in exchange for more economic reforms), banks were sure to get a good amount of their principal back, and the U.S. government avoided increasing international financial instability. The formula between debtors, creditors, and the hegemon of shared risk, shared responsibilities, and mutual obligations eased the debt-service burdens of developing countries and allowed them to break out of their debt traps.

A New Role for the IMF

During the mid-1980s, the United States pushed the IMF to work closely with the World Bank to solve debt problems in the less developed countries (LDCs). During this period the Washington Consensus gradually emerged as the recommended strategy for developing nations (see Chapter 11). According to the neoliberal Reagan administration, debt would be overcome as economies opened up and integrated into the growing global economy.

In addition to helping member states deal with balance-of-payments problems, the IMF became a "lender of last resort" in the international economy to help nations overcome their debt burden. World Bank and IMF loans were made subject to **structural adjustment policies (SAPs)**, a series of actions to which the borrowing government had to agree before receiving a loan.

This IMF **conditionality** is controversial because it involves a number of politically unpopular SAPs designed to restore economic balance. Some of the required polices include *currency devaluation* to generate exports; *price stability* to control inflation and encourage savings; *fiscal austerity* to cut state spending and subsidies while privatizing national industries; *tariff liberalization* to promote competition in the domestic economy; *higher interest rates* to attract investment in the short run; and *sound social programs* for the lower classes to counteract higher import prices, fewer subsidies, and higher taxes.

The IMF-instigated policies were designed to reduce the current account deficit by increasing exports and reducing imports—and simultaneously to help bolster the capital account by stemming capital flight and limiting new borrowing needs. In the long run, these policies were supposed to generate economic growth, allowing a nation to repay its old debts and be less dependent on credit in the future. In the short run, the policies usually lowered living standards and imposed hardship, especially on the poor—in some cases leading to civil unrest. Although in theory the IMF and the debtor-nation governments worked together, in practice their relationship was often conflictual, with the IMF responsible for international financial stability while debtor-nation governments had to suppress domestic forces opposed to SAPs.

The Peso Panic of 1994

The Mexican Crisis of 1994–1995 was the first crisis in the new era of *global* finance and investment, where global financial flows were more volatile and harder to regulate nationally. Economist Paul Krugman applies the term "contagion crisis" to describe a financial crisis that spreads internationally to the point that it threatens to unleash a worldwide depression.

The years leading up to Mexico's entrance into the North American Free Trade Agreement (NAFTA) in 1994 contributed to an investment speculation bubble. Venture capitalists and large investors were convinced that Mexico's membership in the regional alliance would improve its prospects for political stability and economic growth. Capital flowed into Mexico from many sources, including pension funds holding the money of retirees, authors, clergymen, and grandmothers. Everyone felt that the new era of "emerging markets" had arrived—bringing high rates of return in its wake. What followed was a euphoric phase in which the economic ambitions of fund managers and middle-class Northerners were disconnected from political and social realities. Many investors made a good deal of money—at first. As word spread, more investors jumped in, driving up the prices of Mexican real estate, stocks, and bonds.

The wheels fell off the wagon in 1994 when a rebellion broke out in the poor region of Chiapas and the ruling party's presidential candidate was assassinated. Suddenly, foreign investors had doubts about Mexico's political stability. As they began shifting funds out of Mexico, pressure mounted on Mexican officials, who wanted to keep their exchange rate fixed to the dollar. The government had an obligation to give investors U.S. dollars when they sold their Mexican stocks, bonds, and pesos. As this pushed up the value of the dollar, the government knew that Mexican banks would soon run out of dollars. On the other hand, officials wanted to stem the outflow of money from Mexico. To do so they would have to raise interest rates to make rates of return on foreign investments look more attractive. The tradeoff was that this would also slow down the Mexican economy by making bank loans for Mexican borrowers much more expensive.

Inevitably, domestic interests prevailed and the peso was devalued, signaling to foreign investors that they were going to lose lots of money on their investments. They scrambled (panicked) to get out of Mexico before things got even worse. The price Mexico paid for the stampede and the drastic depreciation of the peso was a severe recession. The inflation rate doubled and unemployment jumped to 7.6 percent by August 1995. Mexico's GDP fell off dramatically in 1995, effectively wiping out the short-term economic gains from the NAFTA boom. Exports recovered due to the peso's lower value, but higher interest rates, a credit crunch, and higher poverty gave the country what critics called a "tequila hangover."

THE ASIAN FINANCIAL CRISIS

Less than two years after the Mexican crisis, the Asian financial crisis struck, threatening the financial stability of the entire globe and causing economic damage that lasted for years afterwards in East and Southeast Asia.[7] It demonstrates how easily crises occur—even in states with otherwise sound economic policies—when global market actors lose confidence in a government's ability to manage its finances or live up to external expectations.

The crisis started on July 2, 1997, when Thailand's currency, the baht, suddenly collapsed in value. This **currency crisis** was initially reported only on the back pages of the financial sections of world newspapers. But it started a chain reaction of economic, political, and social effects, together referred to as the *Asian financial crisis*, because it spread like a contagion to Indonesia, Malaysia, Taiwan, Hong Kong, and South Korea.

The Thai government had guaranteed that the exchange rate between the Thai baht and the U.S. dollar would be *fixed* at a rate of 25 baht per dollar. Capital was attracted to Thailand because the country's interest rates were *higher* than those in the United States. The government's pledge of a stable currency value encouraged Thai finance companies to borrow U.S. dollars on global markets, convert them to Thai baht at the fixed exchange rate, and then lend them out at a higher interest rate in Thailand. Banks and borrowers used the funds to expand businesses, purchase property, and even speculate in Thai stocks. Consequently, business bubbles began to inflate in Thailand and other countries in the region.

Problems developed when Thai banks were found to have many bad loans on their books—loans that were unlikely to be repaid on time and perhaps could never be repaid at all. Some of these bad loans were blamed on **crony capitalism**— a system in which the government gave some Thai banks favorable treatment in return for bribes or loans from the banks. In other words, public officials and business elites scratched each other's backs. When the bad loans were revealed, international investors became concerned about the health of the Thai economy and began to pull their funds out of Thailand. This meant that for every 25 baht withdrawn, the Thai government had to give $1 U.S. in return. As the flow of funds out of Thailand increased, the Thai government's supply of dollar reserves was drawn down. Conjecture began that the government would not be able to keep its promise of a fixed exchange rate—what would it do when it ran out of dollars?

This speculation soon turned into a kind of self-fulfilling prophecy. When everyone tried to pull out quickly and unexpectedly, it was impossible for the Thai government to pay everyone their dollars. These conditions were perfect for a **speculative attack,** which is essentially a confrontation between a central bank, which pledges to maintain its country's exchange rate at a certain level, and international currency speculators, who are willing to wager that the central bank is not fully committed to its exchange-rate goal.

Currency speculators can attack a local currency by borrowing huge amounts of it and then selling it on the market for a foreign currency. The central bank can keep its pledge by using its foreign currency reserves to buy up the local currency the speculators are selling. If the central bank keeps its pledge, speculators stand to lose very little because they can buy back the local currency to repay their loans at about the same rate at which they sold it. If, however, the central bank is not willing to intervene to keep its local currency stable, or if it runs low on the foreign reserves it needs to do this, then the local currency's value will depreciate in international markets. Speculators will be able to buy back the local currency at a lower price resulting in great profits after they have paid back their loans in local currency.

Typically, central banks have billions of U.S. dollars of reserves and access to considerably more funds through agreements with other countries' banks. How, then, is it possible to "break the bank" with such apparent ease? It is because global financial markets, when focused on a single country or industry, have even greater resources. Hedge funds are private investment funds that profit from betting on small pricing anomalies between assets such as stocks, bonds, and currencies that are trading at different prices in different places. They must be able to mobilize vast sums of money—hundreds of millions or even billions of dollars—with each dollar invested earning a small but quick return. Tidy profits come from small profit margins on lots of money. Hedge funds can be controversial when speculation zeroes in on a currency that appears to be trading at a higher price than is justified by political-economic conditions. Then the hedge funds can engage in the kinds of speculative currency attacks that were responsible for the collapse of the Indonesian rupiah and the Malaysian ringgit in 1997–1998, as well as the British pound and the Italian lira during 1992–1993. As long as investment capital is freely mobile between countries, currency crises caused by speculative attacks and investment bubbles are likely to occur.

When the Thai government in July 1997 was forced to abandon its fixed exchange rate of 25 baht per dollar, the baht's value fell to about 30 baht per dollar in a matter of days. Seeing the crisis in Thailand, investors "sold Asia," pulling their investment funds out of other countries in the region. The Asian currency crisis continued through the summer and into the fall. When the dust settled, the Thai currency's new exchange rate was about 50 baht per dollar, with similar collapses in other Asian countries. This had a number of serious effects. For Thai citizens, the most direct effect was that foreign goods were suddenly more expensive. A $10 bottle of a U.S.-made prescription drug that used to cost 250 baht was now priced at about 500 baht. But U.S. citizens benefited, for example, when a 100-baht sack of Thai jasmine rice, which used to cost $4, was now just $2. Of course, this also put pressure on U.S. rice farmers to match the lower Thai prices.

However, the biggest effects were in the financial sectors where even Thai businessmen who had made good business decisions or lent money efficiently could not possibly repay their U.S.-dollar loans because it required twice as many baht as expected. Many went bankrupt. Many people in Southeast Asia had acted rationally and worked hard but found themselves deep in debt, their life savings wiped out, and with few prospects for short-term recovery. The losses in Thailand were enough to lower the average per-capita income of the entire country by about 25 percent in one year. For many, the economic collapse was similar to the Great Depression.

The Asian financial crisis had ramifications beyond Asia for a number of years. We will briefly mention three important effects that it had on global financial conditions. First, Russia became the next domino to fall in 1998. It was still struggling from the collapse of communism and had trouble collecting enough taxes to fund government spending. Having spent a lot of money fighting in the breakaway region of Chechnya, it also lost export earnings from oil due to the Asian crisis. As foreign and domestic investors worried about Russia's economic stability, they sold off government securities and rubles and pulled their money out of the country. An IMF bailout worth $4.8 billion failed to help. The stock market tanked 75 percent in the first eight months of 1998 and the country's central bank used up more than $25 billion of foreign reserves trying—in vain—to maintain the value of the ruble. The ruble collapsed, inflation skyrocketed, and Moscow temporarily suspended foreign debt payments. But within a year, Russia was recovering quickly, as devaluation helped local manufacturers and world oil prices rose.

Second, Argentina soon had its own crisis from 1999 to 2002. Since 1991, it had pegged the peso to the U.S. dollar to control inflation, but it had run up a dangerously high foreign debt. A recession beginning in 1999 forced the government to implement a series of budget cuts and IMF-required austerity measures that lasted for two years. By the end of 2001, unemployment was 20 percent and political unrest was becoming unbearable. A run on banks and capital flight forced the government to announce a freeze on all bank withdrawals for a year. It devalued the peso and unilaterally converted dollars held in bank accounts into pesos at the new exchange rate, effectively forcing depositors to lose a large amount of money. In 2002 the government defaulted on more than $100 billion in public debt—much of which was never repaid to foreign creditors. By 2003 robust growth returned, thanks in part to rising prices for commodities exports.

Third, all of these crises badly tarnished the reputation of the IMF and other international financial institutions. IMF bailouts were too little, too late, and the conditions attached to them made the economic downturns even worse.[8] Emerging countries became convinced that austerity, higher taxes, unregulated financial flows, and privatization were the wrong prescriptions for a country during a financial crisis. Even if these measures might have paid off in the long run, in the short run the economic pain and severe political instability were too much for a society to tolerate. Through most of the 2000s, developing countries shunned the IMF as best they could by building up foreign currency reserves in case they faced financial problems. It was not until the global financial crisis that developed countries would begin to understand why emerging markets rejected their Washington Consensus and neoliberal certainties.

THE GLOBAL FINANCIAL CRISIS OF 2007

The current global financial crisis is not a unique event but the latest in a long line of financial crises. By September 2008, the U.S. real estate-mortgage problem had resulted in a full-blown global financial debacle, essentially freezing the circulation of credit within and between states. By the summer of 2009, some of the world's largest financial institutions had either gone bankrupt, been nationalized, or been rescued by the government. Simultaneously, the financial turmoil produced a deep global economic recession with dizzying job losses, record home foreclosures, and a substantial increase in poverty. Public confidence in governments' handling of economic affairs faltered, so much so that ruling parties and coalition governments were ousted in countries such as Iceland, Latvia, and Japan.

Why did this happen—especially in advanced, industrialized countries whose economic institutions were supposed to be some of the most well-regulated in the world? Heated debates on the causes of the crisis have occurred in the halls of officialdom, in the news media, and in academia. Some often-mentioned causes include the following:

- A global economic imbalance rooted in a U.S. balance-of-payments problem
- A U.S. regulatory regime that led to excessive debt and imprudent lending practices by banks, mortgage companies, and other financial institutions
- A myopic ideology that promoted globalization and the "magic of the market" without accounting for market failure and the impact of deregulation on financial institutions
- The irrational, unethical, and even illegal behavior of some individuals and companies
- Weak global governance

What follows is a chronological discussion of the causes of the crisis and the key actors in it.

The Run-Up to the U.S. Financial Crisis

Cyclical recessions have been regarded as one of the side effects of capitalism. As noted in Chapters 2 and 3, from the 1930s to the 1960s, officials in the United States and Europe viewed their economies through a Keynesian lens. In pursuit of socioeconomic and political stability, states used fiscal policy to control inflation, minimize recession, and support rising wages. Beginning in the late 1960s, Keynes's ideas were gradually replaced by more orthodox economic liberal (OEL) ideas, which featured "minimally fettered" capitalism—or a *limited* state role in the economy (see Chapter 2).

In the early 1980s, U.S. President Reagan and British Prime Minister Thatcher reduced taxes and *deregulated* many sectors of the economy, including banking. They insisted that markets—not states—could best redistribute income to those who were most efficient, innovative, and hardworking. By the end of the Cold War in 1990, many Western ruling elites encouraged former Soviet states and developing nations to adopt democracy, open markets, and privatization.

Throughout the go-go 1990s under President Clinton, stock prices skyrocketed and new communications technologies enhanced market activity. Many developing nations competed for huge amounts of unregulated "hot money." As discussed above, these funds destabilized the Mexican economy in 1994 and helped produce the collapse of many Asian economies in 1997. In 1999, the U.S. Congress repealed the depression-era Glass–Steagall Act, thereby allowing commercial banks with deposits insured by the FDIC (Federal Deposit Insurance Corporation) to become affiliated with investment banks that made many high-risk investments. Although a dot-com investment bubble burst in 2000 and 2001, taking with it $7 trillion in assets as technology stocks tanked, the new Bush administration and the Federal Reserve under Alan Greenspan remained adamant about the need for deregulation. They continued to believe that markets were efficient, self-regulating, and good at assessing financial risks and setting prices—beliefs that Nobel Prize–winning economist Paul Krugman says in retrospect were "dangerously simplistic, naïve, and ahistorical."[9]

Mounting structural problems in the U.S. economy played a role in the onset of the financial crisis in 2007. First, the United States was running a huge trade deficit, financed by big exporters like China and Japan that bought enormous amounts of U.S. stocks, Treasury bills, and other securities. In effect, the trade-surplus countries were loaning money to Americans who had an insatiable appetite for cheap imported goods and speculation. Beginning in 2001, the Federal Reserve lowered interest rates, which made it easy for Americans to borrow money and spend more, even though their average incomes stagnated after 1999. The United States gradually built up an unsustainable level of personal and public debt.

Many mortgage companies and big banks that dominated the New York Stock Exchange expanded programs first started in the 1990s to profit from the fast-growing home real estate market. They created new "exotic" loan products such as ARMs (adjustable rate mortgages) and loans with "teaser rates" or no money down to attract first-time buyers and especially those who otherwise might not have been able to purchase a home (so-called NINJAs—people with no income, no jobs, and no assets). With the government unwilling to exercise oversight and prohibit lax lending standards, lenders intentionally signed up mortgage customers they knew would have difficulty making their monthly mortgage payments. In particular, **subprime mortgage loans** (loans made to risky borrowers with weak credit scores who were often allowed to make interest-only repayments early in the loan cycle) are believed to have caused many buyers to make irrational decisions often based on incomplete (hidden) information. Banks were often less interested in the qualifications of the borrower than in "making the deal" to collect lucrative sign-up fees and improve their rating in the eyes of investors. Moreover, many borrowers believed that as the economy continued to grow, the market value on homes would increase and they would be in a better position to borrow against the increased future value of their house or sell the house for a hefty profit.

Things got messy and opaque when banks and lenders packaged risky home loans in bundles and then resold them as securities to other banks, hedge funds, and foreign financial institutions. Investors throughout the international financial system saw these securities as good investments with the potential for high returns, but the securities concealed the weakness of many of the underlying mortgages. Global investors mistakenly believed that they were making safe, "can't lose" bets. Speculation also translated into increased demand for risky mortgages and other assets in countries such as Britain, Spain, Ireland, Lithuania, and Estonia.

With an expectation of making huge profits, banks and other financial institutions (like hedge funds, private equity firms, and insurance companies) kept borrowing more money to make riskier loans and buy big pools of mortgages. Big investment banks like Goldman Sachs, Merrill Lynch, Lehman Brothers, Bear Stearns, and Morgan Stanley became highly *leveraged*—that is, the ratio of loans they made over the amount of funds they kept in reserve grew to unprecedented levels. Based on mathematical models associated with derivatives (see the Coding the Money Tree box that follows), they packaged and bought mortgage-backed securities and other investments whose true underlying values were nearly impossible to measure.

►CODING THE MONEY TREE[a]

Although created to spread default risk over a broad range of assets so as to make them safer to invest in, poorly regulated derivatives contributed to the financial crisis. While a proverbial "money tree" was created on paper, derivatives were used by banks that cared more about their own profits than the security of their clients' investments.

Derivatives were first concocted in financial mathematics research departments. Michael Osinski was the first to create a program that streamlined their production. Looking back on his work, Osinski remarks, "I have been called the devil by strangers and 'the Facilitator' by friends. It's not uncommon for people, when I tell them what I used to do, to ask if I feel guilty. I do . . . ."[b] At first, paper traders could offer highly liquid investments with a negligible default risk and an enormously high return; what wasn't to love about them? Soon everyone wanted them. These instruments shifted from complex

sources of short-term gain to dangerous, volatile, mispriced financial weapons. With an overwhelming demand for these assets in the 1990s and the first decade of the 2000s, investment bankers faced very few consequences from losing increasingly disposable clients. Banks and traders started to roll the dice even more, diversifying into even riskier investment sectors like real estate.

When banks expanded into the subprime housing markets, deciding when, and if, mortgage-backed securities would go under became a difficult task, especially since credit agencies granted many AAA ratings. Yet as Osinski comments, "Throw some epsilons and thetas on a paper, hoist a few Ph.D.'s behind your name, and now you're an expert in divining the future." This mantra took much of the worry out of derivatives and allowed Osinski's program to spread throughout Wall Street.

Regulation is warranted when the rational choices of individuals result in collective failure. In this particular instance, it was best for individuals, banks, and investment firms to pursue short-term profits. Regulators had been dissuaded from doing more to limit derivatives. Yet, many of these institutions seemed to forget that market prices can easily drop. The collapse of many derivatives destabilized the global economy, leading the media to point fingers, first at banks and financial mathematicians for developing these tools, then at traders for misusing them, and finally at economists for promoting the ideology that markets are self-correcting.

However, banks perhaps should not be faulted for misusing tools that regulators and public officials viewed as too complex to regulate. Arnold Kling, a former senior economist at Freddie Mac, once commented that of all the traders he knows, only a small handful actually understand derivatives.

Officials are left with many concerns: How much state regulation is needed to prevent private interests from damaging society? Are some financial processes too complex to regulate? Should society pay to clean up private financial actors' mistakes? Whatever the answers, we can be sure that the bold new world of financial innovation has more surprises waiting for us.

References

[a]Jordan Anton researched and drafted the material for this box feature.
[b]Michael Osinski, "My Manhattan Project: How I Helped Build the Bomb That Blew Up Wall Street," *New York Magazine*, March 29, 2009.

The Bubble Bursts

During the George W. Bush administration, a number of experts, including Nouriel Roubini at New York University and Robert Schiller at Yale University, warned public officials about a growing real estate bubble, but their forebodings attracted little attention until the subprime mortgage market started to crumble in 2006. By early 2007, a slew of large mortgage companies with portfolios of subprime loans worth $13 trillion—20 percent of U.S. home lending—filed for bankruptcy. Mortgage markets in other countries, including the United Kingdom and Japan, began reflecting the same trend occurring in the United States.

Fed Chairman Ben Bernanke and Treasury Secretary Hank Paulson finally expressed alarm about mounting troubles at many financial companies around the world in 2007. Merrill Lynch, Citigroup, and other large financial institutions reported billions of dollars of losses on subprime mortgage investments. Governments responded to these problems in an ad hoc manner. By the end of 2007, the U.S. Federal Reserve and the European Central Bank had lowered interest rates and injected several hundred billion dollars into the money supply for banks to borrow at a low rate. At the same time, some **sovereign wealth funds** from the Middle East and Asia provided capital to markets by buying at least $69 billion worth of shares in financial companies in 2007.

In the first half of 2008, the volatile U.S. stock market suffered big losses. The Federal Reserve helped JPMorgan Chase acquire Bear Stearns, Wall Street's fifth largest and most highly leveraged bank. Because big banks had become so interconnected (interdependent), losses tied to U.S. mortgage securities and other risky investments spread throughout the world banking system.

In the summer of 2008 many analysts recognized that banks would eventually not be able to cover their "toxic securities," making them increasingly riskier investments. Growing corporate and consumer debt added to concerns. The real estate bubble began to tear in July 2008 after panicky investors started unloading their stocks in the government-backed Fannie Mae and Freddie Mac loan agencies, which together owned or guaranteed $6 trillion of the $12 trillion mortgage market in the United States. Congress hastily passed a "rescue plan" to try to assure investors that the loan agencies would remain solvent, but many investors began seeking safer havens for their money. They focused on hot commodities like oil, gold, rice, and wheat, raising fears of higher inflation and negative growth. Oil prices reached $147 a barrel in July 2008, causing increased concerns about the ripple effects of high energy costs on consumers and businesses.

In September, a series of cascading financial crises caused stock markets to plunge and global credit markets to freeze up, almost overnight. Like the Asian crises in 1997, many investors previously willing to take a risk now panicked, causing many stocks and retirement funds to lose a large percentage of their value. On September 7, the U.S. government announced that it would put Fannie Mae and Freddie Mac into "conservatorship"—meaning they would be nationalized. When the U.S. government refused to rescue Lehman Brothers, a big investment bank, the latter collapsed and filed for bankruptcy.

Soon thereafter, the U.S. Fed came to the rescue of the American International Group (AIG), one of the world's largest bank insurers, pumping in $85 billion to become an 80 percent owner of the company. AIG had been heavily involved in issuing **credit default swaps (CDSs)**—contracts that give banks insurance against default by borrowers and that allow investors to bet on the possibility that companies would default on their loans. As subprime defaults and bankruptcies rose, AIG did not have the money to pay claims on CDSs, which were worth over $45 trillion. The Fed's aid to AIG—which eventually became a nearly $150 billion bailout package—was a hedge against the possibility that failure of AIG would cause the entire global financial system to collapse.

Big banks merged or bought up the dying remains of others: Bank of America took over Merrill Lynch and Bear Stearns; JPMorgan Chase absorbed Washington Mutual; and Wachovia merged with Wells Fargo. Ironically, this process made too-big-to-fail banks even bigger! Most of them had billions of dollars of toxic assets (mainly home mortgages) on their books. Likewise, many of them were overleveraged—they had borrowed too much money in relation to their own capital held in reserve. They were reluctant to lend to one another or to smaller banks on "Main Street" who financed local businesses and home sales.

When manufacturers and service providers could not find capital to borrow, they started laying off or firing people. Declines in tax revenues meant that state and local governments had to cut spending on schools and social services. As personal incomes dropped, consumers cut spending significantly, drove up their personal debt by using credit cards to substitute for the loss of pay, and hoarded what cash they had left. One out of ten homeowners in the United States could not make payments on their homes. Mortgage and bank defaults also rose to record levels in England, Ireland, Iceland, Italy, and Eastern Europe. Banks were stuck with properties they were forced to auction off at huge losses. Both the freezing up of credit markets and the downward economic spiral seemed inexorable.

We Are All Keynesians Now

As the fear of not only a deep recession but a second Great Depression mounted, many public officials—including the widely admired former Fed Chairman Alan Greenspan—began to sound more like Keynesian HILs than Milton Friedman-type OELs (see Chapter 2). A temporary coalition of officials and academics agreed that the U.S. Federal Reserve and central banks in other nations would have to become the "lenders of last resort." While many OELs preferred to let the market run its course and cull a number of big banks, most HILs and mercantilist-oriented policy makers supported a quick outlay of new national monies to unfreeze financial markets. The Bush administration (and later the Obama administration) believed that if the U.S. government failed to do something, the global financial system would suffer a total meltdown. With the United States' encouragement, many states did adopt a variety of measures—so-called "stimulus" packages—to restart their economies. These rescue packages flew in the face of the economic liberal ideology that had shaped state–market relations since the early 1980s. They also angered many ordinary folks who felt that the bailouts rewarded the very same financial elites who caused the crisis in the first place.

On October 3, 2008, President Bush signed the Emergency Economic Stabilization Act to create the **Troubled Assets Relief Program (TARP)**, which authorized Treasury Secretary Henry (Hank) Paulson to use up to $700 billion of taxpayer money to buy up bad assets in banks in the hopes of keeping credit moving. Soon U.S. officials injected $250 billion of TARP money into U.S. banks. As the crisis went on, some financial institutions built up their cash reserves rather than lend money and continued to pay their executives generous bonuses. Beginning in late 2008, Paulson also gave TARP funds to AIG, Chrysler, GM, and GMAC (GM's finance corporation). It is important to note that TARP was not a government giveaway; it was primarily a federal government purchase of shares and equity stakes in companies. When it wound down by the end of 2010, TARP had actually disbursed only $415 billion ($245 billion to banks, $68 billion to AIG, and $80 billion to the auto industry). The government got back much of its money through bank repayments and sales of shares. (By late 2012, the government's overall loss from TARP was only about $24 billion, according to the Congressional Budget Office).

Contagion Takes Over

In October 2008, central bank officials and finance ministers of the United States, the European Union, Canada, China, Sweden, and Switzerland met and agreed to further cut interest rates to stimulate the world economy. Meanwhile, the U.S. Dow Jones Industrial Average dropped 22 percent—its worst week ever—with stocks worth $8.4 trillion less compared to the market high in 2007. In mid-November, a handpicked group representing the world's largest economies—the new G20 (not to be confused with the WTO's G20)—met in Washington, D.C. Although they failed to agree on detailed proposals to "reform" international financial markets, the inclusion in negotiations of countries such as China, South Korea, and Saudi Arabia signaled that officials wanted emerging powers to invest in the United States and other industrialized nations. In effect, globalization would work in reverse, helping rescue the developed nations while making them more dependent on the developing nations.

In November, the U.S. Federal Reserve became a "lender of last resort" by extending huge emergency loans to about 700 banks, in the hopes that this new money would encourage them to make more home, student, auto, and small business loans. (By the time the program ended in July 2010, as much as $15 trillion in low-interest, short-term loans had been lent on a rolling basis—without Congress' knowledge—to U.S. and European banks). The Fed ultimately recouped its loans, with interest, so the central bank did not lose money, but the scale of its interventions suggests how deeply dependent the financial markets were on the government.

By December 2008, the global economy was clearly in a recession. The Federal Reserve and the Bank of England began a policy of **quantitative easing**—increasing the money supply by purchasing hundreds of billions of dollars of bonds and other assets from financial institutions. But stock markets in Europe and the United States closed the year having suffered declines of approximately 40 percent in their indexes. In January 2009, companies in the United States and Europe announced huge layoffs of workers.

O'er the Ramparts We Watched

During his inaugural address in January 2009, President Obama said he would impose tough sanctions on banks that had "nearly destroyed the economy." He also said that he would focus on putting people back to work, building a new infrastructure, and supporting middle class priorities in education and health care. His administration quickly ratcheted up the Bush administration's support to Chrysler, GM, and GMAC (GM's finance corporation) from $25 billion to $75 billion by the end of 2009. In February 2009, Congress passed Obama's signature legislation, the American Recovery and Reinvestment Act. This $787 economic stimulus plan—sort of a mini New Deal—included massive spending on infrastructure to boost job creation and consumer demand.

Not unexpectedly, many Republicans and Blue Dog (conservative) Democrats attacked these measures, widening an already deep ideological rift between them and moderate-to-liberal Democrats. The clash between a still-dominant neoliberalism and a resurgent Keynesianism resulted in legislative deadlock. Why?

Congressional Republicans have promoted policies of "fiscal conservatism" that often include the following:

- Cutting the national debt and shrinking the budget deficit (the difference between taxes and spending)
- Shrinking the size of the government
- Cutting spending on Medicare and Social Security

- Opposing new regulations on financial institutions
- Avoiding significant reductions in defense spending
- Decreasing taxes and fighting inflation

They criticized Obama's economic stimulus as an example of wasteful government spending. For example, in 2009 the administration lent $535 million of stimulus money to a solar-panel manufacturer called Solyndra; in August 2011 the company filed for bankruptcy and the loan was never repaid. Deficit hawks believe that to generate growth the government should impose austerity measures such as layoffs of public workers, cuts in social spending, and reductions in expensive retirement and health care programs.

Similarly, Congressional Republicans (and Tea Party ultra-conservatives) blamed the housing bubble on quasi-state finance agencies Fannie Mae and Freddie Mac whose lax standards invited banks to make loans to too many unqualified borrowers. They argued that the best way to clean up the housing mess was to "let the market clear itself." Paradoxically, many of these conservatives support tax incentives for the rich, high defense spending, and government subsidies to energy companies, farmers, and high-tech companies. In other words, they support pro-business government spending but not government regulation.

The Countermovement

Historian Karl Polanyi argued that because economic liberal polices always produce the conditions for their own undermining, a countermovement to these policies can always be expected to emerge. Similarly, neo-Keynesian (HIL) economists such as Paul Krugman, Robert Reich, Brad DeLong, and Joseph Stiglitz—who believe that government must correct the fundamental flaws of unregulated capitalism—often assert the following:

- Austerity lowers incomes and weakens demand, thereby stalling economic recovery.
- Government deficit spending boosts demand and creates jobs.
- Moderate inflation is not a problem in the short run.
- The state should invest heavily in education, infrastructure, and new energy industries.
- The wealthy and major corporations should be forced to pay higher taxes.

According to political scientist Henry Farrell and economist John Quiggin, the spread of the financial crisis opened the door to re-acceptance of these Keynesian ideas amongst a network of expert economists whose policy proposals spread like wildfire to Washington, D.C., Brussels, and Berlin.[10] Neo-classical economists who dominated the U.S. economics profession were suddenly on the defensive as a number of their prominent members, including Martin Feldstein and Larry Summers, publicly supported fiscal stimulus. Europeans who suddenly switched to supporting deficit spending and massive central bank intervention in financial markets included IMF Director-General Dominique Strauss-Kahn and popular *Financial Times* columnist Martin Wolf. Even the conservative European Central Bank went along with stimulus spending.

Yet, many liberals and progressives felt that the countermovement was half-hearted and short-lived. Obama was seen as politically pragmatic to a fault, agreeing with Republicans in 2010 to support an extension of the Bush tax cuts for two more years in exchange for an extension of unemployment benefits for only a few months. HILs specifically criticized him for pandering to economic elites. His selection of Timothy Geithner—a former president of the Federal Reserve Bank of New York—as Secretary of the Treasury and Larry Summers as Director of the National Economic Council raised doubts about the president's commitment to financial reforms. These advisors seemed more interested in reestablishing financial stability than helping Main Street. In her 2012 book *Bull by the Horns*, former FDIC chair Sheila Bair called Geithner a "bailouter in chief" who threw money at banks with almost no strings attached, refused to support mortgage modifications for struggling homeowners, and later watered down reforms in the Dodd-Frank Act.[11]

Little was done to impose tighter limits on executive pay and bonuses in exchange for government bailouts. CEOs' compensation continued to grow during the Obama presidency. In 2011, the "median pay of the nation's 200 top-paid CEOs was $14.5 million."[12] Meanwhile, struggling homeowners failed to receive significant mortgage relief such as a lowering of principal owed. Between September 2008 and September 2012, 3.8 million U.S. property owners lost their homes to foreclosures.

The administration also refused to prosecute Wall Street insiders for apparently illegal improprieties leading up to and during the crisis; in a rare exception, millionaire investor Bernie Madoff was convicted in 2009 of running a Ponzi scheme that defrauded customers of more than $50 billion. After 2008, banks continued to engage in illegal practices such as robo-signing, whereby they foreclosed on homeowners with falsified or unverified documentation. Not until 2012 did the federal government and state attorneys general negotiate a $25 billion settlement over these fraudulent practices with the five largest banks in the United States.

To critics, measures that Congress has adopted to reform the banking and finance sectors are quite timid. Despite Senate Republican opposition, a Consumer Protection Financial Bureau (CPFB) was finally set up to conduct risk assessment of the financial system. In 2010 Congress approved the Dodd-Frank Act, a law that, among other things, requires banks to keep more capital and collateral in reserve and allows the Commodity Futures Trading Commission to regulate some types of derivatives trading. One of the law's most controversial proposals is the **Volcker rule**, which prohibits banks from owning hedge funds and engaging in certain risky trading. Despite these supposedly sweeping changes, JPMorgan Chase in 2012 lost at least $6.2 billion on a complicated hedging strategy that went bust. Trades made in the bank's London office involved the same kind of credit default swaps that contributed to the 2008 crisis. CEO Jamie Dimon had bitterly opposed regulations of the banking system that would limit the use of derivatives, at one point calling them "un-American." He later admitted that JPMorgan Chase had engaged in "dumb risk-taking."

How can we explain the relative weakness of financial reforms under the Obama presidency? Keynesians blame, in part, the banking lobby—what Simon Johnson and James Kwak call a "new American oligarchy" of six megabanks—that spent tens of millions of dollars opposing strong regulations. Even with Dodd-Frank, claim Johnson and Kwak, "The ideology of finance—the idea that behemoth banks peddling increasingly incomprehensible products are somehow good for ordinary people—though shaken, remains dominant in Washington."[13] Structuralist Robert McChesney points out that most politicians turn to vested interests to help finance their election campaigns, creating an undemocratic system of influence peddling—a dollarocracy—whereby corporate lobbies get favorable treatment from lawmakers that exacerbates political and economic inequality.[14]

Another reason may be U.S. political culture. Free-market ideas resonate strongly with public and private elites who have been conditioned to fear potentially authoritarian "big government." There has historically been significant public opposition to a "nanny state" that oversteps its boundaries. Tied to that opposition has been widespread resistance to higher taxes since the early 1980s. In the same vein, the notion that the United States is a "land of opportunity" with high social mobility runs deep—even if it is largely a myth since 2007. As former Republican presidential candidate Herman Cain said in 2011, "Don't blame Wall Street, don't blame the big banks, if you don't have a job and you're not rich, blame yourself."

Occupy Wall Street: "We Are the 99%"

To the delight of many HILs and structuralists, Occupy Wall Street (OWS) seemed to put a dent in the popularity of neoliberalism with its key slogan "We Are the 99%." Beginning with a September 2011 demonstration in New York against big banks, OWS soon spread to other U.S. cities such as Chicago, Atlanta, and Oakland—and later to global metropolises such as London, Rome, Santiago, Madrid, Athens, Sydney, and Toronto. Inspired by mass demonstrations during the Arab Spring, its most important policy recommendations are as follows:

- Reduce inequality by raising taxes on the rich and redistributing wealth
- Re-regulate banks and limit the influence of corporate money in the political system
- Provide bailouts (like mortgage relief, tax cuts, unemployment benefits, and student loan forgiveness) to ordinary families and workers
- Expand the welfare state and workers' rights
- Reject electoral politics in favor of direct political action

The OWS's inchoate mix of populist, anarchist, and anti-capitalist ideals appealed to a segment of middle and working class Americans frustrated with political gridlock and rising inequality. A leaderless social movement, OWS called for a breakup of "too-big-to-fail" banks, the five largest of which controlled $8.5 trillion at the end of 2011—half of all banking industry assets in the United States. Like structuralists, many OWS members have argued that both the Democratic and Republican parties are running a corporate state that reproduces the conditions for the survival and growth of capitalism. Ironically, says public intellectual Chris Hedges, the ruling elites are undermining their own system as they "retreat into hedonism," "pillage their own institutions," and "devote their energies to stealing and exploiting as much, as fast, as possible."[15]

These self-destructive tendencies, according to OWS-leaning scholars, stem in large part from the ruling elite's unwillingness to acknowledge the need for a fairer, more moral political economy. Robert Reich points out that there is an "unprecedented concentration of income, wealth, and political power in the top 1 percent" who control more than 40 percent of U.S. wealth and receive more than 20 percent of national income.[16] According to the Federal Reserve, average family wealth shrank 14.7 percent between 2007 and 2010 and average family income fell 11.1 percent in the same period.[17] Moreover, the U.S. Census Bureau reports that in 2011, 47 million Americans were living below the poverty line (defined as an average annual family income of $22,400).[18]

THE EUROPEAN DEBT CRISIS: IS THE DREAM OVER?

As we write at the end of 2012, the European Monetary Union and the seventeen countries that use the euro as their currency are at a crossroads! For almost five years many European states have experienced intractable debt problems that could easily lead to national defaults—failures to pay back tens of billions of euros to creditors. In particular, five EMU countries—Portugal, Ireland, Greece, Spain, and Cyprus—have had to turn to the "troika" comprised of the European Central Bank (ECB), the European Commission, and the IMF for assistance in meeting their debt obligations and saving their banks (see Chapter 12). Greece received its first EU-IMF bailout worth €110 billion in May 2010. In November 2010, Ireland got an EU-IMF loan of €85 billion; in May 2011 Portugal got a €78 billion EU-IMF loan (see Table 8-1). However, private investors drove up the interest rate on government bonds issued by Portugal, Italy, Greece, and Spain, making it much more costly for these countries to borrow.

Among other things, the troika have required that Portugal, Ireland, and Greece raise taxes and make deep cuts in the number of civil service workers, pensions, education, and social services. For example, in exchange for a second bailout of €130 billion in February 2012, the Greek government was required to lay off more than 150,000 government workers and decrease the minimum wage by more than 20 percent.[19] Even Italy and France have been forced to make painful cost reductions to lower their budget deficits (see The "Bitter Medicine" of Austerity). Germany and many private lenders have argued that austerity is the best medicine to reduce the level of sovereign (national) debt and restore investor confidence.

Yet, as might be expected, the public has strongly resisted these strident policies. Between 2010 and 2012, eleven governments in the seventeen-member Euro zone fell apart or were voted out, an indication of how frustrated voters are. There is a widespread perception that international lenders are inflicting severe socioeconomic pain on people who were not responsible for the crisis.

How events in Europe unfold will have tremendous consequences for one of history's most admired experiments in regional integration. One thing at stake is the viability of the modern welfare state. In an ironic twist, Jin Liqun, the head of China's sovereign wealth fund, said in November 2011 that European countries had a "worn out welfare society" with labor laws that "induce sloth, indolence, rather than hardworking." Scholar Thomas Wright also predicts that a collapse of the euro could damage Europe's soft power in the world, cause a long-lasting global depression, and end multilateral cooperation within the transatlantic alliance.[20]

THE "BITTER MEDICINE" OF AUSTERITY[a]

On April 4, 2012, Dimitris Christoulas committed suicide near the Greek Parliament. He left a note that said his pension had been cut and that he could not bring himself to eat out of trash cans. On May 24, 2012, Antonis Perris, an unemployed musician, and his 90-year-old mother with Alzheimer's both jumped to their deaths from the roof of their apartment building in Athens. Perris had posted a note online saying they had run out of cash.[b] On November 9, 2012, a woman named Amaia Egana in a Basque town leapt to her death from her apartment just before she was to be evicted for failing to make her mortgage payments. Hours after her suicide, thousands of demonstrators marched through her town chanting "Banker, remember—we have rope," "It is not a suicide, it's a homicide," and "We must stop financial terrorism."[c] In response to this and other suicides, the Spanish government on November 15 placed a two-year moratorium on evictions of poor people who have defaulted on their home mortgages.

Similar incidents have occurred all over Europe where many poor and working class citizens blame austerity policies for the extraordinary amount of suffering they are now enduring. The famous European social safety net was designed to help those without jobs, providing them with health coverage and public assistance until they could find employment. But now the welfare state is under attack.

One of the ways to cut the level of government debt is to "sack" (lay off) large numbers of public employees and trim the benefits of those who remain. Simultaneously, many countries have introduced "labor-market flexibility," meaning reducing wages and worker benefits and making it easier to hire and fire. Even countries thought to be relatively insulated from the repercussions of austerity have been feeling the crunch. For instance, France has seen a sharp increase in short-term contract labor, which rarely provides workers good benefits or a decent enough wage to live on. Likewise, some unemployed white-collar workers have taken to living in trailers in French parks.

Many kinds of public services have been cut, including education, elderly care, transportation, and garbage pickup. It is not hard to find lines at local soup kitchens. In October 2012, the Spanish Red Cross launched a public campaign called *Ahora + que nunca* (Now More Than Ever) to raise money to give food parcels to the poor. One of the advertisements it ran on Spanish TV showed a father opening an empty refrigerator, then sharing with his two children an omelette made with one egg.[d]

The working class and poor have been saddled with higher taxes. Greece went out of its way to increase the chances of collecting new taxes by attaching them to everyone's power and water bills. In some cases, people have allowed their utilities to be cut off and have moved in with relatives or friends. Because a large sales tax hike in Portugal has made going out to a restaurant expensive, there has been a "sudden proliferation of the 'marmita,' or lunch box, used by employees to take their home cooking to work."[e]

It remains to be seen if Europe's political elites can weather anti-austerity protests and offer a light at the end of a long tunnel of social suffering.

References

[a]Matthew Pedro, Dave Balaam, and Brad Dillman researched and wrote this box feature.

[b]Ariana Eunjung Cha, "'Economic Suicides' Shake Europe as Financial Crisis Takes Toll on Mental Health," *Washington Post*, August 14, 2012.

[c]Anne Sewell, "Protest in Barakaldo, Spain over Suicide of Evicted Woman," *Digital Journal*, November 10, 2012, at http://www.digitaljournal.com/article/336545.

[d]"Red Cross Issues First Appeal in Spain to Help Those Affected by Crisis," *El País*, October 10, 2012, at http://elpais.com/elpais/2012/10/10/inenglish/1349869331_462240.html.

[e]Raphael Minder, "Austerity Protests Are Rude Awakening in Portugal," *New York Times*, October 14, 2012.

The EMU Debt Trap: Beware the Greeks

When fifteen EMU countries adopted the euro as their common currency in 2002, they began to experience strong growth rates linked to the injection of large amounts of capital into their economies by banks and private investors. However, a sovereign debt problem emerged after the U.S. housing bubble burst in 2007 and recession spread across the Atlantic. What caused the crisis? Many neoliberal analysts have been quick to blame countries like Greece and Italy for reckless government spending, corruption, and lax tax collection. However, the European debt problem cannot simply be attributed to excessive government borrowing; there is actually a more complicated story that involves structural flaws in EU institutions, political constraints, and reckless *lending*.

First, before adopting the euro, each European country could devalue its own currency if it needed to increase its competitiveness; increased exports would then provide more income to service debts. However, by joining together in a monetary union, the seventeen Euro zone countries could no longer individually print money or use devaluation to resolve individual debt problems. Instead, the Frankfurt-headquartered European Central Bank set monetary policies for all members. It has had a free-market orientation and a reluctance to let inflation rise too high.

Although the Maastricht Treaty of 1992 required EMU members to meet specific criteria regarding the size of their budget deficit and government debt, they did not strictly adhere to their own rules. Why would they care about it as long as members were doing quite well economically? For example, Ireland—once one of the poorest countries in Europe—grew so fast between 1994 and 2007 that it attained one of the world's highest per capita GDPs. Multinational financial institutions and private investors bankrolled Europe's IT industries, real estate, tourism, green energy projects, and infrastructure. London, Paris, Barcelona, and Milan were booming metropolises. Reborn after reunification, Berlin sought to claim its status as one of Europe's wealthiest and most cultured cities.

Second, the debt crisis can also be partly attributed to the unwillingness of countries like Italy and Greece to reform their economies so as to increase productivity and competitiveness. They got complacent while the going was good, ignoring potential problems. Let's look briefly at the records of now-troubled countries (also see Table 8-1, which presents data included in Table 12-2):

- While borrowing was easy, Greece kept its official retirement age at 58 and expanded welfare benefits. It invested in a lot of new infrastructure, especially for the 2004 Olympics in Athens.
- The so-called Celtic Tiger, Ireland, adopted policies to attract huge foreign investors such as Microsoft, Intel, Google, and Citi. Yet, the Irish overbuilt new offices, homes, and apartments, generating a speculative bubble that burst in 2007. In September 2008, the Irish government guaranteed all of the €106 billion debt of the six largest banks that had financed the real estate bubble. The government then borrowed €85 billion from the troika to finance its deficit and to pay bank bondholders, making taxpayers responsible for what had been private debt.
- Many neoliberals blame Portugal's socialist government for mismanaging the government for the past forty years. Yet, before May 2011, Portugal had one of the best rates of economic recovery in the European Union. It consistently ranked

TABLE 8-1

Debt and Economic Indicators of Selected European Countries

	GDP (Billions of $U.S., 2011)	Government-Debt-to-GDP Ratio (%, Q2 2012)	Total External Debt (Billions of $U.S., Q1 2012)	EU-IMF Bailout Loans (Billions of $U.S., 2010–2012)	Unemployment Rate (%, Q3 2012)	Projected GDP Growth Rate (%, 2013)
Euro zone						
Greece	299	150	521	317	25.1	−4.8
Portugal	238	118	508	78	15.7	−2.7
Italy	2,195	126	2,514		10.7	−1.8
Spain	1,491	76	2,383	130	25.5	−1.7
France	2,773	91	5,130		10.7	−0.3
Ireland	217	112	2,214	67.5	14.8	1.0
Germany	3,571	83	5,798		5.4	0.4
Comparison Countries						
United States	15,094	73	15,481		8.1	1.9
Mexico	1,155	42	309		4.8	3.4

Sources: World Bank Indicators; Eurostat News Release 150/2012 (October 24, 2012); World Bank Quarterly External Debt Statistics; OECD Harmonised Unemployment Rates, Updated: November 2012; OECD *Economic Outlook* No. 93 (May 29, 2013).

above other member states in measures of high school graduates, exports, and entrepreneurial innovation. However, the state did spend heavily on a public sector with too many well-paid bureaucrats. As bond traders and speculators drove up the interest rate, Portugal had to pay on bonds it issued to raise money for debt repayments. Portugal turned to the EU and the IMF in May 2011.

- Italy has had a history of overspending and widespread tax evasion. Although its banks were not saddled with a lot of bad real estate loans, its high public debt (120 percent of GDP) made foreign investors wary of lending it more money except at high interest rates. In 2011 the government sold off some public real estate, increased the retirement age, and privatized some public services.
- Spain had a healthy budget surplus until 2008. It did not even have a sovereign debt problem: its government debt-to-GDP ratio in mid-2012 was just 68 percent, lower than that of France and Germany. However, many bank loans made during the real estate bubble went sour after 2007, plunging the economy into a recession. Unemployment reached a staggering 25 percent in October 2012. Spain applied to the EU for €100 billion to bail out its struggling banks, effectively raising its debt-to-GDP ratio substantially.

Whatever overborrowing Portugal, Italy, Ireland, and Greece may have undertaken was not a problem as such until the crisis started. Before that, many of the top people in Europe's banks and businesses had "made a killing," as the saying goes. Structuralists point out the irony of private banks and private bondholders "socializing" their potential losses, i.e., transferring the cost of their bad loans to European taxpayers—and liquidating assets in southern Europe as fast as they could. Just as is the case in the United States, the middle class and poor are left to pay the bill.

A third cause of the European sovereign debt crisis is the flip side of the over-borrowing: overlending. Egged on by ratings agencies that masked the riskiness of investments, international and domestic creditors of Portugal, Italy, Ireland, Greece, and Spain extended loans and bought government bonds at low interest rates before the downturn after 2007. They failed to anticipate a systemic crisis in the Euro zone. Germany for many years had been running a huge trade surplus with southern European countries. As southern European companies became less competitive within the Euro zone, they were unable to boost exports through devaluation of their own currency. So trade deficits in these countries were covered with capital inflows from northern European countries that caused excessive indebtedness.[21]

What does the future hold for Europe? We note three potential scenarios that will be touched on in Chapter 12. First, the major players in Europe may continue to muddle through with more austerity. But is this the way out of recession and the debt crisis? Contrary to what was expected, debt levels of Portugal, Italy, Ireland, Greece, and Spain have actually *increased* since the imposition of harsh spending cuts. Therefore, Keynesians believe a better approach is pro-growth stimulus spending with shared sacrifice throughout Europe.

Second, things may get worse if Europe cannot find ways to deal with Greece—the supposed "spoiled child" of Europe—and other big borrowers. Greece partially defaulted on its debt in February 2012 and has been debating whether or not to reissue its own currency, the drachma. Between October 2009 and June 2012, Greeks withdrew an estimated €72 billion from banks. Similarly, between July 2011 and July 2012, Spaniards, Portuguese, Irish, and Greeks together took €326 billion ($425 billion) out of local banks, transferring funds to safer accounts in countries such as Germany, France, and Switzerland.[22] So alarmed were EU officials by these slow-motion bank runs (which pundits called "bank jogs") that in June 2012 they privately prepared contingency plans to impose capital controls in the Euro zone and limit the amount people could withdraw from ATM machines. If contagion spreads, some states might withdraw from the euro, or the EMU could totally collapse.

Third, structural weaknesses of EU institutions might be overcome. European policy makers could either try to extend their reach and power or throw in the towel and return to a less-integrated, less-supranational community. The EU has taken some steps to construct a common fiscal policy, at the cost of Euro zone members giving up more sovereignty to the ECB and Brussels.

CONCLUSION: CRISIS, CHOICE, AND CHANGE

In their famous comparative politics reader *Crisis, Choice, and Change*, Gabriel Almond et al. examined how different societies handle occasional crises.[23] A crisis conditions countries' political, economic, and social institutions in unexpected ways, and some handle their crises better than others. Today the world faces a situation that could easily turn into a global catastrophe. In this conclusion, we discuss some potential corrections and courses.

Rebalancing the Global Glut

Many OELs (also known as austerians or deficit hawks) and some HILs (also known as Keynesians) point out that trade-surplus economies should stop holding huge foreign currency reserves as a form of self-insurance against having to turn to the IMF for loans. Countries like China, Japan, and Saudi Arabia should let their currencies appreciate and increase spending and consumption at home.[24] In Europe, Germany could reduce its trade surpluses by either letting inflation rise or pulling out of the Euro zone and letting a new deutschmark appreciate against the euro. Alternatively, many austerians support a withdrawal of Greece from the EMU, as long as it is done in an "orderly" manner, so that the country can devalue its currency and get out of its debt trap with export growth.

The misaligned balance of payments demonstrates that markets do not automatically self-correct. Thus, relying on other countries to underwrite the mounting debt of the United States, Italy, France, and Spain is not sustainable in the long run.

Regulation of the Domestic Economy

Domestic regulation, or lack thereof, contributed to both the Asian, U.S., and European crises. Most OELs argue that states intervened too much in the market. They blame Asian mercantilist states for restricting investments and using industrial policies that picked winners and losers. The Federal Reserve (with the support of two U.S. presidents) dropped interest rates, making it easier for lending agencies to extend reckless amounts of credit. Governments should limit bailout packages, allow banks to fail, and decrease taxes, especially for higher-income groups.

In contrast, Keynesians like Paul Krugman argue that deficit spending gives "more bang for the buck" to the economy than cutting taxes.[25] Krugman also notes that, historically, the level of debt relative to GDP is low in the United States, and it is unlikely inflation will be a big problem in the future provided the economy grows enough to overcome the debt.[26] HILs wish to strengthen regulation and increase *competition*

as a "disciplining force" over banks. To counter rent-seeking and limit risk taking, big banks should be broken up and required to maintain bigger capital reserves to back up their loans. HILs also stress the urgent need to regulate the so-called **shadow banking system**—a collection of credit intermediaries such as hedge funds, private equity groups, and money market funds that use exotic instruments like derivatives and securitization to borrow and invest trillions of dollars.[27]

Structuralists believe more effort should be made to sever close ties between state officials and the banks they are supposed to regulate. As the crisis worsened, bank mergers and acquisitions increased, leaving only five major banks in the United States—a concentration of capital with negative effects on democracy.

Addressing Economic Ideology and Inequality

Because asset bubbles have driven many financial crises, many HILs have insisted on the need for better economic theories that include a human element. Economists should investigate human psychology and the effects of inequality on political legitimacy, rather than limiting their focus to a rational-choice methodology. They should do more empirical work and test their methods in the real world. Castigating the economics discipline for being "isolated from the ordinary business of life," Nobel Prize-winning economist Ronald Coase stresses that "it is suicidal for the field to slide into a hard science of choice, ignoring the influences of society, history, culture, and politics on the working of the economy."[28]

Keynesians believe that globalization can be made to work but that developing countries must protect themselves, at least until they can compete on a more equal footing with the industrialized states. Like mercantilists, many HILs note that China and India did *not* open up to the global financial system as much as others and yet achieved high rates of economic growth by "cherry-picking" the policies that work best for them (see Chapter 13).

If confidence and trust are to be restored in the financial system, the common good cannot be left to markets that have produced rising inequality in Western societies in the last thirty years. The gap between the rich and poor has significantly widened in almost all the OECD countries—with the top 1 percent earning between 11 and 20 percent of all pre-tax income in 2007 in Germany, Canada, Britain, and the United States. To raise tens of billions of dollars to redistribute to the global poor, a number of European leaders are pressing for a "financial transaction tax"—a tiny tax on all trades of stocks, bonds, derivatives, and currencies.

Joseph Stiglitz has made a compelling case that inequality in the United States is causing economic dysfunction, slowing growth, weakening democracy, and undermining the sense of fair play.[29] He argues that the financial industry has become "rent-seeking"—it tends to speculate, evade taxes, and rip people off with fraud and indecipherable fees. Facing stagnant median wages and high debt, the lower and middle classes cannot raise aggregate demand to fuel growth. The key to solving debt and finance crises, then, is to redistribute wealth downward through a progressive tax system.

In Europe, Keynesians see the need for shared sacrifice between the rich and poor, not more hurtful austerity that by October 2012 caused unemployment to rise to 11.6 percent in the Euro zone—and to 23 percent among youth under the age of 25. The European Union's uncommunitarian and short-sighted financial policies are tragically eroding the model of regional cooperation that Europe offered to the world. It's a Greek tragedy, literally and figuratively.

Global Governance

Lack of management at the global level almost certainly did not *cause* the crisis but rather *contributed* to it. While many OELs prefer *less* global governance and more *laissez-faire* globalization, HILs advocate reforms to the IMF and World Bank that allocate more voting power to the BRICs. Many HILs want regional institutions such as the EU and the new G20 to help states coordinate their national stimulus packages. Reformers would like to see the G20's Financial Stability Board supervise and regulate international financial institutions, especially by imposing capital adequacy requirements on banks and reining in derivatives and hedge funds.

As the world moves from monetary crisis to monetary crisis, the IMF is often blamed for making problems worse. But the greater problem is the inability of member states to square domestic interests with global obligations. For example, they would collectively benefit from suppressing tax competition—a dynamic where each state lowers taxes to attract corporate investment and banking activities.

States must determine how to minimize risk taking and speculative bubbles. The classical solution, which Walter Bagehot presented over a hundred years ago, is to designate an international lender of last resort, to lend when no one else will and hold open the "shutting gate" of *torschlusspanik* to stop the panic.[30] It is clear that the IMF is not and cannot be the global lender of last resort. And yet due to the high degree of international interdependence and integration of capital markets, the global governance structure must expand to match market forces or risk the catastrophic collapse of markets as occurred in the 1930s.

Today's international political economy requires a stable and adaptable finance system. Arguably, the principles and policies that produced the shadow of darkness that has beset the world are, paradoxically, the very same ones that policy makers are trying to preserve through economic recovery programs. If Keynes were here, he might see an opportunity to practice politics as the art of the possible. Undoubtedly, he would suggest that we ask whom we believe the economy ought to serve—the rich and powerful or the poor and weak?

KEY TERMS

structural adjustment policies (SAPs)   183
conditionality   184
currency crisis   185
crony capitalism   185

speculative attack   186
subprime mortgage loans   189
sovereign wealth funds   191
credit default swaps   192

Troubled Asset Relief Program (TARP)   193
quantitative easing   194
Volcker rule   196
shadow banking system   203

DISCUSSION QUESTIONS

1. Compare and contrast the different types of debt problems that were discussed in this chapter in terms of (a) the source of the debt, (b) the interests of major actors in each situation, and (c) how the situation was resolved, if it was.
2. Why so much fuss over speculation? Why do you suppose Keynes would be concerned about it today? Use Chapter 7 to help answer this question.
3. Explain the connection between debt that results from borrowing money and the debt associated with a deficit in the balance of payments. Use examples from the readings.
4. What lessons could Europeans learn from previous crises that could help them resolve their own financial crisis?
5. Explain the role of the IMF in helping to solve balance-of-payments crises. Do you feel the IMF could do more? Why? Why not?
6. If you were to write up a brief outline of how to solve current crises, what measures would you emphasize? Explain.

SUGGESTED READINGS

Barry Eichengreen. *Globalizing Capital: A History of the International Monetary System.* Princeton, NJ: Princeton University Press, 1996.

Financial Crisis Inquiry Commission. *The Financial Crisis Inquiry Report.* New York: Public Affairs, 2011.

Joseph Stiglitz. *The Price of Inequality: How Today's Divided Society Endangers Our Future.* New York: W.W. Norton, 2012.

Johan Van Overtheldt, *The End of the Euro: The Uneasy Future of the European Union.* Chicago: Agate Publishing, 2011.

NOTES

1. Kara Scannell and Sudeep Reddy, "Greenspan Admits Errors to Hostile House Panel," *Wall Street Journal*, October 24, 2008.
2. Cordt Schnibben, "Prison of Debt Paralyzes West," *Spiegel Online*, November 16, 2012.
3. For a good overview of the 1980s' debt crisis, see Benjamin J. Cohen, *In Whose Interest?* (New Haven, CT: Yale University Press, 1986); especially Chapter 8, "Latin Debt Storm."
4. Negative real interest rates exist when inflation rates exceed the interest rate over the term of a loan. This benefits the borrower, because loan repayments have lower real value than the amount borrowed.
5. Susan George, *A Fate Worse Than Debt: The World Financial Crisis and the Poor* (Berkeley, CA: Grove Press, 1988).
6. See Carole Collins, Zie Gariyo, and Tony Burdon, "Jubilee 2000: Citizen Action across the North–South Divide," in Michael Edwards and John Gaventa, eds., *Global Citizen Action* (Boulder, CO: Lynne Rienner, 2001).
7. See, for example, David Vines, Pierre-Richard Angenor, and Marcus Miller, *Asian Financial Crisis: Causes, Contagion, and Consequences* (Cambridge: Cambridge University Press, 2004).
8. Paul Krugman, "How Did Economists Get It So Wrong?" *New York Times*, September 3, 2009.

9. For a readable, well-documented history of the IMF's responses to the financial crises in emerging markets, see James M. Boughton, *Tearing Down Walls: The International Monetary Fund 1990–1999* (Washington, D.C.: International Monetary Fund, 2012), at http://www.imf.org/external/pubs/ft /history/2012.

10. Henry Farrell and John Quiggin, "Consensus, Dissensus and Economic Ideas: The Rise and Fall of Keynesianism during the Economic Crisis," March 9, 2012, at http://www.henryfarrell.net/Keynes.pdf.

11. Sheila Bair, *Bull by the Horns: Fighting to Save Main Street from Wall Street and Wall Street from Itself* (New York: Free Press, 2012).

12. Nathaniel Popper, "C.E.O. Pay Is Rising Despite the Din," *New York Times*, June 16, 2012.

13. Simon Johnson and James Kwak, *13 Bankers: The Wall Street Takeover and the Next Financial Meltdown* (New York: Vintage Books, 2011), p. 230.

14. John Nichols and Robert McChesney, *Dollarocracy: How the Money and Media Election Complex Is Destroying America* (New York: Nation Books, 2013).

15. Chris Hedges, "Why the Occupy Movement Frightens the Corporate Elite," *Truthout*, May 14, 2012, at http://truth-out.org/opinion/item/9112-why-the -occupy-movement-frightens-the-corporate-elite.

16. Robert Reich, "Washington Pre-Occupied," *Huffington Post*, November 4, 2011, at http:// www.huffingtonpost.com/robert-reich/occupy -wall-street-inequality-_b_1075775.html.

17. Jesse Bricker et al., "Changes in U.S. Family Finances from 2007 to 2010: Evidence from the Survey of Consumer Finances," *Federal Reserve Bulletin* 98 (June 2012).

18. Francis Fox Piven, "The War against the Poor: Occupy Wall Street and the Politics of Financial Morality" *Truthdig*, November 7, 2011, at http://www.truthdig.com/report/item/the _war_against_the_poor_20111107.

19. Niki Kitsantonis and Rachel Donadio, "Greek Parliament Passes Austerity Plan after Riots Rage," *New York Times*, February 12, 2012.

20. Thomas Wright, "What if Europe Fails?" *The Washington Quarterly* (Summer 2012): pp. 232–241.

21. Andrew Moravcsik, "Europe after the Crisis," *Foreign Affairs* 91 (May/June 2012).

22. Yalman Onaran, "Deposit Flight from Europe Banks Eroding Common Currency," Bloomberg (September 19, 2012), at http://www.bloomberg .com/news/2012-09-18/deposit-flight-from -europe-banks-eroding-common-currency.html.

23. See Gabriel Almond et al., *Crisis, Choice and Change: Historical Studies of Political Development* (Boston, MA: Little Brown, 1973).

24. For a sophisticated discussion of this argument, see Martin Wolf, *Fixing Global Finance* (Baltimore, MD: Johns Hopkins University Press, 2008).

25. See Paul Krugman, "Bang for the Buck (Wonkish)," *New York Times*, January 13, 2009.

26. See Paul Krugman, "Till Debt Does Its Part," *New York Times*, August 28, 2009; and Paul Krugman, "Bad Faith Economics," *New York Times*, January 26, 2009.

27. An excellent overview of shadow banking can be found in Chapter II of Financial Crisis Inquiry Commission, *The Financial Crisis Inquiry Report* (New York: Public Affairs, 2011).

28. Ronald Coase, "Saving Economics from the Economists," *Harvard Business Review* (December 2012).

29. Joseph Stiglitz, *The Price of Inequality: How Today's Divided Society Endangers Our Future* (New York: W.W. Norton, 2012), p. xxii.

30. Walter Bagehot, *Lombard Street: A Description of the Money Market* (Philadelphia, PA: Orion Editions, 1991), p. 8.

The Global Security Structure

Teach the Children: A Spanish peacekeeper at work in Lebanon.

Ali Hashisho/Reuters

If you lived in the United States, Europe, or the Soviet Union during the 1950s or 1960s, you would have seen World War II film clips of Hiroshima and Nagasaki. You feared that an atom bomb like those dropped on the two Japanese cities would vaporize you in the blink of an eye. This fear heightened during the 1962 Cuban Missile Crisis, when the United States and U.S.S.R. stood "eyeball to eyeball," threatening to use nuclear weapons if their demands were not met.[1] Ultimately, they chose not to use military force. Why? Realists argue that both superpowers anticipated how the use of any military force could easily lead to nuclear war and heavy costs—lives lost and economies damaged. Also, some realists believe that the **bipolar** distribution of wealth and power compelled both nations.

Later, officials and military experts from both superpowers informally accepted the strategic doctrine of **Mutually Assured Destruction (MAD)**, which meant that living under the sword of Damocles (threat of nuclear war) was *acceptable* to both countries as long as both were deterred (i.e., prevented) from initiating a nuclear war.[2] After the Vietnam War, they reached agreements that included limits on the number of weapons in their strategic nuclear arsenals, which helped to further stabilize their political relationship.

The case of the Cuban Missile Crisis highlights five important aspects of the global security structure that correspond to the major topics covered in this chapter. First, since World War II, **realism** has been the most popular outlook applied by academics and security policy makers who address war and peace. Yet, as we explain, other IPE perspectives provide a more comprehensive explanation of security issues. For instance, as structuralists argue, the presence of Soviet missiles in Cuba threatened the U.S. imperial-capitalist domain in the Western Hemisphere.

Second, for better or for worse, realism still influences how major powers' officials and international organizations (IOs) manage Susan Strange's fourth global structure—one we label the **global cyber security structure**. For the purpose of analysis, we define this arrangement as a web of formal treaties, conventions, protocols and other informal rules and norms meant to protect people all over the world from violent and nonviolent threats and actions. Its major players include nation-states, IOs, nongovernmental organizations (NGOs), transnational corporations (TNCs), and other public and private officials who work directly or indirectly on national and international security issues.

Third, U.S. administrations have pursued security policies unilaterally (regardless of allied support) and multilaterally (in cooperation with others). They have either benefited from or sought to construct bipolar, **multipolar**, and **unipolar** configurations of power.

Fourth, today's global security structure agenda reflects a major transformation away from the military-oriented **Cold War** (1947–1991) bipolar security structure to a much broader security agenda of the Obama administration, pursuant to a multipolar systemic order.

Fifth, recent U.S. administrations have increasingly incorporated into the security agenda nontraditional security interests of weaker and poorer states, such as poverty, income inequality, environmental damage, climate change, and immigration. A growing number of IOs, NGOs, and other actors now share the management of a much more fragmented global configuration of wealth and power.

The major arguments we make in this chapter about the new global cyber security structure are the following:

- Realism continues to have a good deal of explanatory power. However, other perspectives provide a more complete understanding of many global security problems.
- Whereas during the Cold War the major threats to national (territorial) security were largely nuclear and conventional weapons, today the major powers are increasingly focused on cyber-based weapons like drones.

- An increasing number of nontraditional security questions such as immigration, the environment, and illicit activities have seeped up from poorer nations to complicate security issues for major powers more than ever before.
- On a day-to-day basis, people in developing nations cannot adjust to these security issues as easily as people in industrialized nations can.
- The major powers will likely continue to intervene in developing countries to fight terrorism, develop natural resources like oil and natural gas, and protect TNC investments.
- However, many major powers are only willing to play a minor role in coordinating the global security structure. They are also not likely to give more authority to other actors, leaving IOs, NGOs, and others without the authority and resources necessary to manage the global security structure.

REALISM LIVES ON: CLASSICAL REALISTS Vs. NEOREALISTS

For nearly seventy years, realism has been the dominant paradigm of state and military officials, and academics, who address national and international security issues. Realists have tended to frame problems in terms of a hierarchy of states based on military power that determines the likelihood of survival against external threats. Since the end of World War II in 1945, the United States has topped the hierarchy of powerful states, along with Great Britain, France, and Russia, who have large conventional (land, air, and sea) and nuclear capabilities. Below we discuss how these major powers endow U.N. agencies, the **North Atlantic Treaty Organization (NATO)**, and other IOs with the authority and capital resources to use force in today's global security structure. Relatively weaker states, lower on the power hierarchy, have included Denmark, Sweden, Italy, Japan, and emerging countries such as Brazil, China, and India. Often, the soldiers of these minor powers are members of U.N. peacekeeping missions and other security forces organized by the major powers.

At the bottom of the hierarchy are weak developing nations burdened with problems such as poverty, hunger, refugees, immigrants, epidemic diseases, and environmental damage. In these states, massive poverty exacerbates tensions between ethnic and religious communities, which often result in human rights violations and genocide, such as the conflict between the Tutsis and the Hutus in Rwanda, or the ethnic tensions among Balkan nations in Eastern Europe. U.N. peacekeeping forces and NGOs such as Amnesty International play active roles at this level. A prominent issue for many of these states is the continued interest (some call it interference) by major powers for supposed security reasons connected to oil exploration and production, counterterrorism, and TNC investments.

Just as with other IPE perspectives, variations in realist thought have important implications for explaining and solving security problems. Events like the Cuban Missile Crisis can be framed by two different versions of realism: **classical realism** and **neorealism**. Classical realism is rooted in the ideas of Thucydides, Machiavelli, Hobbes, and more recently George Kennan and Hans Morgenthau, who emphasize how and why individuals and political institutions acquire power that determines nation-state survival.[3] Classical realists assume the following:

- State survival depends on the power to organize and control armed forces so as to defend institutions, territory, skies, and people.
- No two states have the same national interests, which is the foundation of conflict in the global security structure.
- The drive for security *always* trumps ideological principles and motives.
- Power is thought of primarily in terms of military capabilities and is used to get another state to do something it would not do otherwise, especially in state defense.
- Military tools are the most powerful in the state's arsenal. The economy, particularly industrial capacity, is also important, but not as critical.
- The international security structure conditions, but *does not always determine,* state behavior as much as the *choices and decisions* of security agencies and national leaders.
- State leaders think strategically and often make mistakes or misperceive a situation.
- War is often a *choice* of state leaders, made to readjust the **balance of power** or to establish a new configuration of power.
- Peace can result from cooperative efforts by states and should not be imposed on other states by a single hegemon. Imperial powers become the enemy of all others.

For classical realists, the first and second levels of analysis are more important than the international and global levels of analysis (see Chapter 1). For example, President John F. Kennedy and Attorney General Robert Kennedy did not feel compelled to resort to war and instead chose to "think outside the box" when it came to resolving the Cuban Missile Crisis.

Neorealists criticize classical realists for oversimplifying the motives of states and decision makers—portraying them as cyclically struggling for power, for the sake of power, and to enhance state security. Neorealists put more emphasis on the third- and fourth-level structural features of the security structure and how they condition state and individual behavior.[4] Neorealists generally assume the following:

- The global security structure lacks a single sovereign, which *compels* states to make security their primary objective.
- Because sovereign states can use force whenever they want to, the *absolute security* of any state cannot be guaranteed.
- Each of the 200-plus states in the international system today is a unitary and rational actor.
- Much of what happens *inside* a nation-state's domestic black box is too difficult to theorize about scientifically.
- A change in the global security structure comes with a shift in state power capabilities.

If Kenneth Waltz were to explain the Cuban Missile Crisis, he would suggest that the structural condition of bipolarity forced the superpowers to act out roles assigned to them in the security order. The number of weapons and other hard power indicators are the best indicators of state capabilities. The *relative equality*

A Selected Chronology of Security Developments after World War II

1945	The United Nations Charter signed in San Francisco. United States drops atomic bombs on Hiroshima and Nagasaki; Japan surrenders.
1947–90	The Cold War between the United States and the U.S.S.R.
1949	The U.S.S.R. detonates first A-bomb. NATO created. Communist forces take over China. Bipolarity hardens.
1950–53	The Korean War. Bipolarity becomes entrenched.
1955	The Warsaw Pact created.
1956	Soviets crush the Hungarian revolution.
1962	The Cuban Missile Crisis. The strategic doctrine of MAD becomes entrenched.
1964	United States deploys combat forces in Vietnam.
1968	Soviets suppress dissents in Czechoslovakia. Tet offensive in South Vietnam. Bipolarity weakening.
1972	The United States and U.S.S.R. enter into détente (peaceful coexistence). The SALT I and ABM treaties signed.
1973–74	OPEC raises the price of oil. Energy becomes major security issue. The Third World takes on new significance.
1978	China begins economic reforms. The second OPEC oil crisis begins.
1979	The U.S.S.R. invades Afghanistan. Détente derailed. The Shah of Iran is overthrown and Ayatollah Khomeini comes to power. U.S. embassy employees taken hostage in Iran.
1981	U.S. hostages in Iran released after President Reagan's inauguration.
1983	The United States invades Grenada to rescue medical students and overthrow pro-socialist government.
1984	All major arms control agreements between the United States and U.S.S.R. halted.
1987	The United States, U.S.S.R., and their allies agree to reduce the number of offensive weapons deployed in Europe. START I talks continue.
1989	The United States invades Panama. The Berlin Wall is penetrated.
1990	Iraq invades Kuwait. The globalization campaign takes off. The U.S.S.R. disintegrates. War breaks out in the Balkans.
1991	The Persian Gulf War. The United States heads a UN-sanctioned force to liberate Kuwait.
1992	The United States leads multilateral forces' intervention in Somalia on a humanitarian mission, which turns into a military mission. President Clinton withdraws U.S. forces in 1993.
1993	UN Secretary General Boutros Boutros-Ghali asks for command of a UN military force outside state control.
1994	Genocide in Rwanda. The UN fails to effectively respond.
1992	Fighting breaks out between Serbs, Croats, and Muslims in former Yugoslavia.
1999	NATO forces intervene in Kosovo.
2001	9/11 terrorist attacks on Twin Towers in New York and Pentagon in Washington, D.C. UN and U.S. Senate authorize US–NATO intervention in Afghanistan.

(continued)

2001	President Bush pulls the United States out of both the Kyoto and ABM treaties.
2003	UN-approved, U.S.-led coalition invades Iraq.
2007	The global financial crisis begins in the United States
2010	U.S. forces begin withdrawal from Iraq. Four nuclear power plants in Fukushima, Japan, melt down after being stuck by an earthquake/tsunami. The Arab Spring begins in Tunisia and quickly spreads to Egypt and other countries in the Middle East.
2011	The Libyan uprising begins. Colonel Qaddafi is driven from office.
2012	The Syrian uprising turns into a civil war.

of the power of the United States and U.S.S.R. deterred the use of nuclear weapons; the states acted rationally when they saved both themselves and the state system.

Classical realists would respond that the neorealist perspective has two deficiencies. First, it overlooks the role of individual actors. Second, it does not question the security structure's constraints or permanency. Actors are assumed to *perceive* and *interpret* the significance of other states' actions or capabilities in predictable ways. Yet, as we discuss later, some states and individual actors have attempted to *change* the number of major powers in the security order, which demonstrates that the structure itself does not condition actor behavior as much as it is assumed to.

These theoretical issues have many practical consequences for the global security structure today. A classical realist might inquire as to the motives of former president George W. Bush and his **neoconservative** advisors in war. To neorealists, President Bush did *not* have much choice but to attack Afghanistan and Iraq due to the 9/11 attacks. Classical realists wonder if the Bush administration might have adopted other goals and means to accomplish the same objectives. And President Obama? Has his administration been oriented toward unilateralism, like its predecessors, or multilateralism? Should the United States take up the mantle of an imperial power, promoting unipolarity the way the Bush administration did, and as the economic historian Niall Ferguson suggests it should?[5] If not, what polar order fits the world's distribution of both wealth and military power? We explore these and other political economy questions in this chapter.

THE EARLY COLD WAR SECURITY STRUCTURE

Many classical realist-oriented political historians and political scientists place the origins of the Cold War in the fact that most of Europe and large parts of Asia lay in ruins after World War II. As the British and French empires were crumbling, a power vacuum opened up between the United States and the Soviet Union. The two hegemons had sharply contrasting ideologies (democracy vs. communism) and economic systems (capitalism vs. socialism). Did the Cold War have to occur? Yes, according to many neorealists—there was no alternative; differences between the two hegemons formed a stage upon which the actors knew all their lines. Alternatively, Daniel Yergin argues in his well-documented book *Shattered Peace* that the two hegemons could have prevented the Cold War.[6] Soon after 1945, the

United States faced the choice of either negotiating with the Soviets to pull out of Eastern Europe or sending U.S. troops back into Europe to force them out, an unacceptable political choice for a war-weary nation. Later, the Soviets retreated from Greece, Iran, and Austria without confrontation.

Thereafter, the two superpowers mirrored each other in ways that entrenched bipolarity and organized their political, economic, and military alliances. In 1949, the United States formed a military alliance with Western Europe and Canada— NATO. In 1952 the Soviet Union organized the Warsaw Pact alliance with Central and Eastern European socialist states. In the tight bipolar security structure of the Eisenhower years, in zero-sum fashion each superpower also tried to create political and ideological "spheres of influence" among independent developing nations that detracted from the power and influence of the other hegemon in various regions of the world.

Despite the U.S. monopoly on nuclear weapons until 1949, when the Soviet Union detonated its first atomic weapon, the Soviets refused to withdraw from Eastern Europe. U.S. atomic weapons did not deter the U.S.S.R. from helping North Korea attack South Korea in 1950 either. President Truman worried that anything but a conventional response to North Korea's attack could lead to the use of atomic weapons by the Soviet Union. He organized a United Nations peacekeeping effort to defend South Korea. Likewise, the ever-growing number of Soviet atomic weapons did not stop the United States from intervening in Central and Latin America, the Middle East, and Southeast Asia.

Given the limited military and political utility of nuclear weapons, the United States *accepted* Soviet hegemony over Eastern Europe and *intentionally shifted* its focus to deterring an invasion of Western Europe by threatening the Soviets with massive (nuclear) retaliation if there were such an attack. Until the mid-1960s, the primary U.S. strategic objective was to stay ahead of the Soviet Union in the production of nuclear weapons and strategic (long range) platforms such as B-52 bombers, nuclear submarines, and short- to long-range intercontinental ballistic missiles (ICBMs).

To U.S. and Soviet officials, the Korean War produced two informal rules. First, do not directly engage the forces of the other hegemon because it could generate total war between the superpowers. Second, conflict with your opponent's surrogate should not escalate into nuclear war. These lessons apply to U.S. intervention in Vietnam and to the Soviet Union's intervention in Afghanistan in the 1980s.

Interestingly, noted historian and diplomat George Kennan, whose ideas about "containment" shaped U.S. foreign policy objectives after 1946, severely criticized U.S. policy makers for their unilateral decision to promote a military buildup to solve the essentially political problem of what to do about Berlin and Eastern Europe. This development led to a preoccupation with Soviet capabilities and ideology in an arms race that only engendered more fear—even paranoia—in officialdom and the public.

JFK, the Cuban Missile Crisis, and the Entrenchment of Bipolarity

John F. Kennedy took office in 1961 promising to take a harder stand against international communism than Eisenhower and to close the supposed gap between U.S. and Soviet nuclear capabilities. But he green-lighted a botched, CIA-sponsored invasion of Cuba by anti-Castro patriots at the Bay of Pigs that humiliated the United States. Not long thereafter, Kennedy was eager to restore American resolve and reputation. The opportunity came when the Soviet Union upset the bipolar balance of power by placing medium-range missiles in Cuba, just 90 miles from Florida. Unexpectedly, the president chose *not* to take his military advisers' recommendations to invade Cuba and attack Soviet missile sites. Instead, he ordered a naval blockade of Soviet ships moving missiles into Cuba. This left the Soviets with the choice of risking nuclear war by running the blockade or standing down and looking weak. The tense standoff only ended when the Soviets agreed to remove missiles from Cuba in exchange for a U.S. pledge to remove missiles from Turkey.

The Cuban Missile Crisis impacted the international security structure in important ways. It seemed to confirm the absurdity of MAD; how could each superpower maintain the capability to knock out its opponent's weapons while assuring the opponent that it did not intend to use its weapons? This absurdity became the basis of Stanley Kubrick's classic, darkly comical film, *Dr. Strangelove*. Moreover, many people found the idea of planning to kill millions of human beings morally repugnant, even if the purpose was to deter an enemy from attacking first. Nevertheless, the crisis lent theoretical and political support for the concept of MAD as a basis of further stabilizing U.S.-Soviet relations. It was clear that Soviet strategic weapons capabilities would soon catch up to U.S. nuclear capabilities. Bipolarity had helped lock the superpowers into an arms race, but MAD made it clear that no rational leader on either side would start a war if the costs of engagement outweighed the gains. As a result, the superpowers agreed to limit defense expenditures and cooperate for the sake of enhancing deterrence and co-managing the bipolar security structure.

The Vietnam War and the Road to Multipolarity

To stop the spread of communism in Vietnam and the rest of Indochina, President Lyndon Johnson sent U.S. troops into South Vietnam in 1964, where they stayed until 1973. Although U.S. forces prevailed in many battles, their reliance on conventional forces and tactics like "search and destroy," as well as the high cost of the war in terms of dead servicemen and defense expenditures, would not produce a *political* victory in South Vietnam.[7] As in the case of Korea, political considerations such as North Vietnam's close relations with the Soviet Union and China prevented the United States from using nuclear weapons (which it did consider). Classical realists Kennan and Morgenthau argued that fighting in Vietnam was *not* in the U.S. national interest.

The United States had again staked its fortunes in terms of a military victory rather than resolving a political issue—a country's division. Johnson withdrew his nomination for president in the 1968 campaign, frustrated that "a damn pissant country" could thwart the United States. In 1969, President Nixon bombed parts of Cambodia to try to turn the tide in Vietnam, but he ended up widening the war and weakening the United States' image as the strongest nation in the world. After the war, the Vietnam Syndrome connoted the reluctance of the United States to intervene in weaker, underdeveloped countries like Vietnam unless quick victory was assured without high loss of lives or expenditures.

Nixon's National Security Adviser Henry Kissinger believed that the international security order had shifted away from bipolarity to multipolarity due to the redistribution of economic power that came with the recovery of Western Europe and Japan after World War II and the rapid growth of countries such as South Korea. Modeled on the European concert of power in the nineteenth century, the major powers in the changing order included the United States, the Soviet Union, Japan, Western Europe (as a bloc), and China. For Kissinger, multipolarity required that a *proactive* and contemplative hegemon (the United States) lead in the cooperative management of a variety of increasingly interrelated political, economic, and security issues. Shuttle diplomacy was also required to make multilateralism work, which kept Kissinger busily moving between national capitals to make sure leaders were on the same page.

By 1973, arms control negotiations between the two superpowers became crucial to maintaining rough parity in nuclear weapons and stability in U.S.-Soviet relations. The superpowers started talks on the first Strategic Arms Limitations Treaty (SALT). At Kissinger's urging, Nixon accepted détente (peaceful coexistence) with the Soviet Union, which resulted in grain sales and cultural exchanges. The two sides also informally agreed to not interfere in developing nations in the other's sphere of influence.

Japan's rising wealth, growing share of global trade, and proximity to both North Korea and China made it a major player in the new security structure. Additionally, as Western Europe integrated its economies and political systems, it acted as a single major power. Kissinger convinced Nixon to open up relations with China to promote interdependence between the two countries and to use Beijing as a counterweight to Moscow. Meanwhile, nuclear proliferation emerged as another international security issue when China, India, Pakistan, and Israel began to acquire nuclear weapons.

More so than anything else in the early 1970s, the oil crisis of 1973–1974 triggered by the Organization of Petroleum Exporting Countries (OPEC) destabilized the international security structure. Suddenly, the oil-rich developing countries had a "weapon" against industrialized countries that were dependent on oil imports. OPEC raised the price of oil dramatically, causing a major international recession; unsurprisingly, the U.S. contingency plan was to take over Middle Eastern oil fields. Resource dependency raised awareness of international economic interdependence, which in turn paved the way for many developing nations to play a bigger role in the international political economy. As we discuss in Chapter 11, the G-77 countries called for a new international economic order. Many experts began to reframe the relationship of the developed and developing nations in terms of a North–South conflict. In sum, OPEC tightened the connections between international politics and economies during the 1970s and further loosened bipolarity by weakening U.S. hegemony, contributing to the emergence of more centers of power in the Third World.

Human Rights and "The Hell of Good Intentions"

In 1977, President Jimmy Carter explicitly tried to move away from a realist orientation in U.S. foreign policy toward an idealism whose hallmarks were the promotion of human rights and improved relations with developing nations. Carter insisted that human rights should be a security issue in the United Nations. The problem was how to make human rights work as a foreign policy tool without compromising U.S. security interests. As political scientist Stanley Hoffmann famously wrote, the danger was that human rights would turn into "the hell of good intentions."[8] Four tough issues shaped the global security order during Carter's administration:

- The increasing sophistication of nuclear weapons
- The second oil crisis of 1978–1979
- The Soviet intervention in Afghanistan
- The Iranian revolution

Multiple independently targeted vehicles (MIRVs) capable of striking both an opponent's defensive and offensive nuclear weapons complicated arms control and weakened MAD. Hard-line realists argued that the Soviets might be more likely to preemptively launch a nuclear first strike. The president responded to a second oil crisis in 1978 with efforts to decrease U.S. dependence on Middle Eastern oil, including by imposing energy efficiency measures on the nation. In 1979, the Soviets invaded Afghanistan to support their client regime. Carter threatened to not send the SALT II agreement to the Senate for approval if they did not leave; they did not. Détente was derailed. Carter's National Security Adviser Zbigniew Brzezinski was proven right; the Soviets could not be trusted. Carter again looked weak when Islamic revolutionaries drove the Shah of Iran from power in 1979 and took U.S. embassy officials hostage for 444 days.

Reagan and the Cold War Redux

As Ronald Reagan was sworn in as president in 1980, Iran released the U.S. hostages. Reagan "rode high in the saddle" to "make America proud once again." He intended to reclaim U.S. military, economic, and political supremacy over the U.S.S.R. Labeling the Soviet Union as the "evil empire," his administration also intentionally sought to *reimpose* a bipolar framework on the international security structure. The "cowboy" president was strongly influenced by many hardcore, anti-communist advisors. In reaction to a buildup and modernization of Soviet forces, the United States modernized its own nuclear arsenal of submarines and ICBM MX "peacekeepers." NATO and the Warsaw Pact nations both modernized their medium- and short-range nuclear weapons in Europe. By 1984, all arms control talks with the Soviet Union ceased.

In his second term, Reagan did an about-face and developed a personal friendship with Premier Mikhail Gorbachev that resulted in a series of new arms control agreements. Reagan personally hated the idea of MAD. He intended to take care of the "assured destruction" part of MAD by developing a Star Wars program—a space-based defensive system to knock out long-range strategic weapons before they could reach orbit. Because the plan intimidated the Soviets, he even offered the Soviets a system of their own.

Another goal for Reagan was overcoming the Vietnam Syndrome. The Reagan Doctrine of support for anti-communists led to U.S. intervention in

Grenada; proactive support for pro-Western authoritarian regimes in Nicaragua, El Salvador, and Guatemala; and weapons shipments to anti-communist forces in Afghanistan and Angola. According to the Center for Strategic and Budgetary Assessments defense spending, urged on by defense industry lobbyists, hit a peak of $456.5 billion in 1987 (in projected 2005 dollars), compared with $325.1 billion in 1980.

Economic liberals praised Reagan for supporting capitalism and democracy in developing nations, which, in effect, laid the groundwork for globalization. Since the Reagan administration, the neoliberal policies of the IMF, the WTO, and the World Bank have often served as instruments to achieve various U.S. economic and political objectives. Commitments to open borders, free trade, floating exchange rates, capital mobility, and the magic of the market's invisible hand were meant to help grow the economies of many LDCs—and as a side benefit, enhance U.S. security. Most successful were the East and Southeast Asian economies, which opened up trade and investment opportunities for U.S. businesses.

On the other hand, most structuralists despised the Reagan administration, and argued that neoimperialist policies generated more poverty, labor exploitation, and environmental damage. Reagan's policies were directly responsible for nonconventional wars and conflicts in the developing world. His actions were also seen as concentrating power in the White House by undermining the very democratic principles that his administration claimed to promote in the rest of the world.[9]

THE POST-COLD WAR CONFIGURATION OF POWER

The end of the Cold War opened up channels for economics to play a greater role in security issues. Neorealist John Mearsheimer predicted that we would "soon miss the Cold War" because it had provided a measure of order and purposeful management during a reasonably stable and *relatively* peaceful phase in the history of global security.[10] For Mearsheimer, the collapse of the Soviet Union in 1991 was the watershed event that broke the backbone of the Cold War security structure. In contrast to Reagan, President George Bush (senior) adopted a multilateral approach to the U.S. role in the world. He sent U.S. troops into Somalia as part of a UN peacekeeping mission to deal with starvation and hunger. He also envisioned a bigger role for UN peacekeeping forces in other international security issues as part of what he called a "new world order."

While some realist academics and officials at the time believed that with the Soviet Union out of the way, the United States should capitalize on the opportunity to act unilaterally as a benevolent global hegemon promoting capitalism and democracy everywhere,[11] others argued that the security system was moving toward multipolarity. After Saddam Hussein invaded Kuwait in 1990, Bush persuaded the UN to sanction a U.S.-led multilateral force to liberate Kuwait during the so-called Gulf War. On other issues, Bush was not multilateral in his outlook. For example, he did not support the 1992 Rio Summit that linked economic development to environmental damage.

The Clinton administration viewed the international distribution of power as multipolar, and emphasized cooperation with allies and the use of nonmilitary instruments to deal with "competitors" (as opposed to "enemies") like China and Russia. Clearly fearing the Vietnam Syndrome, Clinton withdrew U.S. forces from Somalia and supported the deployment of UN peacekeepers in places like Bosnia and Haiti. In the Balkans crisis, the United States played a backseat role to European efforts to deal with the situation. Only in Kosovo in 1999 did U.S. forces become directly involved in confronting the Serbian military. The Clinton administration also maintained draconian sanctions on Iraq and militarily enforced no-fly zones over northern and southern Iraq. After terrorist strikes on U.S. embassies in Kenya and Sudan, it launched cruise missiles against suspected terrorist sites in Sudan and Afghanistan.

As noted in previous chapters, Clinton strongly supported international organizations such as the IMF, the World Bank, and the new World Trade Organization (WTO). He worked hard to gain Senate ratification of the NAFTA and WTO agreements. The United States benefited from a relatively open and minimally regulated global economy that complemented its security objectives within the emerging global security structure. Once again, structuralists were quick to point out that the industrialized nations' neoimperialism and neocolonialism—masquerading as globalization—caused violent conflicts in developing regions of the world. The integration of global markets, they claimed, compounded security problems such as famine, poor health, corruption, environmental damage, and human rights abuses in Southeast Asia, the Middle East, Latin America, and Africa.[12]

By the start of the new millennium, integrated financial markets and neoliberal policies had precipitated a major redistribution of global wealth that weakened U.S. (hegemonic) power. First, globalization enhanced the competitiveness of emerging countries that capitalized on increased access to U.S. and European markets. Second, reductions in U.S. foreign aid and increased use of sanctions often engendered hostility toward the United States and its allies because of the impact on the poorest people in targeted countries. Third, the United States continued to accumulate debt that was financed by investments from trade-surplus countries, thereby over-stretching the U.S. economy and severely weakening its "empire."[13]

George W. Bush: Unipolarity and the Neorealist Nightmare

The terrorist attacks on New York's twin towers and the Pentagon on September 11, 2001, propelled the Bush administration to pursue a unipolar global security structure. Muslim extremism replaced communism as the archenemy of the United States. Accordingly, the new Bush Doctrine proclaimed that the United States would preemptively attack countries that harbored terrorists or that looked as if they might attempt to harm the United States. On October 7, 2001, the United States and some of its NATO allies invaded Afghanistan, quickly driving much of the Taliban that was protecting Osama bin Laden and al-Qaeda into the hills of Eastern Afghanistan and Pakistan.

The Bush administration then immediately turned its attention to removing Saddam Hussein from power in Iraq, a goal many neoconservatives had in mind even before Bush took office. The administration received approval from both the U.S. Congress and the UN Security Council to use force against Iraq if Hussein did not allow UN inspections for possible **weapons of mass destruction (WMD)**.

When some of the strongest NATO members objected to the threat of war against Iraq, Secretary of Defense Rumsfeld paternalistically labeled France and Germany as "old Europe." On March 19, 2003, the U.S. and a new "coalition" of forces (mainly Eastern European) invaded Iraq under the guise of finding WMD.

Many classical realists had viewed the 9/11 attacks as acts of terrorism—not a declaration of war against the United States.[14] They took issue with the administration's global hegemonic outlook and belief that the United States was "chosen by God" to lead a moral crusade to save the rest of the world from terrorists. The war in Iraq did not go well due to unexpectedly strong resistance from insurgent groups, including ex-Baathists, foreign fighters, and Sunni and Shia militias. The United States relied heavily on private military contractors (PMCs) to supplement the relatively small U.S. force, a costly move due to PMC propensity to shoot first and ask questions later.[15] As in the Vietnam War, U.S. leaders misidentified the true nature of the threat, adopted an inappropriate joint military-political strategy to "win the war," and failed to develop a coherent nation-building plan.

By 2006, the Iraq War had become a quagmire, if not a fiasco. U.S. unilateralism had alienated coalition partners who began refusing to lend any more financial assistance, troops, or diplomatic support in either Iraq or Afghanistan. Especially problematic was the sectarian violence between Sunis, Shiites, and Kurds, along with Iran's growing influence. Reports that Iraqi males were interrogated and tortured in prisons such as Abu Ghraib damaged U.S. prestige, as did the subjection of suspected al-Qaeda and Taliban militants in Guantanamo Bay, Cuba, to waterboarding and other practices illegal under the Geneva Convention. The United States was also condemned for carrying out rendition—transferring suspected terrorists to places like Egypt and Eastern Europe where laws against torture were ignored and access to the Red Cross was denied.[16]

At the same time, the Bush administration rejected multilateralism after 9/11 by withdrawing from the long-standing 1972 **Antiballistic Missile (ABM) Treaty,** which outlawed the development of space-based missile defense systems. Against Russia's protests, the administration proposed deploying a new version of Reagan's National Missile Defense (NMD) program aimed at destroying incoming ballistic missiles. The United States also irked allies by withdrawing support for the Kyoto Treaty (see Chapter 20) and the International Criminal Court, and by hesitating to support new efforts to enforce the Biological Weapons Treaty of 1972.

Between 2007 and 2008, the Bush administration sent 30,000 more U.S. troops to Iraq as part of a "surge" to reverse deteriorating security conditions. NATO added a paltry 5,000 troops. In an effort to reduce the number of coalition soldiers killed or wounded, the Pentagon began using the **Joint Special Operations Command** (JSOC) for "targeted killings" of suspected terrorists. Comprised primarily of Green Berets, Army Rangers, and Navy Seals, the JSOC sends small groups on commando raids and uses drones for surveillance and airstrikes.

Were these unilateral actions appropriate responses to 9/11? To many classical realists, President Bush tried to construct a security structure that was inappropriate for the twenty-first century. Many realist-mercantilists, HILs, and structuralists agreed that when the Bush administration left office in early 2009, the United States was losing much of its real power like an engine dripping oil.

As in Vietnam, the U.S. military was ill-suited to fighting prolonged guerrilla wars—especially in urban areas. The wars in Afghanistan and Iraq also increased U.S. budget deficits and debt, something former Vice-President Dick Cheney once commented did not matter, on the cusp of the global financial crisis of 2007. So outsized were Washington's hegemonic ambitions and so overstretched was the U.S. economy that the United States ironically depended on China's purchases of U.S. treasuries to help finance the wars.

Structuralists argue that the United States intended to dominate Iraq's oil industry and establish a deep "footprint" in the Middle East. In *The Sorrows of Empire*, Chalmers Johnson asserts that the United States already has an empire in 700-plus military installations and numerous troops it maintains all over the world.[17] For Johnson, the source of U.S. imperial behavior is a "military–industrial complex" that needs to sell military arms and sustain massive U.S. defense spending. Congressional committees, Pentagon agencies, and private arms manufacturers have orchestrated a "feeding frenzy" over newer weapons and technology, often reinforcing tensions or negative views of an enemy to justify sales. In 2011, the United States sold a record $66 billion in weapons overseas—that is, three-fourths of global sales—with more than 80 percent sold to developing countries.[18]

Journalists Dana Priest and William Arkin reveal how 9/11 caused a dramatic proliferation of U.S. intelligence agencies and 2,000 companies that collect and analyze information about terrorists worldwide. Employing well-paid D.C. lobbyists, private security and intelligence companies have won many profitable government contracts. PMCs formerly in Iraq and still in Afghanistan include Xe (formerly Blackwater), Lockheed Martin, Halliburton, KBR, DynCorp, and Triple Canopy.[19]

Obama and the Light Footprint

In his first four years in office, Barack Obama pursued foreign policies that reflected a mixture of President Carter's idealism, Clinton's multilateralism, and Bush's militaristic unilateralism to achieve a variety of security objectives. He worked with Russia to cut the number of strategic nuclear weapons and halt the proliferation of WMD. He negotiated with Iran and North Korea to allow the IAEA to inspect their nuclear-processing facilities. Surprisingly, the Nobel Committee granted him the Nobel Peace Prize in 2009 for his "extraordinary efforts to strengthen international diplomacy and cooperation between peoples."

Yet when it came to tracking down terrorists, Obama became the sheriff George Bush only imaged himself to be. Upon the advice of General David Petraeus and the neocon Secretary of Defense Robert Gates, Obama in 2009 ordered his own surge of 30,000 more U.S. troops into Afghanistan to "finish the job." NATO contributed 5,000 more troops. His strategy de-emphasized conventional counterinsurgency operations and focused on winning the "hearts and minds" of the Afghan people.

As we write in the fall of 2012, the surge in Afghanistan is coming to an end. The administration and the American public have become disillusioned with Afghan state corruption, allied troop losses, and mounting expenses. Political instability has increased, raising doubts about the trustworthiness of Afghan leaders and their chances for survival, let alone for promoting democracy. The U.S. military plans to cease leading operations before 2015.

In his book *Confront and Conceal,* *New York Times* reporter David Sanger describes how Obama's strategic thinking and decision-making capabilities have shaped his policies toward Afghanistan and other conflicts around the world.[20] Since the beginning of his administration, Obama has faced pressure to square the need for cuts in defense spending with the desire to keep the United States in a global leadership position. His solution has been to mix unilateral and multilateral approaches and use a more selective range of weapons. According to Sanger, "When confronted with a direct threat to American security, Obama has shown he is willing to act unilaterally—in a targeted, get-in-and-get-out fashion, that at all costs, avoids the kind of messy ground wars and lengthy occupations that have drained America's treasury and spirit for the past decades."[21]

The **Obama doctrine** relies on a "light footprint" in contrast to Bush's heavy footprint. The administration believes that conventional military solutions to terrorism are increasingly inappropriate in war-torn, fragmented nations like Afghanistan, Sudan, Mali, and Somalia. Moreover, Obama has felt pressed to reduce the number of American casualties and trim defense expenditures during the recovery from the financial crisis. Therefore, he has relied on drones, joint strike forces, and an assortment of offensive and defensive cyber tools. Another potential weapon is the so-called **"bunker buster"** that many believe was designed with North Korea's and Iran's nuclear facilities in mind. It would drop a heavy conventional warhead at high speed to knock out a deep underground installation with the destructive force of a nuclear warhead—literally leaving a deep footprint in the earth!

Drones and Joint Strike Forces

Drones—small aircraft also called **unmanned aerial vehicles (UAVs)**—are used for aerial reconnaissance, taking out suspected terrorists with guided missiles, patrolling U.S. borders, and domestic law enforcement. In 2011, the CIA and the U.S. military carried out hundreds of covert drone strikes in at least six countries: Afghanistan, Yemen, Iraq, Somalia, Pakistan, and Libya. Between 2005 and September 2012, roughly 2,700 people were killed from drone strikes in Pakistan alone. When strikes have killed innocent citizens—as they routinely do—the Pakistani government has insisted that the United States end the strikes altogether. U.S. drones have also been deployed in the Seychelles, the Arab Peninsula, and across South Asia and Africa. Recently, drones helped gather intelligence for the raid on Osama bin Laden's compound in Pakistan and pinpointed targets for NATO jet strikes in Libya—including one that hit Colonel Muammar el-Qaddafi's convoy shortly before his death in October 2011.

A number of factors have contributed to the increasing popularity of drones. First, nine years in Afghanistan and Iraq wore out U.S. and allied troops. Repeated tours, brain injuries, high suicide rates, and sexual violence have taken a toll on military personnel. The use of drones decreases the number of troops needed on the ground and limits collateral damage. Second, in the face of the financial crisis, they help reduce military expenditures. Third, many leaders and some in the public view them as the perfect weapon for taking out "evildoers lurking in the global badlands."[22] However, as discussed in the box The Ethics of a Joystick Warrior, recent controversy about the ethics of using drones has grown.

The Obama administration has made U.S. Joint Special Force Operations (JSFO) another important weapon in the campaign against terrorists. Using drones

THE ETHICS OF A JOYSTICK WARRIOR

If you played a lot of computer games when you were young, you may qualify to serve as a soldier or private contractor in any of the forty-five countries that are now training people to operate their drones. Many drone pilots "fly" small robotic unmanned aerial vehicles (UAVs) thousands of miles away in the Middle East or Africa. Your office will be in a deep bunker somewhere near Langley, Virginia, Las Vegas, Nevada, Denver, Colorado, or one of seventeen other sites. One often cited fact these days in the United States is that there are more people training to fly robotic drones than training to fly military planes. Your desk has screens that receive information from global satellites or from human intelligence sources on the ground. Many supporters argue that because of their precision, drones have helped decrease the loss of life in conventional military personnel who would otherwise engage targeted terrorists. Many ethicists and structuralists would like you to know that just like any other soldier or civilian contractor operating on the ground, drone operators are not free from the duty of making ethical choices, even if they are thousands of miles away from the effects of their work.

Depending on the mission, your drone gathers intelligence by looking "into" developments on the ground through high-powered telescopes. Or your drone hunts down suspected terrorists to "take out" (kill) with one of its small, high-powered, guided missiles. After work, you leave your virtual world and return to your friends and family. And yet just like any other combatant on the field, you are also quite susceptible to post-traumatic stress syndrome (PTSD), depending on how disturbing your job is to you, given the disconnect between working in a virtual world and knowing that the people you may kill or injure cannot see you or may be innocent victims. The Bureau of Investigative Journalism reports that between 474 and

884 civilians have been killed by drones in Pakistan since 2004—176 of whom were children.[a]

Because drones lower the political and psychological barriers to their use, drone operators have an ethical duty to try to separate combatants from noncombatants.[b] Just as in the case of other weapons, drone pilots must also attempt to determine if the war is just in the first place. To the extent that drone strikes constitute intervention in a country such as Pakistan where a state of war does not exit, drone pilots may be complicit in violating international law, if not committing war crimes.

It should be noted that to justify the use of drones and other weapons, the Obama administration dropped the use of the phrase "war on terror" in 2009 and now uses "as a matter of international law" and the right to "use force consistent with our inherent right of national self-defense" in response to 9/11.[c] Finally, some claim that Congress (intentionally?) plays a limited role in oversight of drones, leaving the president a free hand to use them indiscriminately. This blurs the line between the roles of civilians and the military in war and also circumvents the Constitution's mandate that Congress provide oversight of their use.

References

[a]John Knefel, "'Whatever is Left is Just Pieces of Bodies and Cloth': New Report Details the Horror of Living Under Drones," *Truthout*, September 25, 2012.

[b]"The Ethics of Drones," *Religion and Ethics Newsweekly*, August, 26 2011, at http://www.pbs.org/wnet/religionandethics/episodes/august-26-2011/the-ethics-of-drones/9350.

[c]See Michael Gerson, "America's Remote-Controlled War on Terror," *Seattle Times*, May 6, 2012.

and working with intelligence agencies, Special Ops deploy small contingents in the Middle-East, Central Asia, and Africa on missions. According to multiple reports, JSFO worked with Xe (formerly Blackwater) and used drones in "snatch, grab, and assassinate" operations in Pakistan and elsewhere.

Cyberwarfare

In September 2012, hackers in the Middle-East severely disrupted the online banking operations of Wells-Fargo, U.S. Bancorp, and Bank of America.[23] Even though no personal information was lost, the attack sent another warning of cyber threats from states, cybercriminals, and terrorist groups. Information and communications technology plays an increasingly critical role in the command and control of not only conventional weapons and WMD but also drones and Special Ops Forces. For many national security experts today, the threat of cyberattacks and cyberwarfare is one of the most important domestic and international security issues for businesses and militaries in the major powers.[24]

To confront the threat, both defensive and offensive policies involving cooperation between public and private institutions are needed. Business experts claim that the biggest threats to U.S. security come from China, Russia, and organized crime. According to journalists Michael Riley and John Walcott, since 2001 the Chinese have gained access to 760 U.S. companies, universities, Internet services providers, and state agencies to steal information about clean energy, biotechnology, advanced semiconductors, aerospace and telecommunications equipment, pharmaceuticals, and medical devices. China has hacked into an array of corporations in Asia, the United States, and Germany, "using a vacuum cleaner to suck data out in terabytes and petabytes."[25]

In 2010, attacks hit Google, Intel, and Adobe—things corporations don't like to admit for fear of negative investor and consumer reaction. Congress has struggled to agree on a national policy that meets the pro-free market objectives of businesses that are also afraid to share information with state intelligence agencies they cannot trust. Richard Clarke, former security adviser to President Bush, feels strongly that cyber threats are too real and too important to be held hostage to business interests.[26]

The Obama administration has quietly developed more defensive and offensive cyber operations. Most notably, the 2010 computer virus named Stuxnet—developed with Israel—targeted equipment controlling Iranian nuclear centrifuges. In Afghanistan, the Marines used cyber tools to get inside al-Qaeda command and control operations. And the Pentagon's research arm, the Defense Advanced Research Projects Agency (DARPA), is funding contractors to develop "revolutionary technologies for understanding, planning and managing cyberwarfare"—part of an ambitious program called Plan X.[27]

Domestic Cyber-Surveillance and Individual Rights

For classical realists, domestic politics complicates executive decisions about foreign policy. For neorealists, domestic politics exists in a black box that should remain shut. However, in the cases of the Afghanistan and Iraq wars, resulting financial costs have grave consequences for the size of U.S. spending deficits and debt. Most realists have come to accept that globalization has blurred the virtual and real boundaries between domestic and international policies. Additionally, since 9/11, many Americans have a better understanding of how issues such as the global financial crisis, environmental degradation, and cyber surveillance directly affect their security.

Structuralists have been particularly vocal about four interrelated surveillance issues. First, they charge that the NSA, CIA, and other intelligence agencies have been spying on U.S. citizens, with the president and Congress playing major roles in the practice.[28] NSA veteran and whistleblower William Binney maintains that domestic surveillance has become more expansive under President Obama than under President George W. Bush. The NSA compiles trillions of phone calls, emails, and other forms of data that Americans send and receive.[29] Many legal experts charge that intelligence agencies operate without clear authority or even NSA has also collaborated with police to gather intelligence. And new technologies—such as biometric equipment from the Afghanistan and Iraq wars—has been used against Occupy Wall Street movement participants, environmental activists, and Tea Party members.

This raises a second issue that structuralists think Americans *should* consider critical. The public interest law professor Jonathan Turley wonders why Americans consider themselves "free" when there is growing evidence to suggest the contrary—lack of fair trials, torture, and use of secret evidence to imprison individuals.[30] Glenn Greenwald, a columnist at the *Guardian* newspaper, also argues that since 9/11, U.S. civil liberties have been reduced or jeopardized in the name of national security—making the United States a more authoritarian nation.[31] The evidence? The following are just some of the measures the PATRIOT Act and the new National Defense Authorization Act have allowed:

- Monitoring, assassination, and indefinite detention of U.S. citizens
- Arbitrary trials and warrantless searches
- Use of secret evidence and secret courts
- Extraordinary rendition

President Obama has continued the Bush policy of denying prosecution of CIA employees for waterboarding terrorist suspects. Many international lawyers claim this countermands many international laws and treaties. The Obama administration has been also accused of detaining insurgents in Afghanistan in a "black jail" run by U.S. Special Operations Forces. It ordered the killing of Anwar al-Awlaqi and his son—both U.S. citizens—in Yemen in 2011. Under the National Defense Authorization Act, people (including U.S. citizens) accused of terrorism can be detained, stripped of their legal protections, and tried in military or federal court—as determined by the President.

Under the PATRIOT Act, the President can force companies to turn over information related to citizen finances, communications, and associations. Secret courts can issue secret warrants to pursue individuals deemed to be aiding or abetting hostile foreign governments or organizations. Finally, GPS devices can be used to monitor citizens without a court order or review. Clearly, these anti-democratic policies have become the new norm in the American political economy.

A third issue drawing criticism from structuralists is the continued expansion of the military-industrial complex under President Obama. According to a Department of Defense report, the Pentagon has paid $1.1 trillion to defense contractors over the last decade. More than 300 legal cases involving alleged civil and criminal fraud by contractors have totaled only $1 million dollars in judgments.[32] Priest and Arkin are critical of the inefficiency, redundancy, and secrecy that have become routine features of the national security state.[33] Tom Englehardt suggests that this trend serves the wider political-economic objective of providing a bigger role for civilian security contractors and weapons manufacturers in military operations.[34] Finally, structuralists claim that the new national security state is highly capable of blocking efforts to cut defense program budgets, as demonstrated by the defense industry's and Congress's opposition to recent efforts to trim Pentagon spending by $78 billion by 2016. These cuts would have affected areas of "overcapacity" in ineffective or redundant weapons systems. Predictably, a combination of industry lobbying, "generous political donations," and the revolving door of officials between defense industries and the Pentagon was able to limit defense spending cuts by a whopping 2 percent in 2011![35]

Ultimately, these policies may undermine the safety of U.S. troops abroad along with the country's military and economic influence. Neocons and the political right usually claim that these counterterrorism developments are necessary and are angered by the left's implicit rejection of the United States as the world's hegemon. Many critics on the left accuse Obama of selling out America's soul to prevent the country from relinquishing its global position. The Constitution and Bill of Rights limit state power—in both war and peace. Much like the Japanese internment during World War II, efforts to weaken them undermine the foundation of U.S. values and institutions, making the United States more like authoritarian regimes it and the UN criticizes for human rights violations.

The Future Security Agenda

The Obama administration has grappled with other problems that are reshaping the global security structure. First, as neorealists highlight, tensions with Russia and China are likely to endure. Second, the Arab Spring continues to transform the Middle East, bring religion and class to the foreground, and destabilize countries that the United States cannot ignore. Third, a host of non-traditional security problems loom in the background, affecting citizens' sense of personal security and demanding multilateral cooperation.

Additionally, Russian President Vladimir Putin's cooperation with other states has been unpredictable. On the one hand, Russia has shared an interest in fighting terrorism and preventing nuclear proliferation. However, tensions remain over what Russia perceives as Western meddling in its "near abroad"—Central Asia and ex-Soviet republics with substantial Russian-speaking minorities and Russian economic interests. Moreover, Putin resents U.S. and EU pressure over Russia's domestic policies regarding corruption, state control of energy resources, and political opposition. The danger is less Russia's strategic threat to the outside world than its internal destabilization generated by its toxic mix of nationalism and political repression.

China's role in the security structure has also preoccupied officials, especially in Japan, the United States, and Australia. As we discuss in Chapter 13, many realists fear that China is bent on confronting the United States or U.S. allies militarily in the Pacific region, while economic liberals believe globalization will diffuse China's militaristic nationalism and strengthen political cooperation. In 2011, the Obama administration began a strategic and economic "pivot" to the Asia-Pacific region in anticipation of winding down the Iraq and Afghanistan wars.[36] Part of the rationale was reassuring Asian allies and guaranteeing freedom of navigation in vital commercial sea lanes. China perceived the pivot as directed against it, and resented Washington's pressure on currency and trade issue. China has alarmed Asian neighbors and the United States with its rapid military modernization and provocative claims to most of the islands in the South China Sea—where vast offshore energy sources may exist (see Chapter 3).

In keeping with some of the developments in the other three structures, globalization and neoliberal policies have fostered a shift in the distribution of wealth and power in the global security structure, and the United States may no longer be able to sustain its hegemonic military and economic power as it did in the past. China may or may not continue to finance U.S. debt (see Chapter 8).

The Arab Spring confronted the United States with potential security challenges that will not be easy to manage militarily. Although European members of NATO took the lead in ousting the Qaddafi regime in 2011, the United States has been wary of putting troops in Syria or any other Arab country. The danger is that Syria's civil war will drag on, drawing in radical Islamists and spilling over into Lebanon and Jordan, causing sectarian violence in those countries. At the same time, the Syria conflict is creating a deeper Shia-Sunni split in the region, with Sunni-majority countries Turkey and Saudi Arabia aiding the rebels and Shia-majority Iraq and Iran trying to prop up Assad. Hundreds of thousands of Syrian, Iraqi, and Palestinian refugees in the Levant put pressure on host countries.

President Obama has failed to pressure Israel to end its settlements expansion and seriously negotiate a two-state solution with the Palestinians. The Middle East peace process is moribund, with a dangerous combination of a right-leaning Israeli society, devastated Palestinian economy, and well-armed Hamas in Gaza. These factors are a recipe for more regional conflict which will force the United States to choose sides.

The prognosis for better U.S.-Iranian relations is also poor. The United States has cobbled together an international coalition, backed by the United Nations, to prevent Iran from building any nuclear weapons. Assassinations of Iranian scientists, a steady drumbeat of war talk from Israel, and the Obama administration's repeated threats to strike Iran ("all options are on the table") have increased Tehran's sense of insecurity and probably made it more intransigent. Instead of pursuing a grand political bargain with Iran, Washington has orchestrated draconian sanctions that have hurt ordinary Iranians and emboldened the clerical regime.

INTERNATIONAL ORGANIZATIONS

Today's global security structure is marked by a growing number of both traditional and nontraditional security issues that threaten not only nation-states in the realist sense of security threats, but different economic, ethnic, religious, and gender groups of people with violence and death. NATO, UN Peacekeeping Forces, aid and development agencies, the **International Criminal Court (ICC)**, NGOs such as Amnesty International and thousands of other agencies all play an increasingly important role in directing security issues in this increasingly fragmented global security structure.

NATO Peacekeeping

Because security is so sacrosanct to the major powers in particular, they have always been reluctant to give IOs much authority to manage, let alone solve, such problems. Thus, SALT, START, and the Conference on Security in Europe (CSE) talks in 1984 and 1987 involved only the two superpowers (and their allies in the CSE talks) in efforts to increase confidence and reinforce stability throughout Europe. Some twenty-seven members of the Partnership for Peace (PfP) program routinely deal with regional problems such as of peacekeeping, arms control, civil emergencies, and landmine action. Today, NATO has a total of twenty-eight members, seven from the PfP program. As discussed above, after 9/11, NATO members invaded Afghanistan to drive out the Taliban. The invasion of Iraq in 2002 was conducted by newer NATO members that supported the U.S.-led invasion.

Since the end of the Cold War, many critics of NATO have argued that the United States should decouple itself from the costs and political burdens of defending and extending nuclear deterrence over an increasingly larger Europe. Others have criticized NATO for not having a clear military strategy or political objectives in a changing security atmosphere. While public opinion has at times favored the use of NATO's use of force to deal with alleged atrocities, the recent cases of Yemen, Libya, and Syria demonstrate that many allied national leaders have been reluctant to send ground forces into these and other countries for fear that direct intervention or military and economic support for revolutionary forces could worsen the security outlook of their civilian populations.[37]

Many questions linger about NATO's military role and funding. NATO also faces issues of nationalism and ethnic and religious rivalry in member states such as Turkey and nations in-line to become members on its eastern borders. Whether NATO can deal adequately with drugs, terrorism, weapons proliferation, immigration, and other pressing security threats remains to be seen.[38] Clearly, some issues like immigration and terrorism get more attention than others in NATO planning and operations.

The United Nations and UN Peacekeeping Operations

The UN Security Council is authorized under the UN Charter to deal with *any* issue that threatens peace and security. However, in cases involving major security issues between the United States and Soviet Union such as the content and size of their nuclear arsenals, strategic doctrines, or involvement in developing nations, the UN played little to no role—by design. Security issues between the five permanent members of Security Council always involved the possibility of a veto. In effect, this limited the role of the major powers in many conflicts helped keep the permanent members in the Council from leaving it, at the expense of inaction by it.

Only twice since World War II has the Security Council authorized the use of force: in 1950 in Korea, and in 1990 when a coalition of forces drove Iraq out of Kuwait.

However, the UN's role in promoting security treaties between the United States and Soviet Union did pick up near the end of the Vietnam War in the mid-1970s. The superpowers reached an agreement in the ABM and SALT talks and also cooperated with the UN to establish a number of conventions, treaties, and protocols to address the proliferation of nuclear and other WMD. More often since the late 1960s, many minor powers have engaged with the UN in assertive efforts to create new rules and conventions related to the production, deployment, and sale of conventional weapons and, more recently, WMD and their component parts. The United Nations also served as a forum for negotiations that resulted in several security treaties dealing with acquisition of weapons (mostly conventional) through commercial and noncommercial channels. These treaties and conventions have faced several challenges, many from developing nations resenting these limits. As some realists and structuralists note, the objective of nonproliferation often conflicts with two political and economic objectives: to market missiles and other weapons-producing technologies, and in cases such as Pakistan, North Korea, and Iran, to maintain the right to develop nuclear power for energy—and also nuclear weapons to defend themselves.

More notably, however, in certain circumstances the Security Council and General Assembly are both authorized to deploy **peacekeeping operations (PKOs)** to help reduce tensions between conflicting parties. UN peacekeeping is an integral part of the global security structure that involves the periodic use of member-state troops to help settle disputes and resolve conflicts. It often serves a critical management function when states are ineffective, such as early in the Cold War when the Security Council was deadlocked about when to use force. Peacekeeping forces served as a mechanism for dealing with aggression and conflict in situations that would *not* directly involve the superpowers or other permanent members of the Security Council. UN peacekeepers were to serve as a neutral force between warring states, policing cease-fires, enforcing borders, and maintaining order when states requested their presence. Of some sixty-three PKOs, early ones consisted of specially trained soldiers from "neutral" countries such as Canada, Ireland, and Sweden. Since the end of the Cold War, the biggest contributors to PKOs have been developing countries such as India, Pakistan, Bangladesh, Nepal, and Nigeria. These states have tended to look more positively to international and regional organizations rather than to the United States and other major powers to generate norms, rules, or security standards that reflect interests other than those of the major powers.

In 1992, UN Secretary-General Boutros Boutros-Ghali tried to break new ground by suggesting that blue-helmeted peacekeeping forces should play a more assertive and proactive role in peacemaking to deal with the growing number of nationalistic, ethnic, and religious conflicts that intensified after the Cold War. He wrote that "while respect for the fundamental sovereignty and integrity of the state remains central, it is undeniable that the centuries-old doctrine of absolute and exclusive sovereignty no longer stands, and was in fact never so absolute as it was conceived to be in theory."[39] He also suggested that the secretary general should be able to call on all nations to provide soldiers for a UN-led military, an idea that did not go over well with most of the major powers. Under his leadership, however, the UN increased its peacemaking operations in poorer states, including Angola, Liberia, Haiti, Tajikistan, Somalia, and Cambodia. But apart from sanctioning NATO's efforts, the UN played only minor roles in conflicts in Rwanda, Kosovo, East Timor, and recently in Iraq, Libya, and Syria.

Increasingly, critics have questioned the UN's ability to produce peace in a civil-war environment.[40] They argue that some UN operations, such as in Rwanda, were too late to resolve internal conflicts.[41] Furthermore, costs often exceeded estimates, and member states used UN forces instead of their own for expensive campaigns. These and other limitations stymied UN peacekeepers' ability to find political or military solutions to regional conflicts, which diminished the UN's reputation.

TABLE 9-1

Treaty	Effected	Points of Interest
Treaty on the Nonproliferation of Nuclear Weapons (NPT Treaty): created to prevent transfer of nuclear weapons between nations created the International Atomic Energy Agency (IAEA) for inspection of nuclear weapons.	1970	The nuclear states of India, Pakistan, and Israel haven't signed. North Korea withdrew in 1993, and, like Iran, pushes ahead with nuclear development programs.
Biological and Toxic Weapons Convention (BTWC): limits research of biological weapons to defense	1975	100 signers included United States and U.S.S.R., Iraq, Iran, Syria, Russia; at least 16 other countries have been suspected of either researching or producing biological weapons.
Comprehensive Test Ban Treaty (CTBT): would outlaw testing of nuclear weapons	Created in 1996, not taken effect yet	157 states have ratified it, 25 more have signed but not ratified. Doesn't take effect until all 44 states capable of building a crude nuclear weapon have signed and ratified it. The United States, China, India, Israel, Iran, and Pakistan are slow to agree.
Chemical Weapons Convention (CWC): pledged to eliminate all chemical weapons by 2007	1997	Russia, Israel, Egypt, Syria, Libya, North Korea, and Iraq have not signed.
Missile Technology Control Regime (MTCR): prohibits export of missile technology	Created in 1987	Iran, Israel, Saudi Arabia, Pakistan, India, and North Korea (not signers) have been developing short- and medium-range ballistic missiles. China—which has sold missiles to Pakistan—and India have also come under pressure to adhere to this voluntary agreement.

The UN has often been criticized for its ineffectiveness in combating terrorism, which is rarely the product of a single state. So-called state-sponsored terrorists are often financed or supported by governments seeking to influence another nation. Iran, North Korea, Sudan, and Syria, among others, earned reputations as state sponsors of terrorism. Religious terrorists make up one-fourth of all terrorist groups. They mix religious opposition with ideological justifications including the right to self-determination, such as al-Qaeda's transnational operations.[42]

Recently, many states, IOs, and NGOs have committed to cooperating in dealing with terrorism, largely because the weapons readily available to terrorists are so lethal and sophisticated. Many NGOs provide emergency relief, demobilize former fighters, clear landmines, organize and conduct elections, and promote sustainable development practices. UN bodies have passed resolutions urging states to deny financial support and safe havens for terrorists, share information with other states about terrorists, and become party to terrorism conventions and protocols. Specifically, they encourage states to

- criminalize the financing of terrorism;
- freeze without delay any funds related to persons involved in acts of terrorism;
- deny all forms of financial support for terrorist groups;
- suppress the provision of safe haven, sustenance or support for terrorists;
- cooperate with other governments in the investigation, detection, arrest, extradition and prosecution of those involved in such acts; and
- criminalize active and passive assistance for terrorism in domestic law and bring violators to justice.

Since the late 1990s, PKOs have been limited to multidimensional problems that involve military, civilian police, and other civilian personnel working alongside local governments and groups. In sixteen PKOs today, national soldiers and UN peacekeepers in South Somalia, Sudan, Congo, Haiti, Lebanon, Kosovo and others must contend with a wide variety of nontraditional security issues on a day-to-day basis in ways that reflect respect for the local culture. For example, how do peacekeepers ensure that women are not concealing weapons under *niqabs* without violating cultural norms of decency? Also, rival groups habitually target each other with violence during religious holidays or pilgrimages; preventing attacks requires knowledge of holy sites, religious calendars, and specific practices. Any cessation in hostilities can only be sustained if peacekeepers respect local customs.

Acting on its authority under the UN Charter, the Security Council often recommends that parties try to reach agreement by peaceful means. It can undertake investigation and mediation. For example, former Secretaries-General Boutros-Ghali and Kofi Annan have acted as Special UN Representatives in efforts to try to establish a ceasefire for all parties in Somalia and most recently in Syria. Finally, UN workers often toil alongside NGO workers trying to address nontraditional security situations like hunger, poverty, human rights violations, immigration, refugees, and environmental degradation. In most of these cases, both the major and less powerful states have relied on the UN, other

IOs, and NGOs (discussed next) to address these issues. More often than not, however, the UN has not had enough human and economic resources to solve these issues.

Human Rights and the ICC

The connection between security and human rights issues has grown stronger in the new global security structure and IPE studies. Many UN members who cherish their right to self-defense have become more willing, even compelled, to transfer some authority to the UN to manage a variety of human rights violations, especially "war crimes" and "crimes against humanity." This movement dates back to the Nazi war crimes trials in Nuremburg, Germany, after World War II. In the 1990s, the UN established two truly international war crimes tribunals to deal with atrocities in the Balkans and Rwanda and later added a tribunal that focused on atrocities in Sierra Leone, reflecting some agreement about the conduct of nations and individuals in war. Located in The Hague, the Netherlands, Kenya, and Sierra Leone, these tribunals have lacked both funding and authority to arrest suspects.

However, a number of indictments for war crimes involving the rights and treatment of individuals have been handed down. Serbian president Slobodan Milosevic was indicted for crimes against humanity and other war crimes in Kosovo, and died in prison in 2005. Former prime minister of Rwanda Jean Kambanda was sentenced to life in prison for genocide in that country in 1994. In 2012, a tribunal in The Hague sentenced former Liberian president Charles Taylor to fifty years in prison for aiding and abetting those who committed atrocities in Sierra Leone in the 1990s.

By 2000, a permanent ICC was created by a 138-nation treaty to hear cases of post-2002 worldwide genocide, war crimes, and crimes against humanity. The Clinton administration signed the treaty, but the second Bush administration opposed it because U.S. officials could be accused of war crimes for any act of war. Great Britain, France, and Germany are financing and contributing staff to the new court.

Realist critics point out that the new tribunals lack the authority to compel compliance with international laws and conventions of war, because they lack real power to punish nations or groups for violations. To others, the establishment of the tribunals signifies that the issues of conduct and justice during war have moved up on the agenda of states and shifted some authority beyond nation-states to IOs in cases such as genocide and human rights violations. Even if some of these organizations are still dependent on the major powers for authority, they have gradually acquired more clout—albeit in reflection of big-power interests.

NGOs: POOR AND FAILED STATES COME UNDONE

Scholars have used the term "securitization" to describe how problems like climate change, poverty, and resource shortages have in recent years become recognized as threats to national and global security. NGOs like the Red Cross and

WORKING FOR THE INTERNATIONAL CRIMINAL TRIBUNAL FOR THE FORMER YUGOSLAVIA[a]

It has been nearly ten years since I graduated with a degree in International Political Economy, and I have finally landed at a place where I can see many of the theories I learned during my studies put into practice. I am a legal assistant at the International Criminal Tribunal for the Former Yugoslavia, part of the defense team for Radovan Karadzic, in The Hague, Netherlands. The ICTY was created in 1993, nine years before the International Criminal Court was established. It was created to prosecute perpetrators of the most serious crimes committed during the wars in the former Yugoslavia, and it has indicted 161 individuals, from those at the bottom of the chain of command right up to former prime ministers and presidents. Like the ICC, it prosecutes crimes against humanity, war crimes, and genocide.

To work for one of the special international courts, you must be able to keep a long-term perspective. The Karadzic trial, for instance, has been going on for four years and is expected to last another two. In the ten years since the formation of the ICC, only one individual has been sentenced by that court. When coming to work, you pass by those protesting the detention of the accused. At lunchtime, you watch CNN broadcasting about the horrors in Syria. Sometimes you wonder if there is really a point, if international cooperation is really ever going to prevent the most heinous of crimes.

When entering the Tribunal, you are greeted with what is essentially its mission statement: "Bringing War Criminals to Justice, Bringing Justice to Victims." It is a lofty ideal, and one that reflects the organization's vision of its role in both international security and international human rights. While it is true that the court has sentenced many war criminals, the question remains as to whether it has had any sort of impact on peace and security in the Balkans. Many in the region, particularly in Croatia, Serbia, and the Serb-held territory of Bosnia, distrust the Tribunal, often accusing it of bias. Even twenty years after the start of the war, tensions among ethnic groups in the former Yugoslavia still remain.

Of course, beyond the ideals of international justice and global security, it is necessary to remember the actual function of the court: to provide a fair trial. It may be difficult to achieve. At the Tribunal, defense teams are not paid by the United Nations, which funds the rest of the organization. The teams all share a joint office, where workers compete to use one of about twenty computers built in 2005. With such a poor distribution of resources, the question of true "fairness" must be examined.

When the Special Tribunal for Lebanon was created in 2009, the defense was incorporated as part of the institution. So, too, at the ICC, which includes an Office of Public Counsel for the Defence. Such steps are necessary to ensure the long-term viability of the courts and the continued development of international law. The fairer the process, the more likely that states will voluntarily submit cases they are unable to prosecute and that they will cooperate with the courts. While it still might take time for individual citizens to accept their leaders being sentenced by an international court, a fairer trial can only help the court's legitimacy. And as the courts grow in stature, we will start to see their true effect on international security.

[a]Kristen Schlewitz wrote the material for this box.

Red Crescent, Amnesty International, Greenpeace, Doctors Without Borders, and Worldvision—motivated by humanitarian, ideological, and practical concerns— are gaining greater influence in the global security structure. The International Campaign to Ban Land Mines (see the "Landmines" box in Chapter 5) is a good example of how coalitions of NGOs can change security practices. Violence against women and refugees in states such as Afghanistan, Pakistan, Palestine,

Iraq, Yemen, Somalia, North and South Sudan, Nigeria, and the Congo is routine. These states often depend on UN peacekeeping forces and an array of NGOs to mitigate some of the violence.

Many studies attribute conflict and a host of unconventional security issues to the lack of development. Some blame TNCs, natural resources extraction, and the search for markets and cheap labor in developing regions for causing exploitation, poverty, and repressive forms of neocolonialism.[43] Large slums in Rio de Janeiro, Mexico City, Nairobi, Lagos, and Manila suffer significant urban violence. Many terrorism experts contend that *favelas* in cities like these and in failed states such as Afghanistan, Somalia, and Nigeria are hotbeds for ethnic and religious conflict. At the same time, industrial agriculture and monocropping (see Chapter 18) are undermining biodiversity and leaving food production vulnerable to the spread of plant diseases in developing countries. Shortages of arable land, water, and energy may spark future "resource wars" with Darwinian consequences or what Peruvian scholar Oswaldo de Rivero warns will be physical-social imbalances that lead to "the cataclysm of national disintegration" in many poorer parts of the world.[44]

The global security structure today lacks strong institutions to coordinate responses to these problems. And few electorates want to be told they must limit consumption or pay higher taxes to solve the world's ills. However, the proliferation of unconventional security problems around the world can only be halted through multilateral cooperation and political risk-taking. U.S. budget constraints, weak U.S. international credibility, and the global financial crisis are all factors that will stand in the way of concerted problem-solving. If Great Powers try to solve these problems militarily or unilaterally, they will fail. We realize that solutions requiring shared sacrifice are sometimes politically untenable, as they are perceived as infringements on state sovereignty. The result may be that the world muddles through problems or keeps discounting their importance until they turn into full-blown crises.

CONCLUSION: AN EVEN DARKER FUTURE?

Some U.S. administrations after World War II liked the Cold War bipolar balance of power between the United States and the Soviet Union because of its defined structural arrangement. Others preferred a multipolar security structure because it reflected the distribution of wealth and power away from the two superpowers toward emerging countries. Regardless of each administration's orientation toward the distribution of power, the following lessons seem to apply:

- realism still has a good deal of explanatory power, but policy makers should supplement

it with other political-economic perspectives, including structuralism and constructivism in particular.
- under the right circumstances, small nations can overcome larger nations—or at least weaken their resolve to fight wars in places like Korea, Vietnam, Iraq, and Afghanistan.
- the U.S. public is increasingly unwilling to bear the economic and political costs associated with being the world's strongest military power.
- given these two factors, there are major impediments and costs to U.S. military intervention in Iran and Syria.

Globalization brought an emphasis on open markets and economic competition, but also the hope that economic liberal policies would produce democracy and peace in developing nations. However, globalization helped weaken bipolarity and transform the international security structure into a less orderly configuration with more flexible rules and norms. By the mid-1990s, technological innovation had made conventional weapons more lethal and nuclear, biological, and chemical weapons more powerful. At the same time, globalization contributed to the proliferation of these weapons to public and private forces that have helped destabilize many developing nations.[45]

After 9/11 the Bush administration attempted to reorder the security structure along unipolar lines with the United States as the lone global hegemon. With terrorism replacing communism as the main external enemy, U.S. efforts to bring democracy and stability to countries like Iraq and Afghanistan backfired, resulting in the (planned) withdrawal of U.S. and allied forces.

The Obama administration has pursued a more nuanced strategy that relies less on conventional forces and more on unilateral strikes that employ drones and Special Operations forces. The other side of this Janus-faced strategy is a multilateralism that tries to get NATO allies to share the burden of fighting terrorists in Afghanistan, Pakistan, and parts of Africa. Obama also prefers to use soft-power instruments such as improved information and communication systems, cultural globalization, and diplomatic cooperation with a variety of states.

Realists tend not to be surprised by many of these developments, given their belief that conflict is a foundational element of any group or security order. However, a weakness of realism is that it tends to insulate the major powers from a growing list of problems in weaker and poorer states. The powerful countries in today's increasingly fragmented security structure are preoccupied with global terrorism and recovery from the financial crisis. Meanwhile, issues such as poverty, immigration, drug trafficking, and environmental degradation are increasingly impinging on the security of the Western powers. In this view, IOs and NGOs are only as effective as the major powers allow them to be. It is up to states to decide if or when UN- and IO-sponsored treaties are to be adhered to.

Regardless of whether or not the United States remains a global hegemon, if global security is to be achieved in any meaningful sense of the term, the current global security structure can no longer be managed by one power alone. Realists would be the first to point out that unipolarity tends to be unstable. To protect against global threats, the United States and other powers will need to consciously share security management functions with IOs, regional organizations, and NGOs that reflect the interests of a global civil society. Decision makers should focus more on widening the scope of their options and choices rather than conforming to standard practices and ideas.

KEY TERMS

bipolarity 207
Mutually Assured Destruction (MAD) 208
realism 208
global cyber security structure 208
multipolarity 208
unipolarity 208
Cold War 208

North Atlantic Treaty Organization (NATO) 209
classical realism 209
neorealism 209
balance of power 210
neoconservatives 218
weapons of mass destruction (WMD) 218
Obama doctrine 221

bunker buster 221
unmanned aerial vehicles (UAVs) 221
Joint Special Operations Command 222
International Criminal Court (ICC) 227
peacekeeping operations (PKOs) 228

DISCUSSION QUESTIONS

1. Discuss some of the main structural features of the new global cyber security structure.
2. Discuss several ways in which economic developments in the last twenty years have contributed to a weakening of U.S. military and economic power.
3. Outline some of the benefits and drawback of the Obama administration's unilateralist application of force combined with multilateralist outlook about sharing power with other states.
4. Outline some of the security threats and issues that IOs and NGOs deal with. Discuss some of the reasons why they do not have more success solving these sorts of problems. What would it take for them to be more successful?
5. Pick a significant security event and discuss how a classical realist and a neorealist would explain it. Discuss which outlook is closest to your own view and why.

SUGGESTED READINGS

David Calleo. *Follies of Power: America's Unipolar Fantasy*. New York: Cambridge University Press, 2009.

Amy Chua. *World on Fire: How Exporting Free Market Democracy Breeds Ethnic Hatred and Global Instability*. New York: Anchor Books, 2003.

Oswaldo De Rivero. *The Myth of Development: Non-Viable Economies and the Crisis of Civilization*, 2nd ed. London: Zed Books, 2010.

Chalmers Johnson. *The Sorrows of Empire: Militarism, Secrecy, and the End of the Republic*. New York: Metropolitan Books, 2004.

Thomas E. Ricks. *Fiasco: The American Military Adventure in Iraq*. New York: Penguin, 2006.

David Sanger. *Confront and Conceal: Obama's Secret Wars and Surprising Use of American Power*. New York: Crown Publishers, 2012.

NOTES

1. Robert Kennedy, *Thirteen Days: A Memoir of the Cuban Missile Crisis* (New York: W.W. Norton, 1969).
2. For a readable account of nuclear strategy, see Edgar Bottome, *The Balance of Terror: Nuclear Weapons and the Illusion of Security, 1945–1985* (Boston, MA: Beacon, 1986).
3. The classic study outlining the principles of realism is Hans Morgenthau, *Politics among Nations: The Search for Power and Peace*, 3rd ed. (New York: Knopf, 1960).
4. For example, see John Mearsheimer, *The Tragedy of Great Powers* (New York: W. W. Norton, 2001).
5. Niall Ferguson, *Colossus: The Rise and Fall of the American Empire* (New York: Penguin Books, 2005).
6. Daniel Yergin, *Shattered Peace: The Origins of the Cold War and the National Security State* (Boston: Houghton Mifflin, 1977).
7. Frances Fitzgerald, *Fire in the Lake: The Vietnamese and the Americans in Vietnam* (Boston: Little, Brown, 1972).
8. See Stanley Hoffmann, "The Hell of Good Intentions," *Foreign Policy* 29 (Winter 1977–1978), pp. 3–26.
9. See Chalmers Johnson, *The Sorrows of Empire: Militarism, Secrecy, and the End of the Republic* (New York: Routledge, 2005).
10. John Mearsheimer, "Why We Will Soon Miss the Cold War" *Atlantic Monthly* (August 1990), pp. 35–50.
11. See Robert Kagan, "The Benevolent Empire," *Foreign Policy* (Summer 1998), pp. 24–49.
12. Neil Smith, *The Endgame of Globalization* (New York: Routledge, 2005).
13. Ibid.
14. See Thomas E. Ricks, *Fiasco: The American Military Adventure in Iraq* (New York: Penguin, 2006).
15. See Jeremy Scahill, *Blackwater: The Rise of the World's Most Powerful Mercenary Army* (New York: Nation Books, 2007).
16. See Maggie Farley, "Report: U.S. Is Abusing Captives," *Los Angeles Times*, February 13, 2006.

17. See Chalmers Johnson, *The Sorrows of Empire*, p. 182.

18. See, for example, William Hartung and Michelle Ciarocca, "The Military-Industrial-Think Tank Complex," *Multinational Monitor*, January/February 2003.

19. Dana Priest and William Arkin, *Top Secret America: The Rise of the New American Security State* (New York: Little, Brown and Company, 2011).

20. David Sanger, *Confront and Conceal: Obama's Secret Wars and Surprising Use of American Power* (New York: Crown Publishers, 2012).

21. Ibid., p. xiv.

22. Tom Englehardt, "The Arrival of the Warrior Corporation" *TomDispatch*, February 24, 2012, at http://www.tomdispatch.com/archive/175507.

23. Andrew Tangel and Mim Puzzanghera, "Biggest U.S. Banks Fail to Repel Cyber Threat," *Seattle Times*, September 28, 2012.

24. See Jeffrey Carr, *Inside Cyber Warfare: Mapping the Cyber Underworld*, 2nd ed. (Sebastopool, CA: O'Reilly Media, 2011).

25. Michael Riley and John Walcott, "China-Based Hacking of 760 Companies Shows Cyber Cold War," December 14, 2011, at http://www.bloomberg.com/news/2011-12-13/china-based-hacking-of-760-companies-reflects-undeclared-global-cyber-war.html.

26. Richard Clarke, *Cyber War: The Next Threat to National Security and What to Do About It* (New York: HarperCollins, 2010).

27. Scott Shane, "Cyberwarfare Emerges From Shadows for Public Discussion by U.S. Officials," *New York Times*, September 26, 2012.

28. See Shane Harris, "Giving In to the Surveillance State," *New York Times*, August 23, 2012.

29. See Amy Goodman and Juan Gonzalez, "Whistle-blower—the NSA Is Lying: The U.S. Government Has Copies of Most of Your Emails," *Democracy Now*, May 20, 2012. See also, "The Spy Factory," *Nova, PBS*, February 3, 2009.

30. Jonathan Turley, "Ten Reasons the U.S. Is No Longer the Land of the Free," *Washington Post*, January 13, 2002.

31. Glen Greenwald's columns can be read at http://www.guardian.co.uk/profile/glenn-greenwald.

32. See Mike Ludwig, "US Military Paid $1.1 Trillion to Contractors That Defrauded the Government," *Truthout* Report, October 20, 2011.

33. Dana Priest and William Arkin, *Top Secret America*.

34. Tom Englehardt, *The United States of Fear*, (Chicago, IL: Haymarket Books, 2011).

35. Aprille Muscara, "Defence Contractors Insulated from Budget Cuts," *IPS Inter Press Service*, January 19, 2011.

36. For an overview of the U.S. shift to Asia, see Mark Manyin et al., "Pivot to the Pacific? The Obama Administration's 'Rebalancing' toward Asia," (Congressional Research Service), March, 28, 2012.

37. See for example, Joseph S. Nye, "The Intervention Dilemma," *Al Jazeera*, June 15, 2012.

38. This issue is discussed at some length in Moisés Naím, "The Five Wars of Globalization," *Foreign Policy*, 134 (January/February 2003), pp. 29–39.

39. See Boutros Boutros-Ghali, "Empowering the United Nations," *Foreign Affairs*, 71 (Winter 1992/1993), pp. 98–99.

40. See David Rieff, "The Illusions of Peacekeeping," *World Policy Journal*, 11 (Fall 1994), pp. 1–18.

41. An excellent read on the UN's role in Rwanda is Michael Barnett, *Eyewitness to Genocide: The United Nations and Rwanda* (Ithaca, NY: Cornell University Press, 2000).

42. For a more detailed overview of terrorism in general, see Brigitte Nacos, *Terrorism and Counterterrorism: Understanding Threats and Responses in the Post-9/11 World*, 3rd ed. (New York: Pearson Longman, 2009).

43. For a good overview of this argument, see Oswaldo De Rivero, *The Myth of Development: The Non-Viable Economies of the 21st Century*, 2nd. ed. (New York: Zed Books, 2011).

44. For examples of the "resource conflict" prediction, see Michael T. Klare, *The Race for What's Left: The Global Scramble for the World's Last Resources* (New York: Metropolitan Books, 2012); Oswaldo de Rivero, *The Myth of Development*.

45. See Amy Chua, *World On Fire: How Exporting Free Market Democracy Breeds Ethnic Hatred and Global Instability* (New York: Anchor Books, 2003).

The Knowledge and Technology Structure

Pinning our hopes on technology.

Corbis

Have you ever illegally downloaded a song, movie, or video game? If so, you're in good company. Since its founding in 2003, The Pirate Bay, based in Sweden, has attracted millions of Internet surfers looking for copyrighted material for free. Using BitTorrent technology, the site made it simple to find digitized files and share them with almost anyone in the world. By 2008, it was listed as one of the 100 most popular sites in the world, with an average of twenty-five million users per month. It became the bête noire of Hollywood studios and global entertainment companies who repeatedly sued it. In

April 2009, a Swedish court found several of the brash young men running the site guilty of copyright violation and ordered them to pay damages and go to jail. Since then, TPB has managed to survive in the face of attacks by hackers, blocks on access imposed by some governments, and efforts by Google, Facebook, and Microsoft to make it difficult to reach the site. In the furor following the court case, the Swedish Pirate Party, a new political party that advocates limiting copyrights to five years and getting rid of patents, won 7 percent of the national vote in Sweden to gain a seat in the European Parliament. By 2012, a German Pirate Party promoting political transparency and Internet freedom had won seats in state parliaments, and small Pirate parties had sprung up in dozens of countries.

The Pirate Bay saga is one of many examples of high-stakes global struggles over knowledge and technology that are shaping the future of competition, freedom, and security in ever-changing ways. In this chapter, we examine the international knowledge structure—a set of rules, practices, and institutions that determines who owns and can make use of knowledge and technology and on what terms. It profoundly conditions the other structures we have examined—trade and production, finance, and security—by affecting capital flows, where goods and services are produced, and the ability of states to protect themselves from enemies.

In the first section, we define the knowledge structure, the actors in it, and some of the issues at stake. Next, we analyze how states and companies work within it to control information flows and generate technological advances. In a related fashion, we also look at how states struggle to attract highly trained workers. In the second half of the chapter, the focus turns to **intellectual property rights (IPRs)**, especially patents, copyrights, and trademarks. We analyze how developing countries are contesting the rules to more quickly catch up to the world's economic powers. Finally, we contrast different perspectives on whether or not the system that controls IPRs is relatively beneficial and fair.

It is said that knowledge is power. We posit that there are four important trends in the knowledge structure that will affect your life and your country's destiny in unsettling and potentially liberating ways.

First, liberals and mercantilists agree that knowledge and technology have become increasingly important determinants of power. Economic success and military might are less dependent on control of land or natural resources and much more based on human capital and prowess in such areas as engineering, information and communication systems, and basic scientific research.

Second, the pace of technological change has quickened. Profits in the global economy are shifting away from manufacturers to: those who control the knowledge of *how* to produce; those who finance, design, and market new products; and those who control the *distribution* of knowledge-intensive goods and services.

Third, knowledge is increasingly dispersed but interconnected and therefore harder for any one country to control. Countries that maintain openness to global flows of goods and ideas—as advocated by economic liberals—will likely benefit economically. However, mercantilists are right that governments often try to limit certain kinds of information flows and use subsidies, selective protectionism, and intellectual property laws to decisively affect who benefits from interconnected knowledge.

Finally, there is a growing tension globally between owners of IPRs and individuals who believe that many forms of knowledge should be "free" or in the public domain.[1] International intellectual property rules that ignore social demands for low-cost or free music, software, movies, news, and medicines will be virtually impossible to enforce. Intellectual property (IP) holders who want stricter controls face a monumental battle with IP consumers who want freedom of use and a redistribution of social benefits from technology.

THE INTERNATIONAL KNOWLEDGE STRUCTURE: ACTORS AND RULES

The international knowledge structure is a web of rules and practices that determine how knowledge is generated, commercialized, and controlled. *Knowledge* is an umbrella term we apply to many different things, including ideas, technology, information, and intellectual property. Ideas are ethereal; they can be exchanged between people by means of language, education, and cultural practices. Technology is a specific kind of knowledge about the process by which to produce goods and services and how to apply science for useful commercial purposes. Information can be thought of as data and news that people produce, share, and recombine to serve economic, cultural, and political goals. And intellectual property consists of inventions, artistic works, and symbols that governments have granted monopoly rights to for limited periods.

As you can imagine, rules on the flows of knowledge create rights, incentives, and prohibitions for countries, businesses, and consumers. Many of these rules are created by powerful countries and multinational corporations that seek to convince the rest of the world of their legitimacy. At the same time, many social forces resist knowledge controls through political action and lobbying—and sometimes they are willing to defy laws to get what they believe is their due. Rules that we look at include national laws governing freedom of information and intellectual property rights; bilateral and multilateral treaties that determine what obligations a state has to protect the patents and copyrights of other countries; and shared norms about the moral obligations of producers and consumers of knowledge.

Individuals navigate the knowledge structure to educate themselves, enjoy entertainment products, and engage in political action. They tend to view relatively unrestricted access to knowledge as a basic human right. As profit-making entities, companies are keen to commercialize and control the knowledge they produce, and they constantly need new technology to compete successfully. States want to foster their own technological development and force other countries to comply with certain rules. At the global level, international organizations enforce negotiated rules concerning knowledge and teach countries how to cooperate with one another. Also, many NGOs are trying to change the rules to better serve the interests of the poor and the exploited.

The international knowledge structure conditions all IPE relationships, including production, trade, finance, and security. For example, the United States chose a strategy of nuclear deterrence in the early postwar years in part because technology made nuclear weapons appear to be less costly than conventional weapons. The high costs of the arms race, which was also a technology race, contributed to the pressures that brought the Cold War to an end in the late 1980s. Advances in information and communication technology (ICT) have resulted in a borderless, lightly regulated global financial system using complex instruments such as derivatives. The race to develop new energy technologies will determine which countries dominate production of electric cars and solar panels. Innovations in transportation technology like containerization made it possible to shift many manufacturing processes to Asia. Clearly, nations and transnational corporations that want to win—or just hold their own—in the game of global competition will have to gain access to the best technology.

THE IPE OF INFORMATION, INNOVATION, AND TECHNOLOGY ADVANCEMENT

In this section we examine how countries try to regulate information, foster innovation, and turn knowledge into comparative advantage in the global economy. We find a surprisingly large role of the state in coordination of **research and development (R&D)** with market actors. Some developing countries are closing the knowledge gap with wealthier countries while gaining a bigger share of global production, but the United States and the European Union are fighting hard to attract the world's most highly skilled workers.

A key historical and theoretical question is this: What have been the appropriate roles for governments and market actors in fostering innovation and accumulation of knowledge? As we have seen in discussions about the current financial crisis, trade policy, and the environment, a growing number of political economists such as Joseph Stiglitz, Ha-Joon Chang, and Dani Rodrik believe that states need flexibility to craft policies in sync with their particular national needs. With regard to knowledge governance, they argue that one size does not fit all. Some states try to substitute for the private sector in research and development, some partner with it in a variety of ways, and some simply clear away obstacles in the way of private innovators. States find it difficult to balance the interests of producers and consumers of knowledge. They want to nurture those who turn technological innovations into lucrative exports. They also are willing to spread knowledge around the world by educating foreigners in their universities and encouraging outsourcing by their TNCs. But at the same time many nations are intent on staying one step ahead of rivals in innovative fields and in military technologies.

Information: A Double-Edged Sword

The digital revolution has profoundly changed the quantity and quality of information individuals potentially have access to. Information can both empower and disempower: in the hands of citizens it can become the fuel for political revolution, but in the hands of governments it can be used to surveil and police society. We look briefly at some of the global arenas in which the fight over information has played out.

The proliferation of social media has opened up new forms of national and cross-border communication that occur through blogs, podcasts, virtual game worlds, Skype, YouTube, and Facebook. It is not just the mediums of exchange that are changing but also the content and speed of exchanges. The political power of social media became clear during the Arab Spring in early 2011. Internet access and widespread cell phone ownership allowed millions of Egyptians to share information via Facebook and text-messaging, which helped circumvent government censorship and mobilize citizens. Protestors used all of these tools simultaneously and in such a dispersed yet coordinated way that the regime of Hosni Mubarak reacted by shutting down mobile phone and Internet service for a week.[2] Opposition forces in Tunisia, Libya, and Syria also posted YouTube videos online that were picked up by international news media, providing hour-by-hour coverage of events. The shaky videos and photos from cell phones have revealed regime abuses, documented the humiliation of regime leaders, and made martyrs out of ordinary people. The ability of cyberactivists to use these social media has destroyed regime information monopolies and sustained on-the-ground political activism. While authoritarian regimes are weakened, Western governments and international organizations also find it harder not to respond to the outrage of their own citizens and immigrant communities who can gain up-to-the-minute information from Twitter, blogs, and satellite television.

Regimes have fought back through control and suppression of information using advances in technology. China has been relatively successful in building the "Great Firewall" to filter access to politically sensitive information on the Internet. Police and intelligence agencies engage in extensive cell-phone wiretapping and monitoring of communications infrastructures. Where traditional media like television and newspapers are not fully state-controlled, governments in places like Russia and Iran use legal sanctions and harassment of journalists to restrict private media companies. The case of WikiLeaks (see the related box) suggests that even governments in democratic countries are willing to go to great lengths to try to control classified information and punish whistleblowers.

WIKILEAKS

If you want an unvarnished, behind-the-scenes look at the conduct of war, diplomacy, and foreign policy, you might want to peruse some of the millions of secret documents released by WikiLeaks. Your faith in humanity and the moral uprightness of your country might be shaken. You can watch a video of a U.S. Apache helicopter gunship mowing down over a dozen unarmed civilians in Baghdad in 2007.[a] You can read Hillary Clinton's assessment that donors in Saudi Arabia—a close ally of the United States—are the "most significant source of funding to Sunni terrorist groups worldwide."[b] You can find that the International Committee of the Red Cross uncovered evidence of widespread ill-treatment and torture of Kashmiri prisoners by Indian security forces in the first half of the 2000s, leading it to conclude that the Government of India condones torture.[c] You can examine U.S. military documents revealing widespread human rights abuses by Iraqi forces that the United States failed to investigate and numerous incidents of American troops killing Afghani civilians.[d] You can peruse thousands of files documenting commercial transactions between Western companies and many of the most repressive governments in the world.[e] And you can read U.S. diplomatic cables assessing Tunisia's former ruling family as corrupt, nepotistic, mafia-like, and spendthrifty—cables that played a role in sparking Tunisia's 2011 Jasmine Revolution.[f]

(continued)

The guiding force behind WikiLeaks is Julian Assange, a brash Australian committed to government transparency and uncovering conspiracies of the powerful. In effect, he has taken it upon himself to de-naturalize government narratives about foreign affairs. He has relied upon a network of volunteers and whistleblowers to provide his organization secret documents that are published digitally through mirrored websites on servers in many different countries to prevent any particular state from suppressing access to them. At the height of his influence between 2009 and 2012, Assange published hundreds of thousands of U.S. military documents and diplomatic cables dating back almost a decade—leaked by U.S. soldier Bradley Manning—and thousands of sensitive documents and emails from private companies, politicians, the United Nations, and the Syrian government. Assange also: attacked U.S. companies like Google and Yahoo for amassing data about individuals; accused the mainstream media of regularly spreading lies and government propaganda; and singled out Facebook as the "most appalling spying machine that has ever been invented."[9] In a relentless effort to undermine WikiLeaks, the U.S. government successfully pressured PayPal, Visa, Mastercard, and U.S. banks to stop processing supporters' donations to it. After being accused of two rapes in Sweden, Assange fled to Great Britain. When a court ordered him extradited, he fled to the Ecuadoran embassy in London and was granted political asylum.

The WikiLeaks saga has demonstrated the ability of a small group of cyberactivists and whistleblowers to use digital technology to easily spread unprecedented amounts of sensitive information that threaten a country's national security, undermine a TNC's reputation, or potentially endanger the lives of individuals. It is but one example of citizen activists bypassing mainstream journalists to propagate information in the service of explicit political agendas. It has shown the increasing difficulty states have in controlling information and exercising their traditional sovereign powers in cyberspace. It reminds us of the abuses of government power and the conniving of private interests that classical liberals since Adam Smith have warned us about. Even if WikiLeaks dies out, there will still be competitors like the National Security Archive, Cryptome, and OpenSecrets to publish leaked documents and declassified government records with sensitive information.

References

[a]See http://www.collateralmurder.com.
[b]See http://www.guardian.co.uk/world/us-embassy
   -cables-documents/242073.
[c]See http://www.guardian.co.uk/world/us-embassy
   -cables-documents/30222.
[d]See http://wikileaks.org/afg/ and http://wikileaks
   .org/irq/.
[e]See http://wikileaks.org/the-spyfiles.html and http://
   wikileaks.org/syria-files/.
[f]See http://www.scribd.com/doc/44262151/Tunileaks.
[g]"WikiLeaks Revelations Only Tip of Iceberg—
   Assange," May 3, 2011, at http://rt.com/news
   /wikileaks-revelations-assange-interview/.

Democratic and authoritarian regimes are also using technology to collect and manipulate information. They have installed ever more futuristic data-collection and surveillance systems not just to prevent crime but to monitor communications of citizens, gather overseas intelligence, and enhance border control. Closed circuit TV cameras and biometrics are but two of the means by which states gather domestic intelligence that threatens individual liberties. The ruling family of tiny Qatar uses the pan-Arab satellite network Al-Jazeera, which it owns, to shape Arab public opinion and place pressure on other countries, including the United States. Since 2005, the Russian government has funded a Kremlin-friendly international television network called Russia Today (RT) which is available through cable

TV subscription and via YouTube in many countries. Alongside these channels that are gaining global market share are long-established, state-owned European broadcasters such as Britain's BBC and Germany's Deutsche Welle.

The digital revolution also allows private corporations to gather unprecedented amounts of consumer information that can be used in ways contrary to the public interest. Battles between states and TNCs over how this information is used are part of a wider battle over regulation of the market. Some governments worry about how private control of technology can lead to anti-competitive behavior, threats to privacy, and concentrations of power. For example, the European Commission has spearheaded efforts to prevent Microsoft from abusing its control over computer software, to stop Google from undermining its competitors, and to force Facebook to protect users' personal data. Different legal obligations and cultural expectations across countries make it difficult to create global standards. Some states try to harness the power of their information-technology companies to hurt rivals overseas. For example, the United States vigorously promotes a relatively unfettered, uncensored, open architecture for information services dominated by U.S.-based TNCs in the hopes that it will empower civil society in countries like Iran and China. On the other hand, the U.S. House of Representatives' intelligence committee in October 2012 accused two huge Chinese companies, Huawei Technologies and ZTE, which supply equipment used in telecommunications and mobile phone networks worldwide, of being threats to U.S. national security. The committee argued that the Chinese state could use them to spy on American consumers, steal the intellectual property of U.S. companies, and conduct cyberwarfare in the event of a conflict.[3]

Structuralists John Bellamy Foster and Robert W. McChesney worry that corporations have crushed the liberating potential of the communications revolution, turning the Internet into an oligopolistic sphere from which they can extract exorbitant profits. In addition to being a threat to democracy, these corporations are spreading a form of "digital feudalism where a handful of colossal corporate mega-giants rule private empires."[4] Thrown by the global wayside are net neutrality, quality journalism, and the public domain.

However, global civil society is fighting back, promoting new privacy norms such as disallowing companies from gathering and storing certain kinds of customer data. Transnational advocacy groups that are loosely part of the Access to Knowledge (A2K) movement seek to weaken intellectual property rights and make the results of all forms of government-sponsored research freely available. There are even efforts to force companies to allow interoperability of their products with those of rivals to prevent them from monopolizing certain markets. And Yochai Benkler describes the emergence of a new global information ecosystem he calls the "networked fourth estate" in which traditional media interacts with low-cost, decentralized news producers like non-profits, bloggers, and citizen-journalists.[5]

Jennifer Shkabatur points out that new information technologies allow international organizations (IOs) to more easily monitor states' compliance with their international obligations to protect the environment, public health, and human rights.[6] Using webcrawlers, online networks of experts, and data published online by laypersons, IOs can compare state-provided information with independently generated information to determine if state behavior is consistent with the expectations of international regulatory regimes. The effect may be to dramatically increase pressure on states to be more transparent and accountable.

Finally, the politics of information has important implications for the exercise of a country's soft power and protection of commercial interests overseas. In recent years, private media in Europe and the United States have published material that Muslims deem to be offensive. A Danish newspaper's publication of cartoons mocking the prophet Muhammad in 2005 led to a series of violent anti-Western demonstrations in predominantly Muslim countries. Subsequent boycotts of Danish goods in the Middle East caused significant losses for Danish exporters of dairy products and pharmaceuticals. Similarly, the publication on YouTube of the trailer for an Islamophobic movie called the *Innocence of Muslims* in September 2012 provoked anti-Western riots in the Muslim world that empowered radical Islamists and undermined U.S. public diplomacy. The rapid propagation of media products by extremists has the potential to affect the post-Arab Spring democratization process and relations between the West and the Middle East. It forces democratic countries to search for a balance between freedom of expression and norms proscribing hate speech.

Moreover, widespread access in China to information about Japan's actions in September 2012 towards three disputed islands in the South China Sea threatened trade relations and deepened military tensions. In the weeks after the Japanese government bought the islands from their private Japanese owners, virulently anti-Japanese protests in dozens of Chinese cities caused stock prices of some Japanese companies to fall, spurred Japan Airlines to cancel many flights to the mainland, and forced Japanese manufacturers such as Panasonic, Sony, and Honda to temporarily halt production in their Chinese factories. All of these examples demonstrate that globalization of information is a double-edged sword: it has the potential to tie nations together as well as to provoke international tensions and unintended cultural misunderstandings.

Government Innovation Policies in Developed Countries

Technologically advanced countries are playing a game of global "keep-up," not "catch-up." They want to stay competitive in knowledge-based industries and nurture "creative industries," where value added per worker is high and positive spillovers into other sectors of the economy are great. Some of these signature industries include design, arts and entertainment, biotechnology, health care, and defense. Innovation is premised on political openness, vast educational opportunities, labor mobility, and other characteristics that only a limited number of countries can quickly turn to their advantage.

These nations recognize that technological growth has historically been a key determinant of economic growth. For example, in the nineteenth century the U.S. government founded land-grant colleges throughout the country to spur transformation in agriculture, industry, and engineering. More recently, "advances in knowledge" accounted for an estimated 68 percent of the increase in U.S. labor productivity and 28 percent of the growth in U.S. income between 1929 and 1982. While technological innovation is largely the product of investment in research and development by individual firms, governments have tried to nurture it through public spending and subsidies and IPR enforcement (discussed later in this chapter). Building a technology infrastructure is something many states have done historically, often in times of national emergency or interstate rivalry. Massive U.S. investment in the Manhattan Project during World War II gave the country superiority in nuclear technology. As part of its political rivalry with the Soviet Union during the Cold War, the United States boosted its leadership in space technology via the Apollo Project and military spending on satellite systems. From 1990 to 2003, the U.S. Department of Energy and the National Institutes of Health funded the Human Genome Project, which had major benefits for commercial innovation in molecular medicine and the life sciences industries.

Governments often identify new R&D needs and provide resources for huge leaps forward in areas such as energy and medical research. This can be done by direct funding to universities, government research labs, and private companies. Sociologist Henry Etzkowitz stresses how this funding can produce a "triple helix"—a university–industry–government relationship that accelerates innovation.[7] For example, the Bayh-Dole Act of 1980 gave U.S. universities and federal labs the right to gain patents on inventions funded with public money and sell or license those IPRs to private companies. Examples of government-assisted innovation in the United States include Gatorade (developed at the University of Florida and now licensed to Quaker Oats), Google online searching (hatched at Stanford University), and storm-tracking radar (developed at MIT).

In a related fashion, many governments provide "venture capital" to small private firms with promising new technology. In 1958, the U.S. government created an agency within the Department of Defense called the U.S. Defense Advanced Research Projects Agency (DARPA) to finance research by industries and universities into technology of use to the military. Technological spin-offs from its continuing sponsorship of research include the Internet, virtual memory, computer networking, integrated circuit design, and voice-to-text software.

After World War II, the U.S. federal government funded about two-thirds of all U.S. R&D, but in recent decades this has declined to one-third as private industry has boosted its own investment. In the OECD countries, businesses now fund about 70 percent of R&D. For more than fifty years, the United States has led the world in overall combined government-private R&D. In 2009, it accounted for 31 percent ($400 billion) of global R&D spending, compared to 12 percent by China, 11 percent by Japan, and 6 percent by Germany (adjusted for PPP).[8] To gain a sense of how committed a country is to future innovation, we can measure the ratio of its R&D spending to GDP. The United States' robust ratio of 2.9 percent in 2009 lagged behind Japan's 3.3 percent but was much higher than the G20 countries' 2 percent and China's 1.7 percent.[9] This means that the United States and Japan will likely keep their technological lead for many years, even if China's R&D spending grows at a much faster rate. As laid out in its 2000 "Lisbon Strategy" and in its 2010 "Europe 2020" growth strategy, the European Union has also sought to increase research spending to equal at least 3 percent of EU GDP—a level only four of twenty-seven countries had reached by 2010. R&D has become more internationalized since the 1990s, with TNCs shifting some of it to countries like China and India with large markets and large pools of skilled, lower-cost researchers.

Scholars Jakob Edler and Luke Georghiou argue that public procurement has been an important means by which governments generate demand for innovative products by being a direct purchaser ("lead user") of them.[10] Governments also give tax rebates to consumers and businesses that purchase innovative products, thus encouraging faster commercialization of them. One example of this is so-called "green procurement," where consumers get long-term loans and rebates to install energy-saving appliances or get cash rebates for trading up for cleaner, gas-saving cars. Since 2004, Germany has accelerated development of renewable energies by guaranteeing to producers of solar and wind power an above-market price for the energy they contribute to the electricity grid. The subsidies come from a fee on each household's electric bill. Japan adopted a similar pricing system in 2012 to encourage the spread of renewable energy sources to fill the void caused by the shuttering of nuclear power plants after the Fukushima disaster.

In addition to fostering innovation, developed states seek to prevent the diffusion of some forms of advanced technology to other countries. During the Cold War, the United States forbade the export of weapons systems (and information related to them), nuclear technology, and dual-use technologies to the Soviet Union. It also established "deemed export controls" that limit the transfer of export-controlled items or protected technical information to foreigners working or studying in the United States. Universities or private contractors have to obtain licenses to allow foreigners to access this information, particularly if the institutions get federal funding.

By requiring licenses and approvals for certain lists of exports, the United States has slowed the spread of technology that could enhance other countries' military-industrial potential. When sharing advanced technology with close allies like Japan, Britain, and Germany, the United States has sought to ensure that they also restrict its re-export. This has required close multilateral cooperation, especially among NATO members, to harmonize all their export controls.

However, geopolitical and economic changes since 1990 have weakened the West's technological oligopoly. As French political scientist Hugo Meijer argues, "In the post-Cold War era, the mutually reinforcing trends of the lack of a common security threat, a weaker multilateral framework governing export controls, and the globalization and commercialization of military-related technologies have significantly eroded the ability of states to control the transfer of dual-use technologies to potential adversaries."[11] Private companies on the cutting edge of ICT need to find export markets for dual-use products in order to remain profitable. Export controls hamper their ability to compete globally and conduct joint research with non-military firms in other countries.

Closing the Knowledge and Technology Gap

Many innovations result from the individual decisions of millions of companies or as a result of processes inherent in global capitalism. For example, high-tech (knowledge) industries have been termed **Schumpeterian industries**—after economist Joseph Schumpeter (1883–1950). He believed that only firms with some degree of monopoly power would likely have the *incentive* (a large payback resulting from a long imitation lag) and the *ability* (in the form of monopoly profits) to invest in risky, expensive, and long-term R&D projects. Consequently, many key industries were likely to be monopolistically structured. However, over time, technologically audacious newcomers would displace once-dominant firms. "Gales of creative destruction" would destroy established monopolies and create new dominant firms.

Because of economies of large scale (including network economies), competition in many industries today is not for market share but for the market itself—competition becomes a "winner take all" or at least a "winner take most" proposition. This reality has obvious political-economic implications. In order to foster the development of national champions that dominate Schumpeterian industries, mercantilist-minded policy makers will put in place industrial policies that marshal the resources and power of the state to this end. Even liberal-minded policy makers will recognize the importance of creating conditions within their countries that will promote entrepreneurs capable of competing in Schumpeterian industries—conditions described in Michael Porter's best seller *The Competitive Advantage of Nations*.[12] The ability to acquire, create, and control technology has become central to international competition in the twenty-first century.

Political economist Raymond Vernon has discussed another way in which markets diffuse technology around the world. He observed that some of the products that the United States once produced and even exported were eventually produced abroad and became imports. This product life cycle (from export to import) is in part based on the interaction of product and process innovation. The United States has for years been especially strong in product innovation—inventing new products, developing them for the home market, and eventually exporting them to other countries with similar needs.

Other nations such as Japan have shown success in process innovation—the development of more efficient, lower-cost production techniques. As process innovation is applied, production is shifted abroad from U.S. factories. The new producer may be an especially innovative firm in Japan, or it could be a low-cost producer in a newly industrialized country (NIC), especially if innovation has standardized the product and simplified its construction. The cycle is completed when the United States then ends up importing at low cost the item it once exported.

The cycle that Vernon described has accelerated in the last twenty years to produce what we refer to as the globalization of production, and while it is substantially a market-driven process, governments in developing economies now have a much more direct role in managing it. Many product and process innovators are mushrooming in places like China and India. Through partnerships between government and business, investment in education, and acquisition of technology from foreign sources, the Asian "Tigers" now compete head-to-head with U.S. and European firms for world market share in high-value-added goods.

Political economists such as Gary Gereffi analyze more complex, contemporary forms of the product cycle called **global value chains**, which account for "the full range of activities that firms and workers do to bring a product from its conception to its end use and beyond."[13] Many firms are linked in a set of global relationships (or a division of labor) in which Western firms engage in high-value functions such as finance, basic research, design, product branding, and marketing, while developing countries perform low-value functions such as low-wage manufacturing, subcontracting, and raw material extraction and processing. LDCs want to move up the value chain to more profitable activities, but to do so they need to close the technology gap with developed countries by ensuring a rapid transfer of know-how to their societies.

Taiwan and Korea have followed Japan's example for how to move up the value chain to capture more profit. They created national champions through deliberate industrial policy and strategic trade policies, among other things (see Chapters 6 and 11). Their companies started out by manufacturing or assembling parts and components for global corporations. Then their companies began to engage more in product design and upgraded their manufacturing technology. Finally, they became leaders in some industries, accumulating patents and manufacturing their own brands. At this stage, their companies are global players in their own right, like Taiwan's Acer and Korea's Samsung, LG, and Hyundai.

China is following the Japanese and Korean model of creating national champions through deliberate industrial policy. It encourages national companies to conduct more R&D and buy overseas high-tech assets like IBM's PC division, called Lenovo since 2004. The Chinese, Indians, and others in Asia are determined to attract cutting-edge research labs. Singapore is becoming a biomedical research center. China is now a leading manufacturer of solar panels. High-tech and medium-tech manufactured goods represent a significant share of exports for China and Brazil (as for Japan, Germany, Ireland, and the United States). And TNCs are outsourcing high-skill tasks like software development, engineering services, and drug trials to these countries.

Struggles over Education and Skilled Workers

Innovative societies require more than just good institutions and R&D spending; they also need well-educated workers and skilled professionals. The United States, Europe, and many other OECD countries have had the best of both worlds since World War II. Struggles over knowledge embodied in people extend to higher education and visa policies.

Labor mobility is a critical contributor to an innovative society, particularly the ability of individuals to move from one company to another and to set up new businesses. Economists have found a lot of innovation in regional high-tech clusters with high labor mobility like Silicon Valley and North Carolina's Research Triangle. Similarly, innovation is spurred by in-migration from other countries, that is, international labor mobility.

The United States attracts many gifted foreign students to its institutions of higher education. In 2011–2012, there were 764,000 foreign students in American universities, a record high number.[14] Almost 47 percent of these students came from the top three sending countries: India, China, and South Korea. Almost half were studying business, engineering, and physical and life sciences. Foreign students make up a vital percentage of all students in graduate programs in the

United States. They earned one-third of PhDs in science and engineering fields in 2009 and more than half of all doctorates in engineering, physics, and computer sciences.[15]

The U.S. economy benefits from harnessing the skills of these graduates who remain in the United States and enter the labor force, often with permanent residency. In a testament to their importance, former INTEL chief Andrew Grove said once that the government should staple a Green Card to the diploma of every foreign student graduating in the United States! According to Vivek Wadhwa, "During the closing decades of the 20th century, roughly 80 percent of the Chinese and Indians who earned U.S. PhDs in science, technology, engineering, and mathematics (STEM) fields have stayed in the United States and provided a critical boost to the nation's economy."[16] He found that many of these immigrants are employed in companies producing software or providing innovation/manufacturing-related services. In Silicon Valley specifically, half of all start-up companies in engineering and technology between 1995 and 2005 had at least one key foreign-born founder.[17]

Other indicators demonstrate the importance of U.S. ethnic scientific communities to innovation and commercialization of products in high-tech and professional fields. Foreign nationals in the United States have received a large number of U.S. patents. Census data show that in the United States 30 percent of computer software developers are foreign nationals.[18] Twenty percent of engineers and architects and 15 percent of nurses in the United States are foreign-born. And more than 400,000 Europeans with science and technology degrees work in the United States, attracted by better salaries, more funding, and better opportunities for advancement than in the EU.[19] However, U.S. industries complain that the U.S. government does not issue enough H-1B work visas for skilled foreigners.

A changing global economy, however, means that the United States has to compete more than ever for the best students and professionals. China and India now churn out many more undergraduate and graduate students than the United States in engineering, IT, and computer science. From only 3.4 million university students in 1998, by 2008 China had 21.5 million.[20] At the same time, the European Union passed a Directive on Highly Qualified Workers in 2009 designed to attract highly skilled immigrants who otherwise might choose to work in the United States, Canada, or Australia.

Many students are returning home after studying or working in the United States, mitigating a lot of the previous brain drain. Their return is a very important mechanism of technology transfer. Many are working in new research labs set up by the likes of IBM, GE, and Cisco. In 2008 and 2010, Vivek Wadhwa surveyed hundreds of young, professional Indians and Chinese who had returned to their home countries after working or studying in the United States. The vast majority of those surveyed indicated that opportunities for professional advancement were better at home and that they could find a better quality of life and better family values in their native country than in the United States.[21] This indicates the rising standard of living for the upper classes in Asia's rising powers (see Chapter 13). Clearly the "land of opportunity" has a lot of new competition.

Over the long term, the innovative capacity of any country depends on its ability to teach its own citizens the skills needed in knowledge-intensive industries. Not only is it the percentage of students in higher education that counts, but also what they study, how well they learn, and their financial condition at the time of graduation. While the trends look bright in a rising power like China, they appear to be deteriorating in the United States. Between 2002 and 2010, state appropriations per student in U.S. public research universities fell 20 percent, even as college enrollment increased. By 2011—in the midst of the financial crisis—state appropriations per student had dropped to their lowest level in twenty-five years.[22] In addition, rising tuition, stagnant family incomes, and higher student loan defaults indicated that the U.S. university system was eroding. Although the United States still has one of the highest levels of overall education spending as a percentage of GDP, between 2000 and 2009 the ratio barely grew in the United States while it skyrocketed in Korea, the Russian Federation, Mexico, and the United Kingdom. The average growth in education spending as a percentage of GDP rose faster in OECD countries than in the United States, indicating that other countries are working harder to close the gap.[23]

THE IPE OF INTELLECTUAL PROPERTY RIGHTS

In addition to R&D and technology, intellectual property rights (IPRs) are a key component of the knowledge structure today. Patents, copyrights, and trademarks are the most important forms of IPRs, but states have also assigned rights to such things as geographical indications, industrial designs, and trade secrets. IPRs are government-granted rights to control—for a limited amount of time—the use of inventions, creative works, and commercial names and symbols. The kinds of things states deem worthy of granting rights to have varied significantly over the last 200 years, as has the strength and length of protection. Officials struggle over when and under what conditions these rights can be overridden to protect the general public. Control of ideas and the products that are associated with them has important effects on innovation and the distribution of wealth.

There are a number of ways in which countries coordinate their IPR policies, such as through the **Trade-Related Aspects of Intellectual Property Rights (TRIPS)** agreement of the WTO, which requires countries to provide a minimum level of IPR protection and enforcement. However, it is important to remember that individual states define IPRs in different ways that reflect historical differences in their legal traditions and political evolution.

Patents confer the exclusive right to make, use, or sell an invention for a period usually of twenty years (counted from date of filing). Without these rights, many companies would be unable to capture all of the benefits of their R&D expenditures and therefore might not find it worthwhile to invest in scientific research and innovation. While the criteria for gaining a patent vary from one country to another, usually the invention must be new, useful (have some kind of industrial application), and nonobvious to someone who is skilled in the field. In exchange for the temporary monopoly on the use of the invention, an inventor must disclose the details of it in writing to the public. Companies can make their own patent-protected products, license the use of their patents to others, or even sell their patents.

Countries place many restrictions on patents. For example, EU members do not offer patents for computer programs, methods for treatment of the human body, or inventions whose commercial exploitation conflicts with public policy. Governments reserve the right to override patents in some circumstances such as when patent holders abuse their market power by acting like a monopoly or cartel. Governments can issue a compulsory license, which allows a firm to use someone's patent without their permission in exchange for a specified payment to the patent owner. And governments will sometimes override patents in times of national emergency such as war. The United States, Japan, and the European Union each account for approximately 30 percent of the most valuable patents registered in the world annually.

Copyrights protect the *expression* of an idea, not the idea itself. They are provided to authors of artistic works like books, movies, television programs, music, magazines, photographs—and even software in a growing number of countries. Copyrights generally allow an owner to prevent the unauthorized reproduction, distribution, and sale of an original work. The WTO TRIPS agreement requires members to offer copyright protection that lasts at least the life of the author plus fifty years. In the United States and Europe, protection lasts for the life of the author plus seventy years—and in the United States corporate works (works for hire) are protected for ninety-five years. Lengths of protection have grown longer in the last 100 years while the value of trade in copyrighted products has mushroomed. There is a growing debate about whether so many creative works should be kept out of the public domain for so long. In the United States, the major copyright industries— movies, music, book publishing, and software—contribute to about 6.4 percent of overall GDP—more than $930 billion annually.[24]

Governments provide exceptions to copyrights so that we can make use of copyrighted material in certain circumstances without paying or asking permission from the copyright holder. For example, it is considered "fair use" in many countries to reproduce or use a portion of a work for criticism, parody, news reporting, or teaching. Similarly, it is usually legal to reproduce or record a book, song, or TV program for personal, noncommercial use. After all, that's what a photocopier, a digital video disc (DVD) burner, and TiVo are mostly used for! And once we purchase a legal physical copy of a copyrighted item, we are free to sell it or rent it to whomever we want.

Trademarks are signs or symbols (including logos and names) registered by a manufacturer or merchant to identify its goods and services. Protection is usually granted for ten years and is renewable. A trademark gives a company the right to prevent others from using the symbol, name, expression, or slogan. Examples of trademarks include the Nike swoosh, the brand name Kleenex, and MGM's lion's roar. In most countries, one cannot get a trademark for a term denoting kind, quality, value, or origin like "excellent," "extra," "cheap," or "Norwegian."

Trademarks are essential for the efficient functioning of the market. They help prevent unfair competition from imitators and consumer confusion about the true source of a product. They help consumers select products of high quality and reliability. Without a system of adequate trademark protection, consumers will spend more hours attempting to discern quality differences, and producers will be discouraged from investing in the production of quality goods and services. Trademarks also convey information about a buyer and his or her social status.

The Politics of IPRs in Developed Countries

The United States, the European Union, and Japan have largely shaped the global rules governing IPRs. They have defined the scope of IPRs, signed international agreements, and set up multilateral institutions to enshrine the rules in international relations. They seek to enforce these rules, using political lobbying and international diplomacy.

The United States has taken the lead in promoting the protection of IPRs, under relentless pressure to do so in the last twenty-five years from powerful businesses. The Intellectual Property Committee, an ad hoc coalition of twelve major U.S. corporations established in 1986, contended that there was a link between the protection of IPRs and U.S. international competitiveness. Without adequate protection, U.S. firms would find it difficult to profit from product and process innovation. Foreign firms that infringe on IPRs have lower development costs because they are merely copying original technological innovations. Consequently, these infringing firms can underprice the U.S. firms that incurred the original development costs. The IPC members also painted a picture of an epidemic of piracy of entertainment media, and they estimated the overall losses to U.S. business from foreign infringement of IPRs in tens of billions of dollars every year.

As political scientists Susan Sell and Aseem Prakash have documented, the pro-IPRs movement was spearheaded by a network of companies mostly in the software, video, music, agricultural chemicals, and pharmaceutical industries. They also developed alliances with similar companies in Europe to successfully frame IPRs as rights—not government-granted privileges—and to spread a discourse about the dangers of "piracy" to free markets.[25]

Their most important goal was to create a set of enforceable international minimum standards for IPRs. In the 1980s there were already multilateral IPR agreements in existence, including the 100-year-old Berne Convention on copyrights and the Paris Convention on patents and trademarks. In 1967, the World Intellectual Property Organization (WIPO), a UN agency, was created to monitor adherence to these conventions. But the business networks and U.S. and European governments were dissatisfied because the conventions had low standards, did not have enforcement mechanisms, and did not include many developing countries.

During the Uruguay round of trade negotiations from 1986 to 1994, the United States and other developed nations insisted on the establishment of a new treaty called TRIPS, which WTO members would be obliged to accept, along with the new GATS and the revised GATT. TRIPS requires countries to provide a minimum level of intellectual property protection and adhere to the Berne and Paris Conventions. Special concessions were also negotiated for developing countries that need time to amend their IPR laws in order to conform to the minimum standards.

TRIPS was a coup for major intellectual property producers because it tied intellectual property protection to participation in the liberalized international trade system and established a mechanism for binding dispute resolution. Many developing countries did not particularly like the agreement and had little role in crafting it, but they accepted it as a price to pay for gaining other trade benefits within the WTO. TRIPS also expanded the kinds of intellectual property protected to include **geographical indications (GIs)**, plant varieties, and trade secrets (such as the formula for Coke, Colonel Sanders' secret recipe, and lists of customers).

Not surprisingly, the developed nations have also supported U.S. efforts to enhance the international protection of IPRs beyond just the TRIPS standards. They strengthened WIPO, which administers its own convention and some twenty-four international agreements on IPRs. It has an Arbitration and Mediation Centre (WIPO Center) that can resolve disputes between private parties over domain names and cybersquatting. In 1996, WIPO produced two treaties that harmonize the protection of IPRs on the Internet and thereby promote international electronic commerce. In 2000, WIPO also adopted a Patent Law Treaty to harmonize patent application procedures across countries.

Under U.S. trade law, the government can act unilaterally against countries that fail to protect IPRs adequately. Special Section 301 of the 1988 Omnibus Trade and Competition Act requires the United States Trade Representative (USTR) to create annually a "watch list" and a "priority watch list" for countries that have shortcomings in the protection of IPRs. After investigating the policies of an offending country, the USTR may negotiate a bilateral agreement or institute trade sanctions. The USTR's 2012 Special 301 Report includes an assessment of the effectiveness of intellectual property protections in seventy-seven countries. Thirty-nine countries were placed on the priority watch list or the watch list, including the five largest countries in the world other than the United States (China, India, Indonesia, Brazil, and Pakistan) and America's three biggest trading partners—Canada, China, and Mexico. As in the past, it seems that the United States has trouble finding more than a handful of important countries that live up to its self-declared IPR standards.

With the stick of unilateral trade sanctions firmly in hand, the United States has successfully negotiated bilateral and regional agreements with many countries to improve the protection of IPRs. It has also signed free-trade agreements with Central America and about a dozen countries including Chile, Peru, Colombia, Korea, Singapore, and Morocco that provide even more intellectual property protection than the minimum required by TRIPS.

Developed nations have also sought to "harmonize" IPR laws across national boundaries. Separate from the WIPO and the WTO, developed countries negotiated a voluntary agreement called the Anti-Counterfeiting Trade Agreement (ACTA) to ratchet up the fight against counterfeit goods and copyright-infringing actors, especially through border controls and enforcement by customs agencies. Actions like these are part of what Susan Sell has described as an ongoing campaign by powerful political actors and business groups to strengthen global IPR enforcement and tie counterfeiting and piracy to security issues, lost business revenues, and lost taxes.[26] Although the ACTA treaty was signed by the United States, Japan, the European Union, and several other countries in 2011 and 2012, European protests against it in early 2012 stalled ratification. At the same time, two bills in the U.S. Congress—the Stop Online Piracy Act (SOPA) and the PROTECT

IP Act (PIPA)—that would have dramatically expanded penalties for online copyright violations touched off unprecedented social opposition. Wikipedia, Reddit, and BoingBoing went dark on January 18, 2012, while big Internet companies like Google, Facebook, and Craigslist directed millions of users to lobby Washington against these so-called censorship bills—both of which were withdrawn in the face of this first-ever Internet "blackout."

Although developed countries are cooperating in important ways, conflict between them over IPRs still exists to a significant degree, given the centrality of knowledge and technology to competitive advantage. For example, while the United States does not give producers of databases IPR protection, the European Union lets them prevent unauthorized "extraction" and "re-utilization" from their databases for fifteen years. Japan and the European Union also provide protections for fashion designs (of clothing, bags, and accessories) for three and ten years, respectively, but the United States gives no IPRs to fashion designers. The United States has much stronger protection of so-called **publicity rights** than any other country in the world. Famous people and celebrities can ban unauthorized use of their name, image, or identifying characteristics (with exceptions for activities like news reporting). These rights can even be inherited or sold to third parties who want to use them for marketing. For example, Albert Einstein's publicity rights are owned by the Hebrew University in Israel, which has licensed the use of his name and image to Disney (for the Baby Einstein products), to Nestlé (for a Japanese coffee), to Apple (for its early "Think Different" ad campaign), and to dozens of U.S. manufacturers of cheap collectibles.

Geographical indications have emerged as a new bone of contention between the Old World and the New World. The TRIPS agreement defines GIs as "indications which identify a good as originating in the territory of a Member, or a region or locality in that territory, where a given quality, reputation or other characteristic of the good is essentially attributable to its geographical origin." Examples include Champagne, Roquefort, Scotch, Vidalia onions, Florida oranges, Idaho potatoes, and Napa Valley wine. They give a collective monopoly over specific names to producers who are often located in a well-defined area and who use specified ingredients and production methods. One of the main justifications for GIs is that they prevent the public from being misled about the origin or quality of a product.

European countries insist on strong GI protections—especially for wines and spirits—because Europe has the largest number of historically well-known products. They have sought to use the GIs as a form of protection against low-cost agricultural competitors in the United States, Australia, and the New World who want to imitate the original products. The European Union is even trying to "**claw back**" to GI protection the names of several dozen meats, cheeses, and alcoholic goods that are considered generic words, including Parmesan cheese, Feta cheese, and Chablis. Within the WTO it has negotiated for an international register of GIs and an extension of the strong GI protection currently applying to wines and spirits to include other products like food.

In recent years, many countries outside of Europe have begun to warm to the idea of promoting their own GIs, through national laws and bilateral treaties. As the size of global markets has increased, so has the potential market value of GIs like Basmati rice, tequila, Darjeeling tea, and Washington State apples.

GIs can potentially encourage innovation in artisanal markets, promote regional industries, and encourage sustainable growing practices. Some see them as a way of resisting homogenized global brands and protecting "heritage" and diversity of products.[27] Law scholar Madhavi Sunder notes that GIs have the potential to help the poor by giving more value to the collective contributions of farmers and craftspeople.[28]

North–South Conflicts over Intellectual Property Rights

Developing nations have increasingly resisted the IPR norms and policies that developed countries promote. Part of the opposition is to the minimum standards for protection in TRIPS. LDCs want more flexibility to craft their *own* IPR standards consistent with their specific national needs. They have forcefully demanded recognition of their right to make use of already-existing flexibilities in the TRIPS agreement like compulsory licensing of essential drugs. They have also sought to redefine principles of intellectual property law to include promotion of human rights, public health, education, and cultural autonomy. Finally, some countries are seeking to extend IPRs to biodiversity and traditional knowledge.

Although the poorest countries have until 2016 to fully implement TRIPS requirements, Argentina and Brazil spearheaded a Development Agenda for WIPO that was formally adopted by the WIPO General Assembly in 2007. The Agenda is a set of forty-five recommendations under which the WIPO is supposed to encourage technology transfer to developing countries, recognize that intellectual property rules should account for different levels of development, and make sure that IPRs not just focus on economic growth but serve a variety of social goals. A body called the Committee on Development and Intellectual Property (CDIP) is charged with monitoring implementation of the recommendations.

Although there are no guarantees that developing countries will benefit from strengthening their systems of IPR protection, China, India, and Brazil increasingly recognize the need to protect their own companies' patents and copyrights. And for those countries attempting to follow export-oriented development strategies, the risk of trade retaliation and the need to attract FDI provide strong incentives to comply with developed countries' IPR demands. Responding to some of the LDCs' foot-dragging in IPR enforcement, developed countries have signed bilateral free-trade agreements with countries that agree to higher standards of protection than are required by TRIPS. At the multilateral level, the United States has since 2009 been negotiating an agreement called the Trans-Pacific Partnership with countries along the Pacific Ocean that, among other things, requires strong intellectual property protections.

Debates over Patented Medicines

One of the most successful efforts to challenge the TRIPS agreement has been in the areas of compulsory licensing and access to medicines. A **compulsory license** is a license a state grants to a domestic private company or government body, with or without the consent of the rights holder, to produce and sell a good under patent. Although compulsory licensing is allowable under TRIPS if a government first negotiates with the patent holder, many poorer countries after 1994 felt that TRIPS unfairly constrained their ability to issue compulsory licenses for the manufacture of lifesaving medicines that were under patent. In the face of an HIV/AIDS epidemic, South Africa's government voted in 1997 to permit imports of cheap generic antiretroviral drugs from India and to allow compulsory licensing of patented antiretrovirals in South Africa (see the box Patent Rights versus Patient Rights).

A new global coalition called the Access to Medicines campaign led by NGOs and developing countries reframed the discussion of IPRs in light of the HIV/AIDS crisis. They sought to discredit big pharmaceutical companies for focusing on monopoly patents rather than saving lives. They pointed out that in national emergencies a country can override the rights of some patent holders. At the same time that the United States was resisting the campaign's efforts, hypocritically the U.S. Congress threatened to issue a compulsory license for Cipro production in 2001 during the anthrax scare. Bayer—the patent holder of this antibiotic—responded by agreeing to radically reduce prices and expand production.

Under intense pressure from Access to Medicines activists, pharmaceutical companies have pledged hundreds of millions of dollars for HIV/AIDS assistance in developing countries. Major manufacturers of antiretrovirals have drastically reduced the price per dose they charge poor countries for patented HIV/AIDS drugs through a variety of mechanisms like discounting, tiered pricing, and voluntary licensing programs. Private companies have also partnered with NGOs and governments in multilateral initiatives such as the Global Fund to Fight AIDS, Tuberculosis, and Malaria (to increase funding and access for health care) and the Global Alliance for Vaccines and Immunization (to increase research on "neglected" diseases and delivery of patented vaccines at affordable prices). It is hoped that a combination of more generics, more compulsory licensing, more voluntary cooperation by Big Pharma, more foreign funding, and more flexibility in IPR laws can make essential medicines more accessible throughout the world.

▶ PATENT RIGHTS VERSUS PATIENT RIGHTS

In 1998, about one in five adults living in South Africa was infected with HIV/AIDS. Unfortunately, the patent-protected antiretroviral drug "cocktail" that held the disease in check cost about $15,000 per patient per year in the United States. Consequently, only the richest South Africans could afford the treatment. Government subsidization of the drugs, at these prices, would have overwhelmed the budget. Generic versions of the drug cocktail produced in India cost only $200. India did not issue patents on pharmaceuticals, and this allowed the development of

a competitive generic drug industry. South Africa, on the other hand, had long had very strong patent laws.

Faced with this tragic public health crisis, the government of South Africa voted in 1997 to permit generic imports and "compulsory licensing" of these drugs. Thirty-nine pharmaceutical companies from around the world responded to South Africa's Medicines Act with a lawsuit to try to block the law. Activists around the world, incensed by this legal action, rallied against the lawsuit with the slogan, "Patient Rights over

Patent Rights." When the lawsuit finally reached the courtroom in March 2001, the pharmaceutical companies withdrew it in an effort to avoid a public relations debacle.[a]

Developing countries then successfully pressured WTO officials at ministerial meetings in Doha in November 2001 to affirm their right to issue compulsory licenses, especially in the face of national emergencies or conditions of national urgency like widespread HIV, malaria, tuberculosis, and other epidemics. This interpretation of the TRIPS agreement, called the Doha Declaration, was a breakthrough for the poorest countries. However, it still did not resolve many disputes over IPRs and the right to health. Many countries do not have companies with sufficient technological capacity to produce generics under compulsory licenses for their own domestic market.

Developing countries insisted that they should be able to import generic versions of patented medicines from countries such as India and Brazil and as an alternative to issuing a compulsory license locally without violating trade laws. After much hemming and hawing by the United States, the European Union, and Big Pharma, WTO members in 2003 agreed to this waiver, and most members by December 2009 had formally accepted it as a change to the TRIPS agreement. Brazil has been very active in using the threat of compulsory licenses to get price reductions from patent holders. Thailand, however, was put on the U.S. Section 301 Priority Watch list as punishment for issuing compulsory licenses in 2006 and 2007 for several anti-AIDS drugs, anticancer medications, and the heart drug Plavix.[b]

References

[a]The description of these events in this and the following paragraph was drawn from Amy Kapczynski, "Strict International Patent Laws Hurt Developing Countries," *YaleGlobal*, December 16, 2002, at http://yaleglobal.yale.edu /fr/node/285.

[b]For background on this dispute, see Mishka Glaser and Ann Marie Murphy, "Patients versus Patents: Thailand and the Politics of Access to Pharmaceutical Products," *Journal of Third World Studies* 27:1 (Spring 2010), pp. 215–234.

Struggles over Traditional Knowledge

Another IPR struggle between South and North is over **traditional knowledge (TK)**, which is the accumulated knowledge and practices of indigenous communities as they relate to plants, plant uses, agriculture, land use, folklore, and spiritual matters. Indigenous peoples around the world over many generations have developed deep understandings of their physical environments and the plants they use for food and medicine. They have developed and preserved a wide variety of plant diversity through harvesting and breeding practices. In fact, many of the major food crops in North America and Europe originally came from these local communities.

Northern companies have often appropriated TK for their own selfish purposes. As Madhavi Sunder notes: "The poor's knowledge is often considered simply the discovered bounty of nature—age-old knowledge that, remarkably, has remained static over millennia, and thus 'raw material' waiting to be turned into 'intellectual property' by entrepreneurs, largely from the Global North."[29] The economic value of TK is potentially very high. Billions of dollars' worth of prescription drugs sold every year are derived from tropical plants whose medicinal properties were learned from indigenous peoples. Countries like Brazil, India, the Philippines, and Indonesia have begun insisting that those who want to take seed samples or find local plants with chemicals that can be used in medicine must get permission, acknowledge the source of subsequently patented materials, and share benefits with the local communities whose traditional knowledge they initially relied upon. Developed countries have resisted the protection of TK, partly because TK conflicts with historic notions of what is intellectual property and promises to redistribute some of the gains from global innovation to poorer countries.

As the South seeks to valorize its control over biodiversity and medicinal plant uses, many countries are also trying to protect TK from appropriation and misuse by nonindigenous groups. This is an effort to give new cultural rights to indigenous peoples. Through the WIPO and in individual countries like Canada, there are campaigns to give indigenous peoples copyrights over their own folklore and artwork—including stories or sacred texts passed down over generations. Maoris in New Zealand and Native Americans have fought to prevent symbols associated with their people from being used by schools and private businesses. Similarly, some indigenous communities are seeking to establish their own trademarks over collective symbols and to apply design protections for handicrafts and carpets. India is rapidly creating a digital library of its traditional knowledge—including 1,300 yoga poses—so that non-Indians cannot patent, copyright, or trademark it.

Perspectives on Intellectual Property Rights

In light of the struggles over IPRs discussed so far, we conclude by contrasting some key theoretical arguments about IPRs and their effects on the global knowledge structure.

In the economic liberal view, property rights are fundamental to the functioning of a market system because they incentivize the efficient use of resources and establish a direct link between effort and reward. Knowledge is potentially expensive to make, but it is hard to prevent people from copying it cheaply. The knowledge one firm uses can also be used by other firms. This potentially leads to market failure, because there will be free riders—users of knowledge who do not pay for it. Consequently, unless firms can legally deny the use of newly created knowledge to other firms, rapid imitation will eliminate the profits from innovation necessary to recoup investments in R&D.

When a government provides the creators of knowledge a legal, but temporary, monopoly, they can exclude people from accessing their knowledge without paying for it. Creators are remunerated for their effort by gaining adequate returns on their investments in generating intellectual property. As a result, consumers worldwide supposedly get a wider variety of new products at reasonable prices. IPR enforcement also ensures that consumers will have higher quality and safer products than would otherwise be the case. And countries that protect intellectual property tend to attract more FDI and benefit from more technology transfer.

Mercantilists see the process of technological innovation in a much different light. Nations must develop and then closely guard their own technology while simultaneously acquiring other countries' technology. The protection of IPRs for domestic firms is clearly appropriate in order to foster domestic technological innovation, but equal protection for technology owned by foreign firms is not always in the national interest. As early mercantilists Friedrich List and Alexander Hamilton argued (see Chapter 3), free trade benefits the most developed manufacturing nations at the expense of less developed nations. Similarly, international conventions that protect IPRs will benefit those nations with the most advanced technological capabilities at the expense of less technologically developed nations. In this regard, mercantilist and structuralist thought is similar.

Intellectual property law scholar Peter Yu points out that when it comes to technological laggards, they need to fight for more "policy space" in IPRs, that is, the ability to craft their own intellectual property laws based on their own "conditions, capabilities, interests and priorities."[30] From a mercantilist perspective, many countries can make the best use of their limited resources by stealing intellectual property. Why? Because their businesses will save on R&D and absorb technology faster; their citizens will get much cheaper products; and the government will not have to spend money on a bureaucracy to protect the IPRs of foreigners. The Chinese seem to have taken this lesson to heart, just as previous generations of Japanese, Koreans, and Americans did.

Structuralists contend that developed nations use IPRs to monopolize global markets and extract excessive profits from Third World countries. The capitalists that hold IPRs behave like international monopolists and cartels. They are not really interested in competition, which they will sacrifice on the altar of rent-seeking and litigation. As international relations scholar Carolyn Deere Birkbeck notes, 90 percent of global cross-border royalties on intellectual property and technology licensing fees go to just ten developed countries.[31]

Economic geographer Christian Zeller claims that capitalists want to appropriate, control, and commodify intellectual creativity everywhere that it exists.[32] They always seek to create private property rights from "socially-produced knowledge." Capitalists dispossess "researchers, skilled workers, and also rural communities" of the "knowledge and information which they generate in collective work," transferring the rents to "venture capital, investment funds and license companies."[33] In this structuralist vision, the real creators of knowledge—farmers, indigenous peoples, scholars, and hardworking employees—never really reap the fruits of their creativity.

Alternative Perspectives on Intellectual Property Rights

Beyond these three perspectives, there are other complex and overlapping points of view on IPRs from the constructivists, "balancers," and "abolitionists." As we discovered in Chapter 5, constructivists see our social world as constructed: what we value and the interests we have are defined by our shared discourse about them. We have constructed a discourse that something called "intellectual property" is like real "property" and that there are "rights" we should ascribe to that property. While today it may seem natural to see most creative ideas and knowledge-based products as having rights attached to them, historically that was not the case.

Constructivists trace over time how we define IPRs and talk about them; by so doing we better understand whose interests in society are being served by this discourse. Since the 1980s, powerful economic lobbies have defined IPRs as an international trade issue. They frame intellectual property as something that belongs to creative and hard-working people who seek a just reward for their efforts. Creators are pitted against forces described as "pirates" and "counterfeiters" who unjustly take what is not theirs and hurt honest people and companies. In contrast,

Madhavi Sunder argues that if we look at intellectual property through a cultural perspective, we can redefine its purpose to mean empowering the poor so that they can enjoy a livelihood, fairly participate in cultural production, and preserve their cultural diversity from the onslaught of profit-driven, globalized, mass culture.[34]

Constructivists also explain that other social forces are trying to offer an alternative set of ideas about how knowledge is created and circulated in the world. For example, according to legal scholar James Boyle, postmodernists offer us the argument that "all creation is re-creation" and "there is no such thing as originality, merely endless imitation."[35] In this discourse, no one truly owns their creative output because it is built on the ideas of many people who preceded them. As Newton said, "If I have seen further it is only by standing on the shoulders of giants." If creation is cumulative and informed by everyone around us and before us, then it is hard to argue that we should own what we make from shared knowledge.

A different perspective on IPRs comes from "balancers" who want to strike an appropriate balance between individual rights and communal rights. They want to make sure that individuals can be creative and free while still respecting the legitimate economic rights and privacy rights of others. James Boyle, for example, stresses that a large "public domain" and many "fair use" guarantees encourage creative activity in a society. Similarly, Kembrew McLeod and Peter DiCola assert that artistic creativity has always relied upon borrowing, sampling, ripping, and imitating. Therefore, to criminalize these actions when they occur without "permission" is to impede artistic creation itself.[36]

Balancers want to prevent IPR holders from stifling competition or excessively suing others for alleged infringement. Boyle points out that many copyright industries tried in the past to resist new technologies—including the Xerox machine, the VCR, cassette tapes, and TiVo—because it threatened their business model. More recently, cable companies and all the major TV broadcasters are trying to crush an innovative startup company called Aereo by suing it for copyright infringement. Aereo offers a low-cost monthly service that allows customers to capture TV broadcast signals and stream them through the Internet to their home computer or mobile device.

Balancers want to limit the length and scope of IPRs. They abhor the "permission society," where individuals constantly have to ask copyright holders for permission to access almost every cultural product. Instead, balancers like David Bollier assert that societies need to preserve a large knowledge commons or public domain from which everyone can draw freely. He touts the collective generation of valuable content by sharing and peer production through networks where oppressive copyright laws are unenforceable.[37] This resistance to existing IPR laws manifests itself in many forms including the Creative Commons movement, the Open Source movement, mashups, blogs, and social networking.

The last main perspective is that of the "abolitionists," who want to see the elimination or radical reduction of IPRs. Economists Michele Boldrin and David Levine argue that IPRs distort markets, undermine competition, and reduce innovation.[38] They find that in the absence of IPRs, markets still reward innovators who produce goods and services at reasonable prices for consumers. Many economists have found little evidence that IPRs spur more competition, and in many sectors of the global economy such as the fashion industry, database services, software development, and agriculture, there have been significant technological breakthroughs and thriving markets even in the absence of IPR protections.

CONCLUSION

Whether viewed from a liberal, mercantilist, or structuralist perspective, knowledge and technology form an increasingly critical basis of wealth and power. In this era of global competition, companies and policy makers understand that knowledge and technology confer competitive advantage. That the protection of IPRs has risen to the status of a major foreign policy concern for the United States, Europe, and Japan is not surprising. The knowledge structure clearly constrains actors' options and conditions their behavior. It affects which companies and economies will turn innovation into higher productivity, market share, and increased exports. It also helps determine the distribution of benefits by shaping prices, productive capacity, and the quality of goods and services.

The debates and struggles over IPRs will continue for many years. There is greater recognition by some economic liberals that too many

IPRs can have negative consequences for development and the public domain.[39] People insist on being able to share content and network with others around the world, instantaneously. Governments will have a nearly impossible task putting this genie back in the bottle through rigid enforcement of IPRs.

Key questions concerning the knowledge structure include the following: How will the forces of globalization affect the creation and dissemination of knowledge? Will stricter enforcement of IPRs help or hinder the poorest nations of the world? Will piracy and counterfeiting undermine the incentives to innovate? Will the dominance of the United States in science and technology continue, or will it be severely eroded by China and India? Will competition for new technologies lead to a new era of economic nationalism? The answers to these questions will have profound effects on the lives of present and future generations.

KEY TERMS

intellectual property rights (IPRs) 238
research and development (R&D) 240
Schumpeterian industries 246
global value chains 247

Trade-Related Aspects of Intellectual Property Rights (TRIPS) 250
patents 250
copyrights 251
trademarks 251

geographical indications (GIs) 253
publicity rights 254
claw back 254
compulsory license 255
traditional knowledge 257

DISCUSSION QUESTIONS

1. What are intellectual property rights, and why are they important in today's global markets?
2. What are some of the reasons why developed countries like the United States try to restrict or control other countries' access to their technology and intellectual property? Does this behavior contradict economic liberal principles?
3. Describe the nature of the TRIPS provisions. Provide arguments both for and against stronger IPR protections in poor countries.

4. Which countries have been identified as major sources of pirated or counterfeited products? What do you believe are the best ways for developed countries to deal with violations of IPRs?
5. What are some of the most important ways that a country can nurture an innovative and technologically advanced society?

SUGGESTED READINGS

William Baumol, Robert Litan, and Carl Schramm. *Good Capitalism, Bad Capitalism, and the Economics of Growth and Prosperity.* New Haven, CT: Yale University Press, 2007.

Michele Boldrin and David Levine. *Against Intellectual Monopoly.* Cambridge: Cambridge University Press, 2008.

Creative Economy Report 2010. UNCTAD, 2010. At: http://unctad.org/en/Docs/ditctab20103_en.pdf.

Carolyn Deere. *The Implementation Game: The TRIPS Agreement and the Global Politics of Intel-lectual Property Reform in Developing Countries.* Oxford: Oxford University Press, 2008.

Peter Maskus. *Private Rights and Public Problems: The Global Economics of Intellectual Property in the 21st Century.* Washington, D.C.: Peterson Institute for International Economics, 2012.

Susan Sell. *Private Power, Public Law: The Globalization of Intellectual Property Rights.* Cambridge: Cambridge University Press, 2003.

NOTES

1. The programmer and digital activist Aaron Schwartz was one of those individuals who campaigned against Internet censorship and fought to make court documents and academic journals available for free to the public. A co-author of the RSS web feed and founder of one of the companies that became Reddit, Schwartz committed suicide in January 2013.
2. Sahar Khmais, Paul Gold, and Katherine Vaughn, "Beyond Egypt's 'Facebook Revolution' and Syria's 'YouTube Uprising:' Comparing Political Contexts, Actors and Communication Strategies," *Arab Media and Society* 15 (Spring 2012).
3. Siobhan Gorman, "China Tech Giant under Fire," *Wall Street Journal*, October 8, 2012.
4. John Bellamy Foster and Robert W. McChesney, "The Internet's Unholy Marriage to Capitalism," *Monthly Review* 62:10 (March 2011).
5. Yochai Benkler, "A Free Irresponsible Press: WikiLeaks and the Battle over the Soul of the Networked Fourth Estate," *Harvard Civil Rights-Civil Liberties Law Review* 46:2 (2011), pp. 311–397.
6. Jennifer Shkabatur, "A Global Panopticon? The Changing Role of International Organizations in the Information Age," *Michigan Journal of International Law* 33:2 (2011), pp. 159–214.
7. Henry Etzkowitz, *Triple Helix: A New Model of Innovation* (Stockholm: SNS Press, 2005).
8. National Science Board, *Science and Engineering Indicators 2012* (Arlington, VA: National Science Foundation, 2012), p. 4–41.
9. Ibid., p. 4–45.
10. Jakob Edler and Luke Georghiou, "Public Procurement and Innovation—Resurrecting the Demand Side," *Research Policy* 36 (2007), pp. 949–963.
11. Hugo Meijer, "Controlling the Uncontrollable? U.S. Dual-Use Exports in the Post–Cold War Era," *Fiche de l'Irsem* no. 10 (December 2011).
12. Michael Porter, *Competitive Advantage of Nations* (New York: The Free Press, 1990).
13. For more background on GVCs see http://www.globalvaluechains.org/concepts.html.
14. For detailed information on foreign students in the United States, see http://opendoors.iienetwork.org.
15. National Science Board, *Science and Engineering Indicators 2012* (Arlington, VA: National Science Foundation, 2012), p. 2–29.
16. Vivek Wadhwa, "A Reverse Brain Drain," *Issues in Science and Technology* (Spring 2009), pp. 45–46.
17. Vivek Wadhwa, *The Immigrant Exodus: Why America Is Losing the Global Race to Capture Entrepreneurial Talent* (Philadelphia: Wharton Digital Press, 2012).
18. "Immigration and Jobs: Where U.S. Workers Come From," *New York Times*, April 7, 2009, http://www.nytimes.com/interactive/2009/04/07/us/20090407-immigration-occupation.html.
19. Jeff Chu, "How to Plug Europe's Brain Drain," *Time (Europe)*, January 11, 2004, http://www.time.com/time/magazine/article/0,9171,574849,00.html.
20. Ian Johnson, "China Faces a Grad Glut after Boom at Colleges," *Wall Street Journal*, April 28, 2009, p. A1.

21. Vivek Wadhwa, *The Immigrant Exodus*, pp. 39–40.

22. National Science Board, *Diminishing Funding and Rising Expectations: Trends and Challenges for Public Research Universities* (Arlington, VA: National Science Foundation, 2012), p. 10.

23. OECD, *Education at a Glance 2012: OECD Indicators* (OECD Publishing, 2012), p. 236.

24. Stephen Siwek, *Copyright Industries in the U.S. Economy: The 2011 Report* (International Intellectual Property Alliance, 2011), at http://www.iipa.com/pdf/2011CopyrightIndustriesReport.PDF.

25. Susan Sell and Aseem Prakash, "Using Ideas Strategically: The Contest between Business and NGO Networks in Intellectual Property Rights," *International Studies Quarterly* 48 (2004), p. 157.

26. Susan Sell, "The Global IP Upward Ratchet, Anti-Counterfeiting and Piracy Enforcement Efforts: The State of Play" (June 2008), at http://www.twnside.org.sg/title2/intellectual_property/development.research/SusanSellfinalversion.pdf

27. Kal Raustiala and Stephen Munzer, "The Global Struggle over Geographic Indications," *European Journal of International Law* 18:2 (2007), pp. 337–365.

28. Madhavi Sunder, *From Goods to a Good Life: Intellectual Property and Global Justice* (New Haven: Yale University Press, 2012), pp. 141–142.

29. Madhavi Sunder, "IP: Social and Cultural Theory—A Reply to the Question 'Why Culture?'" March 13, 2009, http://uchicagolaw.typepad.com/faculty/2009/03/ip-social-and-cultural-theory-a-reply-to-the-question-why-culture-madhavi-sunder.html.

See also Madhavi Sunder, "The Invention of Traditional Knowledge," *Law and Contemporary Problems* 70 (2007), pp. 97–124.

30. Peter K. Yu, "Intellectual Property Rulemaking in the Global Capitalist Economy," 2008, http://www.peteryu.com/andersen.pdf.

31. Carolyn Deere, *The Implementation Game: The TRIPS Agreement and the Global Politics of Intellectual Property Reform in Developing Countries* (Oxford: Oxford University Press, 2008), p. 10.

32. Christian Zeller, "From the Gene to the Globe: Extracting Rents Based on Intellectual Property Monopolies," *Review of International Political Economy* 15:1 (February 2008), p. 91.

33. Ibid., p. 110.

34. Madhavi Sunder, *From Goods to a Good Life*, pp. 94–100.

35. James Boyle, *The Public Domain: Enclosing the Commons of the Mind* (New Haven, CT: Yale University Press, 2008), p. 154.

36. Kembrew McLeod and Peter DiCola, *Creative License: The Law and Culture of Digital Sampling* (Durham. N.C.: Duke University Press, 2011).

37. David Bollier, *Viral Spiral* (New York: The New Press, 2008).

38. Michele Boldrin and David Levine, *Against Intellectual Monopoly* (Cambridge: Cambridge University Press, 2008).

39. Peter Maskus, *Private Rights and Public Problems: The Global Economics of Intellectual Property in the 21st Century* (Washington, D.C.: Peterson Institute for International Economics, 2012).

States and Markets in the Global Economy

Part III presents four case studies of international political economy (IPE) analysis: the developing countries; the European Union (EU); the rising powers such as Brazil, China, and India; and the Middle Eastern and North African states. Although these studies are informative about four important groups of nations, they are intended to have broader application by exploring particular questions and themes that apply around the globe. Students are challenged to master the specific applications and at the same time appreciate the more general themes that derive from them.

We discuss the development conundrum in Chapter 11, as the chapters that follow connect to the issue of development in one way or another. Development is not a finite process but one that carries on even in the "developed" countries of Europe.

Chapter 12 examines regional integration, one of the most important political and economic trends in contemporary IPE, with specific emphasis on the European Union. Beginning as six nations after World War II, the European Union is now composed of twenty-seven nations, some of which were members of the Soviet-dominated Warsaw Pact during the Cold War. Seventeen nations in the EU now have a common currency that was introduced in 2001. In addition to grappling with a number of policy issues such as immigration and defense, EU institutions today are facing their severest challenge ever: how to save the economies of Greece, Spain, and Portugal while preventing the monetary union from collapsing.

Chapter 13 analyzes the BRICs (Brazil, Russia, India, and China) as they have moved to more market-oriented and, in some cases, more democratic systems of political economy. How have they managed the transition to participation in globalized markets? How do economic reforms affect political decisions? We will also examine the development contradictions and social problems that face these rising powers and some of the former communist countries dominated by the Soviet Union. We contrast different views on how these countries are challenging the power of the United States and its close allies.

Finally, in Chapter 14 we explore patterns of political, social, and economic relations in Middle Eastern and North African states. Although these states share some common institutions, religions, and cultural traits, they differ from one another in ways that are often not communicated in the mass media. Thus, this chapter goes a long way toward dispelling some of the many myths about this region. We show how the region is integrated into the global economy and how it is rapidly changing due to the Arab Spring.

The Development Conundrum: Choices Amidst Constraints

The Challenge of Development: A child is vaccinated against measles in Kenya.

RGB Ventures LLC dba SuperStock/Alamy

Every four seconds a child dies due to poverty-related causes. Eighty percent of humanity lives on less than $10 per day.[1] These facts merely underscore the reality that most of the world's population still do not have their basic needs met, let alone experience economic prosperity. An obvious question is this: Given the great amount of wealth produced in the world each year, why have so many nations remained impoverished, "underdeveloped," or "undeveloped"? This chapter examines various political-economic dilemmas that the less developed countries (LDCs) have struggled with. Development promises an improved standard of living, longer life, and greater status, but it often has a harsh side, raising concerns about the costs and paths associated with this dream.

Aside from the trade-offs involved in pursuing development, LDCs have found themselves in the center of intense debates in IPE about the essential prerequisites to get to the promised land. Can economic liberalism propel the poor to a higher standard of living? Or will the lure of the market and globalization be yet another mirage, raising expectations of impending prosperity only to disappoint?

To better appreciate the development riddle, this chapter begins by describing the common attributes of developing nations. We then outline the period we call "Independence and Underdevelopment" that spans the 1950s and 1960s—the time when many LDCs emerged from colonialism into a world of growing markets, transnational corporations, and the Cold War. Three options presented themselves to LDCs: accept this reality of the international system, try to change it, or drop out of it. Development strategies were influenced by the assumptions and policies associated with economic liberalism, mercantilism, and structuralism. The self-reliance strategy, introduced in this chapter, pragmatically mixes elements of the other two perspectives. The heart of the chapter focuses on these strategies, including their flaws. The final section of the chapter on the Millennium Development Goals (MDGs) discusses UN targets for the poorest countries. We also outline some of the ideas of the development expert Jeff Sachs, who has actively sought an alternative development model not based solely on economic liberal ideas and policies.

WHAT ARE DEVELOPING NATIONS?

The countries commonly referred to as the LDCs, the South, or the developing countries have diverse histories, cultures, economies, and political systems. The characteristics that they do share, however, are important:

- High instances of poverty
- Lack of a sizeable middle class
- Relatively low literacy rates
- Inadequate health care
- Hunger
- High instances of infant mortality
- Lack of infrastructure
- Weak governments
- Dependency on foreign aid and humanitarian assistance

What they often have in common is devastating and persistent poverty. Tens of millions are constantly at the mercy of natural and man-made threats. One measure of the material living standards of a country is income available per person per day to spend on food, shelter, health care, education, and so forth. In industrialized countries, this figure is relatively high. Per capita income in the United States, for example, is about $115 per person per day on average. An income of $115 per day can provide a comfortable and healthy lifestyle by global standards. By comparison, many in the South have a per capita income of $2 per day or less, and hundreds of millions live on less than $1 per day.

Table 11-1 shows the incidence of severe poverty in the global South. The first three columns show the proportion of the population living on less than US $1.25 of income per day in 1990, 1999, and 2008. An income of $1.25 a day is a critical

TABLE 11-1

The Incidence of Extreme Poverty, 1990, 1999, and 2008

Regions	Population (%) Living on $1.25 per Day or Less (in 2005 PPP)			Population (%) Living on $2 per Day or Less (in 2005 PPP)		
	1990	1999	2008	1990	1999	2008
East Asia and Pacific	56	36	14	81	62	33
Europe and Central Asia	2	4	1	7	12	2
Latin America and the Caribbean	12	12	7	22	22	12
Middle East and North Africa	6	5	3	24	22	14
South Asia	54	45	36	84	78	71
Sub-Saharan Africa	57	58	48	76	78	69
Total	37	34	25	58	56	47

Source: Shaohua Chen and Martin Ravallion, "More Relatively-Poor People in a Less Absolutely-Poor World," *Review of Income and Wealth* 59:1 (March 2013): 1-28.

point in discussing real poverty. Less than this amount means inadequate diet, high infant mortality, and shortened life span. In 2008, one fourth of people in the South—nearly 1.3 billion people—lived on less than $1.25 a day. The deepest, most persistent poverty is in sub-Saharan Africa and South Asia. The good news is that deep poverty has declined in several regions, most notably East Asia. The bad news is that the overall figures are still high. Many readers of this book are able to feed their pets better than many LDC parents are able to feed their children.

The next three columns in Table 11-1 show the population percentage with income less than the equivalent of $2 per day in 1990, 1999, and 2008. The difference between existing on $1.25 per day and $2 per day is significant. With $1.25 or less, a person struggles to survive. Two dollars, considering the conditions of poverty we are discussing here, buys a little more than bare subsistence and therefore offers the possibility of better health and human dignity. Of course, $2 a day is so small an amount to most in industrialized countries that it may seem an inadequately modest goal, yet nearly half of all people in the developing countries must try to get by on less than that amount. Note that, according to this indicator, the incidence of poverty is much more geographically widespread, with high poverty rates not just in South Asia and sub-Saharan Africa but also in East Asia and Latin America. Nevertheless, East Asian countries—led by China—managed to cut the proportion of their people in severe poverty by more than half between 1990 and 2008.

There is widespread agreement about the need to improve the living standards of much of the world's population. Escaping poverty is the desirable face of economic development, yet there are many costs that must be borne in economic, social, political, cultural, and environmental terms to achieve this goal.

Independence and Underdevelopment

As colonialism disintegrated during the mid-twentieth century, new nation-states emerged into an international order shaped by the Cold War between the United States with its democratic allies (the so-called First World) and the Soviet Union and its allies (the Second World). For the newly formed nations in Asia, Latin America, and Africa, economic development was practically a universal goal.

In the 1960s, a controversial book entitled *The Wretched of the Earth*, written by Martinique-born psychiatrist Frantz Fanon, emerged as a seminal treatise on the struggle of societies to overcome the shackles of colonialism.[2] In it, Fanon analyzed the struggle against colonial repression with a discourse on imperialism and nationalism. Many students and scholars regarded Fanon's writing as a compelling call for the people throughout the Third World to struggle against—and even to violently oppose—the oppression of Western domination. For our purposes, it is worth noting that Fanon also critiqued the elites in newly independent countries who, as a social class, appeared corrupt and unlikely to genuinely pursue nationwide development.

Fanon highlighted concerns about Third World cultural liberation where, among other things, the language of the colonizer, which the colonized societies had been compelled to adopt, remained a powerful remnant and enduring influence. It was against this cultural and political backdrop that new Third World countries confronted the pressing concerns about development.

Newly independent LDCs often viewed former colonial powers with disdain and suspicion. Many felt that the exploitation they had endured was surely responsible for the economic "backwardness" of their new nation-state. Development—characterized by a growing and prosperous economy—was crucial in order to establish a national identity and ensure political stability. But many LDCs approached development with mixed emotions. The promises of development were an end to poverty and an improved standard of living. On the other hand, development meant exploitation, manipulation, and continued subjugation. This paradox repelled LDCs at the same time as it attracted them. This discord is manifested in the three major forces that shaped the development conundrum for LDCs.

First, because many LDCs approached development both as a response to colonialism and as a resistance to cultural domination by the West, they advocated caution before adopting a Western outlook it.[3] This influential view unified developing countries in the 1970s against the West (see later). Second, proximity to the United States or historical connections to former mother countries often shaped the political and economic development strategies LDCs chose. Pursuing a Western market-oriented development strategy signalled a tacit association with the West in the Cold War. In many cases, association with such Western institutions offered real opportunities for pursuing a partnership with the industrialized nations. Likewise, most LDCs supporting the Eastern bloc of nations preferred non-Western development strategies.

Third, and paradoxically, the economic success of the developed countries provided a strong rationale for some LDCs to follow in their footsteps, or at least to adopt market-oriented prescriptions for economic development. The emergence of new international institutions like the IMF, the World Bank, and the GATT expanded the significance of the market in the world economy. To many, these institutions were largely controlled by the developed countries.

LDCs Mobilizing to Develop

Recognizing that, individually, they were unable to exert much influence on the international system and its institutions, many LDCs attempted to promote a collective identity. The 1955 Afro-Asian Bandung (Indonesia) Conference is regarded as the genesis of what came to be viewed as a Southern perspective, which led to the eventual formation of the Nonaligned Movement (NAM) in 1961. This movement sought to ensure the political independence of remaining European colonies (especially in Africa), to be a vehicle for positioning NAM countries outside the sphere of the Cold War scenario, and to promote the interests of the LDCs.

One of the main concerns of these nations was neocolonialism, or the continued economic domination of LDCs by the industrialized countries. Several leaders and intellectuals argued that, while the colonial era was largely over, LDCs were trapped in a capitalist system dominated by institutions that favored the developed countries.[4] For instance, multinational corporations and their subsidiaries controlled economic resources in LDCs. The wealth and influence of multinationals, often backed by their home-based governments, permitted the industrialized nations to influence international markets for many commodities from LDCs.

Consider the Western oil companies, for example. For much of the twentieth century, seven major oil companies controlled the exploration, processing, and supply of oil in a number of oil-rich regions. These "Seven Sisters," as they were known, often worked to divide the market share, regulate supply, and preserve their control over resources in developing countries. Supported by their respective home governments, these major oil companies also negotiated terms (involving some royalties for the host country) that ensured the companies' dominance of oil exploration and distribution in the international market.[5]

Advocates of this neocolonial argument claimed that compounding such domination by MNCs was a restrictive system of trade, finance, and technology transfer that made LDCs economically vulnerable. In Chapter 6, we discussed the LDC claim that the international terms of trade limited them to be producers of raw materials and primary goods. LDCs were disadvantaged by the lead the industrialized nations had in the production of value-added products and their extensive use of protectionist trade measures. Technological innovations and the related gains in productivity largely occurred in the developed countries, and LDCs found themselves unable to compete in new areas of production. Tight legal controls, patents, and licensing often curbed LDCs' access to such technology. The financial power of multinationals, coupled with the developed countries' control of the international financial system, also meant that they could manipulate the LDCs' access to funds for economic development.

Having failed to influence the international system through their collective action, some LDCs began to doubt that development was even possible within the existing international structure. For example, Argentine economist Raul Prebisch argued that the development dilemma in Latin America was inextricably linked to factors *outside* the region.[6] He and others who were critical of the international division of labor argued that the international trade system reinforced the LDCs' role as exporters of primary products and raw materials, while the developed countries continued to prosper as producers of industrial goods. Further, production specialization perpetuated LDC dependence on the developed countries for capital and technology.

Dependence was considered significant, as it resulted in underdevelopment in LDCs. Early dependency theorists made a distinction between *un*development and *under*development. The former was characterized by lack of development, while the latter was the outcome of a process that *further* undermined LDC economies and simultaneously made the industrialized world more prosperous. Andre Gunder Frank also argued that underdevelopment in LDCs was a *by-product* of the development process in industrialized regions.[7] Osvaldo Sunkel and Pedro Paz argued that "both underdevelopment and development are aspects of the same phenomenon, both are historically simultaneous, both linked functionally and therefore interact and condition each other mutually."[8]

This basic thesis represented the embryo of the dependency theorists' critique during the 1960s and 1970s. For Frank, underdevelopment originated in the colonial order prior to the twentieth century. Through political domination, the colonial powers successfully extracted raw materials and resources necessary for their own development, while impoverishing their colonies. Although decolonization removed the political dominance of the colonizers, the basic economic linkages and division of labor between the two remained largely intact, resulting in neocolonialism. Frank argued that the global capitalist order was organized along the lines of a metropolis-satellite system, in which the metropolis state exploited the satellite by extracting economic surplus and wealth from the latter.

Many dependency theorists suggested that several mechanisms reproduce this relationship. First, through MNCs, profits generated in LDCs are transferred out of those nations. Investments in technology and other innovations are often inappropriate and do not enhance the competitive edge of LDCs. The extensive resources of MNCs enable them to circumvent regulatory measures. Another mechanism is the unequal exchange relationship. The LDCs' "comparative advantage" in primary products and raw materials is vulnerable to international market prices, which are generally rising faster for manufactured goods that LDCs must import. This creates a net outflow of revenue from LDCs to the developed countries.

Other dependency theorists find the international financial and foreign aid system to be exploitative. They claim that foreign banks, for example, are less interested in the development of a country than they are in profiting handsomely from loans. This creates a long-term financial dependence for the indebted country and generous interest receipts for foreign banks. These theorists are also skeptical of foreign aid, arguing that the political and economic strings attached to such assistance often reinforce a dominant–subordinate relationship between the developed and less developed nations.[9]

UNCTAD and the NIEO: LDCs Organize to Change the System

Frustrated by their meager success, many LDCs turned to international organizations to change the IPE structures. In 1964, the **United Nations Conference on Trade and Development (UNCTAD)** was established, spearheaded by the seventy-seven LDCs that became known as the Group of 77 (G-77). They sought to make UNCTAD—which holds a major conference every four years—a mechanism for dialogue and negotiation between the LDCs and the developed countries on trade, finance, and other development issues. For the most part, the developed countries resisted UNCTAD initiatives. Nevertheless, through UNCTAD, LDCs were gradually able to secure some concessions and preferential tariffs for their exports to developed nations.

In 1974, LDCs made a historic attempt at the UN General Assembly to establish a **New International Economic Order (NIEO)**. This initiative was designed to accelerate the pace of development and equalize the economic balance between the LDCs and the industrialized nations. Unlike previous efforts to fine-tune the international economic order, the NIEO was seen by LDCs as an effort to make institutional structures more conducive to LDC development concerns.

Industrialized countries saw demands for a NIEO as a political maneuver by some radical LDCs to undermine the market-oriented global economic system and to redistribute global wealth and power. In the face of this opposition, efforts by LDCs in the 1970s to change the system failed. LDCs were left with the choice of promoting autonomous local development or embracing global markets—and the possibility of dependent development with its associated conundrums.

The Market Unleashed

In the 1980s, the Reagan administration exerted its influence on the IMF, the World Bank, and the GATT to bring LDCs into closer alignment with policies consistent with the free-market ideology and U.S. foreign policy objectives. This period saw the introduction of Structural Adjustment Programmes (SAPs), which contained stringent conditions that LDCs had to adopt to ensure continued IMF assistance in addressing their short-term economic and financial woes. Some of the more controversial measures many LDCs had to carry out include the following:

- Devaluation of currency
- Raising interest rates
- Privatization of public companies
- Reduction of the budget deficit
- Adoption of free-trade policies.

By the 1990s, the collapse of communism gave even more momentum to the Washington Consensus and the liberal market ideology of the West. Globalization—driven in large measure by international trade, finance, and technological interconnectedness—validated a U.S.-led chorus touting the virtues of economic growth through greater emphasis on privatization and free trade. Indeed, it was during the early 1990s that India, China, and the Southeast "Asian Tigers" began to emerge as economic successes in their own right. Yet, as we discuss in the following paragraphs, there is considerable debate about how these countries attained economic growth during this period; free-market policies were not especially central to their development strategies.

The dominant Washington Consensus asserted that developing countries needed to take advantage of global resources and market opportunities. More and more of the resources for development came from financial markets, not from official aid. To repay their debts, with interest, nations had to earn more from exporting—but on what terms?

As during the early 1970s, a consensus emerged among LDCs that the rules of international trade and financial organizations were unfavorable to their interests. Among other things, LDCs were frustrated that their attempts to develop critical agricultural exports were often undermined by, ironically enough, heavily *state-subsidized* agriculture policies in the United States and the European Union. Hypocritically, developed countries were protecting their own markets for sugar, beef, cotton, corn, and fresh produce while demanding that developing countries lower tariffs on imported services and manufactured goods. And once countries like China and Mexico became major *exporters* of manufactured goods, LDCs began to demand more access to rich-country markets, both for manufactured goods and agricultural products.

LDCs brought their demands to the Seattle WTO meetings of 1999 and then more forcefully to the Doha meetings of 2001. They realized that they could not just walk away from global markets, but they also needed rules more favorable to their interests, which were often not compatible with the subsidized agriculture policies in developed nations.

In addition to promoting free trade, the Washington Consensus made a strong case for economic development through capital mobility—the free movement of investment funds into and out of a country. These investment funds come in many forms, including foreign direct investment, commercial bank loans, and purchases of stocks and bonds. Some are long-term and stable, others are short-term and volatile. Some go to purchase productive assets and help companies raise money to expand, while others are simply speculative. Capital mobility means allowing potentially dangerous but remunerative forms of investment along with relatively safe forms, because it is hard to control one without discouraging the other. The risk is that short-term speculative funds—what Keynes called "hot money"—will rush in and out, creating a cycle of booms and busts. With capital mobility came financial instability and the possibility of a devastating crisis necessitating an IMF bailout package.

The Burden of Long-Term Debt

Despite the global spread of the Washington Consensus, by the 1990s many poor countries had failed to reap any of its promised benefits. Instead, forty of the world's **heavily indebted poor countries (HIPCs)**—primarily in Africa—found themselves saddled with long-term debt due to borrowing from the World Bank, the IMF, and some international banks. They simply could not sustain debt repayments. Some of these states complained about **odious debt,** or obligations to outside agencies incurred by a former corrupt regime. Iraq's Saddam Hussein, Ethiopia's Mengistu Haile Mariam, and Chile's Augusto Pinochet allegedly fit in this category.[10] Debt-relief mechanisms of the global finance and monetary structure were not designed for the poorest states.

Since the late 1990s, the UN, NGOs, IMF and World Bank officials, development experts, and even rock stars have campaigned to rectify this problem. In 1996, after pressure from popular movements in both the North and South, creditors launched the **HIPC Initiative** under the direction of the World Bank. The goal was cancellation of the debt of the world's poorest countries, but by 1999 only four countries had received debt relief, and the rise in interest payments owed on the debt wiped out any gains.

In 1999, during massive demonstrations at the G7 meeting in Cologne, Germany, supporters of Jubilee 2000 targeted the inadequacy of neoliberal development policies and, in particular, IMF and World Bank practices. Jubilee 2000 was an effort by a coalition of development-oriented NGOs, churches, and labor groups to pressure the industrialized nations into canceling the debt of twenty countries by 2000 in order to advance global justice. At the G7 meeting, state leaders pledged to write off $100 billion of poor-country debts. As we note later in the chapter, there has been some success with this effort to free up money that can be devoted to poverty reduction.

How to Develop? The IPE Development Strategies

Determining the appropriate strategies for development remains a hotly contested issue in IPE literature. In Table 11-2, we sum up the major elements of the three

TABLE 11-2

The Classic IPE Development Strategies + 1

	Economic Liberalism	Structuralism	Mercantilism	Self-Reliance
Strategy Goals	Economic growth; manufacturing and industry over agriculture	Poverty eradication and equitable income distribution	Economic growth to promote wealth and welfare of the state	Economic growth, but not at the expense of the masses
Policy Tools	Trade as the "engine to growth"; industrial development; the state must be stronger at first to promote change	State-led development; welfare policies; import substitution	State industrial policies that target healthy industries; import substitution and export-led growth	No formal strategy but use of state industrial and trade policies that incorporate open markets when possible
Side Effects	The masses must postpone gratification; democracy comes later	Slow economic growth	State policies often regarded as protectionist and offensive to other states; state investments reflect special interests	Hard to plan; officials must be wise to figure out what tools work best and when
Examples	United States, England, Japan, Asian Tigers, Hong Kong	Cuba, China until 1978, Tanzania, the Czech Republic until 1990, and today Venezuela.	Japan, South Korea, Malaysia, and Indonesia	Most emerging economies today: China, India, Brazil, Indonesia

most popular development strategies. Notice that these three strategies correspond to the three dominant IPE perspectives. The fourth strategy of self-reliance is not a theoretical model of development per se, but rather a response to many failures attributed to the other three. Self-reliance attempts to account for the advantages and disadvantages of each state when it comes to achieving development.

The Economic Liberal Perspective

The economic liberal perspective on development requires that LDCs become integrated into the global market economy, especially through trade. By emphasizing their comparative trading advantages, LDCs are able to capitalize on the benefits of international trade and build a robust economy. Trade enables poorer economies to export their natural resources and (mainly) agricultural commodities, while affording access to manufactured goods from abroad. As these economies grow from export earnings, gradually they will be able to acquire more foreign technology and knowledge to promote new investments in manufacturing. According to this perspective, as "latecomers," LDCs can use the market to develop and industrialize, while learning from the policy mistakes of the now developed nations. Such hindsight translates into less waste of resources and more efficiency, while accelerating the development process.

From the liberal perspective, MNCs are a major source of capital, jobs, and technology. Governments around the world are constantly competing to attract foreign direct investment (FDI). Foreign aid from wealthier nations and IOs is also critical to strengthening the poorer nations' ability to build their economic infrastructure. Some critics have argued that as developing countries compete for FDI, they essentially undercut each other by trying to provide foreign investors with the most lucrative terms in the form of very cheap labor and lax regulation. This generates a "race to the bottom" for wages and working conditions to keep the MNCs and investors from taking their operations to more "investor-friendly" locations. The common images of lowly paid and highly exploited sweatshop factory workers in poor countries producing textiles, leather goods, and footwear are a vivid illustration of this criticism of MNCs and FDI.[11]

According to the liberal model, major obstacles to economic development are LDCs' anemic capital, productivity, and technological base. Other obstacles include poor infrastructure, weak educational systems, and/or traditional value systems. Following this line of reasoning, the neoliberal perspective largely de-emphasizes the importance of *global* structural conditions in mitigating the relative lack of development in LDCs, focusing instead on the aforementioned *internal* conditions. Other variants of this perspective emphasize the *social* aspects of development, such as education, training, and skill-development. At the end of the chapter we discuss the work of Jeff Sachs, who has tried to combine more social factors into the development process.

Marx, who wrote about sweatshop abuses in Great Britain in the 1850s (see Chapter 4), might not be surprised to know that they still exist in the twenty-first century. For many LDCs, sweatshop industries are the most difficult element of the development conundrum. These countries need jobs, investments, technology, and export earnings, but MNCs often bring dangerous and exploitative working conditions. However, the race-to-the-bottom scenario is not the whole story of MNC investment, as Theodore H. Moran has explained. Most MNC investments are North–North in direction, moving from one advanced industrialized country to another, not North–South as is commonly assumed. (Most MNCs invest in industries that pay more than sweatshop-level wages. Even when their investments do go into low-wage and low-skill industries, foreign MNCs frequently do not operate sweatshops directly but rather contract with local suppliers who do, often absolving themselves of responsibility for sweatshop conditions.)

Moran discusses various strategies to improve working conditions in LDCs, such as adopting global labor standards and integrating sweatshop concerns into WTO agreements.[12] He argues that a passive strategy that counts on sweatshop earnings to "trickle down" and eventually create more growth is wrongheaded. Instead, Moran proposes a "buildup" strategy that uses resources created in part by MNCs to improve worker skills and to attract progressively higher-skill industries and jobs. The buildup strategy must be broad-based, not just aimed at attracting MNC funds. He cites experiences in the Philippines, Costa Rica, and the Dominican Republic as evidence that these government programs can help LDCs to move beyond sweatshops.

The economic liberal outlook incorporates Western strategies and assumes that the relationship of rich to poor countries is mutually beneficial. Part of the appeal of this outlook lies in the interpretation that the United States and other industrialized nations went through a series of "stages of growth," which subsequently became benchmarks by which policy makers understood the development conundrum in LDCs. Part of the assumption is that, like the Western industrial nations, LDCs will develop through the workings of an open market system and undergo similar "stages of growth." One of the most influential liberal economic theories of development was the work of W. W. Rostow, who served as an advisor to President Kennedy.

According to Rostow, LDCs must undergo a series of changes in their socioeconomic system in order to develop.[13] These "evolutionary" changes are represented by a series of "stages of (economic) growth" that each society passes through on its way to development. Traditional society experiences low levels of economic productivity due to a lack of technological innovation and a traditional social system where individuals are constrained by rigid social goals and fatalistic values. Increases in education and literacy, entrepreneurship, and investments in raw materials and infrastructure expand the level of commercial activity. Despite the creation of a good deal of disharmony, society is bringing about changes that are compatible with the process of development.

In the "take-off" stage, new industries increase rapidly as the entrepreneurial spirit becomes more dominant. The emergence of a capitalist class accelerates the change by propelling industrialization and the adoption of economic innovation. Conversely, the influence of traditional social values diminishes. Later stages of development are characterized by the use of advanced technology and an increase in savings and investment (approximately 15–20 percent of GNP), which sustains the drive to economic maturity. Countries with a higher level of savings and investments are deemed more likely to develop at a faster rate than those with lower savings. The final stage of mass consumption and self-sustained growth follows when the major sectors of the economy are able to supply goods and services for a large cross-section of the population.

Rostow's theory is largely based on the historical trajectory of Western nations. He perceives the stages of development as universal, arguing that in the long run, the North can model the development process for the South. The historical advancement and diffusion of technology will inevitably lead to changes that are necessary in the early stages of the economic development process in LDCs. Proponents of this model implicitly assume that developing countries will become modern, industrialized nations like England or the United States. It is also assumed that as LDC economies grow and a viable middle class emerges, other changes—such as demands for democracy—will follow.

This development strategy prioritizes open markets and free trade, and hence places a premium on the need for LDCs to adopt export-oriented growth policies based on their natural comparative advantages. Exports would serve as the "engine to growth," with the state guiding the economy toward efficient allocation of resources. While FDI facilitates vital economic activity, foreign aid helps meet important strategic needs. As the processes and linkages associated with globalization have become more intense, proponents of this model have renewed emphasis on the virtues of greater interdependence between the developing and developed nations. While conceding that in the initial stages of development only a small elite will likely benefit from free trade, they are convinced that economic benefits will trickle down to a wider cross-section of society as the economy matures. While the goal of containing poverty may not be an immediate priority of this approach, there is an expectation that over time the trickle-down effect will ease deprivation.

Economic liberal ideas have received considerable attention, related in part to the economic growth achieved by many states, including Japan, the Asian Tigers (Taiwan, South Korea, and Hong Kong), China, Malaysia, Thailand, and Indonesia—all of whom adopted some variant of export-oriented policies. Yet, as we discussed above, there is some disagreement whether these countries adopted an approach squarely consistent with the economic liberal model. Furthermore, both the antiglobalization campaign and the global financial crisis have generated doubts about whether the model is appropriate for most poor developing nations.

The Structuralist Perspective

The Marxist and early structuralist critiques of the development problem begin with the assertion that the core countries dominate the peripheral countries and foster a relationship of dependency. According to this critique, the Western industrial model is inappropriate for LDCs because the developed nations' "neo-imperial" connections to the periphery via trade, aid, and FDI often result in dual economies. One part of an LDC's economy consists of wealthy elites who are well connected to transnational elites in the core, whereas the other part is full of the masses, whose futures remain bleak and who are rooted in local customs and values. For ardent Marxist-structuralists, the liberal trickle-down market model ultimately benefits only elites and core nations and does not produce wider societal development.

The Marxist-structuralist model was closely associated with pro-Soviet models during the Cold War. While many of the former Soviet-bloc countries and their LDC counterparts such as North Korea, Cuba, and Vietnam did prioritize industrialization, they also emphasized self-sufficiency and isolation from the capitalist global economy. LDCs were exhorted to overcome external dependencies by closing the economy (autarchy), rejecting international aid (which furthers dependency), and nationalizing the local holdings of TNCs. Instead of producing for export, LDCs were supposed to impose tariffs to protect local producers, limit expensive imports, and provide subsidies for local industries. Furthermore, rather than waiting for the benefits of free trade to trickle down, the state was urged to eradicate poverty by implementing a more equitable distribution of income and providing strong support for basic health and welfare programs.

During the 1950s, Latin American scholars were increasingly skeptical of the "comparative advantage" road to development, and the dependency critique became an influential framework for development in the Southern Hemisphere. Several Latin America countries opted for **import-substituting industrialization (ISI)**, guided by a belief that the free market system was a threat. Structuralists view the inward-looking and nationalistic *import-substitution* strategy as a way for countries in the periphery to minimize the adverse effects of dependence on foreign capital, technology, and markets. Many were convinced that specializing in primary commodity products was an inherent disadvantage for developing countries in the region. The adverse terms of trade made manufactured imports by LDCs a major foreign-exchange drain. To change this situation, LDCs with a relatively fragile industrial base, such as Brazil and Mexico, had to undertake significant steps to build a viable, home-grown manufacturing sector. Given the large internal consumer market in these countries, a shift from importing manufactured consumer products to producing them locally would translate into new jobs across the economy, improve the adverse balance of payment situation, and promote development.

The first stage of the import-substitution strategy was similar to that followed by the East Asian NICs. By the 1950s, Brazil and Mexico were well into the process of promoting local manufacture of consumer goods (such as processed foods, textiles, and footwear) and curtailing foreign imports. However, significant differences affected the ISI strategies in the East Asian and Latin American cases. Historically, the resource- and agriculture-rich Latin American economies have been more dependent on primary exports than their East Asian counterparts like Taiwan and South Korea.[14] Diversifying from this deeply entrenched, primary-product economy was difficult.

Furthermore, protectionist policies were used heavily in countries like Brazil to displace the foreign share of the consumer market, while in East Asia the focus of these measures was to enhance the international competitiveness of locally produced goods. Hence, by the late 1960s, as South Korea was promoting its exports while maintaining some barriers, Brazil and Mexico were moving into the next stage of intensifying their import-substitution strategy. Ironically, instead of reducing their dependence on foreign capital, the countries had to borrow from abroad to finance the deepening of their ISI. This second stage of import substitution involved expanding the manufacture of labor-intensive consumer goods along with diversifying into capital-intensive goods as well.[15] In this stage, the role of the government and state-owned enterprises expanded. This increasing presence of the state was associated with increased concentration of production in the hands of a few firms (often state-owned) that were not as productive as privately owned enterprises.[16]

However, the performance of these economies was not as strong as that of the export-oriented East Asian NICs. From the 1960s to the 1980s, Brazil and Mexico depended heavily on the domestic consumer market instead of the international market. In order to sustain growth, production reflected the consumption patterns of those with purchasing power. This further aggravated the gap between the "haves" and the "have-nots". By contrast, the income inequality gap within the East Asian NICs narrowed.[17]

Today many structuralists are not so pessimistic about the LDCs' economic linkages to core nations and are open to the idea that export-oriented growth and an aggressive trade posture can reap important benefits for a developing nation. Indeed, China and India, which for decades had been inward-focused, have become more receptive to outward-oriented policies. Other structuralists emphasize greater collective efforts among LDCs to gain leverage in international trade agreements and financial institutions to promote better terms of trade and secure appropriate investments.

The Mercantilist Perspective

Mercantilists consider international trade as essential to national development. However, they are generally not enthusiastic about the laissez-faire and limited-government doctrine, typically associated with the liberal perspective. They believe that each state has a critical role to play in coordinating a trade strategy. Several developing countries in East Asia adopted strategies that, while quite diverse, are generally termed **export-oriented growth.** This mercantilist-oriented strategy calls for the state to strongly emphasize its comparative advantages in selected sectors of the economy and to promote exports from these sectors. However, instead of depending on a noninterventionist state and free-trade policies, the East Asian NICs aggressively pursued specific national and international policies that changed the basic structure and functioning of their economies.

First, the export-oriented East Asian NICs changed the fundamental composition of their production. Prior to the 1960s, like other developing countries, South Korea and Taiwan began promoting manufacturing with a particular emphasis on labor-intensive consumer goods. To accomplish this, the respective governments set up mercantilist-style policies to protect "infant" industries from foreign competition and increase employment.

By the late 1960s, South Korea and Taiwan began the next phase of restructuring. They increased their international market share by promoting the export of domestically manufactured durable goods. State intervention again played a strategic role in launching this export-promotion effort. Selective barriers on imported goods remained in place, although raw material imports necessary for manufacturing were encouraged, and selected domestic manufacturing industries were targeted with fiscal incentives to stimulate the level of exports. By devaluing their national currencies, these East Asian countries made their exports more competitive in the international marketplace and imports less attractive to domestic consumers.[18] Therefore, the NICs purposefully *created* comparative advantages for their manufactured products through these protectionist measures.

During the 1970s, South Korea's manufacturing sector expanded into heavy (technologically-intensive) industries including steel, petrochemicals, and automobiles. These efforts to restructure the economy bore fruit. Manufacturing's share of GDP in South Korea climbed from 14 percent in 1960 to 30 percent by 1980, and has remained stable since then. Agriculture's share decreased from 37 percent to 15 percent over the same period, and by 2012 it had dropped to just 3 percent of GDP. In Taiwan, manufacturing's share of GDP increased from 26 percent in 1960 to a high of about 40 percent in the mid-1980s before settling at about 25 percent after 2000. Correspondingly, agriculture's share of GDP declined from 29 percent to only 2 percent by 2012.[19]

Another major component of this export-led growth strategy involved promoting a high level of savings and investment (including intense efforts in research and development). A combination of factors contributed to this process. In South Korea, the raising of interest rates increased household savings. The government also helped establish private banks and financial institutions, which began to overshadow traditional and informal money markets widely used by consumers and small private companies. This policy allowed the government to increase its oversight of savings in the economy.[20] The growth of financial institutions in Singapore and Hong Kong was also crucial to capital formation—the process of building up a country's stock of equipment, machinery, buildings, and other productive assets. Interestingly, the former developed an approach in which the government maintained tight control over financial institutions, while the latter leaned in the opposite direction of minimal regulation of the financial sector.[21]

The inflow of foreign capital and aid to East Asia also impacted the capital formation process. South Korea's dependence on foreign aid was especially crucial following the Korean War in the 1950s. According to one estimate, approximately 70 percent of South Korea's domestic capital formation came from foreign aid during the 1950s.[22] Taiwan's domestic capital formation also depended heavily on foreign capital during the same period—about 40 percent was externally financed. Recall that this was when South Korea and Taiwan underwent structural transformation by using protective measures to insulate their newly emerging light-manufacturing industries from foreign competition.

Education and human resource development are recurrent themes of development, so it is no surprise that the successes of the East Asian NICs have generated more attention to these issues. The combined impact of investments in education and job training produced a literate and skilled workforce, which was essential to the success of the industrial and investment policies. It also promoted growth in productivity, more industrial flexibility, and greater equality.

As such, we find that the East Asian Tigers didn't simply "roll back the state" and let free competition reign as advocated by the liberal development strategy. The state was instrumental in setting export-oriented development policies to maximize the benefits of industrialization. To take advantage of opportunities presented by global markets, the Tigers relied on strong state policies to limit domestic economic and political disruption.

Self-Reliance

From the above, it should be clear that the first three development models reflect different ideological outlooks, historical circumstances, and state policies. The self-reliance strategy reflects the conclusion reached by many experts and officials that there is no one "magic bullet" approach for development. For any state to rigorously follow any of the standard models is an attempt to fit a square peg in a round hole. In the box Development: A Customized Approach, we have summarized a recent debate between two students of development—a well-known journalist and a university professor—as an example of the different ideas and attitudes that inform development strategies.

DEVELOPMENT: A CUSTOMIZED APPROACH

Martin Wolf, the chief economics commentator at the *Financial Times*, reviewed Cambridge University economics professor Ha-Joon Chang's controversial book *Bad Samaritans* (Bloomsbury Press, 2008).[a] Professor Chang argues that neoliberals have hurt developing nations by opposing their ability to regulate inward direct investments and obsessing about the need for privatization. Many neoliberals also exaggerated corruption, the lack of democracy, and an assortment of cultural issues that presumably act as barriers to change. Meanwhile, neoliberals are famous for pointing out that countries like China reversed course from the use of protectionist industrial and trade policies and promoted (free) trade policies in an attempt to open markets for their exports. These policies capitalized on China's comparative advantage in the export of manufactured goods and facilitated the country's success. Finally, neoliberals argue that, on the whole, import substitution is not good because it creates small-scale, uncompetitive, rent-seeking monopolies.

In critiquing Chang's book, Wolf asks why South Korea developed as fast as it did, while India has taken much longer. His answer is that while protecting its "infant industries" South Korea *rejected* import substitution and adopted a series of *outward-oriented trade policies* that opened it up to the international economy. Until the 1990s, India remained quite sealed off from international competition, was more inward-looking, and more

directed at protecting local industries. However, Wolf goes on to suggest that each state has different circumstances and advantages that can help it develop. He admits that Hong Kong, China, South Korea, Ireland, Singapore, Taiwan, Japan, and Finland were *not* all free traders by any means. Some relied more heavily on FDI than others. But all used the international economy to their advantage and were more outward than inward looking.

Responding to Wolf, Chang clarifies that he is not suggesting that free-trade policies are not good, but that they must be used in conjunction with a variety of protectionist policies (including import substitution) to "create the space in which their producers can build up their productive capabilities before they can compete with better producers from abroad."[b] This is what the Japanese did with their car industries for almost forty years, and South Korea did with steel, shipbuilding, autos, and electronics. Economic liberalism doesn't always work. Many poorer countries suffered low growth practicing free trade. For example, while per capita income in Latin America grew at 3.1 percent during the "bad old days" of protectionism in the 1960s and 1970s, growth in the "good old days" of neoliberalism, from 1980 to 2004, slowed to 0.5 percent.

In essence, Chang and Wolf both agree that developing nations want to rapidly grow their economies, and that for most of the poorer countries, industrialization offers the best chance

(continued)

to earn capital and develop technologies and management capabilities. They also agree that, despite their subtle differences about the benefits of different strategies, there is no "magic bullet" to make any one strategy or combination of strategies work. Free trade and economic liberal ideas alone are not the solution to the problem. South Korea and Taiwan might be exceptions to the rule. What is paramount is recognizing the specific challenges involved in each case and adopting the right balance and combination of options appropriate to the situation.

References

[a]See Martin Wolf, "The Growth of Nations," *Financial Times,* July 21, 2007.
[b]See Ha-Joon Chang, "Response by Ha-Joon Chang," *Financial Times,* August 3, 2007.

Self-reliance moves the debate away from compartmentalized strategies based on the three distinct schools of thought toward a search for what works on a case-by-case basis. This model stresses the importance of taking into consideration the unique circumstances, economic challenges, and resources of each country when considering the combinations of strategies that may be appropriate. Self-reliance allows for the possibility of different outcomes, including one that does not have as its primary objective the narrow goal of achieving economic growth. In most cases, however, it would be hard for officials to reject that goal or to balance it with a variety of social and cultural welfare objectives.

The increasing number of problems poorer states face regarding energy, the environment, political realities, and financial issues will affect their ability to choose different courses of action. Which strategy will be adopted should be decided not on the basis of theory alone, but rather on an assessment of the complex domestic and international factors a particular LDC confronts. As such, while some trade and social policies may have worked for South Korea or Taiwan, it is not necessarily true that these would apply in Gambia or Gabon. Similarly, while strong state-guided industries may not have worked in Vietnam, under different circumstances and in another country they might be relevant and effective.

THE EAST ASIAN MIRACLE AND FINANCIAL CRISIS

What were the lessons learned from the debate between import-substituting industrialization and export-oriented growth? The answer to this question depends on whom you ask and when. By the early 1990s, the evidence seemed to favor an export-oriented strategy based on the dynamic growth experience of the East Asian Tigers and the Southeast Asian "Tiger Cubs" (Thailand, Indonesia, the Philippines, and Malaysia). In *Looking at the Sun,* James Fallows argues that the East Asian system of state-led, export-oriented economic growth proved superior to both the ISI strategy and liberal laissez-faire policies.[23]

The results in Latin America were not as good. It proved impossible to avoid entanglement in international trade and finance. The strategy of borrowing from abroad to build domestic industry created devastating debt crises in Latin America.

The heavy controls adopted to avoid dependency created opportunities for corruption and special-interest manipulation. Latin America experienced less growth and greater inequality.

The World Bank released a study titled *The East Asian Miracle* which sought to assess the lessons learned from import-substituting industrialization versus export-oriented growth.[24] It noted that the "East Asian Miracle"—high growth without great inequality—was due to two basic factors. First, the East Asian countries were successful at "getting the fundamentals right." This is development jargon for avoiding the tremendous economic distortions that the Latin American countries were forced to introduce as they sought inward development. By contrast, the East Asian countries avoided inefficient wage, price, and exchange-rate distortions. They promoted high rates of saving (so that investment was possible without large foreign debts), high levels of education and training, and stable macroeconomic policies. Second, some of the state policies were effective in increasing growth, especially "export-push" policies. According to the World Bank, the contest between state-led import-substituting industrialization and state-led export-oriented growth showed that the key to success was not so much what the government did but what it *avoided* doing. If the state avoids making a number of critical mistakes, development has a pretty good chance.

Many East Asian scholars believed that their state policies were the key to their success. They noted that the World Bank report blamed all failures on the state and credited all successes to natural market forces. They pointed out that many of the positive factors in Asian economic development, such as high savings rates, strong education systems, and relative income inequality, were *dictated by state actions*, not due to the absence of them. In other words, the East Asian economic development was very much the result of carefully crafted mercantilist policies.

The Asian financial crisis that began in 1997 reopened the debate on development strategies. Some argued that the crisis was caused or exacerbated by unwise state involvement in the economy (often called *crony capitalism*). Others claimed that the rapid adoption of Washington Consensus policies, especially free capital markets, was to blame. They believed that "premature globalization"—opening up to global financial markets before necessary domestic institutions and regulations were in place—made the Asian economies unusually susceptible to financial crises.

This was an important issue to resolve. Do laissez-faire policies produce rapid growth, as the World Bank report had suggested? Or do they open up an economy to instability and crises, as the 1997 Asian financial crisis seemed to indicate? In 2001, the World Bank released another study called *Rethinking the East Asian Miracle* that addressed these critical questions.[25] Reading this report, one appreciates that both miracles and crises are complicated phenomena that cannot and should not be oversimplified. The Asian financial crisis was created by a combination of market imperfections, business-government relations that sometimes encouraged financial abuse, and the lack of effective regulation and social safety nets.

In addition, some scholars contend that it is a myth that the developed economies achieved success through the methods they preach to the LDCs today. Instead, writes Ha-Joon Chang, "Almost all of today's rich countries used tariff protection and subsidies to develop their industries. Interestingly, Britain and the USA, the two countries that are supposed to have reached the summit of the world economy through their free-market, free-trade policy, are actually the ones that had most aggressively used protection and subsidies."[26]

In other words, what has worked historically—and also recently, as shown by the experience of several East Asian NICs—are development strategies that effectively incorporate the role of the state in the development process. The key to development in LDCs is not simply more government or less government; rather, it is *good* government. Smaller government (and supposedly a more unregulated market) is not necessarily better government if it sacrifices social goals and institutions. Similarly, big government alone creates many obstacles to successful development. The devil is in the details.

DEVELOPMENT AND GLOBALIZATION

As LDCs entered the twenty-first century, global changes made economic development seem more attainable but riskier and more complex. We often sum up these changes in a single word: globalization. For LDCs, confronting globalization has meant confronting a complicated array of problems and opportunities. The development dilemma is no longer a simple matter of choosing a grand development strategy such as import-substituting industrialization, but rather analyzing how to deal with both the policy choices and critical details that together form the two faces of development today.

The Informal Economy, Microcredit and the Mystery of Capital

Microcredit gives many of the poor a chance to participate in the market economy, often through what is termed the **informal economy**—the part of the economic system that operates outside of direct government control. It often is an important source of opportunity for grassroots entrepreneurship.

However, in many countries, regulations and legal issues make it difficult for people to get started in the informal economy, to take full advantage of its opportunities, and to leverage their success. In his book *The Mystery of Capital*, Peruvian economist Hernando de Soto argues that capital is the key to unlocking grassroots economic growth potential—an idea that the supporters of microcredit agree with.[27] De Soto notes that in many LDCs the poor often have access to capital in the form of land or property that they use but do not own. A small farmer, for example, might live on and till unused land on an absentee landlord's vast estate. Or a city street vendor might slowly build up a structure on a public sidewalk.

The problem, he says, is that because their capital is informal and sometimes illegal, they do not have any *property rights* in it. It can be easily taken away, and it may be costly and difficult to gain formal legal title. And, of course, it is impossible to use this capital to secure credit to expand a business or to build a permanent house. The poor have capital, perhaps as much as $10 *trillion* worth, but they cannot make use of it in the same way that people in developed nations can. If capitalism is to work for the poor, de Soto argues, then the poor need to become capitalists, and that requires that they have rights to the capital they already use.

Recently there has been a realization that development, if it is to succeed, must proceed at all levels at once. That is, LDCs cannot hope to grow if the focus is *only* on policies of the World Bank and the IMF, or *only* on state development strategies. Both types of initiatives must move forward, and even more must happen; development must get down to the grassroots. One of the great errors of grand development strategies was the notion that development financed by "macro-credit" would trickle down from international capitalist institutions or a planning agency to the villages and city streets. The idea of microcredit renewed interest in the possibility that development could grow from the bottom up.

Microcredit is one of the beneficiaries of this "trickle-up" approach.[28] Microfinance seeks to provide credit to people to start their own small businesses, thus enabling the poor to lift themselves from poverty through their own initiative. When they repay their loans, this enables others to access such funds, too. The most famous example of microcredit is the **Grameen Bank**, which was founded in Bangladesh by Professor Muhammad Yunus in 1976. Microcredit loans are very small, often just $20 or $50, but the potential impact is large. Since its inception, the total value of Grameen Bank's loans is in excess of $11 billion, with over 95 percent of the borrowers being women. The reason that microcredit institutions are successful involves overcoming an economic problem called **asymmetric information**. The problem is, who can be trusted to repay a loan, even a small one? If you know whom to trust, you can lend money at low interest rates. But if you cannot tell who is trustworthy (or creditworthy), then you have to charge everyone a high interest rate to cover expected losses. High interest rates, however, discourage trustworthy individuals from borrowing money, thus diminishing the possibility of them starting or expanding a business. The problems of finding out who is trustworthy and the cost of monitoring borrowers limit grassroots development by making credit unavailable or too expensive for the poor, who need it the most.

Microcredit institutions solve this problem by lending money to small groups of people, usually women. Given that each member of the group is individually responsible for repaying the group's loan, it is in each member's interest to work only with productive and trustworthy colleagues who share the same objective. The information problem—whom can you trust?—is thus shifted from the lender to the members of each group. By moving the burden of knowing who is creditworthy from the bank to the borrowing group, microcredit institutions unlock the possibility of credit-financed grassroots economic development.

People who are used to living in societies where credit is readily available may find it difficult to appreciate how even a little credit can benefit people in very poor parts of the world. A small group of women can use a loan to purchase fabric or other raw materials that are then processed and sold in local or regional markets. Without funds for the raw materials, the market value of their labor cannot be realized. The small incomes that are thus generated can change both the economic status of the households and the social status of the women.

Although microcredit institutions often begin with an agenda for socioeconomic change, critics argue that the need to be financially sustainable—to earn interest and achieve high loan repayment rates—sometimes alters these priorities. The concern is that the pressure to be economically sustainable may cause them to avoid loans to the poorest of the poor, who are often the people who most need access to credit. There is also a concern that microcredit institutions, if successful, may introduce capitalist practices and values into indigenous societies.

Development in the New Millennium

Despite years of debates about competing models and strategies, poverty has remained endemic in many parts of the world. Rock stars like Bono have aggressively campaigned for a more meaningful commitment to addressing the dire conditions of many of the poorest nations. The spotlight on poverty, child malnourishment, and disease, especially in sub-Saharan Africa, has served as a glaring reminder that while much about the development landscape has changed over the years, the poor in many parts of the world are still far from being able to meet most basic needs.

Consider the problem of access to health care. Contagious diseases such as malaria, smallpox, and tuberculosis have been virtually eliminated in advanced industrial countries because of action by scientists and public health officials. Vast numbers of people in LDCs are not so lucky. Because of the high cost of research and the low incomes of potential buyers, medical research focuses less on diseases that are widespread in the tropics. Even where drugs are available and medical treatments are well known, the costs of a public-health program are exorbitant. Even governments that are not corrupt often struggle to make public health a high priority.

But the costs of ignoring public health issues are high, too, as the AIDS epidemic in sub-Saharan Africa shows. The Joint United Nations Programme on HIV/AIDS (UNAIDS) reports that although the HIV infection rate in the last ten years continues to decline, sub-Saharan Africa remains the region most severely affected by AIDS. In 2011, for example, 69 percent of all known cases of HIV were concentrated in sub-Saharan Africa, which accounted for 71 percent of all new HIV infections. Lack of money for prevention, treatment, and education is part of the problem. Other elements include the attitudes of some government officials and social and sexual practices that allow the disease to spread. Solving such devastating problems requires citizens to look abroad for assistance and also reflect on their own practices.

To some extent, attention to poverty and health care–related problems increased following the UN's establishment of the Millennium Development Goals (MDGs) in 2000. This initiative helped refocus the international community's commitment to addressing dire economic and human conditions in the poorest nations. The Millennium Development project has pursued the following eight broadly defined goals:[29]

1. To eradicate poverty and extreme hunger by half
2. To achieve universal primary education
3. To advance gender equality and empower women
4. To reduce child mortality by two-thirds by 2015
5. To reduce by two-thirds the maternal mortality ratio
6. To reduce the spread of HIV/AIDS and malaria by half by 2015
7. To secure environmental sustainability
8. To develop a partnership for development that includes an open, rule-based, and nondiscriminatory trade and financial system.

Renowned American economist Jeffrey Sachs was recruited to advise the United Nations. Having advised multiple governments around the world, he has been a strong advocate for greater commitments from industrial nations toward achieving the aforementioned goals. He argues that wealthier nations and international institutions such as the World Bank and the IMF have been partial toward privatization while overlooking the importance of poverty reduction and financial assistance to the poorer countries. He writes:

> Increased foreign financial assistance was deemed not to be needed. Indeed, foreign aid per person in the poor countries plummeted during the 1980s and 1990s. Aid per person in sub-Saharan Africa, for example, expressed in constant 2002 dollars, fell from $32 per African in 1980 to just $22 per African in 2001, during a period in which Africa's pandemic diseases ran rampant, and needs for increased public spending were stark … . Many African countries have heard an earful from the World Bank … about privatizing their health services, or at least charging user fees for health and education. Yet most of the high-income-country shareholders of the World Bank have health systems that guarantee universal access, and all have education systems that ensure access to public education.[30]

Critical of the market-oriented model of development, Sachs believes that the wealthier states can and should provide more aid to the poorest nations. Table 11-3 shows that major donors have increased net Official Development Assistance (ODA), especially since 2000. One motive for this increase is to assist those states helping with the war on terrorism. To those concerned that aid would go to corrupt officials or make matters worse for LDCs, Sachs and the UN both state that LDCs themselves ought to be working toward making government more responsive to the needs of the poor.[31] However, neither Sachs nor the UN are depending on good government alone to solve development problems when issues such as disease prevention, agricultural production, and increasing infrastructure in poor countries are just as important. Sachs is also a vocal proponent for the cancellation of the foreign debts of many desperately poor countries, even suggesting that if the wealthier nations opt not to cancel them, the highly indebted poor nations should refuse to service the exorbitant loans they now carry.

TABLE 11-3

Net Official Development Assistance Disbursements (in billions of dollars)

Donor	1988–1989 Average	2000	2004	2010
United States	8.9	10.0	19.7	26.6
Germany	4.8	5.0	7.5	8.0
United Kingdom	2.6	4.5	7.9	8.0
France	5.6	4.1	8.5	7.8
Japan	9.0	13.5	8.9	7.3
Netherlands	2.2	3.1	4.2	4.6
Spain	0.4	1.2	2.4	4.0

Sources: Organisation for Economic Co-operation and Development, *Statistical Annex of the 2005 Development Co-operation Report* (2006), at http://www.oecd-ilibrary.org/development/development-co-operation-report-2005_dcr-2005-en; Organisation for Economic Co-operation and Development, *Development Aid at a Glance 2012–Statistics by Region* (2012), at http://www.oecd.org/investment/aidstatistics/42139479.pdf.

Since 2000, the IMF, the World Bank, and the developed nations have responded to the goal of debt relief espoused by the likes of Sachs. At the June 2005 G8 meeting (including Russia) in Gleneagles, Scotland, members pledged to fund 100 percent debt relief for eighteen of the world's poorest countries (fourteen of which are in Africa). Obtaining debt relief grew easier as World Bank policy shifted from support for neoliberal "one size fits all" policies to more of a grab-bag approach to development.[32] Yet some countries that could use relief, such as Indonesia, did not qualify as being poor enough, while others, such as Moldova, were not eligible because they were in the former Soviet Bloc of nations. Still, the World Bank estimates that by the end of 2008 the debt of thirty-five poor countries in the HIPC Initiative had been cut by more than 50 percent. A 2009 UN report on the impact of the global financial crisis suggests that the international community was "making notable progress on reducing the external debt burden of developing countries."[33] As Table 11-4 shows, debt as a percentage of gross national income (GNI) in the ten poorest countries in the world is now relatively low.

Sachs' advocacy of the MDGs is based in part in a critique of past strategies—like the structural adjustment programs—pursued by the IMF. In his book *The End of Poverty*, Sachs argues against conventional economic logic and the Washington Consensus, asserting that the "main IMF prescription has been budgetary belt tightening for patients much too poor to own belts. IMF-led austerity has frequently led to riots, coups, and the collapse of public services."[34] He believes that development experts need to emulate a *clinical* approach practiced in medicine. Not unlike individuals, economies are "complex systems," and hence "differential diagnosis" is essential to differentiate between ailments or illnesses even when some common symptoms may be present between two or more cases. Carrying out "differential diagnosis" is critical to being able to diagnose economic problems—and hence the appropriate

TABLE 11-4

External Debt and GNI of the Poorest Countries

Country	External Debt as Percent of GNI (2010)	GNI (2010, Billions of dollars)	GNI per Capita (2010)
Congo, Dem. Rep.	47	12.3	320
Liberia	28	0.8	340
Burundi	34	1.6	400
Eritrea	48	2.1	540
Niger	21	5.5	720
Central African Republic	19	2	790
Sierra Leone	41	1.9	830
Malawi	19	4.9	860
Togo	61	2.8	890
Mozambique	44	9.4	930

Note: Countries shown are the world's ten poorest, ranked by gross national income (GNI) per capita measured in purchasing power parity.
Sources: World Bank, *Global Development Finance Online*; World Bank, *World Development Indicators Online* (accessed June 8, 2012).

case-specific treatment that may be necessary. For Sachs, "clinical economics"[35] can help achieve the broader goals articulated in the Millennium Development project.

Several of Sachs' views about development are currently supported by both the IMF and the World Bank.[36] The latter has always been more focused on development issues than the former, and it has gradually shifted its focus from banking on "top-down" industrial development and market-oriented programs to targeting the poor directly. The IMF and the World Bank now require countries seeking financial aid as well as debt relief through the HIPC Initiative to prepare Poverty Reduction Strategy Papers (PRSPs) that outline how they plan to tackle poverty over a number of years. Because the PRSPs are formulated through a process involving governments, civil society groups, the IMF, and the World Bank, it is hoped that they will support good governance and ensure that the poor benefit from IMF-World Bank funding, rather than bear the brunt of cuts in social spending, as was common under structural adjustment programs.

CONCLUSION

This chapter has demonstrated that since World War II economic development has remained an objective of many different states, IOs, and, recently, NGOs. Different strategies modeled on a subtle combination of policies have resulted in some successes, especially for the NICs of East and Southeast Asia. However, the search for a single solution to development problems has given way to a growing realization that currently there is no one foolproof strategy for all developing nations, nor might there ever be one. Some of the factors that have helped nations successfully develop include their geopolitical position, their colonial past or history, their position in the international economy (what each produces and trades), and a myriad of domestic factors.

In the case of the world's poorest nations, especially those in sub-Saharan Africa, economic development has been modest at best. In many cases, these nations have encountered problems associated with stringent demands made on them by the major powers, the WTO, the IMF, the World Bank, and even the UN. In addition, a myriad of factors within their own societies act as barriers to change, including geographic location, access to water, government corruption, and ethnic and religious differences among social groups.

Acute poverty and political conflicts in Africa remind us that the goal of development is not just having a higher income; it is also about having a better life, with rights and opportunities. Perhaps we should remain optimistic after all. Many states, IOs, and NGOs are heavily invested in trying to promote meaningful change in developing countries, employing a variety of techniques and methods. Indeed, some progress has been made, and certainly lessons have been learned. However, development remains a complicated and frustrating challenge. The development conundrum still remains a pressing reality.

KEY TERMS

United Nations Conference on Trade and Development (UNCTAD)   271
New International Economic Order (NIEO)   272
heavily indebted poor countries (HIPCs)   273

odious debt   273
HIPC Initiative   273
import-substituting industrialization (ISI)   278
export-oriented growth   279
informal economy   284

microcredit   285
Grameen Bank   285
asymmetric information   285

DISCUSSION QUESTIONS

1. How serious is the problem of global poverty today? Explain citing data from this chapter.
2. What four forces have shaped the development process for LDCs? How do these forces create tensions within LDCs and between LDCs and industrial nations?
3. Briefly trace how the issues regarding economic development have changed since the early postcolonial days of the 1950s and 1960s. In particular, discuss the tensions between the UNCTAD and the NIEO, between import-substitution industrialization and export-oriented growth, and between the advocates of the Asian Miracle and those who favor the Washington Consensus.
4. The chapter argues that developing countries need good government more than they need less government or more government. What are the characteristics of good government with respect to economic development? Explain. (Hint: Consider some of the factors discussed in the last section of this chapter).

SUGGESTED READINGS

Paul Collier. *The Bottom Billion.* New York: Oxford University Press, 2008.

Ha-Joon Chang. *Kicking Away the Ladder—Development Strategy in Historical Perspective.* London: Anthem Press, 2002.

Ha-Joon Chang. *Bad Samaritans: The Myth of Free Trade and the Secret History of Capitalism.* London: Bloomsbury Press, 2008.

Hernando de Soto. *The Mystery of Capital: Why Capitalism Triumphs in the West and Fails Everywhere Else.* New York: Basic Books, 2000.

Theodore H. Moran. *Beyond Sweatshops: Foreign Direct Investment and Globalization in Developing Countries.* Washington, DC: Brookings, 2002.

Oxfam. *Paying the Price: Why Rich Countries Must Invest Now in a War on Poverty.* Oxford: Oxford International, 2005.

Jeffrey D. Sachs. *The End of Poverty: Economic Possibilities for Our Time.* New York: Penguin Press, 2005.

Jeffrey D. Sachs. *Common Wealth: Economics for a Crowded Planet.* New York: Penguin Press, 2008.

Joseph E. Stiglitz. *Making Globalization Work.* New York: W. W. Norton, 2006.

NOTES

1. See http://www.globalissues.org/article/26/poverty-facts-and-stats.
2. See Frantz Fanon, *The Wretched of the Earth* (New York: Grove/Atlantic, 1961).
3. See Daniel Chirot, *Social Change in the Twentieth Century* (New York: Harcourt Brace, 1977), p. 173.
4. One of the leading voices of the anti-neocolonial movement was the former president of Ghana, Kwame Nkrumah, who articulated this thesis in his book *Neo-colonialism: The Last Stage of Imperialism* (London: Nelson, 1965).
5. See Joan Edelman Spero, *The Politics of International Economic Relations* (New York: St. Martin's Press, 1981), pp. 246–247.
6. Raul Prebisch, *The Economic Development of Latin America and Its Principal Problems* (New York: United Nations, 1950).
7. Andre Gunder Frank, *Capitalism and Underdevelopment in Latin America* (New York: Monthly Review Press, 1967).
8. Osvaldo Sunkel and Pedro Paz, *El subdesarrollo latinoamericano y la teoría del desarrollo* (Mexico: Siglo Veintiuno de Espana 1970), p. 6, as quoted in J. Samuel Valenzuela and Arturo Valenzuela, "Modernization and Dependency," *Comparative Politics* 10 (1978), pp. 543–557.
9. For a good discussion of this position, see Teresa Hayter, *Aid as Imperialism* (Middlesex, England: Penguin, 1971).
10. Joseph Stiglitz, *Making Globalization Work* (New York: W. W. Norton, 2006), pp. 228–229.
11. For a good video that examines this issue, see "Free Trade Slaves" (1999).

12. Theodore H. Moran. *Beyond Sweatshops: Foreign Direct Investment and Globalization in Developing Countries* (Washington, DC: Brookings, 2002).

13. Walt R. Rostow, *The Stages of Economic Growth: A Non-Communist Manifesto* (London: Cambridge University Press, 1960).

14. See Jorge Ospina Sardi, "Trade Policy in Latin America," in Naya Miguel Urrutia, Shelley Mark, and Alfredo Fuentes eds., *Lessons in Development* (San Francisco, CA: International Center for International Growth, 1989), p. 289.

15. Stephan Haggard, *Pathways from the Periphery: The Politics of Growth in the Newly Industrializing Countries* (Ithaca, NY: Cornell University Press, 1990), p. 26.

16. Youngil Lim, "Comparing Brazil and Korea," in Naya et al., eds., *Lessons in Development,* pp. 102–103.

17. Nigel Harris, *The End of the Third World* (New York: Meredith Press, 1986), pp. 90–91.

18. For example, see Wontack Hong, *Trade, Distortions, and Employment Growth in Korea* (Seoul: Korea Development Institute, 1979).

19. More detailed data is available in Seiji Naya, et al., *Lessons in Development: A Comparative Study of Asia and Latin America* (San Francisco: International Center for Economic Growth, 1987), p. 287; World Bank, *World Development Report 1997* (New York: Oxford University Press, 1997); Carl J. Dahlman and Ousa Sananikone, "Taiwan, China: Policies and Institutions for Rapid Growth," in Danny M. Leipziger, ed., *Lessons from East Asia* (Ann Arbor, MI: University of Michigan Press, 1997), p. 85; CIA *World Factbook*, at https://www.cia.gov/library/publications/the-world-factbook/index.html.

20. William E. James, Seiji Naya, and Gerald M. Meier, *Asian Development: Economic Success and Policy Lessons* (Madison, WI: University of Wisconsin Press, 1989), pp. 69–74.

21. Ibid., p. 81.

22. Haggard, *Pathways from the Periphery*, p. 196.

23. James Fallows, *Looking at the Sun: The Rise of the New East Asian Political and Economic System* (New York: Vintage, 1995).

24. The World Bank, *The East Asian Miracle: Economic Growth and Public Policy* (New York: Oxford University Press, 1993).

25. The World Bank, *Rethinking the East Asian Miracle* (New York: Oxford University Press, 2001).

26. Ha-Joon Chang, "Kicking Away the Ladder: How the Economic and Intellectual Histories of Capitalism Have Been Re-Written to Justify Neo-Liberal Capitalism", http://www.paecon.net/PAEtexts/Chang1.htm. See also his *Bad Samaritans: The Myth of Free Trade and the Secret History of Capitalism* (London: Bloomsbury Press, 2008).

27. Hernando de Soto, *The Mystery of Capital: Why Capitalism Triumphs in the West and Fails Everywhere Else* (New York: Basis Books, 2000).

28. See Muhammad Yunus, *Banker to the Poor: Micro-lending and the Battle against World Poverty* (New York: Public Affairs, 1999).

29. United Nations, http://www.un.org/millenniumgoals/.

30. Jeffrey D. Sachs, *The End of Poverty: Economic Possibilities for Our Time* (New York: Penguin Press, 2005), p. 82.

31. See Jeffrey D. Sachs, "Institutions Matter, but Not for Everything," *Finance and Development*, June 2003.

32. See Dani Rodrik, "Goodbye Washington Consensus, Hello Washington Confusion," *Journal of Economic Literature* XLIV (December 2006), pp. 973–987.

33. See the United Nations, "Strengthening the Global Partnership for Development in a Time of Crisis," MDG Gap Task Force Report (New York: United Nations, 2009).

34. See Sachs, *The End of Poverty*, Chapter 4, pp. 74–89.

35. Ibid, p. 74.

36. See the World Bank, *Economic Growth in the 1990s: Learning from a Decade of Reform* (Washington, DC: The World Bank, 2005).

Toward a More Perfect (European) Union

The Fall of the Berlin Wall: A defining moment in the international political economy.

AP Images/Haley/Sipa

In 2012 the **European Union (EU)** received the Nobel Peace Prize. For many it was a shock that a group of nations would be selected for this distinguished honor instead of a person. Some saw it as a recognition of the people of Europe for achieving one of history's greatest and most interesting experiments: integrating Europe's political, economic, and social institutions. Still others wondered if the award was not a signal coming at a strategic moment during the financial crisis to remind Europeans of what the EU was originally intended for and just how far they had come—lest they give up.

Inspired by the philosophy of Immanuel Kant (1724–1804), some Europeans at the end of World War II hoped that a federation of democratic republics could be the basis for perpetual peace (in stark contrast to the conflicts of the first half of the twentieth century). British Prime Minister Winston Churchill saw a "United States of Europe" that could balance U.S. influence (and possibly prevent U.S. dominance) in the postwar era. French President Charles DeGaulle envisioned a "Europe of States" that would enhance the sovereignty and status of all its members. Many Europeans—especially the French—also supported it to help solve "the German problem"—to entrench Germany in an integrated set of regionally based supranational institutions so that no other country would be dominated by it.

Jean Monnet, a French political-economist, provided the primary motives behind a loose association of European nations. He probably did not intend for what today we know as the EU to be a federated United States of Europe. Rather, his immediate goals included recovery from the war, continued economic growth, and maintenance of peace on a continent that had been ravaged by two long wars over the past thirty-one years. At the time, many European states were modern capitalist economies with budding democratic institutions, which gave the EU's founding fathers good reason to believe they could work together to create common economic and political institutions for their mutual benefit.[1]

Since the early 1950s, the **integration** (combining separate state institutions and processes into single regional bodies and agencies) of a number of West European nations that would be separated from Eastern Europe during the Cold War has gone through a number of mostly successful phases. At times, economic integration has been relatively easier to achieve than political and social assimilation. As membership in the community grew (see Fig 12.1), economic successes on issues like trade "spilled over" into an assortment of agreements on political and social issues. New political institutions were created such as the European Commission, Council of Ministers, European Parliament, European Court of Justice, and the European Human Rights Commission. The Schengen Agreement, made part of EU law in 1997, has allowed uninterrupted, visa-free passage between nations. And yet, the EU's security structure has not developed as much as other institutions, primarily because the North Atlantic Treaty Organization (NATO) almost made it redundant.

While the European community has had several crises in the past, today it faces a critical situation due to the spread of the financial crisis that started in the United States in 2007, to much of the EU. In particular, the debt crisis in the **Economic and Monetary Union (EMU)** states of the EU (often referred to as the **Euro zone**) is at a critical point. Recall that in Chapter 8 we noted that many of these countries are heavily indebted and face the prospect of bankruptcy. They have to figure out how to endure severe cuts in their domestic programs imposed on them by the **austerity policies** of the IMF and EU finance agencies while pushing forward with financial integration by adopting a common fiscal policy that would help them move further along on the road to a truly integrated EU. On the other hand, some EMU members such as Greece who use the euro as their common currency are considering dropping out of the Euro zone so as to be able to return to using their own currency in the hopes of improving their chances of economic recovery.

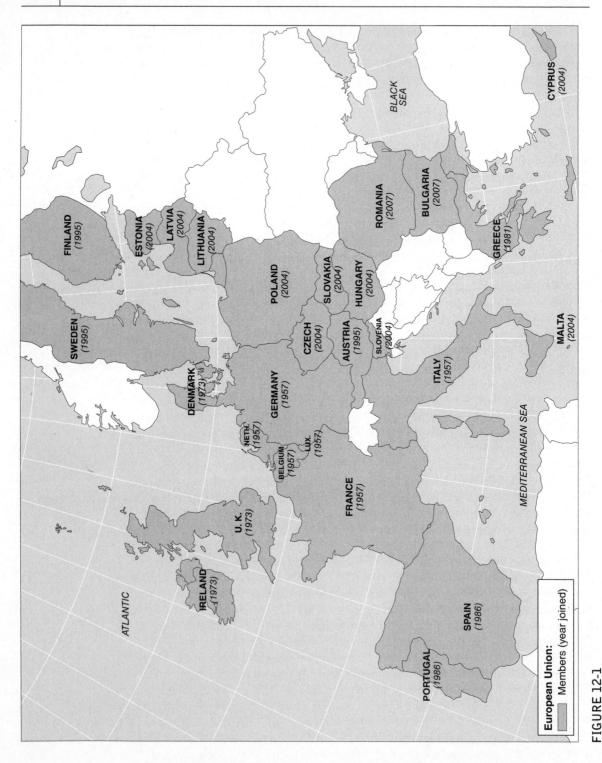

FIGURE 12-1

The European Union, Including Dates of Entry

Also at stake are more than sixty years of political and economic coopera-tion aimed at creating a secure, prosperous Europe. As negotiations on the new EU budget for 2014–2020 progressed, many *Euroskeptics* criticized the EU for costing too much. Some of the northern Euro zone states such as Germany and the Netherlands have encouraged Greece to withdraw from the EMU. Spain has also considered the possibility of discontinuing use of the euro. Even Great Britain, which is a member of the EMU but does not use the euro, is considering leaving the EMU. Critics of integration in all three English-speaking member countries have also called on Prime Minister David Cameron to withdraw Great Britain from the EU altogether.

An irony of history is that Germany now plays a key role in the EMU crisis. Although it lost World War II, Germany over the years has benefited a great deal from economic and political integration. Now many blame it for perpetuating the EMU crisis by insisting that austerity is the best way to deal with debt problems and generate economic recovery. Many worry that austerity could very well drive many of the heavily indebted countries into leaving the EMU. Furthermore, along with Great Britain, Germany could later be accused of helping bring down the entire EU. We try to answer some big questions in this chapter: Why are some EU states seemingly giving up on integration? Is achieving a true European union no longer a common goal? Is cooperation on mutual problems like terrorism, immi-gration, minority-group assimilation, and environmental degradation no longer worth the political and economic price of integration? Has the EU reached its pin-nacle as one of history's most innovative experiments in promoting both capi-talism and democracy? We have no easy answers to these questions, but as you will see in the following discussion, we think that the motivation to integrate is no longer as strong as it once was. Meanwhile the EU seems intent on muddling through the current financial crisis, which could further undermine the goal of integration. Paradoxically, although economic integration was all the rage in the early 2000s, it is economic interconnectedness itself that today is blocking efforts to further many of the Union's objectives related to integration!

THE IPE OF INTEGRATION

Before looking at EU history and some of its institutions, we want to introduce some of the degrees of economic integration that countries can choose to commit to, especially when they are in close proximity in a defined geographical region like Europe. The economic efficiency that comes with shared markets has to be weighed against the loss of some sovereignty associated with a relatively inter-connected system of political and social institutions. For example, a Free Trade Association (FTA) involves a relatively small degree of integration because nations only agree to eliminate tariff barriers to trade in goods and services they pro-duce themselves. But each nation retains the right to set its own tariff barriers with respect to products from outside the FTA. The North American Free Trade Agreement (NAFTA) is an example of an FTA between the United States, Canada, and Mexico. The fact that some goods are tariff-free in FTA transactions but other goods are still subject to differential trade barriers complicates intra-FTA trade and therefore limits overall integration.

A reason for the popularity of integration is its connection to regionalism. Theoretically, by dropping internal trade barriers, members create more trade between themselves. Some of that trade is indeed "generated" by new opportunities provided by barrier-free trade, with no losses elsewhere. Mercantilists would point out, however, that some of the trade is in fact diverted from other non-member countries. For example, when Mexico joined NAFTA, its exports to the United States increased (trade creation), but exports from some other developing countries to the United States fell (trade diversion). Being a member of NAFTA gave Mexico an edge over producers in non-NAFTA countries that were still subject to U.S. tariffs. This resulted in some inefficiencies and economic losses for some non-NAFTA countries that lacked any way to seek compensation.

Economic liberals suggest that economic integration is appealing early on because it is a way for nations to achieve greater efficiency in their use of scarce resources and higher rates of economic growth. In the lingo of economics, integration promotes greater *static efficiency* in two ways. First, with complete free trade each member nation can specialize in producing the goods and services in which it is most efficient. National protective barriers that preserve inefficient industries and promote redundancy are eliminated between member states. Second, a larger, integrated market promotes efficiency in industries with large-scale production or long production runs. These gains from *economies of scale* make products cheaper and more competitive.

However, a more important benefit of integration occurs in the long run when *dynamic efficiency* promotes economic growth. The logic is that a larger, more competitive market is likely to be more innovative. Theoretically, as internal trade barriers are removed, previously protected firms are forced to compete with one another. Firms become more efficient and "nimble." Economic growth rates tend to increase, which in turn raises living standards. Thus, neoliberals assume that economic integration need produce only a little extra growth—one or two percentage points—to have considerable long-term effects on people's lives. These gains from efficient specialization then motivate officials to speed up the integration process.

The fundamental political problem posed by integration is the loss of sovereignty that occurs when nations form regional blocs like the EU. At some point, each member state risks being forced to ignore some of its national interests—political, economic, social, or cultural—as a consequence of maintaining its regional obligations. This tension poses a severe dilemma for states, which tend to value security and autonomy above all else. So why would a nation not only sacrifice its sovereignty but also impose on itself a "democracy deficit" that limits people's choices when it comes to joining regional bodies and paying the economic and political costs stemming from membership in an integrated regional organization?

Several arguments stand out. First, as integrated global markets play a larger role in their economies, many nation-states have found themselves too limited by their territorial boundaries to manage or control the effects of these markets. Second, realists argue that integration enhances the "bandwagon effect" and political power of some states by virtue of their membership in a security alliance. Belgium, for example, is more potent politically as an EU member than if it were simply a small, autonomous nation making its own way in the international political economy. Likewise, integration enhances the division of labor amongst members of the alliance when it comes to security issues. For example, in NATO, the United States has been the major nuclear power, while smaller countries take on different roles depending on their capabilities and expertise with different weapons and in diplomatic situations. Finally, integration is appealing because it represents a way to counter the influence of domestic special-interest groups. For example, when the interests of heavy industry prevent adoption of environmental laws in a country, the responsibility for environmental regulation can be shifted to the regional level. Conversely, national environmental voices will have more influence if other countries in the regional bloc also have strong "green" parties.

THE COMMUNITY BUILDING PROJECT

Considering the diversity of their hopes and fears, how were the Western Europeans (separated from Eastern Europeans after 1947 by the Cold War) able to achieve such an incredible amount of close cooperation? As noted above, the Cold War and economic interests acted as accelerants. The advantages of free trade among partners with similar economic and technological endowments were certainly important incentives for integration. Realists stress that what finally brought them together was the need to find a political solution to the excessive nationalism that had caused the catastrophe of World War II. Moreover, say realists, the Western Europeans were politically motivated to promote security, peace, and political freedom in opposition to the totalitarian security structure established by the Soviet Union in Eastern Europe.

The United States supported postwar European integration because it helped with the political and economic recovery of strong anticommunist allies. From 1947 to 1951, the U.S. Marshall Plan provided European nations with nearly $13 billion in aid (equivalent to more than $90 billion today) for the reconstruction of infrastructure and industries to be used cooperatively by these nations. The Marshall Plan also provided humanitarian assistance to the suffering masses in Europe, in part to prevent the spread of procommunist sentiment amongst the public. Behind the aid was a U.S. condition that the Europeans create a European Payments Union to help distribute the money.

Although Jean Monnet dreamed of a United States of Europe, he began the project with a proposal to build a much narrower alliance along functional economic lines: a zone of free trade uniting the heavy-industry regions that had been contested in previous wars and that spanned the French–German border. The European Coal and Steel Community (ECSC) of 1952 was the critical test case of economic and political cooperation between France and Germany. By all accounts, it was a great success and thereby provided the incentive for further efforts toward Western European integration.

A fuller measure of economic cooperation was achieved in 1957 when the Treaty of Rome created the European Economic Community (EEC) between France, West Germany, Italy, Belgium, the Netherlands, and Luxembourg. The immediate economic objective of the Treaty of Rome was to advance integration from the level of an FTA to a **Common Market**. It did so by creating a **customs union** with three elements. First, EEC members agreed to both tariff-free trade *within* their collective borders and to a common set of external trade barriers. There would be no need for border inspections or custom fees *between* EEC members because of the unified trade structure. Second, they adopted the goal of eliminating quantitative trade restrictions (quotas) and other measures that had the equivalent effect, to ensure the complete free movement of goods. Third and finally, EEC members agreed to pursue the free movement of people (especially employed persons), services, and capital (to a certain extent).

In practice, of course, the elimination of trade barriers was not as complete as theory suggested; some nations retained the right to impose nontariff trade barriers such as health and safety standards on one another. As we discuss below, a true common market remained an objective of the EEC until the 1990s when it was replaced by the goal of a European Union. For the most part, the customs union proved to be an effective step in integration by increasing market size and stimulating growth and efficiency. More importantly, the new members of the EEC gave up more of their sovereignty for the sake of a greater degree of political cooperation necessary to achieve their mutual goals.

The cooperation that came with gradual economic integration was a means to solve other problems that were too big for any one state to deal with. This is reflected in the institutional design of the EEC, which included not only the European Commission as the main executive body ("guardian of the treaties") but also a European Court of Justice (ECJ) and a Common Assembly of national deputies (after 1962 called the European Parliament). These institutions were constructed with a hidden agenda of future growth of other community legislative, executive, and even judicial functions. Furthermore, political, social, and economic cooperation would "spill over" into mutual agreements on such policy issues as immigration, human rights, defense, and the environment.

Great Britain participated in the negotiations for the Treaty of Rome but decided to stand apart from the EEC. There were several reasons for this decision, which was eventually reversed in 1973. First, the British were concerned about the loss of political and economic autonomy that accompanies economic integration. British politicians (and probably most British citizens) were reluctant to cede decision-making power to others or to share it with the French and the Germans. Britain was forced to weigh the trade-offs between self-determination, domestic democracy, and economic growth, which present a constant tension in economic integration. It was also unwilling to give up its "imperial preferences"—preferential trading relations with the Commonwealth nations—or its highly valued "special relationship" with the United States. Although Britain balked at its first opportunity to enter the EEC, it did not want to be isolated from free trade in Europe. It therefore organized a weaker trade alliance called the European Free Trade Association (EFTA). However, the EFTA never became the engine of economic growth that the EEC promised to be. Today, only Iceland, Liechtenstein, Norway, and Switzerland remain members of the EFTA.

The CAP: The Glue That Holds Together the Community

Despite its remarkable success in creating political cooperation, the integration process should not be viewed through rose-colored glasses. As already noted, trade among members was never entirely free. Non-tariff barriers continued to emerge. In violation of the Treaty of Rome, members sometimes refused to accept certain imports from another country due to the influence of domestic groups. To keep states on the road to integration, officials had to reconcile the interests of groups promoting free trade with the interests of unions and other groups that screamed for protection.

A good example of this balancing act is the **Common Agricultural Policy (CAP)**—an EU-wide system of agricultural subsidies financed through taxes imposed by EU member nations.[2] Since 1962, it has been far and away the EU's largest single expenditure and a point of contention both within the EU and in its relations with other nations. The CAP originated at the end of World War II when European governments met to discuss the "farm problem," which was really two problems in one. The first concern was food security—the need to guarantee adequate supplies of agricultural foodstuffs. The second matter was farmers' incomes, which suffered tremendously from the Great Depression, World War II, and postwar economic conditions. Because of the high level of interdependence in Europe, one country's farm policy affected all the others. No single country could solve its problems on its own. For example, France had a more efficient agricultural sector than Germany. Whereas French farmers wanted a customs union that created bigger markets for their foodstuffs, German farmers feared they would not be able to compete after joining the EEC. So why would Germany remain in the EEC if its farmers might be driven off the land? Simply put, German industries would profit from freer trade because they had advantages over French industries. Thus, the dominant special interests of both states were made better off by EEC membership.

At first, the EEC agreed on a system of expensive price supports—which guaranteed farmers high prices—and protective barriers against foreign agricultural produce. These policies helped farmers survive the required adjustments to more rational farm policies and addressed the food security concern. Over the years, however, the CAP's guarantees actually encouraged European farmers to *expand* agriculture production to a vast degree, creating "mountains" of surplus dairy products in Denmark and "lakes" of surplus wine and olive oil in Italy, Greece, and Spain. Without a decline in prices, surplus production could not be eliminated. By the 1990s, CAP was under fire on at least three counts:

- First, the CAP was no longer affordable. It cost more than €40 billion in 2001—almost half of the total EU budget.
- Second, overproduction in the farm sector due to the CAP's vast subsidies was as hard on the environment as it was on the budget. Some farmers cut too many corners to expand subsidized output. Food quality, food safety, and especially environmental sustainability all suffered.
- Third, the CAP harmed poor farmers in LDCs. It limited their access to EU markets. And the EU's surplus farm goods were sold off or "dumped" in foreign markets, driving down farm prices there and, in some cases, driving indigenous farmers out of business. It was said that LDC food security suffered so that the EU's farmers could lead an even more comfortable life. Farm subsidies in countries outside the EU have also made it difficult to address this global problem.

Attempts to reform the CAP were made in 1992 and 2000, but neither made a significant difference to the level of subsidies farmers received. In June 2003, EU agriculture ministers agreed to further changes that were phased in between 2005 and 2012. Instead of receiving subsidies, EU farmers were given a lump-sum called the Single Farm Payment. They were encouraged to produce in response to consumer demand. Farm policy also shifted away from production and payments to focus more on preserving the countryside. When a drop in milk prices caused farmers to protest in 2009, the EU agreed to give the dairy industry €17.9 million between 2010–2013.[3]

In 2013, the CAP is expected to remain at 31 percent of the EU budget (€43.8 billion), down from 71 percent in 1984. Great Britain expects to pay €10 billion, one of the reasons why it argues that it has been subsidizing EU farmers without receiving many CAP funds for its own farmers. New proposals include a Single Payment Scheme that cuts funds to large farms and increases the amount of money transferred to the rural development budget. Other proposals include subsidizing crops for biofuels and abolishing a "set aside" scheme, which paid farmers to leave a part of their land unfarmed to prevent over production. Environmental groups have criticized the termination of the set-aside scheme because it could endanger wildlife in unfarmed areas. A reformed CAP is also likely to include an income insurance scheme for farmers and to spend more on innovation, climate, and energy.

Over the years, there have been many strong arguments against the CAP. EU farmers—particularly in France—have consistently had a lot of political clout and have favored it. France has received the most CAP subsidies, in part because its farmers have also been some of the most vocal, visible, organized, and politically powerful interest groups in Europe, always willing to set up road blocks in Paris, at the Channel Tunnel, and at ski resorts in the dead of winter. The CAP has also been blamed for the stalled WTO trade talks (see Chapter 6). The United States has refused to reduce its agricultural subsidies as long as the EU keeps its CAP. The continuing stalemate between the EU and United States has not been good for taxpayers in these countries and for poor farmers in the developing world, some of whose exports have not been able to gain entry into the EU.

Geographic Expansion

In 1967, the EEC formally joined with the ECSC and Euratom, another pan-European organization, to create an institution with broader responsibilities called the European Community (EC). The change in name signaled an intention to move beyond purely economic issues, although economic concerns continued to dominate EC discussions. An expanded political agenda reflected the prevailing wisdom in Europe that is sometimes summed up as the **bicycle theory** of European regionalism. A bicycle is stable so long as it keeps moving, but once it stops, its stability disappears and it tends to fall over. In the same way, according to Walter Hallstein, the first president of the European Commission, European unity could be sustained only if European nations constantly strived for an "ever closer union." Jean Monnet proposed the economic goal of prosperity through a unified market, and that was indeed enough to get European regionalism's bicycle moving. In the years that followed, Europe sought to keep its momentum going by accepting a series of new challenges.

The EC broadened its geographic vision in several stages. Table 12-1 traces the expansion of European regionalism from the original six nations that signed the Treaty of Rome to the current twenty-seven members of the European Union. Great Britain finally entered the EC on January 1, 1973, along with Ireland and fellow EFTA member Denmark. Britain took the leap only after two controversial referenda and a series of painful negotiations. By all accounts, it entered in 1973 on terms that were distinctly inferior to those offered in 1957. Britain's status as a European nation was determined, but its ambivalence about its relationship to Europe remained. Greece entered the EC in 1981, followed by Spain and Portugal in 1986. In all three cases, EC membership was in part a reward for the triumph of democratic institutions over authoritarian governments. Free trade and closer economic ties were intended to solidify democracy and protect it from potential communist influences.

TABLE 12-1

Chronology of the European Communities/European Union

Year	Month	Event
1951	April	The treaty establishing the European Coal and Steel Community (ECSC) is signed by the Benelux states (Belgium, the Netherlands, and Luxembourg), France, Germany, and Italy, and goes into effect in July 1952.
1952	May	The European Defence Community (EDC) treaty is signed in Paris by the six member states of the ECSC; the treaty is rejected in August 1954 by the French National Assembly.
1957	March	The Treaty of Rome, establishing the European Economic Community (EEC) and the European Atomic Energy Community (EURATOM), is signed by the six member states of the ECSC and goes into effect in January 1958.
1960	May	European Free Trade Association (EFTA) goes into effect.
1963	January	French President Charles de Gaulle announces his veto against membership of the United Kingdom in the EEC.
1965	July	Until January 1966, France (led by President de Gaulle) boycotts the European institutions to protest proposed supranational developments.
1968	July	Customs Union completed: All internal customs duties and quotas are removed, and a common external tariff is established.
1973	January	Denmark, Ireland, and the United Kingdom join the EC.
1981	January	Greece joins the EC.
1985	December	The European Council agrees on the Single European Act, which goes into effect in July 1987.
1986	January	Spain and Portugal join the EC.

(continued)

TABLE 12-1 (continued)

Chronology of the European Communities/European Union

Year	Month	Event
1989	September–December	Communist regimes collapse in Central and Eastern Europe.
1990	October	The reunification of Germany: East Germany becomes part of Germany and the EC.
1992	March	The European Council signs the Treaty on European Union in Maastricht, establishing the EU and (as a part of it) the European Monetary Union.
1995	January	Austria, Finland, and Sweden join the EU.
	March	The Schengen Agreement (which abolishes all border controls) is implemented by seven EU member states: Germany, France, the Benelux states, Spain, and Portugal.
1997	June	The European Council agrees on the Treaty of Amsterdam, which strengthens the institutions of the EU.
2000	December	The European Council agrees on the Treaty of Nice, which prepares the EU for further enlargement.
2002	January	Euro coins and banknotes enter circulation and replace national currencies.
2004	May	Accession of ten new members to the EU: Cyprus, the Czech Republic, Estonia, Hungary, Latvia, Lithuania, Malta, Poland, Slovakia, and Slovenia.
	October	The European Council signs the treaty establishing a Constitution for Europe.
2005	May	The treaty establishing a Constitution for Europe is rejected in referenda in France and the Netherlands.
2007	January	Bulgaria and Romania join the EU.
	Summer	The financial crisis begins in Europe. Iceland and Hungary first hit hard.
2009	December	The Treaty of Lisbon, ratified by the parliaments or people of the twenty-seven member states, goes into effect.
2010		The EC, ECB, and IMF (troika) make austerity their primary objective to deal with the growing debt of Ireland, Greece, Italy, Spain, and Portugal. Greece threatens to default on its debt and gets a $110 billion euro rescue package from the EU and the IMF.
2011		Germany and others suggest that Greece take an "orderly exit from the EMU."
2012		Greece and the troika agree to a second bailout in February, but Greece does not receive the last installment of its bailout until late November.

Sources: Neill Nugent, *The Government and Politics of the European Union* (Durham, NC: Duke University Press, 2006); website of the European Union, at http://europa.eu.

However, the broader market was not in all respects a better market. The entry of Ireland, Greece, Spain, and Portugal (at the time called "the poor four") magnified a variety of tensions within the EC. These less developed nations were less clearly a part of the pan-European market. Lower living standards limited the extent of their trade with richer member states. Finally, the entry of four largely agricultural nations into EC institutions, including the CAP, put severe fiscal strains on the other nations. The broader market was surely in the long-run interest of the EC, but it created stresses in the short run.

The SEA and Economic Union

These economic and political problems reached a peak in the mid-1980s. Higher EC program costs like those in agriculture imposed a disproportionate burden on Great Britain in particular, precipitating a split in the EC. Jacques Delors, the newly appointed president of the European Commission, traveled from capital to capital seeking ways to reunite the governments and peoples of the EC and keep integration moving forward. In the end, Delors concluded that international trade, which Monnet had used to bring the EC together in the first place, was the force most likely to reenergize Europe. In 1985 Delors issued a "white paper" proposing to create a single integrated market by 1992. Under his leadership, the EC identified 200 general areas where agreement on "directives" was needed to achieve the goal of a true common market. The European Council agreed to the **Single European Act (SEA)**, which went into effect in July 1987.

In an economic union, tariff and nontariff barriers are completely eliminated, creating a more fully integrated market. Moreover, members of an economic union agree to four "freedoms" of movement—for goods, services, people, and capital—that significantly limit national sovereignty. It should be noted that the EU is *not* yet an economic union. Plenty of restrictions on trade and services still exist in a variety of sectors. For example, free movement of goods requires much more than the absence of tariffs and quotas; there are hundreds of nontariff barriers that must be addressed. Health, safety, and technical standards can all discourage imports from other countries while encouraging the purchase of domestically produced goods. For economic liberals, these standards must be leveled (or *harmonized*) to allow—to the maximum possible extent—that a good sold somewhere in the group be allowed to be sold everywhere in the Union. The EU applies what it calls the "principle of mutual recognition" when there is no common (European) standard: the standard for a good of one country has to be accepted in any other country—without objections!

Free movement of services, which represents an increasing proportion of world trade, is also more complex than it may seem. Services such as banking, finance, and insurance are traditionally subject to heavy regulation that varies considerably among nations. Free movement of people requires a unified immigration policy, because a person who is free to enter and work in one member of the economic union can, in theory, live and work anywhere in the union. Finally, the free movement of capital requires the dismantling of capital controls and investment regulations, which affect flows of money into and out of a nation. Many nations have traditionally imposed capital controls to encourage domestic investment, promote financial stability, or reduce foreign exchange variations. Although an economic union does not eliminate all of these controls, they must be "harmonized" (or mutually recognized) so that they do not become a barrier to economic activity. Thus, a common administrative organization such as the European Commission is inevitable if one wants to realize an economic union.

Economic integration necessitates some level of political integration. The SEA went beyond improvement of economic freedom in the EC to prepare the big political step forward that was made in the early 1990s with the Treaty of Maastricht. It changed the requirement of a unanimous vote to approve most legislative decisions concerning the single market. The "unanimity vote" had made decisions on European legislation very difficult to make, because it essentially gave a veto to every single member of the Council of the European Community (the meeting of the national ministers of the member states). The SEA introduced a **qualified voting majority (QVM)** rule, meaning that a decision was taken if at least sixty-two of eighty-seven votes (=71.26%) of the Council of the EU were in favor of a proposal. Votes were allotted to the twelve member states on the basis of their size. In addition to its practical advantages, the QVM had great symbolic value. It meant that, at least with respect to single-market legislation, European institutions were gaining in importance because it would be possible to take decisions against the will of some opposing members. The SEA also gave more power to the pan-European institutions (discussed later in the chapter): the European Commission, the European Parliament (EP), and the European Court of Justice.

Delors's single-market initiative posed a real challenge to EC member states. It required each nation to sacrifice its interests on hundreds of small issues—many of which had important domestic political effects—in order to achieve the four freedoms. National sovereignty and economic growth were often in conflict. For example, environmentalism is an important social value in Germany, and the Green Party is a potent political force on some issues. Germany wanted to have its own high environmental standards applied to all EC vehicles, but poorer countries such as Greece and Portugal opposed these environmental regulations as too costly.

The Treaties of Maastricht and Lisbon

Unexpected turns in European politics occurred in 1989 and 1990.[4] With the fall of the Berlin Wall and the collapse of socialist regimes in Central and Eastern Europe, the Western European countries faced a double challenge: reunification of the formerly socialist German Democratic Republic with the Federal Republic of Germany on October 3, 1990; and applications for membership from most of the Central and Eastern European countries. The **Treaty of Maastricht**, which established the EU in 1992, was mainly a result of negotiations during the process of German reunification. Great Britain's prime minister Margaret Thatcher and France's president François Mitterrand were reluctant to accept a unified Germany, which brought back memories of German domination in Europe. France proposed a monetary union that would solve the German problem by chaining Germany to the rest of the EU through a strong link—a common currency—that would force Germany to give up the most powerful symbol of its economic strength, the Deutsche Mark. A second plan, proposed by Germany and France together, was to promote European political integration. France was willing to give up some of its sovereignty in exchange for a European Union that had more control over Germany. Likewise, Germany was ready to give up national sovereignty in exchange for trust in its reunification.

The conference of Maastricht in December 1991 realized both plans. The leaders of the twelve member states decided to establish a monetary union by 1999 and replace their national currencies with one common currency (named the euro in December 1995). They agreed to establish a **European Central Bank (ECB)** that would be independent in its monetary policies from other European institutions and from national governments and would be committed to the objective of price stability. They also agreed that only those countries that fulfilled the so-called convergence criteria—a low inflation rate, low interest rates, and low government debt—would join the Euro zone. In 1997, the European Council made another decision to strengthen the euro by agreeing on a "Stability and Growth Pact" that forces countries to respect a certain discipline in government spending after they join the Euro zone. At that time, the European Council was given the authority to penalize countries running high government debt that risked causing *inflation* in the whole Euro zone. (In the current crisis, inflation has *not* been a product of high levels of debt.)

Although the criteria for joining the single currency were thought to be very strict, in fact twelve of the fifteen countries in the EU in 1998 were set to enter into monetary union. Denmark, Great Britain, and Sweden elected to remain outside the Euro zone. The ECB took control of the Euro zone's monetary policy on January 1, 1999, and three years later, new banknotes and coins were introduced.

The second plan that was realized in Maastricht was to finally move from an economic community to a political union—a step that had already been prepared by the SEA in 1986. The union created one legal and institutional structure for three areas of cooperation:

- A "Single Market" that was started with the EEC treaty in 1957 and formally adopted by the SEA in 1986.
- Cooperation in "Foreign and Security Policy," which began in 1970 but remains difficult even today. Although the EU would have more weight in world politics if it spoke with one voice, the national interests of the bigger members often diverge. This can be seen quite well in the differences among the European states regarding the war in Iraq: whereas France and Germany opposed the U.S. invasion, Great Britain, Italy, and Poland contributed troops to the U.S. occupation.
- Cooperation in "Justice and Home Affairs," which had expanded under the Schengen Agreement that opened the borders between most of the European countries and defined new forms of police cooperation beginning in 1995. By 2006, this agreement had been signed by Germany, France, Belgium, the Netherlands, Luxembourg, Austria, Italy, Spain, Portugal, Greece, Denmark, Finland, and Sweden. Great Britain and Ireland have not joined the agreement; Iceland and Norway joined it without being members of the EU.

Political decision making differed considerably in these three areas, which were called the "three pillars" of the EU. In the Single Market (Pillar 1), EU institutions worked like a national political system with the European Commission as a government and both the Council of the European Union and the European Parliament as legislative bodies that cooperated in the legislative process like the two chambers of a parliament. In Foreign Policy (Pillar 2) and Justice and Home Affairs (Pillar 3), the Council of the EU was the main political institution, and decisions had to be unanimous (not taken with QVM), so that each national government had a veto position. This is why Pillar 1 was called "supranational" and Pillars 2 and 3 were labeled "intergovernmental." Pillar 1 worked like a government beyond the nation-state, whereas Pillars 2 and 3 performed like an international organization in which national governments coordinated their policies.

The process of "deepening" European integration was followed by "broadening": There were big enlargements in 2004 (from fifteen to twenty-five members) and 2007 (with the entry of Bulgaria and Romania, to twenty-seven members). It became clear that the institutional design of 1957 based on six members would hardly work for twenty-seven. In 2002, the EU tasked a European Convention with drafting a constitution for Europe. For eighteen months, 105 deputies of the EU member states (including the states that would join in 2004 and 2007) discussed the EU's institutional future. In 2004, the president of the convention, former French President Valéry Giscard d'Estaing, presented the result: a draft constitution that reflected a compromise between the need to streamline the decision-making processes, the desire for more political integration, and the fear of giving up too much sovereignty to the EU. In referenda in the summer of 2005, 54.5 percent of French voters and 61.6 percent of Dutch voters rejected the draft constitution.

After a period of "reflection" to search for new ways of achieving the necessary reforms, officials in June 2007 decided to draft a new Treaty that would realize large parts of the draft constitution without using the symbolism of a constitution. The **Treaty of Lisbon** (signed in Lisbon in December 2007 and ratified in November 2009) came into effect in December 2009. The treaty also abandoned the 3 Pillars and made the EU a legal instrument of its own. Other important changes stipulated in the treaty were as follows:

- Instead of rotating the presidency every six months, the EU has a President elected for two-and-a-half years (with the possibility of reelection for one term). This change is meant to bring more continuity and efficiency to EU politics.
- A new position called the High Representative of the Union for Foreign Affairs and Security Policy is designed to resolve frequent disagreements among Europeans on foreign policy. The High Representative—together with the new President of the European Council—is supposed to improve the coordination of the EU members in foreign policy and give a face to the EU in the world. Both these two offices are meant to answer Henry Kissinger's famous question in the 1970s: "Who do I call when I want to call Europe?"
- The **European Parliament** is to have equal standing with the Council of the EU in most social, economic, and environmental policies (formerly Pillar 1).

The purpose is to establish in these policy areas a bicameral system, with the EP and the Council acting as two legislative chambers and the Commission working like an executive branch of government. This strengthening of the EP is meant to respond to the democratic deficit.

- After November 2014, qualified majority voting will apply a double majority rule: Decisions will need to be approved by 55 percent of the member states representing at least 65 percent of the EU's population. Most economic and social decisions will be made by qualified majority voting.

EU POLITICAL INSTITUTIONS

European integration has always been as much a political process as an economic one. Since the 1950s, European elites have designed an impressive set of political institutions to make policies, settle disputes, and define their community's values and goals. These institutions have delicately balanced national interests against European-wide interests. With intergovernmental and supranational qualities, they are designed so as not to be dominated by any one power or small group of member states.

- The **European Council**, comprising the heads of state and government of all member states, meets at least twice every six months. It engages in strategic decision making such as setting EU priorities, negotiating EU treaties, and agreeing on the EU's budget.
- The President of the European Council, who is elected for two-and-a-half years, chairs European Council meetings, tries to build EU consensus, and represents the EU in foreign relations (along with the European "foreign minister" who is called the High Representative of the Union for Foreign Affairs and Security Policy).
- The **Council of the European Union** (or Council of Ministers), composed of a single representative from each member nation, is the main lawmaking body of the EU. It makes key legislative decisions—often in cooperation with the Commission and the Parliament. It plays an important role in deciding foreign, fiscal, and economic policies. Each EU member country has Permanent Representatives in Brussels (the EU "capital") who do the day-to-day political and technical work of preparing decisions to submit to the Council of Ministers.
- The **European Commission**, composed of a president and twenty-seven commissioners (one for every member state), acts as the EU's executive cabinet. Like a cabinet minister or department secretary in a nation-state, each commissioner—who is appointed for a five-year term—has a specific "portfolio" of responsibilities such as competition policy, trade, or agriculture. Decisions are taken by absolute majority (with a strong tendency to achieve a *de facto* consensus). The Commission designs policy programs and budgetary proposals, monitors implementation of EU laws, and represents Europe in international organizations.
- The European Parliament, whose members are directly elected by European citizens for five-year terms, has become like a traditional parliament. It has 754 deputies who are organized along political party lines and not according

to national citizenship. It participates in drafting policy programs and European legislation, votes on the EU budget, and approves and controls the European Commission.

- The **European Court of Justice (ECJ)** is composed of twenty-seven judges and eight advocates-general who are appointed to six-year terms. It adjudicates legal conflicts between EU institutions and between the EU and member states. Because its decisions usually emphasize the priority of European law over national legislation, it is an important promoter of European integration.
- The ECB is responsible for monetary policy and price stability in the Euro zone. It manages the foreign reserves of the member states and promotes the smooth operation of payment systems in the Euro zone.

The broadening and deepening of the EU over the past twenty-five years has created real political problems that daily test the strength of its somewhat unwieldy institutions. Deepening forced each member state to cede many economic and political powers to these institutions, resulting in a complex and confusing relationship between European and national legislation. Broadening the size of the Union has tended to reduce the clout of existing members, some of whom complain that they pay more into EU programs than they get back in benefits. Likewise, some complain that increased membership reduces the relative importance of their vote and political influence. Nevertheless, as discussed earlier, individual nation-states who give up some sovereignty—while still retaining distinct political and economic interests—gain benefits associated with economic efficiencies and payoffs stemming from enhanced political and social cooperation.

While these trade-offs sound good in theory, they still cause problems—none greater today than a financial crisis that threatens to break up the EMU, if not the EU itself.

THE FINANCIAL DEBT CRISIS IN THE EURO ZONE

For the past several years, the financial debt crisis in the Euro zone has tested the ability of the European community to coordinate an overall response to one of the darkest times in EU history. Because of the interconnectedness of major banks and economies in the world, the financial crisis that started in the United States in 2007 quickly spread to Europe. The bankruptcy of Lehman Brothers in the United States in September 2008 triggered severe financial turmoil throughout much of the European banking system. Iceland's banking system collapsed almost overnight, angering continental depositors who had thought that Iceland's high-interest-paying banks were safe places to invest. Some British banks collapsed as well, threatening the British economy.[5]

Initially, many states in Europe felt insulated from the crisis. As late as 2008, a number of experts and commentators were still praising the euro as an "astounding success."[6] Yet, the wakeup call for Europe occurred when credit was frozen because many European banks and financial institutions would not lend to one another. It was clear to many officials that the EU lacked the tools to insulate member states or to deal with the shocks the financial crisis had on their economies. The 1992 Maastricht Treaty provided little guidance; in fact, it prohibited the bailout of any member. Although it had limited the amount of debt a state could have in relation to GDP, this rule was waived temporarily to get the EMU launched in 1999. Italy, Germany, and France, among other states, regularly went over the allowed debt-to-GDP ratio. Early on, few people cared little when banks eagerly loaned to businesses and poorer states created sovereign bonds to attract investors.

As the crisis worsened in 2008, European governments hurriedly drafted their own emergency legislation to support their banks as the impact of the crisis spread throughout the community. For instance, in late 2008 Germany, Great Britain, and France decided to grant more than €1 trillion (about $1.4 trillion) as guarantees for bank transactions and €185 billion ($237 billion) as state aid to failing financial institutions such as France's Société Générale and Germany's Commerzbank and Hypo Real Estate. France and Great Britain also responded with large economic stimulus packages in an effort to prevent GDP from falling more than a projected 5 percent in 2009. After their real estate bubbles burst, Ireland and Spain nationalized the debt of their big banks in order to calm investment markets in their countries.

In December 2008, the EU decided on a €200 billion stimulus package (about 1.5% of EU GDP)—which turned out to be mostly the sum of national packages plus some funds that had been reallocated by the European Commission. In addition, the EU participated with Germany, Great Britain, France, and Italy in the meetings of the "Group of 20" to revise regulations on global financial markets. However, national differences about how to handle the crisis became more visible. Many began to doubt whether EU members and institutions could effectively deal with the crisis. Whereas Germany and France promoted stringent new safeguards on financial markets, Great Britain wanted to avoid strong foreign control of the "City"—London's powerful financial marketplace. Germany favored moderate action in order to avoid an excessive increase in state debt (which it argued could generate the next bubble crisis).

By late 2009, Greece began to fall into a severe crisis as investors feared that the country might default on its huge public debt. At first, Germany, the Netherlands, Finland, and Austria refused to bail out the Greeks. Instead, authorities put together a €110 billion bailout package that required Greece to adopt austerity policies that cut government spending on social programs and increase taxes in order to reduce the level of its government debt (see Chapter 8 for more details). For the next three years, Greece and four other indebted states (Italy, Spain, Portugal, and Ireland) were accused of being profligate—spending beyond their means. Some referred to them as the "Club Med group" because, with the exception of Ireland, they all border the Mediterranean. Detractors took to also labeling them the "PIIGS."

Institutional Weaknesses: The Unfinished Union

As far as the market was concerned, the rescue package for Greece was not a comprehensive (EU) solution. Other EMU countries also had sovereign debt problems of potentially crisis proportions. It was clear that the EMU had no real process for dealing with a financial crisis of this magnitude. Because the EMU had a common currency and ECB policy was dominated by Germany—the strongest economy in the region—each country had only a limited number of tools it could use to prevent bankruptcy or help its own economy recovery. None of the seventeen members of the Euro zone could devalue its own currency to increase its own exports. Under these conditions, Euro zone countries became dependent on the EU-ECB-IMF **troika** for financial assistance, making this loose coalition of finance agencies a central player in the EMU financial crisis. As we discuss below, each leg of this financial triumvirate has its own mandate, constituency, and outlook on debt issues, which makes it difficult for them to agree on common solutions to the debt crisis as a whole. The fact that national and troika leaders scrambled to create a firewall between EMU and global markets and new institutions suggests that the Euro zone experiment was flawed at birth: It did not envision the possibility of a systemic crisis or withdrawal of one or more of its members.

In May of 2010, seventeen Euro zone members and representatives of the troika passed another measure creating a three-tiered scheme to deal more directly with the emerging sovereign debt crisis.[7] The top tier of the scheme was a European Financial Stability Facility (EFSF) that could lend up to €440 billion and a €60 billion European Financial Stability Mechanism (EFSM) administered by the European Commission. In September 2012, the EFSF and EFSM were replaced by a European Stability Mechanism (ESM) that could lend up to €500 billion in new funds—called the "bazooka"—to help bailout struggling countries. The second tier of the scheme was an IMF supplement to the ESM of €250 billion.

The third tier was an ECB commitment to intervene in cases where defaults were imminent. Influenced strongly by Germany, the ECB has been responsible for monetary and price stability in the Euro zone. However, under terms of the EMU treaty, it was limited in what it could do, and it had always been concerned primarily with inflation and interest rate adjustments. Its former president Jean-Claude Trichet—a deficit hawk—did not want the ECB to be the EU's "lender of last resort." Trichet argued that financial discipline and austerity would inspire confidence and lead to growth (via investment). For him, Germany was the model country to emulate because in the first half of the 2000s it had successfully reduced its debt and reformed its economy.

Other indirect measures to deal with the crisis included European Commission draft legislation—adopted in January 2011—to create a European System of Financial Supervision (ESFS) that included a European Systemic Risk Board (ESRB) in charge of monitoring the stability of the entire EU financial system. The ESFS legislation also transformed three already existing EC committees into three European Supervisory Authorities (ESAs) with advisory powers over banking, insurance, and securities. Germany has been one of the major keys to solving the crisis because of its ability to provide financial support for the ECB and EC. The troika has negotiated bailouts for Ireland, Greece, Portugal, and Spain (see Table 12-2). Interestingly, Ireland and Portugal were once held up as models of how well austerity measures were working. Greece is another matter though. After it agreed to the terms of a second bailout package from the European Commission, the ECB, and the IMF in February 2012, protestors set fire to 110 buildings in Athens. Since then, there has been a fierce debate amongst debtor countries, the troika, and private investors about conditions attached to borrowing by the heavily indebted states.[8] Led by Germany, supporters of austerity have dug in on their demand

TABLE 12-2

Debt and Economic Indicators of Selected European Countries

Country	GDP, Billions of U.S. Dollars, 2011	Government Debt-to-GDP Ratio, in Percentage, 2009	Government Debt-to-GDP Ratio, in Percentage, Q2 2012	Total External Debt, Billions of U.S. Dollars, Q1 2012	EU-IMF Bailout Loans, Billions of U.S. Dollars, 2010–2012	Unemployment Rate, in Percentage, Q3 2012	Projected GDP Growth Rate, in Percentage, 2013
Euro zone							
Greece	299	130	150	521	317	25.1	−4.8
Portugal	238	83	118	508	78	15.7	−2.7
Italy	2,195	116	126	2,514		10.7	−1.8
Spain	1,491	54	76	2,383	130	25.5	1.7
France	2,773	79	91	5,130		10.7	−0.3
Ireland	217	65	112	2,214	67.5	14.8	1.0
Germany	3,571	75	83	5,798		5.4	1.4
Comparison Countries							
United States	15,094	90	107	15,481		8.1	1.9
Mexico	1,155	45	42	309		4.8	3.4

Sources: World Bank Indicators; Eurostat News Release 150/2012 (October 24, 2012); World Bank Quarterly External Debt Statistics; OECD Harmonised Unemployment Rates, Updated: November 2012; OECD *Economic Outlook No. 93* (May 29, 2013; Eurostat, "Government Finance Statistics: Summary Tables—2/2012 (2012).

that states like Greece must decrease their debt by reducing pensions, health care, and other public welfare programs. Like Germany, other northern European states such as the Netherlands, Finland, and Austria have also been unenthusiastic about rescuing weaker member states for fear that it could perpetuate moral hazard and encourage debtor states to let up on implementing austerity policies.

In 2011 and 2012, there was extensive press coverage of the disagreements and conflicts between German Chancellor Angela Merkel and Greek Prime Minister George Papandreou, Italian Prime Minister Silvio Berlusconi, and French President Nicolas Sarkozy (the latter three of whom were turned out of office). Debt negotiations were often a contest between Northern countries—that disliked bailouts and favored austerity—and the Club Med group—that favored a Keynesian approach of more assistance to deal with their debt and help their economies grow. Some experts argued that Germany could also help debtor countries by increasing its imports of EU goods and spending more on public programs, even if it meant a higher level of inflation,[9] which has yet to appear.

By 2011, some officials and experts—including some Germans—were suggesting that Greece and other countries such as Spain, Portugal, and Italy should drop out of the Euro zone. In turn, many officials in high-debt countries contemplated doing just that—so as to be in a better position to help their countries recover from the crisis. A return to the drachma, for instance, would allow Greece to devalue its own currency, which could increase exports, increase unemployment, and generate economic growth.

Many critics agreed that austerity was proving to be nothing more than a socio-political disaster and a debt trap.[10] Table 12-2 also compares the debt-to-GDP ratios for Euro zone countries in 2009 and mid-2012. It is clear that the ratios have gone up significantly for most countries *since* they adopted austerity measures. An increasing number of economists and national officials argue that deep cuts in state spending have only undermined growth and raised unemployment rates in most EMU countries, making it harder for them to shrink their debt. Many countries increase their debt by borrowing while at the same time their economies are shrinking, worsening their debt-to-GDP ratios, which causes investors to lose even more confidence in them. This drives up the cost of borrowing, which generates the need for more bailout funds from the troika! It seems to be a vicious cycle.

During negotiations over extending more credit to Club Med countries, troika members have had to account for the demands of the German people for more austerity. Chancellor Merkel has pandered to voters who prefer suffering as way to purge Greece and others of their profligate ways. These Germans argue that Greece spends too much, can't collect taxes from the rich, and drags its feet on privatization. It has been helped only on condition that its politicians commit to pro-growth market reforms. Interestingly, many critics have countered that Germany seems too willing to damage Greece, Portugal, and Spain in order to get their attention! Within the troika, Chancellor Merkel has been playing chicken until the last moment. She has let up on austerity only when faced with the possibility that lack of agreement would weaken the EMU as a whole that would have many negative economic consequences for Germany, especially if the EU slides deeper into another recession.

What Can the Troika Do?

It is clear that even if the troika agrees more closely with the Germans, its members also have an incentive to contain the crisis contagion and save their indebted client states; their histories are all bound up together in the history of the EMU and the EU. Recall that the troika is made up of the European Commission, the ECB, and the IMF. Former Portuguese Prime Minister Jose Manuel Barroso heads the European Commission, which implements EU policies and spends EU funds. The EU has a limited capacity to lend to indebted states. It helps national officials establish the terms of loans to countries seeking to borrow from the EU. It has contributed to the European Stability Mechanism fund. Even though the EU has resisted helping Greece and others, it has backed the idea of issuing Eurobonds as a way to deal with the debt of EMU nations.

Mario Draghi of Italy became president of the ECB in November 2011. During interviews, he looked to be a hardliner on inflation. Even if he preferred austerity, he stated categorically that without the ECB's help, the EMU, and quite possibly the EU, could go down in flames. Draghi put the ECB on a very different path, pledging to do "whatever it takes" to save the EMU, while still maintaining the support of political leaders and central bankers. He cut the ECB's main interest rate at least twice and then quietly began providing emergency loans to European banks. The effect was to "flood the financial markets with euros in a Hail Mary attempt to make sure that the region's sovereign debt crisis did not lead to a major financial shock."[11]Draghi argued that the ECB could help banks acquire money cheaply and get loans out, lest they become like the "zombie banks" of Japan in the 1990s—with too many nonperforming loans on their books. But some economists worried that the ECB was gambling too much and merely creating the conditions for another banking crisis in a few years.

Today, Draghi supports regulation of big banks at the European level rather than only at the national level. He has also tried to increase the authority of the bank's president and make the ECB more like the U.S. Federal Reserve.[12] He favors letting the ECB use its funds to help Greece, Spain, and others by purchasing their sovereign debt, as long as they adhere to their commitments to restructure their budgets and economies. Finally, "Super Mario" has also become one of the most influential and charismatic executives in Europe. Many praise his pragmatic outlook and ability to resist political pressure. Still, he lacks the authority necessary to reduce significantly the debt of Euro zone states.

Christine Lagarde became managing director of the IMF in 2011 when Dominique Strauss Kahn was driven from office after accusations of sexual assault. Generally, Lagarde wants to provide some outside financial assistance to the EMU, provided its members can meet the IMF's conditions. At first, she asked G8 nations to build up their IMF reserves for the purpose of helping bail out some EMU states.

Like the IMF as a whole and her personal friend Angela Merkel, Lagarde tends to shuffle back and forth between supporting austerity policies and recommending that their impact be softened to improve the EMU's chances of survival. She warned that governments around the world had systematically underestimated the damage done to growth by severe austerity policies.[13] She has also supported regulations and reforms that promote economic growth and create jobs. However, in an hour-long interview with *The Guardian* newspaper in May 2012, Lagarde was asked her thoughts about Greeks suffering from the effects of austerity. She opined that Greek should "help themselves collectively by all paying their tax." She rather callously said that little kids in Niger "need even more help than the people in Athens."[14]

On the whole, the IMF does not want to get too involved in the debt crisis and does not have much to contribute by way of funds. However, Lagarde does want the agency to play an active role in determining the outcome, especially given the criticism of the IMF's role in past crises (see Chapter 8). The IMF continues to slowly change its role from mainly assisting developing countries to also helping industrialized countries—as if it were the global "lender of last resort."

Mapping the Minefield

As we write in late 2012, the Greeks are finally getting the last installment of a loan negotiated early in the year. Spanish banks have been in big trouble for most of the year. Some officials want to use the ESM's €500 billion bazooka to help their banks survive. However, there is yet to be an agreement on how much and in what ways countries will contribute to raise that amount.[15]

A number of economists suggest that there are still many practical things that can be done to save the EMU.[16] Even if the ECB cannot alone contain the contagious effects of the financial crisis, it could buy the bonds of Italy, Spain, and the other heavily indebted countries.[17] But Germany, the Netherlands, and Finland do not support the move; to them, the ECB has gone rogue if it buys bonds from the Club Med states. The Bank could purchase low-risk covered loans, backed by packages of loans. It could encourage emergency lending, which it did for Greece and Ireland. It could lengthen loan repayment periods. It could also expand the range of securities it accepts as collateral. A different kind of solution to the debt crisis is promoted by the IMF. When Greece accepted terms demanded by the troika and private investors to receive another dose of financial assistance in February 2012, private investors had to agree to take a 75 percent "haircut" (loss on their investments). Indeed, more haircuts may be the only realistic way to actually lower debt in the short run in most countries.

Some believe that solutions like these have not been tried because politicians cater to the Germans who worry a great deal about inflation and bailing out irresponsible southern countries. And yet the stakes seem so high and the choices more limited than ever. Instead of actively promoting more cooperation, Euro zone states seem only to be buying time as the EMU muddles along looking for band aid solutions for what are really structural and political problems.

Three observations can be made about the troika: First, while institutions matter a great deal, so do the people who manage them. Some officials are more constrained by a bureaucracy's rules; others such as the ECB's president Draghi are willing to think outside the box during times of crisis. Second, these three institutions will play a major role in determining if the EMU survives, and yet the troika is only an informal committee that lacks the authority to solve the EMU's underlying structural problems. Third, all parties must also deal with German resistance to any deals that let debtors off the hook. However, if the EMU should fall apart, the troika and Germany are sure to bear a good deal of the responsibility for its failure.

CHALLENGES IN WORLD POLITICS

The EU is often criticized for being too slow or too weak in its reactions to new economic or security challenges it faces in the global political economy. What are the main foreign policy challenges of the EU today? As we discussed earlier, the dominant economic challenge to the EU is the financial crisis that threatens to bankrupt a number of heavily indebted states. In addition to responding on the domestic level to this crisis, the EU is involved in a global response to this and similar issues elsewhere, especially through its involvement in the G20. Among the objectives of the EU in G20 negotiations are the strengthening of the role of the IMF and the tightening of global financial markets regulations. For instance, the EU has pushed for strict regulation of hedge funds and control of offshore banking.

Growing economic competition from countries like India and China is yet another challenge. To keep its technological lead in sectors like machinery and equipment, fabricated metal products, and chemicals, the EU will need to reinforce its research and development efforts with a special emphasis on cross-border R&D cooperation.

A third economic challenge with an important political impact is energy policy. Like the United States, the EU is mainly dependent on fossil fuels. Approximately

37 percent of its energy needs are met by oil, 24 percent by gas, 18 percent by coal, 14 percent by nuclear power, and 7 percent by renewables. Most of the gas used in the EU comes from Russia (about 42 percent), and Russia has shown in recent years that it will not hesitate to use its gas exports for political pressure. Most Russian gas is transported to Europe through pipelines that pass through the Ukraine. In recent winters, Russia has repeatedly accused Ukraine of stealing gas or not paying its debts from gas imports. To pressure Ukraine, Russia stopped its gas exports several times—causing fallout not only in Ukraine but also in other European countries, notably Bulgaria and Romania, where thousands of households were without heat for part of a winter. The EU has tried to diversify its gas imports by building a new gas pipeline called Nabucco, which will transport Central Asian gas through Georgia and Turkey without touching Russian soil. It has also pushed member states to reduce energy consumption by using new technologies and shifting to renewable energies.[18]

The EU is also worried about political developments in Russia. After a period of democratization in the 1990s, for many officials, Russia under President Putin has turned into an authoritarian regime. In a war with Georgia in August 2008, it ruthlessly defended its interests, considering its neighboring states as exclusive zones of interest and openly questioning their sovereignty. EU members Poland and the Baltic states, who suffered for decades under the tutelage of the Soviet Union, are eager to defend their independence from Russia in questions like the deployment of antimissile systems, which Russia considers as a potential security threat.

Another major issue in security policy is the war against international terrorism. Many European member states are involved in NATO activities against terrorism in Afghanistan, the Horn of Africa, and most recently in Libya. However, as in the United States, public support for troop deployment has waned as the situation in Afghanistan has deteriorated. A general question is how independent the EU will be from the United States in its security policy.

Another major challenge for the EU is to define its relations with Islamic countries and with its own Muslim population. This is not just an issue of foreign policy: Between 5 and 10 percent of the population of countries like Germany, the Netherlands, France, and Great Britain is Muslim. Germany has many immigrants from Turkey; France has many North African immigrants; and Great Britain has large Indian and Pakistani immigrant communities. Many EU countries have had fierce debates over issues of freedom of religion and freedom of speech that involve immigrant communities, including a row in 2006 over cartoons about the Prophet Muhammad in a Danish newspaper.

Finally, the relationship between the EU and Islam has been at the core of the debate over Turkey's potential membership in the EU. Turkey has been officially recognized as a candidate for membership in the EU since 1999. In 2005, accession negotiations between Turkey and the EU started. Proponents of an accession of Turkey argue that its membership would help to build a bridge between European and Islamic countries. Critics warn that Turkey's population will surpass Germany's population in the next ten years, so that by the time of an accession, Turkey would be the largest member state. They also stress that, despite a number of political reforms in Turkey, its political and judicial system is still far from meeting European standards for rule of law and religious freedom, particularly in regard to discrimination against members of Christian churches.

CONCLUSION

The EU likes to portray itself as a global peace-maker and a model of integration for other regions in the world. The achievements of European integration after World War II are certainly impressive: Never before in history have Western Europeans experienced a comparable period of peace, freedom, and wealth. In the beginning, the motives behind integration were as much political as they were economic. An assumption since then has been that free markets and the free movement of citizens would help accelerate political integration in a union—albeit not necessarily one similar to that in the United States. The EU has also provided political stability by acting as a negotiator in international conflicts, especially in the Balkans and in Africa. It has been a strong supporter of international institutions like the IMF in the current financial crisis.

On the other hand, the EU's role in international conflicts often appears as weak. Aside from developments related to the current debt crisis in the EMU, during the war between Russia and Georgia in August 2008, the EU was not able to moderate Russia. During the conflict between Russia and Ukraine over gas prices, the EU was not able to secure a continued gas supply for many of its citizens in Eastern European countries. Disagreements among the EU members and insufficient military equipment have weakened the position of the EU in many international conflicts in the Balkans and Africa especially.

Structuralism, realism, and neomercantilism all help explain European integration. This process was made possible by the global security structure provided by NATO and the United States during the Cold War. Without the threat of Soviet aggression and the spread of communism in Western Europe, there would not have been such a willingness to cooperate. Indeed, since the end of the Cold War, political negotiations in the EU have become more complicated—not only because of the rising number of member states but also because of the rise of nationalism. For example, in the elections for the European Parliament in June 2009, the Eurosceptic parties won 180 seats out of 736—close to one-quarter of the seats. With the debt crisis has come an alarming rise of extremist parties on both the left and the right in many of the troubled states. For example, in Greek parliamentary elections in June 2012, the far-left, anti-austerity Syriza party received 27 percent of the votes and the far-right ultra-nationalist Golden Dawn party won 7 percent.

EU countries are now in the middle of the once-in-seven-years process of negotiating a new budget. Many assume that in the face of the financial crisis, subsidies for agriculture and other community programs will be drastically cut. Prime Minister David Cameron is critical of the EC's recommendation of increasing the EU budget by €100 billion (for a total budget of €1 trillion between 2014 and 2020). Many of his Conservative Party supporters—and some Labour Party and Liberal Party members of Parliament—also want Great Britain out of the EU, or at least in a looser relationship with it.

The financial crisis is the EU's biggest challenge at this time, but also one of the biggest challenges to the global political economy as well. It is hard to imagine that despite all the EU's historical efforts, the motivation to integrate further seems to be waning. The EU as a whole is left with states trying to save themselves and others that resist cooperating unless the solution satisfies them completely. In other words, the cost to each state of the public goods provided by the community are too high or the benefits of what cooperation remains is not enough to keep each of them in the game. Surely Germany and the other northern nations must realize that in the bigger scheme of things they are risking a lot: another major recession, loss of trade, and loss of cooperation to tackle major issues like terrorism, immigration, energy, and the environment. In an integrated community, no state succeeds on its own.

Ironically, the neoliberals who promoted economic integration and the euro as win-win propositions in the early 1990s are not speaking up. Do they no longer support the ideas they so enthusiastically preached about the benefits of integration and globalization? While many conservatives support austerity to decrease debt, realist-mercantilists and structuralists are more likely to make the case that an even more integrated EU still serves many worthwhile political and economic goals.

We must remember that the EU is neither an international organization (in terms of its cooperation between independent states) nor a federal state. Rather, it is an entity *sui generis*—a specific mix of supranational and intergovernmental elements. It may yet emerge as something quite distinct from what so many have imagined it to be. It has integrated much further than any other region. Yet, it may not be able to integrate any further—to become what many have said was an unachievable dream. There is a possibility that it will convert itself into two groups of states, those in the north that are better off and those weaker states that are not prepared to integrate their economies any further.

That said, if EU members still want to integrate further it will require more leadership and "political will" to overcome many political-economic barriers. Angela Merkel is not the avid supporter of integration that Jacques Delors, former German Chancellor Helmut Schmidt, and former French President Valéry Giscard d'Estaing were. Politically, Merkel's intransigence signals Germany's doubt that the EMU and the EU are worth committing more German money to. Together with politically unacceptable proposals such as a common fiscal policy, the EU may have reached a dead end.

There is hardly any way for the EMU to go forward without Germany. And yet, there is no way to go backward without all EMU members paying a heavy economic price. Some hold the view that Germany will come around—not for economic reasons alone but because maintaining the stability of both the EMU and EU is still one of its primary national interests. Politics may yet win out over economics. It is hard to imagine that Merkel will want to risk breaking up the EMU under her watch and to stand accused of having sold out Europe.

KEY TERMS

European Union (EU)   292
austerity policies   293
Economic and Monetary Union
   (EMU)   293
Euro zone   293
integration   293
Common Market   297
customs union   297
Common Agricultural Policy
   (CAP)   299

bicycle theory   300
Single European Act (SEA)   303
qualified voting majority (QVM)
   rule   304
Treaty of Maastricht   304
European Central Bank
   (ECB)   305
European Parliament
   (EP)   306
Treaty of Lisbon   306

European Council   307
Council of the European
   Union   307
European Commission   307
European Court of Justice
   (ECJ)   308
troika   310

DISCUSSION QUESTIONS

1. One theme of this chapter is the tension between economic and political integration. Discuss ways in which economic and political integration conflict with one another and generate tensions.
2. Explain the difference between static efficiency and dynamic efficiency. How is each important to the integration process?
3. What is the Common Agricultural Policy (CAP)? Explain how the CAP illustrates the themes of this chapter and also how it creates tensions among EU members and between the EU and its international trading partners.
4. Discuss the impact of the financial crisis on the EMU states and on the likelihood that they will continue to use the euro. Do you agree with those

who feel that the greater the number of states who drop out of the Euro zone, the greater the chances that the EU will come apart?

5. Outline five or six reasons why so many experts and national and regional officials focus on the role of Germany in the financial crisis.

SUGGESTED READINGS

Authoritative website of the EU at http://europa.eu

John Newhouse. *Europe Adrift*. New York: Pantheon, 1997.

Andrew Staab. *The European Union Explained*, 2nd ed. Bloomington, IN: Indiana University Press, 2011.

Johan Van Overtveldt. *The End of the Euro: The Uneasy Future of the European Union*. Chicago: Agate Publishing, 2011.

Antje Wiener and Thomas Diez. *European Integration Theory*, 2nd rev. ed. Oxford: Oxford University Press, 2009.

NOTES

1. For a brief overview of the history of European integration, institutions, and a number of policy issues, see Andrew Staab, *The European Union Explained*, 2nd ed. (Bloomington, IN: Indiana University Press, 2011).

2. For a brief overview of earlier CAP history and a number of policy issues, see Wyn Grant, *The Common Agricultural Policy* (New York: St. Martin's Press, 1997).

3. See "Common Agricultural Policy" at http://www .civitas.org.uk/eufacts/FSPOL/AG3.htm.

4. For a good overview of the dilemmas facing the EC at the end of the Cold War, see John Newhouse, *Europe Adrift* (New York: Pantheon, 1997).

5. See the video *Inside Job* (2010) for an overview of the impact of the financial crisis on Iceland.

6. Cited in Johan Van Overtveldt, *The End of the Euro: The Uneasy Future of the European Union* (Chicago: Agate Publishing, 2011), p. 77.

7. Ibid, pp. 97–98.

8. There are many YouTube videos on the euro debt crisis and individual nations. For example, see: http://www .youtube.com/watch?v=Ahnyd7oZvjw; http://www .youtube.com/watch?v=HZc6oD0WfW8;http:// www.youtube.com/watch?v=yRT3HeQ-fLI; http:// www.youtube.com/watch?v=n6ImKVM_eZU; and http://www.youtube.com/watch?v=W0AaQrykoH0.

9. See Paul Krugman, "Crash of the Bumblebee," *New York Times*, July 29, 2012.

10. See Robert Reich, "The Austerity Death-Trap," October 19, 2011, at http://robertreich.org /post/11660232763.

11. See "Mario Draghi," *New York Times*, November 24, 2012.

12. See Nicholas Kulish and Jack Ewing, "Europe Increases Power of Central Bank's Chief," *New York Times*, July 7, 2012.

13. Claire Jones, "Lagarde Calls for Caution on Austerity," FT.com, October 11, 2012.

14. Decca Aitkenhead, "Christine Lagarde: Can the Head of the IMF save the Euro?" Guardian (UK), May 25, 2012.

15. See James Kanter, "Europe Still at Odds over the Workings of Its Bailout Fund," *New York Times*, October 7, 2012.

16. Jack Ewing, "Economists Warn of Long-Term Perils in Rescue of Europe's Banks," *New York Times*, February 12, 2012.

17. For a detailed discussion of these sorts of micro policy recommendations, see Landon Thomas, "Economic Thinkers Try to Solve the Euro Puzzle," *New York Times*, August 31, 2012.

18. See the website on EU energy policy at http:// europa.eu/pol/ener/index_en.htm.

Moving into Position:
The Rising Powers

The Vortex of Rapid Growth: A woman sells medicinal teas in Beijing's Zhongguancan district –also known as China's Silicon Valley.

Gideon Mendel/Corbis

During his first visit to China in November 2009, U.S. President Barack Obama acknowledged the growing importance of China to the United States and the global economy. Instead of harping on China's protectionism and human rights violations, he emphasized the need to gain its cooperation in putting pressure on Iran and North Korea over nuclear issues, reducing climate change, and letting its currency appreciate to reduce its massive trade surplus with the United States. However, two years later, Obama angered Beijing when he announced plans to station 2,500 Marines permanently in Darwin, Australia as part of a policy to bolster the U.S. military presence in Asia. In the thick of campaigning for re-election in 2012, he also repeatedly criticized China's unfair trade practices. The president's seemingly contradictory approaches to China remind us that China's rapid growth simultaneously benefits and challenges the world's remaining superpower. Now the second largest economy and the biggest producer in the world of steel, coal, textiles, PCs, TVs, and cell phones, China helps U.S. consumers while it hurts many U.S. workers. Its rising military power potentially threatens U.S. allies in the Pacific. Whether or not Beijing leans more toward cooperation or confrontation in the future, we can be confident that the post–Cold War era of U.S. unilateralism and hegemony is rapidly ending.

China, India, Brazil, and Russia are changing economic and geopolitical relationships in the world. As they transition to market-oriented economies, these rising powers are profoundly reshaping where goods are produced, what global poverty trends look like, and how capital flows around the world. Their insatiable demand for raw materials and consumer items is driving up global commodity prices and creating ever more strains on the environment. They are creating a more multipolar world, which some hope will usher in an age of peace but others fear will lead to new arms races and monumental struggles over access to energy and food. Their development will determine whether hundreds of millions of people will be able to enjoy a better future and share more of the global wealth previously denied to them.

Complex transformations in a nation's system of political economy cause stresses and strains at all levels: individual, national, regional, and global. The former states of the Soviet Union are engulfed in the problems of the dramatic transition away from communism. Brazil experienced rapid growth in the 1960s and 1970s, only to falter in the 1980s, with crushing debt. Now it is building on nearly twenty years of growth to find its place as a competitive exporter. Communist China is transitioning to a hybrid system of **market socialism** in which the state retains central control but strongly encourages private economic activities. India is in the unique position of trying to overcome grinding poverty with neoliberal reforms carried out under a long-established democratic system.

In this chapter we present a number of important theses about the rising powers. First, their paths are very different, reflecting variations in countries' history, size, political system, and policy decisions. Second, the experiences of countries in transition lead us to question many assertions in the IPE theories we discussed in the preceding chapters. For example, China shows that economic liberals' belief that capitalism and freedom go together may not always be true.

On the other hand, some countries' phenomenal growth under market-friendly policies suggests that mercantilists overestimate the positive outcomes of state guidance of the economy. Many rapid reductions in poverty belie structuralists' belief that global capitalism locks poor countries into a vicious cycle of underdevelopment.

Third, in most countries transition has been a painful and chaotic process that has, at least in the short run, destroyed valuable social institutions and undermined social stability. Globalization holds out the hope of a higher standard of living at the same time that it threatens institutions, cultural practices, and ways of living that many people value. For a substantial number of people, capitalism has brought sacrifice, crime, and despair. Finally, the rising powers are ineluctably bringing intense competition to Europe, the United States, and Japan—developed nations that are losing more of their labor-intensive manufacturing and some of their ability to dominate international institutions. Consequently, many of the "rules of the game" affecting trade, finance, and security will start reflecting the interests of emerging countries.

TRANSITIONS IN THE FORMERLY COMMUNIST COUNTRIES

Although the Soviet Union came into existence in 1917, most communist or socialist regimes emerged after the end of World War II in Eastern and Central Europe, North Korea, China, Vietnam, and Cuba. For these states, political and economic power was rooted in a single party whose membership was generally limited to about 5 to 10 percent of the population, although a much larger percentage participated in party-led programs and movements. The official ideology of the party touted its revolutionary achievements such as eliminating inequality and promoting rapid growth of heavy industries, infrastructure, and health facilities. Some states developed "personality cults" around leaders like Stalin, Mao, Castro, and Kim Il-Jung, who were venerated for liberating the nation from imperialism, performing heroic deeds, and/or paving the way for rapid economic development.

Most of the means of production—factories, land, and property—were owned by the state on behalf of the people as a whole. The party-state guaranteed employment. A large state bureaucracy determined which raw materials, goods, and services should be produced, in what amounts, at what prices, and for whose consumption. Many consumer goods were of low quality. This cumbersome system of central planning eventually resulted in a myriad of problems such as overproduction of some goods, shortages of others, and misallocation of national resources. It also suffered from what János Kornai has described as "soft-budget constraints": state enterprises had little incentive to turn real profits when they could count on cheap state loans and perpetual debt forgiveness.[1]

It is important to remember that in their heydays from the 1930s to the 1970s, many socialist/communist economies successfully generated high growth rates. The Soviets transformed their agrarian, preindustrial society into a military–industrial powerhouse in less than two generations. Many developing countries and ex-colonies found their model of self-sufficiency, industrialization, educational opportunity, and upward mobility for peasants and the urban poor compelling (see Chapter 11).

Contradictions grew worse throughout the 1970s and 1980s. Declining productivity and an inability to match the pace of technological innovation in the West led leaders such as Soviet General Secretary Mikhail Gorbachev to seek some reforms starting in the mid-1980s. Gorbachev's policies of *glasnost* (openness) and *perestroika* (restructuring) were meant to reform, not eliminate, communism. Along with some leaders in Eastern Europe, Gorbachev hoped that a limited amount of political and economic liberalization would give the populace a greater stake in the system. Instead, popular political demands and divisions among party elites—and the unwillingness of key political and military elites to violently suppress widespread demonstrations and strikes—rapidly led to the unraveling and collapse of the communist regimes beginning in 1989. By 1991, the Soviet Union had broken up into fifteen separate countries.

Two difficult economic transitions started soon thereafter: **marketization** (the re-creation of market forces of supply and demand) and **privatization** (the transfer of state-held property into private hands). In order to privatize factories, shops, land, and apartments, postcommunist governments had to figure out what the assets were actually worth and who should get them—but the results were often unfair and undemocratic. States also had to re-create a market in which competition would determine the value of property, labor, goods, and services. Some argued that changes should be gradual to minimize social disruptions. Others favored a policy called *shock therapy* which included a rapid freeing up of prices and a quick end to central planning and state subsidies. Favored by many liberal Western advisors, this therapy was pioneered in Poland and later attempted in Russia.

NEW POLITICAL AND ECONOMIC LANDSCAPES

How successful have all of these market-oriented reforms been in the past twenty-five years? Almost all postcommunist countries suffered severe economic decline and political upheaval until the late 1990s, when they entered into a phase of rapid growth that lasted until the financial crisis of 2008. Until 2005, their average real GDP had not even recovered to the 1989 level.[2] The World Bank estimates that at the start of the financial crisis in 2008 at least 40 percent of people in the postcommunist states (plus Turkey) were poor or vulnerable, that is, living on less than $5 a day (see the box Waiting for Godot in Coscalia, Moldova). A 2010 survey of 39,000 households conducted by the European Bank for Reconstruction and Development (EBRD) showed the fragility of economic gains after more than two years of global financial crisis. Unemployment in postcommunist countries rose dramatically and many people had their wages cut. As a result, 38 percent of households had to reduce food consumption and more than 60 percent had to ask relatives for loans.[3]

▶ WAITING FOR GODOT IN COSCALIA, MOLDOVA[a]

Although Moldova has been an independent nation-state since 1991, its citizens are still awaiting an external savior. Culturally, most of Moldova's 4.3 million residents identify with their neighbors, the Romanians. They speak the same language, seek blessings from the same Eastern Orthodox saints, and eat the same polenta and sausage dishes. However, Moldova's independence from the former Soviet Union got off to an inauspicious start, when in 1990 a province called Transnistria on the eastern side of the Dneister River broke away, taking with it much of Moldova's industrial base. From 2001 to 2009, a reconstituted Communist Party dominated the political system, undermining democratic institutions. In his 2008 bestseller *Geography of Bliss*, National Public Radio correspondent Eric Weiner deemed Moldova the "unhappiest place on earth."

The rural town of Coscalia is a case study of Moldova's problems and an example of the difficulties many rural villages have faced since the collapse of the Soviet Union. Located in a hilly region, an hour southeast of the capital city of Chisinau, Coscalia has 700 homes and a registered population of 2,000. Its houses have electricity and satellite TV, but not running water. Seasonal vegetables add spice to the inhabitants' otherwise relatively dull diet of corn- and wheat-based dishes, lathered with homemade sour cream and cheese. Meals are washed down with wine that families store in large oak barrels under their houses. The most valuable assets of many families are their cows, worth $1,000 each.

It does not take long in Coscalia to realize that something seems amiss. At markets the numerous elderly lean on their canes and walking sticks, haggling for bright yellow sunflower oil or other necessities with the proceeds of pension checks of $40 a month or less. There are few working-age men. The village is full of nurseries and nursing home. When local schooling ends at the age of sixteen, many young men and increasingly women emigrate to Moscow, where construction workers can earn $400 a month, or Italy, where caring for the elderly

in their homes can pay $800 a month. Less fortunate women end up like thousands of other Moldovans as prostitutes in Italy, Turkey, and Germany.

Coscalians have found it difficult to collectively improve their lot. Cows produce more milk than can be drunk, so it is processed and consumed as cheese in the summer months; the excess goes to waste. Residents recognized the problem and agreed that the solution was a milk-receiving station that could keep milk cool until it could be sent to a nearby cheese-making plant. However, lack of trust meant that there was no way to raise money for the project from local residents. Eventually they found an external donor, but in the manipulations common in Eastern Europe, the grant mostly benefited one recipient rather than the larger community.

Most residents have a let's-make-do attitude which is evident in the patched together nature of shared facilities such as wells. It has not been possible to levy a small tax on the sellers at the weekly market so that they can display their goods on tables set on concrete rather than on the ground or hanging from fences. Residents still detest cooperatives because they remember that the wealthiest today are those who manipulated communist-era co-ops. Coscalia is a sobering reminder that development is hard. Literacy, remittances, and aid have not yet made the town a beacon of hope in a troubled countryside.

Moldovans as a whole oscillate between a nostalgia for communist leaders, who dictated work and put bread on the table, and a desire to enjoy the freedom of a liberated lifestyle. Theirs is not an isolated country: Moldovans every day are confronted with the economic, political, and social successes that benefited Romanians who can travel freely to EU countries. Moldovans have access to radio, TV, and articles in German, Italian, Russian, and English. However, to ensure that dreams of a better life in Coscalia can turn into realities, Moldova still needs trust and vision.

Reference
[a]Jess Martin authored the material in this box. Our thanks to her.

To better understand the variations in postcommunist outcomes, we examine Russia and some of the former republics of the Soviet Union. The Baltic states—Estonia, Latvia, and Lithuania—joined the European Union in 2004, consolidating economic liberalism and social democracy. By the end of 2007, their average GDP was about 50 percent higher than in 1989. However, they took a hard hit from the global financial crisis. For example, Latvia's GDP fell an astonishing 18 percent in 2009, and only 15 percent of Latvians in 2010 thought that the combination of democracy and a market economy was the most preferable system for their country. Despite these setbacks, the Baltic states have generally been successful for a number of reasons: a precommunist history of statehood and significant economic development, historical ties to Western Europe, and rapid growth of civil society and prodemocratic political parties. The likelihood of joining the European Union had a very important role in accelerating reforms. By enmeshing these countries quickly in a dense set of trade, aid, political, and military relationships after 1989, the European Union helped soften the economic transition and provided a clear set of regulations and benchmarks to which reformers could aspire.[4]

The transition results are more mixed in the Commonwealth of Independent States (CIS), which includes most of the ex-republics of the former Soviet Union including Russia, Belarus, Ukraine, Armenia, Azerbaijan, Kazakhstan, Kyrgyzstan, Moldova, Tajikistan, Turkmenistan, and Uzbekistan. On average, it was not until 2007 that the GDP in real terms recovered to 1989 levels in these countries. Even worse, Ukraine's GDP in 2011 was only 60 percent of what it was in 1989, a testament to its prolonged economic decline.

In the CIS countries and the non-EU postcommunist states in Europe, unemployment fell significantly from 12.4 percent in 1999 to an estimated 8.4 percent in 2007, but it edged up to 10.2 percent in 2010 before dropping to 8.2 percent in 2012.[5] These countries have attracted large capital inflows but are poorly integrated into the world trade system. Many are still negotiating membership in the WTO; Ukraine and Russia did not join until 2008 and 2012, respectively. The CIS countries have been stunted by **crony capitalism,** in which some businesspeople have become extremely rich, often through government connections and corrupt practices, while many others have seen their standard of living decline. Democracy is weakly institutionalized or absent, partly because of the legacy of a long period of Soviet rule and the predominance of energy-intensive and heavy industries. Freedom House rates eight countries that used to be part of the Soviet Union as having "consolidated authoritarian regimes."[6]

Russia exemplifies many of the problems—and a few of the successes—in the CIS. The election of Vladimir Putin as president in 2000 brought an end to Russia's tentative experiment with democracy. According to political scientist M. Steven Fish, the failure of democracy in Russia is primarily due to incomplete economic reforms, a weakened legislature, and the curse of natural resource wealth.[7] Putin cracked down on independent media and civil society while suppressing opposition political demonstrations. Following a stint as prime minister from 2008 to 2012 under his presidential successor, Dmitry Medvedev, Putin was re-elected president in 2012. He has surrounded himself with powerful political allies called the *siloviki*—officials in the Kremlin who have backgrounds in the secret police and intelligence services. At the same time, he promoted a muscular form of nationalism in domestic and foreign affairs, which has manifested itself in a brutal counter-insurgency in Chechnya, invasion of Georgia in 2008, and occasional cutoffs of gas flows to Ukraine. An egregious example of the suppression of dissent occurred in 2012 when police arrested three members of a punk rock band, Pussy Riot, for filming an anti-Putin video inside an Orthodox church. Despite pleas from musicians like Sting, Madonna, the Red Hot Chili Peppers, and Paul McCartney that the women be released from custody, a Russian court sentenced them to two years in jail.

Important sectors of the Russian economy were sold in the early 1990s to a handful of local investors with ties to the government and the old *nomenklatura* (senior Soviet bureaucrats). The result was the emergence of "**oligarchs**," a small number of individuals with huge influence in the economy, government, and the media. In the 1990s, Russia suffered a rapid decline in the standard of living as people found their savings wiped out and their salaries unable to keep up with rising prices. Hyperinflation was eventually brought under control, but by 1999 more than one-third of the population lived in poverty. Life expectancy declined precipitously in what can be called a "mortality crisis." In 2009, average male life expectancy in Russia was only sixty-two years, compared to seventy-two years in China and seventy-six years in the United States.[8] Although combined life expectancy for both sexes rose to seventy years by 2011, and fertility rates increased as well, political economist Nicholas Eberstadt argues that the "dying bear's" "demographic disaster" deprives it of the human resources needed to significantly improve its economic performance and military prowess in the future.[9]

Russia's economy turned around by the start of the millennium, growing at a rate of nearly 7 percent a year from 1998 to 2008. But much of its growth was based on exports of oil and raw materials rather than the development of a diversified market economy. Many small private firms have suffered from insolvency and interference from the state bureaucracy. Organized crime and corruption remain serious problems. Putin has found it difficult to eliminate a number of wasteful government subsidies. The state has effectively renationalized much of the oil and gas sector, and state-owned conglomerates are also important in the automobile, aerospace, and defense industries. Oligarchs remain important in energy, minerals, steel, and banking sectors, but many have turned to the Kremlin for help in repaying huge debts they incurred with Western creditors.

For many years to come, Russia will struggle to deal with internal economic and social problems while reasserting its role in a more multipolar world. Putin's strategy of nurturing state-controlled "**national champions**" in energy and mineral sectors is a risky proposition, given the volatility in world energy prices and the neglect of private sector manufacturing. Russia has lost a lot of potential foreign direct investment from multinational corporations fed up with the lack of rule of law and Kremlin interference in the market. For example, although Swedish retailer Ikea has spent $4 billion building fourteen popular malls since 2000, it was so fed up with government corruption and fraud that it suspended all further investments in Russia in 2009.

Scholars recognize that post-Soviet countries play different roles in the global economy. For economic liberals, the integration of some into the European Union is evidence of the triumph of the triumvirate of democracy, capitalism, and peace.

Most ex-Soviet republics enjoyed robust economic growth from the late 1990s to 2008. By contrast, structuralists argue that countries like Russia, Ukraine, and Moldova are worse off now than under communism because of the breakdown of the state and society that accompanied privatization and marketization. Reforms upset established expectations and ways of life. Voters in many countries rose up in a backlash against the reformist agendas, strengthening the power of xenophobic and authoritarian elements.

Realists remain concerned about the security threats from an authoritarian Russia that claims spheres of influence around its borders and uses its oil-and-gas wealth to pressure European neighbors and centralize economic power in the hands of corrupt, Kremlin-friendly elites. Once a proud superpower, Russia now accounts for only 3 percent of global GDP compared to the United States' 22 percent. Realists worry that as Russia becomes an ever more important energy producer, it will cooperate less with other countries. Andrew Kuchins and Anders Aslund point out that its leaders nurse strong grievances about Western interference in their country after the Cold War and want to reassert "hypersovereignty" and "privileged relations" with weaker neighbors.[10] Putin seems to want a world in which U.S. power declines and a proud Russia reasserts its own interests rather than simply conforms to global liberal norms.

Economist Nouriel Roubini even argues that, despite its nuclear weapons and energy, Russia no longer should be considered one of the emerging BRICs (Brazil, Russia, India, and China): "Saddled with a rustbelt infrastructure, Russia further disqualifies itself with dysfunctional and revanchist politics and a demographic trend in near-terminal decline."[11] More likely to replace it alongside Brazil, India, and China as first-tier economic powerhouses, Roubini suggests, are Indonesia, South Korea, or Turkey—all democratic countries with competitive manufacturing and, in the case of Indonesia and Turkey, lots of raw materials and growing populations.

BRAZIL: THE COSTS OF SUCCESS

To some people, Brazil conjures images of white-sand beaches, samba music, the extravagance of Carnivál, and the bikini-clad Girl from Ipanema (immortalized in a Frank Sinatra song). To others, it is better known for its high incidence of gun violence, grinding poverty, and one of the highest rates of income inequality in the world. Both of these idealized, polar-opposite images of Brazil obscure the country's complicated economic, political, and cultural history. Nearly the size of the continental United States, Brazil is home to over 220 different indigenous groups speaking more than 180 distinct languages. Native Brazilians, however, make up only 0.4 percent of the population. Like the United States, it is a country of immigrants who came in successive waves from Europe, Africa, Japan, China, and even North America. Although it is a cultural "melting pot," inequality remains a serious problem. Brazil's changing geopolitical status often throws that inequality into sharp relief. For instance, some residents of Rio de Janeiro's *favelas* (shanty-towns) are facing eviction as the city prepares to host the World Cup in 2014 and the Olympics in 2016. While some call this a much-needed "clean up" of the city's notoriously dangerous slums, others claim that the poor are being swept aside in an effort to create the image of a truly "modern" Rio. Brazil, then, reflects a contradiction common to today's **emerging economies** tremendous economic growth has given it greater influence on the global stage, but lasting legacies of exploitation and poverty have yet to be overcome.

From Colonialism to Modernization

From the sixteenth to the nineteenth centuries, Brazil was a Portuguese colony, enriching the crown with sugar and coffee from vast plantations on the coasts and gold mined by *bandeirantes* in the vast, wild interior. It declared independence from Portugal in 1822, establishing its capital as Río de Janeiro on the Atlantic coast. Most economic activity was concentrated on the coast; the interior of the country was (relatively speaking) sparsely populated. Home to thousands of indigenous communities with rich cultural and economic histories, Brazil's interior presented both a challenge and an opportunity to prospectors and cattle ranchers who saw the remote region as a source of vast potential wealth that was at the same time out of the reach of the federal state.

Beginning in the 1930s, Brazil embarked on a successful program of development based on the principles of import-substitution industrialization (see Chapter 11). From 1945 to 1980, Brazil's average annual rate of growth topped 7 percent. In 1956, President Jucelino Kubitschek made it his mission to integrate the vast countryside with the "modern" coastal cities by moving the capital a thousand kilometers inland. His ambitious plan, called "50 years in 5," was to build a new capital called Brasília from the ground up in the middle of the desert in a single presidential term. The high-modernist city of famed architect Oscar Niemeyer left an indelible mark on both the landscape and the collective consciousness of the nation. Its construction in the interior signaled a step into the era of developmentalism based on the principles of modernization.

A decade later, however, military officers overthrew the democratically elected government of João Goulart, ruling the country as a dictatorship until 1985. Despite political and cultural repression, the country experienced an economic boom in the 1960s and 1970s—creating strong manufacturing, agricultural, and technological sectors. However, growth was fueled by heavy borrowing from international creditors. By 1980, Brazil—like countries throughout Latin America—was on the verge of defaulting on its international debt. The IMF arrived with its classic bargain: financial bailout in exchange for strict structural adjustment.

The 1980s turned into the so-called Lost Decade. Brazil's rate of annual GDP growth fell from 7.5 percent to 2.5 percent. Some state-owned industries were privatized, and the structures of import substitution were dismantled. Although plagued by high inflation and high interest rates, Brazil eventually clawed its way out of crushing debt. Ironically, what helped Brazil regain economic power was the economic infrastructure that had been built during the import-substitution period. State investments in industry, agriculture, and energy created a solid foundation for development when the global economy rebounded in the 1990s with increasing demand for commodities and manufactured goods alike. Then, beginning in 1994, democratically elected president Fernando Henrique Cardoso—a former dependency theorist—accelerated reforms with his "Real Plan" which successfully stabilized Brazil's currency, tamed inflation, privatized more state-owned enterprises, and broke up state monopolies. Nevertheless, these reforms, especially fiscal austerity and tax increases, rankled the country's working poor.

Following the re-election of Cardoso in 1998, Brazil began to be perceived as a model for stability and successful democratization within the Latin American region. It started to emerge as one of the world's most important exporters of agricultural products and ethanol. This moment marked the consolidation of many years of shifting fortunes in its economic development, as the country moved toward a customized mixture of liberalization combined with policies aimed at domestic industrial and social development. It also sought to make its mark on the global trade regime.

At a December 1999 meeting of the World Trade Organization in Seattle, Brazil's Foreign Minister Luiz Felipe Lampreia banded together with leaders of other large "emerging markets" such as South Africa, Kenya, India, and Thailand to criticize U.S. and EU dominance of trade negotiations. In an official statement, he said, "If free and fair trade is the name of the game—and most of us think it should be—we still have much to do to improve the rules by which we play. We all know that the world is no level playing field, but it is imperative that, at the very least, all players can trust that there are rules which apply to all alike, rules which are not written to protect the strong from their own weaknesses and to prevent the weak from taking advantage of their own strengths."[12] Lampreia specifically took rich countries to task for maintaining lavish agricultural subsidies and protecting themselves from imports of farm products while hypocritically asking emerging countries to liberalize their markets even more. While the "Battle in Seattle" street protests outside the WTO meeting ended talks, it was the protests inside the meeting—by a Brazil-led coalition called the G20—that began to change the trade agenda that had dominated negotiations since the WTO was formed in 1994.

The Rise of Brazil under Lula

Brazil's coronation as a major rising power coincided with the election of Labor Party candidate Luiz Inácio Lula da Silva as president in 2002. A long-time union leader, Lula had run on a populist platform that presented a stark contrast with what many saw as Cardoso's neoliberal economic policies. Lula was admired by Brazil's urban poor, having grown up with little formal education and having spent years as a manual laborer in the slums of São Paulo. He famously lost a finger to a lathe in an auto-parts plant at the age of fourteen. His election was part of a wave of victories for leftist Latin American presidents popular with the working class and rural poor, including Hugo Chavez of Venezuela (elected in 1999), Evo Morales of Bolivia (2006), Cristina Fernandez de Kirchner of Argentina (2007), and Fernando Lugo of Paraguay (2008).

Despite his populist credentials, Lula also quietly embraced free trade and free markets. His administration skillfully used the World Trade Organization to reject the protectionism that persisted in WTO agreements like the Agreement on Agriculture by calling for *more* market access and *fewer* trade barriers in the United States and Europe. In this way, then, Lula surprised many analysts who had expected his social democratic government to turn away from economic liberalism. He spent generously on social programs but also pushed for privatization and export-oriented growth. GDP grew at an annual rate of 4.8 percent between 2004 and 2008.[13]

Domestically, however, his crowning economic achievement was the Fome Zero (Zero Hunger) program, which quickly became one of the most comprehensive and well-known public assistance programs in the world. Fome Zero includes a conditional cash transfer program called **Bolsa Família** (family grant), which provides cash assistance to needy families—but only if they meet certain conditions, like school attendance, vaccinations, and regular medical and dental care for children. The program has sharply reduced absolute poverty and improved health and education for young people.

In 2010, *Time* magazine named president Lula the number one "Most Influential World Leader." During his eight years in power, Brazil staked its global political fortunes on speaking out against the United States and Europe on behalf of the "developing world."[14] In return, leaders like U.S. president Barack Obama and British prime minister David Cameron acknowledged Brazil's new-found geopolitical status through strategic partnerships. By 2012, Brazil had surpassed Great Britain to become the world's sixth largest economy.

The Costs of Economic Success

Despite this progress, Brazil's economic rise has not been without conflict and contradiction. Especially controversial have been the environmental and human rights implications of agricultural growth. While Brazil has been a major producer of coffee, tropical fruits and beef, Lula's economic development strategy encouraged the expansion of export-oriented agriculture—mainly soybeans for animal feed and sugar cane for ethanol. Since 2003, the land area in which these two crops are planted has increased by more than 30 percent, mostly in the central-west and northern regions of the country, which are home to the fragile ecosystems of the *cerrado* and the Amazon rainforest. Deforestation is the price Brazil has paid for the expansion of farmland and growth of agricultural exports. In addition, there are more violent conflicts between large producers and rural peasants over access to land. The government has often failed to enforce the meager environmental regulations that exist.

Home to the world's largest "carbon sink" in the Amazon rainforest, Brazil finds itself at the center of major international environmental debates. Many environmentalists believe that Brazil's land use decisions should take into account the "ecosystem service" that the rainforest provides. Some scientists estimate that tropical forests—the "lungs of the world"—absorb as much as 20 percent of carbon emissions from the atmosphere every year. Their loss could drastically accelerate global climate change. However, many Brazilians argue that it is unfair and hypocritical for rich countries—that previously cut down much of their own forest land—to ask Brazil to refrain from exploiting an economic resource. They believe that the United States and Europe need to reduce their own carbon emissions first.

Nevertheless, it is clear that large-scale timber extraction, agricultural expansion, and cattle-farming growth have caused significant deforestation. In response to international pressure, the transnational agribusiness community—which is responsible for processing and exporting nearly all of western Brazil's soybeans—has voluntarily agreed to a "sustainable soy" program whose centerpiece is a moratorium on the purchase of soybeans grown on land cleared after 2006. While there is widespread skepticism that a voluntary agreement among transnational soy brokers will be effective, the federal government's recent crackdown on illegal logging has helped reduce the rate of deforestation by 75 percent since 2004.

Many of the environmental controversies that surround soybean production also apply to ethanol, a fuel Brazilian cars have been running on since 1978. Brazil is currently the second largest producer (and largest exporter) of ethanol in the world. Its producers use sugar cane as a feedstock, which is much more efficient than corn in terms of the net energy yield per acre of crop planted. Ethanol from sugar cane is a renewable fuel and emits fewer greenhouse gases than gasoline. Biofuels in general have been criticized for diverting both land and crops from the food system, leaving fewer resources for food production and indirectly contributing to rising food prices (see Chapter 18). In Brazil in particular, sugar cane plantations and mills are blamed for reducing the land available for food production and diverting massive quantities of water from some of the country's most important watersheds.

Agricultural development policies also often leave small-scale producers and indigenous communities without access to the land upon which they rely for their livelihoods. In response, the grassroots Landless Rural Workers Movement has used both legal and extralegal means to occupy and resettle idle land held by absentee owners. Conflicts over the right to land in the country's interior are often violent, and over the last twenty years more than 1,000 rural activists have been killed in these conflicts. Despite Brazil's impressive economic statistics, millions have been excluded from the country's meteoric rise.

One of the primary obstacles to further economic development in Brazil is the poor transportation infrastructure. Because there is not enough public funding to build all the necessary new roads, the government has entered into partnerships with private entities whereby they pay to create the roadbed (clearing land, construction, and grading) and the government pays for the road surface. In 2012, President Dilma Rousseff announced an ambitious plan to license private companies to build and operate several thousand miles of roads and railways. Critics argue that this approach denies improved infrastructure to poor communities, reinforcing Brazil's famously high rate of inequality. Nowhere is this inequality more evident than in the agricultural frontier. As one drives across the vast plains of the *cerrado* in the state of Mato Grosso, the roads that pass through large soybean farms are in excellent condition, but the asphalt literally stops at the edge of indigenous reserves.

Brazil's economy has suffered ups and downs since the 2008 global recession. In 2009, Lula famously blamed the financial crisis on "white people with blue eyes" who "before the crisis appeared to know everything and now demonstrate that they know nothing" about the global economy. Growth rebounded in 2010 in part because of the relatively quick recovery of commodity prices and sustained foreign investment. Rising global demand for aircraft and basic commodities like food, iron ore, and energy have no doubt helped keep Brazil's exports up. In 2009, China surpassed the United States as Brazil's most important trading partner. Brazil has also been relatively more insulated from international credit markets and has tightly regulated domestic banks. By 2012, it held more than $370 billion in foreign reserves.

Brazil has been proud of its economic model which embraces free markets and foreign investment, but also maintains large state-owned industries in strategic sectors like oil, electricity, telecommunications, and agricultural research. The giant state-owned development bank, BNDES, is the main source of long-term, subsidized credit for large public and private companies. Since discovering huge oil and gas deposits in deep waters off of the Atlantic coast in 2006, the state-owned energy company Petrobas has taken the lead in investing tens of billions of dollars to develop the deposits, while still encouraging participation by foreign energy corporations. It hopes that with more than $400 billion of investments, Brazil will become the fifth largest oil exporter in the world by 2020. Along with social programs like the Bolsa Família, Brazil managed to cut the poverty rate from 38 percent in 2001 to 25 percent in 2009. The growing middle class constitutes a strong domestic market for Brazilian goods and services. Like the other countries profiled in this chapter, Brazil has shown that economic development can occur without complete adoption of the principles of the Washington Consensus.

However, there are still storm clouds on Brazil's horizon. Growth faltered in 2011 and slowed to 0.9 percent in 2012—the worst performance among BRICs— as manufacturing declined and Chinese demand slowed. Inequality remains persistently high, contributing to class tensions. Ironically, Brazil now faces one of the diseases of affluence: obesity. According to a government survey in 2012, 15 percent of Brazilian adults are obese and half are overweight—no doubt due in part to the growing popularity of fast food from the likes of McDonalds (700 restaurants) and Coca-Cola ($8.7 billion worth of soft drinks sold in 2010).[15] Structuralist critics argue that the social and environmental costs of the country's economic success, including deforestation and land concentration, outweigh many of the gains. While none of us has a crystal ball to see the future, we can expect Brazil will work hard to showcase its successes to the world when the Olympics come to Rio in 2016.

INDIA: THE OTHER ASIAN TIGER

While Russia is sometimes viewed as an angry bear, India has often been portrayed as a caged tiger poised to leap to unimaginable economic heights. Since independence in 1947, it has all too often found itself in this poised stance: ready, but just not quite willing to jump. Despite progress in the recent past, this country of 1.2 billion suffers from a massive, inefficient, governmental bureaucracy and poor public infrastructure. To reach its growth potential, India will need to ease barriers to trade, expand the export of manufactured goods, and unleash the energies of the private sector.

From Independence to a Mixed Economy

In the early years of colonization, Britain discouraged Indian manufacturing, and instead the British East India Company made India into a subservient provider of raw materials for the factories of the United Kingdom. Then, during the era of the British Raj from 1858 to 1947, Britain invested in a massive network of railways, roads, canals, bridges, and telegraph links to transport and coordinate India's vast quantities of raw goods for subsequent export, mainly to England. The spread of property rights, the English language, and a broad political and legal framework aided the eventual emergence of India's democratic institutions.

Following independence in 1947, India's first prime minister, Jawaharlal Nehru, promoted a self-reliant, import-substitution-led model of growth that was as independent of foreign capital as possible. Mistrusting the global capitalist system, Nehru drew inspiration from the Soviet Union and chose a path of modernization through industrialization. Although India chose a foreign economic model, the motives of its leaders were nationalist in nature.[16] They stood at the helm of the "commanding heights" of the economy, and all sectors seen as essential to industrialization, such as steel, engineering, water, electricity, mining, and even finance, were dominated by public enterprises. Unlike the Soviet Union, India retained democracy and private property. However, central planning and a large bureaucracy stifled the private sector. A business environment replete with onerous protectionist policies, licenses, and regulations came to be known as the "License Raj." India struggled to improve its agricultural sector, which was not only an important source of revenue and food security but the largest source of employment for India's population.

Nehru hoped that by following a socialist development strategy, India would eventually be able to compete globally once it had built up enough capital and infrastructure.[17] He realized that foreign investment and technology transfer were necessary for an industrializing economy, provided that they served the state's interests. These were the makings of a mixed economy. After experiencing a severe food shortage in the early 1960s, India started to use a new High Yield Variety (HYV) of wheat developed and funded in part by the Rockefeller Foundation. Confident of the potential to drastically increase agricultural productivity, New Delhi imported over 18,000 tons of Mexican HYV seed, distributed it across the Punjab, and made large public investments in agricultural research and agricultural extension services. The results were extremely successful. Eventually (after a hiccup due to crop failure in the early 1970s), the country emerged out of famine and became not only an agriculturally self-sufficient nation but a surplus-exporting agrarian powerhouse. Aside from the high crop yields, this **Green Revolution** played an important role in stimulating auxiliary sectors of India's economy such as irrigation, transportation, and manufacturing of fertilizers and agrochemicals. Additionally, the Green Revolution shifted India's subsistence agriculture to a more capitalist model of farming.

Critics blame Nehru for trying to modernize by mimicking some of the policies of the Soviet Union—an already industrialized and militarily powerful country.[18] The persistence of state planning throughout much of India's first four decades of independence reduced incentives for private investment. Inefficient public enterprises and overbearing restrictions on private enterprises during import substitution slowed the rate of industrial growth, as did India's fighting two wars with its neighbors, Pakistan and China. Despite large-scale capital investment during the first thirty years of independence, India averaged a modest annual economic growth rate of only 3.6 percent, and the annual GDP per capita growth rate was a mere 1.4 percent. These modest figures were sarcastically dubbed "the Hindu Rate of Growth." However, the growth rates were nearly four times greater than those under British colonial rule in the fifty years preceding independence.[19]

As India witnessed some of the destructive powers of a mismanaged socialist economy, the administration under Prime Minister Rajiv Gandhi in the mid-1980s began to flirt with liberalization. Rajiv Gandhi relaxed restrictions on large companies, eliminated price controls on cement and aluminum (which expanded construction projects across the nation), overhauled the tax system, and increased the flexibility of industrial firms, which were previously licensed for specific products only.[20]

Post-Reform Performance

Despite a noticeable acceleration of growth in the 1980s following liberalization and a modest engagement with the global economy, India faced a distortion of trade and aid due to the end of the Cold War and the fragmentation of the Soviet Union, India's primary trading partner. Additionally, the 1990 Gulf War led to a spike in oil prices, driving India's balance of payments into a crisis in mid-1991. India's foreign debt had climbed to $72 billion, making India the world's third largest debtor at the time.

In response to the 1991 crisis, India borrowed $6 billion from the International Monetary Fund and accordingly was required to adopt a series of reforms aligned with the Washington Consensus. The minister of finance at the time (and current prime minister), Manmohan Singh, devalued the rupee, reduced the number of industries reserved for the public sector, and allowed MNCs to have a 51 percent (majority) share in Indian firms. The five years following India's 1991 liberalization registered record high annual growth rates of 6.7 percent. A vibrant world economy was eager to engage with south Asia. The services sector blossomed, overshadowing industry growth levels during this time (see The Case of Bangalore: Epitomizing India's Duality). By 2012, annual exports of software and information technology services alone reached more than $60 billion.

India increased its global presence following reforms, with more than 100 of its companies each reaching a market capitalization value of over $1 billion. Companies such as Infosys Technologies, Reliance Industries, Tata Motors, Wipro, and Jet Airways have become familiar names in the international business community. Over 125 Fortune 500 companies have research and development bases in India. Foreign direct investment grew from less than $100 million in 1990 to $24 billion in 2010. Trade with the United States in goods and services has blossomed: in 2011 India's exports to the United States were worth $53 billion and imports from it were worth $33 billion.

India's new development model tenuously combines protectionist state-led growth with neoliberal, market-driven growth. India has skipped to a service-driven economy, largely bypassing a labor-intensive industrial revolution. Its comparative

THE CASE OF BANGALORE: EPITOMIZING INDIA'S DUALITY[a]

Bangalore, located in the southern state of Karnataka, India, serves as an ideal example of both globalization's successes and challenges within the framework of India's post–1991 neoliberal reforms. The city experienced unprecedented levels of growth due, in large part, to the rapid global expansion of the information technology (IT) sector. At the same time, it suffered overpopulation, rising inequality, and poor governance.

Bangalore was considered a key location for software development and the outsourcing of IT-related industry for a number of reasons, including a large presence of leading universities and research institutions, an English-speaking labor pool, and an existing close-knit relationship between the government and the private sector. Bangalore is home to over 100 research universities and technical institutions, the clustering of which is replicated by that of IT firms in Special Economic Zones (SEZs) on the outskirts of the city. In 1996, when the IT revolution began to take shape, IT employees' salaries averaged six to eight times lower than those of their U.S. counterparts. Bangalore attracted the best elements of India's comparative advantage: high-skilled, English-speaking, low-wage workers.

Bangalore accounts for one-third of India's software exports and nearly one-third of total employment in Indian IT services. In 1996, Bangalore was cited as being "Asia's fastest growing city." Today, however, one sees incomplete flyover structures and buildings, rapid expansion of slums, traffic gridlock, and unbearable pollution. This may not seem an unusual or original story, but indeed,

Bangalore epitomizes India's development character: fast-paced growth driven by the services sector, though constrained by a byzantine bureaucracy.

The city, too, represents the trend of a rapidly urbanizing nation; Bangalore's population exploded from 2.9 million inhabitants in 1981 to 9.6 million in 2011. The economic repercussions of such growth are seen in skyrocketing property rates and a 25 percent increase in wage rates per year. Three new firms enter Bangalore's city limits each week. Over 900 new cars are added to Bangalore's narrow streets *every day*. One might see this as a positive change, but in the context of Bangalore's base for success, MNCs are increasingly discouraged by the rising costs of doing business in the city. Infrastructural development has failed to keep pace with such rapid urbanization. Bangalore was ranked last on a list of seventeen Indian cities in terms of ease in starting a business, according to the World Bank's 2009 *Doing Business in India* report.

Exasperated Bangaloreans and corporations alike are flexing more political muscle to help create an easier future. Nandan Nilekani, one of India's most successful entrepreneurs, notes that the IT industry's 40 percent annual growth throughout the 1990s has created a new class of affluent, "high-impact" urban residents, and thus an increase in demand for shopping malls, better roads, and fewer power cuts.

Reference

[a]Rahul Madhavan authored the material in this box. Our thanks to him.

advantage in information technology services and call centers has certainly given it a global export niche, but these sectors will never be able to create enough jobs to absorb the mass of poorly educated peasants. Only a major increase in factories and manufacturing facilities will provide them with employment opportunities.

Left behind has been the peasantry. Economic reforms in the 1990s included the elimination of most agricultural subsidies, lower prices supports, and encouragement of cash crops like cotton that left many farmers at the mercy of market forces. As many farmers fell deeply into debt between 1995 and 2010, 250,000 of them committed suicide—"the largest wave of recorded suicides in human history."[21]

Despite economic liberalization, businesses complain that rigid labor laws make it very difficult, legally, to fire an employee. Poor public services, underdeveloped physical infrastructure, and an inconsistent supply of water and electricity all place major constraints on India's potential for further rapid development and sustainable urbanization. For example, while China has almost 50,000 kilometers of national, divided highways, India has only 5,000 kilometers of comparable roads. And in late July 2012, the country was hit by a massive power outage that temporarily deprived over 600 million people of electricity. A government commission contends that recurring power failures lower national growth by 1.2 percent a year; businesses big and small have to install costly backup generators to insure a steady flow of electricity.[22] India's rural electric supply is also sporadic and sparse.

Another pressing issue is a substandard education system that deprives many youth of proper primary schooling. Despite reforms beginning in the late 1980s, it was only in 2002 that India legislated the right to free and compulsory education for all children aged 6–14 years. As more MNCs invest in India, they rapidly increase demand for a cheap, skilled, knowledgeable, English-speaking workforce. India has nearly 300 universities and over 12,000 colleges, producing approximately two million degree holders per year, nearly one half of whom are engineering or technology-oriented graduates.

Outlook for the Future: The Crisis and Beyond

Compared to the 3.6 percent annual growth rate during India's first thirty years after independence and the 6 percent rate during the 1980s, GDP grew on average more than 8 percent annually from 2004 to 2011. India's economy was hot, driven in part by foreign capital inflows. However, India is still a very poor country: its Gross National Income per capita in 2011 (in purchasing power parity) was only $3,600, and 69 percent of the population in 2010 made less than $2 a day.

A widely cited comparative statistic between India and China is the percentage of the population in each country that is of working age. Over half of India's population is under the age of twenty-five, and approximately 40 percent are under the age of eighteen. The proportion of the working-age population will continue to rise for the next few decades, whereas in China it is expected to fall. These statistics point to the potential for India to enhance labor productivity, particularly beyond already-vibrant industries such as pharmaceuticals and chemicals. With over 60 percent of Indians employed in low-productivity farming, the need for increased employment opportunities in manufacturing and services is clear.

India has continued to grow amid the financial crisis that swept the world in October 2008. Its financial system has fortunately avoided a bad-loan culture, and its banks are sparsely connected to overseas credit markets. Banks in which the government still retains majority ownership control approximately 70 percent of total banking assets. As a consequence of its historically protectionist policies, India is less dependent on exports and thus less susceptible to global market turmoil.

Despite being somewhat insulated from the financial crisis, India desperately needs to improve its infrastructure, including seaports and airports. Even its security systems are feeble, which was demonstrated in the response to a three-day-long terrorist attack in Mumbai in November of 2008. India ranks an unimpressive 132 out of 183 countries in the World Bank's 2012 "Doing Business" report, a testament to how difficult it is to start a business, get permits, and enforce contracts. If India is to become a global leader, it must reshape the business environment to be conducive to large-scale investment and more exporting.

Scholars have debated whether or not India's democratic system has left it at a disadvantage in generating economic development compared to authoritarian China. Lobbying groups have significant influence over government officials. Economist Amitendu Palit points out that retailers, small manufacturers, and unions have opposed the lifting of protectionist barriers and implementation of reforms that would create more domestic competition.[23] Weak coalition governments and a federal system that gives considerable power to states also make it hard to carry out decisive, transformative policies.[24] Corruption is endemic; since 2010 citizen-activists such as Anna Hazare and yoga guru Baba Ramdev have led large anti-corruption protests.

Most IPE scholars expect that it will take many years for India to become a global power. In the meantime, realists hope it will be a regional buffer against Islamic extremism in neighboring Afghanistan and Pakistan. Moreover, they see it as a close ally of the United States and a counterbalance to China. Economic liberals see in India proof that moving away from a state-dominated economy leads to rapid growth. They also are heartened that it is a model of how democracy and free markets can work even in a very poor country.

Structuralists tend to pooh-pooh the India-rising hype, noting that caste and exploitation still leave most Indians in deep poverty. The flashy IT sector, which employs barely 2 percent of Indians, bypasses most of the population, especially in rural areas and urban slums. The proliferation of ultra-rich businessmen points to growing inequality of wealth. An iconic example of this disparity is the case of Mukesh Ambani, a corporate mogul whose personal wealth is estimated at some $20 billion. His jarring, twenty-seven-story home in Mumbai, completed in 2010, has three helipads, many floors of parking, and six hundred servants. Novelist Arundhati Roy sees this as emblematic of a "trickledown," "gush-up" economy that "concentrates wealth on to the tip of a shining pin on which our billionaires pirouette" and that causes "tidal waves of money [to] crash through the institutions of democracy—the courts, Parliament as well as the media, seriously compromising their ability to function in the ways they were meant to."[25] Even liberal Indian billionaire Nandan Nilekani recognizes some of these problems—along with massive education, health and environmental failures. However, in a recent book he expresses confidence that India has a promising global future due to its embrace of English, **demographic dividend** (a large, young population), embedded democracy, and empowerment through technology.[26]

CHINA IN TRANSITION: AN ANALYSIS OF PARADOXES

Though born out of the structuralist rhetoric of communist revolution, modern China in the last three decades has adopted increasingly liberal economic policies on its way to becoming a manufacturing powerhouse and major player in the global economy. Its strengths, however, are counterbalanced with internal tensions due to constrained social and political freedoms. In its foreign policy, Beijing makes calculated realist decisions about security and economic strategy but finds itself ever more dependent on the success and cooperation of other nations.

This section analyzes several contradictions that have emerged during China's development. First, Chinese leaders are trying to foster a consumer culture while relying on profoundly illiberal social controls and exploitative practices. Second, Beijing has presided over a broadly mercantilist system that nevertheless is fueled by global interdependence. Finally, the Chinese government has fostered cooperative relations with leading powers and adapted to global norms at the same time that it seeks to challenge the Western international order. The tensions inherent in the pursuit of contradictory policies have been thrown into relief by the recent global financial crisis, which has strained China's model and shaken some of its international trade relationships.

The Roots of China's Rise: The Transition to Market Socialism

The transition away from classic socialism began with the death of Mao Zedong in 1976. Mao had presided over nearly three decades of increasingly tenuous rule by the Communist Party. His Great Leap Forward (1958–1960), an attempt to organize citizens into *people's communes* of localized industrial production, undermined agriculture and led to a famine that caused the deaths of tens of millions of people. This was followed by the disastrous Cultural Revolution (1966–1976), in which Mao encouraged Chinese citizens to attack the party-state itself, which he claimed had become too bureaucratic and resistant to revolutionary change. By the late 1970s, China's economy was unstable, and the legitimacy of the Communist Party was in serious jeopardy.

Mao's death instigated a power struggle that Deng Xiaoping eventually won. Deng concluded that ideology alone could not sustain the party-state after the tumult of the preceding decades. In 1978, he unveiled an economic reform program that combined elements of socialism with a greater role for markets and private property. Communal farms were dissolved and farmers were granted increased autonomy in selecting which crops to plant, as well as the ability to sell excess crops in free markets. Food production and farmers' income rose, stimulating the growth of private rural enterprise. At the same time, Deng created what was termed the "open door." Barriers to international trade and finance were lowered, opening China to global markets, foreign investment, and technical know-how. A necessary consequence of these reforms was greater recognition of private property rights: Farmers gained the right to sell their land (with restrictions) in the mid-1980s, and private businesses were gradually legalized.

Unlike in the ex-Soviet bloc, however, the Communist Party did not give up power. Because of the party's centrality in facilitating development, China's transition is most accurately viewed as one from classical socialism to market socialism.[27] Under this system, private enterprise and markets enjoy a more liberal macroeconomic climate but still remain what the Chinese have called "the bird in the cage"—that is, held firmly in the grasp of state control at the level of individual corporations and industry policies.[28] Many state-run companies are kept afloat with government financial support.

Migrants from rural areas have filled many of the new jobs in export-oriented manufacturing facilities, the backbone of China's booming economy. Guangdong province in southeastern China is the largest manufacturing region. In 2007, *The Atlantic* correspondent James Fallows speculated that this one province in the Pearl River Delta employed more factory workers than the entire U.S. manufacturing sector.[29] It produces everything from cheap children's toys to computer motherboards. At its height, the port city of Shenzhen alone shipped these goods around the world at a rate of one standard twenty-foot shipping container every second. A result of the booming export economy was a massive current account surplus that reached $426 billion in 2008. China has used its surplus to buy U.S. Treasury bills and accumulate reserves of dollars and euros. In addition, it has invested in property and stocks overseas, most recently in Africa, where it is pouring billions of dollars into new energy, minerals, and infrastructure projects. This buildup of assets has created tensions with lawmakers in the United States and other nations, which will be discussed in following sections.

Rapid growth has fueled tensions between the Chinese population and the Communist Party leadership. The government has gone to great lengths to censor expressions of dissatisfaction, often with police and military force. This was demonstrated in the 1989 Tiananmen Square crackdown against pro-democracy activists and the suppression of the Falun Gong religious movement in 1999. Beyond direct repression, however, China's leaders also understand that maintaining economic growth and basic services are keys to maintaining political control.

Hu Jintao, who assumed the role of China's Paramount Leader in 2002, advanced a set of policies designed to balance the imperative of rapid growth with the goals of decreasing income inequality and protecting the environment. But officials have struggled to maintain an 8 percent annual growth rate of GDP since the global economic downturn that began to hit China in 2007 and 2008. As the effects of the U.S. real estate and financial crises spread throughout the global financial system, demand for Chinese-produced goods fell. Thousands of factories closed in the Pearl River Delta. An estimated twenty million factory workers in Guangdong province and across the rest of the country were shut out of jobs, with little or no immediate social safety net. Even Dafen, a Guangdong village that produces more manufactured oil paintings than any other location in the world, has been hurt by the U.S. housing crisis: as Americans defaulted on mortgages and new construction ground to a halt, demand for mass-produced art and knockoffs of famous paintings dropped.

The government responded swiftly—both through crackdowns on protests and a massive stimulus plan to boost domestic demand. But that was not enough to stop the decline of China's current account surplus from a whopping 10 percent of GDP in 2007 to just 3 percent in 2011. One of the reasons for China's worsening **terms of trade**—the ratio of prices of exports to the prices of imports—is the rising cost of imported commodities and minerals. In addition, China's rising wages and modest currency appreciation are making its goods relatively less competitive in the world.

Economic uncertainty following the global downturn has put into relief the contradictions arising from China's development strategy. Beijing must nurture its own consumer culture and boost domestic spending—tasks to be delicately balanced against efforts to maintain political control and impose social transformation. It must also balance its mercantilist–realist aspirations with the humbling reminder of its global economic interdependence. At the same time, it must adapt to global norms and institutions that it sometimes sees as standing in the way of its own aspirations for superpower status. We will explore each of these contradictions in the sections that follow.

Contradiction I: Fostering a Consumer Society
Despite Repressive Policies

As Beijing has learned during the global downturn, relying heavily on exports to consumers outside its borders has severe risks. Its long-term challenge of maintaining a minimum level of growth is as much a matter of expanding domestic consumption as it is protecting trade advantages.

Fostering domestic market growth is in Beijing's interest because selling more Chinese goods inside China will provide a more reliable and stable economic model. However, there are many roadblocks on the way. The factories of Guangdong and other producing regions are designed to make products that most Chinese either cannot afford or do not desire in the first place. A shift to more consumption of domestically produced goods will require costly adjustments to the production and logistics infrastructure of the export economy.

Export-led growth has been ingrained with a host of social habits and cultural expectations—not the least of which is modest personal consumption. Even after three decades of growth, Chinese consumers still spend less and save far more than their Western counterparts. A study by private consulting firm McKinsey asserts that the average Chinese household saves 25 percent of its discretionary income, a rate nearly five times that of the average U.S. family.[30]

Still, consumerism has been developing in China's burgeoning metropolises. In the late 1990s, there were only a few malls in the country; there are now hundreds, stocked with high-end Western brands and tagged with equally high prices that are out of reach for many Chinese consumers. By mid-2012, there were 570 Starbucks stores in China and 336 Wal-Mart Supercenters employing 100,000 "associates," a clear indication of the rising income of the middle class. Helen Wang, author of *The Chinese Dream*, estimates that about 300 million Chinese can be considered middle class, most of whom live in big cities along the eastern and southern coasts.[31]

The developing consumer culture can in many ways be traced—ironically— to the rhetoric and policies of the Communist Party. Providing more affordable basic social services may, in the long run, be China's ticket to instigating greater domestic spending. Early in 2009, the government announced that along with its dramatic fiscal stimulus package, it would spend over $125 billion in three years to build a network of government-supported clinics and hospitals aimed at providing medical care to 90 percent of the population.

Late in 2008, Beijing introduced an economic stimulus package worth more than four trillion Yuan (over $500 billion), aimed at curbing the worst effects of the global recession and expanding infrastructure. China had employed this strategy before in the aftermath of the 1997 Asian financial crisis. The recent stimulus seemed to work, with growth hovering above 9 percent from 2009 to 2011. However, problems began to emerge as growth slowed to 7.8 percent in 2012 and easy money drove up inflation. State-owned banks—already saddled with many bad debts—lent more money to risky borrowers, contributing to a housing bubble.

Despite these problems, economist Arvind Subramanian points out that since the beginning of the 2000s, the average Chinese citizen has enjoyed rising consumption. He doubts that China's economic transition can be stopped: by 2030 China will probably be the world's economic powerhouse, based on existing data trends. He predicts that "the economic dominance of China relative to the United States is more imminent (it may already have begun), will be more broad-based (covering wealth, trade, external finance, and currency), and could be as large in magnitude in the next twenty years as that of the United Kingdom in the halcyon days of empire or the United States in the aftermath of World War II."[32]

In contrast, structuralists point out that the middle class has been rising on the backs of the rural population. The government has deliberately exploited peasants to facilitate urban development, thus widening the social and economic gaps between China's coastal areas and its interior. In addition to imposing a highly regressive taxation system in the rural areas, it has deprived as many as forty million peasants of their land since the early 1990s with little or no compensation. More than 200 million farmers have left the countryside to look for work in cities. Members of this "floating population" are, in effect, illegal immigrants in their own country, excluded from many of the social services available to urban dwellers and often exploited by employers without recourse.[33] As the global economic downturn slowed growth in Guangdong and other provinces, China experienced tens of thousands of small protests in 2009 by laid-off workers, those whose land has been reclaimed by the government, and employees with a variety of workplace grievances. Ethnic tensions have erupted violently, including widespread protests by Tibetan minorities and clashes between Muslim Uighurs and Han Chinese in Western China.

Structuralists also argue that in its singular pursuit of industrialization the Communist Party has disregarded the health and safety of its own people, as is evident in the spread of lung diseases, poisonings, tainted products, water pollution, and workplace injuries. Three-fourths of the world's most air-polluted cities are in China, and 70 percent of its rivers are seriously polluted. The Ministry of Environmental Protection has estimated that in 2010 alone, pollution and environmental damage cost the Chinese economy $230 billion—3.5 percent of GDP.[34] And the combination of a one-child policy along with access to ultrasound and abortion has meant that Chinese couples are having more boys than girls, such that the sex ratio imbalance has reached disturbing levels: 120 boys for every 100 girls under the age of fifteen years. Surplus men and disappearing women will have important negative consequences for crime, health, and social stability.

From the military actions in Tiananmen Square to policing of international press coverage during the 2008 Olympics, China has a notorious record of maintaining strict control over public discourse and exercising force when necessary to maintain conformity. The government widely restricts Web access, censors media, and monitors cell phones. The dilemma China faces is that expansive, direct control over media access is increasingly at odds with the values and desires of an educated middle class. In late 2009, the State Council announced plans to invest billions of dollars in the development of news and entertainment companies that have less direct state control and more involvement from private firms. However, in the face of demands that it censor its Internet search engine, Google pulled out of mainland China in 2010 and routed users through servers in Hong Kong.

Decades of economic reforms have not been accompanied by much political reform. In fact, the Communist Party sees its ability to maintain economic growth as intimately tied to its ability to maintain political power. These conditions pose important questions for IPE theories. Does economic liberalism depend on political liberalism and freedom of expression? Are development of a mass consumer culture and widespread inequality compatible with the continued rule of an information-shy, single party? At its General Congress in November 2012, the Communist Party chose Xi Jinping as the successor to Hu Jintao as party secretary. While the public was excluded from any role in picking Xi, China's president for the next ten years, the party is experiencing infighting between different factions, including the military, Maoists, and reformers. Whoever gains the upper hand will have a hard time ignoring the interests of an ever-expanding middle class. For example, a survey in spring 2012 by the Pew Research Center's Global Attitudes Project found that half of the Chinese respondents believe that corrupt officials are a major problem, and four-fifths agree with the statement the "rich just get richer while the poor get poorer."[35]

Contradiction II: Mercantilism That Runs on Global Interdependence

Other key questions are these: How long can China behave like a mercantilist-nationalist power in the face of global interdependence? Will it be able to engage in currency manipulation, violate the intellectual property rights of MNCs, and build up the military while maintaining its pledge to abide by economic liberal norms embodied in international institutions? China's mercantilist policies and trade decisions are intimately tied to—and limited by—its dependence on export markets.

Many Western pundits and politicians accuse Beijing of playing unfairly by keeping the value of the renminbi artificially low, providing export subsidies, and dumping products overseas. They see these mercantilist–realist policies as representing a strategic threat to the economic and security interests of the United States, Europe, and Japan. China's increasing wealth has also led to its emergence as a potential counterweight to the United States in Pacific Rim affairs. This has been a source of concern for many neoconservatives who believe the United States should use its global primacy to spread the values of freedom and democracy.

Realists have a much less sanguine view of China than free-market theorists. They worry that its military modernization will threaten U.S. military hegemony worldwide. The "China price" for manufactured goods is weakening or destroying major industries in the developed world such as textiles, electronics, and green technologies, leading to a major loss of good jobs and rendering developed countries more vulnerable in a potential war. Clyde Prestowitz sees China as a neo-mercantilist power that will undermine U.S. economic primacy and standards of living unless the United States responds to its unfair trade with explicit industrial policies, selective protectionism, and more investments in education and R&D.[36] Political economist Derek Scissors warns that the visible hand of the state is still very important in China, as is evident in numerous price controls, state-owned enterprises, and regulations on foreign investments.[37]

Columnist Thomas Friedman refers to the Sino-American relationship as a "de facto partnership between Chinese savers and producers and U.S. spenders and borrowers."[38] Historians Niall Ferguson and Moritz Schularick coined the term "**Chimerica**" to describe the phenomenon: China not only produces the affordable goods that Americans crave, but its culture of personal saving builds the credit that effectively bankrolls a culture of leveraged debt in the United States.[39] As a result of this partnership and exports to elsewhere in the world, Chinese banks hold vast reserves of foreign currency—$3.3 trillion by the end of 2012. By the beginning of 2013, China owned more than one-fifth of all U.S. Treasury securities held by foreign countries—worth more than $1.2 trillion—making it the U.S. government's largest creditor. Nevertheless, Beijing is well aware that a quick sell-off of these assets, aimed at devaluing the dollar, would have unacceptably negative consequences for China's own economy and financial holdings. Former *Financial Times* journalist Guy de Jonquières goes so far as to assert, "Generally, China has proven a hesitant paymaster, apparently more interested in achieving secure prudential returns on its money than in using it to procure strategic geopolitical advantage."[40]

China has recently been less willing to defer to pressure from Western powers. Since the beginning of the global recession, it has struck a more aggressive position on some issues, suggesting that financial troubles in the United States and the European Union have convinced it of the superiority of its own economic model. For example, self-confidence has emboldened nationalists to slow the appreciation of the renminbi to just 15 percent between 2007 and 2012. More tellingly, Beijing shocked many countries in 2010 when it temporarily halted the export of rare earth metals used in the manufacture of consumer electronics, hybrid car batteries, and military equipment (see the box Struggles over Rare Earths in Chapter 3). With a near monopoly over rare earths production, China drastically raised the price of the metals and forced other countries to open their own mines. Some interpreted its move as an effort to compel some overseas manufacturers to move their factories to China to gain access to the rare earths. For realists, the lesson of the episode is that China cannot be trusted to abide by global trade rules in the future.

There have also been concerns about poor quality control and lack of regulations. Western consumers sometimes buy dangerous products from China such as lead-tainted toys, contaminated pet food, counterfeit drugs, rotten drywall, and, yes, even honey with illegal antibiotics. An estimated 20–30 percent of the U.S. West Coast's mercury, ozone, and air-particle pollution now comes directly from China, which derives much of its electricity from coal-burning power plants.

The prospect of a stronger China, with its repressive political system and human rights practices, worries many realists. Given that a state's internal political configuration shapes its foreign policy, they contend that a more confident authoritarian China is by nature a more assertive China. Other fears are driven by the strategic landscape in Asia, which contains some dangerous flash points—including Taiwan, an independent state over which China claims sovereignty. Realist political scientist John Mearsheimer has stated adamantly that China will inevitably become more aggressive and seek regional hegemony, compelling the

United States to try to slow its rise.[41] A stronger China would have greater capacity to resolve disputes militarily. For example, in the South China Sea, Beijing has recklessly asserted territorial claims over islands and territorial waters very close to the Philippines, Vietnam, and Malaysia.

And its disregard for the rights of its Muslim minorities and Tibetans is mirrored overseas in its expanding relationships with some of the world's worst human rights violators such as Sudan and North Korea. At the UN Security Council, it has given diplomatic support to the government of Sudan, which is accused of contributing to genocide in Darfur, and also to Iran, which is accused of having a secret nuclear weapons program. Both countries export oil to it.

Contradiction III: Adapting to Global Norms and Institutions (While Trying to Change Them)

The last contradiction that we examine is somewhat the reverse of the second. Expressed as a question, it is this: As China becomes a global power, can it spread its own norms while still abiding by the rules of liberal institutions and norms of global governance? Economic liberal scholars and some others argue that we should not fear China; rather, we should recognize that its growth is good for the rest of the world and is likely to reinforce international cooperation. They see China's success in climbing the ladder of development as vindicating their assertion that freer markets and open trading systems lead to rapid growth and mutual interdependence. As China finds a comparative advantage in manufacturing, developed economies reap the benefit of cheaper products. Moreover, according to James Fallows, even as the United States loses low-profit manufacturing, its companies still reap huge profits from control of product design, branding, retailing, and after-sales servicing.[42]

Political scientist Michael Beckley rejects the thesis of Arvind Subramanian and many realists that China's economic growth necessarily means the decline of the United States. He points to empirical evidence suggesting that the United States is actually *gaining* relative to China in areas such as wealth, innovation, and military capacity.[43] For example, in the two decades from 1992 to 2011, U.S. GDP per capita (in PPP) rose from $25,000 to $48,000, while China's rose from $1,000 to $8,000. Both countries grew wealthier—but in fact the absolute gap in wealth between them grew wider.[44]

What's more, China's voracious demand for raw materials provides a boon for countries rich in oil, iron ore, alumina, copper, and arable land. Africa has benefitted most significantly: China is now the second largest trading partner with the continent after the United States. Since at least 2000, Beijing has promised African nations billions of dollars in aid, loans, and debt cancellation in exchange for access to their natural resources and markets. In 2012, it pledged loans to Africa worth $20 billion over the following three years. It has also pitched itself as a low-cost builder of roads, dams, and hospitals. Critics see its engagement in Africa as causing instability and undermining local manufacturing. But according to international development scholar Deborah Brautigam, China should not be interpreted as a "rogue donor" bent on ruthless exploitation of the continent.[45] Rather, it has a "win-win" relationship with its African partners. Aid and investment—without a lot of political and economic conditions attached to them—create opportunities for more business in natural resources and construction. She points out that China is usually no worse than Western donors and MNCs on issues like corporate social responsibility and environmental stewardship. Its lack of emphasis on democracy and labor rights simply reflects its own internal priorities for growth and collective sacrifice, as well as its belief in non-interference in the domestic affairs of other countries.

Ultimately, the realities of global economic interdependence constrain China's ability to act rashly and malevolently in pursuit of own benefit. Deep interconnections with the rest of the world tamper its ability to exercise a realist–mercantilist agenda willy-nilly. Indeed, leaders in Beijing have shown themselves to be pragmatic in foreign affairs. Case in point: China has actually helped pull the world out of the global financial crisis. Adopting a constructivist perspective, scholars Rosemary Foot and Andrew Walter argue that China has moved significantly toward complying with global norms and institutions, many of which it had no role in creating.[46] It is broadly within the global mainstream on issues such as nuclear non-proliferation, climate change mitigation, and regulations on trade and banking. Foot and Walter acknowledge that it resists compliance with rules against exchange rate manipulation, and it does not align its behavior with promotion of human rights and democracy. Nevertheless, they interpret it as generally committed to global order: "China's tolerance of norms, rules and standards produced by global economic institutions in which its influence has been negligible has in fact been remarkable."[47]

Similarly, many liberals believe that China's wealth is strengthening institutions of global governance such as the WTO, the UN, and the G20. In this conception, it is China that is accepting the developed world's consensus, not the developed world that is bending to the "Beijing Consensus." Political scientists Daniel Deudney and G. John Ikenberry argue that capitalist autocracies like China and Russia will eventually not be able to resist pressures for political liberalization.[48] Ikenberry stresses that there is a strong global order based on a commitment to openness, free markets, democracy, multilateralism, and rule-based behavior. Given that China has few close allies in the world, any effort to defy these principles would meet considerable resistance and cost Beijing dearly. Therefore, concludes Ikenberry, "China and other emerging great powers do not want to contest the basic rules and principles of the liberal international order; they wish to gain more authority and leadership within it."[49]

In the realm of security, the U.S. Department of Defense sees little evidence that Beijing is willing to risk a military confrontation with the United States or its neighbors.[50] Its primary military concerns—to deter a Taiwanese declaration of independence and win any conflict in the Taiwan Strait—are hardly malevolent. Its military modernization is focused on dealing with potential threats in its immediate periphery rather than on projecting its forces far overseas. Moreover, the United States enjoys such a dramatic advantage in military technology that even a sustained effort by China to rebuild its military would still leave the United States in a dominant position for many years.

Whatever form China's adaptation to global interdependence and global norms takes, we can be sure that China will be shaped as much by internal changes as by the way it is treated by its rivals in the rest of the world.

CONCLUSION

Most scholars of IPE agree that the countries we have discussed in this chapter are reshaping the global economy and will play much more powerful roles in the coming years. They often disagree, however, on what precisely those roles will be and whether or not they will lead to a more secure and equitable world. Broadly speaking, some IPE theorists fear the emergence of these aspiring powers, while others see their success as laying the foundation for mutual benefit from globalization.

Each of the BRIC countries is finding its global niche. Due to its service-oriented growth model, India has been described as the "back-office" of the world. Because of its large FDI inflows and relatively open trade regime, China has come to be known as the world's "workshop." Russia is a major energy producer and continental power with many nuclear weapons. Brazil is coming into its own as a huge exporter of food and natural resources. It never experienced complete state control of the economy and has benefitted from relatively efficient democratic rule and a diverse economic base.

It was only in the 1980s and 1990s that each of these emerging powers began to undertake its unique version of market-oriented reforms. Along the way, Brazil has faced debt burdens and inequality. Russia has suffered deindustrialization and various social ills, turning into something of a rentier state. India has left too many poor people by the wayside. China cannot shake off authoritarianism.

Nevertheless, China has maintained dramatically better performance since the late 1970s than the other countries. It focused more heavily on education and literacy initiatives than India. Rural reforms were deeper and more immediate than in Brazil. The communist party was better able to effect top–down development as compared to democratic and pluralistic India and Brazil. It avoided Russia's shock therapy and resource curse. Although its paradoxical combination of authoritarianism and consumerism, entrepreneurialism and state intervention, may unravel in coming years, it is likely to be the one that takes on the most global responsibilities. Whatever the paths each of these countries take, their leaders will continue to face demands for freedom, equality, and protection—demands as pressing now as they were on the eve of the Russian Revolution in 1917 or at the end of the Cold War.

KEY TERMS

market socialism   320
glasnost   322
perestroika   322
marketization   322
privatization   322

crony capitalism   324
siloviki   324
oligarchs   325
national champions   325
emerging economies   327

Bolsa Família   329
Green Revolution   332
demographic dividend   336
terms of trade   338
Chimerica   342

DISCUSSION QUESTIONS

1. How are China's reform experiences different from those of Russia, Brazil, and India? China aims to reform its market without a radical alteration in its political system. Is it possible to change the market so dramatically without changing the state? Explain.

2. Which of the three core IPE theories do you feel best explains the paradoxes and contradictions in each country's development model? Why?

3. In many ways, China and India appear to be developing under opposite models—India focused on service industries with a robust democracy and

China emphasizing export-oriented manufacturing with a strong central government. What similarities and differences exist in their models?

4. In what ways has state intervention helped and hindered the rising powers, especially in Brazil and India?

5. Look at the "Made in. . . ." labels on your clothes, electronics, and household possessions. What does this indicate about the role of the rising powers in global manufacturing?

SUGGESTED READINGS

Anders Aslund. *How Capitalism Was Built: The Transformation of Central and Eastern Europe, Russia, and Central Asia.* Cambridge: Cambridge University Press, 2007.

Ivan Berend. *From the Soviet Bloc to the European Union.* Cambridge: Cambridge University Press, 2009.

Andrew Nathan and Andrew Scobell. *China's Search for Security.* New York: Columbia University Press, 2012.

Nandan Nilekani. *Imagining India: The Idea of a Renewed Nation.* New York: Penguin, 2009.

Thomas Skidmore. *Brazil: Five Centuries of Change.* Oxford: Oxford University Press, 2010.

Hugh White. *The China Choice: Why America Should Share Power.* Collingwood, Vic.: Black Inc., 2012.

NOTES

1. See János Kornai, *The Socialist System: The Political Economy of Communism* (Princeton, NJ: Princeton University Press, 1992).

2. EBRD, *Transition Report 2008: Growth in Transition* (Foreword), November 2008, http://www.ebrd .com/downloads/research/transition/TR08.pdf.

3. EBRD, *Transition Report 2011: Crisis and Transition: The People's Perspective,* November 2011, http://www .ebrd.com/downloads/research/transition/tr11 .pdf; *Life in Transition: After the Crisis,* June 2011, http://www.ebrd.com/downloads/research/surveys /LiTS2e_web.pdf.

4. Ivan Berend, *From the Soviet Bloc to the European Union* (Cambridge: Cambridge University Press, 2009), especially Chapter 3.

5. International Labor Organization, *Global Employment Trends-Update,* May 2009, http://www.ilo .org/empelm/pubs/WCMS_114102/lang—en/index .htm; International Labor Organization, *Global Employment Trends 2013,* http://www.ilo.org/global /research/global-reports/global-employment-trends /2013/WCMS_202326/lang—en/index.htm.

6. See Freedom House, "2012 Nations in Transit Data," at http://www.freedomhouse.org/report-types /nations-transit.

7. M. Steven Fish, *Democracy Derailed in Russia: The Failure of Open Politics* (Cambridge: Cambridge University Press, 2005).

8. World Health Organization, *World Health Statistics 2012,* at http://www.who.int/gho/publications /world_health_statistics/EN_WHS2012_Full.pdf.

9. Nicholas Eberstadt, "The Dying Bear: Russia's Demographic Disaster," *Foreign Affairs* 90:6 (November/December 2011): 95–108.

10. Andrew Kuchins and Anders Aslund, *The Russia Balance Sheet* (Washington, DC: Peterson Institute for International Economics, 2009), especially Chapter 8.

11. Nouriel Roubini, "BRICKbats for the Russian Bear," *The Globe and Mail* (Canada), October 16, 2009.

12. The full text of Lampreia's statement can be found at http://www.wto.org/english/thewto_e/minist_e /min99_e/english/state_e/state_e.htm.

13. For a discussion of Brazil's economic and social achievements under Lula, see Albert Fishlow, *Starting over: Brazil since 1985* (Washington, D.C.: Brookings Institution Press, 2011).

14. Riordan Roett, "Toodle-oo, Lula: Brazil Looks Forward with Dilma," *Current History* 110:733 (February 2011), pp. 43–48

15. Rachel Glickhouse, "Supersized Brazil: Obesity a Growing Health Threat," *The Christian Science Monitor* (blog), at http://www.csmonitor.com/World /Americas/Latin-America-Monitor/2012/0730 /Supersized-Brazil-Obesity-a-growing-health-threat.

16. Paul Brass, *The Politics of India since Independence,* 2nd ed. (Cambridge: Cambridge University Press, 1997), p. 273.

17. For a detailed analysis of other significant events in the economic history of independent India, see Arvind Panagariya, *India: The Emerging Giant* (Oxford: Oxford University Press, 2008).

18. Brass, *The Politics of India since Independence*, p. 275

19. V. N. Balasubramanyam, *The Economy of India* (London: Weidenfeld and Nicolson, 1984), p. 43.

20. Panagariya, *India*, p. 83.

21. P. Sainath, quoted in *Every Thirty Minutes: Farmer Suicides, Human Rights, and the Agrarian Crisis in India* (New York, NY: Center for Human Rights and Global Justice, 2011), at http://www.chrgj.org/publications/docs/every30min.pdf.

22. Mark Magnier, "India's Power Outage Puts Its Superpower Dreams in a New Light," *Los Angeles Times*, August 1, 2012.

23. Amitendu Palit, "Economic Reforms in India: Perpetuating Policy Paralysis," National University of Singapore-Institute of South Asian Studies, Working Paper 148-29 (March 2012).

24. Carl Dahlman, *The World under Pressure: How China and India Are Influencing the Global Economy and Environment* (Stanford: Stanford University Press, 2012), pp. 55, 89.

25. Arundhati Roy, "Capitalism: A Ghost Story," *Outlook* (March 26, 2012), at http://www.outlookindia.com/article.aspx?280234.

26. Nandan Nilekani, *Imagining India: The Idea of a Renewed Nation* (New York: Penguin, 2009).

27. Shangquan Gao, *China's Economic Reform* (New York: St. Martin's Press, 1996).

28. Barry Naughton, *Growing out of the Plan: Chinese Economic Reform, 1978–1993* (Cambridge: Cambridge University Press, 1996), p. 120.

29. James Fallows, "China Makes, the World Takes," *The Atlantic* (July/August 2007), pp. 48–72.

30. McKinsey Global Institute, "If You've Got It, Spend It: Unleashing the Chinese Consumer," McKinsey & Company, 2009, at http://www.mckinsey.com/insights/china/unleashing_the_chinese_consumer.

31. Helen Wang, *The Chinese Dream: The Rise of the World's Largest Middle Class and What It Means to You*, 2nd ed. (Charlesston, SC: Bestseller Press, 2012).

32. Arvind Subramanian, *Eclipse: Living in the Shadow of China's Economic Dominance* (Washington, DC: Peterson Institute for International Economics, 2011): 4.

33. Li Zhang, *Strangers in the City: Reconfigurations of Space, Power and Social Networks within China's Floating Populations* (Stanford: Stanford University Press, 2001).

34. Edward Wong, "Cost of Environmental Damage in China Growing Rapidly amid Industrialization," *New York Times*, March 30, 2013.

35. The full survey results are available at http://www.pewglobal.org/2012/10/16/growing-concerns-in-china-about-inequality-corruption.

36. Clyde Prestowitz, *Three Billion New Capitalists: The Great Shift of Wealth and Power to the East* (New York: Basic Books, 2005).

37. Derek Scissors, "Deng Undone: The Costs of Halting Market Reform in China," *Foreign Affairs* 88:3 (May/June 2009), pp. 24–39.

38. Thomas Friedman, "China to the Rescue? Not!" *New York Times*, December 21, 2008, p. 10.

39. See Niall Ferguson and Moritz Schularick, "'Chimerica' and the Global Asset Market Boom," *International Finance* 10 (2007), pp. 215–239.

40. Guy de Jonquières, "What Power Shift to China?" *ECIPE Policy Briefs* no. 4 (2012): 2.

41. John Mersheimer, *The Tragedy of Great Power Politics* (New York: Norton, 2001).

42. Fallows, "China Makes, the World Takes."

43. Michael Beckley, "China's Century? Why America's Edge Will Endure," *International Security* 36:3 (Winter 2011/2012): 41–78.

44. International Monetary Fund, World Economic Outlook Database (April 2012), at http://www.imf.org/external/ns/cs.aspx?id=28.

45. Deborah Brautigam, *The Dragon's Gift: The Real Story of China in Africa* (Oxford: Oxford University Press, 2009).

46. Rosemary Foot and Andrew Walter, *China, the United States, and Global Order* (Cambridge: Cambridge University Press, 2011).

47. Rosemary Foot and Andrew Walter, "Global Norms and Major State Behaviour: The Cases of China and the United States," *European Journal of International Relations* (February 6, 2012): p. 17.

48. Daniel Deudney and G. John Ikenberry, "The Myth of Autocratic Revival," *Foreign Affairs* 88:1 (January/February 2009), p. 90.

49. G. John Ikenberry, "The Future of the Liberal World Order," *Foreign Affairs* 90:3 (May/June 2011), pp. 56–68.

50. For an assessment of China's militarization and its implications, see the *Annual Report to Congress: Military and Security Developments Involving the People's Republic of China 2012*, http://www.defense.gov/pubs/pdfs/2012_CMPR_Final.pdf.

The Middle East: The Quest for Development and Democracy

Continuity Amidst Change: Women walking near a mosque in Dubai, United Arab Emirates.

AP Images/Kamran Jebreili

Mohammed Bouazizi was a poor, unlicensed fruit vendor in the small town of Sidi Bouzid, Tunisia. On December 17, 2010, a police officer seized the apples on his cart and humiliated him in front of a group of other vendors. Although he had been subjected to similar indignities by public officials for many years, this time it was too much to bear. Shortly thereafter he doused his body with paint thinner and lit himself on fire in front of the city hall. He died three weeks later. A video of a small protest in Sidi Bouzid the day after Bouazizi's self-immolation spread through Facebook and eventually was shown on Al-Jazeera, the pan-Arab satellite television station. Protests erupted throughout Tunisia. In an extraordinary turn of events, President Zine al-Abidine Ben Ali fled the country on January 14, 2011, and his regime collapsed. The Arab Spring had begun.

Peaceful protests and some violent demonstrations quickly spread throughout the Arab world, shaking the foundations of authoritarian governments. Three more of the longest-serving Arab dictators would soon lose power. Egypt's president Hosni Mubarak was forced out of office on February 11, 2011, after eighteen days of protests during which hundreds of thousands of Egyptians occupied Cairo's Tahrir Square. An uprising that began in Benghazi, Libya, on February 17, 2011, turned into a bloody conflict that eventually ended with the death of Muammar el-Qaddafi on October 20, 2011. Yemenis forced the resignation of their president Ali Abdullah Saleh in February 2012. Elsewhere, the Bahraini and Syrian regimes clung to power by using massive violence against their own people. As we write, the reverberations of the Arab Spring continue, holding out the tantalizing hope of democracy but also tearing some societies apart.[1]

How the Middle East grapples with the Arab Spring depends on internal economic, political, and social factors as well the region's relationships with the rest of the world. After World War II, the United States became the dominant influence in the area as the European colonial powers withdrew, leaving behind newly independent states. Whether at the beginning of the Cold War or during the recent "war on terror," many in the Middle East have mistrusted the world's hegemon and condemned it for caring more about its own interests than about what is good for people in the region. While the United States struggles to burnish its reputation as a promoter of democracy, women's rights, and peace, its policies on Iran, Iraq, Syria, and Israel-Palestine have fueled animosities.

This chapter begins by examining how the Middle East was historically integrated into the international economy and security structure under European colonialism and during the Cold War. This is followed by a discussion of the causes of conflict and cooperation. We then assess competing claims about whether the region is "falling behind" in the global economy or successfully integrating itself into the global trade, finance, and knowledge structures. Finally, the chapter assesses the challenges for countries swept up in the political revolution beginning in 2011. While you may find the references to so many countries overwhelming at first, we hope that by the end you will have a good understanding of the region's dynamics.

The chapter lays out several broad theses regarding tensions among states, markets, and societies in the Middle East. International markets demand openness, while states jealously guard sovereignty and individuals demand protection from aspects of globalization. Until the Arab Spring, the Middle East had responded to these contradictory pressures by muddling through—adopting some economic liberalism and political reform but resisting fundamental change. Today's expectations of freedom will be hard to fulfill given a long history of unaccountable government and social inequality. Consolidation of democratic governance will depend upon responsible new leaders *within* the region. Outside powers will unleash more horrendous problems if they seek *military* solutions to Syria's civil conflict, Iran's nuclear program, or the Israeli-Palestinian conflict. But *negotiated* solutions to these same problems are fraught with uncertainty and risk that will not necessarily produce a better future either.

AN OVERVIEW OF THE MIDDLE EAST

Which countries constitute the Middle East? This chapter focuses on the region that U.S. social scientists commonly refer to as the Middle East and North Africa (MENA), an area that is tied together by history, self-identification, and economic-political interactions. It includes Israel, Iran, and Turkey (all non-Arab countries) and the numerous Arab states in the *Mashriq* (Syria, Lebanon, Jordan, Iraq, and the Palestinian Territories), in the Arabian Peninsula (Saudi Arabia, Yemen, Oman, Kuwait, Bahrain, Qatar, and the United Arab Emirates), and in North Africa (Egypt, Libya, Tunisia, Algeria, and Morocco). The distance from one end of the region to the other (Rabat, Morocco, to Tehran, Iran) is nearly 3,700 miles. (See Figure 14-1.)

In addition to official languages of Arabic, Farsi, Turkish, and Hebrew, the MENA also has millions of Kurdish speakers (especially in Turkey and Iraq) and millions of Berber speakers (especially in Morocco and Algeria). Arabic is the most widely used language (even Iran, Israel, and Turkey have Arabic-speaking minorities), and the majority of people are Muslims. Of a total regional population of more than 400 million people, there are about 13 million Christians and 6 million Jews. Substantial minorities of Christians live in Egypt, Syria, and Lebanon. Although 75 percent of Israelis are Jewish, 17 percent of Israeli citizens are Muslims. Most Muslims in the MENA are Sunnis, but the majority of the population in Iran, Iraq, and Bahrain is Shi'ite.

MENA countries differ significantly in terms of level of development and relationship to the global economy. For example, Yemen, one of the poorest countries in the world, has a per-capita gross domestic product (GDP) of only $2,200, whereas Israel's per-capita GDP is $32,200—slightly higher than that of Italy or Spain.[2] Grouping countries on the basis of exports, GDP, and population yields four general categories of MENA countries (see Table 14-1). First are the big oil exporters of the Gulf Cooperation Council and Libya, with comparatively small populations and high per-capita incomes. A second group includes big oil exporters such as Iran, Iraq, and Algeria, with large populations and historically highly protectionist economies. Third are non–oil exporters such as Israel, Turkey, Jordan, Tunisia, and Lebanon, with significant agriculture, industrial exports, tourism, and openness to foreign direct investment. Fourth are the countries like Egypt, Morocco, Syria, Yemen, and the Palestinian Territories, with mostly large populations, low per-capita GDP, and high rates of rural poverty.

The Middle East as a whole lags behind every other major region of the world in terms of democracy. Freedom House, an independent organization that annually measures countries' political freedom, ranks only Israel (in the Middle East) as being "free."[3] Seven countries—Turkey, Lebanon, Kuwait, Morocco, Egypt, Libya, and Tunisia—are assessed as only "partly free" because, despite elections, they limit political rights and civil liberties. All eleven other countries (plus the Palestinian Territories) are considered "not free." In the aftermath of the Arab Spring, Tunisia, Egypt, and Libya held fair elections that may propel these countries toward democracy; however, violence and repression in countries like Syria and Iraq seem to foreshadow a darker political future.

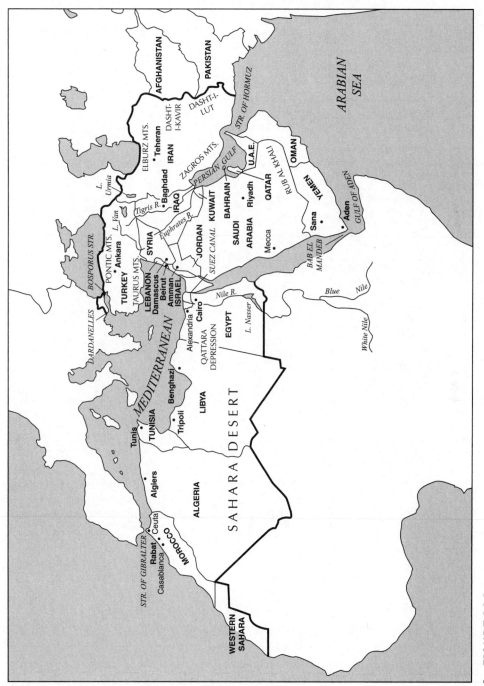

FIGURE 14-1

The MENA States.

TABLE 14-1

Economic and Demographic Differences between MENA Countries

Country	Mid-2012 Population (in millions)	GDP per Capita in 2012 (in U.S. dollars)
High-Income Oil Exporters		
Saudi Arabia	28.7	25,700
United Arab Emirates	8.1	49,000
Libya	6.5	13,300
Oman	3.1	28,500
Kuwait	2.9	43,800
Qatar	1.9	102,800
Bahrain	1.3	28,200
Middle- to Low-Income Oil Exporters		
Iran	77.9	13,100
Algeria	37.4	7,500
Iraq	33.7	4,600
Diversified Exporters		
Turkey	74.9	15,000
Tunisia	10.8	9,700
Israel	7.9	32,200
Jordan	6.3	6,000
Lebanon	4.3	15,900
Low-Income, Significantly Agricultural Countries		
Egypt	82.3	6,600
Morocco	32.6	5,300
Yemen	25.6	2,200
Syria	22.5	5,100
Palestinian Territories	4.3	2,900

Note: GDP per capita figures are in purchasing power parity (PPP). The figure for the Palestinian Territories is for 2008.

Sources: Population Reference Bureau, *2012 World Population Data Sheet*, at www.prb.org /pdf12/2012-population-data-sheet_eng.pdf; CIA, *World Factbook*, https://www.cia.gov/library /publications/the-world-factbook/index.html, accessed March 30, 2013.

THE MIDDLE EAST'S HISTORICAL LEGACY

To help us understand the roots of current conflicts and the structure of current markets, we need to know something about the history of the Middle East's contentious relations with the Western powers. Most of today's Middle East countries (except Iran and Morocco) were once part of the Ottoman Empire, which for hundreds of years was a commercial power in the Mediterranean and a military adversary of the European countries.

The Ottoman Heritage

By the nineteenth century, the Ottoman Empire had turned into the "sick man of Europe." European imperial powers extended their military and economic influence, gaining commercial concessions throughout the empire. France colonized Algeria in 1832, and in the 1880s Britain and France took control of Egypt and Tunisia, respectively, on the pretext that they were no longer able to pay their debts to European creditors. The Ottomans and local rulers in the Middle East tried with very limited success to keep up with the Europeans through **"defensive modernization"**—reorganizing their governments, adopting European military technology and legal codes, and building state-owned factories.

Why was the Middle East unable to compete with Europe? A similar question is posed today by many Arabs and Iranians who wonder why their countries have fallen so far behind the West in terms of technology and have been unable to challenge successfully the military "aggression" of the United States and Israel. In his influential book *What Went Wrong?*, Princeton University historian Bernard Lewis points to a lack of separation of church and state, cultural immobilism, and lack of political freedom (especially for women) as factors that hindered modernization in the Muslim Middle East.[4] Some economic historians point out that Ottoman "capitulations"—special economic privileges and legal rights granted to Europeans over several centuries—prevented the region from imposing high tariffs to protect infant industries. Some Muslim reformist thinkers believed that Muslim societies needed to discard historical accretions in Islam and engage in *ijtihad* (reinterpretation of Islamic legal sources).[5]

Alternatively, political scientist L. Carl Brown argues that the Middle East got locked into a system of international diplomacy called the *Eastern Question Game,* in which outside countries continuously penetrated the region and jockeyed for power. The result of this mercantilist game was that Middle Eastern political leaders tended to favor "quick grabs," eschew bargaining, and treat politics as a zero-sum game.[6] As we will see later in the chapter, the kinds of explanations we have listed here are still in vogue today as interpretations of the roadblocks for Middle Eastern countries trying to adapt to globalization.

Twentieth-Century Colonialism and Its Aftermath

By the end of World War I, the European powers had carved up the region—excluding Turkey, Iran, and Saudi Arabia—into colonies. They drew state boundaries and often exercised strong influence over monarchical regimes in "protectorates" and "mandates." The violence that colonial powers used against inhabitants seeking independence was ferocious, sometimes setting back industrialization and state formation for decades. For example, during the "pacification" of Libya from 1911 to 1933, the Italians killed most of the country's livestock and caused the displacement, imprisonment, or death of a majority of the inhabitants.[7]

Soon after World War II, nationalist movements blossomed across the MENA. The Zionist dream of a Jewish state in Palestine was fulfilled in 1948 when Israel declared its independence and rebuffed an invasion by its Arab neighbors. By the late 1950s, most of the countries in the region were independent. Algerians, however, fought a brutal guerrilla war for independence from the French from 1954 to 1962, during which more than 750,000 people were killed (and many tortured by the French).

Many independent states still had to deal with a colonial legacy of exploitation and the lingering presence of European powers. In the Suez Crisis of 1956, for example, Israel, France, and Britain briefly invaded Egypt after its president Gamal Abdel Nasser nationalized the Suez Canal. The oil industries were dominated by the West's "Seven Sisters," who for decades deprived Middle Eastern countries of a "fair share" of oil revenues.

Ordinary citizens had little role in governance, and there was a huge economic divide between urban and rural dwellers. Poor health care and poor education were the norm, not the exception. For example, at the time of Algeria's independence from France in 1962, less than one-third of Muslim children were enrolled in elementary school. As late as 1970, Oman had only one hospital and ten miles of paved roads.

Arab socialists and military officers who staged a series of *coup d'états* in the 1950s and 1960s sought to break the cycle of dependency and inequality they blamed on the West and its lackeys in the region. They implemented modernization programs, complete with subsidies on basic goods, state-owned industries, and high tariffs. Their success, however, was tempered by the intrusion of the Cold War into the region.

The Cold War to the Present in the MENA

Proxy regimes relied on the superpowers for weapons and economic aid. Washington was more than happy to support authoritarian leaders like Iran's Mohammad Reza Shah Pahlavi as a bulwark against communism and to secure oil supplies. Moscow was eager to detach Third World countries from the Western orbit.

The Cold War had at least two lasting effects on the region. First, it pushed the oil-producing states of the Organization of the Petroleum Exporting Countries (OPEC) to assert control over oil production and pricing. Responding to U.S. support for Israel in its 1973 struggle against Soviet allies Syria and Egypt, Arab members of OPEC nationalized oil companies and temporarily cut off oil exports to the United States. The net results in the 1970s and early 1980s were much higher prices and a massive transfer of wealth from industrialized nations to oil producers. Second, in their struggle against leftist political parties and Soviet proxies, the United States and its Middle East allies often accommodated conservative Islamist movements, even supplying massive amounts of weapons to the *mujahideen* (freedom fighters) in Afghanistan. The "blowback" from this marriage of convenience with Islamists would haunt the West in the 1990s and 2000s.

At the end of the Cold War in 1990, the United States emerged as the unrivaled external hegemon. Violent organizations such as al-Qaeda and Hizballah became the West's new bogeymen. Neoliberal economic policies spread in the face of a deep slump in oil prices that had begun in 1985. The 1993 Oslo Accords promised peaceful relations between Israel and the Palestinians, but the Gulf states and Iran started an arms race. Military spending in the Middle East in the 1990s still averaged about 7 percent of GDP, the highest rate of any region in the world.[8] Unfortunately, a 1990s "peace dividend" never materialized. Instead, MENA countries (excluding Turkey) increased military spending by 62 percent in real terms from 2002 to 2011.

Since 2001, dramatically higher oil prices have flooded the treasuries of oil exporters, allowing them to pay down foreign debt and boost government spending. Respectable growth rates were welcome news for the region's people but did not mitigate inequality. While the impact of the 2008 financial crisis was limited, the Arab Spring and sanctions on Iran have reversed economic progress in many countries.

From September 2001 to January 2011, the geopolitical reality of the MENA states was shaped by the crackdown on radical Islamists. Preoccupied with the war on terror and the occupation of Iraq, the United States suffered a sharp decline in its moral authority. The Obama administration turned its attention to Afghanistan, eventually withdrawing all troops from Iraq. At the same time, Israel in January 2009 launched a devastating attack on the Palestinian Islamist group Hamas in the Gaza Strip. The peace process between Israel and the Palestinian Authority came to a dangerous halt when Prime Minister Benyamin Netanyahu formed a right-wing government following Israel's elections in February 2009.

A new regional dynamic is the flexing of political and military muscles by the Shi'ites in Lebanon, Iran, and Iraq. In Lebanon the powerful Shi'ite Hizballah militia fought a thirty-two-day war with Israel in the summer of 2006. As Lebanon recovered, Hizballah rebuilt its weapons arsenal and gained one-third of the cabinet seats in a unity government following June 2009 parliamentary elections. Iran has continued to develop its nuclear enrichment capability, raising tensions with Israel, the United States, and the European Union, who have threatened military strikes if Iran develops nuclear weapons. By 2012, Iran faced sanctions that limited its oil exports and cut its access to the global financial system. Iran's President Mahmoud Ahmadinejad has been defiant toward the West and has repeatedly issued vituperative statements about Israel. After a rigged presidential re-election in June 2009, Iran's hardline clerical regime brutally suppressed a series of mass street demonstrations led by reformers, provoking widespread international condemnation.

The Arab Spring has also changed the geopolitical environment in some important ways:

- First, U.S. adversaries have suffered severe setbacks: Qaddafi's regime in Libya was overthrown with the help of NATO bombing; Iran is more isolated than ever before; and Bashir al-Assad's regime in Syria faces collapse in the face of armed rebellion.
- Second, two of the United States' close allies in the war against terrorism—the dictators in Egypt and Tunisia—have been replaced by elected governments dominated by Islamists from the Muslim Brotherhood.
- Third, conservative monarchies have survived the Arab Spring so far and are increasingly assertive in promoting the interests of Sunni Muslims, which may fuel more instability in Syria, Iraq, and Bahrain.
- Finally, some states seem to be breaking apart, opening the way for radical Islamism. The proliferation of militias in Syria, Libya, and Yemen, along with

a breakdown of central government authority, promises more sectarian conflict and humanitarian disasters that the international community will have to deal with.

THE ROOTS OF CONFLICT AND COOPERATION

Given the many injustices in Middle East history, it is no surprise that there are lingering grievances that contribute to recent conflicts. To understand why so much interstate and intrastate violence occurs, we will look primarily at political forces operating at the international and domestic levels. Of course, the MENA is not just one vast "arc of crisis"; many forms of interstate cooperation can be identified. By analyzing patterns and causes of both conflict and cooperation, we can better understand the prospects for growth and democracy.

Conventional wisdom holds that ancient hatreds—traceable to Biblical times, the Crusades, or the Sunni–Shi'a split in early Islam—are at the heart of conflicts. This "clash of civilizations" explanation of global problems—popularized by the late political scientist Samuel Huntington—is tempting to accept, especially when we look at the current war on terror. Although modern-day combatants frequently use imagery from holy texts to justify their struggle, we should be wary of using their worldviews as a basis for explaining conflict. It is more accurate to tie regional insecurity to three contemporary political factors: (1) the search by external powers for influence in the region; (2) aggression by regional leaders; and (3) oppressive regimes that foster Islamist violence.

Blaming the Outside World

Meddling by outside powers has often had terrible consequences. Slicing up territories or combining different ethnolinguistic and religious communities to create new states, the Great Powers ensured future strife. They and their allies have even acquired and/or used weapons of mass destruction or other proscribed weapons. Spain was the first country to use WMDs in the region. Sebastian Balfour, a professor of contemporary Spanish studies, has carefully documented Spain's extensive use of chemical weapons—mostly mustard gas—on rebels in Morocco's northern Rif region in the 1920s.[9] France in the late 1950s and early 1960s conducted seventeen nuclear tests in Algeria's Saharan desert during Paris's development of a nuclear weapons arsenal. It used napalm extensively against Algeria's *mujahideen* during the 1954–1962 War of Independence. Israel is the only country in the region that is known to possess nuclear weapons—perhaps 200–300—and a capacity to deliver them against regional enemies. Even the United States has been criticized for using depleted uranium ammunition and white phosphorus incendiary devices during its occupation of Iraq.

During the Cold War, the Soviet Union and the United States sponsored different political forces. Staunchly anti-Israeli regimes found the Soviets eager to sell them military equipment. On the other side, monarchs such as the King of Jordan and the Saudi royals looked to the United States for a security umbrella against pan-Arab socialist regimes. Turkey and Israel earned aid and weapons from Washington by touting their frontline role in the struggle against communism. Although Egypt under Anwar Sadat warmed up to the United States in the 1970s, Iran turned rabidly anti-American after the 1979 Islamic Revolution. Despite the prevalence of anti-Americanism today, the majority of regional governments have close military ties and/or friendly relations with Washington. Yet, Iran, Syria, Hizballah, and Hamas resist **"Pax Americana"**—a supposedly benevolent form of imperialism under which countries are expected to make peace with Israel, end terrorism, and host U.S. military bases (or at least cooperate with the United States on security issues).

Given the United States' deep military penetration of the MENA, most recently in Iraq, countries trying to defy the hegemon's interests face potentially heavy costs. For example, Arab states squandered billions of dollars in their unsuccessful wars against Israel. U.S. weapons and economic assistance to Israel for over forty years have helped ensure that there is no fundamental change in the Arab–Israeli balance of power. Between March and October 2011, NATO launched 9,700 air strikes against targets in Libya in a successful effort to help rebels overthrow the Qaddafi regime. Led by France and Britain (and with U.S. support), this extraordinary bombing campaign marked the first direct military intervention of Western powers in the unfolding Arab Spring.[10]

The United States and its allies have also imposed a variety of economic sanctions on MENA countries, including cutoffs of aid, freezing of assets, trade embargos, and prohibitions on Western investments. Ostensibly designed to foster regime change or "better behavior," these sanctions have usually ravaged vulnerable populations without achieving their political objectives. For example, the UN's punitive (and corrupt) **Oil for Food Program** allowed Iraq to export only a certain amount of oil after 1992, and the profits were to be used to import food and medicine. This program resulted in the deaths of hundreds of thousands of Iraqi civilians between 1991 and 2003, and many more suffered malnutrition, disease, and poor health. According to the philosopher Joy Gordon, who carefully studied the program, so terrible was the humanitarian disaster it caused that the acts of U.S. officials who designed and enforced it are "tantamount to war crimes" under international law.[11] Since 2006, the UN Security Council has imposed increasingly harsh sanctions on Iran, including a ban on arms exports to it, to try to get it to stop uranium enrichment. The United States and the European Union have gone much farther, cutting off Iran's banks from international financial institutions and embargoing Iran's oil exports. Iran's poorest citizens have borne the brunt of the pain: By 2012, hundreds of thousands had lost their jobs, prices of basic foodstuffs were rising quickly, and the value of the rial had plummeted.[12] Only Libya caved in to international sanctions in 2003, owning up to its involvement in the 1988 airplane bombing over Lockerbie, Scotland, and agreeing to dismantle its incipient nuclear weapons program.

Three different measures provide a clear indication of how many people in the Middle East blame outsiders for regional violence. First, conservative analyst Daniel Pipes argues that for decades there has been a widespread political culture of **conspiracism** in Iran and the Arab countries, wherein the "hidden hand" of the West or Israel is seen lurking behind all the region's wars and other ills. This mind-set, he asserts, encourages extremism and "engenders a suspiciousness and aggressiveness that spoil relations with the Great Powers."[13] Second, a discourse shared by some Muslim scholars chastises the West for its nefarious role in the region. For example, at a conference in Egypt in 2000, one prominent Muslim scholar characterized the West in these terms:

> Your globalization, oh you craven braggarts, is an arbitrary hegemony, a despotic authority, an oppressive injustice and a pitch-black darkness, because it is a globalization without religion and without conscience. It is a globalization of violent force, heedless partisanship, double standards, pervasive materialism, widespread racism, outrageous barbarism and arrogant egoism. It is a globalization that sells illusions, leading to perdition and to burying dreams in the depth of nowhere, spreading flowers over the corpses of the hungry.[14]

Finally, public opinion polls reveal a high level of fear of the United States, *even among its Middle East allies*. A Pew Research Center survey in 2009 found that 50 percent of all respondents in Turkey, Lebanon, and Jordan were somewhat, or very, worried that the United States might pose a military threat to their country.[15] Another Pew survey in Spring 2012 revealed that more than 80 percent of Turks, Egyptians, and Jordanians opposed U.S. drone strikes and viewed the United States unfavorably.[16]

Blaming "Aggressive" Regional Powers

The use of terms such as the "Mad Mullahs" (Iran's Shi'ite clerics), the "Butcher of Baghdad" (Saddam Hussein), and the "Mad Dog of the Middle East" (Muammar Qaddafi) implies that these "brutal" or "irrational" leaders were responsible for sparking conflict. Although demonizing Middle East leaders is not good social science, it is clear that aggression by regional powers has been as important a source of insecurity as superpower meddling or transnational terrorism. Aggression takes many forms, including territorial grabs, punitive strikes, threats of invasion, and covert operations against neighbors. These acts may be designed to destabilize political rivals, expand a country's territory, or solidify control over strategic natural resources.

For example, Saddam Hussein's opportunistic 1980 invasion of Iran sparked a terrible eight-year war during which Iraq used chemical weapons against Iranian troops. Iraq's 1990 occupation of Kuwait—partly due to its long-standing desire to gain ports on the Persian Gulf and dominate oil production—prompted a multinational counterattack led by 500,000 U.S. troops. On the other side of the Arab world, Morocco's 1975 takeover of the large but sparsely populated Western Sahara stemmed in part from King Hassan II's desire to boost his domestic legitimacy and control the territory's valuable phosphates and Atlantic fisheries.

When the Shah of Iran was overthrown in 1979, the successor regime under Ayatollah Ruhollah Khomeini sought to spread Islamic revolution by fomenting unrest in Arab Gulf states, supporting Hizballah in Lebanon, and sponsoring terrorist acts in the 1980s and 1990s. Hostile relations with the United States reached a new low in 2002 when President Bush named Iran as part of an "Axis of Evil" along with Iraq and North Korea. During the occupation of Iraq from 2003 to

2011, the U.S. government accused Iran of providing material support to Iraqi insurgents and Shi'ite militias.

Since at least 2008, the threat of violent conflict between Iran, Israel, and the United States has hung over the region. Some scholars argue that Iranian militarism and defiance of international norms are at the heart of the conflict. Iran's development of nuclear energy, ballistic missiles, and uranium enrichment capacity suggests that it is putting together the pieces of a nuclear weapons program. Tehran has repeatedly impeded the work of the International Atomic Energy Agency and refused to agree to UN Security Council demands that, among other things, it halt uranium enrichment. In addition, Iran has threatened Israel and suggested that, if attacked, it would close the Strait of Hormuz—through which a major portion of the world's oil transits.

While most Americans do not perceive Israel as an aggressor, Arabs have long portrayed it as a power intent on territorial expansion at the expense of Palestinians and surrounding countries. Under British tutelage from 1917 to 1948, Palestine witnessed a mass influx of Jewish immigrants who fundamentally changed the demography of the mandate. During its war of independence, Israel fought against invading Arab armies and encouraged or forced some 700,000 Palestinians to flee, gaining control of 78 percent of the mandate's territory—much more than allotted to it under a UN partition plan. Israel's military superiority was proven in the 1967 Six-Day War when the Jewish state seized control of the rest of Palestine (the West Bank and Gaza), Egypt's Sinai Peninsula, and Syria's Golan Heights. It rebuffed an invasion by Egypt and Syria in 1973 but signed a peace treaty with Egypt in 1979. In 1981, it destroyed a nearly complete nuclear reactor in Iraq. No sooner had it withdrawn from the Sinai in 1982 than it invaded Lebanon, occupying the southern part until 2000. It briefly re-invaded and heavily bombed Lebanon in 2006 during a month-long war in which Hizballah launched hundreds of missiles into northern Israel. In 2005, Israel withdrew from the Gaza Strip, but in the face of Hamas rocket attacks it re-invaded the Strip from December 27, 2008, to January 18, 2009. A UN fact-finding commission in September 2009 issued a report (dubbed the Goldstone Report) on the Gaza conflict, accusing Israeli forces and Hamas of committing war crimes—and possibly even crimes against humanity.[17]

While continuing to occupy the Golan Heights, Israel has durable peace treaties with Egypt and Jordan. Its threats since 2009 to take military action against Iran convince some critics that its alleged penchant for interstate adventurism and militarism is alive and well. In contrast, Israeli leaders have consistently justified their military engagements on the basis of their inherent right of self-defense. Before the Oslo Accords, Israel faced many acts of terrorism from groups associated with the Palestine Liberation Organization. In the first half of the 2000s, a horrific series of terrorist attacks and suicide bombings drove Israel to start building a 450-mile long defensive wall/barrier along its border with the West Bank.

Israeli policies toward Palestinians provide the most persuasive evidence that Zionist expansionism is hindering conflict resolution. Israeli leaders have sanctioned the long-term occupation and transformation of Palestinian territories seized in 1967. By 2012, Israel had settled more than 500,000 Jews in the West Bank and East Jerusalem. Whatever the security or religious justifications offered by the Jewish state, its relentless settlement expansion is a violation of international law. Even the Obama administration has pressured Israel—without success—to cease building or expanding settlements, calling them an obstacle to peace.

Sociologist Lisa Hajjar has studied the impact of the Israeli military court system in the Palestinian Occupied Territories.[18] She finds a system of military rule and military "justice" that has regulated the movements of Palestinians and subjected inhabitants to arrest, detention, and humiliation. Since 1967, the military courts have prosecuted more than 500,000 of the 3.5 million Palestinians in the West Bank and Gaza. The reality is one of constant surveillance and constant disruption of normal life. Perceiving themselves as subjected to apartheid-like conditions and slow-motion ethnic cleansing, Palestinians have stiffened their resistance, some of which turned violent as during the *intifadas* (uprisings) in 1987–1991 and 2000–2005.

The West Bank and Gaza for over a decade have experienced economic distress, largely as a result of deliberate Israeli policies to isolate the territories from international trade and prevent Palestinians from working in Israel. Political economist Sara Roy has meticulously analyzed the horrendous economic and social conditions for Palestinians caused by Israel's policy of imposing curfews and travel bans, expropriating land, destroying civilian infrastructure, and uprooting tens of thousands of olive and citrus trees.[19] Israel insists that its punitive actions are triggered by Palestinian terrorism and rejection of compromise. An Israeli blockade of the Hamas-controlled Gaza Strip after 2006, coupled with the Israeli military offensive there in December 2008 and January 2009, has triggered a human crisis in which two-thirds of the population live in poverty.

If one agrees that the Israeli–Palestinian conflict is rooted in incompatible claims of Zionists and Palestinian nationalists to the same territory, its resolution requires the creation of two states alongside each other and mutual recognition of each side's sovereignty. A two-state solution was expected to result from the peace process that Israel and the Palestine Liberation Organization began with the Oslo Accords in 1993. Yet many now argue that a viable Palestinian state is impossible to create if Israel refuses to withdraw settlers, end its occupation, and allow a Palestinian state to control its own water, borders, and airspace.

Blaming Oppression (and Islamist Resistance to It)

Regional conflicts are also fueled by cycles of oppression–terrorism–counterinsurgency within states. Leading participants in these terrible cycles are often dominant ethnolinguistic and religious groups who subjugate weaker groups and minorities and who try to justify their own violence via "myths" that serve as little more than cover stories for the pursuit of self-interest.

For years, secular Arab regimes had claimed that they were fighting retrograde Islamic fundamentalists and terrorists, but when the Arab Spring started it was really mass demands for fair treatment and freedom that they were trying to crush. Ahmed Hashim, a former U.S. adviser to General John Abizaid in Iraq, in 2005 observed that ethnosectarian hatred had grown in Iraq, with Sunnis viewing Shi'a as "primitive and childlike," Kurds holding contempt for non-Kurds, and Shi'a seeing Sunnis as oppressors and Kurds as "arrogant backstabbers."[20] Manichean views such as these do not explain the politics of oppression and resistance at the heart of struggles. Historically, violence has been used by movements seeking independence from colonial rule or outsiders. Noting international norms of self-determination, Kurds, Sahrawis, and Palestinians have struggled for sovereignty (or at least autonomy) over a given territory in which they are currently facing political oppression. Hamas and Hizballah also utilize violence in pursuit of political goals linked to explicit conceptions of liberation. Interpreting these groups as simply using terrorism for terrorism's sake or attacking foreign occupiers because they "hate our freedoms" is a convenient way of ignoring or discounting their stated goals. As sociologist Charles Tilly notes, "Properly understood, terror is a strategy, not a creed."[21]

Some Islamists claim that they are fighting governing elites whose cultural beliefs reflect **"Westoxication"**—a seduction to poisonous, imported Western culture and institutions. Others seek the right to implement conservative social policies they claim are based on Islamic law. Shi'ites in Iraq and Lebanon (and to some extent in the Arabian Peninsula), seeking to reverse decades of Sunni (or Maronite Christian) discrimination, are claiming political power commensurate with their size of the population. Whether governments and occupying powers call their opponents "terrorists," or whether nationalist insurgents and *mujahideen* call their opponents "state terrorists," the fact is that all these combatants mostly injure and kill innocent civilians, not other armed fighters.

Extremist Islamic movements and terrorist groups use religion as a political tool, even if reasonable people agree that they misinterpret Islam. Historically, civil wars involving religious extremists in Lebanon (1975–1990), Algeria (1992–2000), Iraq (2003–2011), and Syria (since 2011) have caused enormous damage, population displacement, and loss of life. Rising unemployment and inequality after the 1970s pushed many poor Muslims to become foot soldiers. In contrast, the leaders of these radical movements often are well educated (many have science and engineering backgrounds) and from the middle class, suggesting that they feel unfairly excluded from the ruling elite.

At another level of analysis, we can see these groups as reflecting a change of ideas within the Muslim world. In the last thirty years, militant Islamist movements have spread a puritanical interpretation of Islam with emphasis on jihadist rhetoric and the application of Islamic law. Why has radicalism spread and attracted adherents? One reason is that millions of Arabs who since the 1970s have migrated (often temporarily) to work in the conservative, oil-rich Gulf states have been exposed there to a more "fundamentalist" perspective on Islam. Second, Gulf regimes and wealthy Gulf citizens have funded *madrasas* (Muslim schools) and charities throughout the Muslim world that have sometimes taught a chauvinistic form of Islam. Third, globalization empowers not just liberal, peaceful movements but their antithesis as well. Extremists are in some ways a reaction to the perceived humiliation of their countries by the Americans, Europeans, and Israelis.

Nevertheless, the MENA is hardly the only region in the world where political groups instrumentalize religion. In Pakistan, Somalia, and Afghanistan, groups claiming to act in the name of their religion or ethnicity have also caused horrible conflict. According to the U.S. National Counterterrorism Center, in the fifteen countries in the world with the most terrorist attacks in 2011, only 27 percent of the attacks occurred in the Middle East.[22] However, in 2011 Iraq alone accounted for one-fourth of all of the world's deaths from terrorist incidents, according to the NCTC.

Cooperation at the Interstate Level

Despite insecurity in some countries, most of the MENA's citizens do *not* face violence daily. In fact, few countries have high crime rates (although domestic violence against women and children remains a big problem). And from 1970 to 2010 there was political stability: only one dictator (Iran's Shah) was overthrown by his own people, and only one regime (in Iraq) was overthrown by an outside power.[23] In the last twenty years there has *not* been widespread political violence in the Gulf Cooperation Council (except Bahrain), Turkey (except Kurdish regions), Iran, or Morocco. The Arab Spring has brought unprecedented demonstrations, but the only places where it has led to thousands of people killed and injured are Libya and Syria. Nevertheless, it is important to remember that terrible insecurity also results from having to flee from one's home. According to the United Nations High Commissioner for Refugees, three million Iraqis are internally displaced or living as refugees in neighboring countries. By January 2013 almost one million Syrians had fled their country.

Drowned out by media coverage of regional conflicts are the many enduring forms of state-to-state cooperation in the MENA and positive relations with Western powers. Almost all the countries in the Middle East have at some time benefited from their security relationship with the United States. In 1787, Morocco and the United States signed a Treaty of Friendship and Amity that is still in force today and that constitutes the longest unbroken treaty between the United States and another country. President Woodrow Wilson supported self-determination for states after World War I, and the United States helped liberate North Africa from fascism in World War II. The United States supported Algerian independence from France, helped Israel defend itself during wars, and liberated Kuwait (with EU support) from Saddam Hussein's occupation.

NATO has undoubtedly secured Turkey, one of its founding members. Since the mid-1990s, the European Union has promoted formal security cooperation with southern Mediterranean countries. In the aftermath of the 2006 Israel–Hizballah War, France and Italy took the lead in contributing troops to a robust UN peacekeeping force in Lebanon. France, Britain, and the United States were joined by Qatar, Turkey, and the UAE in helping Libyan rebels thwart Qaddafi's effort to crush them.

Cooperation among Middle Eastern states is not yet well institutionalized, largely owing to historical rivalries. The Arab League, headquartered in Cairo, represents so many different countries with competing interests that it cannot easily act in concert on major issues. However, in the 2000s it twice offered Israel a comprehensive peace plan to end the Arab-Israeli conflict. It endorsed NATO's involvement in Libya. It has played an active role in Syria since 2011, proposing a peace plan and later rallying international support to remove Bashir al-Assad from power. The Gulf Cooperation Council has probably been the most successful regional organization, coordinating trade and security policies. It deployed troops to Bahrain in 2011 to prop up the Sunni monarchy against a Shi'ite-dominated uprising.

Cooperation at the Human Level

Some of the most robust cooperation occurs within cross-national human networks. On an individual level, emigration and dual citizenship tie the United States and Europe more closely to the Middle East than many observers realize. The U.S. Census Bureau estimates that in 2010 the U.S. foreign-born population included more than 356,000 Iranians, 137,000 Egyptians, 127,000 Israelis, 121,000 Lebanese, and 106,000 Turks.[24] According to Philippe Fargues, a leading French demographer, more than eight million first-generation immigrants from the Arab countries and Turkey are living in Europe, including five million North Africans and three million Turks.[25] For example, an estimated 738,000 Moroccans live in Spain and 1.1 million Algerians live in France. In France, approximately 8 to 10 percent of the population is Muslim, the majority of whom are from North Africa. Many immigrants came to Europe as temporary "guest workers" in the 1950s through the 1970s but stayed and raised families. As is the case in the United States, many immigrants remain connected to their home countries through extended family ties and remittances (see the next section).

Many American citizens live and work in the Middle East, and many Middle Easterners who have become naturalized U.S. citizens retain citizenship in their country of birth. As late as September 2009, more than 124,000 U.S. troops, at least 31,000 U.S. citizens working for private contractors, and 1,000 embassy personnel were present in Iraq. (Conversely, the United States has admitted more than 80,000 Iraqi refugees into the United States since 2007.) In early 2012, there were an estimated 35,000 to 40,000 U.S. troops deployed in the Persian Gulf region, largely with the approval of Arab governments. When war broke out between Israel and Hizballah in July 2006, there were more than 25,000 Americans living in Lebanon. American forces evacuated 15,000 of these scared and displaced Americans, many of whom are dual citizens. At least 160,000 American Jews live in Israel, most of whom have gained Israeli citizenship under the Law of Return (which grants citizenship to Jews from anywhere in the world who settle in Israel). For an examination of how education ties together citizens of the West and the Middle East, see the box "International Education and the Middle East."

▶ INTERNATIONAL EDUCATION AND THE MIDDLE EAST

Having citizens knowledgeable about other regions' languages and cultures is what political scientist Joseph Nye considers a source of a hegemon's "soft" power (see Chapter 9). For a region as important to the United States as the Middle East, it is surprising that so few Americans learn its primary languages—Arabic, Farsi, and Turkish—or study abroad there. In 2009, approximately 35,000 U.S. college students were taking Arabic courses—triple the number since 2002—but they represented only 2 percent of all

(continued)

students taking foreign language classes.[a] The second Bush administration significantly increased funds to train intelligence agents and military personnel in "strategic" foreign languages, but many of those government employees who study a critical Middle East language do not gain fluency or working proficiency.

Studying abroad is another way to increase cultural understanding. Although the number of U.S. students studying in the Middle East steadily increased after 9/11, the overall number of Americans choosing to learn about the region firsthand is low. In the 2009–2010 school year, only 9,803 participated in a study-abroad program in the Middle East and North Africa—just 3.6 percent of the nearly 270,604 U.S. students who studied overseas that year, mostly in Europe and Latin America.[b]

The United States—like Europe—has for decades attracted many of the best-educated Middle Easterners to study in its universities. Many of these students stay in the United States after their undergraduate or graduate training, contributing to the U.S. economy. International political and economic trends dramatically affect which countries in the Middle East send how many students to the United States. At the height of the second oil boom in the early 1980s, Middle East oil exporters flooded U.S. schools with students pursuing scientific and technical degrees (and English-language proficiency). By contrast, 9/11 caused a short-term decline in the number of Arabs studying in the United States, many of whom felt unwelcome or had trouble getting visas. In 2005, there were only 3,000 Saudis studying in the United States, an example of how U.S. security policies conflict with other U.S. interests. But what a difference a few years and a lot of oil revenues make: in the 2011–2012 school year there were 34,139 Saudis studying in the United States—more than the number of Canadians. There were also 11,973 Turkish students, bringing the total number of students from the Middle East to about 74,000.[c]

Many Middle Easterners return home with their U.S. or European degrees, taking up important positions in the government and the business community. Europe and the United States hope that some of these individuals will become secular surrogates for the West. Tunisia's president Moncef Marzouki studied medicine at the University of Strasbourg in France. Egypt's president Mohamed Morsi has a Ph.D. in engineering from the University of Southern California. And the Emir of Qatar, Sheikh Hamad bin Khalifa Al-Thani, attended England's Sandhurst Military Academy. In addition, U.S.-style, English-language universities are popping up like mushrooms in the region. This new trend derives from the desire to modernize higher education and the need to have citizens master language and technical skills that are vital to participating in the global economy. In addition, dozens of Western universities have set up branch campuses in Arab countries or entered into cooperative agreements with Middle Eastern institutions of higher education. All of these educational ties have the potential to foster long-term cooperation and understanding between the West and the Middle East.

References

[a]Nelly Furman, David Goldberg, and Natalia Lusin, "Enrollments in Languages Other Than English in United States Institutions of Higher Education, Fall 2009," December 2010, http://www.mla.org/pdf/2009_enrollment_survey.pdf.

[b]Calculated from data in Institute of International Education, "Host Regions and Destinations of U.S. Study Abroad Students, 2008/09 – 2009/10." Open Doors Report on International Educational Exchange, 2011, http://www.iie.org/opendoors.

[c]See Institute for International Education, *Open Doors 2012 "Fast Facts,"* November 2012, at http://www.iie.org/Research-and-Publications/Open-Doors/Data/Fast-Facts.

FACING THE GLOBAL ECONOMY: INTEGRATION OR MARGINALIZATION?

There is a significant debate among scholars about whether the MENA is "keeping up" with globalization or "falling behind" the rest of the world. In this section, we discuss two different hypotheses about economic processes in the region. The first suggests that the MENA is successfully integrating itself into the global economy and preparing for a sustainable future. The second asserts that the region is becoming increasingly uncompetitive and marginal, failing to switch to high-growth economies that can resolve sociocultural problems. As will become evident, the MENA is a very diverse region with many kinds of ties to the global economy.

Oil, Industry, and Growth

Growth in many parts of the MENA is tied to hydrocarbons. The years 1973–1984 were a golden age for oil exporters that raised incomes dramatically. Adjusted for inflation, oil prices from 1985 to 1999 fell into a slump, lowering growth rates throughout the region. But since 2000, prices have recovered nicely as a result of OPEC oil production cuts and rising demand from China. At the end of 2012, the price of OPEC oil was $108 a barrel. According to the World Bank, growth in the MENA (not including Turkey and Israel) averaged 5.1 percent from 2000 to 2007, one of the best spurts since the late 1970s. Despite the global financial crisis, growth from 2009 to 2010 in Iran and the Arab countries (not including Iraq, Libya, the Palestinian Territories, Qatar, and the UAE) averaged almost 3.5 percent. The turnaround in oil and gas revenues, which could last for many years, allows many countries to rebuild infrastructure and boost employment.

Saudi Arabia has taken advantage of its abundant hydrocarbons to expand into energy-intensive industries that benefit from subsidized domestic oil. The country has become an exporter of cement, steel, and, especially, petrochemicals that China is gobbling up. Moreover, the Middle East in 2011 supplied 22 percent of the United States' crude oil needs, 51 percent of China's, and 87 percent of Japan's, making it vital to the global economy.

Some non–oil exporters seem to be finding their own successful growth models based on a variety of paths. For example, in the space of less than twenty years, Dubai has transformed itself from a desert backwater into a transportation, financial, and tourist hub (see Dubai: The Las Vegas of Arabia). Tunisia has adopted an export-oriented strategy that looks as if it were borrowed from Asia. Turkey, Tunisia, Morocco, and Egypt have world-class tourism sectors. The financial crisis did not result in dire consequences for non–oil exporters because they have relatively low levels of foreign debt and were not exposed to the U.S. subprime market. However, they have fared much worse since the Arab Spring due to diminished exports, a plunge in tourism, and a loss of foreign direct investment. In 2011, GDP suffered negative growth in Egypt, Tunisia, Yemen, and

Syria, according to the World Bank.[26] In 2012, average growth of GDP in non-oil exporters was a sluggish 2.5 percent, partly due to the effects of the Euro zone crisis on exports.[27] There is a real danger that continued instability will hamper economic recovery.

DUBAI: THE LAS VEGAS OF ARABIA

Two generations ago, Damascus and Cairo were the "happening" places in the Middle East in terms of political ferment, economic dynamism, and cultural attraction. A generation ago, Beirut, the so-called "Paris of the Middle East," was the place to go for tourism and trade. Now the most dynamic city-state in the entire Middle East is Dubai, a small desert patch on the conservative Arabian Peninsula. It is a wheeler-dealer's kind of place, open to big ambitions and grandiose schemes. How did this backwater become a fast-growing financial, trade, and tourism hub in just three decades?

Dubai is one of seven sheikdoms that make up the loosely federated United Arab Emirates (UAE). It has a coastline only 45 miles long. Before the UAE's independence in 1971, Dubai City was a sleepy town known for pearl diving that was connected to a surrounding Bedouin population. Oil was discovered in the 1960s, and the emir at the time—Sheikh Rashid bin Said al Maktoum—invested proceeds in an international airport and dredged the main harbor for international shipping.[a] He encouraged investment in high-rises and hotels and established a modern telephone system. His sons—part of the ruling Maktoum family—have invested government funds heavily in basic infrastructure. Realizing that limited oil supplies would soon diminish, they set up free-trade zones, established incentives for international container business, and made sure there were no income or corporate taxes. Theirs has been a vision of a global *entrepôt,* attracting business from any company in the world.

Openness to the world has been only part of the city-state's recipe for fast growth. Equally important has been the Maktoum family's own

private investments throughout the emirates and their strong reliance on state ownership. As one author has noted, "Dubai is a leading case study in successful state capitalism....[The Maktoum family's] city state has been aptly described as a family conglomerate run by Sheik Mohammed as ruler and CEO. He is the visionary behind the leading enterprises in Dubai, including investment, media and hotel companies, as well as Emirates Air."[b]

The results on the ground stagger the imagination. The sheikhdom headquarters Al Arabiyya, a satellite TV network that is a strong rival of Al-Jazeera for the Arab news market.[c] It has two of the largest shopping malls in the world, two indoor ski slopes, and Burj Dubai, the tallest building in the world (which is twice as tall as the Empire State building). At least two large real estate developments are being built on huge artificial islands off the coast; one—called The World—consists of "several hundred man-made islands representing regions of the world in their respective continental groups. There are to be private-estate islands, resort islands, [and] community islands."[d] Despite a population of only two million people (mostly expatriates), there were 9.3 million visitors in 2012. In addition, Dubai is building the $8 billion Al Maktoum International Airport, which will supposedly become the biggest passenger and cargo airline hub in the world.

In Dubai, we see the conflation of mercantilist, liberalist, and structuralist forces.[e] The state has made growth possible through its investments and policies. The international market has swarmed in to take advantage of the city-state's deregulated, Las Vegas–style economy. But the whole edifice, a structuralist would point out, rests on exploitation of hundreds of thousands of poor Asian workers and thousands of prostitutes with no unions or political rights. Like the real Las Vegas, Dubai has been hard hit by the global financial crisis since 2007. Real estate prices crashed, construction slowed or stopped on many big projects, many laborers left, tourism dropped, and the city-state was saddled with debt. Dubai's risky marriage with globalization now seems to be on the rocks.

References

[a]Jeremy Smith, "Dubai Builds Big," *World Trade*, April 2005, p. 58.

[b]William Underhill, "The Wings of Dubai Inc.," *Newsweek*, April 17, 2006, p. 34.

[c]Lee Smith, "The Road to Tech Mecca," *Wired*, July 2004.

[d]Tosches, "Dubai's the Limit," *Vanity Fair*, June 2006.

[e]For an overview of the keys to Dubai's success, see Martin Hvidt, "The Dubai Model: An Outline of Key Development-Process Elements in Dubai," *International Journal of Middle East Studies* 41: 3 (August 2009), pp. 397–418.

Israel and Turkey are standout cases, more globalized than other MENA countries. Israel has transformed itself into a diversified economy exporting mostly high-technology products, including advanced weaponry. Since the U.S. technology boom in the 1990s, more than 100 Israeli companies have raised significant capital by listing on the New York Stock Exchange. Some Israel-based companies are global players. For example, Teva is the largest generic drug manufacturer in the world. And Israel's Strauss Group, in partnership with PepsiCo, produces the hugely popular Sabra Hummus brand. Israel has some of the highest numbers of engineers, scientists, and patent holders per capita of any country in the world. In their popular book *Start-up Nation*, Dan Senor and Saul Singer attribute Israel's economic dynamism to factors such as immigration policies, a unique combination of individualism and egalitarianism, and the effects of military service.[28]

Turkey's economy has performed remarkably since 2002, with GDP growing at over 5 percent per year on average. Under Prime Minister Recep Tayyip Erdogan, Turkish companies have invested heavily in the Middle East and Central Asia in construction and transportation. They are major exporters to Europe of manufactured goods like home appliances, televisions, clothing, and steel. More than thirty-one million tourists visited Turkey in 2011—eleven million of whom came from Germany, Russia, and the UK—generating revenues of $24 billion. Turkey's leading political economist, Ziya Öniş, describes Turkey's current development phase as "regulatory neo-liberalism," whereby a popular ruling party, the Justice and Development Party, enforces macroeconomic reforms like privatization of state enterprises, grants power to independent state agencies, welcomes foreign investment, and prods big Turkish companies to transnationalize (expand markets overseas and partner with foreign multinationals).[29] He notes that Turkey weathered the financial crisis without having to turn to the European Union or the IMF. Its advantages as an "emerging tiger" include its "young population, geopolitical position, level of entrepreneurship, and the quality of human capital." But he argues that a "deepening of liberal democracy" is necessary for sustained growth in the future.

Trade and Investment with the World

MENA countries are being integrated into the global economy through the World Trade Organization and various free-trade agreements. Collectively, their most important trade and investment partner by far is the European Union. Beginning in 1995, the European Union flexed its soft power by offering Arab Mediterranean countries more market access, billions of dollars of aid, and billions of dollars of loans from the European Investment Bank. China, Japan, India, and the United States are also important trade partners of the MENA. The United States has signed bilateral free-trade agreements with five close MENA allies, including Jordan and Morocco. The region is a major importer of U.S. machinery, aircraft, cars, grain, and engineering services. Since 2001, it has become a boom market for companies like Microsoft, Cisco, Bechtel, Boeing, and General Electric that have garnered contracts to supply, build, and operate many new infrastructure projects. However, the combined effects of the Euro zone crisis, the global financial crisis, and the Arab Spring have caused net foreign direct investments in the MENA to decline by more than 50 percent—from $30 billion in 2008 to just $14 billion in 2012.[30]

The Middle East is also a major importer of weapons from the United States, Europe, and Russia. From 1996 to 2003, U.S. arms sales agreements with Middle Eastern countries totaled $35 billion. From 2004 to 2008, the United States supplied more than 50 percent of the conventional weapons bought by Middle East regimes. In 2011, the United States agreed to sell Saudi Arabia 154 fighter aircraft worth $30 billion. Marxist economists Jonathon Nitzan and Shimshon Bichler have argued that U.S. arms sellers (the "Arma-Core") have a common interest with U.S. oil companies (the "Petro-Core") in the periodic outbreak of wars in the Middle East, because the resulting hike in oil prices after conflicts boosts their profitability.[31] In other words, when conflicts cause oil prices to rise, Middle Eastern countries almost inevitably use the windfalls to buy more weapons. That is good for trade, but not necessarily for MENA growth.

Middle East oil exporters recycle some profits back to oil-consuming countries in the form of investments in stock markets, purchases of real estate, and deposits in Western banks. This **petrodollar recycling**, first witnessed in the 1970s (see Chapter 8), jumped into high gear again after 2000, tying the economic fortunes of some MENA countries closely to the international financial system. Dubai Ports World, a Dubai-based company that manages port facilities around the world, is an example of the greater role of the Middle East in overseas services. Many Middle East investments come from **sovereign wealth funds** (**SWFs**), which are large investment pools controlled by the governments of resource-rich countries. In 2012, the SWFs of Abu Dhabi, Saudi Arabia, Kuwait, and Qatar controlled global assets worth an estimated $1.6 trillion. Qatar's SWF, for example, owns London's The Shard, the tallest building in Europe. When the financial crisis hit in 2007, MENA SWFs poured tens of billions of dollars into Western banks and companies. They purchased Barney's New York and bought large equity stakes in Daimler (maker of Mercedes cars), Volkswagen, Barclays Bank, Merrill Lynch, Citigroup, and New York's Chrysler Building. The liquidity was badly needed, but some U.S. and EU politicians—already concerned about dependence on OPEC oil—worried that MENA governments would use the SWFs to gain political leverage over their countries and potentially threaten national security.

Remittances—money transferred by foreign workers to their home countries—also strongly integrate people in Europe and the Middle East. Countries in North Africa rely on billions of dollars of annual remittances from workers in Europe to help with their balance of payments and to supplement the incomes of the poor. Since the 1960s, Turkish workers in Europe have remitted at least $75 billion back to Turkey, providing financial security to many families. Egyptians in Europe, the Arab countries, and North America sent $14 billion back to Egypt in 2011 and $18 billion in 2012. Lebanon received $7.5 billion from expatriates in 2011, equivalent to a staggering 20 percent of its GDP. Without remittances, labor-exporting countries would have significantly worse current account deficits.

Globalization in the Gulf Cooperation Council

The six countries in the **Gulf Cooperation Council (GCC)**—Saudi Arabia, the United Arab Emirates, Kuwait, Oman, Bahrain, and Qatar—are deeply integrated into the global economy not just through oil exports and SWFs but also via their labor markets. Alongside the indigenous population are expatriate (foreign) workers who make up more than 70 percent of the entire workforce in these six countries and nearly half of the 47 million people living there in 2011.

Where do the expatriates come from? During the 1970s oil boom, three-fourths of immigrant workers came from fellow Arab countries. By 2004, only one-third of foreign workers were Arabs, joined by a growing number of Indians, Pakistanis, Bangladeshis, Filipinos, and other Asians. However, the post–2000 oil boom has increased demand for more Arab workers.

Although the GCC benefits from the skills and low labor costs of its internationalized workforce, the region's ruling families are increasingly worried about the political and cultural dangers from heavy reliance on foreigners. Expatriate grievances have provoked some strikes and unrest. Asian women who work as nannies and domestic helpers often complain of physical and sexual abuse by employers. Gulf leaders worry that children raised by Asian nannies and taught by foreigners will lose their Arab and Islamic identity. They are also concerned about the large number of illegal aliens and "stateless" residents who are politically loyal to foreign countries.

Non–GCC countries are also turning to expatriate labor, which can usually be taken advantage of more easily than domestic workers. According to an extensive investigation by the U.S.-based National Labor Committee (NLC), tens of thousands of guest workers from Bangladesh, China, and India are working in Jordanian textile factories that export garments duty-free to the United States.[32] Many of these (often Asian-owned) companies, in which workers are frequently exploited in sweatshop conditions that the NLC asserts constitute forced labor, supply Wal-Mart, Target, L.L. Bean, and other U.S. retailers. Jordan, like its GCC neighbors, has found that importing Asian workers (especially Chinese) fuels export growth. Algeria now has more than 40,000 Chinese workers—almost half of all foreigners in the country—building highways, railroads, and public housing. In May 2012, a Chinese construction company in Algiers started work on what will be the third largest mosque in the world—able to hold 120,000 worshippers! The presence of so many non-national, non-unionized workers may be hampering the development of a powerful labor movement within civil society. Expatriate workers have also suffered from the disorder of the Arab Spring: in Libya, more than half a million of them—mostly Tunisians and Egyptians—had to flee.

The Falling Behind Thesis

Despite the MENA's seemingly successful integration into the global economy, there is a powerful counterargument that it is falling behind other modernizing countries and failing to move up in the global hierarchy. Many countries' economies are still dominated by inefficient state-owned enterprises and unprofitable public banks. Periodic conflict and lack of industrial dynamism have stunted foreign investment. In a powerful analysis of these problems, a team of Arab social scientists published the *Arab Human Development Report 2002*, which identified the Arab MENA as suffering a gap with the rest of the world in terms of knowledge, freedom, and women's empowerment.[33] More recently, UN-Habitat identified problems compounded by rapid urbanization, including lack of adequate housing and serious water scarcity. Neglect of agriculture means that half of the MENA's caloric needs are met by imported food, making it vulnerable to rising global food prices.[34]

The Challenge of the Historical Legacy

Some of the region's inheritance from the past seems to be hampering its adaptation to globalization. As mentioned earlier, colonial powers left many unfortunate legacies. Some states' overdependence on a single, exported commodity, such as oil, cotton, or phosphates, slowed economic diversification. Colonial regulations stifled educational opportunities and growth of an indigenous private sector.

After independence, many countries adopted development policies that were beneficial in the short term but that eventually, by the 1980s, had outlived their usefulness. Agrarian reform and land redistribution lowered agricultural productivity. High tariff barriers protected inefficient domestic companies. Government subsidies, price controls, and overvalued currencies all contributed to a misallocation of resources. Nevertheless, Middle East growth rates in the 1950s and 1960s were quite remarkable in countries such as Israel, Syria, and Iran, and most countries dramatically increased literacy and access to health care. The 1970s witnessed another growth spurt fueled by oil revenues.

Development troubles came to a head in the early 1980s, when neoliberalism and economic reform began sweeping through many parts of the world. From 1980 to 2000, per-capita GDP in the MENA (excluding Israel and Turkey) *failed to grow at all*, while in East Asia during the same period it expanded at an annual rate of 4.1 percent.[35] The wave of Western private investment spreading to Latin America and Asia simply bypassed the region. When was the last time you read about a U.S. company outsourcing to the Middle East? When oil prices began to tumble in 1983, countries had trouble servicing their foreign debt.

Beginning in 2002, the recovery in crude oil prices (adjusted for inflation) helped many economies grow. However, gains in per-capita GDP before the financial crisis are now threatened by the Arab Spring. Growth of GDP per capita slowed after 2008 and turned negative in 2011 and 2012. In 2012, the youth unemployment rate in the MENA was 28 percent. In 2012, the overall unemployment rates in North Africa and Middle East were 10.3 percent and 11.1 percent, respectively, higher than in any other region of the world, according to the International Labour Organization.[36] One can expect that newly elected governments in places like Egypt and Tunisia will have a very difficult time trying to improve the economic conditions of society's most vulnerable.

As of mid-2012, only a handful of countries in the world had yet to join the World Trade Organization, and a surprisingly large number are in the MENA: Algeria, Iran, Iraq, Yemen, Syria, Sudan, Libya, and Lebanon. As a whole, the region also has high average tariff levels. This indicates that many regimes are reluctant to adjust rapidly to international trade rules. The MENA has not significantly diversified its exports. Eighty percent of its exports to the United States consist of oil, gas, and minerals. Although trade openness can bring long-term benefits, the short-term consequences are politically unpalatable. Many Arab businesses—especially in textiles and consumer goods—will not be able to compete with European or Chinese imports.

Surprisingly little trade occurs *between* MENA countries (although the GCC countries have become major investors in other parts of the Arab world). Arab countries' main exports are to the industrialized countries, and the main products they need to import are not produced regionally. Regional integration will remain a hostage to war and historical grievances, forcing countries to look for commercial opportunities with the West and China rather than in their own backyard.

Societal Problems

It has become increasingly fashionable to blame sociocultural factors such as underutilization of female human capital for the Middle East's catching-up problems. Few countries in the world have as dismal a record of female employment as the Arab Gulf countries, where women with citizenship constitute less than 10 percent of the total workforce. Even large countries such as Algeria and Iran have comparatively low female employment rates. In 2012, although three-fourths of MENA men participated in the labor force, less than one-fourth of women did.

It is inaccurate, however, to say that the Middle East lacks a culture of entrepreneurship. Economic dynamism in the private sector is particularly strong in Israel, Lebanon, Turkey, and Morocco. This may be due in part to the fact that large emigrant communities from these countries are present in many parts of the world, forging strong trade and investment links with partners "back home."

The worst economies in the region are Yemen and the Gaza Strip. They will be hard-pressed to recover anytime soon from the tribulations of war and endemic poverty. Yemen has a large, poor rural population. A majority of Yemeni males habitually chew *qat*, a mild narcotic, thereby lowering productivity and depleting family finances. And Yemen's government—which has never had strong control over its territory—is facing serious armed resistance since the Arab Spring.

The Gaza Strip faces a different problem: a blockade imposed by Israel in 2007 (and assisted by Egypt) drastically reduced trade in all but food and basic goods. An easing of some restrictions since 2010 has done little to allow economic reconstruction in a territory where 80 percent of residents rely on food aid.

THE CHALLENGE OF DEMOCRACY

A "Third Wave" of democratization that swept through much of the world from the 1970s to the 1990s bypassed the Arab countries. Until 2011, Israel and Turkey were the MENA's only electoral democracies, but even their political systems are not models of Western "liberalness." Iran's clerical regime was the first in the region to face a large pro-democracy movement following a 2009 presidential election whose results were manipulated. A brutal crackdown on reformists brought an end to demonstrations that seriously challenged the regime's legitimacy. However, the unexpected eruption of the Arab Spring opened up a new era of political change in the Arab world.

How can we explain why most of the region's countries were authoritarian for so long? And what will determine whether fledgling new regimes become the vibrant democracies so many protestors hoped for? Scholars have identified four main structural factors that have historically limited democratization and may yet stand in the way of political freedom: the West, oil, weak civil society, and Islam. We look at each of these factors as we explain how the Arab Spring has evolved and the directions in which we see it headed.

Potential Impediments to the Spread of Representative Government

Europe and the United States bear some of the blame for lingering authoritarianism in the region. After all, it was the European powers that colonized the region and created many "artificial states." Rashid Khalidi, a historian at Columbia University, argues that when European powers entered the region in the late nineteenth and early twentieth centuries, they actually halted an indigenous, incipient movement toward constitutional government and rule of law. After World War II, the United States nurtured close relations with antidemocratic royal families in Iran and the Arabian Peninsula as a means of securing access to oil. In the context of the Cold War, the United States supported anticommunist leaders, going so far as to orchestrate a *coup d'etat* in Iran in 1953. Fear of Soviet expansionism led the United States to reward friendly dictators and turn a blind eye to their human rights violations. Until 2011, the United States tolerated regional allies' repression of Islamist parties.

When the Arab Spring broke out, there was a surprising disconnect between Western publics and their governments. Ordinary Europeans and Americans were electrified by the historic scenes unfolding night after night on television and spreading virally through social media. As during the collapse of the Berlin Wall, it seemed that the ordinary people were finally claiming their freedom. Citizens in the West were reminded of the power of direct action to sweep aside political inertia. But the Obama administration and the French government initially hesitated to abandon friends and military elites in the region. While they and EU leaders later supported transitions in Tunisia, Egypt, Yemen, and Libya, they turned their backs on Bahraini demonstrators who were crushed. They also failed to put any pressure on monarchical regimes—or Iraq and Algeria—to respect human rights and allow fair treatment of opposition political forces. Critics argue that this demonstrates the West's continuing hypocrisy on the issue of democracy: supporting the overthrow of rogue regimes, embracing political change in a few countries, but continuing business as usual with royal families. When Western powers have used military means to induce democratic change—by invading Iraq, bombing Libyan targets, and giving arms and logistical support to Syrian rebels—the unintended consequence has been to provoke sectarian civil wars that make the prospects for stable democracy less likely.

Dependence on oil is another seemingly important reason for resistance to political change. Scholars use the term **rentier state** to describe a country whose government derives a large percentage of its revenues from the taxation of oil exports.[37] Iran, Iraq, Libya, Algeria, and the GCC countries meet the definition of a rentier state. Because they do not need to tax their citizens heavily, demands for representation are generally weaker. Oil concentrates resources in the hands of a small elite who buy political loyalty and foster political dependency. Support for this explanation comes from the fact that with the exception of Libya, every other regime either overthrown or facing overthrow in the Arab Spring lacks significant oil and gas exports: Tunisia, Egypt, Yemen, Bahrain, and Syria. The curse of "black gold" is that the government controlling revenue from it seems to be much more resistant to democratization. Conversely, the non–oil exporters that have been least affected by the Arab Spring (Israel, Turkey, Morocco, Jordan, and Lebanon) are democracies or already have significant political pluralism.

Weak civil society may also explain why so many MENA countries have scored low on Freedom House's annual ranking of political freedoms and civil liberties in the world. Civil society is made up of autonomous social groups such as private businesses, the press, labor, and voluntary associations that historically have been forces for liberalization. These groups face significant legal restrictions in the MENA (except in Israel and Turkey) and often do not have the finances to sustain a long confrontation with the government. It could also be argued that powerful barriers to the entry of women into the workforce and lack of leadership roles for women in religious institutions have prevented a strong, representative civil society from emerging.

The Arab Spring has demonstrated both the benefits of stronger civil society and the dangers where it is weaker. In Egypt and Tunisia, growing middle classes and assertive trade unions have helped form the underpinnings of a democratic transition. Moreover, in October 2011, women gained almost 23 percent of the seats in Tunisia's freely elected Constituent Assembly—a higher percentage than in the U.S. Congress or the British Parliament! By contrast, in countries with very weak civil societies like Libya, Yemen, and Syria, people have turned to tribal or ethno-religious identities during political upheaval, with the result that civil war may be more likely than democracy.

Religious and cultural explanations of democratic weakness in the MENA are quite prevalent, but should be viewed with much caution. Political culture in predominantly Muslim countries, to the extent that it reaffirms patriarchy, delegitimizes minority rights, and devalues secular thought, may create an inhospitable environment for political competition. Governments often claim that Islamists are undemocratic forces that believe in "one man, one vote, one time." In other words, the Islamists support the idea of free elections if the elections will help them, but once in power they will presumably impose harsh Islamic law. Thus, authoritarian regimes (and secular political parties) argue that these allegedly undemocratic movements cannot be allowed to come to power through democratic means. Casual observers of the Middle East tend to believe that Islamic political parties are prone to violence and anti-Westernism. Hamas and Hizballah, terrorist groups linked to al-Qaeda, and militias in Iraq have engaged in numerous acts of violence that undermine the rule of law.

Nevertheless, most of the large, "mainstream" Islamist movements such as the Muslim Brotherhood behave like political parties everywhere in the world, seeking to build large coalitions to win elections and improve their societies. Although their leaders draw upon the language of Islam, they are modern political entrepreneurs. Many of the parties are very conservative on gender issues and frustrated with Western policies, but they frequently espouse a commitment to free elections, rule of law, and social equity. Their private welfare programs fill a large gap left by the state's breaking of its social contract since the 1980s. Their leaders usually have the technical and organizational skills required to govern modern states.

The Arab Spring provides us a unique opportunity to assess the role that moderate Islamists might play in budding democratic systems. In Egypt, the Muslim Brotherhood's Freedom and Justice Party won 47 percent of parliamentary seats at the end of voting in January 2012. Its candidate Mohamed Morsi was elected president in May 2012. However, Egypt's Supreme Council of the Armed Forces has increased its own power, setting up a potential long-term struggle with Islamists to dominate key political decisions. In Tunisia, Ennahdha, a long-repressed but moderate Islamist party headed by Rachid Ghannouchi, won 41 percent of the votes for a constituent assembly in October 2011. It formed a coalition government with two leftist political parties, focusing mostly on economic reform and constitution-writing. In Libya's July 2012 elections for a General People's Congress, Islamist parties fared poorly, beaten out by liberal parties and independent candidates.

Results from Egypt, Tunisia, and Libya suggest three potential trajectories involving Islamists: domination of parliament; a large role in government via coalition; or marginalization from formal politics. It is too early to know how trends will play out, but we can be confident that in many countries Islamists will adapt to democratic norms and procedures. They do not preside over monolithic movements; rather, they are all wracked by internal disagreements. Some are eager to reduce government economic regulation and wipe out corruption, which makes them much more neoliberal than revolutionary! For example, Turkey's democratically elected, Islamist-leaning governing party has worked to prepare the country for eventual membership in the European Union by passing legislation to strengthen minority rights, religious freedom, and economic reform.

Optimists dispute the assertion that nondemocratic values are pervasive in the region. Public opinion polls indicate that fundamental democratic values (with the exception of equal rights for women) are supported by large majorities in the MENA, even if there are disagreements about the most appropriate political institutions. Social mobility may increase support for democratic institutions. Globalization and technological change are undermining information monopolies that governments held until quite recently. Social media, satellite television, and citizen journalism played an important role in mobilizing protesters early in the Arab Spring, and they will help hold new politicians more accountable.

The countries that have made the most democratic progress have for the most part not done so because of Western political or military interference. Foreign "carrots" have induced more lasting political change than the blunt foreign "sticks" of aid cutoffs or military threats. In Turkey, for example, the European Union's offer of potential EU membership has created powerful incentives for Turkey's military and Islamist parties to adopt more democratic institutions. Royal families in Kuwait, Jordan, and Morocco seem to have calculated that moves toward competitive elections will increase political stability. And Islamists in Egypt and Tunisia have responded positively to Western acceptance of their democratic potential and the promise of financial aid.

CONCLUSION

There are many contradictory trends in the MENA's political economy. Each country has its own unique set of state–society–market tensions. Some countries—like Israel and Turkey—are faring much better than the others, open to modern ideas and global interchanges. Some (like Iraq) are locked in the jaws of deep social divisions; some (like Iran) are unable to free themselves from the specter of the past. All face structural pressures from the international community. Forces from within society are clamoring for a role in reshaping governance, even if they disagree over what an ideal nation should look like. The genie of direct political participation and fair elections is unlikely to go back in the bottle in countries swept up in the Arab Spring.

Each of the main IPE perspectives interprets developments in the Middle East differently, based on different assumptions about history and what motivates actors. A mercantilist would probably attribute many of the conflicts and development outcomes discussed in this chapter to the struggle by states for power and protection of national interests. Economic liberal theorists stress the inevitability of MENA change as a result of global market forces. The dynamism of Dubai and Israel, as well as the democratic advances in Egypt and Tunisia, could be proof that people open to the world's ideas and goods are most likely to thrive. Structuralists could point to the MENA's weak industrialization and great disparities of wealth as evidence of the exploitation inherent in global capitalism.

Each of the IPE perspectives gives us insights on the Middle East, but none can tell us how soon and how far democracy, peace, and development will spread. The threat of more violence and disorder looms in places like Syria and Yemen. Our analysis of the region, nevertheless, does allow us to have optimism. History does not have to repeat itself; the new generation in many countries is capable of overcoming old grievances. Fears of a civilizational clash are overblown: most Islamists are reconciled to modernity, and the ties with the West are deep. The Middle East's future will ultimately depend not on the actions of foreigners but on what Middle Easterners do to, and for, themselves.

KEY TERMS

defensive modernization 353
mujahideen 354
Pax Americana 357
Oil for Food Program 357
conspiracism 357

intifadas 360
Westoxication 361
petrodollar recycling 368
sovereign wealth funds (SWFs) 368
remittances 369

Gulf Cooperation Council
  (GCC) 369
rentier state 373

DISCUSSION QUESTIONS

1. Compare and contrast the economic conditions and development strategies of several MENA countries. Which countries are most prepared to face the challenges of globalization? Explain.
2. Are most of the MENA's security problems due to foreign meddling or to the bad decisions of domestic political leaders? How much should we blame "history" for today's woes?
3. What characteristics of the Arab Spring are likely to facilitate or hinder the spread of democracy?

What are the most appropriate ways in which the Western countries could encourage democracy?

4. What are the most important "human connections" between the Middle East and the rest of the world? Are individuals and nongovernmental organizations able to influence changes in the region?
5. How do you think that past and present human tragedies will shape the perceptions of the next generation in the MENA?

SUGGESTED READINGS

François Burgat. *Face to Face with Political Islam.* London: I. B. Taurus, 2003.

James Gelvin. *The Israel–Palestine Conflict: One Hundred Years of War.* 2nd ed. New York: Cambridge University Press, 2007.

Clement Henry and Robert Springborg. *Globalization and the Politics of Development in the Middle East.* 2nd ed. Cambridge: Cambridge University Press, 2010.

Rashid Khalidi. *Resurrecting Empire: Western Footprints and America's Perilous Path in the Middle East.* Boston, MA: Beacon, 2004.

Alan Richards and John Waterbury. *A Political Economy of the Middle East.* 3rd ed. Boulder, CO: Westview, 2008.

NOTES

1. For a valuable survey of the Arab Spring and its consequences, see James Gelvin, *The Arab Uprisings: What Everyone Needs to Know* (Oxford: Oxford University Press, 2012).
2. The GDP figures are calculated on the basis of purchasing power parity (PPP).
3. See Freedom House, *Freedom in the World 2013*, at http://www.freedomhouse.org.
4. Bernard Lewis, *What Went Wrong? The Clash between Islam and Modernity in the Middle East* (Oxford: Oxford University Press, 2002).
5. See Suha Taji-Farouki and Basheer M. Nafi, eds., *Islamic Thought in the Twentieth Century* (London: I. B. Taurus, 2004).
6. L. Carl Brown, *International Politics and the Middle East: Old Rules, Dangerous Game*

(Princeton, NJ: Princeton University Press, 1984), pp. 16–18.

7. For a detailed examination of Libya under the Italians, see Lisa Anderson, *The State and Social Transformation in Tunisia and Libya, 1830–1980* (Princeton, NJ: Princeton University Press, 1986).
8. Fred Halliday, *The Middle East in International Relations: Power, Politics and Ideology* (New York: Cambridge University Press, 2005), p. 153.
9. Sebastian Balfour, *Deadly Embrace: Morocco and the Road to the Spanish Civil War* (Oxford: Oxford University Press, 2002).
10. For a description of the effects of bombing on Libyan civilians, see C.J. Chivers and Eric Schmitt,

"Libya's Civilian Toll, Denied by NATO," *New York Times*, December 17, 2011.

11. Joy Gordon's brilliant and unsettling analysis of the U.S. role in sustaining the brutal sanctions on Iraq is *Invisible War: The United States and the Iraq Sanctions* (Cambridge, MA: Harvard University Press, 2010).

12. For an overview of the sanctions on Iran, see Eskandar Sadeghi-Boroujerdi, "Sanctioning Iran: Implications and Consequences" (London: Oxford Research Group, 2012), at http://www.oxfordresearchgroup.org.uk/publications/briefing_papers_and_reports/sanctioning_iran_implications_and_consequences.

13. Daniel Pipes, *The Hidden Hand: Middle East Fears of Conspiracy* (New York: St. Martin's, 1996), p. 27.

14. Quoted in Fauzi Najjar, "The Arabs, Islam and Globalization," *Middle East Policy,* 12 (Fall 2005), p. 95.

15. *Confidence in Obama Lifts U.S. Image around the World* (Washington, D.C.: The Pew Research Center, July 2009), p. 16, at http://pewglobal.org/reports/pdf/264.pdf.

16. *Global Opinion of Obama Slips, International Policies Faulted* (Washington, D.C.: The Pew Research Center, June 2012), pp. 2, 11, at http://www.pewglobal.org/files/2012/06/Pew-Global-Attitudes-U.S.-Image-Report-FINAL-June-13-2012.pdf.

17. A copy of the contentious report is available at http://www2.ohchr.org/english/bodies/hrcouncil/specialsession/9/FactFindingMission.htm.

18. Lisa Hajjar, *Courting Conflict: The Israeli Military Court System in the West Bank and Gaza* (Berkeley, CA: University of California Press, 2005).

19. Sara Roy, *The Gaza Strip: The Political Economy of De-development,* 2nd ed. (Washington, DC: Institute for Palestine Studies, 2001).

20. Ahmed S. Hashim, *Insurgency and Counter-Insurgency in Iraq* (Ithaca, NY: Cornell University Press, 2006), pp. 72–73.

21. Charles Tilly, "Terror, Terrorism, Terrorists," *Sociological Theory,* 22 (March 2004), p. 11.

22. National Counterterrorism Center, *2011 Report on Terrorism*, p. 9, available at http://asdwasecurity.files.wordpress.com/2012/10/2011_nctc_annual_report_final.pdf.

23. Although Kuwait's rulers fled their country in the wake of Iraq's invasion in 1990, the United States reinstated their government at the end of the Gulf War.

24. U.S. Census Bureau, *2010 American Community Survey*, at http://factfinder2.census.gov/faces/tableservices/jsf/pages/productview.xhtml?pid=ACS_10_1YR_B05006&prodType=table.

25. Philippe Fargues, ed., *Mediterranean Migration: 2008–2009 Report* (European University Institute, 2009), p. 2, http://cadmus.eui.eu/handle/1814/11861.

26. World Bank, *Global Economic Prospects June 2012 (Middle East and North Africa Index)* (Washington, D.C.: World Bank, 2012).

27. World Bank, *Global Economic Prospects January 2013 (Middle East and North Africa Index)* (Washington, D.C.: World Bank, 2013).

28. Dan Senor and Saul Singer, *Start-up Nation: The Story of Israel's Economic Miracle* (New York: Twelve, 2009).

29. Ziya Öniş, "Crises and Transformations in Turkish Political Economy," *Turkish Policy Quarterly,* 9:3 (2010): pp. 45–61.

30. World Bank, *Global Economic Prospects January 2013.*

31. Jonathon Nitzan and Shimshon Bichler, *The Global Political Economy of Israel* (London: Pluto, 2002).

32. Charles Kernaghan, *U.S. Jordan Free Trade Agreement Descends into Human Trafficking and Involuntary Servitude* (New York: National Labor Committee, 2006), at http://www.globallabourrights.org/admin/documents/files/Jordan_Report_05_03.pdf.

33. *The Arab Human Development Report 2002: Creating Opportunities for Future Generations* (New York: United Nations Development Programme, Regional Bureau for Arab States, 2002).

34. United Nations Human Settlements Programme, *The State of Arab Cities 2012: Challenges of Urban Transition* (2012).

35. Dalia S. Hakura, "Growth in the Middle East and North Africa," *IMF Working Papers 04/56* (2004), p. 3, available at www.imf.org/external/pubs/ft/wp/2004/wp0456.pdf.

36. International Labour Organization, *Global Employment Trends 2013* (Geneva: ILO, 2013).

37. For an overview of the "rentier state" concept, see Michael Ross, *The Oil Curse: How Petroleum Wealth Shapes the Development of Nations* (Princeton: Princeton University Press, 2012).

Transnational Problems and Dilemmas

It is increasingly clear that many problems in international political economy are more than international: They are global in nature. That is, these problems are not just conflicts or tensions between and among nation-states. They transcend the boundaries of nation-states and have become truly global in their effects. The final part of this book looks at six aspects of these global problems. All show us the complex interactions between individuals, markets, governments, and international institutions. The global financial crisis has already exacerbated some of these problems. Whether global actors will increase cooperation to tackle them or resort to ever more conflictual policies in the face of them remains to be seen.

Chapter 15 surveys illicit transactions in the global economy, emphasizing that illegal flows of goods, services, and people across borders pose important challenges to governments. Although IPE focuses on states and markets, it is fundamentally about people, as Chapter 16 makes clear. This chapter analyzes migration, tourism, and human networks from an IPE perspective.

Chapter 17 tackles a particularly controversial aspect of North–South IPE: transnational corporations (TNCs). Some see them as engines of growth, others as tools of exploitation. We look at how they have in the past helped define the North–South debate and then go beyond this framework to consider the key issues surrounding TNCs today.

Chapter 18 examines the IPE of food and hunger, with special emphasis on the roles of states and markets in contributing to food and hunger problems. Chapter 19 highlights oil and energy trends, which have become more contentious with the rise of oil prices in the last decade and the serious efforts to switch to green energy. Finally, Chapter 20 presents an analysis of the IPE of the global environment, perhaps today's most serious global issue. Global warming and the Copenhagen Climate Change Conference of 2009 are highlighted as part of a strategic moment for environmental policies that must also grapple with other threatening issues such as deforestation. As will become evident, the problems of food, energy, and the environment are increasingly entangled and inseparable, threatening humanity and creating new international obligations. A glossary of key IPE terms used in the text follows Chapter 20.

The Illicit Global Economy: The Dark Side of Globalization

Young prostitutes in the brothel district of Tangail, Bangladesh.

Gary Hinton/Alamy

Behaving as if only the licit side of IPE exists because it is the easiest to measure and quantify is the equivalent of the drunkard saying that the reason he is stumbling around looking for his keys under the streetlight is because it is the only place where he can see. What we need are better flashlights so that we can also look for our keys down the dark alleys of the global economy.[1]

Peter Andreas

In early 2006, U.S. immigration agents discovered a half-mile-long underground tunnel linking warehouses in Tijuana, Mexico, and Otay Mesa, California. Equipped with electricity, ventilation, a concrete floor, and water pumps, the tunnel—dubbed *El Grande*—probably took two years to build.[2] Agents suspected that it was used for drug smuggling: They found two tons of marijuana inside. They also worried that illegal aliens, terrorists, and weapons of mass destruction could have transited into the United States through this 80-foot-deep corridor. Since September 11, 2001, agents have discovered dozens of tunnels along the U.S.-Mexico border. Other parts of the world have smuggling tunnels, too. Facing an Israeli blockade after July 2007, Palestinians in the Gaza Strip dug dozens of tunnels under the border with Egypt to bring in everything from gasoline and cement to medicine and missiles. All together, the tunnels are the largest non-governmental employer in Gaza.[3] And in mid-2012, authorities uncovered a 700-meter tunnel under the Ukraine–Slovak border equipped with a small train. Given the 2.6 million contraband cigarettes also found, they suspect it was used to import "death sticks" into the European Union without paying customs duties.[4]

El Grande and the other tunnels are but small links in the vast illicit global economy, a network of international trade relationships that brings goods, services, and people across borders every day in defiance of the laws of at least one state. Law enforcement officials occasionally give the public a glimpse of the world of illicit actors and the threats they pose. Nevertheless, illicit international exchanges usually occur in a shadowy world that most consumers never see directly.

This chapter analyzes a broad range of illicit actors and activities that pose significant challenges to governments and legitimate businesses throughout the world. The illicit global economy consists of markets that states cannot easily regulate or tax. A variety of adjectives are commonly used to describe these global markets: *illicit, illegal, informal, black, gray, shadow, extrastate, underground,* and *offshore*. The processes going on in these markets generally fall into categories such as smuggling, trafficking, money laundering, tax evasion, and counterfeiting. The actors conducting these transactions make profits by breaking laws, defying authority, ignoring borders, and often using violence to exploit other people. In previous chapters, we suggested that illegal behavior by financial elites (i.e., men and women behaving badly) was one of the causes of the global financial crisis. Ironically, the global recession has also increased illicit transactions as more desperate and vulnerable people fall prey to traffickers and as struggling businesses try to cut costs by skirting the law.

Until recently, IPE scholars left the study of the illicit global economy to other social scientists. Criminologists have for years studied transnational organized crime groups. Sociologists have looked at the social effects of criminal activities such as drug trafficking and prostitution. International relations experts have been examining closely the connection between money laundering and terrorism since 9/11. Comparative politics specialists have studied the effects of corruption and clientelism on political development. And anthropologists have conducted research on informal markets in developing countries.

IPE scholars have increasingly recognized the theoretical and practical implications of the illicit realm. They have begun to synthesize the work of the other disciplines and branch out beyond the study of what is legal and easily measurable in the global economy. They realize that a close look at the illicit global economy helps us garner new insights into the relationships among states, markets, and societies.

Political scientist Peter Andreas notes that existing IPE perspectives help us understand some—but not all—of what we witness in the shadows.[5] Realists help us understand why security-obsessed states invest so much money and resources in international law enforcement. Liberal theorists help us understand under what conditions multilateral cooperation against crime will occur. Constructivists highlight the role that transnational nongovernmental groups play in changing the public's perception of illicit transactions. And structuralists point out that countries that rely on exports of illegal drugs and "blood diamonds" are stuck in a dependent, exploitative relationship with the "core" countries.

However, the illegal economy also provides a challenge to the three main IPE perspectives. Although mercantilists stress the primacy of the nation-state, the illicit global economy is full of nonstate actors that sometimes thwart the best intentions and institutions of even powerful countries. Whereas liberals focus on the market's invisible hand and individual freedom, the illicit global economy is full of powerful, manipulative criminal hands. The open commercial interchange and deregulation that liberalism promotes are supposed to lead to peace and prosperity, but in the illicit realm unfettered trade can spread horrible conflict, pervasive coercion, and social decay. Structuralists tend to portray capitalist, developed countries as exploiters of the developing countries, but in the illicit global economy, developing countries can sometimes take revenge on the rich North, as when China steals intellectual property or when **secrecy jurisdictions** (places with strong bank privacy laws) in the Caribbean attract billions of dollars from wealthy tax evaders.

In this chapter we make several arguments. Far from reducing black market activity, globalization gives criminals new ways to profit from their cross-border business. Well-intentioned attempts by governments to stop the supply of illicit products sometimes cause more harm than good. International cooperation against transnational crime is hard to sustain and often ineffective. Consumers bear as much responsibility as international suppliers for nurturing illegal commerce. The threats to national security, social well-being, and legal commerce seem to keep growing.

THE ILLICIT ECONOMY IN HISTORICAL PERSPECTIVE

Illicit transactions did not suddenly appear a decade or so ago; there have been many illicit activities in history that have fundamentally shaped relations among states. Centuries ago, European rulers and Barbary Coast potentates authorized pirates to seize other countries' ships and split the booty with them. European countries colonized many parts of the world, seizing the territory and the property of their inhabitants. Although at the time the colonial powers tried to justify colonialism as a kind of civilizing mission, their activities amounted to little more than theft.

Historians Kenneth Pomeranz and Steven Topik argue that violence used to be an important way to gain "comparative advantage" and important commercial benefits in the world. Great Britain, Spain, other European countries, and the United States moved up the rungs of the ladder of development by engaging in land grabbing, slavery, looting, and dope peddling in what we now call the less developed countries (LDCs). As both authors argue, "Bloody hands and the invisible hand often worked in concert: in fact, they were often attached to the same body."[6] They recount how Britain once forced China to buy opium; Belgium brutalized millions of Congo inhabitants and slaughtered elephants for ivory; Spain and Portugal literally plundered the Aztec and Inca civilizations; and U.S. entrepreneurs trafficked in slaves for decades.

Marxists, too, have long recognized that the development of capitalism is rooted in processes of **primitive accumulation,** whereby the upper classes coercively or violently seize assets (such as land) from other actors. Sociologist Charles Tilly famously asserted that state-making is quite similar to organized crime.[7] Just like crime bosses, would-be leaders centuries ago used violence against their rivals and extracted "protection money" that they used to expand their territory and make war. Eventually these state-makers gained legitimacy as kings and turned extortion into legal taxation, masking their sometimes violent and thuggish beginnings.

History shows us that leaders of states have often participated in or sanctioned violent illicit activities. At the same time, these leaders have the power to define *what* is legal or illegal and *who* is a legitimate entrepreneur or an illegitimate one. We see that illicit activities can be very beneficial to some states while being simultaneously disastrous for others. Capitalism in its early stages was more like the Wild West than a contemporary, well-planned industrial park.

Illicit transactions today often mirror, replicate, or repeat these historical processes, even though we often tend to give new names to modern processes. For example, human trafficking is a modern-day form of slavery practiced around the world. Today's drug lords expropriate from peasants and addicts alike, expanding their turf and productive apparatus as would-be kings once did. Corrupt leaders in places such as Nigeria and Iraq have stolen massive amounts of public resources, just as European powers stole from the colonies that they were supposed to be helping. Some leaders in recent decades, such as Slobodan Milosevic in Serbia and Charles Taylor in Liberia, ran their states like criminal enterprises, working in cahoots with *mafiosos* to keep their kleptocracies running before they were ultimately ousted by foreign countries. Israel's seizure for decades of Palestinian real estate and farmland is little different from state-sanctioned theft by pirates and imperialists hundreds of years ago. States and entrepreneurs today still sometimes use violence and coercion to harm their competitors. Although we like to think that the excesses of the past are limited today by international law, good government, and even globalization itself, the reality is that illicit history repeats itself (albeit with new names, new faces, and new *modus operandi*).

THE STAKES AND THE ACTORS

How big and how important is the illicit global economy? There are many disagreements about the answers to these questions, partly because extralegal transactions are so difficult to measure. Governments and multilateral institutions often engage in hyperbole, sometimes either to tout their supposed achievements against the "bad guys" or to heighten threats for political reasons. Canadian economist R. T. Naylor warns us against having too much faith in estimates of the illicit economy's size, which often are based on bad information and false assumptions. For example, he notes that a widely cited estimate of annual global sales of illegal drugs at $500 billion was concocted by a UN official giving a speech in 1989 to grab public attention.[8]

Based on a 2011 meta-analysis of various crime studies, the United Nations Office on Drugs and Crime (UNODC) estimates that the annuals proceeds of drug trafficking and transnational organized crime are equal to 3.6 percent of global gross domestic product (GDP)—or about $2.1 trillion.[9] This estimate may be inflated because it includes the amount of taxes that multinational corporations and investors evade by shifting their money around different jurisdictions. Raymond Baker, a fellow at the Center for International Policy in Washington, DC, gives us a different calculation of "dirty money" that results from public corruption and criminal activities (other than tax evasion).[10] He estimates that annual cross-border sales (in 2005) of illegal drugs and counterfeit goods may amount to as high as $320 billion. Revenues from human trafficking could amount to $15 billion annually. International smuggling of arms, cigarettes, cars, oil, timber, and art may be worth as much as $110 billion annually.

"Guesstimates" though these figures may be, they indicate that the scale of the illicit problem has important implications for development, democracy, and security. The stakes are high. Baker believes that growing illegality is a major contributor to inequality and poverty in the world: "With common techniques and use of the same structures, drug dealers, other criminals, terrorists, corrupt government officials, and corporate CEOs and managers are united in abuse of capitalism, to the detriment of the rich in western societies and billions of poor around the world."[11] Likewise, Moisés Naím, the former editor of *Foreign Policy* magazine, does not believe that democracy can emerge in countries dominated by powerful criminal networks.[12] The illegal economy can also undermine fragile new democracies by putting money into the hands of rivals of the central government, corrupting institutions such as the judiciary, and decreasing government efficacy. In all democracies, it lowers social trust and the belief that one shares the same values as one's fellow citizens.

Who are the central actors in the high-stakes illegal networks? We all have a tendency to believe that the main actors are *mafia* dons, drug lords, and other organized crime figures. The ruthless criminals of Hollywood movies do exist, but full-time gangsters are only one part of a much wider puzzle. Many participants have one foot in the legal world and one in the illegal world, making it difficult to create a profile of the typical illicit actor. Participants include soldiers who loot, government officials who extort, CEOs who evade corporate taxes, bankers who loan to Third World dictators, and consumers who buy fake Louis Vuitton handbags. Even humanitarian workers in war-torn African countries have been known to participate in diamond trafficking.

Just as law-abiding citizens sometimes dabble in the black market, well-trained, "normal" economic actors such as accountants and computer programmers sometimes lend their skills to unethical or criminal operators. For example, anthropologist Carolyn Nordstrom has pointed out that "smugglers today are more likely to be armed with a degree from a leading ICT/computer technology course than an assault rifle."[13] The work skills that the world of international trade demands are also needed in the shadow economies.

There is often no clear wall between the licit and the illicit global economy. Buyers may not know (or not care to know) from whom their suppliers get products. A consumer may illegally download music at night and pay for licensed videogames the next day. A multinational corporation paying almost no taxes in the high-tax country where it is headquartered could be scrupulously paying corporate taxes in low-tax countries where its affiliates operate. Products that start out in some kind of shady operation often enter the "regular" market at a later point. Items produced in the legal market (such as cigarettes) may end up being smuggled across borders. Machine guns sold legally to an army in one country may end up in the arms of insurgents in a neighboring country.

STUDYING THE ILLICIT ECONOMY: KEY FINDINGS

Studying cross-border illegal activities helps provide deeper insights into problems we see in the global economy. Consider the following questions: Why is it so hard to prevent nuclear proliferation? Why don't economic sanctions work well in changing the behavior of rogue regimes? Why aren't governments winning the war against drugs? Why did millions die from war in resource-rich Congo after 1998? In this section we examine six important analytical findings about the illicit global economy that help us answer important questions like these. These findings demonstrate the role that consumers, law enforcement, and globalization play in the growth of black markets. They also explain how illicit transactions affect war, development, and cooperation among states.

Six Degrees of Separation

"I am bound to everyone on this planet by a trail of six people," says one of the characters in John Guare's play *Six Degrees of Separation*.[14] In illicit markets, producers and consumers are also related to one another through a small number of people living in many parts of the world. Between a procurer and consumer are other actors, including financiers, processors, shippers, importers, distributors, and retailers. If we look at international transactions involving the movement of goods and services, we see a global chain along whose links many points of illegality can occur.

The human connections in the chain reveal that none of us is completely divorced from the illegal world. Whether at the beginning, middle, or end of a chain of market interactions, we wittingly or unwittingly are involved in a process that may have been part of the extralegal world. Sometimes we can see our part in the chain, as when, for example, American parents hire illegal aliens from Mexico to care for their children but do not pay social security tax on behalf of these employees. At other times, our part in the chain is largely invisible, as when someone buys a cheap piece of Chinese-made furniture that contains wood from an illegally logged region in Russia's Far East. The greater our degree of separation from the illicit part of a global commodity chain, the less we feel responsible for it.

Carolyn Nordstrom points out that ordinary consumers around the world are deeply complicit in smuggling. She found that in the African war zones where she did research, everyday, mundane commodities such as rice, cigarettes, vegetables, and antibiotics constitute a big chunk of unofficial trade.[15] One can hardly survive in some of these areas without buying smuggled, untaxed items in the informal economy. In developed countries, consumers of software, downloaded music, drugs, vehicles, art, and jeans, to name just a few products, often know that the products they are buying are knockoffs, pirated copies, untaxed items, or stolen property.

However, a countertrend is emerging. Multinational corporations and retailers are taking into consideration that increasing numbers of consumers want to widen the degree of separation between themselves and any potential unethical or illegal practices. The fair-trade coffee movement and the antisweatshop movement have conditioned consumers to think about the ultimate effects of their domestic purchases on overseas workers. Similarly, businesses are keen not to be tainted by ties to illegal activities overseas that transnational advocacy groups are publicizing. Lowe's was one of the first home improvement retail chains to introduce a wood procurement program to help ensure that the company bought timber only from sustainable forests and not from forests that were being harvested illegally in the Third World. In the face of criticism that diamonds from some African countries were fueling wars, the De Beers company participated in a global scheme to track the origins of rough diamond purchases so as to weed out those coming from conflict zones. (See the box De Beers and "Blood Diamonds.")

▶ DE BEERS AND "BLOOD DIAMONDS"

Thanks to years of advertising by De Beers Consolidated Mines, the world's largest diamond multinational company, most consumers are familiar with the phrases "A diamond is forever" and "Diamonds are a girl's best friend." In the last decade, nongovernmental organizations that are critical of the connection between the diamond trade and African civil wars have spread two alternative slogans: "An amputation is forever" and "Diamonds are a guerrilla's best friend." They argue that the diamond industry has helped to finance rebel groups in places such as Sierra Leone, the Congo, and Angola, where millions of people have been killed, mutilated, raped, or displaced during civil war. The recent attention to blood diamonds (also called "conflict diamonds") has forced the diamond industry, as well as governments of diamond-producing and diamond-receiving nations and multilateral institutions, to better regulate the international trade.

It is estimated that 500 tons of diamonds have been mined in the last 100 years, with one-third of them mined in the 1990s alone.[a] The company

(*continued*)

responsible for a large portion of diamond mining and wholesaling is De Beers, cofounded in 1880 by Cecil Rhodes, who formed a syndicate with the ten largest diamond merchants in South Africa.

De Beers established the London-based Diamond Trading Company (DTC), which sells diamond parcels at ten annual "sights" to approximately 125 "sightholders" who then take the diamonds to other cities, where they are repackaged for further sale to companies that then cut, polish, and resell the diamonds to independent retailers. The diamond industry operates in relative secrecy. As of 2002, De Beers reportedly controlled two-thirds of the world's annual supply of rough diamonds.[b] With De Beers' level of control of the market, close to 60 percent of the world's diamonds will go through the DTC in a given year.[c] De Beers' share in the market has declined over the decades, but the rest of the industry still relies heavily on the marketing scheme to convince international consumers that diamonds are as rare as the love that inspires them to buy one.

Diamonds are perhaps the most highly concentrated form of wealth in the world. Because of the difficulty of tracing the origin of any particular diamond and the ease with which diamonds can be moved, these gems have become a key form of currency among illegitimate actors in the international market. Until the 1980s, De Beers was involved directly in Sierra Leone and maintained an office in Freetown. In the 1990s it purchased diamonds in neighboring Liberia, Guinea, and Cote d'Ivoire—countries that were transit points for diamonds smuggled from war-torn Sierra Leone. Rebels in Sierra Leone also smuggled gems through Lebanese, West African, and Eastern European intermediaries. Sometimes raw diamonds were smuggled directly to the main international market in Antwerp, Belgium.

How did diamonds contribute to Sierra Leone's bloodshed? In 1991 a group of Libyan-trained rebels in Sierra Leone formed the Revolutionary United Front (RUF) and began attacking government forces. They seized some government-run diamond mines and over the next decade ran an illicit economy, smuggling diamonds to neighboring nations and trading them for weapons and drugs. The RUF also cut off the limbs of thousands of civilians. In 1999 the international community could no longer ignore the tiny West African country that was becoming one of the most dangerous locations on the globe. The civil war unleashed by the RUF had caused the death of more than 50,000 and the displacement of more than two million people. In January of that year the RUF attacked Freetown, Sierra Leone's capital, and conducted Operation No Living Thing—murdering, raping, and mutilating hundreds of civilians.

The United Nations helped broker a weak peace accord between the RUF and the government of Sierra Leone. The UN Security Council adopted a diamond embargo that banned the direct or indirect import of rough diamonds not sanctioned by the government of Sierra Leone through a certificate-of-origin regime. From July to October 2000 the government of Sierra Leone and the Belgium Diamond High Council created a system under which each diamond arriving in Antwerp from Sierra Leone required a certificate of origin printed on security paper, registration through an electronic database, and electronic confirmation upon arrival. The RUF was quick to find a way around the new requirements, using Liberia and Guinea as cover for the export of their diamonds into the legitimate market. This prompted the Security Council to impose sanctions against Liberia in May 2001, which included a harsh ban against the export of rough diamonds.

In the face of the blood diamond problem, civil society groups such as Britain's Global Witness and Canada's Partnership Africa Canada joined diamond companies such as De Beers, the World Diamond Council, and dozens of governments to establish the Kimberly Process Certification Scheme (KPCS) in January 2003. KPCS members voluntarily cooperate and collaborate to prevent illegal diamonds from entering international trade networks and to shun countries and companies that cannot ensure that their diamonds are conflict-free. The Kimberly

Process is a significant example of a global public–private partnership to combat an illicit activity. Although it is not a panacea, KPCS has helped to foster peace in Sierra Leone and Angola, boost government revenues from legitimate exports, and make consumers more knowledgeable about where their products come from.

References

[a]Ingrid J. Tamm, "Diamonds in Peace and War: Severing the Conflict-Diamond Connection," *World Peace Foundation Report* (Cambridge: World Peace Foundation, 2002), p. 5.
[b]Ibid.
[c]Ibid., p. 4.

A fascinating new global trend is the rise of **socially responsible investing**. This is an effort to allow ordinary citizens to put their money in investment funds that avoid companies or countries that are perceived as being socially or environmentally unethical. Financial markets are offering new instruments for ethical investors. Related to this are a host of divestment-type movements led by some local governments, pension funds, and boardrooms to avoid investing in places where the capital will benefit dictators or criminals. These types of divestment strategies often indirectly target companies and countries linked to illicit activities such as land expropriation and oil corruption. Sometimes they go beyond divestment and turn into bans on doing any business or trade with certain companies and countries. Divestment strategies are basically a form of boycott that challenges economic liberal principles governing trade and capital flows.

The Unintended Consequences of Supply-Side Policies

Another pattern is a strong tendency of governments to adopt policies targeting the sources of illicit products. These policies can be described as interdiction, repression, and eradication. Political leaders like to target suppliers in foreign countries rather than demanders in their own country, even though this focus has been shown in many cases to be more expensive and less effective. For example, the United States spends enormous funds trying to stop illegal aliens from crossing the border with Mexico but significantly less money or effort punishing U.S. businesses that hire undocumented workers. Similarly, money and labor-hours expended trying to stop drug production and smuggling in Latin America far exceed U.S. federal spending on the treatment of drug users. In the global sex industry, law enforcement has a long history of cracking down on prostitutes rather than on the johns who pay for their services.

The reasons states mostly go after the supply side of the problem have a lot to do with the powerful political, economic, and cultural interests in a society. Governments often feel obliged to balance entrenched special interests with the public interest. There is often a sacrifice of efficiency and social goals when powerful actors force governments to attack illicit problems in "someone else's backyard." When law enforcement tries to stop or interfere with the supply side of robust global markets, it often does not achieve the intended results. In fact, there are often perverse consequences. An illicit activity can simply be displaced from one place to another, as when a ratcheting up of policing on one part of a border causes smugglers to move to a less secure part of the border. A supply-side crack-down might drive an illegal activity further underground, making it even harder to control. And a campaign against suppliers can often increase violence and "turf wars" in a society.

Phil Williams points out that efforts to restrict activities create a **restriction-opportunity dilemma**: The more that countries try to impose arms embargoes or ban substances such as drugs or Freon, the more they "provide inroads for the creation of new criminal markets or the enlargement of existing markets."[16] Eva Bertram and her colleagues illustrate a similar unintended outcome they call the **profit paradox**.[17] When states use law enforcement to try to prohibit drugs, the reduction of supply tends to drive up prices. This bolsters the profits of those entrepreneurs willing to take the risk to keep on supplying the black market. And the higher price encourages other would-be criminals to get into the business. One result is that, after a temporary lull, supply climbs up again as criminals find more ingenious ways of getting around prohibitions—and the price goes back down. Another possible result is that the most ruthless and violent criminals gain even more dominance of the illicit market. This dilemma is evident in many areas, leading some to argue in favor of decriminalization of certain types of illicit activity.

Globalization: The Double-Edged Sword

Liberal theory touts the positive aspects of freer international markets. For example, columnist Thomas Friedman portrays a heady new stage of globalization in which changes in technology empower individuals and companies that collaborate and compete peacefully across increasingly invisible borders.[18]

However, from studying illicit markets we learn that globalization is a double-edged sword: Open markets may increase global efficiency, but they also empower the bad guys. Although we still do not know if the ratio of illegal to legal business in the world is increasing, we can be sure that in some countries the ratio has risen. Technological change, which has become something of an object of devotion in Western societies, can also be a false idol. For each potentially desirable trend in neoliberal globalization, there is a criminal downside. This does not mean that the bad outweighs the good, rather that any compelling analysis of global change must account for negative externalities.

Naím points to the dark side of the end of the Cold War: The breakdown of the Soviet Union and the proliferation of weak, postcommunist states created new homes for illegal operations.[19] The transition to market economies gave rise to powerful *mafias*, influence peddling, and old-fashioned gangsterism. And some of the weak states that emerged from the collapse of the Soviet Union became smugglers' lairs. A case in point is Transdniestra, a sliver of Moldova that claimed independence in 1992 (even though no country has recognized its claim). It became a hub for trafficking of weapons, contraband, and stolen cars. And at the end of the Cold War, ex–Warsaw Pact countries off-loaded many small arms into Third World markets.

Many scholars identify global deregulation and privatization as culprits in the rise of the illicit. Deregulation of airlines and shipping industries since the 1980s has fueled some forms of trafficking. The rapid-fire sale of state enterprises has contributed to widespread corruption. Regional integration based on free-trade agreements weakens border control. The opening of capital markets has facilitated the flow of "hot" money around the world. And businesses looking for technical solutions to smuggling, such as by embedding radio frequency emitters in products, often find themselves outsmarted by criminals.

Whereas new technologies of globalization are used by shadow actors, Peter Andreas points out that states are also taking advantage of technological innovations to police the bad guys. For example, digitization enables government database mining, biometric identification, and better electronic eavesdropping.[20] Currency-printing innovations help governments stave off counterfeit paper money. And global positioning system (GPS) technology helps governments track criminal activities such as illegal timber harvesting and illegal waste disposal.

The Problem with Coordination between States

One of the important questions that IPE examines is why states succeed or fail in cooperating with one another. As we learned in earlier chapters, realists view states as constantly competing with one another, whereas liberals stress the ability of governments to coordinate their interactions peacefully. Another of the major findings from the study of illicit markets is that state sovereignty makes coordinated policies against the shadows very difficult. Why is this so?

One major reason is that states are jealous of their sovereignty. They do not like interference in their domestic affairs, and they do not want to be responsible for enforcing the laws of other states. In fact, they will sometimes take advantage of illicit activities outside their borders. Although illicit markets can threaten sovereignty, sovereignty can also shield black markets. For example, some states have become havens for criminal operations. They charge global outlaws a fee for protection behind their sovereign cocoon. In this kind of failed state, leaders can issue diplomatic passports to dubious businessmen, offer **flags of convenience** (places to register ships and airlines that actually conduct all their international business somewhere else), and allow the establishment of servers to conduct Internet gambling or pornography distribution. In exchange for a payoff, they may look the other way as criminals use their territory to smuggle goods.

These activities are part of a wider phenomenon that Ronen Palan calls the **commercialization of sovereignty**—the renting out of commercial privileges and protections to citizens and companies from other countries.[21] A state can market itself as a place to disguise the origin of dirty money. For example, dozens of mostly small countries and territories are **tax havens** (also referred to as offshore financial centers or secrecy jurisdictions), where foreigners can park their money and conduct international financial transactions with very little regulation by local officials. These places—such as the Cayman Islands—attract money launderers and tax evaders who want to stay entirely out of the reach of their home governments. These sovereign jurisdictions benefit both indirectly and directly from global crime (as well as from legitimate international business).

In his book *Treasure Islands*, Nicholas Shaxson stresses that these havens are ubiquitous and integral to the operations of global capitalism. They are to be found in many developed countries, including Switzerland, British overseas territories, and U.S. states such as Delaware and Nevada. He argues that they "provide wealthy and powerful elites with secrecy and all manner of ways to shrug off the laws and duties that come with living in and obtaining benefits from society—taxes, prudent financial regulation, criminal laws, inheritance rules, and many others."[22]

Pressure on pariah states is one way of trying to shut down illicit networks, but it is not necessarily the most effective. The technique often backfires. Leaders of pariah states do not always want to get rid of illicit transactions (especially if these leaders themselves are participating in illegal activities). Even if these leaders really do want to reduce corruption or shadow activities, they might not have the capacity to do so; or if they try to, they may end up being overthrown. In this latter case, punishing a government for not cooperating may have the unintended effect of weakening institution-building in poorer countries. The World Bank under its former president Paul Wolfowitz instituted a punitive model of anticorruption: cutting off aid to countries that failed to stop criminal activities that siphoned off (sometimes indirectly) foreign loans and development aid. The model was halted, in part, because it may have deprived weak but well-intentioned leaders of the very resources and assistance they needed to fight the "bad guys" in their economy.

This raises the bigger question of under what conditions one country has the "right" to use force against another country in which illicit activities are occurring. If a government allows terrorists to launder money through its nation's banking system, does an offended country have the natural right to use force against that government? Can one country use force to prevent massive counterfeiting of its currency in another country? North Korea, for example, is a sophisticated counterfeiter of U.S. currency. If a country allows massive piracy and counterfeiting of intellectual property to occur, is it really stealing other countries' property? Is this tantamount to grabbing another country's territory?

There are many other reasons why states do not cooperate against crime. For one thing, illicit cross-border activities often occur precisely because laws differ from one state to another. Combating this would require states to better harmonize their legal systems, which is politically unpopular. Second is a problem of defection: How to guarantee that a state will actually carry out its commitments to another? Third is a question of privacy. Effective international cooperation requires sharing information about one's citizens and companies, something states have always been reluctant to do. This is a classic mercantilist impulse. States are worried about how rival states will use this information, however well-intentioned the initial cooperation.

Fourth, rival states sometimes encourage black market activities to undermine their enemies. For example, the Reagan administration sought to undermine the Soviets and leftist regimes by pouring weapons into places such as Afghanistan, Angola, and Latin America, fueling arms bazaars that remained long after covert programs ended. R. T. Naylor reminds us that, as part of their mercantilist economic warfare hundreds of years ago, European powers tried to undermine rival states by encouraging counterfeiting, pirating, and the development of smuggling centers.[23] And Peter Andreas recounts some of the ways in which states instrumentalize illicitness to help themselves: by busting economic sanctions (Iran);

by stealing nuclear technology (Pakistan); by engaging in covert operations (the United States); and by turning a blind eye to counterfeiting (China).

Fifth, it is hard to obtain serious cooperation from police forces and governments that are sometimes themselves complicit in illicit activities. In many weak states, officials may protect crime syndicates, be on the payroll of syndicates, or simply look the other way in exchange for payoffs. And sometimes they are simply too afraid to take on powerful criminal organizations and drug cartels. Former Colombian drug kingpin Pablo Escobar, for example, conducted a violent campaign against the government when it came after his cocaine empire in the 1980s and early 1990s. He ordered dozens of assassinations of judges, police, and reporters and bombings of public facilities.

In the absence of effective state cooperation, private companies and international civil society are stepping up to the plate to change norms and practices related to illicit activities. These voluntary efforts are not always successful, but they do put pressure on governments to do more, and they are influencing public opinion. The private sector—worried about bad press and potential legal liability—has taken the lead in establishing codes of conduct and standards of behavior for big players. For example, some of the world's largest private banks have voluntarily adopted regulations to minimize money laundering and other financial crimes. This is part of a broader, post–9/11 shift by multinational corporations to **know-thy-customer rules**, whereby they more carefully screen their depositors, suppliers, and contractors. Even so, since 2011 U.S. officials have charged large banks—including Citigroup, HSBC, and Standard Chartered—with laundering the funds of drug traffickers, potential terrorists, and the government of Iran.

Name-and-shame campaigns bring international attention to illegal and unethical practices. Transparency International is a prominent example of a group whose annual index of corruption—derived from surveys of businesspersons who conduct business in other countries—can pressure governments into trying to get out of the bottom of the list. The Tax Justice Network is part of a coalition of activists trying to crack down on and embarrass tax havens and TNCs that use shady global practices to avoid corporate taxes. Multilateral institutions can also blacklist countries that fail to adopt international financial standards. Whitelisting is another inexpensive way for civic groups and governments simply to publicize companies with clean records in hopes that the market will shift toward their products and practices.

War and Natural Resources

It has become increasingly clear since the 1980s that black market influences on natural resources have important effects on the global security structure. Weak governments and rebel groups in developing countries need money to buy weapons, pay off supporters, and finance activities within their borders. Controlling the extraction and export of natural resources is an important way to guarantee a revenue flow. Insurgents also know that if they deprive the government of control over natural resources, they can achieve important political goals. International commodities dealers generally do not have any compunction about buying from criminal insurgents or corrupt governments.

In Sierra Leone, several factions in the civil war that devastated the country in the 1990s financed their fighting in part by illegally controlling diamond mining. (See the box De Beers and "Blood Diamonds" earlier in the chapter.) Cambodia's Khmer Rouge relied on illegal timber and gem exports from the territory they controlled to fight the government in Phnom Penh in the 1980s and 1990s. Colombia's FARC (*Fuerzas Armadas Revolucionarias de Colombia*) rebels tax the drug trade to finance their rebellion.

In a particularly tragic case beginning in 1998, the Democratic Republic of the Congo was torn apart by militias and neighboring armies that jockeyed for control of rich mineral deposits. Armed groups with no legitimate claims to sovereignty engaged in the illegal extraction and export of minerals such as coltan, which is refined into tantalum, a high-value, strategic metal used in cell phones, computer chips, and aircraft engines. Facing intense scrutiny from global environmental and human rights groups, major cell phone manufacturers like Nokia, Motorola, and Samsung have pressured their suppliers to avoid purchasing coltan/tantalum from the Congo, afraid that they will be accused of being responsible for some of the slaughter. Scholar Michael Nest alerts us to the power of consumers in the biggest Western markets for electronics to pressure MNCs not to buy raw materials from conflict areas. But he finds that China—with more than 600 million cell phone users—has unfortunately been eager to do business with illegal coltan suppliers in Africa, counteracting the efforts of MNCs.[24] Nevertheless, more governments around the world believe that pressuring companies to eliminate conflict minerals in their supply chains is an effective way to reduce violence and war in parts of Africa. As part of the 2010 Dodd-Frank Act, U.S. companies will be required to report to the Securities and Exchange Commission whether products they sell contain tantalum, tungsten, gold, or tin likely to have come from a conflict region.

Corruption Is Hampering Development

Political economists have spent decades trying to explain why some countries develop and others fall behind. They have correlated many factors with development, including the degree of trade openness, levels of political stability, and even the "squiggliness" of borders. Corruption is another key factor that is hampering poor countries. For example, former leaders of Indonesia, the Philippines, and Nigeria skimmed billions of dollars from government coffers, leaving their countries indebted and unable to attract foreign investment. An especially egregious example is the tiny country of Equatorial Guinea, ruled by dictator Teodoro Obiang. Despite being the third largest oil producer in Africa with a population of less than 700,000—meaning it has one of the highest per capita GDPs in the world—the country has a poverty rate of more than 75 percent. Most of the oil wealth—produced by the likes of Exxon Mobil and Marathon—falls into the hands of Obiang and his family. The World Bank has launched an international campaign to promote *good governance* in countries like Equatorial Guinea.

Analysts of the illicit global economy agree that corruption is a big problem, but they argue that the cause of corruption is not simply bad leaders in developing countries. In other words, they find that corruption is a transnational process in which many legal and illegal actors are complicit. Therefore, the fight against it must focus on global actors. Economist William Easterly argues in his book *The White Man's Burden* that foreign aid is frequently eaten up by corrupt governments, and he calls on "utopian social planners" in wealthy countries to adopt much more humble programs to help developing countries.[25] Raymond Baker and R. T. Naylor criticize Western governments and businesses for encouraging corruption.

CASE STUDIES IN THE ILLICIT GLOBAL ECONOMY

Thus far we have looked at six significant analytical findings in studies of the illicit international economy. We have also estimated the stakes involved and identified some of the key players. Now we turn to some case studies—smuggling, drug trafficking, and human trafficking—to illustrate some of the general themes and to specify how and why illicit activities occur and with what consequences for societies.

Smuggling

Smuggling is one of the oldest professions in the world. Enterprising individuals seek to profit from transporting goods across borders in defiance of the rules that political leaders have imposed on exchanges. The objects of smuggling are as numerous as the techniques to avoid getting caught. Some of the most important smuggled items are oil, tobacco, counterfeits, antiquities, animal parts, and military technology.

Cross-border transactions are illegal only if states say they are illegal. In other words, states define what is smuggling and what is not, and these definitions often change over time. A product may be legal in the source country and illegal in the receiving country. Or it might be illegal in the source country and legal in the receiving country. Or it might be illegal in both countries. The particulars of each case will affect the scale of smuggling and the likelihood that states will cooperate to fight it.

What are the motives of those who engage in smuggling? Greed is an obvious reason. Smugglers are willing to take risks because they want to make higher profits than they could achieve through legal trade. However, keep in mind that mercantilist states also engage in smuggling for purposes of security. For example, when the United States tries to restrict the sale of high technology to China, Chinese officials encourage the theft of this technology and its transfer to their country. Governments also feel that they have a right to defy sanctions and embargoes imposed on them by hostile powers. Despite facing strict UN sanctions, Saddam Hussein smuggled oil out of Iraq and garnered billions of dollars to keep his regime afloat in the 1990s.

How do smugglers justify their actions? Many have self-serving rationales that mask greedy impulses. Nevertheless, there are other justifications. Often, smugglers simply do not recognize the legitimacy of the political authority that is regulating trade or the legitimacy of a law that makes a particular type of trade illegal. For example, importers fed up with paying bribes to customs officials may see smuggling as legitimate avoidance of a predatory government. Similarly, some smugglers feel that import taxes are too high. Some smugglers simply do not recognize borders drawn by colonial powers. Others believe that they are supplying poor people with a product at a lower price, thus offering a sort of social service. In failed states or war zones, smuggling is sometimes the only way people can get access to food, medicines, and other necessities.

Smugglers take advantage of differing laws and regulations in neighboring countries to engage in **arbitrage**—buying a product in a lower-price market and selling it in a higher-price market. This opportunity for smuggling arises from price differentials that sometimes result from cross-border variations in taxes, regulations, and availability. When governments restrict the supply of goods and services in the name of morality, public health, and environmental protection, they unintentionally encourage smuggling. For example, the U.S. government bans the individual reimportation of prescription drugs from Canada and Mexico, partly out of a concern for the safety of U.S. consumers and partly to protect the profits of U.S. drug companies. However, the lower prices of prescription drugs in Canada and Mexico have enticed many elderly Americans to look north and south for technically illegal sources. In a classic case, U.S. Prohibition in the 1920s spurred smuggling of alcohol from Canada. Borders in North America have always been quite porous.

Tobacco is one of the most important smuggled products in the world. It is estimated that 11.6 percent of all cigarettes consumed in the world are smuggled and/or illegally produced, depriving governments of some $40 billion in taxes they are owed.[26] Once cigarettes are "in transit" in the global trade system, smuggling allows distributors to avoid all taxes, thus enhancing profitability. Cigarettes are often exported legally to duty-free zones outside the United States and then diverted to other countries. For many years, major U.S. and European tobacco companies were actually complicit in the smuggling, because it was a way of opening up new markets.[27] In some developing countries, cigarette manufacturing, importing, and distribution are a state monopoly. Thus, competition from contraband cigarettes cuts into an important source of government revenue. (Developed countries often forget how much their treasuries relied on "sin" taxes on alcohol and tobacco before World War I. Today many U.S. states, for instance, continue to raise their taxes on cigarettes.)

In a study of cigarette smuggling between the United States and Canada, Margaret Beare found that traffickers include Indian tribes, diplomats, soldiers, and tourists, who take advantage of special privileges they have under the law to move tobacco products across the border.[28] Canadian consumers have been very willing participants, partly because they view high taxes on cigarettes as unfair. Since 2003, the Canadian government and the European Union have sued major U.S. and Japanese cigarette manufacturers to force them to take steps to prevent smuggling of their products. This is a move to force manufacturers to take more responsibility for knowing what wholesalers do with tobacco products and what the chain of trade is from factory to the consumer. The World Health Organization has even proposed that every pack of cigarettes have an electronic mark on its packaging.

Another major impetus to smuggling is differential taxation—when taxes on the same product differ significantly from country to country. Even tax differences between states within the United States are an important cause of domestic black market operations. After 9/11, officials broke up many rings of people who were buying low-taxed cigarettes in North Carolina and Virginia and transporting them to high-tax states such as Michigan and New York, where they were sold at a markup in the black market. Since 2003, the U.S. Bureau of Alcohol, Tobacco, and Firearms has investigated more than 1,000 cases of cigarette bootlegging.

Antiquities are also big business for smugglers. Countries as widespread as Greece, Italy, Bolivia, and Thailand have laws that severely restrict the export or sale of antiquities, which are considered part of the national patrimony. Nevertheless, the huge demand for art and antiquities in wealthy countries supports a thriving transnational trade in stolen cultural property. Simon Mackenzie points out that art dealers and collectors have a strong sense of entitlement to enjoy and preserve cultural items, and they take insufficient steps to verify the legal provenance of objects they purchase.[29]

The most important international agreement designed to control antiquities looting is UNESCO's 1970 Convention on the Means of Prohibiting and Preventing the Illicit Import, Export and Transfer of Ownership of Cultural Property. Some progress has been made in mitigating black market trade through the International Council of Museums' Red Lists of threatened archaeological objects. And the United States has in recent years signed Memoranda of Understanding with countries such as Peru, China, and Greece to ban importation of broad categories of archaeological items likely to have been looted. It remains difficult for countries to recover antiquities, in part because it is usually impossible to prove that they were stolen or where the illegal excavations occurred. In recent years the Italian and Turkish governments have aggressively put pressure on major museums such as the Getty and New York's Metropolitan Museum of Art. An unfortunate side effect of the Arab Spring has been large-scale looting of major archaeological sites in Libya, Egypt, and Syria.

The illegal timber trade is causing massive deforestation in places such as Indonesia, Malaysia, and South America. Interpol and the United Nations Environment Programme estimate that illegal logging accounts for between 15 to 30 percent of all global logging, with higher rates in tropical countries.[30] Timber harvested illegally on state-owned land or in defiance of national regulations finds a hungry market in Japan, China, and the United States. The insatiable demand for paper and wood worldwide drives the market, which takes advantage of corrupt governments, civil conflict, and lax policing of enormous forested areas. The expansion of palm oil plantations in Indonesia and cattle farming in Brazil also contributes to illegal deforestation. Much illegal timber gets mixed with legitimately harvested wood at the time of export, making it difficult for importers to trace the true source of the product.

As countries like Indonesia and Thailand have been stripped of valuable forest cover, illegal logging has shifted to new areas like the Greater Congo Basin, Burma, and Papua New Guinea. This illicit market causes many follow-on problems that the global community must grapple with, including loss of biodiversity and increased global carbon emissions. Moreover, governments lose billions of dollars of tax revenue. Unfortunately, international efforts to suppress illegal deforestation have had limited effects. One treaty that countries have used in the fight is the Convention on International Trade in Endangered Species of Wild Fauna and Flora (CITES), which obliges signatories to regulate the import and export of certain types of endangered tree species (as well as thousands of plant and animal species). In the United States, an amendment in 2008 to the **Lacey Act**—a long-standing environment protection law—criminalizes the importation of wood that was illegally harvested overseas and requires importers to declare the type of wood being brought in and its country of origin (see the box Gibson Guitar and the Lacey Act). Although many big retailers like Home Depot, Walmart, and Ikea now have much better supply chain systems to buy from sustainable forestry producers, wood from tropical countries still often comes from illegal sources.

◢ GIBSON GUITAR AND THE LACEY ACT

Some of the biggest names in rock music play Gibson guitars: Eric Clapton, The Edge, Jimmy Page, Keith Richards, Angus Young, and Neil Young. So it was something of a surprise when in 2009 and again in 2011 agents from the U.S. Fish and Wildlife Service raided Gibson Guitars' factories in Nashville and Memphis, seizing wood used in guitar-making. What had such an iconic American company done wrong? Federal authorities charged Gibson with importing ebony and rosewood in violation of the Lacey Act, a long-standing law amended in 2008 to prohibit the importation of any wood product illegally sourced in a foreign country.[a] Gibson's CEO Henry Juskiewicz vehemently contested the charges, but his company reached an out-of-court settlement in August 2012 in which it admitted to wrongdoing and paid penalties of over $600,000. This case reveals how illicit logging collides with American manufacturing, environmental law, and U.S. domestic politics.

Rosewood and ebony have been used in guitars for a long time because of their durability and tonal quality. Unfortunately, the tree species these tropical woods come from are globally endangered due to overexploitation and illegal deforestation. Gibson imported ebony from Madagascar and ebony and rosewood from India, even though both countries have banned the export of unfinished lumber to try to stop illegal logging in their own countries. Among other things, the Lacey Act was designed to support forest conservation overseas and to shield U.S. sustainable forestry companies from having to

compete unfairly with illegally sourced wood that drives down global prices.[b]

Gibson and its supporters took their case to the court of public opinion. They argued that Gibson did not know where the imported wood had originally come from and had assumed that it was from legal sources. How were they supposed to know whether or not one of their suppliers, or one of their suppliers' suppliers, had broken laws somewhere else in the world? They noted that because the Lacey Act *did* allow the import of finished ebony and rosewood (like fingerboards) but not unworked planks of wood—and because Madagascar and India allowed the export of finished but not unfinished wood—the net effect was to privilege wood crafters overseas using illegal wood and disadvantage wood crafting companies like Gibson in the United States. American companies thus lost high-skilled jobs, and countries with unenforced laws and corrupt governments could grow their workforce. Gibson claimed it was being "bullied" by an "out-of-control" Federal government that was unfairly targeting small businesses. Juskiewicz made his case on conservative radio shows and Fox News, gaining support from Republican lawmakers.[c]

Gibson's critics blamed the company for profiting from an illegal market, deliberately mislabeling import records, and conveniently pleading ignorance about its supply chain.[d] They argued that it is the responsibility of any company to know where its supplies come from and to obey the laws that other countries have to protect their own forests. To deny that responsibility would open the door to any company to import overseas stolen goods, whether they be plundered antiquities, poached animals, or illegally sourced logs.

Before Gibson settled with the government, conservatives in Congress introduced bills in 2012 that would have watered down parts of the Lacey Act. An unlikely alliance of environmental groups, musicians, and U.S. timber companies lobbied to keep the Lacey Act strong.[e] The U.S. timber industry liked the Lacey Act because it served as a form of protectionism. Environmental groups like Greenpeace saw it as a tool in the global fight against deforestation. Even the Dave Matthews Band, Sting, Jack Johnson, Jason Mraz, Willie Nelson, and Maroon 5 signed a pledge supporting the Lacey Act and encouraging the use of only legally and sustainably harvested woods in musical instruments.[f] In the end, the Lacey Act was unchanged. The question remains whether most companies have the money or even the ability to police their supply chains back to the source of raw materials overseas. And will most guitar aficionados give up sonorous ebony and rosewood for sustainable tonewoods like maple, sapele, and African blackwood?

References

[a]Craig Haviguhurst, "Why Gibson Was Raided by the Justice Department," National Public Radio (August 31, 2011), at http://www.npr.org/blogs/therecord/2011/08/31/140090116/why-gibson-guitar-was-raided-by-the-justice-department.

[b]Patricia Elias, "Logging and the Law: How the U.S. Lacey Act Helps Reduce Illegal Logging in the Tropics," Union of Concerned Scientists (April 2012).

[c]Jonathan Meador, "Does Gibson Guitar's Playing the Victim Chord Stand Up to Scrutiny?" *Nashville Scene* (October 20, 2011), at http://www.nashvillescene.com/nashville/does-gibson-guitars-playing-the-victim-chord-stand-up-to-scrutiny/Content?oid=2656825.

[d]Ibid.

[e]Jake Schmidt, "House Committee Votes to Allow Illegal Loggers to Pillage World's Forests: Undercutting America's Workers & Increasing Global Warming," June 7, 2012, at http://switchboard.nrdc.org/blogs/jschmidt/house_committee_votes_to_allow.html.

[f]http://www.reverb.org/project/lacey/index.htm.

Smuggling of animals and animal parts is having a devastating effect on many species around the world. One of the difficulties in stopping wildlife trade is that the more endangered the animal, the higher the price for it and the greater the incentive to poach it, which accelerates its move toward extinction. The illegal ivory trade is responsible for drastic reductions of the stock of elephants and rhinoceroses in Africa and Asia. After a multinational treaty to ban the trade of ivory came into effect in 1989, an unintended effect was an assault on hippopotamuses and walruses, whose tusks became a substitute for ivory.[31] R. T. Naylor argues that all those who consume animal products are part of the chain of responsibility for poaching and illegal trade. Blame must be pointed in the direction of the fashion and cosmetics industry, tourists who buy trinkets made from animal parts, pet owners, and zoos.[32]

Sadly, many of the most magnificent creatures in the world are headed for extinction, despite strict trade restrictions under the CITES Convention. Avarice and covetousness drive much of the poaching, argues R.T. Naylor in his book *Crass Struggle*.[33] For example, only a few thousand tigers still exist in the wild, and they face the threat of being killed for their pelts and bones to use in "tiger wine." The graceful chiru, a small Tibetan antelope, is being hunted to extinction for its wool, which is smuggled into India and Nepal to make high-value shahtoush scarves. Black bears in North America are hunted illegally for their gall bladders, the bile of which is exported to Asia for use in traditional Chinese medicine. Given how much legal trade in animals and animal parts there is globally, law enforcement agencies do not consider it a high priority to try to crack down on the illicit side of the trade. There are only a few degrees of separation between us and those who are destroying animal species.

Drug Trafficking

Drug trafficking is one of the most entrenched and lucrative illicit activities in the world. Although many drug plants, such as coca, marijuana, and poppies, are grown in developing countries and the refined drug products are mostly consumed in rich Northern countries, marijuana is one of Canada's largest cash crops, and in some states in the United States, it is also a key cash crop. The United Nations Office of Drugs and Crime estimates that between 3.4 and 6.6 percent of the world's adult population used illegal drugs at least once in 2010 (compared to 20 percent using tobacco, which helps explain why cigarette smuggling supplies a much larger market).[34] Most of the profits from the drug trade are at the retail end (in the North), where the markup on products is the greatest.

The global fight against drugs illustrates the enormous costs and limited success of supply-side policies. Between 2000 and 2011, the United States spent $7.5 billion on Plan Colombia, an elaborate program to drastically reduce coca production in Colombia. Owing to massive aerial spraying and assistance to Colombia's military, the amount of coca cultivation in Colombia dropped by more than half, but there was no drop in the amount of global consumption, partly because cultivation expanded in Peru and Bolivia.

Eva Bertram et al. have attributed these kinds of disappointing outcomes to the **hydra effect,** whereby an effort to stop drug production or trade in one area simply causes it to sprout up somewhere else.[35] Whatever success there has been in breaking up big cartels in South America has been offset by the spawning of a larger number of smaller trafficking groups. Colombian traffickers have resorted to using makeshift submarines to transport huge cargoes of cocaine to the United States. Mexico has also become a drug production and transit center as a result of crackdowns in South America. Mexican cartels now supply an estimated 70 percent of drugs imported by the United States, and the violent turf wars between Mexican traffickers caused more than 47,000 deaths in Mexico between 2006 and 2012. The fight against the drug trade is straining the Mexican army and spreading more crime into the United States. With the trafficking come other social ills in Mexico, including widespread corruption and extortion.

Drug production and trafficking have had very negative effects on society, security, and government in developing countries (and in developed countries as well). Colombian economist Francisco Thoumi has documented the pervasive effects of drugs on the economies of the Andean countries (Colombia, Bolivia, and Peru).[36] Drug revenues have funded unsustainable real estate booms and other speculative investments. There has been a sharp decline in social trust, which makes it more costly for everyone to conduct normal business. Traffickers use drug export networks simultaneously to import contraband and weapons.

Thoumi argues that programs to encourage farmers to switch to alternative, legal crops have largely failed. Returns to farmers from illegal crops usually surpass potential revenues from food crops. The United States has seen a similar problem in Afghanistan, where poppy production since the 2002 invasion has skyrocketed. The illicit industry also has profound environmental consequences. Drug production has spurred the destruction of rain forests as growers move into new territory. And in Yemen, the poorest Arab country, widespread cultivation of *qat*—a tree whose leaves are chewed for their narcotic effect—has put a strain on water resources and reduced the amount of acreage devoted to food crops.

In many parts of the world, guerrilla groups and paramilitaries have turned to drugs as an important source of revenue. Rebels in Colombia, Cambodia, and Afghanistan have all used drug revenue to buy weapons and finance their insurgencies. In Latin America as a whole, gun crime and violence tied to the drug trade have ravished major cities. A significant proportion of those who end up in prison in developed countries have some connection to drug offenses.

Can drug trafficking be stopped? Probably not. David Mares points out that Northern countries have not had much success with unilateral threats to withhold aid from countries that fail to fight drugs seriously.[37] The United States sometimes threatens to "decertify" countries that do not adhere to U.S. priorities and to cut off aid and trade privileges. Multilateral police cooperation, border controls, spraying, and anticorruption programs may have some marginal benefits, but they rarely make a dent in overall drug flows. Even when crops are successfully sprayed and criminals jailed in supplying countries, corruption impedes criminal justice systems, and the profit motive leads to rapid relocation of destroyed crops and facilities.

Ultimately, any supply-side effort to combat elements of the drug production cycle faces two core challenges: weak governments that struggle to implement and fulfill policies, and an end-user demand that has maintained tremendous financial incentives to continue producing at every level of the illicit supply chain. The European Union has focused many of its policies on the demand side, decriminalizing small-scale sales and use of marijuana. Many public policy specialists believe that demand reduction or harm reduction in consuming countries through public spending on health and education can be least costly and most effective in the long run. In 2011 a Global Commission on Drug Policy, whose commissioners included Kofi Annan, Paul Volker, Richard Branson, and former heads of government in Europe and Latin America, issued a report advocating an end to the war on drugs, replacing it with policies of harm reduction, decriminalization, and regulation of legal drug sales.[38] These ideas are beginning to find a more receptive audience in the United States, where many states allow medical marijuana and voters in Colorado and Washington in 2012 legalized marijuana possession.

Human Trafficking

According to the International Labour Organization (ILO), 21 million people globally are subjected to forced labor, including 4.5 million victims of forced sexual exploitation (mostly women and children).[39] According to the U.S. State Department, an estimated 14,500 to 17,500 people are trafficked to the United States annually.

As many as 150,000 non-Japanese work in Japan's sex industry. Organized crime groups play an important role in the sex business. They include the Russian Mafia, the Chinese Triads, and the Japanese Yakuza. The former Soviet Union has been an important source of trafficked women since the collapse of communism sent economies in Russia, Ukraine, Moldova, and Belarus into a tailspin. Burma, Nepal, India, and Thailand are also important suppliers to the world's brothels. The trade is usually from poor countries to wealthier countries.

The roots of sex trafficking are in economic incentives, patriarchy, and poverty. Louise Shelley, an expert on transnational crime, argues, "Traffickers choose to trade in humans...because there are low start-up costs, minimal risks, high profits, and large demand. For organized crime groups, human beings have one added advantage over drugs: they can be sold repeatedly."[40] Where women and minors lack political rights, education, and legal protections, they tend to be victims of organized criminal networks. Global and national economic crises tend to disproportionately affect women and children, who are pushed into the international sex industry against their will. Child trafficking is practiced in many countries, in which poor families place children into debt bondage or indentured servitude to an employer in another country. Even government officials and corrupt law enforcement personnel have become direct and indirect supporters of the exploitation of women and children by sex predators. Cuba and Burma, for example, have promoted international tourism and concomitantly acquiesced in the growth of a private sex industry in order to attract foreign currency.

Illegal migration is another large and growing part of the human trafficking problem. David Kyle and John Dale point out a paradox: The more tightly a country controls its borders, the more would-be illegal aliens have to turn to traffickers to get across the border, and the higher the profits of professional smugglers.[41] Employers of illegal aliens in Europe and the United States share much of the blame for human trafficking. Powerful businesses need low-cost labor and are willing to break the law, absent credible threats of punishment. The United States and Europe are caught in a contradiction: Mercantilists and xenophobes want to restrict the flow of immigrants, but liberals who want flexible labor markets and low wages favor more immigrants—legal or illegal.

How can human trafficking be diminished? One way is to build fences on borders and beef up interdiction at sea. An amnesty for illegal aliens and an expansive "guest worker" program are other possibilities. Advocates for prostitutes argue that if trafficked women in the sex industry were provided immunity from prosecution and protection from deportation, they would provide extensive evidence and testimony against organized crime figures. Some believe that consensual, commercial sex between adults should be decriminalized. R. T. Naylor, for example, believes that personal vice done voluntarily by adults should not be criminalized because there is no clear victim. A structuralist would argue, however, that personal choice is not really voluntary, especially in the case of poor people who are compelled to participate in illicit acts in order to obtain an income. Liberal theorists increasingly argue that labor migration is an inherent part of globalization, and states can reduce illicit flows by simply allowing more legal flows. Labor-importing countries would gain valuable, young, low-cost workers, and labor exporters would boost remittance flows to their economies.

International organizations, governments, and nongovernmental organizations (NGOs) have taken significant, albeit insufficient, steps in the last decade to tackle trafficking in persons. In 2000 the United Nations adopted the Convention on Transnational Crime and a related Protocol to Prevent, Suppress, and Punish Trafficking in Persons, Especially Women and Children. The United States ratified the convention and protocol in October 2005, joining more than 150 countries that are party to the convention. Other organizations that cooperate to combat the scourge of trafficking include the ILO and the Organization for Security and Cooperation in Europe.

Individual states have taken unilateral action to address the problem. In October 2000, the United States passed into law the Victims of Trafficking and Violence Protection Act, which, among other things, allows the president to impose sanctions on countries that do not meet minimum standards in fighting human trafficking. In 2012 the U.S. State Department determined that seventeen countries had serious human trafficking problems and were not making concerted efforts to meet minimal standards for eliminating them, while forty-two more had significant trafficking problems. Of the seventeen countries, President Obama imposed full sanctions on Cuba, Eritrea, Madagascar, and North Korea, but he waived sanctions on Libya, Saudi Arabia, Algeria, Kuwait and three others on national security grounds.[42] More than thirty countries—including the United States and many European countries—have extraterritorial laws that make it a crime for their citizens to engage in sex with children overseas.

NGOs have been very active against the sex trade and sex tourism industries. They publicize the poor records of governments, help women and children in danger, and lobby for better national and international legislation. End Human Trafficking Now, Amnesty International, and Anti-Slavery International are important organizations with anti-trafficking networks around the world. Many international charitable organizations also have programs to help victims. *New York Times* columnist Nicholas Kristof has for years raised awareness of sex trafficking, including in his co-authored, bestselling 2012 book, *Half the Sky: Turning Oppression into Opportunity for Women Worldwide*. Finally, UN.GIFT (the UN Global Initiative to Fight Human Trafficking) works with governments and NGOs to coordinate anti-trafficking initiatives.

CONCLUSION

This chapter has examined illicit international transactions that are sometimes overlooked by IPE scholars, who have only recently begun to draw on the work of criminologists, anthropologists, and legal scholars. It has shown that many illicit activities shaped the history of the global economy. The chapter also stresses that illicit activities are sometimes an unanticipated result of global free trade, and that the well-intentioned efforts of governments to halt black markets sometimes have unintended negative consequences. Unless we recognize the terrible human exploitation that often takes place in the shadows, we cannot adequately assess the moral and ethical consequences of globalization. Furthermore, as the financial crisis throws more people into poverty, it increases the risk that they will suffer at the hands of illicit actors.

The illicit global economy has important effects on the world's security, trade, and growth.

It challenges the power of sovereign states and makes global governance more difficult. It is a network through which the world trades a wide array of products that threaten corporate bottom lines and public health. It often fuels conflict and violence, hinders development, and threatens the environment. It has the power to make the world both more equal and less fair. It shows us that globalization and technological innovation are not necessarily forces for the global good.

The illicit global economy blurs the line between the legal and illegal worlds of production, trade, and distribution. It makes it necessary for international organizations to establish and enforce new regulations and codes of conduct. It forces businesses to ask: Do I know my customers? How can I protect my property and my reputation? It forces consumers to ask: Am I responsible for knowing where the products I buy come from? What degree of separation is there between me and others I am tied to in global commodity chains? Increasingly, international civil society is mobilizing to tackle illicit activities. NGOs realize that with pressure (and support) from the grassroots and from consumers, states and businesses can make more progress against illegal actors.

States still tend to rely on supply-side approaches to illicit problems. Their mercantilist reflex to repress and interdict clashes with the hidden hand of the market and the not-so-hidden power of transnational criminals. However, this hardly means that political authorities are helpless. Governments in Europe and North America are increasingly receptive to newer strategies such as decriminalization, harm reduction, and partnerships with civil society groups. As developing countries institutionalize democracy, increase transparency, and strengthen market regulation, they should be better able to keep illicit transactions in check.

KEY TERMS

secrecy jurisdictions   381
primitive accumulation   382
socially responsible investing   387
restriction-opportunity
      dilemma   388

profit paradox   388
flags of convenience   389
commercialization of
      sovereignty   389
tax havens   389

know-thy-customer   391
name-and-shame campaigns   391
arbitrage   394
Lacey Act   396
hydra effect   398

DISCUSSION QUESTIONS

1. List some of the reasons why people participate in illicit markets.
2. How does a focus on illicit transactions help us explain development problems in the Third World? Is illicit activity an inherent aspect of global capitalism?
3. How are licit and illicit markets tied to each other? Are all those actors who benefit directly or indirectly from illicit transactions—even if they themselves don't engage in illegal acts—to be considered "guilty"? What responsibility do consumers and legitimate businesses have for illegal transactions and illicit networks?

4. On balance, does technological progress make illicit activities easier or harder? How can governments and corporations use technology to protect themselves from shadow actors?
5. How do the major findings about the illicit global economy confirm or challenge the key tenets of mercantilism, liberalism, and structuralism?
6. What are some of the unintended consequences of efforts to regulate the illicit global economy? How can states more effectively reduce the negative consequences of black markets?

SUGGESTED READINGS

Peter Andreas and Ethan Nadelmann. *Policing the Globe: Criminalization and Crime Control in International Relations.* New York: Oxford University Press, 2006.

Kevin Bales. *Understanding Global Slavery.* Berkeley, CA: University of California Press, 2005.

H. Richard Friman, ed. *Crime and the Global Political Economy.* Boulder, CO: Lynne Rienner, 2009.

R. T. Naylor. *Wages of Crime: Black Markets, Illegal Finance, and the Underworld Economy.* Ithaca, NY: Cornell University Press, 2002.

Carolyn Nordstrom. *Global Outlaws: Crime, Money, and Power in the Contemporary World.* Berkeley, CA: University of California Press, 2007.

Louise Shelley. *Human Trafficking: A Global Perspective.* Cambridge: Cambridge University Press, 2010.

Ian Smillie. *Blood on the Stone: Greed, Corruption, and War in the Global Diamond Trade.* New York: Anthem Press, 2010.

NOTES

1. Peter Andreas, "Illicit International Political Economy: The Clandestine Side of Globalization," *Review of International Political Economy*, 11 (August 2004), pp. 651–652.

2. "Trafficking: 24 Hours on the Border" (Anderson Cooper 360 Degrees), May 19, 2006, *cnn.com*, available at http://transcripts.cnn.com/TRANSCRIPTS/0605/19/acd.01.html.

3. Nicolas Pelham, "Gaza's Tunnel Complex," *Middle East Report* 261 (Winter 2011): 30–35.

4. Martin Santa, "Smuggling Tunnel Found under EU Border with Ukraine," July 19, 2012, at http://www.reuters.com/article/2012/07/19/us-slovakia-ukraine-tunnel-idUSBRE86I0ZO20120719.

5. Andreas, "Illicit International Political Economy," p. 645.

6. Kenneth Pomeranz and Steven Topik, *The World That Trade Created*, 3rd ed. (Armonk, NY: M. E. Sharpe, 2013), p. 161.

7. Charles Tilly, "War Making and State Making as Organized Crime," in Peter B. Evans, Dietrich Rueschemeyer, and Theda Skocpol, eds., *Bringing the State Back In* (Cambridge: Cambridge University Press, 1985).

8. R. T. Naylor, *Wages of Crime: Black Markets, Illegal Finance, and the Underworld Economy* (Ithaca, NY: Cornell University Press, 2002), p. 33.

9. United Nations Office on Drugs and Crime, *Estimating Illicit Financial Flows from Drug Trafficking and Transnational Organized Crimes* (October 2011), at http://www.unodc.org/documents/data-and-analysis/Studies/Illicit_financial_flows_2011_web.pdf.

10. Raymond Baker, *Capitalism's Achilles Heel* (Hoboken, NJ: John Wiley, 2005), p. 172.

11. Ibid., p. 206.

12. Moisés Naím, *Illicit: How Smugglers, Traffickers, and Copycats Are Hijacking the Global Economy* (New York: Doubleday, 2005).

13. Carolyn Nordstrom, "ICT and the World of Smuggling," in Robert Latham, ed., *Bombs and Bandwidth: The Emerging Relationship between Information Technology and Security* (New York: The New Press, 2003).

14. John Guare, *Six Degrees of Separation: A Play* (New York: Vintage, 1994).

15. Carolyn Nordstrom, *Shadows of War: Violence, Power, and Profiteering in the Twenty-First Century* (Berkeley, CA: University of California Press, 2004).

16. Phil Williams, "Crime, Illicit Markets, and Money Laundering," in P. J. Simmons and C. de Jonge Oudrat, eds., *Managing Global Issues* (Washington, DC: Carnegie Endowment, 2001).

17. Eva Bertram, Morris Blachman, Kenneth Sharpe, and Peter Andreas, *Drug War Politics: The Price of Denial* (Berkeley, CA: University of California Press, 1996).

18. Thomas Friedman, *The World Is Flat: A Brief History of the Twenty-First Century* (New York: Farrar, Straus & Giroux, 2005).

19. Naím, *Illicit*, pp. 24–30.

20. Peter Andreas, "Illicit Globalization: Myths, Misconceptions, and Historical Lessons," *Political Science Quarterly* 126:3 (2011), p. 13.

21. Ronen Palan, "Tax Havens and the Commercialization of State Sovereignty," *International Organization*, 56 (Winter 2002), pp. 151–176.

22. Nicholas Shaxson, *Treasure Islands: Uncovering the Damage of Offshore Banking and Tax Havens* (New York: Palgrave Macmillan, 2011), p. 11.

23. R. T. Naylor, *Economic Warfare: Sanctions, Embargo Busting, and Their Human Cost* (Boston, MA: Northeastern University Press, 2001).

24. Michael Nest, *Coltan* (Malden, MA: Polity Press, 2011), pp.168–172.

25. William Easterly, *The White Man's Burden: Why the West's Efforts to Aid the Rest Have Done So Much Ill and So Little Good* (New York: Penguin, 2006).

26. Luk Joossens and Martin Raw, "From Cigarette Smuggling to Illicit Tobacco Trade," *Tobacco Control* 21 (2012): 230–234.

27. Ibid.

28. Margaret Beare, "Organized Corporate Criminality—Corporate Complicity in Tobacco Smuggling," in Margaret E. Beare, ed., *Critical Reflections on Transnational Organized Crime, Money Laundering and Corruption* (Toronto, ON: University of Toronto Press, 2003).

29. Simon Mackenzie, "Dig a Bit Deeper: Law, Regulation and the Illicit Antiquities Market," *British Journal of Criminology*, 45 (May 2005), pp. 249–268.

30. Christian Nellemann, ed., *Green Carbon, Black Trade: Illegal Logging, Tax Fraud and Laundering in the World's Tropical Forests* (INTERPOL Environmental Crime Programme, 2012), p. 13.

31. R. T. Naylor, "The Underworld of Ivory," *Crime, Law, and Social Change*, 42:4–5 (2004), pp. 261–295.

32. Ibid.

33. R. T. Naylor, *Crass Struggle: Greed, Glitz, and Gluttony in a Wanna-Have World* (Montreal: McGill-Queen's University Press, 2011).

34. United Nations Office of Drugs and Crime, *2012 World Drug Report*, 2012, p. 7, at http://www.unodc.org/unodc/en/data-and-analysis/WDR-2012.html.

35. Bertram et al., *Drug War Politics*.

36. Francisco Thoumi, *Illegal Drugs, Economy, and Society in the Andes* (Baltimore, MD: The Johns Hopkins University Press, 2003).

37. David Mares, *Drug Wars and Coffeehouses: The Political Economy of the International Drug Trade* (Washington, DC: CQ Press, 2006).

38. See Global Commission on Drug Policy, *War on Drugs* (June 2011), at www.globalcommissionondrugs.org/.

39. *ILO Global Estimate of Forced Labour 2012: Results and Methodology*, International Labour Organization (2012).

40. Louise Shelley, *Human Trafficking: A Global Perspective* (Cambridge: Cambridge University Press, 2010), p. 3.

41. David Kyle and John Dale, "Smuggling the State Back In: Agents of Human Smuggling Reconsidered," in Rey Koslowski and David Kyle, eds., *Global Human Smuggling: Comparative Perspectives* (Baltimore, MD: The Johns Hopkins University Press, 2001).

42. "Presidential Determination 2012–16 With Respect to Foreign Governments' Efforts Regarding Trafficking in Persons," September 14, 2012, at http://www.state.gov/j/tip/rls/other/2012/197803.htm.

Migration and Tourism: People on the Move

Waiting for Work: Chinese citizens stand in line before entering Macau.

dbimages/Alamy

As noted in Chapter 1, international political economy (IPE) is not just about states and markets. Movements of people are every bit as controversial and important as flows of corporate bonds, auto parts, prescription medications, or arms. Indeed, their consequences shape how states, international organizations (IOs), nongovernmental organizations (NGOs), and local communities perceive and negotiate their relationship to people inside and beyond national borders. Whether it is the global circulation of unskilled migrant laborers, technology industry professionals, political refugees, tourists, terrorists, or NGO activists, new patterns of human flows have been a central feature of IPE.

The United Nations estimates that about 214 million people, or almost 3.1 percent of the world's population, are migrants living away from their native country.[1] Their movement can be related to the collapse of governments; efforts to gain "guest worker" privileges in another country; the need to escape war, poverty, or natural disaster; or simply the search for freedom and prosperity. Unlike migrants, most tourists travel for reasons related to leisure and recreation. To many people, travel is merely an escape from the routines of everyday life. However, the tourist industry now plays a central role in both the domestic economy and global standing of many nations. Taken together, migration and tourism highlight both the opportunities and inequalities that shape regional development and undergird new global connections in the current context of economic uncertainty.

These different forms of global movement raise questions about some of the basic precepts of IPE. For example, what is the impact of transnational human flows on economic development in both home and host countries? What happens when people increasingly define their identities, communities, livelihoods, politics, and leisure activities in terms other than those related to the nation-state? And what effects do these movements have on the four structures of IPE (security, production and trade, knowledge and technology, and money and finance)?

In response to these questions, this chapter examines how migration and tourism shape the behavior and outcomes of international and national actors and policies. It highlights the inequalities and contradictions that continue to structure the direction and effect of global human flows. It also examines the new strategies employed to regulate human flows and protect individual rights as people increasingly live, work, and play in places other than their nations of birth.

ON THE GLOBAL FAST TRACK: THE IPE OF MIGRATION

We frequently hear stories about how our globalized world has allowed mobile, enterprising migrants to access resources and opportunities unimaginable in their home country. This perspective chalks up immigrant success or failure, belonging or marginalization, to individual actions and values that are sometimes extended to an entire ethnic or national group. In this section of the chapter, we question the assumptions and implications of that perception. For example, which forces govern who migrates, how, and to where? How is the migration experience shaped by a person's race, gender, education, or nationality? How do certain patterns of migration reproduce inequalities between regions and groups rather than transcend them? Although increased global migration seems to point to expanding opportunities for individual autonomy and mobility, immigrants' experiences ask us to reconsider the ongoing structural inequalities that condition their movement and ultimate migration outcomes.

While human movement is a common feature of our world, the notion of migration can be something of a moving target. In its simplest sense, **migration** refers to movement from one place to another—to a nearby city, another region, or another country entirely. Migration may be temporary or permanent; there is nothing about the notion of migration itself that guarantees either the length of residence or the strength of the commitment to the migratory destination. The reasons for migration are diverse: People may not have permanent work or sufficient resources to sustain themselves in their home environment. They may wish to pursue advanced educational or professional opportunities. They may not be able to express their ideas or practice their religion in the way that they choose. They may face environmental devastation or threats to their personal safety. They may be separated from family members. Therefore, when we speak of migration, we are referring to a wide variety of circumstances, motives, and experiences, each with different implications for individuals, states, and the international community as a whole.

Migration has long been an integral force in shaping both individual nation-states and their relationships to one another within the global landscape. **Internal migration**—movement from rural to urban areas or from one area of the country to another—has been a central feature of IPE theories of development (see Chapter 11). In these theories, migration within the nation has often been seen as a crucial step toward modernization (see "China: Bringing Development Home").

CHINA: BRINGING DEVELOPMENT HOME

China's road to modernization can be charted through its citizens' changing migration paths over the past two decades. Domestically, the introduction of the market economy and the shift from collective to household production systems made many Chinese rural farmers "surplus" labor. In response to these changes, and the growing economic opportunities in the cities, many rural residents have taken part in a large-scale exodus from the countryside. By 2003, China's rural–urban migrants, known as the "floating population," were estimated to have reached 140 million.[a] In the cities, successful rural migrants have started informal businesses such as those found in Beijing's growing garment industry. More commonly, they have filled the ranks of the urban workforce whose low wages underwrite the success of China's exports in the global market. Migrants' contributions to China's national development were made especially visible in the 2008 Beijing Olympics, where venues

were constructed in large part by former farmers, who represent 70 percent of the construction industry.[b]

Globally, China has produced a large number of professional migrants who are contributing to national development in a very different way. In 2006, Chinese immigrants constituted 4.1 percent of immigrants to the United States. Overall, these Chinese immigrants were more likely to be working in science and engineering occupations, with one quarter of the men working in management, business, finance, or informational technology.[c] Because of their high education level, these migrants have played a central role in economic and job growth in the U.S. technology industry (Chapter 10). However, instead of constituting a drain on Chinese human resources, they have increasingly become a source of human and economic capital gain for their nation of origin as well. In a 2009 study titled "America's Loss Is the World's Gain," 72 percent of the U.S.-based, professional

(continued)

Chinese migrants interviewed indicated that they thought professional opportunities were now better in China than in the United States.[d] In the context of the global economic recession, many Chinese professionals were thus returning home to job and capital markets that were still growing, rather than shrinking. Validating this perception, many return migrants reported faster movement up the management ladder, better compensation, and more professional recognition in China. Therefore, while the current economic downturn has been global in scope, for China's mobile professionals, migration to the United States has increasingly served as more of a career detour than a destination, with the road to prosperity leading home.

References

[a]See People's Daily Online, "China's Floating Population Tops 140 Million," July 28, 2005, http://english.people.com.cn/200507/27/eng20050727_198605.html; and Li Zhang, *Strangers in the City: Reconfigurations of Space, Power and Social Networks within China's Floating Population* (Stanford, CA: Stanford University Press, 2001).

[b]Xinhuanet, "Beijing Increases Migrant Workers' Salary for Construction of Olympic Venues," January 19, 2007, http://en.beijing2008.cn/27/97/article214009727.shtml.

[c]Terrazas, Aaron Matteo, and Vhavna Devani, "Chinese Immigrants in the United States," *Migration Information Source*, June 13, 2008, www.migrationinformation.org.

[d]Wadhwa, Vivek, A. Saxenian, R. Freeman, and G. Gereffi, "America's Loss Is the World's Gain: America's New Immigrant Entrepreneurs, Part 4," March 2009, http://ssrn.com/abstract=1348616.

Global migration rose to unprecedented numbers at the end of the nineteenth century; however, it has been in the latter part of the twenty-first century that the volume, reach, and pace of global migration have taken on their current intensity.[2] Whether we are talking about unskilled labor or highly educated professionals, **transnational migration** describes the now-frequent process by which people cross state borders in search of temporary work or for other reasons. Breakthroughs in technology and travel have allowed a broad array of people to move across borders and time zones as part of (or to ensure) their daily lives. Both men and women have blazed new migration trails and contributed to the construction of vibrant multicultural communities that extend across the globe. In the countries with the highest share of migrants in the total population, migrants constituted 22.4 percent in New Zealand, 40.7 percent in Singapore, and 86.5 percent in Qatar.[3]

The increased scale and frequency of transnational migration of the last four decades has been accompanied by new patterns of movement. Whereas previous travel routes were characterized by journeys east and west, or colonial forays south, current migration is characterized by more south–north or even south–south migration. One-third of international migrants moved from developing to developed countries (often from former colonies), while another third moved from developing to other developing countries. Nearly six of every ten international migrants now live in high-income countries that include developing countries such as Bahrain, Brunei, Kuwait, Qatar, the Republic of Korea, and Saudi Arabia.[4] And since 2008, many migrants from developing countries like India, Mexico, and China have returned home.

People were once presumed to migrate in order to take up permanent residence in their destinations; this kind of movement *into* a new country for the purpose of settling and becoming a resident of that country is called **immigration.** Contemporary migration, however, is now less unidirectional, and often more fluid in terms of its duration. **Circular migration** refers to the process by which migrants' movement shifts back and forth between home and work communities in response to different economic opportunities, employment conditions, and family responsibilities. For example, every September, thousands of young men from Mali and Niger travel to the Cote d'Ivoire and other West African countries to seek wage-labor opportunities along the coast. They remain in these jobs until the spring, when they return home to attend to their crops.[5] Similarly, women from the Philippines and mainland China migrate to Hong Kong to work as domestic labor for wealthier, professional families. When their employment contract term is up, they must return home; however, they often solicit a new contract to revisit Hong Kong for another cycle of labor.[6]

The scale and frequency of temporary labor migration is also encouraged by growing transnational networks of kin and neighbors on whom migrants can depend to find residence and work. This pattern of **chain migration,** whereby a migrant "links" up with social networks abroad, promotes the concentration of migrant communities in enclaves or gateway cities, which are oriented around immigrant culture and practical needs. In these enclaves, it is possible for a migrant to speak his or her native language, buy "home-style" food, make quick wire transfers to people back home, and practice local customs.

For example, Roger Rouse studied the large numbers of Mexicans who moved between Aguililla, Michoacan, and Redwood City, California.[7] The concentration of migrants moving between one small town in Michoacan and Redwood City had become so marked by the mid-1990s that many people began referring to parts of Redwood City itself as Aguililla. Indeed, most men in the community spent a portion of their lives moving back and forth across the border between what were, in essence, the two communities of Aguililla. Community members were able to draw on a deeply embedded transnational network to facilitate ongoing transfers of people, money, and resources.

Migrating toward Development

Transnational migration circuits and the social networks on which they are built are an essential part of the changing economic conditions and political relations associated with globalization. As global capitalist production becomes more mobile, migrant workers tend to move to labor markets where there is high demand and low domestic supply. For this reason, migrants often fill jobs at both ends of the labor market. Engineers and scientists take highly specialized professional positions within the technology or aerospace industries. Unskilled workers fill labor and service jobs that few native workers will do—for example, in the food service and garment industries, meatpacking, domestic labor, or agriculture. Furthermore, declining population growth in countries like Japan and in much of the European Union (EU), including Germany, Italy, Austria, and France, has increased the need for workers in general, thus making them a prime destination for foreign labor migrants.[8] From Saudi Arabia to Spain to the United States, changing economic and demographic conditions have required most developed countries to make some accommodations for migrant labor within their borders.

The current global pattern of transnational migration has created new opportunities and challenges for individual migrants and states alike. States with high demand for foreign workers, such as Singapore, Kuwait, or Germany, have developed temporary foreign worker, or **guest worker**, programs that regulate the provisional admission, residence, and employment of a specific class of migrant labor. In many cases, these migration policies usually do not allow whole families to enter the country or provide for long-term residence. For the most part, guest worker programs are aimed at maximizing cheap labor and then keeping migrants moving, rather than creating new nationals.

A prime example of this kind of program was the U.S. Bracero Program. Between 1942 and 1964, the initiative permitted the entry of temporary workers from Mexico to fill U.S. wartime labor shortages in the agricultural sector. By the 1950s, however, the United States sought to deter the permanent settling of Bracero workers and the entry of new Mexican migrants, to prevent the expansion of immigrant labor into nonagricultural sectors, and to curb the rising levels of unemployment among domestic laborers.

As these examples suggest, migrants are subject to different degrees of privilege or prejudice as they move between labor markets. Because of their conditional labor and residency status, guest workers can be especially vulnerable to labor rights violations, discrimination, and abuse. In a recent study of Jordanian garment factories, Bangladeshi workers who were interviewed reported that their employers had confiscated their passports, forced them to work forty-eight-hour periods, provided insufficient sleeping accommodations, and refused to pay mandated overtime pay.[9] The situation for undocumented workers can be just as bad or worse, as these workers often have no recourse in filing complaints against employers who abuse or fail to pay them.

At the international level, migrant rights come under the purview of the Office of the United Nations High Commissioner for Human Rights. However, as people increasingly live their lives in places outside their place of birth, states and IOs alike have recognized the need for new forms of global governance that can regulate human flows and protect individual rights. International treaties like the United Nations 1990 International Convention on the Protection of the Rights of All Migrant Workers sought to clarify migrant worker categories and reiterate receiving states' responsibility to protect migrants' rights. This convention built on previous resolutions passed by the International Labour Organization (ILO) that "advocate the principles of equal treatment, equality of opportunity and non-discrimination" for all workers.[10] In 2006, the United Nations sponsored the High-Level Dialogue on International Migration and Development, at which member states actively debated "how to maximize the development benefits of international migration and minimize its negative impacts."[11] This event spawned the formation of the Global Forum on Migration and Development as a consultative body through which states could address migration issues and develop partnerships.

Despite these developments, much of the work to protect migrant rights and resolve migration conflicts has tended to fall to bilateral and regional negotiations over residence and labor conditions in particular countries. For example, the South American Conference on Migration ("Lima Process") and the Regional Conference on Migration ("Puebla Process") are two regional groups that have worked to protect migrants and facilitate their remittances in Latin America. In Asia, the Ministerial Consultations on Overseas Employment and Contractual Labour ("Colombo Process") has sought to promote legal migration and intergovernmental cooperation.[12] While these consortiums have created regional standards and promoted collaboration on migration, it is often still at the level of bilateral diplomacy that the concerns of specific national origin migrant groups are addressed. Therefore, when U.S. president Obama met with Mexican president Felipe Calderón and Canadian prime minister Stephen Harper at the "three amigos" summit in Mexico in 2009, the question of how to regulate the flow of migrants, trucks, and epidemics constituted the main focus of conversation.

On the other end of the labor spectrum, educated professionals are often highly coveted by both sending and receiving states alike. Indeed, many developing nations have lamented the loss of their most talented citizens through transnational migration. **Brain drain**—a process by which educated members of a society migrate to more developed nations where there are higher salaries and more employment opportunities—has been responsible for reducing the human resources necessary for many states' own development. In response to a grave shortage of domestic nurses in 2006, U.S. lawmakers decided *not* to place limits on the number of visas allotted for foreign nurses. The move, however, frustrated residents in the Philippines and Fiji, who feared that their most valuable health care resources would be wooed away.[13] As a result of conflicts like these, some developing countries have instituted sanctions to keep their professionals at home or to ensure their return from education abroad in order to guarantee the repatriation of valuable knowledge and technology.

Perhaps the biggest reason why migration can be attractive to both migrants and sending states is the opportunity for **remittances**—income earned abroad that is sent back to the home country. Global remittances reached $351 billion by 2011, up 8 percent from 2010, to represent the first rise in remittance flows to all developing regions since the global financial crisis began.[14] Of those flows, the largest remittances went to India ($58 billion), China ($57 billion), and Mexico ($24 billion).[15] At the macrolevel, remittances shore up a nation's creditworthiness and provide foreign currency to prevent balance of payment crises. At the microlevel, remittances are used to supplement individual household incomes, but they are also important for offsetting the cost of education and health care. Furthermore, in some cases, hometown associations—formed by migrants from a single community—have consolidated their remittances to finance infrastructure and development projects in their home communities.[16] For these reasons, even IOs such as the United Nations and the World Bank have promoted "mainstreaming" migration as a central feature of global development efforts.[17]

Some states have developed diverse legal and financial incentives to keep their mobile populations invested in economic and political processes at home. Mexico and Guatemala are among a growing number of states that have instituted dual citizenship designations in order to maintain allegiance among their citizens abroad. India created a new citizenship category altogether for its emigrant citizens—non-resident Indian (NRI). To further encourage capital flows from residents abroad, some states have enabled foreign currency holdings and enacted "matching funds" programs that reward migrants for investing at home. The Mexican government in particular has collaborated with Wells Fargo and Bank of America to allow its citizens to open U.S. bank accounts with a Mexican national identification card that it grants through its consular agencies in the United States. The Central Reserve Bank of El Salvador authorized Salvadoran Banks with branches in the United States to serve as remittance agencies.

The recent global economic recession has illustrated the risks involved in relying on migrant remittance income as a central source of local, national, and regional development efforts. States like Japan, South Korea, Spain, and Dubai—recipients of large migrant labor flows—have begun instituting programs that encourage guest workers to return to their home countries. In what some economists have called the "biggest turnaround in migration flows since the Great Depression," some migrants themselves are choosing to forego emigration or, if already abroad, to return home (see "China: Bringing Development Home").[18] Non-resident Indians and other one-time migrants now see new industries and high economic growth in India as powerful incentives to return home rather than stay abroad. Mexico, the largest source of migrants to the United States, is a case in point. Mexican census data released in 2009 documented a 25 percent decline in the number of Mexicans migrating to the United States compared to the previous year. Furthermore, the recession that wracked the U.S. economy beginning in 2007 contributed to a 25 percent decline in **remittances** to Mexico by the end of 2009. Remittances remained flat in 2010, only recovering in the last three quarters of 2011.[19] Clearly, the new opportunities brought by migration can also breed new challenges for states that have grown dependent on remittance income.

Transnational migration has clearly become a defining quality of global capitalist production. The economic benefits it offers to individual migrants, sending states, and receiving nations have generated new and different patterns of human flows across the globe. Nonetheless, as described earlier, the global fast tracks to economic development are often built along lines of global inequality in terms of who can move, who benefits from that movement, and how sustainable those benefits might be. Therefore, it's important to explore the social and political dimensions of transnational migration to understand what other forces shape the nature and consequences of global human flows.

Citizenship and the Politics of Belonging

Can a person be a citizen in more than one country and, if so, how does he negotiate multiple political allegiances? What role do cultural and social differences play in shaping the conditions for citizenship? A closer look at global flows forces us to question the assumption that national identity, politics, or even development is rooted within the boundaries of the nation-state. With the help of new information technologies and a highly mobile population, national identity politics may be enacted across the globe. Furthermore, transnational communities formed around beliefs, identities, or politics that are not tied to a particular state reflect new kinds of human connections that raise new challenges for both the states that contain them and the international political economy in general.

Some of the most heated debates about migration in the United States and Europe have centered on the social and political implications of migrants. Given that one of the chief functions of the modern state is to control its borders and protect its citizens' rights, some see unauthorized migrants as a threat to the political sovereignty and security of the nation. Rather than getting the necessary work permits before entering the country, **irregular migrants** enter a country without visas or stay on after their work visas have expired and thus lack the necessary documentation to remain in the country legally. Senegalese and other sub-Saharan migrants have been entering Spain in large numbers over the past few years through the Canary Islands (a Spanish territory just off West Africa) or Malta. In 2006, their large numbers caused a humanitarian crisis in the Canary Islands and also protest from native Spanish residents who saw them as a threat to economic stability and national security. In the United States, anti-immigrant legislation in southern states such as Arizona and Alabama illustrates how economic pressures have resulted in new efforts to regulate migrant flows and assert tighter control over national borders.

The EU has grappled with this issue as it has extended membership to some post-Soviet states and now contemplates Turkey's admission. With the inclusion of poorer Eastern European members in 2004, many of the original EU members imposed migration limits to mitigate the prospective flood of migrants that they feared would move westward. Indeed, anti-immigrant campaigns invoked the "Polish plumber" as a symbol of the cheap migrant labor they claimed would take over local jobs. While studies show that Eastern European migrant numbers did increase substantially, their employment fueled growth and did not depress wages, as feared.[20] What is more, non-EU nationals outnumbered migrants from new to old EU countries. Therefore, one of the main points of opposition to Turkey's inclusion has been the ongoing fear of waves of cheap labor from Asia and the Middle East. These fears grow in part out of the fact that Turkey, like Spain, is no longer defined by outmigration of its citizens but rather by inmigration—in this case, of migrants from Afghanistan, Bangladesh, Iraq, and Iran, as well as former Soviet states. These irregular migrants often move to transit states such as Turkey, as a first step toward greater economic opportunities in more affluent countries of the EU. In the context of increasing regional migration, the migration policies of individual EU member states thus come to matter greatly.

Citizenship is a legal category that entitles a person to full and equal rights within a given state, perhaps most importantly including the right to vote. However, states have various means of assigning that status. Citizenship may be granted based on birth, ethnicity, or naturalization. Anyone born on U.S. soil is eligible to apply for citizenship. Furthermore, once immigrants to the United States obtain a "green card," they can eventually earn the chance to be naturalized as citizens. Because they provide immigrants the opportunity to become permanent residents, countries such as the United States or Australia are known as **settler states.** By contrast, people born on German soil do not necessarily receive citizenship. Instead, German citizenship is granted through one's parents: One must have a German mother or father, or a parent with established permanent residence, to become a German national. Restrictive migration policies in countries such as Japan and Saudi Arabia make it even harder for migrants to become citizens of those countries.

Another way that people can make a claim for permanent residence in a country that is not their own is through refugee status or asylum. Indeed, refugees currently account for approximately 16 percent of all international migrants in the less developed countries (LDCs).[21] **Refugees** are displaced people who are unable or unwilling to return to their country of origin because of fear of persecution on account of race, religion, nationality, membership in a particular social group, or political opinion. A Sudanese victim of factional violence who has moved to a temporary camp in Chad could be considered a refugee. Often the UN High Commission on Refugees may be responsible for negotiating a permanent resettlement destination—either in Chad or in another country—for this Sudanese refugee. In 2010, Afghan refugees constituted the largest group of refugees—29 percent of the global population—followed by Iraqis. By the end of that year, developing countries hosted 8.5 million refugees or 80 percent of the global refugee population. Pakistan alone hosted 1.9 million refugees—the highest number.[22]

People who seek **asylum** are also permanently displaced people who face persecution in their home countries. These immigrants, however, often make their claims for protection to a court within the nation in which they hope to reside, usually from within that nation's territory. Although over 850,000 individuals filed for asylum in 2010, that number constituted a 10 percent decline in petitions from the prior year. South Africa was the largest recipient of individual asylum applications.

Citizenship and asylum are more than just legal categories; they are also the highly politicized subject of geopolitics. A recent legal study showed that the U.S. government has granted political asylum to 80 percent of Cuban asylum applicants, but only 10 percent of Haitian applicants. This discrepancy in asylum rates reflects the U.S. government's policy of recognizing Cubans as political refugees fleeing an authoritarian, communist regime, while Haitians tend to be seen as economic migrants rather than refugees.[23]

Even when foreigners acquire legal residence or citizenship in their adopted countries, states often struggle with integrating them into the social fabric of their new homes. One reason for this struggle is that instead of following a process of **assimilation**—whereby an immigrant takes on the values and customs of the new prevailing culture—immigrants may retain a strong connection to their culture or nation of origin. **Diaspora** refers to communities that have retained a common identification with their homeland, despite being displaced and dispersed. The Jews' expulsion from Babylon in the fifth century B.C. and the transatlantic African slave trade during the sixteenth to nineteenth centuries established the Jewish and African diasporas as the original diasporic communities. In both of these cases, peoples' forcible displacement from their homeland produced transnational communities that continued to identify with a common history and identity even though they might speak different languages and be citizens of other states.

Today, the concept of diaspora has expanded to refer to a much broader array of transnational communities. We can talk of the Indian, Iranian, Filipino, Chinese, or Haitian diasporas as communities created through an intense process of migration and global dispersion. Diasporic communities may be linked to a specific nation-state—such as the case of the Irish diaspora—or may be a stateless nation—such as the Kurds. Regardless of type, diasporas are increasingly significant both for the new kinds of social, political, and economic organizations they represent and also for the effects they have had on political and economic processes in their home countries. For instance, Haitian migrants in New York see their long-term residence and labors abroad as part of a concerted campaign to improve and support their homeland, something Nina Glick-Schiller and Georges Fouron have called "long-distance nationalism." In this formulation, the Haitian community is defined not by its residence on Haitian soil but rather by its common Haitian blood and obligation to the homeland.[24]

New information technology has played an important role in supporting diasporic communities. Now, even when immigrants cannot easily or frequently travel between origin and adoptive countries, they can keep abreast of local news through online media, participate in virtual chatroom conversations with other diaspora members, and manage individual and group finances through Internet banking. Many local communities have created Web pages to keep residents living abroad informed about local needs and goings-on, as well as to stimulate outside investment and participation in local events. The global expansion of cellular phone service to rural areas, as well as Internet conferencing services, has facilitated real-time communication between immigrants and their kin in historically remote areas. All of these technologies allow people to maintain social connections across borders, preserving community language, identity, and politics at any distance.

Many receiving states have had to contend with the complex political implications of diaspora. In February 2006, when a Danish newspaper published a cartoon satirizing the Prophet Muhammad, a group of Denmark's fundamentalist Muslim clerics lobbied the embassies of eleven "mostly Muslim" countries to demand a meeting with Denmark's prime minister. The Danish prime minister's refusal provoked a boycott of Danish goods across the Middle East, as well as violent protests against European offices, media, and tourists throughout the region. This example demonstrates how a transnational community can be mobilized not simply on the basis of a common national identity but also on the basis of a common religious identity. With Islam as Europe's fastest-growing religion, the social and political implications of an increasingly active Muslim diaspora have become the source of much debate across the continent.

Even when migrants actively embrace their new host society, discrimination and inequality can deprive migrants of everyday privileges afforded to native residents. Often this marginalization coincides with perceived differences in language, customs, and cultural values. In some cases, higher population growth rates among immigrant families have meant that the immigrant population is growing faster than the native-born population, leading nativist constituencies to worry about becoming a minority in their own country. Consequently, immigrant struggles for social recognition and political inclusion have fueled some of the major social and political conflicts in recent years. The term **cultural citizenship** effectively describes immigrants' demands within these conflicts—that is, they seek a sense of social belonging that is not contingent on assimilation, but rather is built on a respect for diversity.

Two weeks of rioting by youth in Paris suburbs during 2005 illustrate this point. The clashes between youth and the French police were attributed largely to the extreme social marginalization and impoverishment experienced by North African immigrants and their descendants, despite their official French citizenship. This contradiction prompted a *New York Times* article to raise the important question, "What makes someone French?"[25] Because the French have always insisted on a secular national identity, they have glossed over racial and cultural distinctions rather than try to address their social and political effects. The French government's 2004 ban on the wearing of head scarves or other religious paraphernalia in public schools illustrates just such an attempt to suppress the visibility of cultural differences. Nonetheless, many of France's European counterparts are trying to find a way to recognize diversity, both to create a more multicultural society and to defuse the move by disenfranchised immigrant youth toward radical or fundamentalist organizations.

As the French case makes clear, the increasingly multicultural societies created by transnational migration require new ways of thinking about what makes someone an authentic citizen of the nation and thus bring into focus contradictions in the definition of the nation itself. Porous state borders and fluid patterns of human movement challenge the assumption that the modern nation is defined not only by a sovereign state but also by a singular, common history and culture. This challenge is true in the United States, as well, although immigration is a central feature of U.S. national identity. For example, in 2006 a musical collaboration produced the first Spanish-language version of the U.S. national anthem ("The Star-Spangled Banner"). "Nuestro Himno," as the track is called, emerged at a moment of intense national debate over the immigration question. It called attention to what many view as the increasingly diverse and politicized reality of U.S. national culture. However, it also perturbed many pundits who saw the song as an attack not only on the United States' primary language—English—but also on the Anglo values and identity that they claimed defined U.S. history.

Both the French and the U.S. immigration debates highlight the importance not simply of cultural values, but also of race, in defining the terms of national identity and citizenship. To explain the marginalization of immigrant groups, many scholars of U.S. immigration history have compared the experience of early twentieth-century immigrants from Europe with the experience of post-1965 immigrants from Asia and Latin America. Although earlier immigrants were originally identified as distinct races—Irish, Italian, Jewish—their "racial" difference largely disappeared as they assimilated to Anglo values and became upwardly mobile. Consequently, these European immigrants have increasingly been seen as "white." By contrast, later immigrants with darker skin or other phenotypical differences have been unable to shed their racial identities even when they assume "American" values, speak English, and acquire middle-class status.[26] In these cases, it is the perceived racial difference, as much as or more than cultural difference, that explains specific groups' lack of cultural citizenship.

While new patterns of international human flows are often celebrated as evidence of the emancipatory potential of globalization, a closer look at the contours of those flows demonstrates how racial, gender, class, and national differences (among others) continue to exert a strong influence over individual and group mobility and the outcome of that movement. In other words, does the fact that Dominicans emigrate in high numbers and remit large amounts of money to the Dominican Republic evidence growing individual freedom and a globalized form of national development or ongoing dependency and underdevelopment? Certainly many individual Dominicans and even the Dominican national economy as a whole have benefited greatly from migrant labor in the United States. Nonetheless, the lack of domestic jobs in the Dominican Republic and the nation's reliance on the United States for its development accentuate the ongoing inequalities that shape transnational migration. These are the contradictions inherent in the new forms of human movement and connections emerging through globalization.

The IPE of Transnational Human Flows

Clearly, then, new global migration and settlement patterns present many opportunities and challenges. Politicians, policy analysts, academics, and community members often debate these trade-offs in terms that invoke IPE theories. For example, orthodox economic liberals (OELs) argue that migrant labor is a natural part of the free-market system and therefore should be allowed to flow freely. From this view, foreign labor supports economic growth in industries in which domestic labor is too expensive or unavailable. Even if immigrant labor displaces small numbers of native labor, depresses wages, or requires benefits, neoliberal perspectives highlight these facts as economic trade-offs that are outweighed by the lower prices enjoyed by consumers, the higher profits enjoyed by employers, and the generalized levels of economic growth that result from immigrant labor. Supporting this view, a recent study estimated that legalizing the more than twelve million irregular migrants in the United States would cost approximately $54 billion in benefits between 2007 and 2016; however, those costs would be offset by $66 billion of new revenue that immigrant workers would add to the Treasury through income and payroll taxes, Social Security withholding, and fines and fees required by law.[27]

Heterodox interventionist liberals (HILs) also tend to support migration on the basis of their belief in the individual's right to freedom of movement as part of a bundle of basic human rights. This view is especially prevalent in cases of migrants fleeing repression or violence in their home country because, according to liberal political philosophy, our obligations as humans extend beyond national borders. What many HILs call for, then, is simply more effective ways of regulating the flow of immigrants across borders. The work of the ILO and the UN's High-Level Dialogue on International Migration and Development are two examples of efforts to formulate these regulations and global standards.

Some of the most strident opposition to migration these days comes from economic national-realist types who claim that migrants pose a threat to national security in the form of lost domestic jobs and lower wages, especially for low-skilled native workers. Many critics claim that immigrants place a heavy toll on health care, schools, and other state services.[28] This perspective has fueled vigilante groups such as the Minutemen in Texas and Arizona, who claim that their efforts to patrol and actively deter immigration along the U.S.-Mexico border are born of a sense of patriotism and defense of U.S. sovereignty.[29] Similarly in

Europe, conservative politicians in Italy, France, the Netherlands, and Britain have made nativist politics and opposition to immigration a central feature of recent elections.[30] This perspective is mercantilist because of its economic nationalist sentiment and use of comparative advantage to justify limits on the mobility of labor. In its current ideological manifestation, mercantilist positions also tend to equate domestic political security with economic security, worrying that migrants represent serious breaches to both.

Structuralists may also oppose some dimensions of migration, but for radically different reasons than their mercantilist counterparts. They view increasing migration as a result of the underdevelopment produced by global inequality. From this standpoint, the global division of labor is responsible for creating impoverished nations whose citizens have no choice but to migrate in order to support their families. Free-trade zones flood local markets with foreign goods, destroying local production and local enterprises so that workers must migrate to find new labor opportunities. Furthermore, structuralists often criticize the exploitation of these unskilled migrants within the richer countries as further evidence of the need to restructure the terms of global capitalist production and trade (see Chapters 4 and 6).

Constructivist theory (see Chapter 5) would also point to multiculturalism and citizenship as elements in the political and economic debates on immigration. North American society has struggled to assimilate its large numbers of Latino and Asian immigrants—a task that some claim has been made easier by the shared faith between immigrants and natives, as well as the active role that churches play in integrating new arrivals. In Europe, large numbers of Muslim immigrants from Northern Africa and the Middle East have made cultural assimilation more difficult and, in a post-9/11 world, the stakes higher. In both places, states and citizens are grappling with how to reconcile democracy's values with changing demographics and cultural politics.[31]

In today's highly mobile landscape, global migration is clearly an important subject for IPE. As the aforementioned debates evidence, the question is rarely whether or not global migration should happen, but under what conditions and with what ends. Both individuals and states can benefit from transnational human flows, but they raise the questions such as Does transnational movement represent growing freedom or ominous challenges to security? Who bears responsibility for migrants—the sending or receiving states? What new forms of global governance would be effective in regulating migrant movement and rights? Resolving the cultural politics that emerge from the increasingly diverse constituencies that transnational flows produce and the economic challenges that arise from economic downturn highlight the double-edged sword of these human dimensions of globalization.

GOING MOBILE: THE POLITICAL ECONOMY OF INTERNATIONAL TOURISM

Like migration, tourism refers to the movement of individuals from one location to another, but unlike temporary and permanent migrants, most tourists travel for reasons related to leisure and recreation. Voluntary travel across international borders produces the single largest transnational flow of human beings in the world. According to the United Nations World Tourism Organization (UNWTO), international tourist arrivals grew from 25 million in 1950 to 980 million in 2011.[32]

The growing transnational flow of tourists stems from the same technologies and institutional arrangements associated with the global flow of goods, ideas, and money. To a large degree, discrepancies in wealth and power between individuals and countries, and interactions between states and markets, determine the distribution of benefits and costs of tourism. Further, many economic liberals portray tourism as a path to development, political legitimacy, and peace, while structuralists see tourism as a destructive force. Mercantilists meanwhile eschew the moral debate and instead focus on how to promote national security while at the same time attracting more tourists and tourism revenues than other states. As political economists like to point out, tourism involves unavoidable trade-offs that benefit some while hurting others. Tourism generates revenues, but comes with a price. When faced with the choice of whether or not to participate in tourism, all but the most isolationist states in the world accept certain trade-offs as a worthy price to pay. Despite the slowdown in the growth of international tourism caused by the late 2000s global economic recession, the flow of tourists crisscrossing the globe is in the long term almost certain to continue.

Engine of Economic Growth or Tool of Exploitation?

In the decades following World War II, the reconstruction of war-torn Europe, the growing prosperity of the North American and Western European middle class, and the implementation of policies aimed at encouraging economic growth led to the rapid expansion of international tourism. In the early days of the modern tourism boom, economic liberals argued that countries should use their comparative advantage in cultural traditions, historical sites, or attractive natural landscapes in order to attract tourists and the money that they bring. Few questions were asked about the potential harmful consequences of tourism, particularly because the economic benefits of tourism promotion seemed so significant and lasting.

There is no doubt that tourism produces tangible economic benefits. The most obvious and attractive to governments around the world is the creation of direct revenues that flow from tourist spending both before and during their trip, as well as from tourist payments of taxes while traveling in the host country. International tourism receipts, defined by the World Trade Organization (WTO) as all payments made by international tourists for goods and services (such as food, drink, accommodation, airfares, souvenirs, and entertainment), stood at $919 billion worldwide in 2010.[33] As direct revenues circulate and are re-spent in the local and national economy, backward linkages to other sectors of the economy, such as transportation, construction, and agriculture, also take place as tourists stimulate demand for certain goods and services.

Tourism is an important source of revenue for governments of tourist-receiving countries. Globally, the travel and tourism industry generates roughly 3 percent of total GDP. When tourism's indirect impact on economic activities is included, this figure rises to 9 percent.[34] For many LDCs that depend on just one or two primary commodities for the bulk of their export earnings, tourism represents an opportunity to diversify the economy. Moreover, for economies heavily burdened by external debt, tourism provides a valuable source of foreign exchange by producing direct revenues for businesses and various levels of government. The ILO points out that tourism ranks as a top three export for thirty LDCs and is the leading services export in LDCs, accounting for one-third of all LDC exports.[35]

The creation of employment is an important and highly visible economic benefit of tourism. It is estimated that roughly 100 million people work in the travel and tourism industry around the world.[36] The travel and tourism industry accounts for roughly 3 percent of total world employment. Although most employment in the travel and tourism industry is concentrated in hotels, tour operators, airlines, and travel agencies, tourists also stimulate indirect employment in other sectors that meet the needs of tourists, but that are not dependent on tourism alone. For instance, since hotels require many goods and services, including marketing, security, and catering, companies that offer these services are induced to hire workers, thereby creating more employment.

As a result of its association with the economic benefits discussed earlier, tourism is seen by the vast majority of governments, organizations, and tourists themselves as an economic panacea and "smokeless industry," providing income and employment without requiring the construction of polluting factories. This represents the liberal view of tourism as a progressive force; communities and countries take advantage of their natural or cultural comparative advantage and contribute to a positive-sum game whereby tourism provides benefits for tourists and hosts alike. The OEL perspective asserts that states should take a laissez-faire approach to tourism and allow the travel and tourism industry to develop naturally since doing so will most likely maximize the inevitable economic benefits produced by participation in international tourism. In many ways, this approach to tourism reflects the wider economic liberal assertion that globalization offers enhanced financial opportunities for poor individuals and countries.

The economic liberal view on tourism is today still common in the marketing activities of travel and tourism businesses and government "tourist boards," as well as in promotional organizations such as the UNWTO and the World Travel and Tourism Council (WTTC). Those who espouse an OEL perspective also support the General Agreement on Trade in Services (GATS), a WTO agreement that establishes rules governing trade in services, including the "Tourism and Travel-Related Services" cluster. GATS requires that members of the WTO grant foreign-owned companies free access to domestic markets in services and avoid giving preferential treatment to domestic companies over foreign-owned services firms.

In the late 1960s and early 1970s, the economic liberal approach to tourism was challenged by critics who began depicting tourism as a destructive force that promises many benefits, but in practice creates more problems than it solves. While some proponents of the critical perspective on tourism are HILs wishing to use government intervention to minimize some of the costs created by natural market activities in tourism, most are structuralists who believe that the exploitation and inequality inherent to capitalism and global economic relations poison tourism, particularly for developing countries.

Structuralists point out that the direct revenue so touted by boosters of tourism growth is offset not only by direct expenditures such as advertising but also by **revenue leakages** which result in tourism receipts being leaked out of an economy as repatriated profits to foreign-owned multinational tourism corporations. Revenue leakages are also caused by payments for imported goods and services required by the tourism industry (such as bathroom fixtures in hotels) or tourists themselves (such as luxury food items not grown locally). Most estimates of revenue leakages suggest that over half of all tourist-related spending leaks out of, or never even makes it to, destinations in the developing world.[37] Further, the majority of economic benefits associated with tourism are concentrated in the hands of the economic and political elites who have the capital and political connections to utilize the opportunities afforded by investment by tourism multinationals.

Structuralists argue that the jobs made available by tourism are low skilled, are often dangerous, and feature little room for advancement because of poor pay and few benefits. Structuralists also complain that tourism is a notoriously fickle industry. Small changes in tourist tastes, or more significant events within the destination itself such as political instability or natural disasters, can severely damage a country's tourism industry. Coupled with the seasonal, casual, and part-time nature of much tourism in most destinations, the vulnerability of tourism to changes in demand often weakens the potential of tourism as a development strategy.

Structuralists also liken modern international tourism to neocolonialism, whereby formally independent states still suffer from unfair relationships associated with colonialism. Dependency theory links the development of the industrial, wealthy core countries of the world to the exploitation and underdevelopment of the poor, weak, and dependent former colonies in the periphery of the world system (see Chapter 4). Based on a dependency approach, structuralists point out that tourist destinations in the developing world serve as the **pleasure periphery** for core countries. For North American tourists looking for a cheap sunshine holiday, the islands of the Caribbean region serve the role of a pleasure periphery. Similarly, Southeast Asia and the Mediterranean basin (southern Europe and North Africa) provide pleasure peripheries for Japan/Australia and Northern Europe, respectively.

Economic liberals argue that travel is directly linked to economic prosperity. In particular, affluence leads to higher levels of discretionary household income. As the number of individuals with discretionary income grows, demand for travel services also grows. A clear indication of the connection between economic prosperity and travel is the recent explosion in domestic and international tourism in and from China. China's rapid economic growth since the 1980s has resulted in a dramatic growth in domestic tourism, as well as a surge in outbound tourism. By 2020, China is projected to be the fourth largest source of international tourists in the world.[38] Improved infrastructure, government policies that encourage openness to the outside world, and economic growth in neighboring countries have also made China a major tourism destination. In 2010, China was the third most popular tourism destination in the world (56 million international arrivals), surpassed only by France (77 million) and the United States (60 million).[39] China is set to become the world's number-one tourism destination in terms of arrivals by 2020.

The global economic recession of the late 2000s temporarily halted the virtually uninterrupted growth in international travel and tourism that the world had seen since the 1950s. Just as travel always increases as societies grow more productive and wealthy, people always cut down on travel in difficult or uncertain economic times. As a result of the recession facing most industrialized countries, international tourism arrivals declined by nearly 4 percent between 2008 and 2009. By 2010, however, the number of international arrivals quickly bounced back, growing by 7 percent over 2009 levels to reach 940 million.[40] Although many destinations around the world saw a dramatic decline in 2009 in international tourism demand because of the erosion of consumer confidence, the quick return to normal patterns of rapid growth demonstrates the resiliency of tourism in the face of barriers to its growth. At a broader level, the questioning of market fundamentalism that the financial crisis has prompted has been largely absent in discussions of tourism: States affected by a reduction in tourism continue to hold a free-market perspective on tourism and show no signs of challenging the "more-is-better" philosophy underpinning state tourism policies.

State Management and Promotion of Tourism

Though popular tourist destinations are usually positioned naturally to attract visitors because of unusual geographical landscapes or exotic cultural attributes, tourism destinations are in fact created, not born. In other words, it takes both states and markets—and specifically states acting to influence market forces—in order for a location to become attractive and accessible. One such case is Cancun, the famous sunspot destination located on the northeast coast of the Yucatan Peninsula in Mexico. In 1967, the Mexican government identified Cancun as a **growth pole**, a deliberately chosen location meant to serve as an engine of economic growth in the surrounding region. This growth pole strategy quickly transformed Cancun from a sparsely populated coconut plantation and site of small Mayan ruins into a globally renowned beach resort destination with almost half a million permanent residents, hundreds of hotels, and three million visitors per year.[41]

With few exceptions, governments around the world prefer policies that promote tourism growth, placing top priority on maximizing tourist arrivals and expenditures despite the negative costs associated with hasty tourism development. States, therefore, often intervene directly in the economy to create financial, regulatory, and social environments conducive to rapid tourism growth. The exception to this growth-at-all-costs pattern is the Himalayan mountain kingdom of Bhutan, which, unlike the overwhelming majority of other states, particularly those in the developing world, heavily restricts the growth of tourism through policies that exclude all but the wealthiest tourists. The Bhutanese government demands that every tourist pay daily tariffs, surcharges, and expenditures totaling a minimum of $250 per night, and issues visas only to those on expensive organized group tours. By tailoring tourism toward a wealthier clientele, Bhutanese tourism authorities are able to generate greater per-tourist revenues while at the same time limiting the social, cultural, and environmental impact of tourism in Bhutan.

For states that promote tourism, there is a risk of becoming too popular as a destination. Without state management and regulation of tourism growth, destinations tend to become loved to death by eager tourists. The very natural attractions that draw tourists in the first place often become threatened as visitors quickly exceed the destination's carrying capacity. During the 1980s, governments, tourists, and tourism businesses responded to concerns about the negative tourism impacts by shifting toward **alternative tourism,** a form of tourism that provides alternatives to mass tourism experiences based on the standard "sun, sea, and sand" formula. The most popular example of alternative tourism is **ecotourism,** defined by the International Ecotourism Society as "responsible travel to natural areas that conserves the environment and improves the well-being of local people."[42] In addition to drafting appropriate laws, and enforcing existing ones, in order to minimize the environment impact of tourism, states can promote ecotourism by restricting the number of tourists in sensitive areas. States can also create national parks and wildlife reserves that provide the locations for many ecotourism activities. Unfortunately, with rare exceptions, governments having to choose between rising tourist arrivals, and therefore profits, and environmental protection almost always pick the former.

The mercantilist approach to tourism is important when one considers other ways states limit access to travel within their borders. States determine which nationals are allowed entry and under which conditions (permissible length of stay, for example). Countries that enjoy a close relationship, usually reflected in high cross-border traffic among its citizens, allow each other's visitors to enter easily. Until 2009, Canadians wishing to visit the United States required only a valid driver's license. On the other hand, some states forbid or heavily restrict the entry of the nationals of particular countries. Several countries—including Algeria, Brunei, Iran, Libya, Pakistan, Saudi Arabia, Somalia, and Sudan, among others—refuse to recognize passports from Israel, thereby precluding travel to those countries by Israeli citizens. On the whole, tourist access to other countries varies widely. Citizens of Denmark, Finland, and Sweden can enter 173 countries and territories without needing a visa, but tourists from Afghanistan, Iran, Lebanon, Nepal, and Pakistan enjoy this privilege in fewer than forty countries.[43]

Perhaps the most important role played by states insofar as tourism is concerned is the management of a country's international image. Changing tastes and preferences among international tourists makes it difficult for tourism planners to predict whether a destination will remain popular in the future. Tourist demand depends heavily on prevailing perceptions of a destination. Thus, anything that alters perceptions in a negative manner carries enormous implications for the travel and tourism industry in host societies. Natural disasters, political stability, and terrorism are all examples of forces that can dramatically shift demand away from a destination. States therefore often focus a great deal of energy and resources on countering the negative impacts of such events.

Natural disasters make popular headlines in newspapers and television news reports. As a result, despite how geographically limited the impact of a natural disaster may be, the average person with a limited knowledge of the affected country naturally forms a negative mental association with that country and becomes much less inclined to travel there. The damage unleashed by the natural disaster is then compounded by the loss of income created by a drop in tourist demand. For example, the Indian Ocean tsunami in December 2004 that killed over 200,000 people resulted in extensive damage to the infrastructure of several tourist-dependent economies, including the Maldives, Sri Lanka, southern Thailand,

and India's Andaman and Nicobar Islands. The immediate drop in tourism to these regions only made things worse, as tourism revenues rendered even more necessary by the tsunami dried up overnight. More recently, the Fukushima Daiichi nuclear disaster, caused by a massive earthquake and tsunami off the coast of Japan in March 2011, led to a 60 percent plunge in tourist arrivals the following month; for 2011 as a whole, tourists arrivals dropped 28 percent compared to the previous year.[44]

The means by which tourists are able to travel from one country to another are also employed by individuals intending to commit acts of terrorism. In addition to combating terrorist organizations that target their citizens, states also attempt to counter the damage done by terrorism to their tourism industries. Terrorists favor tourists as targets for several reasons: some tourists travel to remote, dangerous locations that serve as the base of terrorist groups; tourists are much "softer" targets than heavily defended military or political sites; the killing of tourists generates extensive international media coverage; and terrorism disrupts economies dependent on tourism revenues, thereby helping to cripple unpopular regimes.[45] Since the late 1990s, tourists have become especially popular targets for terrorist organizations. In 1997, terrorists killed close to sixty foreign tourists at Luxor in Egypt. In 1999, seventeen tourists visiting Uganda's Bwindi Impenetrable National Park were kidnapped (and eight later killed) by Hutu extremists from Rwanda. In 2011, a suicide bomber killed eleven tourists in a popular tourist café in Marrakech, Morocco. In the decade following September 11, 2001, terrorists have continued to carry out attacks against tourists in many countries, including Chad, Egypt, Ethiopia, India, Indonesia, Kenya, Mali, Mauritania, Pakistan, and the Philippines.

States that experience terrorism within their borders usually react immediately to restore their international image in order to lure back tourists. The United States after September 11, 2001, stands as an exception. Because the majority of the nineteen hijackers who carried out the attacks on the World Trade Center in New York and the Pentagon in Washington, DC entered the United States on tourist visas, concerns were raised that freedoms given to tourists to visit the country were being abused by individuals who intended to participate in terrorist acts against Americans. As a result of domestic political pressure, the U.S. government implemented several measures aimed at better screening and monitoring of visitors to the United States: This includes, since 2004, the requirement that all visitors with a visa entering the United States at air and sea ports have fingerprints and photographs taken. Due to deteriorating global perceptions of the United States, and the more stringent entry requirements imposed by the U.S. government on visitors, the number of international tourists visiting the United States fell by 20 percent between 2000 and 2003; it took six full years after the attacks of September 11, 2001, for the number of international tourists visiting the United States to reach pre-9/11 levels.[46]

Economic liberals are quick to point out that quick action on the parts of business and government can reverse the initial losses associated with tragic events, such as natural disasters, outbreaks of disease, and acts of terrorism; the evidence seems to confirm this view. Despite suffering a 23 percent drop in tourist arrivals in the year following a devastating terrorist attack that left 161 foreign tourists dead in 2002, the island of Bali in Indonesia quickly returned to pre-bombing levels and, by 2004, exceeded the number of international tourists in 2002 by 13 percent.[47] Further, following a subsequent (but far less deadly) terrorist attack in 2005, tourist arrivals in Bali initially dropped, but by 2008, arrivals had exceeded 2005 levels by 42 percent.[48] By 2010, just five years after the second terrorist attack, nearly 2.5 million international tourists visited Bali—an 80 percent increase over 2005 levels.[49] The persistent growth in global tourism praised by economic liberals is so assured, it seems, that even fear of death at the hands of terrorists is not enough to thwart our desire to travel.

Social and Cultural Dimensions of Travel and Tourism

Social status has long underpinned motivations for travel, from the 1840s, when Thomas Cook first took English industrial workers to seaside resort towns, to contemporary travelers who seek out locations off the beaten track as markers of superior taste and style. Social class also determines who can afford to travel in the first place. Culture is also a crucial component of travel to many destinations for two reasons. First, throughout history, tourists have been motivated to visit cultures perceived to be exotic and unfamiliar. A desire for cultural authenticity has long characterized tourism, and some scholars have even argued that modern tourism is premised on the search for authenticity. As the global proliferation of Western material goods seemingly erases cultural differences, tourists strive to experience a level of cultural authenticity that lies beyond the superficial, and supposedly inauthentic, "front stage" where hosts perform mostly for tourist consumption. Second, despite the role played by cultural "otherness" in luring foreign tourists, the majority of international tourists visit countries with similar cultural traits, particularly in language or religion. Cultural affinity is the reason that the British are the second largest inbound tourist market in Australia, and why U.S. residents made over 11.5 million trips to Canada in 2011.[50]

Tourist demand stimulates both the rejuvenation of cultural traditions and the rehabilitation of historical architectural monuments. Funds that are collected as entry fees and donations at historical sites can be put to use on the site itself, but more importantly, the interest shown in historical sites by tourists motivates governments to allocate resources to the rehabilitation and maintenance of such sites. Without the incentives created by tourism revenues, historical sites such as Angkor Wat in Cambodia, Machu Picchu in Peru, and the ancient city of Timbuktu in Mali would likely have remained crumbling ruins, or at least would have received far less attention and funding. In many cases, governments wishing to restore an historical site for tourism or other purposes succeed in acquiring funds from the United Nations Educational, Scientific, and Cultural Organization (UNESCO), which maintains a World Heritage list of cultural and natural properties deemed essential components of global heritage.

Critics of the unregulated nature of global tourism argue that the presence of highly conspicuous tourists in local communities increases criminal activity, especially in destinations whose residents are much poorer than the tourists visiting them. Several factors make tourists good targets of criminal activity: They are likely to mistakenly stray into unsafe areas or become lost; tourists are more likely than locals to be taken advantage of due to their lack of familiarity with local norms or procedures; a holiday mentality makes tourists more trustful and less alert; and tourists are apt to display objects of value such as money, jewelry, and cameras openly and without caution.

Another cost associated with the interaction of rich tourists and poor locals is the way in which tourism tends to have a **demonstration effect,** whereby some locals, especially youth, come to desire the material objects—and emulate the values, lifestyles, and behavior—of wealthier foreign tourists. As youth who interact with tourists adopt foreign, usually more modern, cultural values, social tension can occur between older members of the community who worry about the loss of traditional values and those who interact directly with tourists and wish to reject or modify traditional cultural practices. Aside from possibly fostering a sense of inferiority due to creating a desire for, but inability to purchase, expensive material objects possessed by tourists, the demonstration effect is especially a concern when locals interact with tourists who exhibit sexual promiscuity or the open use of drugs and alcohol.

Tourist demand for cultural artifacts and traditions perceived to be exotic transforms certain aspects of host cultures into commodities to be bought and sold. The **commodification** of culture initiated by tourism ultimately strips the original meaning and purpose from cultural objects, customs, and festivals as locals respond to commercial pressures and incentives. Critics of tourism-induced cultural commodification decry the production of "airport art," bastardized versions of traditional arts and crafts sold as cheap tourist trinkets in airports and shopping malls. Rather than being allowed to evolve naturally, according to indigenous needs, cultural performances change in substance, timing, or length in response to the entertainment demands and short attention spans of most package tourists.

Most structuralists disagree with the rosy view that tourism promotes peace, security, and tolerance. The reason is that the vast majority of tourists receive information from enormous multinational tourism companies that are concerned more with profit than accurate or balanced representations of host cultures. Though states can change perceptions abroad through their actions, governments are limited in their ability to change tourists' deep-seated cultural preconceptions because stereotypes are created or at least maintained by tour operators and travel agents that reduce complex cultures to a few recognizable, palatable nuggets for tourist consumption.

Though economic liberals agree that tourists may have inaccurate or simplistic ideas about the cultures of their hosts, the interactions between tourist and host that travel permits nevertheless help to foster better cross-cultural understanding. Again, structuralists would suggest that this may be possible under the right circumstances, but in practice, tourists and their hosts are positioned unequally in wealth and power, especially when tourists from wealthy countries visit destinations in developing countries. Tourism is a service industry and thus demands a certain level of servility. Since tourism centers on pleasure and recreation, there is even greater pressure for employees to ensure that the customer is satisfied. Moreover, tourists tend to travel in an "environmental bubble" where encounters with locals outside the tourism industry are rare, fleeting, and predictable. Instead of challenging servile and demeaning views of their people, states and local tour operators often perpetuate the problem by reassuring tourists in brochures and other advertisements that locals will cater to their every whim.

The most visible social cost of tourism in many destinations is prostitution. Several factors help to explain the connection between tourism and prostitution. People on vacation tend to spend money much less cautiously than when at home. A holiday frame of mind, characterized by inversions of normal routines and patterns of behavior, also encourages some tourists to engage in activities, such as paying for sex, that are normally avoided at home. Irregular patterns of spending and behavior, combined with the spatial concentration of tourists in conspicuous locations of consumption and hedonism, create a market for local sexual services. It is therefore no surprise that in virtually all popular destinations, especially in poor countries, sex is easily available for purchase by tourists. Even in strictly controlled societies such as Cuba and Burma, the sex trade is supported partly by certain segments of tourists.

An insidious side of the tourism–prostitution relationship is the sexual exploitation of children by tourists. Though some tourists who purchase the sexual services of locals may be unaware of the young age of the sex worker, most tourists who engage in such activities with minors are fully aware of what they are doing. A lack of alternative means of survival, sexual abuse, and the collusion of corrupt government officials and police officers help to sustain this trade. In response to the moral condemnation generated by images of tall male Western foreigners walking hand in hand with young Cambodian, Costa Rican, or South African girls (or boys), countries such as the United States, Australia, and New Zealand have begun to enforce laws that allow them to prosecute citizens who travel abroad to purchase sex from minors.

In sum, to those who are fortunate enough to afford it, travel is an escape from the routines of everyday life, but tourism should, in addition to providing pleasure, receive serious academic and policy consideration due to its widespread and growing global significance. Tourism is fundamentally an IPE issue, with political, economic, social, cultural, and environmental implications. Patterns and trends in the global travel and tourism industry closely mirror, and in some cases magnify, such features of the world system as global integration, inequality, and the clash between traditional and modern culture. In short, tourism is the perfect embodiment of the interconnections, tensions, and benefits associated with globalization.

CONCLUSION

Migration and tourism represent two of the most significant forms of contemporary human flows, each with important consequences for IPE. These forms of movement are shaped by different motives, ranging from the migrant's drive for economic gain, the refugee's flight from persecution, and the tourist's desire for recreation and exploration. Each also denotes different temporalities, such that while a tourist's travels are temporary, a migrant's sojourns may extend out for several years or even a lifetime. For all their differences, however, the two phenomena are related. It is no coincidence that poor laborers often leave the very places that wealthy Northern tourists seek out as exotic tourist escapes, while the migrants seek jobs in the industrialized countries that wealthy tourists flee in search of recreation. Therefore, global flows crystallize many of the inequalities inherent in globalization. Both forms of movement are structured by national security considerations, global markets, emerging technologies, and capital flows. Consequently, they draw our attention to the changing sources of labor and resources in a shifting landscape of production and distribution. Both have the potential to serve as powerful sources of economic development, yet they also demand new strategies for governance that can facilitate economic flows and protect vulnerable constituencies across borders. Taken together, both provide us with a clear sense of how human flows intersect with IPE structures to create new opportunities and challenges for a variety of international actors.

IPE theories are useful for making sense of the stakes of these global human flows. Economic liberals might see merit in the unfettered movement of both migrants and tourists across the globe because of the important roles that they play in the global marketplace and for the freedoms that their movement embodies. Structuralists, on the other hand, often criticize both of these forms of human movement because of the way they reflect and reproduce global economic inequalities. Mercantilists would evaluate the impact of migration and tourism in relation to the state's political economic interests. In either case, highlighting the interaction between human flows and political economic forces allows us to discern how the same global connections that bring economic prosperity can also be tenuous and potentially unsustainable forces for long-term economic development. More importantly still, they allow us to appreciate the implications of these flows not just for states and international institutions, but for the very people who are on the move in this age of uncertainty.

KEY TERMS

migration 406
internal migration 407
transnational migration 408
immigration 409
circular migration 409
chain migration 409
guest worker 410
brain drain 411

remittances 411
irregular migrants 413
citizenship 413
settler states 413
refugees 414
asylum 414
assimilation 414
diaspora 414

cultural citizenship 415
revenue leakages 421
pleasure periphery 421
growth pole 422
alternative tourism 423
ecotourism 423
demonstration effect 426
commodification 426

DISCUSSION QUESTIONS

1. What is the difference between a migrant and an immigrant? Under what circumstances is that distinction useful?
2. What trade-offs are involved in "mainstreaming migration" as a national development strategy? Explore the different stakes of such a strategy for countries such as the Philippines, Senegal, India, or El Salvador.
3. Compare a female Cambodian refugee living in Wisconsin with a male irregular migrant from the Dominican Republic living in New York City. What similarities and differences might characterize their (a) reasons for coming to the United

States, (b) their economic opportunities within the United States, and (c) their experience of cultural citizenship within the United States?
4. What makes tourism an attractive option for the state? How does tourism create risks for the state? Why is it necessary for destination states to be concerned about making tourism environmentally sustainable?
5. What are the rewards and risks of tourism according to liberals, mercantilists, and structuralists?
6. What are the political, economic, and social trade-offs associated with tourism?

SUGGESTED READINGS

Migration

Caroline Brettell and James Hollifield, eds. *Migration Theory: Talking Across the Disciplines.* New York: Routledge, 2000.

Stephen Castles and Alistair Davidson. *Citizenship and Migration: Globalization and the Politics of Belonging.* New York: Routledge, 2000.

Monica DeHart. *Ethnic Entrepreneurs: Identity and Development Politics in Latin America.* Stanford, CA: Stanford University Press, 2010.

David Fitzgerald. *A Nation of Emigrants: How Mexico Manages its Migration.* Berkeley and London: University of California Press, 2009.

Ruben Martinez. *The New Americans: Seven Families Journey to Another Country.* New York: The New Press, 2004.

Tourism

Sharon Gmelch. *Tourists and Tourism: A Reader.* Long Grove, IL: Waveland Press, 2004.

Kevin Hannam and Dan Knox. *Understanding Tourism: A Critical Introduction.* Los Angeles: SAGE, 2010.

Martin Mowforth and Ian Munt. *Tourism and Sustainability: Development and New Tourism in the Third World*, 3rd ed. London: Routledge, 2009.

Richard Sharpley. *Tourism, Tourists and Society*, 4th ed. Huntingdon, UK: ELM Publications, 2008.

David Weaver and Laura Lawton. *Tourism Management*, 4th ed. Milton, Australia: John Wiley, 2010.

NOTES

1. United Nations, Department of Economic and Social Affairs, Population Division (2009), *Trends in International Migrant Stock: The 2008 Revision* (United Nations database, POB/DB/MIG/Stock/Rev.2008).

2. Giovanni Gozzini, "The Global System of International Migrations 1900 and 2000: A Comparative Approach," *Journal of Global History*, 1:3, pp. 321–341.

3. Migration Policy Institute, "Top Ten Countries with the Highest Share of Migrants in the Total Population," http://www.migrationinformation.org/datahub/charts/6.2.shtml, based on figures from the United Nations, Department of Economic and Social Affairs, Population Division (2009), *Trends in International Migrant Stock*.

4. Ibid.

5. T. Painter, S. Dusseini, S. Kaapo, and C. McKaig, "Seasonal Migration and the Spread of AIDS in Mali and Niger," International AIDS Conference, Amsterdam, 1992, 8:D425, www.aegis.com/conferences/iac/1992/PoD5228.html.

6. Nicole Constable, *Maid in Hong Kong* (Ithaca, NY: Cornell University Press, 1997). Also see Sze Lai-Shan, "New Immigrant Labor from Mainland China in Hong Kong," *Asian Labor Update*, no. 53 (October–December 2004), at http://www.amrc.org.hk/alu_article/discrimination_at_work/new_immigrant_labour_from_mainland_china_in_hong_kong.

7. Roger Rouse, "Mexican Migration and the Space of Postmodernism," *Diaspora*, 1 (1991), pp. 8–23.

8. Jeffrey Fleischman, "Europe in Immigration Quandry," *Seattle Times*, June 7, 2006, p. A3. Also see Edward Alden, Daniel Dombey, Chris Giles, and Sarah Laitner, "The Price of Prosperity: Why Fortress Europe Needs to Lower the Drawbridge," *Financial Times*, May 18, 2006, p. 13.

9. Steven Greenhouse and Michael Barbaro, "The Ugly Side of Free Trade," *New York Times*, May 3, 2006, p. C1.

10. See the standards set forth by the ILO's International Migration Programme at http://www.ilo.org/public/english/protection/migrant/areas/standards.htm.

11. United Nations General Assembly (2008), "International Migration and Development: Report of the Secretary General," 63rd session, at http://www.unhcr.org/refworld/docid/48e0deca2.html.

12. Ibid., p. 17.

13. Celia Dugger, "U.S. Plan to Lure Nurses May Hurt Poor Nations," *New York Times*, May 24, 2006, p. A1.

14. The World Bank, Migration and Remittances Unit, "Migration and Development Brief," December 1, 2011, at http://econ.worldbank.org

/WBSITE/EXTERNAL/EXTDEC/EXTDECPROS
PECTS/0,,contentMDK:21121930~menuPK:314
5470~pagePK:64165401~piPK:64165026~theSit
ePK:476883,00.html.

15. See Ernesto Lopez-Cordova and Alexandra Olmedo, "International Remittances and Development: Existing Evidence, Policies and Recommendations," paper prepared for the G-20 Workshop on Demographic Challenges and Migration, August 27–28, 2005, in Sydney, Australia, at http://www.iabd.org.

16. Manuel Orozco, "Mexican Hometown Associations and Development Opportunities," *Journal of International Affairs,* 57 (Spring 2004), pp. 33–34.

17. H. E. Sheikha Haya Rashed Khalifa, "Closing Statement by the President of the 61st Session of the General Assembly," High-Level Dialogue on Migration and Development, United Nations, September 14–15, 2006, at http://www.un.org/migration/gapres-speech.html.

18. Barta, Patrick and Joel Millman, "The Great U-Turn," *Wall Street Journal* (Eastern Edition) New York, June 6, 2009, p. A-1.

19. The World Bank, Migration and Remittances Unit, "Migration and Development Brief," December 1, 2011, http://econ.worldbank.org/WBSITE/EXTERNAL/EXTDEC/EXTDECPROSPECTS/0,,contentMDK:21121930~menuPK:3145470~pagePK:64165401~piPK:64165026~theSitePK:476883,00.html.

20. "EU Thumbs-Up for Polish Plumber," BBC World News, November 28, 2008, at http://news.bbc.co.uk/2/hi/uk_news/7735603.stm.

21. United Nations, Department of Economic and Social Affairs, Population Division, *Trends in International Migrant Stock.*

22. United Nations Refugee Agency (UNHCR), *Statistical Yearbook 2010*, p. 8, at http://www.unhcr.org/4ef9cc9c9.html.

23. Rachel Swarns, "Study Finds Disparities in Judges' Asylum Rulings," *New York Times*, July 31, 2006, p. A15.

24. Nina Glick-Schiller and Georges Fouron, *Georges Woke Up Laughing* (Durham, NC: Duke University Press, 2001).

25. Craig Smith, "France Faces a Colonial Legacy: What Makes Someone French," *New York Times*, November 11, 2005, p. A1.

26. See Aihwa Ong, *Buddha Is Hiding: Refugees, Citizenship, and the New America* (Berkeley: University of California Press, 2003). Also see

Karen Sacks, "How Did Jews Become White Folks?" in Steven Gregory and Roger Sanjek, eds., *Race* (New Brunswick, NJ: Rutgers University Press, 1994), pp.78–102.

27. June Kronholtz, "Politics & Economics: Immigration Costs Move to the Fore; Differing Estimates Open New Battleground Over Senate Bill," *Wall Street Journal*, May 24, 2006, p. A4. See also Edurdo Porter, "Illegal Immigrants Are Bolstering Social Security with Billions," *New York Times*, April 5, 2005, p. A1.

28. Ibid.

29. Diego Cevallos, "U.S.-Mexico: 'We'll Do it Ourselves,' Say Immigration Vigilantes," Inter Press Service, June 14, 2006.

30. See, for example, Mark Rice-Oxley and James Brandon, in "Britain, Far-Right Push Threatens Tony Blair," *Christian Science Monitor*, May 6, 2004, p. 1; "World Briefing Europe: The Netherlands: Government Resigns," *New York Times*, July 1, 2006, p. A6; Peter Keifer and Elisabetta Povoledo, "Illegal Immigrants Become the Focus of Election Campaign in Italy," *New York Times*, March 28, 2005, p. A8.

31. Alden et al., "The Price of Prosperity."

32. UNWTO, *UNWTO World Tourism Barometer*, June 2012, p. 3, at http://dtxtq4w60xqpw.cloudfront.net/sites/all/files/pdf/unwto_barom12_01_january_en_excerpt.pdf.

33. UNWTO, *Tourism Highlights 2011* (Madrid: UNWTO, 2012), p. 2, at http://mkt.unwto.org/sites/all/files/docpdf/unwtohighlights11enhr_1.pdf.

34. World Travel and Tourism Council (WTTC), *Travel & Tourism 2011* (London, WTTC, 2012), p. 3, at http://www.wttc.org/site_media/uploads/downloads/traveltourism2011.pdf.

35. International Labour Organization (ILO), International Labour Office Sectoral Activities Programme, *Poverty Reduction Through Tourism* (Geneva: ILO, 2011), p. 1, at http://www.ilo.org/wcmsp5/groups/public/@ed_dialogue/@sector/documents/publication/wcms_159257.pdf.

36. WTTC, *Travel & Tourism 2011*, p. 2.

37. Martin Mowforth and Ian Munt, *Tourism and Sustainability: Development and New Tourism in the Third World*, 3rd ed. (London: Routledge, 2009), p. 186.

38. David Weaver and Laura Lawton, *Tourism Management*, 2nd ed. (Milton, Australia: John Wiley, 2002), p. 90.

39. UNWTO, *Tourism Highlights 2011*, p. 6, at http://mkt.unwto.org/sites/all/files/docpdf/unwtohighlights11enhr_1.pdf.

40. Ibid., p. 4.

41. Laura Del Rosso, "Cancun Airport Sets Arrivals Record in 2011," *Travel Weekly*, January 18, 2012, at http://www.travelweekly.com/Mexico-Travel/Insights/Cancun-Airport-sets-arrivals-record-in-2011/.

42. The International Ecotourism Society, "What Is Ecotourism," at http://www.ecotourism.org/what-is-ecotourism.

43. Henley and Partners (an international consulting firm) has complied a Visa Restriction Index, which ranks countries according to the freedom of international travel that their citizens enjoy. See http://www.henleyglobal.com/visa_restrictions.htm.

44. Lucy Birmingham, "Is Post-Fukushima Japan Safe for Tourists?" *Time World*, November 10, 2011, at http://www.time.com/time/world/article/0,8599,2099119,00.html; Japan Tourism Marketing, *Statistics of Visitors to Japan from Overseas, 2012*, at http://www.tourism.jp/english/statistics/inbound.php.

45. Weaver and Lawton, *Tourism Management*, p. 104.

46. Office of Travel and Tourism Industries (OTTI), "International Visitors (Inbound) and U.S. Residents (Outbound)—International Travelers to /from the United States, 2000-2008," at http://tinet.ita.doc.gov/outreachpages/download_data_table/2008_Visitation_Report.pdf.

47. Bali Tourism Authority, *Direct Foreign Tourist Arrivals to Bali by Nationality by Month in 2005*, at http://bali-tourism-board.com/files/By-nationality-2001-2005.pdf.

48. Bali Tourism Board, *Tourist Arrival*, at http://www.balitourismboard.org/stat_arrival.html.

49. Ibid.

50. Canadian Tourism Commission, *Tourism Snapshot*, at http://en-corporate.canada.travel/sites/default/files/pdf/Research/Stats-figures/International-visitor-arrivals/Tourism-monthly-snapshot/tourismsnapshot_2011_12_eng.pdf.

Transnational Corporations: The Governance of Foreign Investment

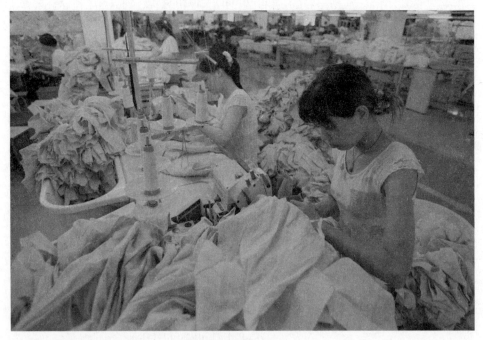

Laboring for TNCs: Garment workers in Shenzhen, China.

Rob Crandall/SCPhotos/Alamy

In the twenty-first century, transnational corporations (TNCs) have been the main engines underpinning the expansion of global capitalism. We constantly see them in our daily lives and in the news. Most major cities have stores owned by global retailers like McDonald's, Starbucks, Wal-Mart, and Ikea. Energy giants sell us gasoline and pollute the environment, as witnessed during the disastrous BP oil spill in the Gulf of

Mexico in 2010. Transnational banks and financial institutions like JPMorgan Chase and the Royal Bank of Scotland contributed to the global financial crisis. Manufacturing champions like Apple, Samsung, and Sony produce many of the electronic items we can no longer do without. But activists and some nation-states have begun to challenge powerful TNCs—and the liberal capitalist system itself. For example, the Occupy Wall Street (OWS) movement has focused popular attention on the inequality that invariably accompanies the spread of TNCs and lightly regulated capitalism. And fast-developing countries like China, Brazil, and India have created giant state-controlled companies that *The Economist* magazine claims represent a form of "state capitalism" and "the most formidable foe that liberal capitalism has faced so far."[1] The durability and impact of these challenges are unclear at this time, but there is little doubt that TNCs will remain important actors in the global economy.

TNCs have always been controversial because their global reach makes them difficult for nation-states to regulate or control. Perceptions of TNCs have evolved as international political economy (IPE) has changed over the past fifty years. TNCs have been perceived as agents of capitalist imperialism, tools of U.S. hegemony, and actors engaged in "triangular diplomacy" with states and other TNCs. With the rise of the BRICs (Brazil, Russia, India, and China) as important economic powers and homes of fast-growing TNCs, new perceptions of TNCs may emerge.

This chapter looks at the contemporary patterns of TNC investment and answers a number of important questions: What exactly are TNCs? Where do they operate and why? How much power do they have? And to what extent can their activities and interactions with nation-states and workers be regulated by formal global regimes? Finally, we also consider how increased global competition and the severe economic crisis that began in 2007 might impact **foreign direct investment (FDI)** and the globalization juggernaut.

The main points this chapter makes are as follows: First, TNCs are critical actors in the international economy because they operate in markets that span national borders and often transfer badly needed resources and know-how to developing countries. Second, these corporations engage in FDI for a variety of reasons: to exploit a competitive advantage they have; to gain access to cheaper labor and natural resources; to circumvent trade barriers and mitigate the effects of currency instability; to be close to their customers; and to respond to the strategic moves of other TNCs. Third, FDI has grown dramatically over the last sixty years, fueled by technological changes facilitating international transportation and communication and the spread of economic liberalism across the globe.

Fourth, for much of the post–World War II period, the bulk of FDI flowed from rich, northern countries to other rich, northern countries. Today things are changing, as BRICs have become significant hosts of FDI—and foreign investors themselves. TNCs headquartered in BRICs and other developing countries may begin to have a substantial impact on economic competition and political relations among states. Fifth, many TNCs are powerful enough to engage in negotiations with states and can from time to time win such favorable concessions that structuralists see them as neoimperialist exploiters. Finally, new kinds of TNC are emerging, ones that are either more globally integrated with complex supply chains or owned by national governments.

WHAT ARE TNCs?

Before we begin, however, we must deal briefly with terminology. Businesses that compete in global markets have been given different names at different times and in different fields of study. Once they were called simply *international businesses*, to distinguish them from firms that operated in local or national markets. For many years, the term **multinational corporations (MNCs)** was applied to firms that operated in several different national markets. As global markets and production structures have emerged, the accepted term has become **transnational corporations (TNCs)**. The prefix *trans* means *to go beyond*, and the markets where these businesses compete are regional—as in North America or the European Union (EU)—or global, thus transcending national markets.

You might not have encountered the term *transnational corporations* before, but you certainly are familiar with the businesses that wear that label, the items they produce and sell, and the markets where they function. It is estimated that there are about 103,000 TNCs in the world today with 892,000 foreign affiliates. Together they account for about one-quarter of global gross domestic product (GDP) and one-third of world exports. Table 17-1 displays a list of the twenty largest nonfinancial TNCs in 2011, as compiled by the United Nations Conference on Trade and Development

TABLE 17-1

Twenty Largest Nonfinancial Transnational Corporations (TNCs) in 2011, Ranked by Foreign Assets

Rank	TNC	Headquarters Country	Market
1.	General Electric	United States	Electrical and electronic equipment
2.	Royal Dutch Shell	Netherlands/United Kingdom	Petroleum
3.	BP	United Kingdom	Petroleum
4.	Exxon Mobil Corporation	United States	Petroleum
5.	Toyota Motor Corporation	Japan	Motor vehicles
6.	Total SA	France	Petroleum
7.	GDF Suez	France	Electricity, gas, and water
8.	Vodafone Group	United Kingdom	Telecommunications
9.	Enel SpA	Italy	Electricity, gas, and water
10.	Telefonica SA	Spain	Telecommunications
11.	Chevron Corporation	United States	Petroleum
12.	E.ON AG	Germany	Electricity, gas, and water
13.	Eni SpA	Italy	Petroleum
14.	ArcelorMittal	Luxembourg	Metal
15.	Nestlé SA	Switzerland	Food, beverages, and tobacco
16.	Volkswagen Group	Germany	Motor vehicles
17.	Siemens AG	Germany	Electrical and electronic equipment
18.	Anheuser-Busch InBev NV	Belgium	Food, beverages, and tobacco
19.	Honda Motor Co Ltd	Japan	Motor vehicles
20.	Deutsche Telekom AG	Germany	Telecommunications

Source: United Nations Conference on Trade and Development (UNCTAD), *World Investment Report 2012: Annex Tables.*

(UNCTAD), ranked according to foreign assets owned. (Rankings of TNCs vary according to year and whether the list is based on assets, revenues, or number of employees. The seating order varies, but the names for the most part remain the same.)

TNCs IN PERSPECTIVE

TNCs have existed for hundreds of years; some of the earliest ones were state-chartered organizations such as the East India Company, which was granted a monopoly on trade with the East Indies by Queen Elizabeth I in 1600. These firms neatly combined visions of a business empire with the imperial territorial ambitions of the home states. TNCs today typically are private business firms that compete in regional and global markets. They are distinguished by the foreign investment that they undertake as part and parcel of their operations. Because TNCs operate in markets that span national borders, they necessarily invest in production, research, distribution, and marketing facilities abroad, often transferring technology in the process.

It is tempting but dangerous to generalize about what the 103,000 TNCs are and how they behave, beyond saying, as we have here, that they are creatures of transnational markets that have command of valuable FDI resources. A certain stereotyped image of TNCs has been formed in the press and elsewhere, however, and it is important to take a close look at it. Stereotypes are usually distortions based on a few exceptional cases, and this is true of TNCs as well. Here are some "facts" commonly associated with TNCs:

- They are gigantic business organizations that dominate production, investment, sales, and employment worldwide.
- They exploit the cheap labor and natural resources of less developed countries (LDCs).
- They are the most powerful actors in the world today, dwarfing all but a few states.

Let us look at these stereotypes to see how well they explain the actual pattern of TNC activities today.

How Large Are TNCs?

Some TNCs are *very* large, but in general, TNCs come in different sizes and compete in markets of different scales. For example, the U.S.-based company General Electric, the largest TNC in the UNCTAD rankings for 2011, owned $503 billion in foreign assets. By comparison, the firm ranked 20th, Deutsche Telekom AG of Germany, had foreign assets of just $102 billion. The 100th ranked TNC, British aircraft maker BAE Systems plc, had foreign assets of $30 billion. If we were to continue down the list, we would come to some very small firms indeed. These businesses might be TNCs, and they might even be quite large compared to the typical firm competing in a local market, but they are of an altogether different scale from the "giants."

When we talk about giant TNCs, then, we are really talking about the largest 200 or so firms, not about TNCs generally. These business organizations are very large, as has been said before, because they often make huge investments and compete in global markets for goods and services such as electronics and electrical equipment (including computers), oil and gas, telecommunications, motor vehicles and parts, food and beverages, and pharmaceuticals.

There are several ways to measure the relative size of TNCs, and it is useful to look at several of them to get a better perspective on the competitive landscape. UNCTAD lists TNCs according to the value of their foreign assets, a good approach because it stresses the effects of FDI. But large firms that do not invest abroad and therefore do not own foreign assets would not appear on this list at all. The *Financial Times*, the distinctive pink-toned British newspaper, publishes a Global 500 listing based on the total value of company shares on world stock markets. Firms need not be TNCs to appear on this list, since rankings are based on share value, not FDI, but in practice many of them are TNCs. The financial crisis caused a 42 percent drop in the market value of these 500 companies from $26.8 trillion in 2008 to $15.6 trillion in 2009, but by 2012 total market capitalization had recovered to $25.3 trillion. Table 17-2 lists the top fifteen firms from the *Financial Times* list for 2012. While in 2009 Apple was 33rd in the Global 500 listing with a market value of $93.6 billion, in 2012 it had leapt to first place with a value of $559 billion, largely due to the spectacular popularity of its iPhones and iPads. In 2003 there were no Chinese companies in the *Financial Times'* top fifteen, but by 2012 there were four (including two banks)—a clear indication of China's rising power and ability to weather the financial crisis relatively well. The list is dominated by three types of TNCs: those in banking, energy, and electronics/communications sectors. It is notable that the only non-U.S., non-Chinese TNCs in the top fifteen are Royal Dutch Shell and Nestlé.

TABLE 17-2

Largest Global Companies by Market Value, 2012

Company	Country	Market Value (billions of dollars)	Total Employees
1. Apple	United States	559	63,000
2. Exxon Mobil	United States	409	82,000
3. PetroChina	China	279	553,000
4. Microsoft	United States	271	90,000
5. IBM	United States	242	433,000
6. Industrial & Commercial Bank of China	China	236	409,000
7. Royal Dutch Shell	United Kingdom	222	90,000
8. China Mobile	Hong Kong	221	175,000
9. General Electric	United States	212	301,000
10. Chevron	United States	212	61,000
11. Wal-Mart Stores	United States	208	2,200,000
12. Nestlé	Switzerland	207	328,000
13. Berkshire Hathaway	United States	201	271,000
14. China Construction Bank	China	193	329,000
15. AT&T	United States	185	256,000

Source: Financial Times, Global 500 2012, March 30, 2012.

Microsoft, the fourth most valuable firm in the *Financial Times'* Global 500, competes in a global market and is a technology leader, but it does not in fact engage in a great deal of foreign investment, so it does not even appear among the top 100 firms in the UNCTAD rankings. Microsoft forms partnerships with foreign firms and sells to foreign customers. This is a fundamentally different strategy from FDI.

Wal-Mart Stores is a big firm (number 11 by market value) and also a major foreign investor (number 34 on the UNCTAD list), but it is perhaps most noteworthy because of its large global workforce, estimated at about 2.2 million workers in 2011. Many TNCs, however, do not employ as many workers as one might suppose given their economic scale. They are more important for the technology they can supply (Microsoft) or the FDI they can provide (Exxon Mobil) than for the absolute number of jobs they can create.

In conclusion, the largest TNCs are very large indeed, but not all TNCs are large businesses. Many of the world's largest businesses do not engage in substantial amounts of FDI and do not, therefore, rank among the leading TNCs. The key aspect of TNCs to keep in mind is not their size, which varies, but their ability to provide FDI.

The Recent Rise of TNCs

TNCs have become more pervasive in recent years. According to UNCTAD, the total amount of inward FDI flows increased dramatically from an annual average of about $225 billion worldwide in the period 1990–1995 to nearly $1.9 trillion in 2007. Because of the global financial crisis, inward FDI flows dipped to $1.2 trillion in 2009, but they rebounded to $1.5 trillion in 2011. This rise in TNC investments reflects the growth of regional and global markets. UNCTAD identifies three forces driving this transnational market growth: policy liberalization, technological change, and increasing competition.

More and more countries have sought to attract FDI inflows to create jobs and encourage economic development. Since the early 1980s, many LDC governments have adopted the "Washington Consensus" policies, which facilitate open trade and free capital mobility. These policies create an environment more conducive to TNC investments. Countries that enter the main regional economic groups—NAFTA and the European Union—adopt especially liberal trade and investment rules. China's entry into the World Trade Organization (WTO) in 2001 accelerated its inward FDI flows. Countries such as India and Japan that have been slow to abandon mercantilist policies are disadvantaged in the competition for FDI, though that seems to be changing with India. FDI is still controversial, but virtually all nations now actively seek it to advance their economic agendas.

Technological change has also accelerated FDI by reducing transportation and communication costs. Taken together, technological change and policy liberalization have expanded the domain of transnational markets relative to markets that are mainly domestic. This means that firms face greater competition than ever before, which further accelerates the FDI process. Unlike the first TNCs, which benefited from monopoly power, most TNCs today are driven to invest abroad by the competitive environment found in transnational markets, the policy liberalization that encourages that competition, and the technological changes that make foreign investment more efficient.

The Patterns of TNC Operations

For many years there was a widespread perception that most TNCs were North-based businesses that shifted production to the less developed South to take advantage of cheap labor and natural resources. But the facts did not support this perception. For much of the post–World War II period, most TNC investment was North–North rather than North–South. FDI mainly originated in rich countries in the industrialized North (the United States, Europe, and Japan) and flowed predominantly to Europe and the United States. Consider that in 1990 developed countries originated 95 percent of all outward FDI and were hosts to 83 percent of all inward FDI. These were the regions that had the largest, most technologically advanced and competitive corporations. They also had the richest markets and most skilled labor forces. The high wages of their workers were matched by their high productivity.

These long-established patterns are rapidly changing. FDI outflows from rich, developed countries dropped from 95 percent in 1990 to 81 percent of overall outflows in 2011 as firms from developing countries entered global markets and acquired foreign business assets. Five TNCs on UNCTAD's top 100 list are headquartered in newly industrialized countries: Hutchison Whampoa and CITIC Group (diversified businesses in China); Vale (a Brazilian mining company); Petronas (a state-owned Malaysian petroleum producer); and Cemex (a Mexican cement producer). The change is even more dramatic when we notice that inflows of FDI to developed countries dropped from 83 percent in 1990 to only 47 percent of overall inflows in 2011. Emerging economies in Asia, Latin America, and the Caribbean have become attractive locations for TNC operations. China and Hong Kong, for example, received almost half as much FDI in 2011 ($207 billion) as did the whole of the European Union ($421 billion). India and Russia, which still have domestic regulatory regimes that are perceived to be biased against foreign investment, have had a steady and significant inflow of FDI since 2007.

Other developing countries like Brazil and Mexico also attracted large amounts of FDI ($67 billion and $20 billion in 2011, respectively), but the whole of sub-Saharan Africa saw an inflow of only $35 billion in 2011, with few nations attracting FDI of more than a few hundred million dollars. Excluding FDI in natural resources extraction, Africa is essentially ignored by TNCs because these countries do not have large markets and significant skilled labor, or because political and social instability makes them an undesirable investment target.

Despite recent changes, a great deal of FDI is still regionally based, flowing out of countries in the EU into other EU countries and out of countries in NAFTA and into other NAFTA countries. This makes sense because TNCs tend to evolve and expand to compete in particular markets. While markets for some commodities are truly global, especially petroleum and some primary products, much recent market growth has been regional, driven by EU and NAFTA expansion. The European Union and NAFTA combined accounted for over 33 percent of all inward FDI in 2011. The United States, Japan, the United Kingdom, and Germany remain the biggest investors in the world today.

Most "global" businesses are not really global at all, it seems, but instead channel investment to particular regional markets, leaving out large parts of the world, especially in Africa. But as we have seen, the North–North pattern is changing, with developing economies in Asia and Latin America becoming important hosts and homes for FDI. A survey of 3,000 TNCs by UNCTAD in 2011 found that China, the United States, India, Indonesia, Brazil, and Australia—in that order— were seen as the most attractive locations for *future* FDI.

What Determines Where TNCs Invest?

The stereotype that TNCs invest only where labor and natural resources are cheap is clearly not a good general explanation of TNC behavior, although it does apply to some specific situations. As noted above, a great deal of FDI goes from rich, high-wage countries such as Germany to other rich, high-wage countries such as the United States. And, in any case, the theory that TNCs go where labor is cheap is at best an incomplete theory because it does not tell us why TNCs invest in a *specific* low-wage country like China instead of another low-wage country like Kenya. The question of why TNCs invest where they do is thus a very interesting one. Since there are thousands of TNCs in the world, it is unlikely that a single theory can explain all of their behavior. Here are several explanations that attempt to account for different aspects of TNC behavior.

Product Cycle Theory

Why do TNCs invest abroad, especially in other high-wage countries, when they face so many obvious disadvantages in doing so? A U.S. company setting up operations in France, for example, must deal with different laws and regulations, different labor practices and union restrictions, a different language and culture, and a variety of other difficulties. It would seem that a French firm that is already equipped with "local knowledge" would have a distinct competitive advantage. Why wouldn't a U.S. company simply reach an agreement to have a French firm produce and sell products under license?

TNCs do not make much sense in highly competitive markets with standardized products and technology, where everyone has equal access to resources and decisions are made on the basis of cost or price alone. In markets like these, the disadvantages of operating abroad would doom any foreign firm. TNCs make sense, however, if they possess some particular knowledge or advantage that compensates for other disadvantages. Raymond Vernon's **product cycle theory** provides one explanation for TNC investment behavior.

Vernon was particularly interested in TNCs that produce technologically sophisticated products and in the surprisingly common phenomenon of trade reversals, where the country that invents a product sometimes finds itself a few years later importing that same item from abroad. His three-stage product cycle theory explains how this can happen and how TNCs are created in the process.

In the first stage of the product cycle, a firm in a high-income country identifies a need that can be satisfied with a technologically sophisticated product. For example, the modern mobile phone satisfies the needs of people who want to remain in communication in many locations. The United States, Japan, and the EU members have the technology resources to address this sort of need and the income to pay for the products, which are often very expensive in the early stages. In the first stage, therefore, companies like Motorola (United States) or Nokia (Finland) invest millions of dollars in research, development, and manufacturing of products to satisfy a home-country need.

Once the product has been developed and a market created at home, it is possible to export to other countries where consumers or businesses may have similar incomes and living standards. In the second stage, therefore, mobile phones may be exported to other high-income areas of Asia, Europe, and North America. The firms become multinational or transnational in this stage, according to Vernon's theory, as they establish sales offices and some production or distribution facilities abroad. Some of the North–North FDI that was discussed earlier occurs in stage two. Finally, the technology becomes standardized to the point where the product may be produced more efficiently in a newly industrialized country such as Mexico or Malaysia. At this point production moves abroad and the TNC makes another foreign investment.

Note that technology and market factors are important elements of the product cycle explanation of TNC behavior. Products are invented and developed where technology is abundant and incomes are high. The market expands to other high-income countries once the product has been developed, and FDI follows as firms rush to compete in the bigger market. Finally, when the technology matures, production spreads around the globe via FDI flows.

Appropriability Theory

Developed by Richard Caves and others, **appropriability theory** helps explain why firms invest abroad rather than license production to a local firm or take on a local partner. The appropriability theory argues that some firms become TNCs because they have too much to lose if they enter into partnerships or licensing agreements with foreign companies, which might in fact appear more profitable in terms of a simple dollars-and-cents calculation. This is especially true if a firm has some specific "intangible assets" such as valuable trademarks or patents, new technologies, trade secrets (such as Coca-Cola's formula), or efficient management techniques.

The fear is that these advantages or technological innovations will be stolen, copied, or otherwise "appropriated" by the competition if a firm does not retain full control over them. If a firm gives up control of foreign production, distribution, or sales, it risks losing control of its key competitive advantage. For example, once the foreign partner or licensee learns how to manufacture and sell the product itself, it might go into competition with the originating firm.

The only way to be sure that the key competitive factors are protected (and not appropriated by foreign firms) is to keep full control of the process by sending FDI to foreign markets and creating wholly-owned subsidiaries. Rather than licensing agreements, TNCs engage in FDI, according to this theory, as a defensive measure.

TNCs AND UNDERDEVELOPMENT

Stephen Hymer, a political economist with a Marxist-structuralist perspective, was among the first to see that TNCs sometimes exist to protect and exploit unique advantages such as those just discussed. Hymer argued that the desire to retain monopoly power, exploit foreign markets, and earn excess profits caused TNCs to engage in patterns of FDI that do not foster economic development, but rather lead to the "development of underdevelopment" (see Chapter 4).

If executives in corporate headquarters fear that their company's competitive assets will be appropriated or diluted, they will tend to keep control of them at home and be sure that strategic decisions are made by home-country, not host-country, executives. This creates what is called the **branch factory syndrome,** whereby critical technology and the most productive assets remain securely at headquarters while inferior technology and less productive assets are transferred abroad, to the branch factory. FDI that builds branch factories may transfer technology and create jobs, in this theory, but the technology will always be inferior and the jobs will never be as good as in the headquarters firm.

Hymer's theory goes further than appropriability theory by linking TNC strategy to an international division of labor that privileges the industrial core and systematically prevents periphery countries from catching up. Hymer adopts a structuralist perspective on TNCs and FDI, conceptualizing the international economy as an arena of conflicting interests between actors with unequal power.

Politics and Protectionist Barriers

Political factors can also be important in TNC strategies. TNCs depend on open international markets. They need to be able to invest abroad, of course, but they also depend on the ability to import and export. Trade barriers make their internal operations less efficient and disadvantage them compared with protected domestic firms. This explains in part why so much FDI is regionally based, such as FDI within the EU or within NAFTA. The lower trade and investment barriers within the regional blocs encourage intra-bloc FDI compared with other patterns of FDI.

Interestingly, however, trade barriers can also encourage certain types of TNC behavior. Some FDI is an unintentional result of mercantilist policies designed to keep out foreign products. A foreign firm can get around a country's tariff barriers by establishing a factory in that country; in a sense, this transforms the foreign firm into a domestic firm. In the early 1980s, for example, the United States negotiated a voluntary export agreement with Japan that was intended to protect U.S. automobile firms while they developed more fuel-efficient models. The agreement put numerical limits on car exports from Japan to the United States. The limits did not apply, however, to automobiles assembled in the United States and sold by Japanese firms, so long as most of the parts came from the United States or Canada. Honda, Toyota, and Nissan all began to invest in production facilities in North America so that they could expand their market shares despite the trade barriers.

In the U.S.-Japan automobile agreement case, a policy that was intended to keep out foreign cars instead attracted foreign FDI and probably strengthened the Japanese firms. Of course, it is not always possible or profitable to employ FDI to get around protectionist trade barriers, but where it is, it helps us understand why firms invest abroad.

Politics can affect FDI patterns in other ways as well. The Boeing Company, for example, markets its commercial aircraft to many airlines that are owned by governments or whose decisions are strongly influenced by government policy makers. Boeing often finds that, to get a large order for its aircraft, it must accept "offsets," which are agreements that certain components will be produced in the country buying the airplanes. Sometimes investments are made and technological know-how is transferred in exchange for purchase orders. In situations like these, as IPE scholar Susan Strange pointed out, TNCs may become so involved in international politics that their negotiations, with host states and home states as well as with other TNCs, are more like diplomacy than simply business.

Currency Instability

TNCs are especially susceptible to the effects of unstable foreign exchange (FX) rates because they often have costs that are denominated in one group of currencies and earn revenues in other currencies. An unexpected shift in exchange rates can raise effective costs and reduce revenues. Some international businesses have seen profits collapse and foreign markets disappear due to exchange rate swings. In 2003, the world's largest food company, Nestlé, announced that profits had fallen by half despite a higher quantity of goods sold, due to the unexpected appreciation of the Swiss franc. What Nestlé gained through its increased sales, it lost many times over in the FX markets.

There are many ways to reduce this exchange rate risk, including the use of complex financial instruments. One very direct way is to establish production facilities in each major market so that costs and revenues largely accrue in the same currency. The problem of currency instability is a factor that drives TNCs to behave more like national firms than like global giants.

The combination of trade barriers and exchange rate factors encourages firms to produce goods in the countries where they are sold rather than simply export them from a central location. The globalization of markets, therefore, is sometimes associated with what might be called "multi-local" production and a corresponding pattern of TNC investment. That is, the corporation is regional or global, but its operations in different countries are configured along more national or local calculations in order to minimize or avoid trade barriers and currency problems.

Another pattern of FDI occurs when FX rates are misaligned (either undervalued or overvalued), as explained in Chapter 7. When a currency is overvalued, for example, imported products are systematically less expensive than domestic goods. This can be a strong incentive for firms to invest in foreign production facilities. The foreign factories may be more or less efficient, but they benefit from advantageous FX rates.

For example, because the U.S. dollar was considerably overvalued during the early 1980s, U.S. firms had an incentive to set up offshore production facilities. And in the late 1980s, a situation called *endaka*—meaning an overvalued Japanese yen—forced Japanese firms to set up production networks throughout East Asia and Southeast Asia and to ruthlessly cut costs at factories in Japan. *Endaka* was very stressful for Japanese businesses, but it forced them to evolve into super-efficient TNCs. More recently, the weak dollar (it depreciated by approximately 30 percent against the Euro between 2000 and 2012) has driven many European companies to set up operations in the United States.

Location-Specific Advantages

FDI may also be influenced by location-specific advantages. Some of these advantages are obvious, such as access to natural resources that are available only in specific areas—a powerful impetus for a lot of Chinese FDI in Africa and Latin America. At other times, the advantages are more complicated. For example, if a company wants to compete in the computer software market, it would need to set up shop where the best people are. This means that it would invest where many other firms have also located, so that it can benefit from the pool of highly trained individuals in that area and the intense competition and constant innovation that is built into this environment. It would channel FDI to Redmond, Washington (Microsoft's home), the Silicon Valley of California, Israel, and probably Bangalore, India. These and just a few other places in the world have the right technological and human environment to make a firm very competitive.

In the same way, if a company wanted to compete in the world market for eyewear such as designer sunglasses, it would probably open a facility near Belluno, Italy. As Michael Porter explains in his book *The Competitive Advantage of Nations*, this region of northern Italy is where the world's top eyeglass design and manufacturing facilities are found and where the world's pickiest eyeglass customers live, too. It is impossible to compete successfully in the global market without being exposed to the intense and innovative competition in this local market. Most of the quality eyewear in the world is manufactured by companies that have at least some of their facilities in Belluno.

Competition

Finally, it is important to remember that TNCs are transnational because the markets where they compete are throughout the world. In some cases, a firm may be driven to invest abroad because of simple competitive pressures: If one firm does not contest this market, other firms will, and they may gain an advantage from doing so. In this regard, firms may act a bit less like rational profit-maximizing enterprises and a bit more like mercantilist states, which see an opponent's gain as their own potential loss.

To summarize, some TNC investments are driven by the desire to exploit low wages or cheap natural resources but, given the types of products that TNCs manufacture and their actual pattern of FDI, other factors are much more important. TNCs invest abroad to protect a competitive advantage, to exploit a monopoly position, to get around trade barriers, to avoid currency problems, to take advantage of special production environments—and because they are driven to do so by their competition with other TNCs.

HOW POWERFUL ARE TNCs?

Many people assume that TNCs are very powerful because they are such large organizations and because, through their FDI flows, they influence the global distribution of investment and technology. Some people go so far as to assert that TNCs are as powerful as states—or more powerful than states.

One commonly cited "fact" is that around half of the top 100 "economic entities" are corporations—and the other half are countries. This statistic is based on comparisons of the GDPs of countries with the total revenues of corporations. But to make these comparisons is to misunderstand what a TNC is and also to misunderstand what a state is.

From a technical standpoint, comparing countries and TNCs this way is comparing apples with oranges. The GDP of a country is not equivalent to the total revenues of a corporation. Wal-Mart has high revenues, to be sure, but why are its revenues the correct measure of Wal-Mart's power and not its wage bill, its net profits, its employment total, its FDI resources, or the technology that it can potentially offer a host country? One suspects that total revenues are selected simply because they make Wal-Mart appear larger than states. TNCs do have tremendous influence over economic resources, but not so much as this biased methodology suggests.

The second problem is that this analysis compares TNCs and nation-states in strictly monetary terms, ignoring many factors that really matter a great deal more. This focus on one factor, money, is ironic because many critics of TNCs criticize corporations for ignoring important nonmonetary factors, such as security or the environment. States possess territory and make laws; they have sovereignty, citizens, and armies and navies. They have legitimacy, too, which means that the international community accepts their right to make important social decisions. TNCs have none of these things, unless you think that employees or customers are the same as national citizens. Even the giant Wal-Mart, which has over two million employees, has fewer workers than most countries have citizens, if we want to use this as our measure. States are fundamentally different from TNCs, and attempts to compare their power and influence based on simple numerical indicators must inevitably distort reality. Both states and TNCs have power, and so sometimes they must negotiate and engage in diplomacy, but their powers differ and so their relationship is complex and evolving.

CHANGING REACTIONS TO TNCs

Apart from business leaders and economists, who tend to view the growth of TNCs as the natural consequence of emerging regional and global market structures, most authors interpret the expansion of TNCs as a decisive shift in the balance of power in the global economy. They argue about who will benefit from this shift and how. Several quite distinctive viewpoints have emerged that we will discuss in this section: TNCs as a form of capitalist imperialism, TNCs as a tool of U.S. hegemony, and TNCs as state-level actors in IPE.

TNCs and Capitalist Imperialism

TNCs and FDI were distinctive elements of the first modern era of globalization, which reached its zenith about a hundred years ago and ended with the opening shots of World War I. V. I. Lenin famously characterized this era in a book title as *Imperialism: The Highest Stage of Capitalism*. Lenin focused on "finance capitalism," not TNCs *per se*, but his approach and many of his conclusions are easily applied to TNCs. Lenin argued that colonial imperialism had been replaced by economic imperialism. Foreign armies and occupying forces were no longer necessary because the same result (exploitation by and dependency on the capitalist core) could now be accomplished by foreign investors and business corporations.

If you read Lenin's famous little book on imperialism, you will quickly appreciate that it is very much a creature of a particular time and place, full of references to long-forgotten people and events. It was not a book written for the ages but rather an argument written in the present tense. His indictment of international investment as a form of imperialism, however, does live on through books such as William Greider's *One World, Ready or Not: The Manic Logic of Global Capitalism*.[2]

Stephen Hymer draws a direct link between TNCs and imperialism today, as was discussed earlier in this chapter. Hymer's path-breaking theory of TNC behavior suggests that many TNCs engage in FDI because they wish to exploit a monopoly position while protecting a key asset, such as a patented process. Their profit-maximizing strategy is to exploit the foreign market in favor of higher profits at home. In terms of financial strategy, terms of trade, and technology transfer, Hymer predicts that TNCs will engage in a pattern of behavior that is imperialism in everything but name.

TNCs as Tools of U.S. Hegemony

TNCs came to be viewed by many as tools of U.S. hegemony during the Cold War era. There were several reasons for this association. First, U.S. TNCs were especially active and focused on foreign expansion in the immediate post–World War II years. U.S. foreign policy seemed to be directed in part to creating opportunities for U.S. firms to expand abroad. And once FDI had taken place, U.S. investments abroad created economic interests favorable to U.S. policies. So it seemed as though the United States promoted its TNCs, and they in turn supported U.S. policies.

IPE scholar Robert Gilpin, writing in his 1975 book *U.S. Power and the Multinational Corporation*, argued that American-based TNCs were a tool of U.S. hegemony. Citing a famous international economist, he asserted:

> As Jacob Viner has pointed out, from the initial movement of American capital and corporations abroad the State Department and the White House have sought to channel American investment in a direction that would enhance the foreign policy objectives of the United States. With respect to the foreign expansion of the multinational corporation, these objectives have been seen as maintaining America's share of world markets, securing a strong position in foreign economies, spreading American economic and political values, and controlling access to vital raw materials, especially petroleum.[3]

One example of Gilpin's thesis is found in the role that Boeing played in U.S. relations with China in the 1970s. President Richard Nixon went to China in 1972 in a move to solidify U.S. hegemony relative to the USSR (an event so dramatic that it is even cited in *Star Trek VI: The Undiscovered*

Country: "There is an old Vulcan proverb: Only Nixon could go to China"). He also went to sell airplanes, specifically Boeing 707s. Although American and Chinese officials made endless toasts, it was the aircraft sale that sealed the deal by providing meaningful economic benefits to both countries. Chinese purchases of Boeing aircraft later in the 1970s were symbolic of China's commitment to modernization and the U.S. government's commitment to closer diplomatic relations with China, as was paramount leader Deng Xiaoping's 1979 tour of Boeing assembly facilities near Seattle.

By the mid-1970s, when Gilpin's book appeared, U.S. hegemony seemed to be in decline. U.S. wealth and power had not declined in *absolute* terms, but Europe and Japan had closed the gap, resulting in a *relative* decline in U.S. influence. Ironically, Gilpin viewed this as a consequence of the strategic use of U.S. FDI:

> From a political perspective, the inherent contradiction of capitalism is that it develops rather than that it exploits the world. A capitalist international economy plants the seeds of its own destruction in that it diffuses economic growth, industry, and technology and thereby undermines the distribution of power upon which that liberal interdependent economy was rested.[4]

Gilpin was concerned that the relative decline of U.S. hegemony would bring an end to the international political environment that had made the expansion of U.S. TNCs and the reconstruction of Europe and Japan possible. He feared a return of protectionism as had occurred when British hegemony declined at the end of the nineteenth century.

Nearly forty years after Gilpin's book was published, the viewpoint that American TNCs are tools of U.S. hegemonic strategy no longer dominates the debate, but it has not entirely disappeared. U.S. media conglomerates have global influence, U.S. films and television shows are seen around the world, and U.S.-based content providers and social media companies have a large presence on the Internet. For example, Hollywood movie studios control approximately two-thirds of worldwide box office sales. At the beginning of 2013, Menlo Park, California-based Facebook had more than one billion users, and San Francisco-based Twitter had 200 million active users and 500 million registered users. To the extent that these TNCs present world events and ideas in ways that cast a favorable light on U.S. policies and U.S. values and interests, they are a source of what Joseph Nye calls "soft power."[5] Some have argued that this soft power advantage is even more important to U.S. foreign policy in the long run than is U.S. military dominance.

TNCs as State-Level Actors

The decline of U.S. hegemony did not end the era of TNC expansion, as Robert Gilpin suspected, but it did change its pattern. TNCs based in the "triad" of Japan, the EU, and the United States intensified their foreign investment activities. The United States, which had become accustomed to its position as a "home country" for U.S.-based TNCs, found itself also a "host country" to major TNCs based in Japan and Europe. The previously accepted distinction between home and host countries was starting to disappear, replaced with the realization that we are all host countries now.

The list of potential host countries expanded dramatically with the collapse of communism in 1989. Many countries, including even Russia, opened their doors to FDI and the resources and technology that it promised. Other events brought even more countries into the world economy. The end of apartheid in South Africa, for example, attracted inward FDI and allowed South African firms an opportunity to expand abroad. SABMiller, formerly South African Breweries, is now the world's second largest beer producer, with production facilities in more than forty countries. And perhaps most consequential of all, economic liberalization in China and India opened the two largest countries in the world to inward flows of FDI.

In their 1991 book *Rival States, Rival Firms*, John Stopford and Susan Strange coined the term *triangular diplomacy* to describe the pattern of state–TNC relations that they saw emerging. In the past, they wrote, firms had competed with other firms, and states had engaged in diplomacy with other states.[6] By 1990, they said, the largest TNCs had more power relative to states and relative to competitive markets, too. Diplomacy—where actors bargain with each other—was a more accurate description of where the world was heading. Although large TNCs were still in competition with each other, they also often bargained with each other much as states did. More and more often TNCs would form alliances or other working arrangements to develop technologies and spread the risk of new investments (see the box Outsourcing and the Globally Integrated Enterprise later in the chapter).

An example of firm-to-firm diplomacy was New United Motor Manufacturing, Inc. (NUMMI), a joint venture between fierce competitors Toyota and General Motors (GM). NUMMI was established in 1984 when Toyota agreed to take over operations in GM's least efficient factory, located in Fremont, California. Using Japanese management techniques, Toyota soon had the NUMMI factory running at world-class quality and efficiency, churning out cars for both Toyota and GM. The NUMMI alliance, just one of many among automotive companies, allowed GM and Toyota to share risk, share markets, and combine strengths even as they competed for the same customers.

State–TNC bargaining is the third side of the diplomacy triangle. Both states and TNCs control valuable resources, and they need each other. States would like the investments and technologies that TNCs can offer. TNCs, for their part, desire access to the natural resources and skilled labor that states control and, of course, they also seek access to national markets for the goods and services that they produce. (A state that fails to adequately educate and train many of its citizens and thus offers mainly unskilled labor has little to bargain with and can expect to attract sweatshop-type FDI.) Since each side has much to offer and much to gain, it would seem that mutually advantageous agreements should be easy to achieve. But it is not as simple as that.

Because TNCs compete with each other for transnational markets, they have a strong incentive to attempt to negotiate the most favorable terms possible for their FDI projects. TNCs typically seek favorable tax treatment, state-funded infrastructure, and perhaps even weakened enforcement of some government regulations. A weak state, or one with few productive resources and a weak market system, may be at a fundamental disadvantage in such negotiations. Competition from other states may force it to grant many concessions to attract FDI. This is true both in LDCs and in advanced industrial economies.

In the early 1990s, for example, the German automaker Mercedes-Benz announced that it would build a factory in the United States to produce a Mercedes sports-utility vehicle (SUV). Mercedes-Benz had much to offer in this FDI project, although perhaps its most valuable bargaining chip was its reputation for quality. The ability of a state or locality to satisfy Mercedes-Benz would be a sign to other companies that the area could meet high quality standards. More FDI would be likely to follow. The stakes, therefore, were very high in bargaining over this investment.

Mercedes-Benz increased its bargaining power by creating competition for its FDI. It published its requirements for the FDI project and invited a large number of state and local governments to make bids for the factory. By 1993 the list was narrowed to three potential factory sites in South Carolina, North Carolina, and Alabama. All three states had right-to-work laws that limited union power. North Carolina offered $108 million of investment incentives. South Carolina offered a package similar to the one that had previously attracted a BMW factory; the total value was about $130 million. Alabama won the bidding, however, by pledging to Mercedes a package worth $253 million.

The Alabama–Mercedes story highlights the bargaining power TNCs often have in negotiations with states. Alabama gave Mercedes tax abatements on machinery and equipment, improved highways and other infrastructure the company needed, and spent money on education and training that would benefit the company. The University of Alabama even agreed to run a special "Saturday School" to help the children of German Mercedes managers keep up with the higher standards in science and math back home in Germany. All this was paid for by the taxpayers of Alabama. The governor of North Carolina was particularly upset by a tax break the Alabama legislature passed (labeled by some the "Benz Bill"), which allowed Mercedes to withhold 5 percent of employees' wages to pay off Mercedes debts.

The wooing of Mercedes went beyond financial incentives. It included an offer to name a section of an interstate highway "the Mercedes-Benz autobahn," airplane and helicopter tours for Mercedes-Benz executives, and the governor driving a Mercedes as the official state car. It is not surprising that a Mercedes executive claimed it was "Alabama's zeal" that was the deciding factor. In return, 1,500 workers got good-paying jobs, with the likelihood that thousands of other new jobs would be created in supplier firms, restaurants, and the like.[7]

The lesson seems clear: TNCs are "footloose" and have many possible investment options, whereas states are rooted, like trees, in the territory they control. When a TNC has unique resources to offer while the state has few and faces stiff competition from other states, the TNC has a tremendous advantage and the diplomacy can be very one-sided. However, this need not always be the case; if states make their own investments in education, resources, infrastructure, and so forth, then they can have the upper hand. The competition that TNCs face from each other can press them to make concessions, too. For example, several European countries held auctions for third-generation (3G) wireless telecommunications rights beginning in 2000. At stake were a limited number of slots in the part of the electromagnetic spectrum reserved for cutting-edge wireless communications networks. The bidding among telecom TNCs for these licenses was intense, and the sums that were paid to the European governments were astronomical—about $108 billion just for the right to set up the networks.

It is clear today that the telecom TNCs overbid for the 3G rights; the payments were much higher than justified by potential revenues. Did the states "win" the diplomacy? In a dollars-and-cents view, yes, it appears they did. In the long run, however, the outcome is less clear because the states do need the TNCs (and their resources) as much as the TNCs need the states (and their resources). When competition drives a bargain too far on either side, it puts the other party at risk and suddenly the whole enterprise is in jeopardy.

This is what bothered Raymond Vernon when he wrote his 1998 book *In the Hurricane's Eye: The Troubled Prospects of Multinational Enterprises*. Vernon was concerned that competition among TNCs was forcing them to squeeze states for more and more concessions. Although we say that the states are squeezed, it is of course the citizens of the states who feel the pressure from higher taxes or reduced government services, lower labor standards, and lax environmental enforcement. How would they react? One possibility is that they would put political pressure on their governments to adopt protectionist measures generally. This was Vernon's fear. Although Vernon wrote prior to the protests at the 1999 WTO meetings in Seattle, the chaos of those protests is very much the eye of the hurricane he was describing.

TNCs thrive in a liberalized global climate. Many observers were predicting the endless expansion of TNCs, as indicated by the title of Kenichi Ohmae's influential book *The Borderless World*[8] and the title of David Korten's book *When Corporations Rule the World*.[9] In contrast, Vernon saw the potential for a great collapse. *The Hurricane's Eye* concludes with this warning:

> The great sweep of technological change continues to link nations and their economies in a process that seems inexorable and irreversible. . . . Yet the basic adjustments demanded by the globalization trend cannot take place without political struggle. Too many interests in the nation-states see the economic risks and costs of the adjustments involved, even if justified in the longer terms, as unfairly distributed and deeply threatening. . . . But a prolonged struggle between nations and enterprises runs the risk of reducing the effectiveness of both, leaving them distracted and bruised as they grope towards a new equilibrium. To shorten that struggle and reduce its costs will demand an extraordinary measure of imagination and restraint from leaders on both sides of the business-government divide.[10]

A GLOBAL FDI REGIME?

In the mid-1990s, the Organization for Economic Co-operation and Development (OECD) sponsored talks between business and government leaders with "imagination and restraint" over a Multilateral Agreement on Investment (MAI). The intent was to create a regime to govern FDI in the same way that the WTO governs international trade. What kind of governance? The goal of the MAI talks was to set norms and standards for state–TNC negotiations.

Both sides of the table had something to gain from an international investment agreement. TNCs, for example, want to be assured of "national treatment." Under WTO rules, nations can impose certain trade restrictions at the border, but once a product enters a market it cannot be discriminated against in favor of domestic products. National treatment in trade prevents domestic discrimination against foreign products.

National treatment for FDI would mean that, while a state has the right to regulate inward investment at the border, once that investment has been made the state must treat the local subsidiary of the foreign TNC the same as it treats similar domestic firms. There must be no domestic discrimination against TNC affiliates, even if this means giving them tax preferences and subsidies intended for domestic firms only. TNCs believe that recognition of this principle would make FDI more efficient and less vulnerable to political forces.

TNCs would also benefit if nation-states coordinated or harmonized their regulations on big businesses. As we have noted, TNCs are forming more alliances and merging operations in order to be competitive with other TNCs. But because of their broad reach, TNCs often find themselves subject to antitrust or competition regulation in several different jurisdictions. For example, the United States and the European Union have adopted different norms for business mergers, and when TNCs wish to join operations, they frequently need to gain approval in both places. In 1996, EU competition regulators initially opposed approval of a merger between two U.S.-based aircraft firms, Boeing and McDonnell Douglas, which had been given a green light by U.S. authorities. It was suddenly clear that the EU could veto an agreement between two U.S.-based firms if they both had important operations in Europe. Subsequently, the EU did veto a merger in 2001 between General Electric and Honeywell—both U.S.-based TNCs—despite prior U.S. government approval because EU officials feared that the merger would reduce competition in the markets for aviation electronics and airplane engines.

Although TNCs cannot escape government regulations on things such as approval for mergers and acquisitions, they would clearly benefit from being subject to just one set of rules instead of several contradictory ones. For their part, states have important interests that could be served by a multilateral investment agreement. These might include a set of standards for TNC behavior (to prevent labor rights abuses, for example) and rules on transfer pricing. When a TNC transfers resources (say, auto parts) from one subsidiary to another, it has to set an internal price, called the **transfer price**, which is used to calculate the profits and therefore establish the tax liability of operations in each country. It is well known that transfer prices can be manipulated to create artificially low profits in jurisdictions where tax rates are high and artificially high taxable income for operations in countries where tax rates are low. Transfer price manipulation is essentially a way for TNCs to lower their tax burden and deprive states of tax revenues.[11] An investment agreement could prevent this.

A multilateral agreement would also be useful if it prevented states from getting caught up in bidding wars for TNC projects. If states agreed to abide by rules about what incentives they could provide, all might benefit in the long run.

Some studies suggest that state incentives and giveaways are ultimately not very important in the pattern of FDI location, except perhaps on the margin. Typically, market factors tend to be more important in the decision to invest abroad at a particular location than all the goodies that states offer to entice foreign firms. In the end, FDI largely goes where it would have gone, but with the bonus payments thrown in. The only way to stop this, however, is for all the states involved to agree to tie their own hands, and that is what international treaties and agreements are supposed to do.

The OECD's attempt to negotiate a final version of the Multilateral Agreement on Investment failed in 1998, perhaps predictably. Instead of binding rules, all that could be agreed on was a set of voluntary guidelines. Why did the MAI negotiations collapse? The short answer is that states were unwilling to give up the right to pursue their national self-interest. They wanted to be able to discriminate in favor of domestic firms when this seemed prudent and to bid lavishly for TNCs' factories when the opportunity was presented.

Instead of one global agreement on FDI, UNCTAD reports that as of 2011 there were over 6,000 separate International Investment Agreements (IIAs) between TNCs and nation-states, creating a complex hodgepodge of rules and standards. This system of IIAs does nothing to reduce the incentive for states to engage in "beggar thy neighbor" bidding wars to attract TNCs, nor does it facilitate enforcement of uniform labor and environmental standards in TNC operations. In the absence of *multilateral* agreements to regulate TNC behavior, NGOs have stepped into the breach and mounted campaigns to pressure TNCs to treat their foreign workers fairly. TNCs have responded by adopting more corporate social responsibility standards. The success of these is a matter of intense debate as compliance is hard to monitor and enforce (see the box TNCs, Global Commodity Chains, and Accountability).

▶ TNCs, GLOBAL COMMODITY CHAINS, AND ACCOUNTABILITY

Traditionally, many TNCs had one of two types of organizational structure. They were either vertically integrated or horizontally integrated firms. More recently, a new TNC structure has appeared: the globally integrated enterprise based on a **global commodity chain** (also referred to as a global supply chain), whereby the TNC does not own most of the elements of its foreign operations. With improved information technology, some TNCs can "outsource" vital functions to foreign-owned firms. The TNC builds a transnational network of contacts and contracts that it coordinates to create a regional or global business presence.

Nike, for example, is a high-profile TNC, but you will not find it ranked near the top of the FDI rankings of firms. It owns very few production assets either outside or inside the United States. Most Nike products (its line of baseball caps is a notable exception) are manufactured and distributed by foreign-owned firms under contract to Nike. Everything from production of raw materials, to apparel sewing to distribution is coordinated by Nike through chains of contracts and business relations with other firms. The assets that Nike absolutely controls and guards jealously are its brand name, its image, and the famous "swoosh"

(continued)

trademark. Similarly, Apple outsources most of the manufacturing and assembly of components for iPhones and iPads to companies in countries like China, Japan, and Taiwan while maintaining firm control over the design and reputation of its iconic products.

Global commodity chains raise all sorts of interesting questions in IPE. Are TNCs accountable for what is done in their subcontracting firms? When Nike was criticized for labor conditions in factories in its chain, it did eventually change them. More recently, Apple has come under increasing pressure to improve conditions at one of its major suppliers, Foxconn, a Taiwanese-owned company that employs 1.2 million workers in China.[a] A TNC like Apple or Nike might not be legally accountable for its suppliers' actions, but in competitive market environments it sometimes must establish accountability for actions of other firms in order to have credibility in the marketplace and legitimacy in its negotiations with other actors that are concerned about corporate social conduct.

The issue of sweatshop conditions in some apparel global commodity chains illustrates this point. Some of the NGOs that have targeted sweatshops supplying TNCs and focused on improving working conditions in them are Global Exchange, Clean Clothes Campaign of Europe, Co-op America, Sweatshop Watch, and the United Students Against Sweatshops. Some university groups are part of a large network of more than 110 academic institutions focused on generating a code that permits only "sweat-free" clothes to bear their name. In September 2002, some twenty-six apparel companies signed an agreement to establish a monitoring system that would oversee working conditions in their subsidiaries in developing countries. Some 250 U.S. companies, including Apple and Nike, have created codes of conduct for their subcontractors.[b]

Many TNCs have taken the issue of accountability very seriously. The NGO Business for Social Responsibility (BSR) defines its goal as "achieving commercial success in ways that honor ethical values and respect people, communities, and the natural environment." BSR argues that **corporate social responsibility (CSR)** can have a positive effect on businesses by reducing operating costs, enhancing brand image, increasing sales and company loyalty, and raising productivity and quality.[c] Companies that have been recognized for their commitment to CSR are the Co-operative Bank, Starbucks Corporation, B&Q, and Novo Nordisk.

It remains to be seen, however, whether the CSR movement will create widespread change in TNC behavior. Some scholars have questioned the effectiveness of CSR, seeing it as window dressing by a few high-profile TNCs and therefore likely to result only in marginal changes in business conduct.[d] Robert Reich, for example, argues that "companies are neither moral nor immoral" and that what drive the behavior of TNCs are deeper structural forces and not the ethics of their top executives. Reich and others advocate multilateral and national regulations that would apply to all corporations. As global commodity chains become more important in transnational production, the question of their accountability and how to respond to them will continue to be a central issue on the public policy agenda.

References

[a]See Charles Duhigg and David Barboza, "In China, Human Costs Are Built into an iPad," *New York Times,* January 25, 2012.

[b]Robert Collier, "For Anti-Sweatshop Activists, Recent Settlement Is Only Tip of Iceberg," *San Francisco Chronicle,* September 29, 2002. See also John Miller, "Why Economists Are Wrong about Sweatshops and the Antisweatshop Movement," *Challenge* 46 (January–February 2003), pp. 93–112.

[c]See the website of Business for Social Responsibility, at www.bsr.org.

[d]See David Vogel, *The Market for Virtue: The Potential and Limits of Corporate Social Responsibility* (Washington, DC: Brookings Institution Press, 2005); and Robert Reich, *Supercapitalism: The Transformation of Business, Democracy, and Everyday Life* (New York: Alfred A. Knopf, 2007). For a critical view on Nike's claim that it has complied with its agreement to monitor its facilities, see Richard Read, "Nike's Focus on Keeping Costs Low Causes Poor Working Conditions, Critics Say," *Oregonian,* August 5, 2008.

CONCLUSION

TNCs Today

Change and uncertainty are the hallmarks of this period of transition in the global economy and international relations. Nevertheless, we can identify some powerful currents that are likely to affect the pattern of FDI flows and perhaps the behavior of TNCs. The developments we discuss here raise many crucial questions, making this an exciting time for students of IPE and TNCs.

A potentially game-changing development, as we have alluded to already, is the spectacular economic growth of countries like China and India. Just as the rise of Japan and the newly industrialized countries spawned successful competitors to Western TNCs in previous years, we are now seeing enterprises from countries like Brazil, Russia, India, and China (the BRICs) challenge the dominance of Western TNCs. A recent book by members of the Boston Consulting Group argues that the process of globalization has advanced so far that we are now in a condition they call "globality." Whereas global business used to be a "one-way street" benefiting Northern TNCs, it is now a two-way process, with TNCs from the North and the BRICs "competing with everyone from everywhere for everything."[12]

Partly in response to this intensified competition and partly in response to changes in communication and transportation technologies, we are beginning to see the arrival of what Samuel Palmisano, the former CEO of IBM, calls **globally integrated enterprises** that are adept at linking together multiple partners and suppliers from around the world to collaborate and share in the finance, design, and production of new products.[13] In contrast to the pressures to internalize activities implied by the appropriability theory and the branch factory syndrome we discussed earlier, TNCs are increasingly externalizing some of the activities they used to conduct in-house.

There are several reasons for adopting "nonequity modes" (NEMs) of international production, the term UNCTAD uses to describe what TNCs do when they coordinate global commodity chains without owning most of the firms in the supply chains. One is to spread the potential risks of operating in a more competitive and uncertain environment. Another is to increase TNCs' flexibility to respond to changes in demand. Disentangling themselves from relationships with suppliers is often easier and less costly than closing a wholly-owned affiliate. And depending on the complexity of the product, TNCs can gain cost and skill advantages by outsourcing sizeable chunks of their operations. TNCs can outsource much of the production of simple products like toys or garments to lower cost suppliers. Producers of sophisticated products can tap into pools of talented labor across the globe. The following box focuses on the production of Boeing's new airplane, the 787, and provides a striking example of this process at work.

OUTSOURCING AND THE GLOBALLY INTEGRATED ENTERPRISE: BOEING'S 787 AIRPLANE

Boeing, one of the two leading producers of airplanes, launched the development of its new airplane, the 787 "Dreamliner," with a revolutionary new business strategy. The plane would be made primarily of composite material rather than metal, and 70 percent of it would be produced by suppliers and subcontractors located all over the United States and the world (among the countries involved are Japan, China, South Korea, Australia, Russia, Canada, England, France, Sweden, and Italy). What is notable about its new strategy is that certain key partners, known as "tier one suppliers," are responsible for all

(*continued*)

the design, engineering, manufacturing, and assembly of various sections of the airplane. So, for example, the wings, at one time considered by Boeing to be key sources of its competitive advantage, are now being produced by Japanese firms with help from Boeing. Below these firms are hundreds of "tier two suppliers" and their subcontractors who feed smaller parts up the line of a long and complex global supply chain. Boeing now sees system integration and final assembly as the source of its competitive advantage.

The outsourcing, according to Leslie Wayne, "is so extensive that Boeing . . . has no idea how many people around the world are working on the 787 project."[a] Not to be outdone, Boeing's rival, Airbus, itself the creation of four European countries, plans to outsource 60–70 percent of the value of the new planes it produces, with much of this work— and therefore many jobs—going to non-European countries. The advantages to such a business strategy are clear for Boeing, Airbus, and other TNCs. They can gain access to large pools of skilled and talented employees around the world, sometimes at lower cost, as with Boeing's use of Russian engineers in Moscow. They can sweeten their relations with foreign governments by building up the technological and managerial expertise of their suppliers, thereby facilitating better state–TNC interactions and in Boeing's case, bigger sales of its airplanes. And they can reduce their financial risk when embarking on expensive new products and projects by sharing the cost with partners around the world (some 40 percent of Boeing's $8 billion development cost is apparently being borne by partners).

But the consequences for the home country are less clear. Boeing workers are especially worried about what this extensive outsourcing means for their jobs. A recent study of Boeing workers, for example, found that some two-thirds of engineers thought that outsourcing threatened their future job security. Interviews with Boeing workers revealed deep anxiety about what this new business strategy meant for the future of the company and the availability of good jobs for Americans. Employees talked about

"giving away the farm" or losing "hard-learned and expensive know-how" and worried about how such outsourcing might damage Boeing's long-term viability and shrink the middle class and the "national tax base."[b] Boeing has recently acknowledged that it overdid the outsourcing and that the supply chain was too complex and extensive. To avoid the kind of delays (three years) and cost overruns (worth billions of dollars) that occurred on the 787, it indicated that the production of future planes will involve less outsourcing.

The emergence of such globally integrated corporations raises several questions for students of IPE. Will the interests of TNCs and home countries become even more complex and decoupled than they already are? Will such cross-national business partnerships and collaboration in production and finance help form a fledgling "global governing class" that shares interests and power but is increasingly deaf to the needs of the citizens of their putative home countries, as Jeff Faux argues in *The Global Class War*?[c] Will the fact that offshore outsourcing increasingly threatens the jobs of service workers and skilled professionals such as accountants, computer programmers, and engineers—and not just blue-collar workers and the unskilled—create sufficient political heat that politicians will respond with measures to slow the process or assist the vulnerable? And will the spread or export of "good" jobs across the world by these global corporations help raise living standards in developing countries, or will they exacerbate class inequalities?

References

[a] Leslie Wayne, "Boeing Bets the House" *New York Times*, May 7, 2006, p. BU7.

[b] Edward Greenberg, Leon Grunberg, Sarah Moore, and Pat Sikora, *Turbulence: Boeing and the State of American Workers and Managers* (New Haven, CT: Yale University Press, 2010).

[c] Jeff Faux, *The Global Class War* (Hoboken, NJ: Wiley and Sons, 2006).

Whereas some political, economic, and technological developments are pushing TNCs to delink their interests from those of their home countries, others are raising concerns about a stealth return of mercantilism or "state capitalism" into the global economy. For example, state-owned TNCs, as their name implies, are majority or wholly owned by a country's government. About two-thirds of China's outward FDI is controlled by the Chinese state.[14] This control enables the Chinese state to underwrite the development of "national champions" to compete against traditional TNCs in world markets and to direct foreign investment to resource-rich countries, thereby ensuring access to the minerals, energy, and agricultural products that are necessary to fuel China's spectacular economic growth.

The rapid growth of **sovereign wealth funds (SWFs)** (from $500 million in assets in 1990 to almost $5.1 trillion in 2012) and state-owned TNCs (accounting for 11 percent of total FDI in 2011) worries many commentators. Often lacking accountability to shareholders, regulators, or voters, their secrecy and potential investment in strategically important industries poses risks.[15] Larry Summers, the former director of the National Economic Council in the Obama administration, sees a potential threat to the liberal global system from mercantilist actions by foreign governments which, as he puts it, might ask an "airline to fly to their country, want a bank to do business in their country, or want a rival to their country's champion disabled."[16] Defenders of SWFs and state-owned TNCs point out that they have been operating for some time with no evidence that they are pursuing anything other than healthy financial returns.

Does the emergence of the BRICs, SWFs, and state-owned TNCs as important sources of FDI change the role of privately-owned TNCs in the global economy? Can FDI originating from China, a country still ruled by the communist party, still be characterized as an instrument of imperialism? Will the state-owned TNCs act with greater concern for labor and environmental rights than long-established TNCs or will they be compelled to behave like all the others by the pressures of global competition? Whether SWFs and TNCs from emerging countries end up rewriting the rules of the liberal global system or not, there is little doubt that they symbolize a rebalancing of power relations in that system.

Finally, we have to ask what kind of long-term impact the severe economic recession that began at the end of 2007 is likely to have on FDI and TNCs. Is support for globalization among elites and citizens around the world so shaken that we might be in for a period of retrenchment, with less open borders, less international trade, and less FDI? Have popular protest movements like OWS raised enough public skepticism about the actions of large corporations and banks, including TNCs, to galvanize politicians to more severely regulate their activities? Although UNCTAD sees no signs of a major transformation in world investment trends, it is making its best judgment based on current conditions. As the global economy recovers, we can expect underlying economic and technological forces to drive the expansion of FDI and TNCs, but perhaps with less enthusiasm for free-market nostrums. But if the crisis lingers or deepens, the likely fallout becomes more uncertain. History reminds us that in response to severe economic crises, political forces can reshape the international order, as they did for example in the 1930s. Prognostication is therefore a dangerous game.

KEY TERMS

DISCUSSION QUESTIONS

1. What are TNCs and how are they different from other business firms?
2. Why do TNCs engage in foreign direct investment? Explain whether or not the following statement accurate: "Most TNCs invest in less developed countries because of the low wages that they can pay there."
3. How and why have reactions to TNCs changed in the last half century?
4. How would an international agreement on governance of FDI benefit TNCs? How would such an agreement benefit states? What prevents such an agreement from being realized?
5. Explain recent changes in the pattern of FDI and in the organization of TNCs. What are some of the implications of these changes?
6. Considering the severity of the financial crisis that began in late 2007, what do you think might be some of the consequences for FDI and TNCs over the next ten years? Will liberal economic policies and open borders beat a retreat or does the crisis mean just a temporary setback for the forces of globalization?

SUGGESTED READINGS

Robert Gilpin. *The Challenge of Global Capitalism: The World Economy in the 21st Century*. Princeton, NJ: Princeton University Press, 2000.

William Greider. *One World, Ready or Not: The Manic Logic of Global Capitalism*. New York: Simon & Schuster, 1997.

Stephen H. Hymer. *The International Operations of National Firms: A Study of Direct Foreign Investment*. Cambridge, MA: MIT Press, 1976.

David C. Korten. *When Corporations Rule the World*. West Hartford, CT: Kumarian Press, 1996.

Raymond Vernon. *In the Hurricane's Eye: The Troubled Prospects of Multinational Enterprises*. Cambridge, MA: Harvard University Press, 1998.

NOTES

1. *Economist*, "Special Report: State Capitalism," January 21, 2012.
2. See William Greider, *One World, Ready or Not: The Manic Logic of Global Capitalism* (New York: Simon & Schuster, 1997).
3. See Robert Gilpin, *U.S. Power and the Multinational Corporation: The Political Economy of Foreign Direct Investment* (New York: Basic Books, 1975), p. 147.
4. Ibid., p. 260.
5. See Joseph Nye, *Soft Power: The Means of Success in World Politics* (Cambridge, MA: Perseus Books Group, 2004).
6. See John Stopford and Susan Strange, *Rival States, Rival Firms: Competition for World Market Shares* (Cambridge, England: Cambridge University Press, 1991).
7. David N. Balaam and Michael Veseth, *Introduction to International Political Economy*, 2nd ed. (Upper Saddle River, NJ: Prentice Hall, 2001), p. 361.
8. See Kenichi Ohmae, *The Borderless World* (New York: Harper & Row, 1990).
9. David C. Korten, *When Corporations Rule the World* (West Hartford, CT: Kumarian Press, 1996).
10. Raymond Vernon, *In the Hurricane's Eye: The Troubled Prospects of Multinational Enterprises* (Cambridge, MA: Harvard University Press, 1998).
11. Useful information about transfer pricing, including links to current articles about it, can be found on the website of the politically active organization called Tax Justice Network, at http://www.taxjustice.net/cms/front_content.php?idcat=139.
12. Harold Sirkin, James Hemerling, and Arindam Bhattacharya, *Globality: Competing with Everyone from Everywhere for Everything* (New York: Business Plus, 2008). A different view is offered by

Panjat Ghemawat in *World 3.0: Global Prosperity and How to Achieve It* (Boston: Harvard Business Review Press, 2011). He argues that geography and culture still matter and that TNCs remain much more tied to their domestic and regional markets than some commentators on globalization imply.

13. Samuel Palmisano, "The Globally Integrated Enterprise," *Foreign Affairs* (May–June 2006).

14. Nargiza Salidjanova, "Going Out: An Overview of China's Outward Foreign Direct Investment" (U.S.-China Economic Security Review Commission Research Report), March 30, 2011.

15. *Economist*, "Special Report on Globalization," September 20, 2008.

16. Tim Weber, "Who's Afraid of Sovereign Wealth Funds?" *BBC News*, January 24, 2008.

Food and Hunger: Market Failure and Injustice

Global Hunger Continues: A man suffering from severe malnutrition in Eritrea.

Mike Goldwater/Alamy

After World War II, there were periods of massive hunger, primarily in developing nations. For the last half century, however, the world food problem has been viewed primarily as one of *excess supply* and *weak demand* for agricultural commodities and foodstuffs. In the summer of 2008 and then again in 2011, the international community was caught off-guard by a combination of low levels of commodity reserves and high food prices. Increased volatility in food markets has become the new norm. The United Nations (UN) frequently warns that another "food crisis" is on the horizon, marking the beginning of a new era in the global political economy of food.

Beginning in late 2005, food prices steadily increased, benefiting many farmers but also increasing the number of poor and hungry. The UN's Food and Agriculture Organization (FAO) reported that world food reserve stock levels reached a record low of a fifty-five-day supply. Before long, protests and riots over high food and gasoline prices broke out in many countries, including Mexico, Indonesia, and Ivory Coast. In Haiti, the prime minister was driven from office. In some countries, hoarding and panic buying resulted. Major food outlets in the United States limited rice purchases. To encourage production, some states responded to the crisis with new farm subsidies. At least forty-seven nations, including Russia, China, and India, either imposed bans on agricultural exports or dropped trade tariffs to encourage imports to help protect their consumers from hunger. In 2011, similar spikes in food prices contributed to political unrest in North Africa and the Middle East that became known as the Arab Spring. Likewise a series of drought conditions in the United States, Russia, Australia, and other states also drove up food prices.

These recent world food crises have generated intense debate over their causes and effects. State officials, international organizations (IOs), media outlets, and academics offered many explanations for the crisis including: a weak U.S. dollar that helped draw down commodity reserve levels; environmental events that placed a natural limit on commodity production, particularly in developing nations; income and population growth in the newly emerging countries, which sparked renewed fears of famine and starvation throughout the world; requirements for biofuel production that reduced the amount of commodities available for food consumption; and investment speculation on agriculture commodities. The world food crisis also incited debate over possible solutions, which included new **genetically modified organisms (GMOs)** and production techniques; a new Green Revolution; UN World Food Program (WFP) efforts to increase food aid to the neediest nations; the reduction of trade barriers; measures to improve food distribution while overcoming conflict and war in many poorer countries; and an emphasis on **food sovereignty** as a strategy to democratize the food system and strengthen local food economies.

This chapter attempts to answer several overarching questions about the "perfect storm" that resulted in a new world food crisis that began in the spring of 2008 and that continues to the present day. First, what explains the dramatic, sudden changes in global supply and demand conditions between 2005 and 2012? Second, when too much food and the *lack of demand* for it were viewed as major policy issues before 2005, why weren't the excess supplies of food fed to those who needed them the most? Third, why were food and hunger problems not dealt with more effectively, causing hunger and starvation to remain predominant features of the international political economy? Finding answers to these questions will help clarify the roots of the recent food crisis, which we argue are part of a perpetual feature in the global food production and distribution system.

After stating our theses in this chapter, we outline some of the political, economic, and social structural elements of the global food production and distribution system. In a brief history section, we then discuss some of the important recent developments in food and hunger conditions and policies. We then use the three dominant IPE perspectives (see Chapter 1) to explain the primary factors that experts and policy officials suggest contributed to the latest world food crisis. The chapter ends with a short overview of popular proposals to solve the crisis and a discussion of some of the implications of our work for management of global food and hunger problems.

We present three main theses in this chapter. First, despite arguments to the contrary, it is clear that the current world food crisis is *not* primarily a product of lower commodity supplies accompanied by a dramatic rise in both income and population. Actually, the imbalance between supply and demand merely begs the question of why prices increased so much over roughly a three-year period *before* the crisis was acknowledged and why commodities ended up in short supply so suddenly. We argue that the seeds of the global food and hunger problem remain rooted in poverty, a mismanaged food distribution system, and policies that encourage the production of highly processed foods that are harmful to both human health and the environment.

Second, despite different macroeconomic conditions, hunger and starvation are *permanent structural* features of the global political economy. The recent world food crisis only magnifies the extent to which political, economic, and social structures of power reign over the market. Poor people have *consistently* lacked access to adequate food supplies, while most people in developed countries have access to relatively inexpensive agricultural commodities and food products. However, these inexpensive food products tend to be high in fats, sugars, and salt, and therefore contribute to increasing rates of chronic diseases like diabetes and obesity. Poorer countries increasingly face a "double burden" of hunger and chronic disease as these processed foods become more accessible.

Third and finally, we contend that management of the food production and distribution system suffers from the conflicting *interests and values* of different food actors, including states, IOs, multinational corporations, and subnational groups. These actors form networks that are not insulated from complicated economic development, energy and environmental issues, or security problems, making it nearly impossible to create an effective global food policy to overcome hunger.

AN IPE OF FOOD AND HUNGER

An IPE of hunger helps explain how a combination of political, economic, and social factors affects national and international food and hunger issues. Realists view the world as a self-help system in which nation-states must compete for power and wealth to improve their relative security. States regulate both national and international markets to serve state interests. Nations with the capacity to produce large agricultural surpluses, including the United States, Canada, France, Australia, Brazil, and Argentina, often benefit from the dependency of other nations on their food exports. Surplus commodity producers also employ *export subsidies* and other trade-enhancing measures to clear *local markets*, generate new markets, and earn foreign currency.

On the other hand, major commodity *importers* sometimes adopt production-enhancing and trade protectionist measures to enhance their own food security. These measures often complicate international trade negotiations such as those in the current Doha round of the World Trade Organization (WTO) (see Chapter 6). Many states are concerned about being dependent on agricultural exporters during a time of crisis or war, when cutting off food supplies may weaken their nation's security. For many nations in Asia or Africa, accessibility to limited amounts of exported rice can mean the difference between maintaining a healthy diet and slipping into a state of malnutrition and hunger.

Many experts agree that **transnational agribusiness corporations (TNACs)** such as Archer Daniels Midland, ConAgra, and Monsanto can both help and hinder food systems. Most industrialized countries have chosen not to seriously restrict agribusiness practices. Regional organizations such as the EU protect farmers with production enhancements, tariffs, and subsidies that distort global supply and demand, possibly contributing to world hunger. IOs such as the UN's FAO and the WFP are often accused of not doing enough to resolve hunger. However, many nongovernmental organizations (NGOs) such as Bread for the World and *Médecins Sans Frontières* (Doctors Without Borders) work effectively to combat hunger throughout the world. Finally, subnational groups like the U.S. National Family Farm Coalition and alternative market mechanisms like **community-supported agriculture (CSA)** play key roles in food policy, production, and distribution at the local level in some countries.

Economic liberals stress that farmers, special interest groups, and agribusinesses in the major grain-producing countries often "capture" the policy-making process in order to enhance farm income through subsidies, trade tariffs, and/or exports subsidies. U.S. and EU politicians often justify these support measures on the basis that they also keep food prices lower than they would be under "free-market" conditions. However, farm supports compensate for low "farm-gate" commodity prices and can lead to excess production and speculation, distorting the market's automatic supply–demand adjustment mechanism.

From the late 1970s to the crisis of 2008, many orthodox economic liberals (OELs) viewed the world food and hunger problem as a failure of market forces to balance supply with demand. *If* markets were depoliticized—the state's role was limited and the market decided policy outcomes—enough food would be produced to feed everyone in the world and would be distributed through trade to those who needed it. For heterodox interventionist liberals (HILs), the picture is more complicated. They are skeptical that states can resolve the myriad conflicting domestic and international interests that give agricultural trade its quasi-protectionist flavor. Policies that support farmers but create minimal distortion of the international market are preferred over free trade, partially to account for the impact of trade policies on society and food security.

Finally, structuralists tend to view the current world food crisis as an extension of a food quandary dating from the 1950s: Low income and lack of access to land have been the major causes of hunger, not overpopulation or lack of production. They charge that the cheap food policies of major producers have benefited the rich to the detriment of the urban working class and rural peasantry. In many countries, officials promote the production of some commodities based on factors such as producer ethnicity, religion, class, history, and other political interests. In Ethiopia, Somalia, the Darfur region of Sudan, Congo, Kenya, and Zimbabwe, social and political factors have resulted in groups of people intentionally being underfed or even starved to death. However, some structuralists would *support* "multifunctional" protectionist trade policies to help promote local producers of indigenous crops and enhance state independence while insulating local production from the vagaries of the international political economy. Agrarian reform—providing landless rural workers with access to land to produce their own food—is also a structuralist prescription for addressing hunger particularly in countries where a large portion of the population still lives in rural areas.

A BRIEF HISTORY OF GLOBAL FOOD AND HUNGER ISSUES

In the twentieth century, most industrial nations saw production subsidies and new agricultural production technologies increased commodity surpluses while demand stayed weak. Farmers in the major grain-growing nations, including the United States, Canada, the European Community (now the EU), and Australia, often complained about low food prices and low farm incomes. They pressured their legislatures for subsidies and protectionist trade measures in order to bring farm incomes up to the level of nonfarm workers. Depending on the country, farm programs included support for wheat, corn, soybeans, sugar, cotton, feed grains, and a small number of other crops. Many farmers benefited from a combination of deficiency payments or direct income support, subsidized loans, conservation policies, and national commodity storage programs that removed commodities from the market.

A farm-food policy network composed of farm groups, agribusinesses, legislators, and executive agencies such as the U.S. Department of Agriculture (USDA) had a vested interest in sustaining farm incomes above what they would have been under free-market conditions. But taxpayer-funded policies were expensive and economically inefficient. As oversupply continuously drove down farm prices, the pressure on states to sustain farm incomes only intensified. Legislators in the world's leading democracies felt compelled to help their farm constituents, even if it meant employing inefficient protectionist measures. Production surpluses helped accomplish a variety of political, economic, and social objectives. For example, in the 1960s and 1970s, surplus corn, butter, cheese, and other commodities played a major part in subsidized U.S. school lunch programs. Domestically, "cheap food" policies increased consumption of especially wheat, corn, and feed grains and were politically popular with commodity farmers and low-income groups.

Food was also an important element of state power. Food-importing states were vulnerable to food-exporting states. The United States routinely used food as a tool to achieve a variety of foreign policy objectives. Aid efforts helped the United States unload its commodity surpluses overseas. U.S. Public Law (PL) 480 and the "Food for Peace" program made food aid easily available to states that were anti-communist and whose economies were potential markets for future sales of U.S. commodities and commercial products.

Throughout the second half of the twentieth century, the UN estimated that an average of 800 million people, primarily in the least developed nations, did not receive the required amounts of protein and calories to fight off diseases such as kwashiorkor and marasmus associated with malnutrition. Hunger came to be viewed as the result of inadequate food production coupled with overpopulation, a problem that seemed endemic to developing nations. The solution seemed fairly simple: The industrialized food surplus countries should help less developed countries (LDCs) adopt Western industrial production techniques to produce more of their own food for export. This in turn would earn these poorer countries the foreign currency they needed to buy industrial goods on the international market, all the while encouraging them to lower their population growth rates. Many officials (especially from states with large commodity surpluses) also suggested that foreign aid would help governments overcome production shortfalls and infrastructure problems, making it easier for LDCs to eventually overcome their hunger problems as their economies modernized. The World Bank and other financial institutions funded development projects that promoted industrialization modeled on Western nations. In the 1960s, the Ford and Rockefeller foundations supported **Green Revolution** research to help LDCs increase production and develop new varieties of wheat in Mexico and rice in the Philippines. To this day, many experts claim that the Green Revolution helped millions of people in developing nations avoid hunger.

Yet none of these measures could overcome the malnutrition and starvation that routinely occurred in India, parts of Southeast and East Asia, and Africa. In addition, overpopulation and rising birth rates were predicted to wreak havoc on countries like India and China. In his work entitled "Lifeboat Ethics," biology professor Dr. Garrett Hardin suggested that the industrialized nations were not likely to transfer a sufficient amount of resources to poorer-overpopulated developing nations to stave off their hunger.[1] Hardin proposed that if the industrialized nations (which were in an imaginary lifeboat) did not want to be swamped by the growing masses in developing nations, they were ethically obligated to cut off food aid and other assistance to save themselves. Food aid was an *unethical* disservice to those whose lives would end when it was discontinued.

Many critics argued that Hardin's analogies were flawed. Even if the world did have a finite amount of resources, the earth had not reached the point where there were just enough resources available for a certain number of people to live comfortably while others perished. Critics asked: Must those in the industrialized nations live as lavishly as they do compared to people in developing nations? Might the "haves" share more with the "have-nots"? How can the major commodity producers such as Canada, the United States, and the EU justify their huge surpluses while so many people in the developing regions of the world are malnourished or starving?

A World Food Crisis and a Paradigm Shift

During the 1972–1973 world food crisis, another explanation of hunger and food insecurity emerged. In 1972, the FAO announced that supplies of world grain reserves had reached record low levels and surpluses usually available to food-import-dependent nations were no longer available. For the next two years, hunger increased in some of the poorest regions of the world. The crisis began when, following a shortfall in Soviet wheat production, the United States subsidized sales of wheat and other grain to the Soviet Union as part of an effort to improve U.S.-Soviet relations, driving up prices and drawing down U.S. wheat stocks.

In 1973, the United States devalued its dollar, which made U.S. grain exports more attractive to nations that wanted to upgrade their diets to include more wheat. Many major grain corporations stood to gain from the shipment of these grains to commercial buyers. Just when poorer countries found themselves most dependent on commodity exports, wheat and feed grains were rerouted to industrialized nations that could more easily afford them. The nations that had relied on food aid imports to meet basic needs were no longer able to afford the higher prices of traded commodities.

Concurrently, the OPEC (Organization of Petroleum Exporting Countries) oil cartel embargoed shipments of oil to the United States and dramatically raised the price of oil (see Chapter 19). Many non-oil-exporting LDCs reluctantly adopted food self-sufficiency policies and limited food imports to pay their higher oil bills. Some food-dependent poorer nations were also crippled by routinely occurring monsoons in Asia and drought in the Sahel region of Africa where almost a million people starved to death when food relief efforts were intentionally blocked.

In the mid-1970s, Frances Moore Lappé, Joseph Collins, Susan George, Colin Tudge, and others challenged Hardin's assumption that overpopulation was the root of the hunger problem. What became known as the **Food First** argument claimed that hunger resulted more from income inequality and a lack of democracy in the food system than from reduced production and overpopulation.[2] Food Firsters cited demographers who maintained that population growth rates decreased in developed nations when their economies transformed from an agricultural to an industrial base. According to the **demographic transition** theory, as people lived longer and per capita income increased, population growth rates naturally slowed. With development and higher personal income, financial security would take away the incentive of poorer people to have more children.

These Food Firsters also pointed out that people in LDCs often adopted measures to control population growth during times of drought or severe food shortages. With the possible exception of China, massive social intervention programs to control population growth did not work. Moreover, in India and elsewhere, these programs were viewed as another example of Western imperialism because they blamed developing nations for overpopulation instead of focusing on income distribution or Western overconsumption. Furthermore, limiting population growth would *not* necessarily guarantee that food would be available to poorer members of society, as the number of hungry in developed societies demonstrates. Estimates showed that enough food was produced in the world to feed each person more than 2,700 calories a day. What developing societies lacked were distribution channels necessary to ensure that all individuals received the daily minimum requirements of nutrients and calories, and the financial resources to either produce or purchase what they needed.

Many Food Firsters also drew attention to hunger and food security from an increasingly global IPE perspective. They outlined some of the political, economic, and social factors that have made it difficult to solve the poverty and food distribution problems that create global hunger. Food Firsters and other structuralist critics also tended to share the belief about the necessity of food security arguing that hunger was *not endemic* to LDCs but rather a by-product of their political and economic relationship to the industrialized nations, shaped by *asymmetrical international interdependence*. In fact, before colonization, developing regions of the world were relatively food self-sufficient. Colonization and interaction with the industrialized nations via trade, aid, and investment had "immiserized" their local economies. The developing nations such as South Korea and Taiwan that overcame poverty and hunger were the exception to the rule, given huge amounts of aid they received due to their strategic relationships with Western powers.

In response to this understanding of the roots of hunger, small farmer and peasant movements around the world began mobilizing to demand greater autonomy to shape local and regional food systems, and to make policies independent of the requirements of international trade agreements. They called for (and sometimes received) land reform that would allow them greater access to land to produce food for themselves and their local community. While many of these land reform programs were deeply flawed and led to an overall reduction in food production, many others—notably in Latin America—succeeded in increasing the food security of the rural poor. This movement would later coalesce internationally as the "food sovereignty" movement, discussed later in this chapter.

Hunger Amidst Plenty

After the food crisis of the 1970s ended, food security conditions did not improve for people living in LDCs. Instances of mass starvation mounted during Bangladesh's civil war. Food was intentionally used as a weapon in other wars, including Ethiopia and the "killing fields" of Cambodia. Throughout most of the 1980s, the Sahel region of Africa experienced several more rounds of mass starvation and hunger. Yet producers continued to reduce food aid and shift it into concessional (trade) channels.

Efforts by international food relief organizations such as the FAO and Office of the UN High Commissioner for Refugees (UNHCR) resulted in few victories when it came to dealing with hunger in the most ravaged nations. In 1992, the United States set a new precedent by sending its forces (backed by a UN resolution) into Somalia to feed millions of starving people besieged by civil war. But following an ambush that killed seventeen U.S. soldiers, the multilateral force withdrew from Somalia. Today, Somalia has become a prime example of a "failed state" known for not only hunger and famine but also instability and war.

During the rest of the 1990s and into the early 2000s, civil war contributed to the deaths of millions by starvation in Rwanda, Sudan, Angola, Ethiopia, Sierra Leone, and Liberia. Meanwhile, Tanzania, Namibia, Botswana, Malawi, Mozambique, Lesotho, Swaziland, Zambia, and Zimbabwe regularly face hunger due to drought. Many of these states also must overcome high incidences of HIV infection, which has worsened their hunger problems. Private organizations, including World Vision, *Médecins Sans Frontières*, and Oxfam, have been unable to do much to halt the spread of hunger and starvation on the continent. In 1996, the FAO sponsored a world food conference in Rome, where 187 states pledged to halve the number of hungry people in the world within twenty years, to approximately 400 million. As of 2012, more than fifteen countries in Latin America, Asia, and Africa had met this goal, and many more had made significant progress. However, the food and financial crises that began in 2008 still threaten that progress.

AN IPE OF THE GLOBAL FOOD CRISIS OF 2008

In the spring of 2008, a "perfect storm" of factors resulted in the most recent global food crisis, unexpectedly producing shortages and abnormally high prices for agricultural commodities and food products worldwide. The following is a list of the seven factors most often cited as causing the crisis:

- An *undervalued U.S. dollar* that led to a severe drawdown in U.S. commodity stocks.
- Natural *resource limits*, including drought, lack of water, and other types of climate change that contributed to commodity production shortfalls throughout the world.
- Increased consumption of animal protein (meat, dairy, eggs) in Asia and Latin America that diverted grain from human consumption to animal feed, and intensified water use—also called "meatification."
- Unusually high levels of *speculation* (investments) in agricultural production that helped drive up commodity and food prices.
- The increased use of new technologies such as *biofuel* production in the United States and the EU that diverted food away from developing regions.
- The *overreliance* of many developing nations on *cheap food policies, inappropriate development strategies*, and *inappropriate technologies* to relieve hunger.
- The continued presence of *war, disease, corruption*, and other unfavorable political and economic conditions that severely weaken food production and distribution systems.

In this section, we employ the three IPE perspectives to explain how each of these factors contributed to the supposed crisis, as well as some possible solutions proposed by a variety of experts, organizations, and agencies.

An Undervalued U.S. Dollar

An undervalued dollar was not the main cause of the World Food Crisis of 2008 but an intervening variable that exacerbated it. A weak U.S. dollar made U.S. grain more affordable, causing other nations to import more of the commodity. As U.S. supply levels dropped to record lows, food prices rose, driving speculation and increasing the probability of an investment bubble in agricultural commodities.

And yet this hardship for both consumers and the world's hungry was viewed as a blessing by many U.S. farmers who had faced low commodity prices for decades. Farmers in grain-producing nations expected to be able to increase production to meet both the future demand related to rising populations and higher incomes in countries like China and India and the increased demand for biofuels. An increase in commodity exports would also improve the U.S. balance of trade. Former USDA official Robert Lewis called for quadrupled world grain production to feed the world's growing population *at the level of U.S. average consumption.*[3] Lewis recommended that U.S. and EU farmers continue to receive production subsidies because they were caught on "an economic treadmill" and deserve higher wheat prices to cover fixed production costs for land, diesel, fertilizers, and other inputs associated with skyrocketing oil prices in the spring of 2008.

Natural Limits, Population Growth, and the Return of Malthusian Nightmares

Against this background many experts also blamed recent production shortfalls on some combination of droughts, lack of water, and global warming in different grain-growing regions of the world. Some identified increased demand for more resource-intensive food products in "newly emerging" nations such as China and India. Some of them theorized that global climate change and the earth's rising temperature led to declines in yields of wheat, rice, and corn. In 2005, the UN's FAO warned that global warming was likely to increase drought and desertification in Africa, decreasing farmland by 1.1 billion hectares (2.6 billion acres) by 2080.[4] Lester Brown, head of the Earth Policy Institute in Washington, DC, reports that water shortages are a major cause of the world food crisis. Beginning in 2005, droughts and unexpected bad weather in the United States, the EU, Russia, Ukraine, and Argentina contributed to record low commodity stockpile levels. Over the last decade, Australia has been hit by intense droughts that have made it difficult to generate its usual commodity surpluses of wheat. Shrinking groundwater levels occurred both in China and in India's Punjab state. Aquifers in the Sahara and in the southwest of the United States were also at record low levels.[5]

Brown expects that by 2050 the planet will have three billion more people— totaling at least nine billion. Although he acknowledges that population growth rates have *slowed* from 2 percent in 1970 to 1.2 percent in 2005, he predicts that global population will soon outrun global commodity supplies. Many of the poorer countries of Asia, Latin America, and Africa (especially the Democratic Republic of the Congo, Rwanda, and Tanzania) are expected to grow their populations by an estimated seventy-four million (the size of two Canadas) per year. This combination of production shortfalls and population growth raises the possibility of another "Malthusian nightmare" of too many mouths to feed.

As noted earlier, most structuralists disagree that the world does not have enough food to feed everyone. The Food Firsters Lappé, Collins, and Rosset argue that while there could be seventy-four million more mouths to feed every year, more people are buying more meat and more food is going into biofuel production. Similar arguments are made by some HILs and neomercantilists, who argue that as China and India have rapidly developed their industrial sectors, they have *deliberately* slowed grain production, becoming more dependent on commodity imports in order to meet a dramatic increase in the demand for soybeans, feed grains, meat, and non-traditional commodities and food. Many HILs would argue that this was a rational economic strategy on the part of Chinese and Indian officials. Other experts are certain that market forces accompanied by a second

Green Revolution—fueled by new production technologies—will help food production keep pace with population growth and higher incomes.

The Role of Speculation

When investors purchase stock in agricultural commodities, they often bid up its value, which translates into higher commodity and food prices. For three years before the world food crisis, huge investment firms began pouring billions into booming markets for corn, wheat, and soybeans. Many TNACs invested in grain elevators, ethanol plants, fertilizers, and farmland in the United States, Brazil, sub-Saharan Africa, Argentina, and even England.[6] This development was part of a global tendency toward investment in other nonagricultural commodities, including oil but also natural gas, gold, copper, aluminum, zinc, and other resources. Driving market prices higher was the industrialization of China and India but also Saudi Arabia and Russia.[7] Another interesting development has been the purchase of land and investment in commodity production by Saudi Arabia, China, South Korea, Kuwait and others in Sudan, Pakistan, Cambodia, Ethiopia, and the Democratic Republic of Congo to export back to the home country.[8] Many structuralist critics have noted the extent to which these foreign operations contribute to sociopolitical tensions in countries whose resources are being used to feed people in other states while locals are driven out of agriculture or remain hungry.

OELs argue that speculation in agricultural commodity production played only a *small* role in driving up food prices. They claim markets were merely responding to record population and income growth rates in China, India, and Saudi Arabia, where higher income also generated demand for more expensive and higher protein-content foods. Speculation helps agribusinesses and other TNCs earn income for the country in which they originate, which may in turn help feed and provide people with jobs. Speculation can also be a *good* thing because it locks in higher food prices and provides farmers with incentives to increase production in places such as Russia, Ukraine, Kazakhstan, and Brazil. In both the United States and the EU, many farmers even asked to roll back conservation programs that limited commodity production.

Yet many HILs remain skeptical of speculation. It helped generate another economic bubble, similar to the industrial bubble in Southeast Asia during the later 1990s, the hi-tech bubble in the United States in the late 1990s, and the recent housing bubble in the United States. The poor have always been hurt the most by "artificial price increases," which undermine the positive effects of speculation. Still another concern was that, given state and local distribution policies, the benefits of speculation were not guaranteed to help the hungry. Finally, if demands for energy and oil continued to grow in China, India, Russia, and Mexico, food prices could be expected to rise to the point of ultimately producing a global fight between food and energy.

Most structuralists condemn speculative investment derivatives in agricultural production for pushing food prices beyond the impact of normal supply–demand conditions and increasing the chances of hunger in developing nations. Two recent studies of the impact of speculation on agricultural commodities show that "increases in futures-trading volume drove cash-price volatility up," which had "causal effects on inflation."[9] Agricultural commodities are fungible, which means that they can be used to make many different products. Market mechanisms will deliver corn, for example, to the most profitable market—which could be ethanol or animal feed—even when people around the world are starving. When investors predict that demand for ethanol or beef will increase, speculators bid up the price of corn, which in turn drives up food prices. Speculation, then, helped to lessen the possibility of achieving the UN's Millennium Development Goal of halving hunger by 2015.

Biofuels

Ninety percent of the world's **biofuel** production is currently bio-ethanol made largely from sugarcane and maize (corn) and used as an additive to gasoline. The remaining 10 percent of biofuel comes from plant oils such as rapeseed, soya, and palm and is turned into biodiesel. Up until 2007, many government officials, agri-businesses, and farmers were thrilled at the prospect of biofuels. They hoped they would reduce dependency on oil imports and as the market grew, biofuels would eat up their surplus agricultural commodities. Farmers would have an opportunity to maintain production and price levels for their agricultural commodities, which would weaken farm pressure on governments to maintain expensive domestic sub-sidies and agricultural trade protection.

As commodity prices increased steadily between 2005 and 2008, the United States, the EU, and Brazil (which together produce 90 percent of the world's biofuels) assertively promoted biofuel production. In 2010, global production of biofu-els had increased 17 percent due to high oil prices, new laws, and mandates in Argentina, Brazil, Canada, China, and the United States, among other countries.[10] Today, the United States and Brazil remain the two largest producers of ethanol at 57 and 33 percent of total global output, respectively. In the United States, corn is the primary feedstock, and sugarcane the dominant source of ethanol in Brazil. In 2007, the U.S. Congress imposed a 35 percent biofuel supply requirement by 2020. Recently, mandates for biofuel have also been established in Argentina, Brazil, Canada, China, and the EU. The European Parliament is calling for 10 per-cent of road transport fuel to come from renewable sources by 2020. The world's largest biodiesel producer is the EU, accounting for 53 percent of all biodiesel pro-duction in 2010. According to the International Energy Agency, biofuels have the potential to meet more than a quarter of world demand for transportation fuels by 2050.

Today, biofuels remain a heavily politicized issue. Studies have raised ques-tions about their efficiency and connection to rising food prices. Two World Bank officials argue that biofuels were the biggest single contributor to the overall rise in grain prices, while an agency report claimed they contributed to a 75 percent rise in food prices.[11] Even the USDA's ex-chief economist Keith Collins suggested that ethanol was a "foot on the accelerator" of corn demand, leading to higher commodity prices by an estimated 50 percent between 2000 and 2006.[12]

Many economic liberals remain undecided about biofuels and their connec-tion to hunger. When the food crisis began, gas, oil, and other energy costs were at record highs. Many HILs believe that biofuels warrant tax incentives, preferential government purchases, and state-sponsored research grants. In cases such as Brazil's Petrobras, public–private business relationships have generated preferential purchases of biodiesel feedstock from small farmers. In some developing countries, biodiesel fuel sources using marginal land could make sense. For example, honge oil nuts can be grown along roads or jatropha grown along rail lines. Malaysia and Indonesia are planting oil palm at a fast pace to supply the rising demand for biodiesel fuel in Europe and other markets. The cost of producing palm oil biodiesel fuel is less than one-third of the production costs of rapeseed biodiesel, which in turn is less that the cost of using soybeans, corn, and other crops. In poor regions with hostile climates, they are an alternative energy source that helps improve lives. In India and China where sustained economic development is emphasized, they also result in a net reduction of greenhouse gas emissions.

Others argue that still not enough is known at this time about the efficiency, effects, and costs of biofuels.[13] More than a few experts (including the libertarian-oriented CATO Institute in Washington, DC) question the greenhouse emissions associated with biofuels. Growing soybeans and other plants and converting them into biofuels can use more energy than the bio-ethanol or biodiesel generates.[14] Biofuels have also led to the destruction of large tracts of the rainforest. They also tend to be a major problem for nations with large economies that do not have adequate arable land to produce enough fuel to meet their nation's energy requirements. Finally, biofuels have contributed to major water shortages in the Rio Grande, China's Yellow River, and India's Punjab state.

Mercantilists Cross Paths with Economic Liberals.   Mercantilists tend to either support or reject biofuels based on their impact on national political and economic interests. In the United States for instance, ethanol accounted for only 6 percent of U.S. corn production in 2008, but was expected to absorb as much as one quarter of the crop for bio-ethanol production in the next five years. Soybeans made up 40 percent of U.S. acreage. This shift in production decreased the volume of wheat being produced and contributed to higher international wheat prices. Because the United States supplies a quarter of the world's wheat, U.S. food donations to the WFP and other aid organizations decreased but have only recently picked up again.[15]

In response to these conditions, many countries, including Ukraine, Argentina, Kazakhstan, and Vietnam, embargoed commodity exports in order to meet local demand. China had been the world's largest soybean exporter but, to meet rising demand, it became a major importer of soy to feed its pigs and cattle. Likewise, in response to the growing international ethanol market, China also limited its own exports of corn and, as noted earlier, invested heavily in agricultural commodity production in many African nations. For many mercantilist-realist state officials, these policy moves raised concern about the impact of decreased soy imports from China for a number of poorer developing ("failed") states, many of whom have direct ties to terrorist groups.

In order to produce more political and economic stability in biofuel markets, some mercantilists favor establishing governance and sustainability standards with other nations. The EU attempted to coordinate state efforts in the community to produce sustainability criteria for land-use requirements for biofuels, and the G8 created a Global Bioenergy Partnership (GBEP) to facilitate international collaboration on bioenergy and energy security, food security, and environment sustainability. An international Biofuels Forum included producers and consumers from Brazil, China, India, South Africa, the United States, and EU. At the 2008 Rome Food Summit, the Organization for Economic Cooperation and Development (OECD) argued for fewer protectionist trade policies so that farmers could benefit from higher food prices, while calling on all states to phase out mandates for biofuels. Structuralist elements of the Food Summit report called for making food security, protecting poor farmers, promoting broad-based rural development, and ensuring environmental sustainability the primary goals of state biofuel policies.[16]

In "The Future of Alternative Biofuels," we discuss some of the second- and third-generation research projects related to renewable biofuel resources researchers are working on presently and which have application in developing countries as one of their objectives.

THE FUTURE OF ALTERNATIVE BIOFUELS

Today, many researchers are working on the development of so-called second-generation sources of biofuel such as biobutanol and synthetic diesel derived from switchgrass, garbage, and algae, instead of agricultural commodities.[a] Experiments are being conducted all over the world. Some of the more well-known involve cellulite biomass derived from non-food sources, such as wood chips, sawdust and other tree waste, citrus peels, and switchgrass, are actively being developed as a source of ethanol production. Other experiments include fungus from rainforests in Patagonia. Some single-celled fungi have been used as biodiesel fuel research by a group at the Russian Academy of Sciences in Moscow. They have efficiently separated large amounts of lipids from these fungi.

Much research on biodiesel fuel is being done by the U.S. Natural Renewable Energy Laboratory in Golden, Colorado, that involves experiments with algae that has a 50 percent more natural oil content than other sources.[b] These algae can be grown on algae ponds at wastewater treatment plants. The production process has not yet been undertaken on a commercial scale. However, many companies are pursuing algae bio-reactors for research on biodiesel fuel with the intent to scale up biodiesel production

to commercial levels. Because it requires neither farmland nor fresh water, algae culture, unlike crop-based biofuels, does not threaten a decrease in food production. Some researchers recently have successfully produced biodiesel fuel from oil obtained from used coffee grounds, which after extracting the oil undergoes conventional processing into biodiesel. The estimated cost of producing biodiesel by this method is about $1 per gallon. Researchers estimate that several hundred million gallons of biodiesel could be made annually using this technique.

To generate demand for renewable sources of energy for biofuels, the U.S. Environmental Protection Agency (EPA) recently dramatically lowered the country's production target for cellulosic ethanol. The EPA's main argument was that second-generation biofuels were a technical challenge and too expensive to commercialize. The EPA's new target will be 25 million liters instead of the 950 million liters required under the 2007 Energy Independence and Security Act.[c] A Spanish company called Ecofasa is making biodiesel fuel from trash from general urban waste which is then treated by bacteria to produce fatty acids, and later used to make biodiesel. Scientists working with the New Zealand company

(continued)

Lanzatech have developed a technology to use industrial waste gases, such as carbon monoxide from steel mills to produce ethanol. In October 2011, Virgin Atlantic airlines made headlines when it joined with Lanzatech to commission a demonstration plant in Shanghai to produce aviation fuel from waste gases from steel production.[d]

Scientists in Minnesota have developed co-cultures of *Shewanella* and *Synechococcus* that produce a long chain of hydrocarbons directly from water, carbon dioxide, and sunlight.[e] The technology has received ARPA-E (Advanced Research Projects Agency–Energy) funding from the U.S. government. The Naval Facilities Engineering Service Center at Port Hueneme, California, is involved in developing biodiesel technologies for the U.S. Navy and other branches of the military.

A major issue for these new technologies will be the application in developing countries that are sorely in need of energy to produce and process commodities and food products. Cuba has spent a good deal of time and money working on such issues.

References

[a]http://www.berkeleybiodiesel.org/efficiency-biodiesel-fuel.html.

[b]http://www.berkeleybiodiesel.org/current-research-biodiesel.html.

[c]Worldwatch Institute, "Biofuels Make a Comeback Despite Tough Economy," August 30, 2011.

[d]http://www.ieabioenergy.com/IEABioenergy.aspx.

[e]http://www.license.umn.edu/Products/Co-cultured-Synechococcus-and-Shewanella-Produce-Hydrocarbons-without-Cellulosic-Feedstock__20100084.aspx.

Lack of agreement on a new international set of biofuel standards has been rooted in a variety of conflicting national and domestic interests and pressures. Many states argued that regulation measures are restricted by national farm support measures. Just before the food crisis, most farmers in surplus-producing states were pleased with higher prices linked to the strong demand for the corn and soy used to produce biofuels. During the crisis, however, consumer groups became more critical of declining reserve supply levels and food price hikes. President Bush and Congress continued to set even tougher standards for future biofuel production and fuel mixture levels. Different U.S. states pursued different policies. California governor Schwarzenegger's executive order established a Low Carbon Fuel Standard (LCFS) or goal of a 10 percent decrease in carbon-intensity biofuels by 2020. The Bush administration opposed the measure, but the Environmental Protection Agency under the new Obama administration accepted it.

Structuralists. Some mercantilist concerns about biofuels overlap with those of structuralists who worry that increasing support for biofuels will eventually concentrate land ownership and corn production on industrial farms while emptying the breadbaskets of the United States, China, Argentina, and Brazil.[17] This could weaken food security by decreasing domestic production and increasing dependence on agricultural imports still further. Many structuralists also share the mercantilist concern that industrial agriculture decreases the number of small farmers, which could weaken both individual and national self-sufficiency. A classic example is the development strategy of Brazil, where increased soybean production for biofuels and exports parallels an attempt to develop renewable sources of biofuels.[18] For now, President Rousseff's farm policy (a continuation of the policies implemented under former president Lula da Silva) privileges large, highly concentrated industrial farms over small family farms, which results in many peasants being pushed off of the land that they rely on for their livelihoods. These large farms take over degraded pasture, which pushes cattle ranchers further and further into the Amazon rainforest, damaging its ecological system, polluting ground and river water with excessive amounts of water, pesticides, and chemicals, and threatening indigenous tribes. Brazil and other states can expect to remain vulnerable to Middle Eastern tensions and conflict as well as drought and other weather-related phenomena. Finally, as dependence on corn increases, input costs will also increase, creating new investment bubbles in areas such as fertilizer and land.

Finally, many worry that attempts to diffuse biofuel production throughout the developing world will increase environmental damage and widen income gaps, both within developing nations and between the rich North and poor South. To critics such as Raj Patel, these trends ultimately enhance the economic power of agribusinesses and their influence in developing nations.[19]

It is unclear how much biofuels alone were responsible for food crisis of 2008. Like speculation, biofuel production increased pressure on the market by shifting agricultural commodities away from food for consumption. Although there was not a commodity shortage, the amount of commodities devoted to food production increased, spiking the cost of food and the number of hungry. When food prices fell, the controversy diminished. Many supporters *and* detractors of biofuels wait for the development of new technology that converts biofuel from nonagricultural to biomass, algae, and other energy resources. Meanwhile, given the conflicting state and nonstate actor interests at stake, states have not been anxious to either regulate biofuel production or agree to international standards.

Genetically Modified Organisms and Industrial Agriculture and Development Models

Since the end of World War II, many neoliberal-oriented Western development experts have argued that economic growth and coordination between industry and agriculture would gradually transform the food system and solve hunger problems. Recently, GMOs have become one of the most popular and yet controversial elements of the agro-industrial model. Many experts believe that first Green Revolution in the 1960s produced enormous benefits in Asia, Latin America, and parts of Africa.[20] Today, consumers are expected to benefit from a second "gene revolution" that is spreading transgenic organisms from North America into many developing countries. Currently, GMO foods are produced in twenty-nine countries and included in 75–80 percent of processed food in the United States. Their supporters often cite increased efficiency and nutritional value along with a decrease in environmental impact as their immediate benefits. GMO crops include plants engineered to be drought-resistant, allowing them to grow in arid areas such as sub-Saharan Africa. In nations such as Uganda, where growing conditions are poor, GMO crops like disease-resistant maize are viewed as necessary to feed the large number of hungry Ugandans.[21]

Two ardent supporters of the popular agro-industrialization model are Alex and Dennis Avery. They and other economic liberals believe that due to environmental limitations, the only way to produce enough food for a growing population is to allow TNACs to intensify production through industrial processes.[22] Ricardian neoliberal trade theories support the idea that GMOs could help many developing nations produce bananas, coffee, sugar, tea, and other commodities specific to their geography. Agricultural exports help earn foreign exchange, which in turn helps food-deficit nations import corn, wheat, and rice produced more efficiently in other nations. Large plantations devoted to soybean production in Brazil and the increase in chicken farms in the Philippines are examples of how the application of modern technology enhances production, earns foreign exchange, brings millions out of poverty, and supposedly increases food security.[23] Furthermore, food aid should be used only in short-term emergencies and as part of humanitarian relief efforts, as aid can easily distort local and global markets. Long-term aid, and food aid in particular, is likely to contribute to corruption and be a disincentive to both local food production and distribution, especially in developing nations.

Industrial production methods that include GMOs require capital-intensive, rather than labor-intensive, agricultural systems, which reduce inefficiencies and lead to wider profit margins. Laborers are then freed to move into other employment opportunities, often created by TNAC foreign investment. GMOs also help save on fertilizer use, transportation, and marketing. TNAC contracts with local farmers are a "form of risk aversion between farmers and companies" like Cargill and ConAgra, which help smaller farmers ensure a more stable and reliable income. The vast majority of GMO crops are engineered to resist either insects or herbicides. While some argue that herbicide-resistant GMOs can decrease farmers' use of the chemicals, others claim that the widespread adoption of the technology has actually increased total herbicide use. Despite reports to the contrary, scientist William Atkinson argues that there have been no documented adverse effects of GMO food on humans.[24]

HILs Shift the Food and Hunger Agenda. In the last decade, HILs have become much more critical than OELs of the supposed benefits of the agro-industrial development model. Most HILs would agree with the primary assertions included in a recent UN report by the International Assessment of Agricultural Knowledge, Science and Technology for Development (IAASTD), which suggest that industrial agricultural systems are contributing to the destruction of ecosystems, are exacerbating global warming, are too dependent on fossil fuels, and are likely to widen the gap between rich and poor.[25] Yet when it comes to GMOs, HILs have mixed views. Some view them as necessary to provide enough consumable commodities. For example, Paul Collier claims that the ban on GMOs has slowed down the application of technology to agriculture, leading to lower yields and higher food prices. For Collier, there is no better alternative in the face of overpopulation and environmental change.[26] For some HILs, however, the argument that GMOs produce more food than their traditional counterparts may have been made in haste. In a series of studies carried out over the past three years, researchers at the University of Kansas found that "GM soya produces 10 percent *less* food than its conventional equivalent, contradicting assertions by advocates of the technology that it increases yields."[27]

Recently researchers on GMOs have put less emphasis on hunger solutions in science and more on altering food distribution channels and addressing social inequalities.[28] They reference studies that state that modified crops decrease ecological diversity, contribute to an increased reliance on industrial methods, and actually increase poverty. Many of the modified crops have not been subjected to comprehensive tests enough to determine their safety on either the environment or humans. In fact, plants that have been genetically engineered to be resistant to herbicides have a negative impact on the environment, as farmers are more likely to spray indiscriminately across their fields, creating a greater likelihood of pollution in both the soil and water runoff. Also, evidence shows the emergence of "superweeds": plants that are closely related to the GMO crop species and take on the herbicide resistance through interbreeding. The most common instance is mustard—a common weed—interbreeding with canola and developing resistance to the very herbicides that farmers rely on to keep it out of their fields.

Structuralists. Many structuralists trace hunger in developing nations back to the colonial policies of the developed nations. Today's rich core states have dominated trade networks since the sixteenth century, colonizing and exploiting peripheral regions of the world for their resources and labor. Dependency theorists (see Chapters 4 and 6) have argued that increased connections to the West in the 1950s and 1960s focused on support for the urban-industrial sector of the economy, while the poorer enclaves, including agriculture, became *more* impoverished and *less* likely to have adequate food supplies. Since the mid-1960s, the major commodity exporting nations have disposed of their huge commodity surpluses as part of their trade and aid programs. In the mid-1970s, developing nations were encouraged to borrow money to finance their industrial development programs. When development did not occur as anticipated, borrowers were pressured into rescheduling their debt and submitting to the International Monetary Fund (IMF) and World Bank's Structural Adjustment Programs (SAPs) that favored investment in high value crops, including soybeans in Brazil, vegetables in Mexico, beef in Costa Rica, chickens in the Philippines, and peanuts in Senegal. Money earned from these crops was meant to service the mounting debt of these countries. Yet, as exports increased, so did interest payments as a percentage of expenditures, and investment in agriculture plummeted. Many states that had been food exporters were forced to rely on imports to feed their people. Cheap imports also undercut the price of domestic commodities, helped drive smaller farmers out of business, and increased dependence on food imports. As Walden Bello aptly puts it, these conditions and other have more than proven that the industrial agricultural model not only is inappropriate for most developing nations but actually helped "manufacture" the current food crisis.[29]

Today, many structuralists are concerned that many African agricultural systems are going through the same transformational process that began during the colonial period. Recently, productivity has increased in Niger, Tanzania, Rwanda, and other countries, yet hunger has risen commensurate with food price hikes. In many situations, hunger has not been the result of any specific food crisis. Before and during the recent crisis, local agro-industrial producers contracting to companies such as Cargill, Archer Daniels Midland, Tesco, and Carrefour recorded huge profits.[30] Many companies focused on export markets; in many cases, GMOs played a major role in increasing commodity production. Meanwhile, the locals predominately subsisted on substandard diets and the remainder of local staple crops.[31] In many cases, GMOs also played a role in cases of fiscal mismanagement, corruption, income disparities, a collapsed currency, and the loss of personal savings.[32]

Many structuralists are exceedingly more suspicious of neoliberal trade and foreign aid policies than HILs, as both can lead to increased dependency on major grain exporters and food aid donors, even when there is no hunger emergency. Many TNACs employ GMOs as part of an effort to shift LDC consumer tastes away from locally grown crops, toward GMO wheat, corn, and soy, the seeds of which are owned, cultivated, and marketed by selective producers who practice industrial agricultural production techniques. Unlike traditional agriculture, GMOs are a business controlled by large agricultural corporations. Their crops are patented as intellectual property of firms such as Syngenta that operate in Bangladesh, China, India, Indonesia, the Philippines, South Africa, and Vietnam, which charge high prices for specialized inputs purchased from the manufacturer.

Another problem is that as more and more TNACs encourage governments of poorer nations to plant GMOs, more small and family farms disappear. Plots of land that previously featured crops such as sorghum, pearl millet, and chickpeas are now devoted to wheat, rice, and soybeans, decreasing ecological diversity and increasing the risk of crop failure. In addition, the excess from these plantations is funneled into the trade markets rather than being sold at low prices to those most in need.

De-peasantisation routinely occurs in countries like Mexico, the Philippines, and Brazil where massive numbers of people have been forced to abandon their agricultural heritage for urban slums. Brazil lost five million farmers in the early 2000s and the Philippines half its grain farmers.[33] Many poorer states have been left vulnerable to an investment opportunity for TNACs and local officials to modernize their agricultural sectors. Paradoxically, incidences of hunger have actually *increased* and poorer states found themselves more food insecure and dependent on imported commodities.

Finally, many structuralist critics have also argued that both state and IO officials have not focused enough on the relationship of aid to poverty, on its impact on small farmers, and on the factors that deter local food production and left states reliant upon importing food or receiving it as aid. The Gates Foundation has also been cooperating with the FAO and WFP to generate a second green revolution in Africa that includes support for GMO crops. According to Vandana Shiva, Gates is the "greatest threat to farmers in the developing world" because these programs stand to greatly benefit major firms like Monsanto and Syngenta whose primary interests include promoting industrial agriculture.[34]

In a 2009 speech to the FAO, former U.S. president Bill Clinton said "we blew it" on global food aid by sending in-kind food aid to countries in need.[35] Farmers in hungry countries could not compete with the cheap U.S.-grown commodities that flooded local markets, driving them out of business and off their land. After that speech, the UN's WFP began to encourage donor countries to contribute funds rather than in-kind donations. Rather than flooding local markets with cheap (including GMO-based) commodities from abroad, the organization shifted to using monetary donations to purchase food locally, which supports local and regional production rather than undermining it.

Finally, some HILs but many more structuralists are spearheading a shift to the IPE of global food production and distribution on two distinct, but interrelated fronts. First is the promotion of food sovereignty in many developing nations, which is distinctly different from the goal of food security. While food security emphasizes economic access to food and macro-level policies that either produce or import enough food to meet basic nutritional standards, food sovereignty emphasizes access to and control over the means to produce one's *own* food.[36] These means include access to land and investment in technologies that benefit small farmers and help them to feed their own communities, rather than technologies that benefit large industrial producers. *Control and decision-making* in the food system is as much a local as it is national or international issue.

On the ground, the international grassroots peasant movement **La Via Campesina** (The Way of the Peasant) brings local and national small farmer organizations together to advocate, protest, and demonstrate for major changes in the control over the inputs of food production along with its distribution at both the local and international level.[37] The principles of food sovereignty are not anti-trade or anti-technology. Rather, advocates argue that trade and more mid-level technology should be deployed in the interests of small farmers and the hungry, rather than as ends-in-themselves. *La Via Campesina* rejects agricultural processes related to GMOs, for instance, that are harmful to the health of people and the environment. Campaigns against GMO are being waged by other groups usually in poorer parts of the world with similar objectives as their Latin peers. Food sovereignty also prioritizes local self-sufficiency over global markets. It rejects free-trade agreements (including obligations under the WTO) that force countries to open their markets to foreign competition and eliminate agricultural protections. Communities and countries should be free to make policy governing food and farming without the constraints of a supra-national agreement or institution. Interestingly, the new farm bill in the United States makes it easier for corporations like Monsanto to stem the tide of GMO foods on the shelves of supermarkets in the United States.[38]

While there are many problems for developing nations to overcome related to agro-industrialization, many of these same concerns have arisen in the industrialized parts of the world where a second front has gradually opened up related to GMOs and to control over food production away from major food companies and TNACs and back to small farmers, at least those who want a voice in the issue. Since the mid-1990s, many critics of globalization and neoliberal policies have tried to broaden the food and hunger agenda to include the sustainability of both food and the environment along with issues of equality and social justice. Others have continuously questioned the viability of industrial agriculture, challenging its assumptions of production efficiency and the impact of industrial production on the environment. However, this broader agenda includes many issues related to immigration, access to food by the poor and elderly, and even the quality of food itself.[39]

Support for a more sustainable food system and promoting greater food security often take place locally and not just in the meeting rooms of the WTO or USDA. In the recent presidential election in California, a referendum to force food processors to label their foods as containing GMOs was ahead in the polls until a week before the election when "Big Food" companies poured millions into the state in opposition to the measure. Participating in growing one's own food in a home garden or community garden, donating or sharing excess within the community, asking for local and organic produce at the grocer, shopping at farmer's markets, eating in season, and joining a CSA farm are just some of the ways consumers are joining with producers within their local communities to build the foundation of political reform.[40] Cities from Chicago to New York and from Shanghai to Mexico City host a proliferation of programs designed to bring the bounty of urban agriculture to the hands of the people, while innovative development programs are returning traditional forms of agriculture and varieties of crops to regions previously dominated by industrial monocropping.[41] A number of groups even focus on the preparation and eating of foods. The popular Slow Food Movement that started in Italy in 1996 has spread to over 150 countries since then.[42] Its goal is promote the production and consumption of sustainable foods along with opposition to the globalization of agricultural products.

Many structuralists raised questions about the extent to which market-oriented food policies served the interests of those who were most hungry. Recently, more experts have accepted the idea that markets alone are not likely to solve the problem of hunger, and that rather than access to markets, the rural poor need access to land and technology to grow food for the local community. How much these efforts actually help feed more of the world's poorest remains to be seen, but more people have become aware of the connection between what they eat and bigger political-economic trends that determine who eats what, when, and how.

Mercantilists.   Mercantilists view the agro-industrial model and its component parts of trade, aid, and use of GMOs as being both helpful and damaging to domestic and international objectives. Like other technologies, GMOs are usually regarded as politically neutral, even if they help complicate many national wealth and security situations. For example, mercantilists are usually divided about the utility of food aid and its connection to hunger. Some supported efforts to use food aid to help contain communism during the Cold War. In the early 1980s, President Reagan cut grain sales to the Soviet Union when it invaded Afghanistan. Food aid and selective trade measures were used as instruments to pressure Asian nations, including Japan, South Korea, and Bangladesh, into cooperating with the United States and its allies. Aid also served as a disposal mechanism for commodity surpluses, benefiting wealthier farmers and agribusinesses.

By the late 1980s, the U.S. State and Commerce Departments and USAID officials were actively promoting the agro-industrial model as a method of integrating poorer economies into the global political economy. Support for foreign aid declined and emphasis was put on "trade instead of aid." LDCs were encouraged to grow their economies by promoting industrial goods for export while importing cheap food from developed nations. After the fall of the Soviet Union in 1990, realists emphasized the links between the agro-industrial model and national interests, including open-market policies, globalization, and the promotion of democracy in states that were susceptible to authoritarian regimes.

Today, many mercantilist-realists have mixed views of development efforts by IOs and civil society to resolve issues of poverty and hunger through economic development. Some suggest that it might be in the interest of the industrialized nations to increase food aid and agricultural assistance to states like Pakistan and Afghanistan, where poverty and hunger undermine social stability and strengthen terrorist groups. Others worry that these measures end up assisting al-Qaeda and other terrorist groups. Meanwhile socialist leaders in Venezuela, Bolivia, and Ecuador, for example, suggest that the promotion of agro-industrial and economic liberal policies and aid continue to contribute to widespread poverty and hunger, an outcome that the United States intended all along.

After 9/11, realists were more than willing to use food aid as a counterterrorism tool. Food served a number of security objectives in Sudan, Somalia, North Korea, Iraq, and Iran. Other realists question the ability of food aid to achieve those objectives. In many cases, aid supplies were often targeted at groups that support government policies, to the detriment of the poor and hungry. In Ethiopia and Sudan, it is hard to target and coordinate food aid with security operations. As aid is considered a strategic resource for combatants, it is often stolen or captured by insurgents and sold to businesses or officials in other states. Food aid shipments are often redirected to other national ports during shipment, especially during emergency periods when food prices are higher.[43]

War, Disease, Corruption, and Government Mismanagement

Many experts and officials point to these four interrelated factors that in some cases exacerbated, if not caused, hunger during the world food crisis of 2008. All four usually appear together, especially in the poorest countries, most of which are in Africa.

OELs usually focus on corruption and government mismanagement more than the other two conditions. William Easterly for one focuses on both foreign aid and national officials in poorer countries who are in league with corrupt businessmen or investors.[44] Often large bureaucracies provide jobs to people who fail to accomplish the simplest of tasks. These positions also offer opportunities for nepotism and siphoning off funds to those they are supposed to regulate. One example is the ministries of agriculture at the federal state and local levels in Nigeria that drain off public funds to elites and their friends when it comes to lucrative programs for fertilizer imports, subsidization, and food distribution.[45] Officials and their associates often meet in expensive hotels and dine on expensive foods imported from Europe and the United States.

For Easterly, corruption and poor management are significant barriers to economic development. He and other neoliberal-oriented experts assume that economic development of these states would significantly relieve hunger. However, in a fascinating account of an IO contractor titled *The Economist's Tale*, Peter Griffiths would largely agree with Easterly about the impact of corruption and poor management on hunger. And yet he arrives at the opposite conclusion.[46] In one instance, Griffiths conducted a study in Sierra Leone to determine if people would be able to feed themselves during another bad harvest season. He soon discovered that it was hard to figure out the price of rice in the country, let alone how much of it was stored where. Much of it that was imported was often reshipped to other countries in the region to earn more for either the state or their business partners. At the time, Senegal had both an agricultural commodities board and a separate rice board that determined rice prices and reserve levels. Different parts of the country grew different types of rice alongside other indigenous crops that made it hard for IOs and NGOs to determine the severity of supply and demand. In many cases, past IO and NGO projects had failed miserably, only to be replaced by other well-intended efforts to deal with hunger. Often these projects were not directed at hunger alone but at education and health care.

Griffiths and many structuralists agree with HILs and mercantilists that corruption usually benefits not only local elites but international corporations and shipping companies. More importantly, though, it was the ideological environment of neoliberal ideas at the time during the Reagan administration that promoted economic growth and deregulation of the domestic and international economy that spurred on a good deal of corruption and mismanagement. Walden Bello supports this same argument about the role of ideology. He suggests that when states practice neoliberal policies, the result is often that private companies crowd out competition from other companies when the state is withdrawn.[47]

Some neomercantilists such as Ha-Joon Chang suggest that in certain cases corruption can actually help developing countries in any number of ways that include the delivery of services to service clients and moving around bureaucratic barriers.[48] Of course, it is usually difficult to know precisely when a bit of corruption is warranted over improving bureaucratic efficiencies.

When it comes to diseases and wars, most scholars agree that they are directly responsible for hunger, if not starvation. As noted earlier in the history part of the chapter, food is routinely used as a strategic weapon. *The Economist* reports that in the Horn of Africa region that includes Somalia, Ethiopia, and Kenya, 17.5 million people were starving because of a combination of long-term drought and civil and ethnic conflict.[49] While the WFP has been trying to feed people, fighting in Ethiopia's Ogaden region makes it hard to help. Food prices are high, in part because food convoys are highjacked.

War is also a notable feature of Central Africa where Tutsi forces in Congo who escaped Rwanda in 1994 have fought government forces over control of minerals and other natural resources, leaving scores of people hungry and seeking shelter in refugee camps. Civil wars and local violence have also occurred in Kenya, Somalia, and Sudan. One of the most notorious cases has been the Darfur region of Sudan where over 300,000 people have died in the past eight years. The connection of war to hunger and other systemic diseases such as AIDS is obvious. People who are hungry are least likely to respond to medication, if they can afford it. Most experts also point out that when these societies and their governments collapse, civil strife, violence, hunger, and other calamities are most likely to result.

CONCLUSION

The IPE of hunger and food issues touches on at least seven of the main themes of the text (see Chapter 1). After World War II, the issue was framed primarily as one of whether supply would be able to keep up with increasing demand. Issues of production outweighed those of distribution until the 1970s, when Food Firsters focused on political and economic factors that determined who would eat, how much, and at what price.

From the early 1980s until now, officials have emphasized economic liberal market solutions to hunger. Food itself has often been used to achieve a variety of state political and economic objectives. As the number of hungry people in the world remained relatively constant, the role of IOs in helping to feed more people was relatively weak and ineffective because states were not willing to give IOs much authority.

Bigger than normal food shortages between 2005 and 2012 that supposedly contributed to a global food crisis helped clarify a few issues related to food and hunger policy. The dramatic spike in prices was not related to real production shortages as much as it was to a perfect storm of factors, including speculative investment, increased pressure on production due to water shortages, income growth in many of the emerging economies, biofuel production, and the persistence of war, famine, and disease. However, record-breaking droughts in the U.S. breadbaskets in 2012 and other countries have shown that as the food system becomes more vulnerable, these environmental shocks have even more dramatic and rapid impact than ever before on the price and availability of food, especially for the world's poorest.

Meanwhile it remains hard to separate solutions to hunger from state interests and food security from economic growth. Food is recognized as a right in words only. In the short run, the influence of politics on market forces is not only acceptable, but necessary, as the many causes of hunger make it exceedingly difficult to find a single solution that includes overcoming poverty and the impact of distribution. Policy issues to be addressed include decisions about the impact of biofuels made from agricultural commodities; the cost and benefits of state support for food production; the use of GMOs blended with more traditional crops and methods to maintain soil fertility and drought relief that come with modern approaches to crop science; and the role of trade in development policies.

The food sovereignty movements in both the developing and industrialized nations are evidence that the global financial crises have only generated more interest in ways to re-embed the market back into society at the local level and do more to proactively solve food and hunger problems, for everyone's sake.

KEY TERMS

food sovereignty   459
genetically modified organisms
   (GMOs)   459
transnational agribusiness
   corporations (TNACs)   461

community-supported agriculture
   (CSA)   461
Green Revolution   463
Food First   464
demographic transition   464

biofuels   469
de-peasantisation   476
La Via Campesina   477

DISCUSSION QUESTIONS

1. Do you agree with the Food Firsters that population and lack of production are as important as poverty and political issues when it comes to the causes of world hunger? Explain.
2. Explain in some detail why OELs in particular looked at food and hunger problems in the 1990s the way they did? Do you agree with the authors that those ideas and policies have not been all that successful when it comes to dealing with hunger? Explain.
3. Discuss at least three connections between the world food crisis and the current global financial crisis.

4. Discuss at least three connections between hunger, energy, and environmental issues—depending on whether or not you have read either Chapter 19 or Chapter 20.

5. Are you optimistic or pessimistic about efforts to promote self-sufficiency or self-reliance and food sovereignty through local markets to deal with hunger issues? Why or why not?

SUGGESTED READINGS

Milan Brahmbhatt and Luc Christiaensen. "The Run on Rice." *World Policy Journal*, 25:2 (Summer 2008).

Robert Gottlieb and Anupama Joshi. *Food Justice*. (Cambridge, Mass: MIT Press, 2010).

Peter Griffiths. *The Economist's Tale: A Consultant Encounters Hunger and the World Bank*. New York: Zed Books, 2003.

Frances Moore Lappé, Joseph Collins, and Peter Rosset. *World Hunger: Twelve Myths*, 2nd ed. New York: Grove Press, 1988.

Raj Patel. *Stuffed and Starved: The Hidden Battle for the World Food System*. New York: Melville House Publishing, 2008.

Hannah Wittman, Annette Aurelie Desmarais, and Nettie Wiebe, eds. *Food Sovereignty: Reconnecting Food, Nature and Community*. Fernwood/Food First/Pambazuka Press, 2010.

NOTES

1. Garrett Hardin, "Lifeboat Ethics: The Case Against Helping the Poor," *Psychology Today*, September 1974, pp. 38–43 and 124–126.

2. Frances Moore Lappé, Joseph Collins, and Peter Rosset, *World Hunger: Twelve Myths*, 2nd ed. (New York: Grove Press, 1988).

3. Robert G. Lewis, "What Food Crisis?: Global Hunger and Farmers' Woes," *World Policy Journal*, 25:24 (Spring 2008), p. 34.

4. See Shaena Montanari, "Global Climate Change Linked to Increasing World Hunger," *World Watch*, September/October 2005, p. 18.

5. Lester Brown, "Voices of Concern," interview on Nova, PBS at www.pbs.org/wgbh/nova/world balance/voic-brow.html.

6. Diana B. Henriques, "Food Is Gold, and Investors Pour Billions into Farming," *New York Times*, June 5, 2008.

7. See Clifford Krauss, "Commodities' Relentless Surge," *New York Times*, January 15, 2008.

8. Thalif Green, "Land Grabs for Food Production Under Fire," October 23, 2009, at http//ipsnews.net/news.asp?idnews=48979.

9. See Noemi Pace, Andrew Seal, and Anthony Costello, "Has Financial Speculation in Food Commodity Markets Increased Food Prices?" *Lancet*, No. 371 (May 17, 2008), p. 1650.

10. See Worldwatch Institute, "Biofuels Make a Comeback Despite Tough Economy," 2011.

11. Milan Brahmbhatt and Luc Christiaensen, "The Run on Rice," *World Policy Journal*, 25:2 (Summer 2008), pp. 29–37.

12. See Andrew Martin, "Food Report Criticizes Biofuel Policies," *New York Times*, May 30, 2008; and Peter Brabeck-Letmathe, "Biofuels Are Indefensible in Our Hungry World," *Wall Street Journal*, June 13, 2009.

13. See Susan S. Lang, "Cornell Ecologist's Study Finds That Producing Biofuels and Ethanol from Corn and Other Crops Is Not Worth the Energy," Cornell University News Service, July 5, 2005.

14. See, for example, Suzanne Hunter, "Biofuels, Neither Savior nor Scam: The Case for a Selective Strategy," *World Policy Journal*, 24 (Spring 2008), pp. 9–17. See also http://www.berkeleybiodiesel.org/current-research-biodiesel.html.

15. See http://documents.wfp.org/stellent/groups/public/documents/research/wfp232961.pdf.

16. For a brief overview of this issue, see Andrew Martin and Elisabeth Rosenthal, "U.N. Says Food Plan Could Cost $30 Billion a Year," *New York Times*, June 4, 2008.

17. Elisabeth Rosenthal, "U.N. Says Biofuel Subsidies Raise Food Bill and Hunger," *New York Times*, October 8, 2008.

18. Clemens Hoges, "A 'Green Tsunami' in Brazil: The High Price of Clean, Cheap Ethanol," *Der Spiegel*, January 24, 2009.

19. Raj Patel, *Stuffed and Starved: The Hidden Battle for the World Food System* (New York: Melville House Publishing, 2008).

20. Terri Raney and Pirabhu Pingali, "Sowing a Green Revolution," *Scientific American*, September 2007, pp. 104–111.

21. Jeremy Cooke, "Could GM Crops Help Feed Africa?" May 30, 2008, at http://news.bbc.co.uk/1/hi/world/africa/7428789.stm.

22. Alex Avery and Dennis Avery, "The Local Organic Food Paradigm," *Georgetown Journal of International Affairs,* 9 (Winter–Spring 2008), pp. 33–40.

23. Byeong-Seon Yoon, "Who Is Threatening Our Dinner Table? The Power of Transnational Agribusiness," *Monthly Review,* 58:7 (2006).

24. William Atkinson, "The High Tech Menu," in Andrew Heintzman and Evan Solomon, eds., *Feeding the Future* (Toronto, ON: House of Anasi Press), 2006.

25. See the International Assessment of Agricultural Knowledge, Science and Technology for Development 2008 report for a detailed discussion of hunger, agriculture, global warming, and the agro-industrial model at http://www.agassessment.org/.

26. Paul Collier, "The Politics of Hunger," *Foreign Affairs,* 87 (November–December, 2008).

27. Geoffrey Lean, "Exposed: The Great GM Myth," *Independent UK*, April 20, 2008.

28. See, for example, Miguel Altieri, *Genetic Engineering in Agriculture*, 2nd ed. (Oakland, CA: Food First, 2004).

29. Walden Bello, "Manufacturing a Food Crisis," *The Nation*, June 2, 2008.

30. David Kesmodel, Lauren Etter, and Aaron O. Patrick, "Grain Companies' Profits Soar as Global Food Crisis Mounts," *Wall Street Journal*, April 30, 2008. See also Grain, "Making a Killing From Hunger," April 2008, at http://www.grain.org/articles/?id=39.

31. Byeong-Seon Yoon, "Who Is Threatening our Dinner Table? The Power of Transnational Agribusiness," *Monthly Review* 58:6 (November 2006).

32. See Sara Miller Llana, "Gap Between Rich and Poor Widens in Argentina," *Christian Science Monitor*, January 27, 2008.

33. See Marco Visscher, "Fatal Harvest," *Ode Magazine*, at http://www.odemagazine.com/doc/4/fatal_harvest/.

34. Vandana Shiva's comment was made at a talk in San Francisco, California, in February, 2009. See http://www.thebreakthrough.org/blog/2009/02/is_bill_gates_a_menace_to_poor.shtml. For a discussion of the relationship of hunger to the issue of the Gates Foundation support for a second Green Revolution, see Eric Holt-Gimenez, Miguel A Altieri, and Peter Rosset, "Ten Reasons Why the Rockefeller and Bill and Melinda Gates Foundations' Alliance for Another Green Revolution Will Not Solve the Problems of Poverty and Hunger in Sub-Saharan Africa," Food First Policy Brief No. 12, October 2006.

35. http://www.cbsnews.com/2100-202_162-4542268.html.

36. See, for example, Hannah Wittman, Annette Aurelie Desmarais, and Nettie Wiebe, *Food Sovereignty: Reconnecting Food, Nature and Community* (Oakland, CA: Fernwood/Food First/Pambazuka Press, 2010).

37. For an overview of the movement, see Annette Aurelie Desmarais, *La Via Campesina: Globalization and the Power of Peasants* (Winnipeg, Manitoba: Fernwood Publishing, 2007).

38. See Corey Hill, "A Farm Bill Only Monsanto Could Love" *Yes! Magazine*, October 5, 2012.

39. See, for example, Eric Schlosser, *Fast Food Nation: The Dark Side of the All-American Meal* (New York: Houghton Mifflin, 2001) and the documentary film, *Food Inc.,* directed by Robert Kenner, 2010.

40. See, for example, Tanya Denckla Cobb, *Reclaiming Our Food: How the Grassroots Food Movement Is Changing the Way We Eat* (North Adams, MA: Storey Publishing, 2011).

41. See Lester R. Brown, "Feeding Eight Billion People Well," in *Plan B 4.0: Mobilizing to Save Civilization* (New York: W.W. Norton & Co., 2009).

42. See, for example, Carlo Petrini, *Slow Food Nation: Why Our Food Should Be Good, Clean, and Fair* (New York: Rizzoli, 2009).

43. See, for example, Laura Blue, "On the Front Lines of Hunger," *Time International*, June 30–July 7, 2008.

44. William Easterly, *The White Man's Burden: Why the West's Efforts to Aid the Rest Have Done So Much Ill and So Little Good* (Cambridge: Cambridge University Press, 2006).

45. See "Nigeria: Let Us Close Down Agriculture Ministry," January 22, 2009, at http://allafrica.com/stories/200901220209.html.

46. See Peter Griffiths, *The Economist's Tale: A Consultant Encounters Hunger and the World Bank* (New York: Zed Books, 2003).

47. See Walden Bello, "Destroying African Agriculture," *Foreign Policy in Focus*, June 3, 2008.

48. See Ha-Joon Chang, *Bad Samaritans: The Myth of Free Trade and the Secret History of Capitalism* (New York: Bloomsbury Press, 2008), especially pp. 160–181.

49. "The Tragedy of the Decade?" *Economist*, October 30, 2008.

CHAPTER 19

The IPE of Energy Resources: Stuck in Transition

Drill, Baby, Drill: The "Ocean Guardian" oil rig near Invergordon, Scotland before leaving for the Falkland Islands in the South Atlantic.

Andrew Dowsett/EPA/Newscom

You hear on the late-night news that gas prices will soon be going up due to an attempted coup in a major Middle Eastern oil-producing country. The very next morning you drive to your local gas station and find out the prices are already up 20 cents a gallon—and three days later another 30 cents! Do you feel ripped off? You wonder, "Did the owner of the station buy higher priced gas just last night, or is he taking advantage of expected higher prices to profit from the news?"

You are environmentally conscientious and decide to buy a new Jeep that uses biodiesel fuel, only to discover less than six months later that biodiesel isn't as efficiently produced as originally thought. Now your friends joke about your contribution to global hunger because biodiesel is derived from corn and other plants that compete with food production. Luckily, your Jeep burns regular diesel as well.

You meet with your friends and can't help but ask them, "With fuel supplies and prices being so erratic lately, wouldn't you think that more alternative sources of energy would have been developed by now? Don't government officials and major oil companies want to get away from petroleum? Don't they care that continued use of nonrenewable resources is contributing to global environmental problems? Does what I do to cut down on carbon emissions even matter?"

To answer these reasonable questions, one needs a fairly clear road map explaining how these developments and inconsistencies came about. In the past few years, many commentators have pointed out how supply and demand volatility in today's global energy markets causes gyrations in the price of petrol at the pump.[1] As recently as 2008, global fossil fuel production was down. Experts were predicting major shortages of oil and higher gas prices. Many countries and oil corporations poured more money into fossil fuel development to achieve "energy independence." Others invested in renewable resources to "get off oil."

However, in just the past few years global energy supply conditions have changed dramatically, reflecting an unexpected *increase* in oil (and especially, natural gas) production. New technologies have made it easier to drill for oil in deeper waters off the coasts of the United States, Canada, Brazil, Mexico, and other countries. **Hydraulic fracturing (fracking)** has opened up large liquefied natural gas (LNG) fields in the United States and elsewhere. Investments by major oil corporations, pension funds, hedge funds, and small companies have also contributed to the surge in fossil fuel production. One effect has been an energy investment bubble, much like the one in the housing and finance market that resulted in the recent financial crisis.

Surprisingly, some experts have suggested that the United States is likely to become the world's biggest fossil fuel producer and exporter by 2020, replacing the **Organization of Petroleum Exporting Countries (OPEC)** as the world's energy hegemon.[2] Energy independence and lower fuel bills are supposedly just around the corner. But to no one's surprise, some companies are now backing off from investing in LNG production as natural gas prices decline. Others are attempting to slow down the long-term shift to sustainable energy. Ironically—and quite unexpectedly—some people in the industrialized nations are beginning to feel the damaging effects of natural gas production on their local environment and their community's social fabric. As has been the case in many developing nations, what was once thought of as a blessing is now turning into a **resource curse**.

This chapter explains some of the factors that have shaped these serendipitous and unlikely circumstances. We chronicle the actors and conditions since the early 1970s that have impacted the supply and demand for fossil fuels (coal, oil, and natural gas) and the development of renewable energy sources (nuclear, wind, solar, and biomass). First, we examine conditions leading up to the OPEC oil crisis of 1973—which generated a recession in the West and shifted the international energy paradigm about resource scarcity. For the next twenty years, OPEC made oil importers feel vulnerable by using oil production and pricing as strategic weapons in pursuit of its members' domestic objectives.

Second, we look at connections between global energy, war, and the environment. The Iran–Iraq War (1980–1988) and the Persian Gulf War (1990–1991) triggered some oil shortages that further convinced oil-importing states to make energy independence a national goal. In the 1990s, concern about the connection between carbon emissions, global climate change, and other environmental issues increased (see Chapter 20). The Rio Conference (1992) and the Kyoto Protocol (signed in 1997) focused attention on the need to reduce global reliance on fossil fuels and increase use of renewable resources.

Third, we examine efforts by the George W. Bush administration to reconcile its wars on terrorism in Afghanistan and Iraq with its efforts to keep oil spigots open in the Middle East and Caspian regions. In 2006, former Vice-President Al Gore released an extraordinarily successful documentary film called *An Inconvenient Truth* that popularized the idea that continued reliance on fossil fuels is causing dangerous and irreversible global climate change. Even though his argument set the tone for many state energy policies, some politicians, business elites, and segments of the populace never totally embraced the scientific claims behind it. The onset of the financial crisis in 2007 postponed efforts to deal with complicated energy and environmental issues. Meanwhile, some developing nations continued to experience the inequality, political instability, and environmental damage associated with an oil resource curse. Ironically, some developed countries are also now experiencing the effects of the "devil's excrement."

Fourth, we explore the symbiotic relationship between energy corporations (publically and privately owned) and state officials who have so generously rewarded the corporations over the years. Together they have spurred commodity speculation and the fossil fuel boom. Fifth, we conclude with a look at three potential global energy policies in the future: heavy investments in fossil fuels; reliance on free-market solutions; and a reinvigorated transition to renewable resources.

There are several interrelated theses in this chapter:

- In a tight global market, energy self-sufficiency does not equal energy independence. Because oil prices reflect global market conditions, single actors have limited influence on petrol prices at the pump.
- State- and privately-owned oil corporations play a major role in setting retail gasoline prices.
- While many states and energy corporations have doubled down on the production of petroleum and natural gas, they have also tried to deter the production and development of renewable energy sources to meet increasing global demand.
- While states have an incentive to regulate the large corporations that extract and process global energy resources, more often they find themselves either in a symbiotic relationship with or co-opted by these TNCs—most of whom have a vested interest in sustaining higher gasoline prices.
- In developing countries, increased resource extraction tends to enrich wealthy elites and major energy companies at the expense of the working class and the poor.
- In many countries, fossil fuel production helps sustain the military power and economic wealth of authoritarian leaders.

OPEC RULES

Since the 1910s, petroleum has been a major fuel of Western industry. Although coal was more readily available, oil was more efficient and had fewer environmental externalities. Until the 1940s, the United States was also the world's largest producer of oil, but its supply could not keep up with demand. So it turned to oil imports to feed a military arsenal that would help defeat Germany and Japan. After World War II, access to oil and coal played a strategic role in the recovery of industries in Europe, the Soviet Union, and especially Japan. While in the early 1960s coal still accounted for 51 percent of global energy consumption compared to 29 percent for oil, today coal makes up only 30 percent of consumption compared to 33 percent for oil. Natural gas production has grown at a rapid rate only in the last decade.

Historically, the production, processing, marketing, and pricing of oil was dominated by seven major multinational oil corporations—the "seven sisters"— five American, one British, and one Anglo-Dutch company.[3] Host nations often felt exploited by the oil companies, so in 1960 major oil-exporting nations—most in the Middle East—formed the OPEC **cartel** to advance their common interests and gain more control over the oil located under their territory.[4] The precedent for a new relationship between host governments, the oil companies, and the industrialized nations was established in 1969 when Libya pressured Occidental Petroleum, a small U.S. company dependent on Libyan supplies, into granting Libya new price concessions. Afterward a host of countries were able to gradually elicit bigger concessions from the oil companies. Libya demonstrated that royalties for host countries could also be raised by increasing oil prices.

The year 1973 was a turning point for energy markets in the international political economy. For many baby boomers, the events surrounding the oil crisis still burn in the back of their minds. A number of Arab states within OPEC imposed a successful oil embargo on the United States and the Netherlands for supporting Israel in the October 1973 war. Almost overnight, OPEC's "oil weapon" increased the price of a barrel of oil in the international marketplace from $2.90 to $11.65—a jump of over 400 percent—resulting in a recession in the Western industrialized nations that severely disrupted the lives of people.

Many non-oil-exporting developing nations also faced dramatic increases in their oil import bills. The major oil companies themselves went along with OPEC price hikes because they could easily pass royalty expenses and the higher gas prices on to consumers. Collectively, cartel members agreed to output quotas lower than the amount that would be produced under competitive market conditions. By the mid-1970s, OPEC controlled oil prices, production levels, and royalty taxes as the developed world's reliance on petroleum imports increased.

To complicate matters, the first Great Recession of the 1970s *weakened* not only the economies of the industrialized nations, but also their demand for oil. One popular saying was that "OPEC had everybody over a barrel" (ar ar!), and yet OPEC also found itself in a vulnerable position. First, it was not in its interest to "break the bank" when it came to weakening the industrial economies that would surely limit their oil imports. A weak U.S. dollar as payment for oil also weakened the value of Saudi investments in the West. As we note in Chapter 7, many of the

U.S. dollars that went to OPEC to pay for oil imports flooded back into Western banks, which in turn loaned money to oil corporations and states investing in new fossil fuel production in Mexico, Venezuela, Angola, Nigeria, and the North Sea—a process commonly referred to as **petrodollar recycling**. Although finding and producing oil in the stormy North Sea and the frozen Alaskan North Slope were technically challenging and enormously expensive at the time, the high price and uncertain supply of oil made these expenditures politically and economically attractive.

The Oil Crisis and the Energy Paradigm Shift: Scarcity and Vulnerability

The OPEC oil price hikes of 1973–1974 and 1979–1980 were like earthquakes—with short, sharp jolts that shook many nation-states and international institutions and changed the global landscape for years to come. One important effect of these policies was a paradigm shift in the way many state officials and consumers understood international energy issues. This change in the dominant beliefs about energy incorporated two critical facts.

First, many developed and developing nations had become *dependent* on and politically *vulnerable* to Middle Eastern oil supplies. In real terms, OPEC had a strategic weapon it could wield to not only enhance the wealth of its members but also attain a variety of geostrategic goals. What complicated matters was that the United States benefited from its alliance with Saudi Arabia, which because of its large oil and capital reserves dominated OPEC. From time to time the Saudis were willing to adjust production in consideration of mutual U.S.-Saudi interests, which included making sure that the Saudi royal family remained in control of its country.

Second, war and conflict destabilized oil markets. OPEC and its hegemonic leader Saudi Arabia set oil production quotas and prices at levels that reconciled their interests with the goal of stabilizing international market conditions. However, percolating below the surface of the oil-as-strategic-weapon story was another story about resource scarcity. Until the 1970s, supplies of oil and other fossil fuels were assumed to be unlimited. The OPEC oil crisis brought about an appreciation that the earth's resources were not infinite after all. It popularized the argument that industrialization was exhausting the earth's resources and ruining the planet's air, land, and water ecosystems. Predictions that oil supplies would run out in twenty-eight years paralleled studies by Donnella Meadows and others that there were "limits to growth."[5] President Nixon did consider a plan to invade the Middle East to protect the oil fields, but instead of risking a war with the Soviet Union, the United States and Western Europe adjusted their consumption habits and suffered through a recession.

Instead of using force to counter OPEC's influence, the Carter administration adopted a series of measures to counter and adjust to higher costs of oil and energy. In a famous speech on U.S. energy policy given in April 1977, the president labeled conservation efforts in the United States "the moral equivalent of war." (Until the late 2000s, it remained common for presidents and other world leaders to call for energy independence.) With the president's backing, the U.S. Congress offered a series of tax incentives to those who reduced energy consumption by insulating their homes, and the highway speed limit was reduced to 55 miles per hour. The United States also created a Strategic Petroleum Reserve (SPR) that would release oil to the market in the case of another crisis. However, many realists criticized President Carter's efforts as "kowtowing" to OPEC and weakening U.S. geopolitical interests in the Middle East and elsewhere.

Carter was the first U.S. president to raise concerns about consumption habits and how they contributed to inefficient use of energy resources. Sustainability and efficiency began to play bigger roles in comprehensive energy planning. Another of his goals was to develop renewable energy resources (discussed later in this chapter). During his presidency, many college classes required students to read E. F. Schumacher's book *Small Is Beautiful: Economics as if People Mattered*, which argued that modern economies running on cheap energy were unsustainable and that smaller, appropriate technologies would help confront energy scarcity.

When Iranian fundamentalists succeeded in toppling the U.S.-backed Shah of Iran in 1979, the ensuing panic in world oil markets due to the fall in Iran's oil production threw the international economy into disarray. Then the onset of the Iran–Iraq War in 1980 again destabilized oil markets and led to a 10 percent decrease in international production, pushing up the price of a barrel of crude to $42. In less than a decade, the oil-dependent economies of the world saw their import bills for petroleum leap by almost 1,200 percent. The outbreak of the Iran–Iraq War increased discussion of how long oil supplies would last.

During this period, prices for oil that was traded on the international **spot market** were much higher than prices set by long-term contracts. The primary beneficiaries of this situation were the major oil companies, whose long-term contracts gave them a supply of oil at a relatively cheap, stable price, which they could then sell at higher spot market prices. Non-OPEC oil producers also benefitted because they could put as much oil into the market as they wanted and receive a good spot price. Some OPEC members began to break long-term contracts in order to sell their oil on the more lucrative spot market. The Saudis tried to keep the others in line, but the momentum would become inexorable. As individual members expanded output to raise more revenue, they collectively drove the price of oil way down by 1982.

In sum, the unified efforts of OPEC in the 1970s demonstrated how much economic and political power a small group of nations could have when they were able to exercise control over a scarce resource. However, OPEC's influence was ultimately limited due to many of the structural issues related to maintaining a cartel. Had Saudi Arabia not been a strategic partner of the United States, industrialized nations might have faced much worse energy market conditions. An increasingly complex interdependence among nation-states and markets made it difficult for any nation (even powerful Saudi Arabia) to completely control world oil prices.

THE 1980S AND 1990S: THE IRAN–IRAQ AND PERSIAN GULF WARS

Dependency, vulnerability, and scarcity would continue to shape international global energy policies in the 1980s. But a more chaotic oil regime and falling oil prices would also be the hallmark of OPEC's declining control. International oil production was interrupted by a series of wars, including the Iran–Iraq War (1980–1988) and the Persian Gulf War (1990–1991). These conflicts did not immediately have the shock effects of the two crises of the 1970s, but they helped weaken OPEC's power and influence.

Under President Reagan, there were several reasons why OPEC gradually lost more control over oil prices:

- A decrease in the demand for oil following the OPEC-induced recession.
- The release of more oil onto the market by new producers, resulting in long-term surpluses and downward pressure on prices.
- Increased competition among OPEC producers and defectors who released oil onto the spot market.

In 1983, with more oil coming on line, OPEC actually reduced the price of its "benchmark crude" for the first time in the organization's history, which contributed to its erosion as an effective, cooperative, price-setting cartel. Fed up with other OPEC members, Saudi Arabia produced over quotas in 1985, flooded oil markets, and drove crude oil prices down to $10 a barrel. Low oil prices through the rest of the 1980s caused economic problems in highly indebted oil producers such as Nigeria and Algeria. Lower prices also punished nations like Mexico and Venezuela that had invested in high-cost oil production based on the assumption that high prices would stay. By the end of the Iran–Iraq War in 1988, in "real terms" oil prices were actually below their 1974 level. Lower prices were also a boon to oil consumers, of course. In fact, some realists argue that it was the drop in oil prices that turned around the U.S. economy during the first Reagan administration, and not the president's free-market policies.

Low, stable oil prices helped many of the emerging economies—especially the Asian Tigers and China—grow and compete with most of the industrial economies of the North. And weaker prices softened the demand for alternative energies like nuclear, solar, and wind. At the time, political pressure to develop alternative resources was based on increasing evidence that industrialization and globalization were poisoning the earth's lands, bodies of water, and air. Also notable was the 1987 release of the UN's Brundtland Report, which linked economic development in the world with a sustainable environment. Opinion polls in the industrialized nations indicated that a majority of people supported raising taxes to deal with some of the environmental side effects of industrialization associated with "cheap oil."

The 1990s: Iraq and the Gulf War

It was déjà vu all over again when oil prices shot up in August 1990 due to military conflict in the Middle East. This time the dispute was between Iraq and Kuwait. Oil was both a source of the discord and a tool used to fight the war. Iraqi president Saddam Hussein was particularly incensed by what he took to be Kuwaiti cheating on the oil production quotas set by OPEC, which Baghdad figured cost the Iraqi state treasury billions of dollars in lost oil revenues. President Hussein also accused Kuwait of duplicitously taking more than its share of oil from the neutral zone between the two countries and pushing too hard for repayment of loans made to Iraq during the Iran–Iraq War. Some Arab states worried that had Iraq gained control of either Iran's or Kuwait's oil fields, its influence as a regional and global power might have grown immensely. The addition of either neighbor's oil reserves to Iraq's own would have made Iraq a close second to Saudi Arabia as the world's premier oil producer. Leading a UN-sanctioned coalition, the United States used military force in Operation Desert Storm to liberate Kuwait.[6]

The impact of the Gulf War on oil prices was short-lived. Oil prices doubled in the wake of the Iraqi invasion of Kuwait, but dropped back to their previous low levels after Iraq was routed in February 1991. Saudi Arabia remained the linchpin in OPEC and a primary security interest of the United States. However, the Gulf War further reduced OPEC solidarity by driving a wedge between Saudi Arabia and Iraq. Many oil companies invested heavily in the development of new oil reserves in non-OPEC nations, which generated increased oil supplies that would continue to push down on oil prices and also affect OPEC's price-setting ability.

Oil remained the world's biggest source of energy, even though it dropped from 45 percent of the world's total energy consumption in 1973 to 35 percent in 1996 as new sources of energy such as nuclear power came on line. For much of the 1990s, oil prices remained relatively low—roughly $10 a barrel less than they were in the 1980s—despite some price spikes in short periods of time. OPEC nations were greatly concerned and adopted a number of strategies to try to stabilize oil prices and maintain their profits. Non-OPEC production (not counting oil from Russia and the United States) rose from 9 million barrels per day in 1976 to 26 million barrels per day in 1995. In 1998, in the middle of the Asian financial crisis (see Chapter 8), the price of oil dropped to $9.64 a barrel. Shortly thereafter, OPEC finally dramatically cut production quotas to push the price of a barrel of oil back up to $26.

For most of the 1990s, a relative calm characterized the relationship between oil-dependent states and OPEC. With the collapse of the Soviet Union in 1990 and the Gulf War victory, the United States had more of a free hand to influence developments in the Middle East oil-producing countries. Globalization was in full swing. Under the Clinton administration (1993–2001), deregulation and the opening of markets led to increased economic growth in the United States and the rest of the world. What had been an "international" energy system was quickly becoming global in scope. Low oil prices allowed U.S. industries to prosper, but also increased their dependence on oil. Consumers benefited from cheaper energy, gasoline, and manufactured goods.

STUCK IN TRANSITION: THE ENERGY BOOM AND VOLATILE MARKETS IN THE 2000S

After the turn of the twenty-first century, the energy picture gradually became cloudy and increasingly unstable. Oil price hikes reflected dramatic growth in world consumption—driven largely by China, India, Brazil, Saudi Arabia, and other emerging economies (see Table 19-1). Increased demand also raised prospects that energy markets were a solid investment opportunity. From 2001

TABLE 19-1

Top Oil Consumers and Hydroelectricity Producers, 2011

	Oil Consumption		Hydroelectricity (Production)
Country	Millions of Barrels per Day	Country	Billion Kilowatthours
United States	18.9	China	687
China	8.9	Brazil	424
Japan	4.5	Canada	373
India	3.4	United States	325
Saudi Arabia	3.0	Russian Federation	163
Brazil	2.8	India	131
Russian Federation	2.7	Norway	120
Germany	2.4	Venezuela	83
Canada	2.3	Japan	82
South Korea	2.2	Sweden	66

Source: U.S. Energy Information Administration, "International Energy Statistics," at http://www.eia.gov/cfapps/ipdbproject/IEDIndex3.cfm. (accessed December 18, 2012).

to 2011, China's oil consumption alone nearly doubled from 4.9 to 8.9 million barrels a day. And China's growing economic success provided it with the income it needed to develop oil in other countries and invest in alternative energy resources at home. Against this backdrop of slowly improving chances for renewable energy, most countries failed to make progress in achieving their goals of getting off oil, establishing energy independence, and promoting environmental sustainability.

Oil and Intervention in Afghanistan and Iraq

After the terrorist attacks of September 11, 2001, there were fears that production in the Middle East would decrease because of the invasion of Afghanistan and then Iraq. The price of oil did dramatically jump at the start of the Iraq war in 2003 and climbed steadily afterward, interspersed with intermittent spikes and drops in prices. Saudi Arabia periodically stepped in to increase production so as to stabilize the oil market.

Meanwhile, some structuralists and realists criticized the United States for pursuing wars in Afghanistan and Iraq in order to promote U.S. oil interests. "No blood for oil!" was the chant at many anti-war demonstrations in 2003. The press made much of the fact that when U.S. troops arrived in Baghdad they protected Iraq's oil ministry while the national museum was looted. Some of these critics argued that the United States wanted to establish a "footprint" in the region in order to influence developments in the Caspian region, where new oil fields were being developed and where pipelines connecting Central Asia to Europe originated. Michael Klare made the case that this required the establishment of U.S. military bases. Given Saudi Arabia's refusal to allow U.S. bases on its soil, the United States resorted to positioning bases in Kyrgyzstan, Uzbekistan, Afghanistan, Iraq, and Pakistan, along with those already in Kuwait, Oman, Bahrain, Qatar, and Turkey.[7]

When the George W. Bush administration took office in 2001, it withdrew U.S. support for the Kyoto Protocol (see Chapter 20), signaling its resistance to Al Gore's arguments about the urgency of slowing global warming by reducing fossil fuel burning. (Ten years later, Canada withdrew from Kyoto, and other big polluters refused to implement caps on carbon emissions.) Even so, support for the shift away from nonrenewable fossil fuels to renewable sources of "green energy" was advancing in many places in the world, albeit much more modestly than some state officials and environmental groups had hoped for. Gore's efforts to explain the scientific evidence behind global warming and climate change in his book *An Inconvenient Truth* resulted in a documentary by the same name, and in 2007 he was awarded a Nobel Peace Prize jointly with the Intergovernmental Panel on Climate Change (IPCC).

In the early 2000s, the high price of imported oil—driven by increased demand in the emerging economies such as China, India, and Brazil—incentivized the United States, Canada, and Russia to produce more of their own fossil fuels and develop new oil fields. States started importing significantly more oil from non-OPEC producers. Despite a desire in some countries to develop more nuclear energy, only China and Russia significantly expanded the amount of nuclear power they generated. For the world as a whole, the amount of nuclear power consumed in 2011 was the same as it had been in 2001.

Between 2004 and 2007, global investments in renewable energy more than quadrupled, with solar, wind, and biofuels receiving 82 percent of this money.[8] Emerging economies such as China, India, Pakistan, and the Philippines set up national programs to promote renewable energy resources such as wind, solar, and nuclear power to meet the demands of their growing populations and larger middle classes. China's solar panel and wind turbine industries provided more value-added jobs domestically and exported attractively-priced products that were very competitive in global markets.

The Devil's Excrement

News media and documentaries began to focus attention on yet another "inconvenient truth" that some countries were discovering: instead of being a blessing, oil turned into the "devil's excrement."[9] As discussed in "The Nigerian Resource Curse," Nigeria is a prominent example of a country where "black gold" turned out to be a "resource curse" that resulted in corruption, violence, tremendous environmental damage, and war between neighboring nations. Nigeria, Equatorial Guinea, and Angola have been particularly vulnerable to the problem of oil-fueled corruption.[10] African oil exporters such as Nigeria, Angola, Chad, and South Sudan have experienced civil war or low-level violence for decades in part over territorial disputes in oil-rich regions. In Sudan, a 2005 settlement that divided up oil revenues between the North and South briefly ended two decades of fighting, but conflict erupted again in 2011. Oil companies that choose to operate under such circumstances often become targets of protest and violence.

THE NIGERIAN RESOURCE CURSE

In a small town in Eastern Nigeria, it could cost 4,000 naira (about US$25) to fill a gas tank. Overnight, however, the cost could more than double to 10,000 naira—even though the government of Nigeria claims it subsidizes the price of oil to keep consumer costs low. Nightmarish social, political, and economic issues like this have plagued Nigeria since the 1970s. The West African nation is one of many countries that are possessed by a resource curse—a paradoxical condition many of the locals refer to as being blessed while at the same time being cursed by the "devil's excrement."

According to the IMF, the Nigerian economy is heavily dependent on the oil sector, which accounts for over 95 percent of export earnings and about 80 percent of government revenues.[a] The country grosses more than $50 billion a year from oil exports, and yet has a poverty rate of 70 percent. Nigeria exports to foreign entities through the work of various major oil corporations such as ExxonMobil, Chevron Texaco, and Shell. It possesses roughly 3 percent of the world's proven oil reserves. It began producing oil in the 1970s when many developing nations were targets of international investors. When international market prices collapsed in the 1980s, Nigeria's debt mounted and investments slowed. Since then the country's wealth has ebbed and flowed with the oil market. Consistent throughout it all has been a growing division in wealth and power between the haves and the have-nots.

Most of the drilling takes place in Niger Delta, which creates many transportation, environmental, and socio-political problems. Much of the coastline of the region has been damaged by the seepage of oil into the water, which impacts fish, fowl, and plant life. Shell launched a massive campaign to clean up the mess, but it is clearly a situation of too little, too late.

The former capital Lagos is also one of most overpopulated and poverty-stricken cities in the world. Income inequality, hunger, disease, poor education, and lack of housing are intractable problems. Because of the wealth generated by oil,

Lagos experienced a real estate boom "during the good times," as did other major cities of oil-exporting nations. Paradoxically, Lagos is also one of the most expensive cities in Africa. Critics charge that the government has displaced locals to construct housing projects for the well-off. It is well-known that there is rampant corruption, money laundering, and racketeering within the government. Economic liberals tend to blame the state for deterring even more foreign investment. Many structuralists blame the state for delayed or nonexistent efforts to improve Nigeria's water supply, roads, and telecommunications systems. The rule of law is weak. For example, some of the videos cited show footage of an incident when some seventy people were killed after they illegally tapped into a gas line.[b]

Both the state and Shell Oil claim that these sorts of problems are the reason why so many Nigerians are poor. On the other hand, a number of revolutionary groups around the country are openly attacking oil installations and abducting oil executives for ransom. The government has fought back in ways that included trying and hanging the indigenous peoples' activist Ken Saro-Wiwa in 1997. In 2009, Shell finally settled a $15 million lawsuit filed by his son alleging that Shell collaborated with the former military government to make an example of Saro-Wiwa.

References

[a]Azam Ahmed, "Wall St. Giants Seek Piece of Nigeria's Sovereign Fund," New York Times, October 25, 2011.
[b]See http://www.youtube.com/watch?v=zalqYjcjA2Y
http://www.youtube.com/watch?v=pLpDmh4BU8w&feature=related
http://www.youtube.com/watch?v=ZGMB9Z4t5Xc&feature=related
http://www.youtube.com/watch?v=AsuYhZq_1m0&list=LP4xx9qGwte6g&index=1&feature=plcp
http://www.youtube.com/watch?v=7OHeR7X2-G4&feature=BFa&list=LP4xx9qGwte6g
http://www.youtube.com/watch?v=ejym4mKelhM&feature=related

2008: The Financial Crisis and the Energy Boom

The financial crisis started a major recession in the United States and Europe that many felt was sure to weaken the demand for oil. Instead of a gradual decrease in production caused by less demand, the financial crisis fed the volatility of energy markets. Oil prices had steadily risen since 2002, and then in July 2008 they suddenly peaked at $147 per barrel—nearly six times what they had been at the beginning of the Iraq war. By December 2008, they had bottomed out at $33 per barrel. Alarmed, OPEC members agreed on strictly lower production quotas, which had the desired effect on oil prices. A year later OPEC had managed to stabilize the price of oil at their "Goldilocks" (desired) price of $70 per barrel. Then in 2011 and 2012, prices stabilized within a range of approximately $85 to $110 per barrel. Oil-exporting countries shifted to having huge trade surpluses, while many oil importers had to spend increasingly more to meet demand and help with their recoveries.

U.S. automakers GM and Chrysler filed for bankruptcy when fewer Americans purchased new vehicles. Airlines were hit with rapid increases in fuel prices. The rise of gas prices to more than $4 a gallon in the United States ate up more and more discretionary income. The spike in oil prices also increased the cost of transporting goods, which translated into higher prices for many agricultural commodities and higher food costs (see Chapter 18). Likewise, in many poorer countries, imported food staples doubled in price, sparking civil unrest and destabilizing many already fragile governments.

With real estate markets in ruins in many of the industrialized nations, private investments flowed into the oil and natural gas sectors. Many investors also diverted their funds away from renewable resources toward natural gas because new technologies were making natural gas extraction and processing much easier all the time. As oil prices continued to climb, state producers and major oil and natural gas producers doubled down on increasing production.

As late as 2008, some predicted that the "tipping point" of **peak oil** had been reached and that supplies would increasingly be in short supply, driving up prices even further. Geophysicist M. King Hubbert, working at the Shell Oil Company in the 1950s, first proposed the controversial idea that the world would run out of oil at some point. Based on what is now referred to as the Hubbert Curve, he predicted a summit in U.S. oil production between 1965 and 1970. After 1970, U.S. oil production did decline until a small uptick occurred when oil was discovered in Alaska. Peak oil advocates believed that in countries such as Argentina, Australia, Colombia, Cuba, Egypt, Iran, Libya, Russia, South Africa, and Yemen, oil production *may* have already passed its peak. Once the tipping point is reached, from that point onward there will be less and less of it available and its cost could skyrocket if sufficient alternative sources of energy are unavailable. For believers in peak oil, it will become harder and more expensive to find and process new sources of oil. This will generate more domestic conflict and exacerbate global security problems and inequality.

Responses to peak oil vary by country and within them. For example, since losing oil imports from the former Soviet Union, Cuba has been forced to realize a post-peak oil society in the past fifteen years.[11] The island nation now utilizes less oil-based transportation, has moved people to more rural areas, and has created many small organic farms which do not use petroleum-based fertilizers or gas-guzzling large farm machinery. Other groups that have responded to the problem of peak oil include "head for the hills" survivalists and those who use alternative energy sources to mitigate climate change. Some people are enthusiastic about a transition to a post-peak oil future where societies must re-localize, cooperate, and live a slower-paced life.[12]

In many industrialized nations, the financial crisis weakened support for the argument that peak oil is a major problem. Moreover, a slew of technological changes related to drilling has reduced investment risks and costs in fossil fuel production and emboldened those who view new technologies as helping overcome the problem of oil scarcity. New technologies have made the search for oil more scientific and reliable—leading some experts to claim that there are more oil reserves than ever before.

As oil-dependent states spent more to increase fossil fuel production or to develop alternative energy resources that would decrease their dependency on imported oil, Saudi Arabia saw the writing on the wall and stepped up its own investments in renewable energy technologies. In fact, the Gulf region quickly became a hot spot for green technology on several fronts, hoping to preserve its role as a leading energy exporter.[13] Because demand from the United States, China, India, and Southeast Asia was expected to continue to increase, Russian leaders attempted to portray their firms as reliable suppliers poised to displace OPEC (read Saudi Arabia) as the key energy supplier to the West. Despite its pretentions, Russia could not play a hegemonic role in the global oil regime because it only accounted for 5 percent of the world's total oil reserves in 2001.[14] Almost half of its hard-currency export earnings that year came from oil exports, and the United States got only 3 percent of its oil imports from Russia. In contrast, 60 percent of China's oil imports came from the Middle East. Nevertheless, Russia has become a more important player in recent years, bolstering its share of global oil production from 8.7 percent in 2000 to 11.7 in 2012.

"Drill Baby Drill": Doubling Down on Fossil Fuels

Prior to taking office as U.S. president in 2009, Senator Barack Obama said, "[We should] free America from its dependence on foreign oil. We must take concrete steps to move us toward energy independence including requiring that 20 percent of the nation's power supply portfolio come from renewable sources like wind, solar, biomass and geothermal energy by 2020, and that a percentage of our nation's fuel supply is provided by renewable fuels such as ethanol and biodiesel."[15] Senator John McCain, Obama's opponent in the 2008 presidential election, agreed with him about the need for energy independence. However, in the 2012 campaign neither the president nor his opponent Mitt Romney stressed renewable resources. Both agreed that the United States should adopt an "all of the above" policy (discussed later in this chapter) that promoted increased production of nonrenewables like oil and coal and some renewable resources. Gone were concerns about peak oil and the environmental costs of unconditional drilling. Why the change in these candidates' bipartisan energy policies?

There were two important developments between the 2008 and 2012 elections. First, the financial crisis led to massive layoffs and high unemployment.

Many government officials believed that one of the ways to rectify these problems was to ramp up the production of fossil fuels like coal, oil, and natural gas, even if it meant increasing dependency on these energy commodities. Second, there were dramatic improvements in technological instruments used to extract and process oil and natural gas. The result was a massive boom in the production of these fuels to meet ever-increasing demand for energy from China, India, and other emerging economies. As we also discuss later in this chapter, many claim that these changes in global markets for fossil fuels are also jeopardizing the progress made in using renewable energy to help overcome energy deficits and deal with climate change.

Oil drilling spread to new areas of the United States, Canada, Brazil, Iraq, the Arctic, and the Gulf of Mexico (when a moratorium on drilling imposed after the 2010 BP oil spill was lifted), bringing more oil onto the market. Meanwhile, natural gas production increased in the Middle East and China, but especially in the United States. Fracking—a method to extract gas from shale rocks—has made major headlines since 2008 because it has succeeded in generating tremendous supplies of natural gas while supposedly causing disastrous human and environmental effects. Chemically treated and pressurized water is forced down into the earth both vertically and horizontally where it breaks open shale and other rocks to release different types of oil and natural gas. The product is collected and sent back to the surface where the chemicals in it are removed. Natural gas has been produced for quite a while in places like Russia, Canada, Iran, Algeria, and Qatar. Development of huge natural gas fields in North Dakota, Texas, Pennsylvania, and New York allowed the United States in 2009 to overtake Russia as the world's largest producer of natural gas (see Table 19-2).

Many experts suggest that U.S. natural gas fracturing has the potential to

- Create 3.6 million new jobs by 2020
- Decrease the U.S. trade deficit 60 percent by 2020
- Reduce greenhouse emissions
- Replace gasoline in U.S. autos
- Cut the costs of transportation, shipping, heating, and cooling
- Decrease companies' use of coal and nuclear energy
- Benefit chemical, pharmaceutical, and fertilizer industries
- Help the United States achieve energy independence

Estimates of how long the U.S. reserves will last vary from seventy to seventy-five years. However, an Energy Information Administration report in 2012 estimated that there is actually 40 percent *less* natural gas than originally predicted in 2011.[16] Major press coverage of oil production and the natural gas "boom" suggests that the United States will shift from being currently the world's biggest consumer of oil to possibly its biggest exporter by 2020. The United States could also soon achieve energy independence.[17] In addition, it might even replace OPEC as the world's energy hegemon.[18]

"Big Oil" companies like Exxon Mobil and BP have been keen to sell U.S. LNG to countries in Asia and Latin America. There has also been an ongoing effort to enhance energy *efficiency*; natural gas has higher conversion efficiency than "dirty coal" and nuclear power. In 2011, the U.S. government issued new fuel economy standards requiring automakers to double car fuel efficiency to

TABLE 19-2

Largest Producers of Coal, Oil, and Natural Gas, 2011

Coal Production		Oil Production		Natural Gas Production	
Country	Million Short Tons	Country	Millions of Barrels Daily	Country	Trillion Cubic Feet
China	3,829	Saudi Arabia	11.2	United States	28.6
United States	1,094	Russian Federation	10.2	Russia	23.7
India	637	United States	10.1	Iran	7.9
Indonesia	437	China	4.3	Algeria	6.7
Australia	436	Iran	4.2	Canada	6.7
Russian Federation	372	Canada	3.6	Norway	5.1
South Africa	282	UAE	3.1	Qatar	4.6
Germany	209	Mexico	3.0	China	3.6
Poland	153	Brazil	2.7	Saudi Arabia	3.6
Kazakhstan	128	Kuwait	2.7	Indonesia	3.3
Colombia	95	Iraq	2.6	UAE	2.9

Source: U.S. Energy Information Administration, "International Energy Statistics," at http://www.eia.gov/cfapps/ipdbproject/IEDIndex3.cfm (accessed December 18, 2012).

54.5 miles per gallon by 2025. The financial crisis also forced Americans to buy fewer cars and drive less. From 1999 to 2010, U.S. imports of crude oil and petroleum products *decreased* from 23 to 15 percent of all imports.

There are plenty of benefits to U.S. trade and national security from the increased production of natural gas and oil. These potentially include

- Lower U.S. dependence on Middle Eastern oil
- Reduced need for U.S. military protection of oil resources in the Middle East
- Overtaking Russia in exports of gasoline, diesel, and other nonrenewables
- $3 billion more per year in profits for U.S. producers and exporters of LNG
- The ability to use fossil fuels as leverage in negotiations (for example, to give privileged access to U.S. gas in exchange for concessions from another country)[19]

In contrast, opponents of the recent oil and natural gas rush have argued that there are a number of problems:

- Contaminated water is discharged into local streams, ponds, and lakes.[20]
- Chemicals used in fracking could escape into the giant water aquifer under Iowa and Kansas.
- Fracked wells leak 40 to 60 percent more methane than conventional wells.
- Fossil fuel companies do not create that many jobs.
- Extension of the Keystone XL pipeline to carry "tar sands" oil from Alberta to the Gulf of Mexico would damage ecosystems and pollute water supplies along its route.

- Much of the natural gas and oil is likely to be exported, which weakens U.S. energy independence.
- Greater fossil fuel use undermines investments in renewable resources, raises greenhouse gas emissions, and hastens the arrival of peak oil.

The following box discusses some of the effects of fracking on local economies and ecosystems.

▶ FRACKING: THE U.S. RESOURCE CURSE?

In its many reports and commercials, the natural gas industry praises itself for its new technology, the jobs it creates, and its contribution to "securing America's energy future." But others believe that the hype about fracking is insidious. There is a television spot on a man who lights his tap water on fire. Another shows a well-off retired couple who abandon their beautiful farm because the river that runs through it is polluted with fracking chemicals.[a] Another news story shows Richard and Thelma Payne, whose home was blown off its foundation.

One of the biggest criticisms of fracking is that it employs excessive amounts of water that contains many harmful chemicals. Under pressure, the water can reach the surface where it can seep into wells and reservoirs.[b] Because fracking leads to dramatically higher use of natural gas—and thus significant carbon emissions—it contributes to the effects of climate changes such as polar ice melting, coastal flooding, and changes in the salinity of the sea.

Aside from natural gas, the extraction process also emits toxic water with carcinogenic chemicals that critics charge contaminates groundwater and produces methane gas that makes people living in the area quite sick with headaches and skin lesions.[c] In many cases, drinking water, ponds, streams, lakes, and aquifers have been contaminated through the ground or had contaminants dumped in them. Earthquakes registering 4.0 on the Richter scale have occurred around Youngstown, Ohio.[d] Finally, many residents of small towns in rural areas have been overcome by higher food and housing prices

due to the lack of infrastructure such as roads and adequate housing to deal with the boom effect on local communities.

In 2004, the Environmental Protection Agency found that fracking was of little risk to humans. A year later its findings were challenged by one of its own engineers who charged that the investigative panel was unduly influenced by industry members who sit on it. In 2005, the U.S. Congress passed the Halliburton Loophole—at the behest of Vice-President Cheney—that exempted gas fracking from the Safe Water Drinking Act in order to promote big business and oppose environmental policies. The EPA is writing new rules for emissions standards and waste water disposal. Fracking has been outlawed in France, while South Africa has imposed a temporary moratorium on it.

References

For a brief visual explanation of the fracturing process, see "Chesapeake Energy Fracturing Hydraulic Method," at http://www.youtube.com /watch?v=73mv-Wl5cgg.

[a] "The Fuss Over Fracking: The Dilemma of a New Gas Boom," at http://www.time.com/time/video /player/0,32068,876880045001_2062814,00.html.

[b] Abrahm Lustgarten, "New Study Predicts Frack Fluids Can Migrate to Aquifers Within Years," *ProPublica*, May 1, 2012.

[c] Walter Brasch, "The Perils of Fracking," *Truthout*, March 19, 2012, at http://www.counterpunch .org/2012/03/19/the-perils-of-fracking.

[d] Steven Mufson, "Can the Shale Gas Boom Save Ohio?" *Washington Post*, March 3, 2012.

The Energy Independence Pipe Dream

With so much oil and natural gas produced, why has the price of gasoline at the pump remained so high? Likewise, why hasn't the United States become energy independent? As noted earlier, some experts and commentators speculate that the United States will unexpectedly soon reach energy independence. Energy security ranks high for those who were around for the two oil crises in the 1970s and who loathe OPEC's seeming stranglehold on the industrialized nations.

While the United States may become "self-sufficient" in energy production, several reporters have pointed out that "U.S. customers would still be suscepti-ble to surges in global oil prices."[21] In effect, if the intention is for the United States to be separate from the rest of the world when it comes to its energy imports and prices, self-sufficiency does not energy independence. While some mercantilists would certainly welcome true independence, most economic liberals would not.

New York Times reporter Floyd Norris helps clarify the situation.[22] Until recently, two different markets have existed for oil and natural gas. Because oil is sold in a *global* market, small changes in supply and demand almost anywhere in the world can easily spike oil prices. The United States can be "relatively self-sufficient," but it is hard to hide resources such as reserve supplies from the market. For example, Norway is a net exporter of oil but also has high gasoline prices.

The market for natural gas is becoming more globalized all the time; prices vary in different regions, depending on problems related to access, processing, and transportation costs. This is one of the reasons why states and corporations have been trying to adjust trade in natural gas to reflect price competition in different parts of the world. The state of Alaska, for example, wants to sell gas to Asia on contract instead of sending it south to the lower forty-eight. Qatar has been shifting its exports to Asia. Japan's demand for natural gas has gone up since the Fukushima disaster. British companies are contracting for U.S. natural gas. All of these trends bother those who worry that natural gas exports will weaken energy independence.

No state leader has the power to decrease gas prices at the pump. As we dis-cuss later in this chapter, oil interdependence and globalization are working well for some countries and many major oil companies. However, it is clear to many structuralists and other critics that industrial society remains addicted to fossil fu-els. They believe that greed is winning out over reason, thereby destroying the global commons and corrupting public and private institutions.

King Coal and Nuclear Power

Energy is not without risks to the environment. Oil drilling and natural gas fracking increase greenhouse gas emissions that lead to more global warming. Coal also releases methane gas, a major contributor to greenhouse emissions. Many argue that the environmental hazards from continued reliance on fossil fuels justify supporting renewable energy.

For now, coal poses a conundrum. It constitutes 21 percent of the United States' overall energy and 44 percent of its electricity production. Coal is still king in China; in 2011, the country produced and consumed half of all the world's coal (see Table 19-2). According to Peter Galuszka, global coal production is expected to increase by 50 percent by 2035, and coal could overtake oil as the earth's primary fuel.[23] As of mid-2012, China and India were proposing to build a combined total of 818 new coal-fired plants. In search of coking coal needed to make steel, Brazilian, Indian, Korean, Japanese, and Russian companies are investing in remote regions of Mongolia, Mozambique, and Botswana. South Africa and Australia are two of the world's biggest exporters of coal.

Because natural gas is lowering the need for coal in the United States, there is more coal to export. For example, the federal government has leased Powder River Basin fields in Montana and Wyoming to strip mining companies that intend to ship the coal by train to the coast of Washington state, where it will be exported to Asia and sold for a high markup. Environmental groups and ecologists oppose this plan because the mining does not create many good jobs and the coal-hauling trains will spew coal dust and diesel along the way.[24]

Some hope that so-called "clean coal" can reduce pressures on the environment. However, coal **sequestration** has yet to be perfected. Sequestration refers to the process whereby carbon dioxide emissions from burning coal are captured and stored underground. The first large-scale sequestration plant is still under development. According to an article in *Scientific American*, China has a few hundred sequestration projects in place across the country.[25] Some of the captured carbon is liquefied and used to feed microalgae which can be used for biofuel. Critics argue that sequestration is not yet a proven technology, nor would it do much good if there were no global carbon tax or cap-and-trade policy to go along with it (to pressure states to decrease production or shift to alternatives). For now, that is precisely the rub, as states have chosen to avoid dealing with greenhouse emissions and global climate change (see Chapter 20).

Nuclear power produces 21 percent of electricity consumed in the United States and 12 percent of the world's electricity output. Despite the argument that nuclear power is dead, most experts and commentators agree that that claim is exaggerated (see Table 19-3).[26] As of 2012, China was building twenty-six new nuclear reactors, hoping to double the amount of electricity from nuclear power by 2015, and Russia was in the process of building ten more reactors. U.S. Senator Lamar Alexander (R-TN) has proposed that the United States build 100 new nuclear reactors in the next few years. Meanwhile, the Nuclear Regulatory Commission in 2012 granted permission for the first new nuclear reactor to be built in the United States in over thirty years.

Aside from the argument that the demand for energy will continue to rise, proponents of nuclear energy point out that it is much "cleaner" than coal and other fossil fuels because it does not emit CO_2. Many environmentalists debate the claim that nuclear power is clean, especially given that there has been no resolution of the problems associated with safely disposing of highly radioactive waste. Three Mile Island, Chernobyl, and the meltdown of the four Fukushima power plants after an earthquake and tsunami in 2011 continue to scare people all over the world. Japan shut down its fifty-four plants after the tsunami (although some have been restarted), and Germany has pledged to permanently close all its nuclear reactors by 2020. For now, the nuclear industry is planning to build new

TABLE 19-3

Top Ten Renewable Energy Producers

Solar Energy Generation[a]		Nuclear Energy Generation[b]		Wind Generation[a]	
Country	Kilowatt-hours, million	Country	Kilowatt-hours, billion	Country	Kilowatt-hours, billion
Germany	4,420	United States	807	United States	55.7
Spain	2,578	France	408	Germany	40.6
United States	2,450	Japan	279	Spain	32.2
Japan	2,251	Russian Federation	155	China	13.1
Republic of Korea	285	Republic of Korea	142	United Kingdom	7.1
Laos	193	Germany	133	Denmark	6.9
Italy	193	Canada	85	Portugal	5.8
China	172	Ukraine	84	France	5.7
Australia	160	China	77	Italy	4.9
Belgium	42	Spain	59	Netherlands	4.3

[a]Wind Electricity/Solar Electricity, Energy Statistics Database, UN Data, http://data.un.org.
[b]World Nuclear Generation and Capacity, Nuclear Energy Institute, nei.org.

smaller reactors with emergency cooling that relies on gravity, evaporation, and convection rather than power-operated pumps and valves that require a lot of electricity.

"BIG OIL" MAJORS: SPECULATION AND LOBBYING

Many experts have written on the topic of how speculation by oil corporations keeps oil prices and corporate profits high, and how cozy relationships between public officials and corporate elites shape legislation, weaken government oversight, and suppress competition in the market. The "Big Oil" or major energy companies include ExxonMobil, Royal Dutch Shell, BP, Total S.A., Koch Industries, Chevron Corporation, and ConocoPhillips. The dominant utility and natural gas companies include General Electric, Southern Co., FirstEnergy, and the Edison Electric Institute. There are many reasons for the growth in oil and now natural gas investments:

- While real estate tanked during the financial crisis, many investors shifted into the energy sector based on growing demand for energy.
- A certain amount of volatility and speculation in energy markets can lead to big profits.
- Oil, natural gas, and some renewables get big government subsidies.
- National and state legislatures derive political and economic benefits from supporting Big Oil and other energy projects.

The major energy companies have been earning high profits lately. President Obama asserted that in 2011 "the three biggest U.S. oil companies took home more than $80 billion in profits. Exxon pocketed nearly $4.7 million every hour. And when the price of oil goes up, prices at the pump go up, and so do these companies' profits."[27]

A number of critics contend that large-scale speculative trading plays a major role in keeping oil prices high and prices volatile. Joseph P. Kennedy II rejects the economic liberal argument that speculation on oil is good because it increases liquidity (the amount of money in the market), better distributes risk, and protects hedgers against future shifts in oil prices. Instead, Kennedy differentiates between investors and "pure speculators" who buy oil "futures" to help drive up oil's price. As in the case of real estate bubbles, when prices rise, speculators often buy more to push up the price—then sell their stock when prices peak in the market, earning huge profits. Kennedy suggests that speculation contributes to 40 percent of the price of oil or as much as $1 for every gallon of gas at the pump. Meanwhile, 90 percent of trading on oil commodity markets involves only trading "paper" with other speculators.

Robert Pollin and James Heintz note that commodity trading has been around for some time and that airlines' bets on large purchases of oil and energy commodities reduce risk against future fluctuation in supply and prices.[28] However, the amount of trading in 2011 was about 400 percent higher than in 2001 and 60 percent higher than in 2009. Today's traders have more money behind them from banks like Goldman Sachs and UBS. Oil futures are often mixed in with stocks, bonds, and other derivative assets. Furthermore, commodity futures are not regulated as much as some other products and services.

There are other ways that multinational and independent energy companies influence energy policy in the United States: by lobbying Congress and executive agencies and by donating to political campaigns. Between the 1990 and 2010 election cycles, individuals and political action committees affiliated with oil and gas companies donated $239 million to candidates and parties—75 percent of which went to Republicans. The week before the 2012 presidential election, Mitt Romney received a $2.5 million (gift!) check from Chevron. Table 19-4 indicates the relatively low "effective federal corporate income tax rates" of major oil companies in the United States (the nominal corporate tax rate is 35 percent), suggesting that Big Oil receives favorable tax treatment from Congress.

High-paid lobbyists usually enjoy strong influence in Washington, DC, especially when it comes to energy policy. Oil industries tend to be the most powerful. Major companies favor "drill baby drill" policies and are critical of environmental regulations designed to mitigate climate change. They claim that regulations are too onerous, hamper exploration, kill jobs, and have little effect.

Corporate influence is also aimed at repealing or weakening industry oversight by Congress and executive agencies. During the George W. Bush administration, the oil and gas industry had trouble winning enough support to repeal bans on drilling in the Arctic National Wildlife Refuge. However, in 2008, thanks to pressure from President Bush and Vice-President Cheney (both oil men), Congress finally voted to lift a ban on offshore drilling in the Arctic National Wildlife Refuge, an environmentally sensitive area. The Environmental Protection Agency (EPA) has been slow to come up with new regulations on carbon emissions standards

TABLE 19-4

Effective Federal Corporate Income Tax Rates, 2008–2010

Company	Rate (in percent)
Devon Energy	5.5
Chesapeake Energy	8.1
ExxonMobil	14.2
Marathon Oil	15.8
Occidental Petroleum	18.9
Chevron	24.8
ConocoPhilalips	26.9

Source: Corporate Taxpayers and Corporate Tax Dodgers, 2008–2010, Citizens for Tax Justice; Institute on Taxation and Economic Policy (November 2011), at http://www.ctj.org/corporatetaxdodgers.

for U.S. refineries. Frank O'Donnell, president of Clean Air Watch, says that the "EPA is engaged in regulatory triage" during an election year so as to appear to not be a strong regulatory agency.[29]

State-Owned Oil Companies

Russia and Venezuela are both considered rebellious "petrostates" because they have tried to use their oil as a political weapon. For example, in January 2009 Russia cut flows through a Ukrainian gas line serving many parts of Europe. But **national oil companies (NOCs)** play a much more complicated role in the IPE of energy than the mischievous role covered by the press. Fifteen of the twenty biggest NOCs are owned by nation-states, many of which were hit hard during the financial crisis. And 80 percent of oil reserves are under state control.[30]

Well-known NOCs like Saudi Aramco, China's CNOOC, Brazil's Petrobras, Angola's Sonangol, and Algeria's Sonatrach have ready access to capital. Some sell their own crude and keep the profit after paying state taxes and shareholder royalties. They can finance their own oil projects. Other companies like the National Iranian Oil Company, Mexico's Pemex, and the Nigerian National Petroleum Corporation lack access to sufficient capital and are susceptible to swings in oil prices. In Iraq, NOCs now own 75 percent of the oil and recently have given foreign oil investors better terms to upgrade their refineries.[31] Many Middle Eastern and African petrostates have used oil revenues to pacify burgeoning populations with subsidized food, gas, and other basic necessities. Energy policy often plays a major role in state development strategies. In other cases—especially places where oil is a resource curse—revenues often go into government coffers and are used by leaders to fund arms purchases, extravagant lifestyles, and kickbacks to foreign investors instead of to fund generous education and social services.

The Renewables: Slowdown vs. Reinvigoration

The recent doubling down on fossil fuel production has dampened enthusiasm for clean energy and derailed efforts to wean nations off wasteful habits. Media outfits like Fox News and the *Wall Street Journal* that tend to be climate-change skeptics have given renewables a bad rap, which has helped block support for green energy resources. The mainstream media has also overlooked examples where solar, wind, geothermal, and biomass energy are doing quite well (see Table 19-3).

In the Obama administration's $787 billion stimulus package, $90 billion was allotted to wind, solar, biomass, battery, and other energy projects. The bill gave $11 billion to modernize the U.S. electrical grid, $14 billion in tax incentives for businesses to invest in renewables, and $6 billion to support efficiency initiatives. Nevertheless, the financial crisis in 2007 and a dramatic increase in natural gas production conspired with doubts about energy resource scarcity and the effects of fossil fuels on climate change to weaken the argument for renewable resources. Other arguments that worked against promotion of renewables include the following:

- Increasing fossil fuel production to support recovery from the financial crisis should take precedence over increasing dependency on renewables.
- The government cannot afford to keep loaning to renewable projects during the financial crisis.
- Renewables cannot meet the growing energy needs of industrialized and developing nations.
- The effectiveness and practicality of renewables have reached their limits.
- Corporate subsidies for renewables are not used efficiently.
- State support for renewables makes the United States look bad in the WTO.
- The state should not be "picking winners and losers" in the energy industry.
- Support for alternative energy hurts trade with Canada and Mexico.

During the first Obama administration, many conservative groups in the United States raised doubts about the need to address global climate issues, in part because they tended to have anti-science, evangelical Christian views and anti-big government ideologies. The conservative think tank The Heartland Institute—which is funded by climate change skeptics and major oil companies—spread the message in K-12 schools that "the topic of climate change is controversial and uncertain," dissuading some teachers from teaching widely accepted scientific findings.[32] A core mission of this organization is to discredit established climate science. Heartland receives funding from a network of wealthy individuals—including the Koch oil billionaires, Microsoft, and R. J. Reynolds Tobacco. Heartland also has a team of experts working to undermine the findings of the UN climate body, the IPCC.

Many major oil corporations have lobbied politicians to oppose promotion of renewable resources. Some critics charge that renewables cannot meet the growing energy needs of industrialized and developing nations for at least other three or more decades. Others contend that because of technical problems, the U.S. electric grid is not well-equipped to handle intermittent sources of energy such as wind and solar energy. Germany has had problems running small renewable energy projects, and China has laid off thousands of workers in solar panel factories because of excess production. Scholars David Victor and Kassia Yanosek argue that alternative energy projects based on biofuels, solar, and wind are in a state of crisis because they simply are not cost-effective or sustainable without government subsidies.[33]

Banks have also become increasingly hesitant to give loans to renewable energy entrepreneurs. Stimulus packages of governments in China, Germany, Spain, India, Italy, and Abu Dhabi have attempted to bypass this obstacle by providing a variety of tax incentives for companies looking to invest in renewable energy. Diane Cardwell points out that even though the U.S. Congress has created a special program to help finance clean energy projects, states and local governments are not using the Qualified Energy Conservation Bonds associated with it. Analysts and bankers say that the small program is not worth the trouble, has few tax benefits, and has confusing requirements.[34]

Finally, the bankruptcies of the solar energy companies Solyndra, Abound Solar, and A123 Systems in 2011 and 2012 made major headlines when opponents of President Obama cited them as examples of bad state investments. Furthermore, government loan guarantees, cash grants, and contracts often result in large profits for investors like Goldman Sachs and conglomerates like General Electric—precisely the kind of actors that should not need government subsidies.[35]

On the other side of this coin, many renewable projects are doing quite well. The 2009 Stimulus Bill did help solar energy a great deal, generating needed capital. For example, the Department of Energy's Loan Guarantee Program helped many solar and wind projects. The DOE program's costs were covered by fees from projects in 2011. Supporters of renewables suggest that they are at a disadvantage because they are still "infant industries" that cannot compete with many of the fossil fuels producers. Renewable supporters note that major energy companies continually receive numerous subsidies such as research grants, tax write offs, and the use of federal land to lower the costs of resource extraction.

Many renewable supporters believe that we cannot drill our way out of our energy problems. Some contend that instead of subsidizing the oil industry, the government should end every single tax break the fossil fuel industry currently receives and require every oil company with over $1 billion in quarterly profits to pay 1 percent of its revenues to finance alternative energy research and infrastructure. Others like Pollin and Heintz suggest that we need to reach a global cap-and-trade agreement to curb carbon emissions as a way of providing an incentive for corporations to invest in renewable resources. Pollin and Heintz also want the government to increase the efficiency of cars, encourage public transportation, and support wind, solar, and other green measures.[36]

Amory Lovins, the chief scientist at the Rocky Mountain Institute, believes that the costs of oil dependency, oil price volatility, and the security of military forces in the Middle East outweigh the benefits of oil and natural gas.[37] There are as many hidden costs in natural gas as there are in oil, some which we outlined earlier. Lovins envisions an epic energy shift on the order of the 1973 OPEC oil crisis that would include *radically* boosting automotive efficiency, increasing the efficiency of buildings and factories, and "modernizing the electric system to make it diverse, distributed, and renewable ... so that it is clean, reliable, and secure."[38] He also praises Germany for its work on solar power.

Many of those sensitive to the politics of energy would suggest that Lovins relies too much on future renewable energy technologies to solve many political and social problems. One might ask why a scientist would overlook the advantages of fossil fuels when renewable technologies either have proved to be unworkable or will not produce enough to meet future demand. To his credit, Lovins lays out a road map for what *could* be achieved if industries and countries merely tried to profit from retrofitting their energy policies. In so doing, he raises many good questions that could serve as the foundation for a major global debate about these issues.

CONCLUSION: THREE FORKS IN THE ROAD

So, let us get back to the dilemma we outlined at the beginning of this chapter. When you drive up to the pump and see that the price of gas has spiked, don't blame the President of the United States—or anyone else, for that matter; he or she alone cannot control oil prices. Global energy markets are tightly integrated. The United States consumes 20 percent of the world's oil but has only 2 percent of global oil reserves.[39] It might help to have more oil reserves, assuming that greater reserves could actually push down prices at the pump. But oil companies have a variety of ways to maintain prices: lobby Congress, speculate on fossil fuels, and try to influence the media.

Big Oil doesn't mind the occasional price hike or spike. When it comes to cutting carbon emissions, it is a more complicated issue. Some would argue that Big Oil is part of the solution, and that it could be even more efficient if the state did not regulate it so much. Others blame Big Oil and the government for not doing more to promote renewable resources.

Many experts and commentators believe that there has not been a consistent set of energy policy recommendations for at least the past decade. In the U.S. presidential election of 2012, both President Obama's and Mitt Romney's outlooks on energy and the environment were nearly identical—or so Obama made it seem that way. Both proposed to continue an "all of the above" approach that encourages the production of fossil fuels *and* renewable energy resources. Both tied support for renewables to recovery from the financial crisis. As expected, where they seemed to differ most was in how much the state should assist renewable industries and in how strong regulations should be to protect both producers and consumers.

This mixed approach appears to have taken hold in nations with significant manufacturing such as Canada, Australia, China, India, and Brazil. Many developing nations also continue to invest heavily in fossil fuel resource production. Over the last thirty years, countries like Brazil have used a mix of regulation and direct government investment to develop a biofuels industry; 70 percent of Brazil's new vehicles run on sugar-based ethanol.

A second path is the one supporters of Mitt Romney and conservative leaders in other parts of the world like: let the free market figure out a way to solve global energy problems with only a small amount of state regulation. Too much regulation stifles innovation. Solutions are most likely to appear through the development of new technologies; witness breakthroughs that enable once-unreachable oil and natural gas deposits to be tapped. Opponents of this path would point out that these new technologies only solve short-term problems, not the probable environmental disaster down the road that will occur if we do not move beyond oil.

A third path to the future requires reinvigorating the transition-to-renewable-resources movement that gained momentum in the 1990s. Because efforts to resolve the financial crisis focus on promoting industrial recovery and use of cheap fossil fuels, a profound shift in values is needed at this critical point in time. The consequences of not switching to renewable new energy sources could be disastrous—a topic we take up in Chapter 20.

Supporters of this path see Democrats as dragging their feet on supporting transition as much as the Republicans. President Obama and other leaders see renewables as a means to an end, but not an end in itself. Balancing economic recovery and energy production with the environment is not the equivalent of letting the environment drive energy policy. Former Peruvian diplomat Oswaldo DeRivero contends that the rest of the world cannot reach the U.S. standard of living based on a U.S. energy-intensive "California" model without destroying the planet.[40] Mass consumption in China,

India, Brazil, and other emerging nations, when added to high energy use in industrialized countries, will bring us all down. Germany, Denmark, Sweden, and a few other states are trying to make it possible to grow their economies without excessively damaging the environment. At least they are willing to test that idea with their laws and tax revenues. Yet, with more severe droughts all the time, the melting of polar ice caps, and hurricanes like Katrina and Sandy, Mother Nature is likely to have the last say.

Hang on for the ride!

KEY TERMS

hydraulic fracturing
(fracking)   485
Organization of Petroleum
Exporting Countries
(OPEC)   485

resource curse   485
cartel   487
spot market   489
peak oil   495
petrodollar recycling   488

sequestration   501
national oil companies
(NOCs)   504

DISCUSSION QUESTIONS

1. In this chapter, we purposely limited our use of the IPE labels economic liberals, mercantilists, and structuralists. Pick a section of the chapter and discuss which of these perspectives would support different arguments in that section.
2. How are the oil crises of the past different from the spike in oil prices in 2008? What were the major causes and effects of increases in oil prices in each case?

3. Define fracking and use the IPE perspectives to discuss some of its more controversial aspects in a recent newspaper article on the topic.
4. Many claim that the United States will soon replace OPEC as the major energy hegemon in the world. Do you agree or disagree with that assertion? What recommendations would you give to the U.S. president and the Department of Energy about this issue? Explain.

SUGGESTED READINGS

Gavin Bridge and Philippe Le Billon. *Oil*. Malden, MA: Polity Press, 2013.

Josh Fox, director. *Gasland*. New York: Docurama Films, 2010.

Jad Mouawad. "Fuel to Burn: Now What?" *New York Times*, April 11, 2012.

E. F. Schumacher. *Small Is Beautiful: Economics as if People Mattered*. New York: Harper & Row, 2010.

Josh Tickell, director. *Fuel*. Canoga Park, CA: Cinema Libre Studio, 2010.

Daniel Yergin. *The Quest: Energy, Security, and the Remaking of the Modern World*. New York: Free Press, 2011.

NOTES

1. See Daniel Yergin, "It's Still the One," *Foreign Policy* (September/October 2009); and Jad Mouawad, "Fuel to Burn: Now What?" *New York Times*, April 11, 2012.

2. Elisabeth Rosenthal, "U.S. Is Forecast to Be No. 1 Oil Producer," *New York Times*, November 13, 2012.

3. For a detailed account of the role of oil companies in the Middle East, see Daniel Yergin, *The Prize: The Epic Quest for Oil, Money, and Power*, 2nd ed. (New York: Simon & Schuster, 2011).

4. The members of OPEC in 1973 were Iran, Iraq, Kuwait, Saudi Arabia, Venezuela, Abu Dhabi, Algeria, Libya, Qatar, the United Arab Emirates, Nigeria, Ecuador, Indonesia, and Gabon. Ecuador and Gabon left OPEC in the 1990s, Angola joined in 2007, and Indonesia suspended its membership in 2009. Not all oil-exporting countries are members of OPEC. Russia and Mexico, for example, are non-OPEC oil exporters.

5. Donella Meadows, Dennis L. Meadows, Jorgen Randers, and William W. Brehens III, *The Limits to Growth: A Report for the Club of Rome Project on the Predicament of Mankind* (New York: Universe Books, 1974).

6. For a detailed account of Operation Desert Storm, see Kendall W. Stiles, *Case Histories in International Politics*, 3rd ed. (New York: Pearson Longman, 2004), pp. 133–152.

7. See Michael T. Klare, *Blood and Oil: The Dangers and Consequences of America's Growing Dependence on Oil* (New York: Metropolitan Books, 2004), pp. 152–175.

8. United Nations Environment Programme (UNEP), "Global Trends in Sustainable Energy Investment 2009," at http://www.unep.org/pdf/Global_trends_report_2009.pdf.

9. In 1975, the Venezuelan oil minister Juan Pablo Pérez Alfonzo coined the term *devil's excrement* to describe how oil became a curse rather than manna from heaven in Venezuela. For more background on how oil exporting distorts economies, see Terry Lynn Karl, "Ensuring Fairness: The Case for a Transparent Fiscal Social Contract," in Macartan Humphreys, Joseph Stiglitz, and Jeffrey Sachs, eds., *Escaping the Resource Curse* (New York: Columbia University Press, 2007), pp. 256–285.

10. See Jad Mouawad, "Oil Corruption in Equatorial Guinea," *New York Times*, August 19, 2009.

11. *The Power of the Community: How Cuba Survived Peak Oil*, Arthur Morgan Institute for Community Solutions, 2006 (DVD).

12. Rob Hopkins, *The Transition Handbook: From Oil Dependency to Local Resilience* (White River Junction, VT: Chelsea Green Publishing, 2008).

13. Elisabeth Rosenthal, "Gulf Oil States Seeking a Lead in Clean Energy," *New York Times*, January 12, 2009.

14. Shibley Telhami and Fiona Hill, "America's Vital Stakes in Saudi Arabia," *Foreign Affairs* 81 (November/December 2002), pp. 167–173.

15. http://www.ontheissues.org/2012/Barack_Obama_Energy_+_Oil.htm.

16. Ian Urbina, "New Report by Agency Lowers Estimates of Natural Gas in U.S.," *New York Times*, January 29, 2012.

17. Rich Miller, Asjyln Loder, and Jim Polson, "U.S. Closing in on Energy Independence," *Seattle Times*, February 8, 2012.

18. See Maouwad, "Fuel To Burn."

19. See Mark Scott, "The Big New Push to Export America's Gas Bounty," *New York Times*, October 24, 2012.

20. Richard H. Thaler, "Why Gas Prices Are Out of Any President's Control," *New York Times*, April 1, 2009.

21. Rich Miller et al., "U.S. Closing in on Energy Independence." See also Rosenthal, "U.S. Is Forecast to Be No.1 Oil Producer."

22. See Floyd Norris, "Why One Gas Is Cheap and One Isn't," *New York Times*, March 3, 2012.

23. Peter Galuszka, "With China and India Ravenous for Energy, Coal's Future Seems Assured," *New York Times*, November 13, 2012.

24. Michael Riordan, "The Cost of the Coal Boondoggle," *Seattle Times*, August 2, 2012; Scott Learn, "Coal Clash: The Powder River Basin, Where Coal Is King," *Oregonian*, June 30, 2012.

25. Coco Liu and Climatewire, "China Seeks Mastery of Carbon Capture and Storage," *Scientific American*, August 24, 2012.

26. Matthew Wald, "Nuclear Power's Death Somewhat Exaggerated," *New York Times*, April 11, 2012.

27. Cited in "Private Empire: Author Steve Coll on the State-Like Powers, Influence of Oil Giant ExxonMobil" (interview with Juan Gonzalez and Amy Goodman), at http://www.democracynow.org/2012/5/4/private_empire_author_steve_coll_on#transcript.

28. Robert Pollin and James Heintz, "How Wall Street Speculation Is Driving Up Gasoline Prices Today," PERI Research Brief (June 2011).

29. Elizabeth McGowan, "EPA Puts Greenhouse Gas Rules for Refineries on Backburner," *Inside Climate News*, March 8, 2012.

30. Valerie Marcel, "States of Play," *Foreign Policy* (September/October 2009).

31. Eric Nordland and Jad Mouawad, "Iraq Considers Giving Oil Investors Better Terms," *New York Times*, March 18, 2011.

32. Suzanne Goldenberg, "Leak Exposes How Heartland Institute Works to Undermine Climate Science," *Guardian*, February 14, 2012.

33. David Victor and Kasia Yanosek, "The Crisis in Clean Energy: Stark Realities of the Renewables Craze," *Foreign Affairs* (July/August 2011).

34. Diane Cardwell, "Few Seize on a U.S. Bond Program Backing Green Energy," *New York Times*, May 8, 2012.

35. See Eric Lipton and Clifford Krauss, "Rich Subsidies Powering Solar and Wind Projects," *New York Times*, November 11, 2011.

36. Pollin and Heinz, "How Wall Street Speculation...."

37. Amory Lovins, "A Farewell of Fossil Fuels: Answering the Energy Challenge," *Foreign Affairs* 91 (March/April 2012): pp. 134–146.

38. Ibid., p. 136.

39. Thaler, "Why Gas Prices Are Out of Any President's Control."

40. Oswaldo De Rivero, *The Myth of Development: Non-Viable Economies and the Crisis of Civilization*, 2nd ed. (London: Zed Books, 2010).

The Environment: Steering Away from Climate Change and Global Disaster

The Toxic Cauldron: Scavengers at the Olusosun dump in Lagos, Nigeria after a fire.

Finbarr O'Reilly/Reuters

"We may get to the point where the only way of saving the world will be for industrial civilization to collapse."

Maurice Strong

This text ends even more darkly than it began. Chapters 18 and 19 dealt with the interrelated issues of food and energy and this one concludes with an examination of what some would argue is an even more critical problem, globally speaking—the environment, and in particular, the issue of **climate change**. This topic has dominated the debate about the environment for the past decade. Climate change has been front and center in shaping the current global political-economic debate on environmental policy in general.

As we saw in Chapter 19, many corporate executives and government officials are worried that the world will not have enough food and energy to sustain the industrial societies we live in or seek to create. However, today the National Aeronautics and Space Administration (NASA) Goddard Institute for Space Studies climate specialist James Hansen argues that there is no doubt that there is now "no other explanation (for high temperatures) than climate change," which he asserts is due to human causes.[1] Other experts from the Intergovernmental Panel on Climate Change (IPCC), World Bank, International Energy Agency (IEA), PricewaterhouseCoopers, and many public and private agencies and groups agree that enough irrefutable evidence has been gathered to conclude that average world temperatures are projected to increase between 1.8 and 4.0 degrees Celsius by the end of the twenty-first century.

Aside from heating up and cooling down different parts of the earth, other effects of climate change include

- rising sea levels,
- El Nino and ocean temperature variability and extremes that lead to more intense and greater numbers of hurricanes, tornadoes, and typhoons,
- ocean acidification that destroys coral reefs and phytoplankton,
- melting ice sheets and glaciers,
- the threatened extinction of polar bears and other animal species,
- and an assortment of environmental problems in developing nations.

In the summer of 2010, high temperatures were recorded in the United States, over much of Europe, and in Russia where some 55,000 people died from the effects of smoke and smog. In 2012, even higher temperatures were recorded in these same parts of the world. Over the last decade, decreased rainfall and droughts have threatened U.S. agricultural production in the Western states and Great Plains' breadbasket along with growing conditions in Europe and many developing nations, all the while impinging on global food security. Australia also suffered a severe drought over the last ten years. There has been some international press coverage of melting glaciers and a rise in sea levels that are damaging groundwater supplies and producing large numbers of refugees from coastal regions in Bangladesh, China, Egypt, and island nations in the Pacific. Flooding and warmer temperatures have been associated with an increase in the occurrence of food-borne illness and infectious diseases transmitted by mosquitoes. The IPCC concludes that humans are likely contributing to the growing number and intensity of tropical storms in the Atlantic such as Katrina (which started in the Atlantic and moved into the Gulf of Mexico in August 2005) and Sandy (which slammed into the Jersey Shore and New York in October 2012).

For many experts and government officials, time is running out to do something about "overheating the planet," which not only despoils the earth but is bringing about the extinction of humankind. Former Director of the UN Environment Program

Maurice Strong's aforementioned comment seems a more suitable way to think of things every day. Currently, an environmental paradox is exacerbating that situation. In order to overcome their financial crisis caused by recessions, much of Europe and the United States are trying to generate economic growth by reinvigorating their industries, which is contributing to global warming. Meanwhile, the emerging economies of China, India, Brazil, and most developing countries seek to maintain their recent economic success or to achieve more of it. All the while many of these nations find themselves facing a variety of environmental issues that promise to despoil and deplete their environments now and for future generations.

As we write, the eighteenth session of the Conference of the Parties (COP 18), the latest in a series of international meetings to deal with the pressing issue of climate change, has just ended in Doha, Qatar. Its major goals were to finalize a new agreement between nations to limit greenhouse emissions such that global temperatures would not rise about 2 degrees Celsius. Another goal was to extend the Kyoto Protocol that was agreed to in 1997 and that required industrialized countries to reduce their greenhouse gas emissions by more than a third by 2012, or 5.2 percent below the 1990 level of emissions.

For the past twenty years, however, a number of weak interim agreements have been reached that left the details about how to reduce greenhouse emissions to be filled in at a future COP meeting. The United States, the EU, China, Brazil, India, and South Africa have all put measurable reduction targets and a variety of other measures on the negotiating table in these COP sessions. For all intents and purposes, however, the problem of what to do about climate change kept getting "kicked down the road" time after time. Conflicting state and regional interests, differences over how much climate change is a problem, and a variety of other factors have made it increasingly more difficult all the time to deal with climate change, let alone other significant environmental problems.

In this chapter, we use the three IPE perspectives to identify and explain many of the causes of different global environmental issues, with particular attention to the problem of climate change. The chapter has four major parts. First is a chronology of major developments leading up to the situation today. Second is a brief history that discusses the broadening scope of many environmental issues for states, international organizations (IOs), nongovernmental organizations (NGOs), epistemic communities, and even some influential environmental "personalities."

Third, we discuss some of the evidence for and against the idea that climate change is so harmful and why it and several other related problems have been so difficult to manage. Fourth and finally, we explore a variety of proposed solutions to environmental problems, focusing on the roles that states, markets, technology, and even ethical values play in reform efforts.

The chapter presents four significant theses. First, most environmental problems including climate change are now global in nature. While one effect of this development has been that management of issues has become more democratic—that is, more actors have a say in these issues all the time—the downside is there are more conflicting interests to reconcile if problems are going to be solved in a cooperative fashion. Second, because of the environment's impact on national economies and security, states and IOs are facing unprecedented global political-economic pressure to grapple with climate change and other environmental problems. Third, market-based or one-size-fits-all solutions alone will not effectively resolve most environmental issues, especially those associated with global warming. Fourth and finally, an alternative constructivist paradigm (see Chapter 5) about the relationship of people to the environment is needed that weds modern industrial societies and their national and subnational cultures with the necessity to preserve what is left of the global environment—in this case one that requires either a cut in CO_2 emissions or some other measure that holds down the earth's temperature.

CHRONOLOGY OF SIGNIFICANT ENVIRONMENT AND CLIMATE CHANGE EVENTS AND AGREEMENTS

1972   The UN hosts the Conference on the Human Environment in Stockholm, Sweden. The conference announces an Action Plan for the Human Environment.

   The United Nations Environmental Program (UNEP) is created to help developing countries with environment issues.

   The Club of Rome issues its *Limits to Growth* report.

1973   OPEC raises the price of oil, generating concerns about energy scarcity and the impact of industrialization on the environment.

1980   U.S. President Jimmy Carter commissions *The Global 2000 Report to the President*, predicting continued population growth, depletion of natural resources, deforestation, air and water pollution, and species extinction. Julian Simon and Herman Kahn respond with *The Resourceful Earth: A Response to Global 2000*.

1987   The Brundtland Report links development to environment damage.

   The UN-sponsored Montreal Protocol to control chlorofluorocarbons that damage the earth's ozone layer comes into effect.

1992   The Earth Summit meets in Rio de Janeiro to focus on "sustainable development"—generating wealth and development while preserving the environment.

   Two conventions are produced: the Convention on Biological Diversity and the Framework Convention on Climate Change (FCCC), which later became the basis of the Kyoto Protocol. Eighteen COPs will be held over the next twenty years to negotiate a global agreement on climate change.

1997   The Kyoto Protocol is negotiated at the third COP dealing with global climate change.

   It requires industrialized countries to reduce their greenhouse gas emissions by more than a third by 2012, or 5.2 percent below the 1990 level of emissions. Two key proposals are the use of emission credits and carbon sinks as part of a cap and trade system. The Kyoto Protocol is to be renegotiated in 2012.

2009   The 15th COP meeting in Copenhagen produces a weak accord that once again *begins* the process of reaching a number of binding agreements on greenhouse emissions, deforestation, verification, and shielding poor countries from the impact of climate change.

2011   The United Nations Climate Change Conference in Durban, South Africa ends with an agreement to start negotiations for a new legally binding climate treaty to be decided by 2015, and to come into force by 2020. Negotiators also agree to a second commitment period under the Kyoto Protocol.

2012   The 18th COP meeting in Doha, Qatar results in no significant agreement on climate change.

THE WIDENING SCOPE OF ENVIRONMENTAL PROBLEMS: A BRIEF HISTORY

Beginning in the eighteenth century during the industrial revolution, science and technology were harnessed to produce new labor-saving devices, industrial machines, and goods for mass consumption. Karl Marx and many of his contemporaries in the mid-nineteenth century complained of the damaging effects that "satanic mills" had on labor and the physical presence of England's bigger cities (see Chapter 4). Manufacturing industries in Europe were fueled by great quantities of inexpensive natural resources and raw materials. On the European continent, air, water, and soil pollution spread beyond local areas. The development of the gasoline-powered engine at the end of the nineteenth century shifted demand away from coal and steam to oil and petroleum-based energy resources. Resources remained plentiful and relatively inexpensive—transportation being the biggest expense.

As industrialization spread throughout Western Europe and the United States, industrial pollution gradually became a bigger international problem—that is, it covered several or more nation-states. For instance, in the 1920s, the United States and Canada argued about the residue of lead and zinc smelting in British Columbia that was carried down the Columbia River into the United States. For the most part, however, environmental issues in the industrialized world were viewed as nation-state-based problems.

The global magnitude of environmental problems was not fully realized until the 1960s. In the United States, global resource depletion became one of the issues of the student movement and the environmental movement that developed at the same time. As the absolute amount of pollution discharged worldwide grew, so did scientific knowledge and public awareness.[2] In 1972, the Club of Rome issued a shocking study, *The Limits to Growth*, arguing that if post–World War II levels of economic activity and environmental abuse continued, it would be the *environment*, not land, food, or other factors, that would limit global progress.[3] The OPEC oil embargo of 1973 and resulting high oil prices also pushed the issue of energy resource scarcity onto the agenda of many nation-states (see Chapter 19). Many developed and developing nations became aware of their dependence on oil to sustain industrialization and economic growth but also on some of the negative effects it was having on the environment.

Meanwhile, the UN made its debut as an important actor in the debate on the environment in 1972, hosting the Conference on the Human Environment in Stockholm, Sweden. The conference announced an Action Plan for the Human Environment with 109 recommendations for governmental and international action on a wide variety of environmental issues. More importantly, it created an organization called the **United Nations Environment Program (UNEP)** to draft treaties, provide a forum for cooperation, and create databases for scientific assessments of the environment. The first UN agency to be headquartered in a Third World capital—Nairobi, Kenya—UNEP has over the years built an extensive network of smaller organizations around itself while coordinating action within the UN on environmental problems. It works on joint ventures with other agencies and organizations, including NGOs. UNEP has always had a funding problem, receiving significantly less than other UN agencies. With a staff of only 300, it cannot muster the authority to coordinate larger agencies. It also has to rely on national governments to implement its policies—actors that may see UNEP as merely another voice for frustrated ex-colonies.

From the 1980s onward, environmental problems continued to gain political recognition. In 1980, President Jimmy Carter commissioned *The Global 2000 Report to the President*, which predicted continued population growth, depletion of natural resources, deforestation, air and water pollution, and species extinction.[4] Even British Prime Minister Margaret Thatcher and Soviet Foreign Minister Eduard Shevardnadze gave speeches connecting the environment to global security. According to Shevardnadze, the environment is a "second front" that is "gaining urgency equal to that of the nuclear-and-space threat."[5] National and international attention to environmental issues reached new heights in response to notorious ecological (mis)management such as oil spills, acid rain, nuclear reactor incidents, droughts, deforestation, and oil, chemical, and toxic waste spills.

In the United States, however, environmentalism met increased resistance. Oil supplies gradually became more plentiful and their price declined or held steady, weakening interest in resource scarcity and environmental problems. In a rebuke to the 1980 report commissioned by President Carter, Julian Simon and Herman Kahn wrote *The Resourceful Earth: A Response to Global* 2000.[6] Kahn went on to refer to the fatalistic outlook of the ecopessimists as "globaloney." Presidents Reagan and Bush senior aligned themselves with optimists who downplayed threats to the environment, arguing that more studies needed to be done. They also claimed that many of the measures proposed to protect the environment were too costly and unfairly penalized businesses. Many U.S. officials adopted a neoliberal position that technology and markets could better solve these problems than coordinated efforts by nation-states in international forums.[7]

Despite the broad range of perspectives at the time, the UN made its way to the forefront of the debate in 1987 by publishing a report entitled "Our Common Future" that shifted attention to the connection between the environment and the survival of developing nations. Sometimes referred to as the Brundtland Report because the chair of the UN commission was Gro Harlem Brundtland (who later became the prime minister of Norway), the report linked hunger, debt, economic growth, and other issues to environmental problems. That same year diplomats also signed the UN-sponsored Montreal Protocol on Substances that Deplete the Ozone Layer which required states to reduce **chlorofluorocarbon (CFC)** production by one-half by 2000. This treaty was in response to the 1985 discovery of a hole in the stratospheric ozone layer over Antarctica in 1985.

CFCs, which are used in many industrial products and processes, were targeted as the largest source contributing to **ozone depletion.** CFCs were long used in refrigerants, aerosol propellants, cleaning solvents, and blowing agents for foam production, but the chlorine atoms in these compounds destroy ozone. The effects of a depleted ozone layer around the earth are global in scope, including a dramatic increase in the incidence of melanoma skin cancer and cataracts, as well as damage to crops and ocean phytoplankton. Scientists estimate that even if CFCs were completely banned, the ozone-layer problem would last at least another 100 years given the present level of atmospheric CFC concentration. The **Montreal Protocol** was later amended to call for a complete halt to CFC production. To this day, the treaty is considered one of the most successful treaties on the environment. It has been amended seven times and ratified by 197 UN member states and the EU.

THE PROLIFERATION OF ACTORS

In the last 300 years, as environmental problems have gone from being local and often temporary to being global and possibly permanent, the actors associated with managing them have also increased in number along with, in some cases, the scope of their interests, jurisdiction, and constituencies. These actors include nation-states, NGOs, IOs, and international businesses, along with a number of individuals identified with particular issues.

More actors and more interconnections among them have on the one hand made the decision making at the global level more democratic in one sense but also complicated the management of many environmental problems.

Many nation-states deal with environmental problems in ways that reflect their different institutions and their political, social, and economic systems. State environmental regulations are prevalent in many Western European nations. In some EU nations, "green" and other political parties influence state environmental policy in this direction. However, in many developing countries environmental issues often divide those who support economic development and those who favor some combination of income redistribution, conservation, and sustainable development. One group of experts reports that by the mid-1980s, 110 LDCs and thirty developed nations had created environmental ministries or agencies.[8] However, there is much evidence that these agencies often did not comply with regulations or have been simply ineffective.

One theory forwarded by Detlef Sprintz and Tapani Vaahtoranta is that in some cases non-compliance might be intentional for some states. Some states tend to be "pushers" of environmental policies while others are "draggers" to the extent that they support or oppose them or fail to implement them fully.[9] When it comes to more controversial issues where the potential consequences are uncertain or immeasurable, states are more likely to act as draggers. As discussed later in the chapter, when it comes to addressing the issue of climate change, for many years the United States has tended to be a dragger for any number of reasons including denying or intentionally downplaying many of the scientific facts put forward to demonstrate that climate change is real.

NGOs have played an increasingly bigger role in policy making and implementation in environmental and climate change issues. Some have annual budgets far exceeding the GDPs of many nations. The largest NGOs work in international humanitarian aid, addressing a variety of environmental issues such as development, water, education, and the preservation of rainforests. Well-known NGOs working strictly on environmental issues include the World Wildlife Fund (WWF), Greenpeace International, the National Geographic Society, Friends of the Earth, the National Audubon Society, and the Sierra Club. Dealing with climate change are the Global Environmental Facility (GEF), CARE, and WWF. The Climate Action Network (CAN) is an umbrella worldwide network of over 700 NGOs in over ninety countries promoting government and individual action to limit human-induced climate change to ecologically sustainable levels.[10]

Some of these groups focus strictly on fundraising and organizing environmentally related projects or awareness campaigns, while others such as Greenpeace aim to influence national and international environmental legislation. The size, cohesiveness, and effectiveness of all these groups vary in different nations, depending on the extent to which environmental causes permeate not only politics but also popular culture and even religion. For many environmentalists in developed countries, the environmental cause has become another basis on which to attack the alienated individualism of a consumption-oriented capitalist society.

IOs have helped states to overcome the free-rider problem (see Chapter 2) to the extent that, by promoting cooperation and assigning costs to organization members, problems can be worked on in a collective fashion. When the environmental movement was first taking off in the late 1960s, Garrett Hardin in his article the **"Tragedy of the Commons"**[11] described the challenges of protecting **collective goods** that are shared by everyone and owned by no one, in particular the environment. His thesis is that many resources are prone to abuse because property rights and freedom both rationally compel, but also allow us, to (over) produce and consume as much as we can. Hardin's analogy of why the earth's resources are overused and fouled typifies the debate over climate change and resource abuse as harm to the atmosphere is shared by all the earth's inhabitants.

Given that one of its objectives is development, the UN has been more active than any other IO in dealing with environmental problems and policies. Aside from UNEP, the UN has several other agencies whose work either directly or indirectly influences the environment. A few of these bodies are the Food and Agriculture Organization (FAO), which monitors global hunger and poverty in developing nations; the UN Population Fund, which supports population-control programs in South Korea, China, Sri Lanka, and Cuba; and a variety of UN population conferences.

The environment's connection to investment and trade policies has been a topic of negotiations in the General Agreement on Tariffs and Trade (GATT) and World Trade Organization (WTO) rounds. The WTO implemented a series of provisions referred to as Multilateral Environmental Agreements (MEAs) that were to accommodate the use of trade-related measures and the environment. In some cases, developing countries were exempted from GATT articles and WTO agreements so they could place national environmental goals ahead of their obligation not to use protectionist measures.[12] Lower environmental standards often translate into lower production costs, thus giving these countries an advantage on the world market.

The World Bank established a Global Environment Fund (GEF) to help developing nations bring proposed projects in line with international environmental standards and goals. However, as noted in several other chapters, it has been criticized for its lack of aid and for support of Structural Adjustment Policies (SAPs) which stress economic growth over the environment.[13]

Many international businesses also play major roles in environmental activism in general but also climate change issues in particular. Large international conferences on the environment have attracted large companies looking to contribute their knowledge on the topic, bridging an unlikely partnership between entrepreneurs and policy officials. Until recently, their attitude has been that environmental rules and regulations are annoying and lead to inefficiencies, to say the least. Many oil corporations such as British Petroleum (BP), ExxonMobil, and Shell, to name a few, claim to make protection of the environment one of their corporate goals. In the case of global negotiations on climate change, most major corporations are on record for opposing these sorts of measures, arguing that they are inappropriate for the hard financial times we live in or unnecessary given new technologies that promise less emissions from more efficient production techniques and processes.

THE SCIENCE AND DISPUTED FACTS OF CLIMATE CHANGE

The issue of global climate change and greenhouse gas emissions has gradually become the most important issue framing international debate on the environment. For decades scientists have been researching the ability of greenhouse gases to trap heat in the earth's atmosphere, but it has only recently become widely accepted that the earth's temperatures are in fact increasing over time as a result of increases in the earth's greenhouse gases. Many of these gases, which include carbon dioxide, nitrous oxide, methane, CFCs, ozone, and other infrared-absorbing gases, naturally occur in the atmosphere. As noted in the introduction to this chapter, many scientists believe that *human* sources of greenhouse gases, such as carbon dioxide produced by the burning of fossil fuels (coal, oil, and natural gas) and the burning and clearing of land for agricultural purposes, make up the largest concentration of the greenhouse gases, and are thus the main causes of global warming. The Mauna Loa laboratory, whose estimates are regarded as some of the most accurate, puts carbon dioxide levels in the atmosphere at 387 parts per million, up 40 percent since the Industrial Revolution, and the highest level seen in the last 650,000 years.[14]

In October 2006, Lord Nicolas Stern issued a 700-word report[15] on the economics of climate change that got a lot of press attention. His findings include

- All countries will be affected by climate change, but the poorest countries will suffer earliest and most.
- Average temperatures could rise by 5 degrees Celsius from pre-industrial levels if climate change goes unchecked.
- Warming of 3 or 4 degrees Celsius will result in many millions more people being flooded. By the middle of the century, 200 million may be permanently displaced due to rising sea levels, heavier floods, and drought.
- Warming of 2 degrees Celsius could leave 15–40 percent of species facing extinction.
- Deforestation is responsible for more emissions than the transport sector.
- Climate change is the greatest and widest-ranging market failure ever seen.

Stern's recommended actions include

- Three elements of policy for an effective response—carbon pricing, technology policy, and energy efficiency.
- Carbon pricing, through taxation, emissions trading, or regulation, to show people the full social costs of their actions.
- Expansion and linking of emissions trading schemes, like those operating across the EU.
- Full integration of climate change into development policy, and rich countries honoring pledges to increase support through overseas development assistance.

In his report Sterns also asserts that another 325 million people, mostly in the developing world, are being seriously impacted by the effects of global warming. His report also accepts the conclusion that global warming is a crisis and estimates that it could cost the world 5–20 percent of its economic output "forever," but that trying to forestall the crisis would cost only 1 percent of the world's GDP.

One of the biggest names in the global warming debate is former U.S. Vice-President Al Gore. During his tenure, Gore became very active in raising public awareness of environmental problems. In 2006, he was featured in a film that documented his activism, outlined evidence of global warming, and warned of its potential catastrophic risks. *An Inconvenient Truth*[16] went on to win an Academy Award, and in 2007 Gore shared a Nobel Peace Prize with the IPCC.

Another recent activist on the environmental scene is Thomas Friedman, the *New York Times* op-ed writer known for his books that explore globalization. In his latest book, *Hot, Flat, and Crowded*, he argues that the United States has surprisingly not fulfilled the role that it should as a world energy leader.[17] Globalization, 9/11, and Hurricane Katrina have brought the issues of environmentalism and energy to mainstream America, if not the world. However, most experts and commentators agree that the United States has not done enough to promote a green technological revolution that is necessary to combat global warming. Interestingly, some critics of Friedman's work on the environment note some of the contradictions between promoting neoliberal policies and business practices and Friedman's argument that the United States in particular should play a greater role in protecting the environment.

Climate Change Skeptics

Some experts remain skeptical about the extent of global warming and climate change. For example, Richard Lindzen, Professor of Atmospheric Science at MIT, suggests that although levels of carbon dioxide in the atmosphere have increased by 30 percent since the turn of the last century, these claims "neither constitute support for alarm nor establish man's responsibility for the small amount of warming that has occurred."[18] Recent weather patterns simply reflect natural variability. Unusually high volcanic activity between 1940 and 1975 may help explain the release of abnormal amounts of sulfate particles. Others argue that carbon dioxide is less potent than other greenhouse gases because half of it is absorbed by oceans, green plants, and forests (the so-called **carbon sinks**).

On a side note, carbon sinks are really part of a broader debate on two other major environmental issues: oceans and forests. Deforestation means less vegetation to help absorb carbon dioxide. Scientists are also studying how forests' ability to absorb carbon dioxide is affected by temperatures. Deforestation is predominantly occurring in developing nations that are heavily dependent on income from the timber that forests generate. Aside from its impact on the atmosphere, deforestation harms biodiversity of both plants and animals, and thus the development of future pharmaceuticals. It leads to increased watershed runoff, which has been known to desertify countries such as Somalia and Sudan as well as exaggerate the effects of flooding by reducing the earth's ability to absorb water.

Scientists have also recently concluded that warming ocean temperatures are decreasing the ocean's ability to absorb carbon dioxide. If temperatures continue to increase, so will the inability of oceans to absorb greenhouse gases, only exacerbating the current situation. However, even if the oceans are not losing their ability to absorb greenhouse gases, increasing levels of carbon dioxide in the ocean have led to ocean acidification, which threatens coral reefs and many delicate ecosystems and food sources around the world. Acidification inhibits the ability of many sea creatures to properly form their shells. In the event that these creatures become unable to survive, there will be a massive disruption to the ocean food chain. Coral reefs are also thought to protect the land from storm surges and hurricanes.

A number of skeptics about climate change base their arguments on their religion and/or their disbelief in math or scientific analysis.[19] In the United States, in particular, many skeptics are members of orthodox denominations of Christian churches whose theological criticisms vary but have in common opposition to "secular" (non-Christian) arguments about the environment. Still others—many of them right-wing political conservatives—are not convinced by hard "scientific models" that climate change even exists.

Finally, some skeptics argue that temperature readings supporting the theory of climate change have been distorted by their proximity to urban areas, which have a tendency to be warmer. Even if this were not the case, computer models cannot accurately account for complex interactions of oceans with atmosphere, cloud behavior, and the role of water vapor. These critics sometimes point to the occasional decrease in average world temperatures on an annual basis, as well as recent events like the appearance of snow in Baghdad. Still other skeptics believe in climate change but argue that there may be possible benefits to warmer climates such as increased farming capacities in cooler areas. Some even go so far as to argue that the existence of greenhouse gases in the atmosphere will stave off the next ice age.

GLOBAL MANAGEMENT OF CLIMATE CHANGE

The Rio Meeting

Despite some continued skepticism in the scientific community to this day, international efforts to deal with global warming have been around for some time. The first multilateral negotiations occurred at the 1992 **Earth Summit** in Rio de Janeiro.[20] Officially titled the UN Conference on the Environment and Development (UNCED), 178 national delegates, 115 heads of state, and more than 15,000 environmental NGO representatives focused their attention primarily on **sustainable development**, or ways to accomplish what seem like contradictory objectives: generating wealth and development while preserving the environment. Agenda 21 laid out plans for states, IOs, NGOs, and special interest groups to achieve a variety of new goals related to different environmental issues.

The Earth Summit resulted in the creation of several conventions including the Rio Declaration on the Environment and Development, the Convention on Biological Diversity, and most importantly, the **United Nations Framework Convention on Climate Change (UNFCCC)**, which later would serve as the basis of the **Kyoto Protocol.**

One of the intellectual and political brains behind the Earth Summit in Rio was Maurice Strong, an environmental extremist and admitted overpopulation doomsayer who was well regarded by world leaders and touted as one of the most well-connected men on the planet. Strong had an extensive web of high-level international connections. This Canadian entrepreneur, under-secretary to the UN, and diplomat fostered the concept of a new "global ethic."

The Kyoto Protocol

In December 1997, a much anticipated meeting of the third COP, the signatories of the Earth Summit's FCCC treaty, was held in Kyoto, Japan, where 2,000 representatives from 159 countries met to strengthen the treaty.[21] This meeting resulted in the creation of the Kyoto Protocol, which required thirty-seven industrialized countries (including twenty-seven from the EU) to reduce their greenhouse gas emissions by more than a third by 2012, or 5.2 percent below the 1990 level of emissions. A popular key proposal of the Kyoto Protocol was the use of **emission credits** as part of a **cap and trade** system whereby limits on greenhouse gas emissions were to be assigned each country based on their 1990 emissions levels. The Kyoto Protocol established operational rules for carbon trading, accounting methods, and carbon offsets—projects such as reforestation that could be substituted for the purchasing of carbon credits. Rules regarding the distribution of emission allowances within a country were left up to individual countries to decide. The governments of most signatories to the protocol could auction off their allowances in the form of "permits" to energy-intensive businesses that could buy and sell or swap them on the international market. Economic liberal advocates maintained that this system addressed a key problem underlying climate change by establishing overall limits on greenhouse gases and forcing producers of CO_2 to pay for its negative externalities, while simultaneously permitting the flexibility of the market to set prices on the credits.

One of the most serious challenges immediately encountered by the Kyoto Protocol was that many other details of the treaty were initially left undefined. An option discussed in future COP meetings was for the United States to either cap its production of emissions or buy its way into compliance with the Kyoto Protocol by paying Russia and other countries to cut their emissions more than required. The United States, the EU, Canada, Russia, and Australia, among others, also wrangled over such issues as the use of carbon sinks such as forests that absorbed CO_2 to enable countries such as the United States, Russia, and others to escape real reductions in the use of fossil fuels.

It is important to note that developing nations as a whole generated serious attention during the Kyoto talks. Nearly all of the countries in the Southern hemisphere became parties to the Kyoto Protocol. However, opposition voices from many developing nations echoed many of the same sentiments of the Group of 77 (G77) who opposed the developed states in the early 1970s. Many African and Latin American countries were supportive of a treaty that limited their emissions, but wanted guarantees that they would get their share of aid from the developed nations to help them cut emissions. Part of the agreement gave many developing nations more time to develop and adjust to emissions targets; they were only encouraged to adopt target levels of their own. For the next two decades, the issue of how much and when developing nations like China and India would be bound by the climate treaty became a major source of tension between developed and developing nations. Meanwhile, the United States and other developed nations resisted transferring any more financial resources to developing nations as a condition for their support for an agreement.

The United States, represented by the Clinton administration, originally signed the Kyoto Protocol in November 1998. To the surprise of many, the U.S. Senate passed a resolution 95–0 informing then President Clinton that it would *not* ratify the treaty unless the same limitations put on the United States and other industrialized nations applied to developing countries such as China and India, or unless the developing nations committed themselves to a complex scheme for trading emission permits and credits.

In the spring of 2001, the new George W. Bush administration suddenly withdrew entirely from the Kyoto Treaty. It claimed that the new treaty would cost the United States $400 billion and 4.9 million jobs. U.S. officials went on to cite natural gas and fossil fuel shortages as reasons to *expand* U.S. energy supplies. The administration also remained skeptical that there was enough evidence that power plant emissions contributed to global warming or that global warming itself was a serious problem.

The Bush administration's response to global warming mirrored its reaction to many security issues, which was to "go it alone" mixed with suspicion of IOs and charges that international agreements such as the Kyoto accords limited state sovereignty. It went on to announce its own plan for an 18 percent cut in greenhouse gases by providing businesses with incentives to invest in cleaner technology. The Bush administration also promoted voluntary compliance with a variety of efficiency-enhancing measures that would purportedly take seventy million cars off the road or remove 500 million metric tons of greenhouse gases from the atmosphere. Meanwhile, the development of hybrid cars, biodiesel fuel, and alternative energy sources was quietly and quickly emerging in reaction to consumer demand for cleaner and more sustainable sources of energy.

After five COPs and much debate over many interrelated issues, in 2002 moderate concessions were eventually made that resulted in more countries ratifying the Kyoto treaty. These countries included more than half of the world's twenty-five most populated countries, and all fifteen EU members at that time. Still, Russia and the United States did not ratify the treaty. In January 2005, the EU bloc implemented the first phase of its own "emission trading scheme." Shortly thereafter Russia finally ratified the Kyoto Protocol and it went into effect, even without U.S. ratification.

Ironically, at the same time some nations such as Canada were "backsliding" on their willingness or ability to comply with the protocol and rejected its original Kyoto emission targets. Australia finally ratified the Kyoto Protocol in late 2007, leaving the United States as the only major industrialized developed nation to withhold participation. However, the United States and other developed states have since failed to enact meaningful legislation to curb greenhouse gas emissions and remain the highest per capita polluters in the world (see Table 20-1). As expected, these developments of the major industrialized nations weakened the commitment of many other nations to meet their emissions goals, which we discuss in the following paragraphs.

Copenhagen

Before the Copenhagen meeting in December 2009, there seemed to be widespread agreement amongst world leaders who supported the Kyoto agreement that in order to stave off serious climate change, a 50 percent reduction in world emissions (from the 1990 baseline) was necessary by 2050. Yet this would not be possible without an agreement by the United States, China, and other major emissions producers to adhere to emission targets. In a new agreement, developing nations would also need to set limits to their emissions and be bound to an international carbon control regime. Furthermore, developed nations would need to provide some assistance to developing nations to shift away from emissions-producing industries and deforestation in their development strategies.

Before the meeting, China was not receptive to establishing verifiable emissions limits. From 2000 to 2008, its greenhouse gas emissions increased by nearly 120 percent compared with the United States, whose emissions grew by 16 percent in the same period, making China the largest net emitter of greenhouse gases in the world.[22] China had taken some initiatives on its own, setting strict fuel-economy

TABLE 20-1	
Biggest Contributors to Carbon Dioxide Emissions, 2010	
Country	CO_2 Emissions (million metric tonnes)
China	8,321
United States	5,610
India	1,696
Russian Federation	1,634
Japan	1,165
Germany	794
South Korea	579
Iran	560
Canada	549
United Kingdom	532

Source: U.S. Energy Information Administration, "International Energy Statistics," at http://www.eia.gov/cfapps/ipdbproject/IEDIndex3.cfm?tid=90&pid=44&aid=8 (accessed December 18, 2012).

standards and energy-efficient building codes and developing wind energy and other alternative energy sources. India had already implemented measures of its own.[23] India's proposal was more modest than China's because its emissions and GDP were about 30 percent of China's. India also strongly supported efforts to fend off significant emissions increases, but gave in only if it were to receive major financial assistance from the developed world.

In response to mounting pressure from the developed world to cut emissions, China, India, South Africa, and Brazil formed another Basic Group to represent their collective interests. They pointed out that most of the greenhouse gases in the atmosphere were the result of cumulative damage over the years from the industrialized-developed world. They also argued that, while collectively their greenhouse gas emissions were significant, their per capita emission output was still far behind that of the United States and other developed nations. It was the Basic Group that rejected the possibility of a binding agreement, at least in the near future. Above all, they protested the unfairness of limiting carbon emissions for them when developed nations had ample time in the past to grow their economies without environmental restraints.

Brazil and Indonesia, the fourth and fifth most populated countries and large greenhouse gas emitters, argued that they were unlike China and India in that their carbon dioxide emissions came mostly from nonindustrial sources such as deforestation. They were willing to cooperate but would require aid from developed countries to help phase out the practice.

Amongst the developed nations, two different coalitions emerged: the EU and the Umbrella Group. Although there was no official list for the Umbrella Group, it included the United States, Canada, Australia, Great Britain, and Japan. Even Japan, which had difficulty meeting its Kyoto targets, finally met its reduction targets for the first time in 2009.[24] The Umbrella Group was comparatively less willing to adopt measures that the rest of the world considered acceptable.

Just before the Copenhagen meeting the Australian government defeated legislation to implement a cap and trade system which would result in a 5 percent reduction for this same time period. Japan offered to cut its emissions by 25 percent of their 1990 levels by 2020, but conditioned it on the participation of countries like China. Realistically, the offers made by developed nations did not meet what is generally accepted as sufficient to hold back serious climate change.[25]

Media coverage of the run-up to the Copenhagen meeting was overshadowed by events surrounding the global financial crisis, which left many states unclear as to how the crisis would impact their environment policies. Many businesses and governments were forced to reevaluate their budgets, priorities, and risk-taking in consideration of the financial crisis. At first the Obama administration took some steps to promote a green U.S. economy, but under the umbrella of its economic stimulus package where 10 percent went toward the financing of green projects. The financial crisis also diminished the willingness of the developed nations help them pay for the negative impact of the environment on their economies.

After two weeks of intense negotiations at Copenhagen, 193 countries produced what once again most experts viewed as a rather weak accord that in principle only *began* the process of reaching a number of binding agreements on greenhouse emissions, deforestation, verification, and shielding poor countries from the impact of climate change. The following were the main points of agreement that were *not* legally binding:[26]

- Developed countries would reduce emissions levels individually or jointly based on pledges made before the conference.
- Developing countries were to monitor emissions and compile data "with provisions for international consultations and analysis."
- Developed countries would raise $100 billion a year by 2020 to help poor countries fight climate change.
- New funds would be provided to help pay countries to preserve forests.
- The increase in global temperature should be kept below 2 degrees Celsius.

Most criticisms of the agreement came from the EU members and poorer nations that felt left out of the negotiations. Small island nations complained that the 2-degree-Celsius target was still too high and that soon many of them would be completely wiped out. Many experts and commentators suggested that the whole effort helped to further divide the northern rich states from the poorer developing nations.

Supporters of the agreement included the Basic Group states that managed to keep the accord nonbinding. At one point, President Obama and Secretary of State Hillary Clinton "crashed" a meeting of the other delegates and joined in the discussion, demonstrating what some claim to be needed leadership on these sorts of issues. The president cobbled together a face-saving "Copenhagen Accord" made up of voluntary agreements that "committed no one to anything" and that lacked an enforcement mechanism.[27]

At this time, Al Gore proposed the idea of a **carbon tax** he believed would be simpler to implement and enforce. He argued that a cap and trade system is in practice no different than a carbon tax system whereby the cost of greenhouse gas emissions is ultimately passed on to the consumer in the form of higher prices. Gore advocated "tax what you burn, not what you earn," but also acknowledged that a cap and trade system in the United States would be easier to coordinate with the policies of other countries.[28] It is unclear if U.S. voters would have countenanced a carbon tax. Critics of cap and trade regimes also pointed out that in Europe heavily lobbied governments ultimately gave away many permits, passing up potentially significant sums of money.

Durban: SNAFU

Predictably, the UN Climate Change Conference in Durban, South Africa, at the end of 2011, ended with an agreement to start the negotiations on a legally binding climate treaty to be decided by 2015 that would come into force by 2020. This agreement would extend the Kyoto Protocol that ended in 2012 which dealt with the initial design of a Green Climate Fund agreed to at Copenhagen the year before. Many environmental groups say the agreement did not do enough to deal with the climate crisis. Kate Horner, a policy analyst at Friends of the Earth International, suggested that the Durban COP was "a further milestone in a very long history of the wealthy world backtracking on their existing promises and reneging on existing obligations."[29] Horner expected the platform to delay action for five to ten years while a new treaty was being negotiated and ratified. It would also attempt to shift the burden of this problem on to developing countries that have contributed less to it than developed states. Others criticized the UN climate summit for being especially damaging to Africa. As in previous cases, many believed that the outcome of the talks produced a very weak agreement that lacked ambition, equity, and justice.[30]

Of special note to many delegates were conditions in Africa that seemed to be increasingly more vulnerable to the effects of climate change. India has only one-tenth of the emissions of the United States, and its water supply is in danger from the Himalaya glacier melts. Routinely, it also has monsoons that kill many people and damage livestock and agricultural commodities. Even so, India and a number of smaller nations were blamed by the wealthier nations for blocking progress on the talks. On the other hand, many structuralist critics argued that the United States tried to weasel out of every promise that it has made, including to take on comparable action to other developed countries in line with its historic responsibility for contributing to this problem. The United States also prevented any further discussion of long-term financing for developing countries.

The 18th COP at Doha: Down and Dirty

In this case, not much was expected, not much happened, nor did the international press give much coverage to the 18th COP in Doha, Qatar, in December 2012. Once again the primary goals of the meeting were to reduce global greenhouse emissions, limit global temperature rise to no more than 2 degrees Celsius, and avert catastrophic climate change. The only real progress in the meeting was to agree to deal with the issue of emissions targets in 2014.

Journalist and activist Bianca Jagger attended the meeting and took extensive notes on the negotiations.[31] She and other structuralists reprimanded negotiators for lacking the political will to deal with the climate change crisis head on and for representing the interests of global businesses over the many poorer states that will have to deal with the continuing negative effects of climate change.[32] Most reporters who covered the meeting noted the growing evidence and effects of climate change by October 2012. November was the 33rd consecutive month that global temperatures were above the twentieth-century average. The atmospheric concentration of CO_2 has risen by 31 percent since 1750. And it is now the highest in 420,000 years. Hurricane Katrina killed 1,836 in 2005, Hurricane Sandy 100, Typhoon Bopha over 700, and so on.

Of some note was the World Bank report "Turn Down the Heat: Why a 4°C Warmer World Must Be Avoided," that the new World Bank President Dr. Jim Yong Kim sent into boardrooms and discussed with reporters.[33] Kim too feared that Kyoto was just barely alive and that what was proposed at Durban—the Durban Plan for Enhanced Action—could be too little, too late. Today, many officials continue to call for a legally binding climate agreement "applicable to all, equitably instituted and responsive to science." However, they are all aware that what seemed obvious and doable in 1992 now appears increasingly more out of reach all the time.

Another confrontation between rich and poor states developed at Doha over extending the Green Climate Fund, established at Copenhagen in 2009. According to the developed states, they were to provide $10 billion a year for the next three years and then $100 billion a year by 2020. Many developing nations interpreted the agreement such that aid would gradually increase after 2012 until 2020 when $100 billion a year in assistance would kick in. The United States and Europe both argued that the financial crisis had made it difficult to generate new funds.[34] Some developing countries demanded $60 billion between 2013 and 2015—the same amount President Obama asked to deal with Hurricane Sandy. Some EU countries were willing to contribute a total of €8.3 billion by 2015. However, many sources blamed the United States for blocking language in the text that might have resulted in an agreement.

Based on the results of past COP meetings, the following factors played a role in support for or against a new climate change agreement:

- Continued conflicting state interests and values.
- Public opposition to national and international leaders who would support a new agreement.
- The financial crisis which pressured states to postpone an agreement.
- Special interests such as the coal and oil industries that campaigned for access to the Arctic, the tar sands in Canada, and more coal mines in Indonesia.
- Skepticism, if not disbelief, in climate change.
- The lack of an identifiable leader such as Maurice Strong in the 1950s and 1960s to support a new agreement.

Many debate whether in a political-economic environment in which pressure on the earth's resources is likely to grow, especially in the face of the current global crisis, nation-states and international businesses will be willing to commit themselves to objectives that do not require excessive amounts of CO_2 emissions and natural resource consumption. Which new technologies help solve environmental problems or simply make them worse? This raises an even more fundamental question: How do actors reconcile political, economic, and social values that emphasize economic growth and consumption with those values that are more environmentally friendly?

SOLUTIONS: A GREEN IPE?

Some of the most popular solutions to environmental problems are

- Limits on population growth
- Development and reliance on new technologies
- Let markets solve environmental problems
- Create a new world order composed of national and global agreements

Limit Population Growth

Many studies demonstrate that (over)population can play a role in damaging a local environment.[35] However, there is still no conclusive evidence that overpopulation itself is a problem of *global* proportions at this point (see Chapter 18). The world population has indeed grown significantly since World War II and is expected to level off in 2050, but the unknown relationship of population and GDP makes it equally difficult to understand the implications of limiting population as environmental policy. China provides an interesting case study of this relationship because of its domestic policies on reproduction. While China's population has grown by approximately 4 percent since 2000, as cited earlier, its greenhouse gas emissions have grown by about 120 percent in this same time period. This indicates that income may have a much stronger relationship to environmental degradation than population. Studies that purport to show that income levels for all people in LDCs have risen since the early 1990s include India and China in their calculations, distorting the calculations for all developing nations. However, when it comes to demographics, it is these two countries that worry officials the most.[36]

Even without policies that limit population growth, the **demographic transition,** which accounts for population growth rates, could slow down naturally as people's income and standard of living increase. Assuming this is true, the global population problem is actually more a problem of unequal distribution of wealth between the have and have-not nations and of unequal distribution of income within developing societies. This explanation strongly echoes the sentiments of many structuralists. In other words, places with relatively low population growth rates have relatively high consumption rates, and thus have a more profound impact on the environment. The reverse would also be true of places like developing countries with relatively high population growth rates.

Does that mean that nothing should be done about current overpopulation problems in some nations? In the short term, many nations *should* make efforts and receive help to slow their population growth rate because of the economic burden more mouths place on their societies. Many have done this through education and by providing people with a means of birth control. For many humanists and culture experts, the empowerment of women and society's guarantee of political rights based on democratic principles are the best solutions to poverty and overpopulation problems.

In all cases, better income distribution is likely to slow population growth rates naturally. However, the point is that if slowing population growth rates are accompanied by an increase in income, population control alone will not solve most environmental problems and may even exacerbate them. For most experts, then, other policies and measures regulating patterns of consumption are needed to curb emissions and promote environmental sustainability.

New Technology

New technologies have offered some hope for significant changes in the way people consume. Since global warming has become the number one threat to the environment, renewable energy has become a trendy area of technological innovation. "Super grids," or high-tech networks that can transmit electricity in high volumes across long distances, are likely to replace outdated electrical grid systems in countries like the United States, allowing for more efficient transmission, distribution, and storage of energy. This system is much better suited for the prevailing renewable energy sources like wind and solar power, encouraging further investment in renewable energy. Several different automakers have released hybrid vehicles that get as many as 48 miles per gallon. The Nissan Leaf runs only on a rechargeable battery.

The use of biofuels as an efficient and viable source of energy is also being heavily explored, making more renewable nonfossil fuel resources to generate energy (see Chapter 19). Roughly 20 percent of U.S. landfills are now collecting the methane produced by waste to generate electricity.[37] The University of Minnesota is developing two cohabitating organisms, one which converts carbon dioxide into sugars and another that transforms sugars into diesel. MIT has been developing a liquid battery that will smooth out intermittent flows of energy from sources like solar and wind power. United Technologies has been studying ways to use low energy sources like enzymes to absorb carbon dioxide emissions from power plant stacks.[38]

A nation's access to modern technology affects more than just its carbon output. Technology is not politically or socially neutral. It often involves the use of dangerous chemicals and potentially damaging processes, but it has also helped cut down on pollution and solve a number of other, related problems. With the development of biofuels, for example, critics have also questioned the morality of using edible products in the production of energy when so many people in the world go hungry (see Chapter 18). Economic liberals in particular like to focus on technology as a factor that can do more good than harm when it comes to the environment, yet many businesses refrain from investing in technology until the government has first provided substantial grants and subsidies for research. As with anything, public support for government involvement can sometimes be difficult to gain. Even with government aid, many new technologies are unaffordable, especially in relation to older, more readily available technologies. Globalization and technology sharing have helped to overcome this problem, but many believe that globalization was also the mechanism by which world consumption was able to increase so dramatically, testing the earth's environmental limits.

In the case of technology, appropriateness is a major issue. Many poorer countries do not need or want more sophisticated technologies until they are better equipped to use them. In many cases, what markets produce in new technologies are not yet appropriate for many of the poorer LDCs. Access to this technology in developing countries has seen recent improvements in part as a response to the explosion of microcredit as a development tool. Many microfinance banks are now partnering with organizations like MicroEnergy Credits and KickStart to create green microfranchises for loan clients. KickStart, for example, requires that its products be highly profitable, affordable, portable, storable, easy to use, durable, made from common materials, culturally appropriate, and environmentally sustainable.[39] Its people are "in the field" and can assess what works best for people in different cultural and political settings.

▶ A HYBRID SOLUTION: MICROENERGY CREDITS[a]

As the number of actors involved in international environmental issues increases, the traditional categories describing the *types* of actors involved have in some instances become less relevant. MicroEnergy Credits (MEC), a Seattle-based "social enterprise," is an excellent example of this trend. They address a number of issues confronting LDCs by facilitating partnerships between businesses and NGOs, while capitalizing on agreements negotiated by IOs and states.

As described in the chapter, when Kyoto took effect in 2005, all the developed countries that participated became subject to limits on carbon emissions. Many businesses in these countries subsequently faced decisions about whether to limit their emissions or buy credits on the international market. MEC was established to help LDCs profit from the developed world's sudden demand for these carbon credits. By promoting clean technology, MEC has been able to reduce carbon outputs in LDCs and then sell these energy savings as carbon credits on the international market.

While the concept of using technology to free up credits is fairly common, the methods by which MEC has accomplished this are quite innovative. The first step in its unique system is forging a partnership with a microfinance institution, or an organization specializing in the banking needs of the poor. These banks are most well known for microcredit programs in LDCs, whereby entrepreneurs can obtain loans for as little as $25 in some places. MEC enters into a contract with the bank, helping them to develop and market green technologies for microloan clients. The clients are then able to purchase a piece of equipment that permits them to conduct business in a more energy efficient way and/or allows the clients to sell clean energy to others in the vicinity.

Once the bank has finalized information on the number of clients using this technology, MEC conducts an audit to determine the resulting reduction in carbon emissions. MEC purchases these carbon credits from the bank, aggregating and packaging them from their various bank partnerships so that they may be sold on the international market.

(continued)

In order to actually sell these credits, MEC has partnered with EcoSecurities, a larger company that specializes in the buying and selling of credits from developing countries. EcoSecurities then purchases these credits from MEC and securitizes them for the carbon market.

Such a system would not be possible without collaboration between many different actors. In this example, the details of the Kyoto Protocol were worked out through an IO, UNEP. Credit allowances were divided up on a per state basis (with the exception of the EU). Both MEC and EcoSecurities are technically for-profit businesses, taking a percentage of profits from each sale. However, many microfinance banks still rely heavily on donations to cover the high overhead costs involved in doing business in the developing world. Thanks to this system, MEC's partner banks now have an additional source of income. The combined efforts of these actors not only have resulted in the reduction of LDCs' carbon footprint, but have also directly impacted the lives of many impoverished individuals by providing them with access to energy, income, and even improvements in health.

[a]Georgina Allen researched and drafted the material in this box using information from MicroenergyCredits.com.

Some of the least technical solutions to global warming are actually considered to have some of the largest potential. Given that carbon sinks absorb roughly 60 percent of carbon emissions, their preservation seems an important factor in staving off major carbon accumulation in the atmosphere.[40] With the creation of a cap and trade system, companies selling carbon offsets in the form of reforestation have generated steam. These companies are also being hired to offset the carbon emissions of things that are not regulated by cap and trade. For example, some vacation companies are now offering zero carbon footprint trips. Additionally, depending on the location and the chosen method of reforestation, there are likely to be long-term financial benefits of reforesting.

Markets for the Environment

Despite the popularity of economic liberal ideas and globalization, the increasing severity of energy and environmental problems has raised many questions about the ability of markets to solve these problems. Kyoto ultimately resulted in the creation of a market-based system. Given the limited debate on the effectiveness of cap and trade, it seems likely that any successor to this treaty will continue to employ this system. The privatization of environmental problems has helped to reduce greenhouse gas emissions while generating significant amounts of wealth. The explosion of green, organic, and local products is readily apparent, with many big vendors now offering eco-friendly products. The entrance of green products into both household and financial markets is certainly a step in the right direction.

More businesses are taking into account objectives other than purely economic ones such as the "public interest" in supporting the environment. "Green products" and "fair trade" items have in fact become big business. Likewise, enterprises that specialize in the production of environmentally friendly items have become big investment opportunities. In an article titled "Will Big Business Save the Earth?" Jared Diamond describes the ways that three big American businesses are making a difference. Wal-Mart has dramatically reduced the fuel consumption of its truck fleets, eliminated packing waste, and phased out products like wild fish that are unsustainable. Coca-Cola is cutting back on water usage and using organic materials instead of petroleum to make bottles. Chevron is using cleaner practices as a way of avoiding future potential expenses in the form of oil spill cleanups, lawsuits, and retrofitting.[41]

In the case of NGOs, Lovins and Boyd make the case that nonprofit agencies have largely overlooked the ways in which business enterprises can also play a major role in dealing with climate change.[42]

Even so, free markets are not an end-all solution to environmental problems for a number of reasons. Economic costs of pollution are often hard to calculate. Some authority like the state has to impose sanctions on violators or assign property rights. Commodifying environmental problems makes them subject to the whims of the economy. As we saw in Chapter 19, the financial crisis has slowed investment in renewable energy. Furthermore, the cap and trade system in the EU has made permits subject to speculation, which as we also know from the financial crisis can have serious consequences.

In sum, the role of businesses as actors on environmental issues is consistent with the economic liberal IPE perspective that markets will ultimately provide the best solution to environmental problems. Some HILs believe that environmentally unfriendly products will eventually become undesirable, either because their true cost will be reflected in the price or because the preferences of consumers will change in favor of new green products. Mercantilists tend to believe that the state must play a more aggressive role in addressing environmental problems by outlawing environmentally damaging activities and taxing goods that are known to cause harm to the environment. Structuralists view environmental degradation in terms of elite control over scarce resources.

More National and Global Agreements: Yet Another New World Order

Given the hypercapitalistic nature of the world economy today, it is no surprise that the Kyoto treaty produced a market-based solution. Critics have always been cynical about capitalism and its effects on the environment. Although no comprehensive, post-capitalist system has been developed, the idea of sustainable development is beginning to take root among officials and NGOs dealing with the interrelated issues of development, food and hunger, energy, and the environment.[43]

Despite broad agreement about the worthiness of sustainable development, actually achieving it is another matter. The failure thus far to develop a global political economic system that encourages environmentalism, or even to negotiate a realistic successor to Kyoto, cannot be taken as evidence of ultimate failure. In the United States, many cities are adopting climate change mitigation or other environmental measures of their own.[44] In China, protests in many cities against big government projects are aimed at pressuring both the national and state governments to give local groups a bigger role in pollution and land use policies.[45] This is not to say that IOs are no longer at the mercy of nation-states. Whether states will endow them with more authority to act over the heads of their creators, however, is yet to be seen.

Even so, the lack so far of an adequate solution to global warming has left many pessimistic about the potential of IOs to solve these problems, especially given the competitive nature of states and markets in the global political economy. But with more being asked of countries of varied developmental stages, creating an all-encompassing successor to the Kyoto treaty has become a very complex task. A number of scientists in Germany and experts elsewhere have put forward the argument that it is time to move away from finding a successor to Kyoto and focus on other ways to deal with climate change.[46]

As in the case of most global negotiations, agreement usually comes down to the dominant major powers, and in this case that will inevitably be the United States, the EU, Japan, Canada, and Australia but also China, Brazil, India, and a number of other emerging countries. In this case, time is not running out, but rather the objective changes from preventing a global crisis to adjusting to what is sure to be one.

CONCLUSION: PLAN FOR A WORLD WHEN THERE IS NO GOING BACK

Since World War II, environmental issues have shifted from issues dealt with mainly by intermittently cooperating nation-states. With accelerated industrialization and globalization in the 1980s, environmental problems became more global and interconnected with development, energy, and security. Until recently, cooperative efforts to solve international environmental problems have ended up on the rocks of history either due to the unwillingness of states to sacrifice domestic interests for the sake of international cooperation or because of the confrontational political-economic relationship of the North to the South.

In the 1990s, the magnitude of scientific data and stories of remarkable weather changes pointed to global warming as a scientific fact. Meanwhile, globalization increased industrial production and world consumption, releasing unprecedented levels of emissions into the atmosphere. These developments fostered a sense of urgency around the issue of climate change and developing alternative energy sources to oil, helping spread awareness of the impact of climate change and other environmental problems along with raising public support for action. Many suggest that with the onset of these events,

a perfect storm has formed that threatens the planet and humankind.[47]

The onset of a financial crisis in 2007 also made addressing environmental issues all the more financially difficult and hard to socially adjust to. Many nation-states continue to have major difficulties reconciling their domestic needs and interests with pressures to cooperate with other states, IOs, and NGOs, to solve environmental problems. This has been demonstrated by the incredible difficulty the world has had in negotiating a successor to the Kyoto accords.

In this situation, the question of *cui bono* is still on the mind of policymakers, businesses, and the public alike. Agreement at Doha assumes that these actors still have choices to make about how to solve this problem. While IOs can help coordinate policy, their overall effectiveness is still quite limited. We suggest that they must not be viewed as the only—let alone the primary—vehicles of change, as communities, states, NGOs, and businesses can all influence the choices of governments and individuals. Solutions to pressing environmental issues require something more dynamic and complicated than open markets alone.

We suggest that the primary issue now is not how much time the world has left to establish a new global order—one that steers the earth away from the risks associated with the ongoing game of chicken between those who don't believe in climate change and those who do. Rather, the evidence is increasing that the earth is relatively speaking quickly moving into a crisis. The climate change crisis raises many issues of efficiency but also equity, social justice, and fairness. Primarily it is a security threat to the planet as a whole. How and what to do about it should be the new main objective of the next COP meeting. A major issue to be dealt with will be a shift in political, economic, and social values.

In the opening session of the Rio Earth Summit, Maurice Strong commented: "The concept of national sovereignty has been an immutable, indeed sacred, principle of international relations. It is a principle which will yield only slowly and reluctantly to the new imperatives of global environmental cooperation. It is simply not feasible for sovereignty to be exercised unilaterally by individual nation states, however powerful. The global community must be assured of environmental security."[48] Given the global threat at hand, Strong's comments make one wonder how much globalization there really is, or if states cannot appreciate enough the extent to which their interests are threatened by environmental issues they like to think they have control over. Realists would caution them that there are times to consider cooperation as the best means of achieving their self-interests.

One would think that scientific hard evidence about how warm temperatures are and how bad off the environment is would have more weight than the assuredness behind speculation related to how much energy is left buried in the ground. Obviously it is politically easier to deny something that we do not want to believe could happen than to care about it and cooperate to find ways to deal with it. And yet as in the case of the tragedy of the commons, the situation is made worse by the *freedom* to do so.

In this sense, it would be a tragedy to know all along what the earth is in for if not more is done to adjust to the impact of global climate change. When is skepticism rational or realistic in the face of so much evidence that humankind may soon be unable to inhabit the earth? As Keynes and others note, quite often rational choices (at the time) do not result in good outcomes for all of society. In this case, cooperation would be necessary, right, and just.

KEY TERMS

climate change   512
United Nations Environment
    Program (UNEP)   516
chlorofluorocarbon (CFC)   517
ozone depletion   517
Montreal Protocol   517
Tragedy of the Commons   518

collective goods   518
carbon sinks   521
Earth Summit   522
sustainable development   522
United Nations Framework
    Convention on Climate Change
    (UNFCCC)   522

Kyoto Protocol   522
emission credits   522
cap and trade   522
carbon tax   526
demographic transition   529

DISCUSSION QUESTIONS

1. Discuss the tragedy of the commons. In what ways does this concept contribute to our understanding of environmental problems?
2. The authors assert that environmental problems have become increasingly global in scope.

What factors—political, economic, and social—contributed most to this trend? Explain. (*Note:* The category *economic* includes items such as trade and finance and also the role of knowledge and technology.)

3. Do you believe that climate change poses a serious threat to the planet? Discuss the roles that the financial crisis, rapid technological innovation, dramatic increases in world consumption, and international security play in solving global warming. How is each of these things beneficial and detrimental to environmentalism? Explain.
4. In considering the outcome of the Copenhagen, Durban, and Doha talks on climate change, do you think nation-states are capable of solving global environmental problems, or should we look to IOs such as the United Nations to play a larger role in dealing with these issues? What conditions or barriers limit the effectiveness of states, IOs, and NGOs when it comes to these problems?
5. What responsibility, if any, do developing nations have for solving global environmental problems? Do you believe that their participation inevitably means sacrificing economic growth, or environmental catastrophe? Ditto the developed states.

SUGGESTED READINGS

Lester R. Brown. *Plan B 4.0: Mobilizing to Save Civilization*. New York: W. W. Norton, 2006.

Thomas Friedman. *Hot, Flat, and Crowded: Why We Need a Green Revolution and How It Can Renew America*. New York: Picador, 2009.

Paul Gilding. *The Great Disruption*. London: Bloomsbury Press, 2011.

Bill McKibben. "Global Warming's Terrifying New Math." *Rolling Stone*, August 2, 2012.

Detlef Sprinz and Tapani Vaahtoranta. "International Environmental Policy," *International Organization*, 48 (Winter 1994), pp. 77–106.

NOTES

1. See http://blogs.scientificamerican.com/observations/2012/10/30/did-climate-change-cause-hurricane-sandy/.
2. See, for example, Rachael Carson, *Silent Spring* (Boston, MA: Houghton Mifflin, 1962).
3. Donella H. Meadows, Dennis L. Meadows, Jorgen Randers, and William W. Brehens III, *The Limits to Growth: A Report for the Club of Rome Project on the Predicament of Mankind* (New York: Universe Books, 1974).
4. See the Council on Environment Quality and Department of State, *The Global 2000 Report to the President: Entering the Twenty-First Century* (New York: Penguin Books, 1982).
5. Cited in Jessica Tuchman Matthews, "Environmental Policy," in Robert J. Art and Seyom Brown, eds., *United States Foreign Policy: The Search for a New Role* (New York: Macmillan, 1993), p. 234.
6. Julian Simon and Herman Kahn, eds., *The Resourceful Earth: A Response to Global 2000* (Oxford: Basic Blackwell, 1982).
7. See World Resources Institute, "Climate Change: A Global Concern," *World Resources 1990–1991* (Washington, DC: World Resources Institute, 1990), p. 15, Table 2.2.
8. See Matthews, "Environmental Policy," p. 239.
9. See Detlef Sprinz and Tapani Vaahtoranta, "International Environmental Policy," *International Organization*, 48 (Winter 1994), pp. 77–106.
10. See: www.climateactionnetwork.org.
11. Garrett Hardin, "The Tragedy of the Commons," *Science*, 162 (December 1968), pp. 1243–1248.
12. See the World Trade Organization website at www.wto.org for a detailed description of WTO activities that deal with the environment.
13. See www.worldbank.org.
14. See Bianca Jagger, "COP18 Failed to Turn Down the Heat," *Common Dreams*, December 12, 2012.
15. See *The Stern Review on the Economics of Climate Change*, October 2006.
16. *An Inconvenient Truth* (Los Angeles, CA: Lawrence Bender Productions, 2006).
17. See Thomas Friedman, *Hot, Flat, and Crowded: Why We Need A Green Revolution* (New York: Farrar, Straus, and Giroux, 2008).
18. Richard Lindzen, "Climate of Fear," *Wall Street Journal*, April 12, 2006, p. 1.
19. See James Broder, "Climate Change Doubt Is Tea Party Article of Faith," *New York Times*, October 20, 2010.

20. See http://www.un.org/geninfo/bp/enviro.html.

21. For a detailed description of the Kyoto Protocol, see "Kyoto Protocol to the United Nations Convention on Climate Change," at http://unfcc.int/resource/docs/convkp/kpeng.html.

22. CIBC World Markets Inc, "StrategEcon—March 27, 2008," March 27, 2008, at http://research.cibcwm.com/economic_public/download/smar08.pdf.

23. "What India Has to Offer in Copenhagen," *Economist*, December 3, 2009.

24. See John M. Broder, "5 Nations Forge Pact on Climate; Goals Go Unmet," *New York Times*, December 19, 2009.

25. For a more detailed discussion, see Michael A. Levi, "Copenhagen's Inconvenient Truth: How to Salvage the Climate Conference," *Foreign Affairs*, 88 (September/October 2009), pp. 92–104.

26. See Broder, "5 Nations Forge Pact on Climate; Goals Go Unmet."

27. See Bill McKibben, "Global Warming's Terrifying New Math," *Rolling Stone*, August 2, 2012.

28. John Broder, "From a Theory to a Consensus on Emissions," *New York Times*, May 16, 2009.

29. See http://www.democracynow.org/2011/12/12/climate_activists_durban_deal_is_very.

30. McKibben, "Global Warming's Terrifying New Math."

31. See Jagger, "COP18 Filed to Turn Down the Heat."

32. See Jagger, Ibid, and McKibben, "Global Warming's Terrifying New Math."

33. See http://www.huffingtonpost.com/2012/11/18/world-bank-climate-change-report_n_2156082.html.

34. John M. Broder, "At Climate Talks, a Struggle Over Aid for Poorer Nations," *New York Times*, December 12, 2012.

35. Ibid.

36. See, for example, David Dollar, "Globalization, Poverty, and Inequality," in Michael Weinstein, ed., *Globalization: What's New?* (New York: Columbia University Press, 2005), pp. 96–128.

37. Al Gore, *Our Choice: How We Can Solve the Climate Crisis* (Emnaus, PA: Melcher Media and Rodale, 2009).

38. Matthew Wald, "Energy Department Aid for Scientists on the Edge," *New York Times*, October 25, 2009.

39. See KickStart's website for a description of their products at http://www.kickstart.org/products/.

40. John Timmer, "Have We Started to Fill Our Carbon Sinks?" *ARS Technica*, November 18, 2009, at http://arstechnica.com/news/2009/11/have-we-started-to-fill-our-carbon-sinks.ars.

41. See Jared Diamond, "Will Big Business Save the Earth?" *New York Times*, December 5, 2009.

42. L. Hunter Lovins and Boyd Cohn, *Climate Capitalism: Capitalism in the Age of Climate Change* (New York: Hill and Wang, 2011).

43. See, for example, Paul Gilding, *The Great Disruption* (London: Bloomsbury Press, 2011).

44. See Juliet Eilperin, "Cities, States Aren't Waiting for US Action on Climate," *Washington Post*, November 8, 2006.

45. See Keith Bradsher, "Saying No to Growth in China," *New York Times*, November 7, 2012.

46. Diet Zeit article.

47. See Gilding, "The Great Disruption."

48. See http://unfcc.int/resource/docs/convkp/kpeng.html.

GLOSSARY

Agro-industrial model   The approach to agricultural production that has been most popular in the industrialized nations. It emphasizes production efficiency gained by the application of new (high) technology and fertilizers, and farming on big parcels of land to increase commodity production. Controversy surrounds its usefulness and impact on developing nations. See *De-peasantisation*.

Alternative tourism   An alternative to mass tourism experiences of the standard "sun, sea, and sand" formula. Ecotourism is an example of alternative tourism meant to promote responsible travel to natural areas that conserve the environment and improve the well-being of local people.

Anti-Ballistic Missile (ABM) Treaty   A 1972 agreement between the United States and the Soviet Union not to deploy more than one defensive missile system each. The rationale behind the agreement was that it enhanced strategic deterrence and mutual assured destruction. See *Mutually Assured Destruction*.

Appreciate   A term used in foreign exchange markets to describe the rise in value of one currency relative to another. Currencies tend to appreciate when the demand for them increases. If a country's currency appreciates too much, it will cause that country's exports to decrease. See *Depreciate*.

Appropriability theory   A theory that transnational corporations engage in foreign direct investment in order to keep firm-specific advantages from being appropriated or acquired by competitors.

Arbitrage   Buying a product in a lower price market in order to sell it in a higher price market. Price differences between markets are often the result of differing laws, taxes, and regulations. When legislative action increases the price of a good that is available in neighboring jurisdictions at a cheaper price, smuggling is encouraged, which fuels a black market for the good.

Assimilation   A process by which one adopts the customs and values of another culture. Relative to migration, assimilation implies that a person's original culture is replaced by the prevailing culture in the destination country.

Asylum   Refuge for a displaced person who cannot return to his or her country of origin because of fear of persecution on account of race, religion, nationality, membership in a particular social group, or political opinion. An asylum seeker solicits permanent residence in another country through application to that country's courts, often from within that state's territory.

Asymmetric information   A problem that exists especially in rural credit markets, in which a lender does not know what borrowers all know, which is who is trustworthy and who is not. This lack of information forces lenders to charge high interest rates, which discourages borrowing in general.

Austerity   Deep cuts in government spending—especially during a recession—designed to reduce a government's budget deficit or free up resources to repay debts to creditors. Austerity policies typically include increased taxes, layoffs of state workers, and reductions in spending on public goods, social programs, and pensions that disproportionately hurt the poorest segments of society.

Balance of payments (BoP)   A financial tabulation of all international economic transactions involving a nation in a given year. How much money flows into or out of a country annually impacts the value of its currency, interest rates, and trade policy, among other things. Ideally, countries would earn as much as they spend. One of the main roles of the IMF until the 1980s was to manage the international balance of payments.

Balance of power   A popular and controversial realist theory that ascribes to states a certain amount of power based on a variety of tangible and intangible factors. In theory, states cluster (or ally with one another) based on shared national interests—in opposition to states with conflicting interests. Peace among nations is usually associated with an *approximate equilibrium* in the distribution of power between nations in this system. This distribution of power results in a bipolar (2), tripolar (3), or multipolar (3+) structure. Others argue that peace is achieved when a hegemon, or dominant power, orders the security structure—referred to as unipolarity or hegemony. See *Bipolarity* and *Hegemony*.

Benign mercantilism   A defensive strategy that seeks to protect the domestic economy against damaging international political and economic forces. What one nation intends as benign can be interpreted by another as malevolent (hostile).

Bicycle theory   A theory stating that, just as a bicycle must keep moving to maintain its balance, the European Union must constantly move forward (in terms of regional integration) in order to maintain political unity. The term is also applied to trade policies in the context of continuing to bring down tariff barriers for fear of protectionism setting back in (the bicycle falling over).

Biofuels   Alternatives to petroleum that are made from plants high in sugar or vegetable oils. Many politicians hope to reduce dependency on oil imports by absorbing surplus agricultural commodities and providing farmers with an opportunity to maintain production and price levels for their agricultural commodities. Experts disagree about how efficient biofuel production is.

Bipolarity   The condition of an international security structure managed by two centers of power. Theoretically, each dominant state or "pole" and those states in its "sphere of influence" compete with others to keep the distribution of power relatively equal between them. See *Cold War*.

Bolsa Família   A widely praised Brazilian anti-poverty program begun in 2003. The Brazilian federal government provides low-income families a monthly cash grant on the condition that their children attend school and get all required vaccinations.

Bourgeoisie   In Marxian analysis, the bourgeoisie is the capitalist class, made up of those who own the means of production. In everyday language, this term often refers to the wealthy and cultural elites of society who have the preponderance of political power. See *Proletariat*.

Brain drain   The exodus of highly-educated, professional migrants out of their country of origin toward economic or social opportunities in another country. This phenomenon is especially significant for Third World countries, whose most skilled residents often move to the First World.

Branch factory syndrome   A syndrome where the headquarters of many major transnational corporations fear losing information to a rival firm if it is transferred to subsidiaries of the corporation in other countries. Therefore, what information that is transferred tends to be less important.

Bretton Woods system and conference   Bretton Woods, New Hampshire was the site of a series of meetings in July 1944 among representatives of the Allied Powers of World War II (including the United States, Britain, France, Canada, the Soviet Union, and many smaller states). The Bretton Woods agreements sought to create a post–World War II international liberal economic order managed by the International Monetary Fund, the World Bank, and (later) the General Agreement on Tariffs and Trade.

Cap and trade   A controversial policy proposal put forward by some states in the Kyoto accord and at the 2009 Copenhagen meeting that allows countries to buy and sell or swap emission production quotas with one another in the international market. States would not be allowed to go over their emissions limit without purchasing (or trading for) a portion of another state's emissions quota. Some view cap and trade as a market solution to an environmental problem.

Capital controls   Government rules and regulations that seek to limit or control inflows and outflows of money or international investment funds in one or more nations. The goal of capital controls is to maintain orderly international capital movements and prevent financial and foreign exchange instability.

Capitalism   A political ideology identified with the owners of capital and society's wealth. Today, however, it usually refers to a market-dominated system of economic organization based on private property and free markets.

Carbon sinks   Typically, forests and large bodies of water that absorb considerable amounts of carbon dioxide from the atmosphere. Planting forests became an acceptable method of offsetting carbon emissions for countries that are party to the Kyoto Protocol.

Carbon tax   A controversial policy that levies a tax on the amount of carbon produced by an industry or nation–state, thereby improving air quality while requiring air polluters to pay more for the negative effects of carbon-based energy.

Cartel   A group of firms or nations that cooperate with one another to control the production and price of a commodity or a particular product. The Organization of Petroleum Exporting Countries (OPEC) is an example of an oil cartel that in 1973 drove up the price of oil to punish states that supported Israel during its Six-Day War with Arab states.

Central bank   The chief monetary institution of a nation. Central banks regulate domestic financial institutions and influence domestic interest and foreign exchange rates. The central bank of Great Britain is the Bank of England, which issues British currency.

Chain migration   A process in which migrants move to "link up" with family members or social networks in their new community or society.

Chimerica   Niall Ferguson's term that accounts for the growing interdependence between China and the United States. China has made a good deal of money based on exports to the United States, which in turn needs China's investments in U.S. businesses and U.S. Treasury securities to offset growing debt. Meanwhile, China is also under pressure to invest more in its own economy so as to overcome many of its own socio-economic problems.

Chlorofluorocarbons (CFCs)   CFCs are compounds of atoms of chlorine, fluorine, and carbon found in cleaning solvents, refrigerants, and aerosols. They are known to deplete the ozone layer around the earth and to contribute to global warming.

Circular migration   Back-and-forth migration between two or more locations; part of an ongoing pattern of temporary emigration from and return to the country of origin.

Citizenship   A legal term related to one who owes allegiance to a particular nation or government. Recent controversy surrounds the issue of citizenship requirements for immigrants, asylum seekers, and other groups of people who seek to live and work in another country.

Classical mercantilism   Historically, state policies that focused on intentionally gaining national wealth and power at the expense of other states. These measures included export subsidies, import barriers, and other efforts to generate trade surpluses and protect domestic producers.

Classical realism   A theory that asserts that the most important actors in international relations are states, which cause wars and international conflicts as they promote their national interests and seek to enhance their power over other countries.

Claw back   An EU effort to turn certain generic names and icons associated with recognizable goods such as "champagne" into registered geographical indications.

Climate change   An increase in the temperature of the earth's atmosphere that results from the greenhouse effect. A hotly debated topic at the December 2009 meeting in Copenhagen as to how much climate change is caused by human-made and natural forces.

Cold War   A phrase first used by Bernard Baruch in 1948 to describe the military and political confrontation between the United States and the Soviet Union and their respective allies that did not turn into a (hot) military conflict, many theorists argue, because of the devastation associated with the use of nuclear weapons. Nonetheless a period of great tensions and *threats* to use military force.

Collective goods   Tangible or intangible goods that, available to all members of society or consumers of the goods, can be denied to no one. The issue of collective goods raises questions about who should pay for these goods when they are provided to the entire group. No single person or entity has an incentive to pay for them and thus enjoys a "free ride" when others do help pay. Examples include clean air, parks, roads, and national defense.

Colonialism   The practice of the major European powers (and later the United States, Germany, and Japan) of taking over or otherwise controlling weaker states or regions. See *Neoimperialism.*

Commercialization of sovereignty   The process of one state renting out commercial privileges and protections to citizens and companies from another state. Examples include offering flags of convenience and serving as tax havens.

Commodification   The process whereby a price is established for a commodity or item that can be bought and sold. Karl Polanyi and others argue that commodification of land, labor, and capital was necessary in England in the seventeenth and eighteenth centuries to make capitalism work. In the context of tourism today, commodification refers to the transformation of cultural objects and values into commodities in response to tourist preferences and demands.

Common Agricultural Policy (CAP) Agricultural export subsidies, tariffs, and income-support measures that the European Union employs to help EU farmers. While many big farmers and agribusinesses support these measures, consumer groups oppose them for claiming a large part of the EU budget and driving small farmers out of the market.

Common market A level of economic integration in the European Community (now the EU) beyond a customs union. See *Customs union*. A common market promotes the freedom of movement of capital, labor, goods, and services. Until the 1990s, the common market was also the popular name of what was essentially the European community.

Community supported agriculture (CSA) Small local food producers, marketers, or collectives who distribute produce to their customers on a weekly or biweekly basis. Part of an effort to encourage local food production, sustainability, and the enhancement of local markets.

Comparative advantage See *Law of comparative advantage*.

Compulsory license A license that a government grants to a local private company or state agency, with or without the consent of the rights holder, to produce and sell a good under patent.

Conditionality A controversial policy of the International Monetary Fund that ties short-term loans to certain conditions designed to improve *current account* balances. In general, the making of loans subject to domestic economic reforms that also promote economic liberal policies and values. See *Structural Adjustment Policies*.

Conspiracism A political culture widespread in Iran and Arab countries that blames covert Western and Israeli manipulation for regional or national problems. Some scholars worry that this mind-set encourages extremism by engendering a mind-set of permanent suspicion toward the West and Israel.

Constructivism A school of thought in international political economy arguing that international structures and institutions have no intrinsic causal power distinct from the values, beliefs, and interests that underlie them. States are not only political actors, but also social actors insofar as they adhere to rules and norms that reflect society's values and beliefs. These values are not static but are the result of ongoing social construction.

Contagion The spread of a financial crisis from one national economy to other national economies through international linkages such as currency, money, commodity markets, and shifting market psychology.

Copyrights Government-granted rights to artists and creators to prevent others from reproducing or publishing their work without permission. This legal protection is granted to the producers of books, movies, television programs, music, magazines, photographs, software, and databases.

Core A term used in Modern world system analysis in reference to the developed capitalist part of the global economic system, also known as the North. The *periphery*, or South, refers to the less developed regions of the system. See *Modern world system*.

Corn Laws Protectionist trade barriers that reflected the interests of the land-owning farmers from 1815 to 1846 and that restricted agricultural imports into Great Britain. When the interests of manufacturers gained control of the Parliament the Corns Laws were repealed, signifying the emergence of economic liberal ideas about free trade.

Corporate social responsibility A term used to describe the efforts of TNCs (and domestic businesses as well) to behave in ways that demonstrate respect for communities and nature. Corporations such as Nike often adopt these practices because they generate business for the corporation.

Council of the European Union A main lawmaking body of the EU, composed of a single representative from each member nation. Ministers from different states specialize in a variety of issues. The main functions of the Council are to decide European legislation that often requires cooperation with the Commission and the Parliament. The Council's most important areas of decision-making powers are in foreign policy, fiscal policies, and economic policies.

Credit default swaps Schemes in the United States whereby investors could, in effect, buy insurance against the possibility that big banks would default on repaying their loans. Many investors covered themselves by betting that the banks would both fail and not fail. When subprime defaults and bankruptcies rose, the banks and AIG did not have the money to pay claims on CDSs, which helped precipitate the U.S. financial crisis.

Crony capitalism　A derogatory term applied to close business–government relations in Asian and other countries, especially when these links foster corruption. Often offered as an explanation for financial crises or as a reason for failure to achieve development.

Cui bono? (kwee bo no)　A term that literally means "who benefits?" Susan Strange advised us to use the question as a place to start when analyzing any IPE issue. As benefits drive actions, so we should "follow the money" to discover in whose interest are the actions and institutional processes under study.

Cultural citizenship　An understanding of citizenship that refers not simply to legal rights but also to a sense of belonging and entitlement that is achieved through cultural difference rather than assimilation.

Currency crisis　A condition that occurs when a nation's currency suffers a substantial short-term drop in its value as a result of a financial bubble, a speculative attack, or another international financial situation. Some economic historians argue that currency crises are endemic to capitalism.

Currency exchange rates　The amount of money or goods a currency of one country will buy when converted to the currency (money) of another country. Exchange rates continuously change as a result of the supply and demand for money, which in turn helps establish the price of goods and services in each country.

Customs union　A group of nations that agree to eliminate trade barriers among themselves and adopt a unified system of external trade barriers. The Treaty of Rome created a customs union in the form of the European Economic Community.

Defensive modernization　Efforts to catch up with other states by reorganizing the government, military, economy, legal system, and other institutions. During the nineteenth century, the Ottoman Empire pursued defensive modernization in order to match Europe's growing imperial power but met with limited success. The inability of the Middle East to modernize is variously blamed on a lack of separation of religion and state, cultural immobilism, and lack of political freedom.

Demographic dividend　Future economic growth caused by a rapidly growing young population in countries such as India and Turkey.

Demographic transition　The point at which population growth rates decrease as birth rates decrease and per-capita income levels rise. The argument often made by those who reject the idea that limiting population growth alone will lead to economic development or solve global hunger.

Demonstration effect　A sense of inferiority related to the desire for, but inability to purchase, expensive material objects possessed by tourists. This happens usually in the case of tourism where locals, especially youth, come to desire the material objects—and emulate the values, lifestyles, and behavior—of wealthier foreign tourists.

De-peasantisation　When peasants or small farmers are driven off the land by government policies or agribusiness practices that lead to low income for producers. A variety of trade practices are often cited for having the same effect on peasants.

Dependency theory　A theory of the relationship between industrialized (*core*) nations and less developed (*periphery*) nations that stresses the many linkages that exist between them to make less developed countries dependent on richer nations. These linkages include trade, finance, and technology.

Depreciate　A term used in foreign exchange markets to describe when the value of one currency falls relative to the value of another currency. See *Appreciate* and *Devaluation*. Currency depreciation can be both a benefit and cost to a nation.

Devaluation　Also termed currency depreciation. A situation in which the value of the domestic currency is reduced relative to that of foreign currencies. Devaluation increases the prices of imported goods, while making exports relatively less costly for foreign buyers.

Developmental capitalism　A term used to describe the system of political economy of postwar Japan where state policies encouraged industrial growth, especially through export expansion. Japan's policies became a model for other developing nations, especially in Southeast Asia.

Developmental state　An interventionist government whose bureaucracy uses financial, fiscal, and investment policies to foster rapid industrialization. It guides private sector investments, supports industries most likely to promote national development, and encourages exports by private companies. The term is usually used to describe four post–World War II Asian states: Japan, South Korea, Taiwan, and Singapore.

Dialectical process　A process whereby contradictions between two conditions or opposing forces result in something new. A thesis, countered by its antithesis, produces a synthesis of the two. This idea was made popular by Karl Marx and many of his followers who subscribed to his philosophy and ideals.

Diaspora   A transnational community whose members share a common homeland, history, and ethnic identity despite their citizenship in other countries. Diasporas may be tied to a particular nation-state or simply reflect a particular national identity.

Discourse analysis   A tool often used by constructivists who trace changes in language and rhetoric in the speeches and works of important officials or actors on the state or international level. The focus is on officials who talk their state's interests into existence, sometimes by adopting a discourse that resonates with an important lobbying group or sector of public opinion.

Dispute Settlement Panel (DSP)   A panel of the World Trade Organization composed of impartial trade experts who rule on trade disputes. The panel can authorize trade sanctions on member states that violate WTO rules and do not comply with a DSP's recommendations.

Double burden   A situation facing low- and middle-income countries in which there is simultaneously significant malnutrition and obesity amongst the population. While some poor people must deal with lack of food and infectious diseases, others suffer from overnutrition—obesity and associated chronic diseases such as diabetes—due to consumption of fatty, high-calorie, processed foods.

Earth Summit   The 1992 meeting in Rio de Janeiro—officially titled the UN Conference on the Environment and Development—that focused on ways to sustain economic development while preserving the environment. The meeting produced a Biological Diversity Treaty and set in motion an agreement on greenhouse emissions cuts that resulted in the Kyoto Protocol in 1996.

Economic integration   The process by which a group of nation-states agrees to reduce protectionist measures, thereby exposing their industries to more competitive producers, for the sake of creating a larger and more tightly connected system of markets. See *Integration*.

Economic liberalism   The ideology and IPE perspective that holds that nations are best off when the role of the state in the economy is minimized. Economic

liberalism derives in part from fear of state abuse of power and in part from the philosophy of individualism and liberty of the Enlightenment. Economic liberal ideas have been popular since the late 1970s and served as the foundation for the policies associated with globalization.

Economic nationalism   A variation of mercantilist ideas. Economic nationalism holds that states have to intervene in the market for the sake of their wealth and power. Alexander Hamilton and Friedrich List are two famous proponents of economic nationalism.

Economic union   A degree of economic integration that goes beyond that found in a customs union. An economic union eliminates both tariff and nontariff barriers to trade and finance among a group of countries. It also relegates a good deal of political and economic authority to a central political agency or group of institutions. See the *European Union (EU)*.

Ecotourism   Responsible travel to natural areas that conserves the environment and improves the well-being of local people. Ecotourism has become a profitable business venture in different parts of the world.

Embedded liberalism   Under the Bretton Woods economic system, states were to be responsible for management of the domestic economy but within an economic liberal international system that brought down trade barriers and opened up states to the freer movement of finance and capital. As states gradually pursued these policies, this compromise would become *implanted* in the minds of actors, institutional procedures, and society. *See Keynesian compromise.*

Emerging economies   Nations making a transition from state-controlled systems of political economy to more market-oriented policies. Includes China, India, Indonesia, Malaysia, the Philippines, South Korea, Thailand, Argentina, Brazil, and the Russian Federation. By the late 2000s, many of these nations played an increasingly large role in different international institutions and agencies.

Emission credits   An implementation mechanism for the Kyoto Protocol, which allows countries to buy and sell carbon dioxide production quotas. See *Kyoto Protocol*. Many experts support the idea because it establishes a market for these credits, and makes markets part of the solution to climate change.

Epistemic communities   Networks of experts working on a particular international problem who often frame the issue for policy makers and the public, and offer solutions. For example, an epistemic community has mobilized around the issue of global climate change, with many scientists, nongovernmental organizations, and the media bringing attention to the threat and advocating solutions.

Euro zone Another term for the seventeen countries in the European Monetary Union that use the euro as their currency.

European Central Bank (ECB) Established in 1998, the ECB works with national banks to define and implement the single monetary policy of the European Monetary Union. It conducts foreign-exchange operations and manages foreign reserves with an objective of promoting financial stability.

European Commission An unelected body created in 1967 whose commissioners are appointed by member states but who are not responsible to them. The EC implements the treaties agreed to by EU member states. Commissioners propose new laws and run the day to day operations of Community affairs.

European Council A body made up of the heads of state and government of EU members that makes strategic political decisions regarding foreign relations, dispute resolution, and amendments to the EU treaties.

European Court of Justice (ECJ) The highest court in the European Union, made up of one representative from each member state. The ECJ's official function is to ensure that European Union law is applied uniformly in each member state.

European Economic Community (EEC) The original European "Common Market" of six countries created by the Treaty of Rome in 1957—France, (West) Germany, Italy, Belgium, the Netherlands, and Luxembourg—that reduced trade barriers amongst one another and established a common tariff around the community to protect its producers. In 1967, the EEC merged with the European Coal and Steel Community and the European Atomic Energy Commission to become the European Community.

European Free Trade Area (EFTA) Promoted by Great Britain in 1960, it was comprised of states that did not belong to the European Economic Community. Its members removed trade barriers among themselves, but maintained the right to levy tariffs on third countries.

European Monetary Union (EMU) Also called the Economic and Monetary Union. The agreement of many European countries to adopt a common currency—the euro—which was introduced in 2002.

At the time of this printing, there are 17 members of the Euro zone. The global economic crisis has generated some reconsideration by a number of states as to whether they can comply with conditions established to stay in the EMU.

European Parliament (EP) An institution unlike a traditional parliament. Its elected representatives from European Union member states sit with their peers from the same party in other states, rather than with their national colleagues. Socialists from all EU nations act together, for example, as do conservatives, Christian Democrats, Greens, and other party groups. The EP's main political functions are, first, to participate in drafting policy programs and European legislation; second, to cooperate with the Council of Ministers in European legislation; third, to vote on the EU budget, which is negotiated by the Council; and fourth, to approve and control the European Commission.

European Union (EU) Successor organization to the European Community as defined by the 1992 Maastricht Treaty. Note that the EU is not yet a union in the formal sense. For now it preserves some member states' rights. At the same time, in some policy areas true supra-national institutions with authority independent of states do exist within the EU.

Export subsidies Government payments to producers that effectively reduce the price of an exported product, making it more attractive to potential foreign buyers.

Export-oriented growth A tactic for economic growth that focuses on bolstering exports and integration into global markets. Popular amongst many emerging market economies such as China. Contrast this policy with *Import-substituting industrialization.*

Fair trade Often presented as an alternative to free trade, fair trade mixes protectionism and free trade to "level the playing field" for domestic producers. The fair trade movement is also defined as an initiative spearheaded by international nongovernmental organizations to provide higher prices to producers of certified commodities such as coffee, cocoa, and timber in developing countries.

False consciousness A belief of the workers in the legitimacy of capitalism. The superior financial resources of the capitalists typically means that procapitalist messages—the benefits of free trade, the need for low taxes on the rich, the problems with unions, and so on—will be stronger than those favored by workers. According to Marxists, capitalists not only exploit workers but manipulate the beliefs of workers so that they are ignorant of, or apathetic about, their own exploitation.

Flags of convenience   Legal businesses and criminals are permitted to register their airplanes and ships in a country even though they will conduct most of their business (licit or illicit) elsewhere. In exchange, host countries typically receive lucrative registration fees, payoffs, or "protection money."

Flexible-exchange-rate system   Theoretically, fixed exchange rates are determined by international agreements among states, while flexible exchange rates are determined by market forces. See *Currency exchange rates*.

Food First   A thesis introduced in the 1970s by Frances Moore Lappé stating that hunger is actually caused by deficiencies in income and land distribution, rather than lack of food production or overpopulation. According to the proponents of this theory, hunger is *not endemic* to less developed countries, but is a *byproduct* of their political and economic relationships with the industrialized nations.

Food security   An element of national security that expresses concerns about the security of a nation's food supply.

Food sovereignty   A concept stressing the rights of farmers in developing countries to control their own land, seeds, and water and to grow diverse and nutritious foods. It also includes the right of local communities to control their own systems of food and agricultural production and consumption in the face of pressures from transnational agribusinesses.

Forcing effect   A situation where a market for a product will be created when demand for it is high enough. Growing demand for large, environmentally-friendly building projects has spurred the creation of certain green building supplies.

Foreign direct investment (FDI)   Investments made by a company (often a transnational corporation) in production, distribution, or sales facilities in another country. The term *direct* implies a measure of control exercised by the parent company on resources in a host nation.

Foreign exchange rates   See *Currency exchange rates*.

Fracking   See *Hydraulic fracking*.

Framing   A term that constructivists use to describe the process by which global actors define the essence of a particular global problem—what is causing it, who is involved, its consequences, and how to resolve it—for the purpose of promoting a particular explanation or outlook about this problem.

Free trade   One of the most popular policies advocated by economic liberals. In keeping with the *laissez-faire* notion that government intervention in the economy undermines efficiency and overall wealth, free trade removes protectionist measures (tariffs, quotas, etc.) that are designed to insulate domestic producers from international competition. It has been a major goal of most international trade institutions since 1947.

General Agreement on Tariffs and Trade (GATT)   An international agreement in 1947 that became the basis of international trade negotiations to reduce trade barriers among its many member nations. GATT negotiations took place over a period of years and were termed "rounds," as in the Kennedy round and the Tokyo round, which reduced trade barriers for manufactured goods. The Uruguay round aimed to create freer trade in services and agricultural goods. GATT was incorporated into the World Trade Organization in 1995.

General Agreement on Trade in Services (GATS)   One of the WTO agreements that came into force in 1995. It liberalizes the trade in services between WTO members and establishes rules members must follow in the treatment of foreign companies delivering services in sectors such as insurance, telecommunications, banking, and transport.

Genetically modified organisms (GMOs)   Also labeled GMs. Living organisms that have had their genetic code altered for commercial or scientific gain. For example, a crop might be genetically modified to enhance desirable nutritional qualities. Critics of GMOs worry about the loss of native biodiversity, the accompanying shift to monoculture farming techniques, and a greater reliance on herbicides.

Geographical indications (GIs)   A term used in the TRIPS agreement for products that comes from specific locales with some characteristics attributable to those locales. Examples are French cognac, champagne, and scotch.

Glasnost   Russian term for the policy initiated by Soviet Premier Mikhail Gorbachev in the late 1980s that involved opening up the Soviet state to political reform. It was meant to complement economic reform, or *Perestroika*.

Global bioenergy partnership (GBEP) Promoted by the FAO, the GBEP is a partnership between public, private, and civil society groups committed to promoting bioenergy for sustainable development in developing nations.

Global civil society Another term for nongovernmental organizations and social movements whose focus is usually the improvement of political, economic, and social conditions in developing nations.

Global commodity chains Networks of firms that produce, distribute, and market various products.

Global Cyber Security Structure A term describing the international security structure since the beginning of the new millennium, where countries like the United States rely more heavily on cyber-based weapons like drones and use or prepare to use cyber-attacks against enemies. It is also a structure in which states increasingly try to protect themselves and their citizens against the potentially devastating results of computer viruses, cyber hacking, identity thefts, and cyber-based espionage.

Global governance The rules, institutions, and processes that affect international cooperation in a specific issue area and management of transnational problems like climate change, environmental damage, and organized crime. The concept emphasizes that mechanisms affecting cooperation involve many state and private actors and many international, regional, and local levels of governance.

Global value chains An update on product cycle theory that accounts for "the full range of activities that firms and workers do to bring a product from its conception to its end use and beyond." Different firms in different countries are linked in a set of relationships (or a division of labor) that leads to the delivery of goods and services. Many Western firms' part in these chains deals with finance, basic research, design, product-branding, and marketing. LDCs want to move up the value chain from low-wage manufacturing to more profitable activities.

Globalism The ideology underlying economic globalization. Popular among supporters of economic liberalism, integration, and globalization.

Globalization A process of global economic integration and growth driven by economic liberal ideas and policies. Globalization also connotes increasing economic interdependence as well as the spread of Western (U.S.) cultural influence all over the world.

Globally integrated enterprise Increasingly, TNCs do not in fact own most of the elements of their foreign operations. With improved information technology, some TNCs such as Boeing and IBM can easily "outsource" vital functions to foreign-owned firms. Many TNCs build their own transnational network of contacts to create a regional or global business presence.

Grameen Bank An important microcredit bank founded in Bangladesh by Mohammad Yunus in 1976. These kinds of banks are an increasingly popular method of helping usually poor women in poor countries create small business enterprises.

Green Revolution Scientific and economic programs in the 1960s that increased food production in India, the Philippines, and other developing countries by introducing fertilizers, hybrid plant and seed strains, and modern farming techniques.

Growth pole A strategically-selected location meant to serve as the center of economic growth for surrounding areas. Through investments in infrastructure and incentives meant to attract capital and labor, governments stimulate economic development by concentrating resources in the growth pole.

Guest worker A nonresident foreign worker. Guest workers are employed temporarily within a foreign state, but both the length of their residence and the conditions of labor are stipulated by that state, which also prohibits the possibility of their permanent residence or citizenship.

Gulf Cooperation Council (GCC) An economic and security grouping composed of Saudi Arabia, the United Arab Emirates, Kuwait, Oman, Bahrain, and Qatar. These six countries share a heavy reliance on foreign workers, which make up a significant proportion of their combined workforce.

Hard currency A currency of known value that can readily be traded on foreign exchange markets and is therefore generally accepted in international transactions. Examples of hard currencies today include the U.S. dollar, the Japanese yen, the euro, and the Swiss franc. See *Soft currency*.

Hard power Military, and in some cases, economic power. Hard power refers to state tools to directly influence, persuade, or coerce other states. See *Soft power*.

Heavily indebted poor countries (HIPCs) A designation for forty-one of the world's poorest countries, mostly in Africa. These countries suffer from high poverty and high incidences of HIV/AIDS.

Hegemonic stability theory   A theory positing that one country that is unusually rich and powerful dominates other states or the entire international system for a length of time, during which it establishes and enforces a set of rules that regulate behavior in the international political economy.

Hegemony   Dominance or leadership, especially by one nation (the hegemon) over other nations. The theory of hegemonic stability holds that the international system achieves growth and stability only when one state acts as the hegemon, dominating the others but also paying the costs associated with counteracting problems in the international system.

Heterodox interventionist liberals (HILs)   Those who support more than a minimum amount of state intervention in the economy—so as to preserve the market and make it work more efficiently and effectively for the majority of people in society.

HIPC Initiative   An effort beginning in the late 1990s to cancel the debt of the most heavily indebted poor countries.

Historical materialism   The idea, central to Marx, that social and political institutions are built on a physical foundation of the economy, not ideas alone.

Hydra effect   Describes a situation in which a crackdown on an illegal commodity (e.g., drugs) in one area triggers its movement to a different area. U.S. antidrug efforts in Latin America have spawned new organizations in Mexico and Puerto Rico.

Hydraulic fracturing   Also called fracking. A process whereby highly pressurized fluids are injected into underground rock formations to fracture the rocks and release natural gas that is then collected at the earth's surface.

Immigration   Movement into another country with the intention of becoming a permanent resident there.

Imperialism   Associated with the works of J. A. Hobson, V. I. Lenin, and R. Luxemburg. Classical imperialism is often associated with historical periods of conquest and colonization of developing territories by industrialized nations. Neoimperialism today often reflects control over another country as a result of trade or foreign direct investment.

Import quotas   Limits on the quantity of an item that can be imported into a nation. By limiting the

quantity of imports, the quota tends to drive up the price of a good while at the same time restricting competition.

Import-substituting industrialization (ISI)   An economic development tactic that attempts to encourage domestic industrialization by restricting imports of industrial products. Contrast this strategy with *Export-oriented growth*.

Industrial policy   Economic policies designed to guide or direct business investment and development. Such policies often include support for businesses and trade protection.

Infant industries   New industries in any nation that are at a disadvantage relative to older, more efficient, foreign industries. Most mercantilists and even some economic liberals suggest that protective measures are justified until the newer industries have time to compete fairly with more mature industries.

Informal economy   The part of an economy that is unregulated and usually does not pay taxes. In a less developed country, most street vendors, for example, would be classified as "informal."

Insourcing   When a corporation that had moved manufacturing overseas decides to resume manufacturing a product in its own factories in the country where it is headquartered, we say that it is insourcing. In other words, it makes new investments and hires workers in its home country so that it no longer uses a contractor in a foreign country such as China to make or assemble a product.

Integration   The process whereby nation-states agree to unify or coordinate some political and economic activities. Economic liberals tend to support integration because it enhances efficiency and productivity.

Intellectual Property Rights (IPRs)   Patents, copyrights, trademarks, and other rights to control inventions and expressed ideas. Many structuralists argue that IPRs should be eliminated or weakened significantly, so as to enable developing nations to acquire necessary technology and low-priced goods.

Interdependence   Usually thought of as interconnectedness between nations and other actors through trade, aid, finance, and investment. Interdependence forces states to cooperate more often but engenders vulnerability and sensitivity to actions of other states.

Internal migration   Migration of an individual or group within a single nation-state, often from one region to another or from the rural to urban locations.

International Criminal Court (ICC)   Since the 1990s a number of international courts have been established to adjudicate the behavior of states and especially individuals accused of violating human rights during war and conflict. The ICC meets in the Hague in the Netherlands and has prosecuted cases related to violations in places such as the Balkans, Rwanda, and Liberia.

International Monetary Fund (IMF)   Created as part of the *Bretton Woods* system, the IMF is an organization of over 150 member states charged with stabilizing the international monetary system. The IMF makes loans to member states when they experience severe *current account deficits*. These loans are made subject to enactment of economic reforms, a practice called *conditionality*.

International political economy (IPE)   The interdisciplinary social science that examines the dynamic interactions between markets, states, and societies, and how the tensions and conflicts between these arenas both affect and reflect conditions outside the nation-state and society.

Intifada   An Arabic word for the "uprising" of the Palestinians against Israeli occupation of the West Bank and the Gaza Strip. There have been two intifadas—the first beginning in 1987 and the second starting in 2000.

Intraregional trade bloc   A trade agreement where nation-states in a particular region remove barriers to trade with the other members of the region. The Asia Pacific Economic Cooperation Forum (APEC) is an example of an intraregional trade bloc that aims to integrate eighteen Asian and Pacific nations into a nonbinding arrangement that would gradually remove trade barriers among members by 2020.

IPE structures   Susan Strange's categories of networks of actors, institutions, and processes that manage the affairs and problems in each of four distinct foundations of the global political economy: production and trade, knowledge and technology, money and finance, and security.

Irregular migrants   Migrants who reside and work in a foreign country without the appropriate legal documents. These workers may have entered the country without permission or entered with a visa but then stayed on past the limits of that permission.

Joint Special Operations Command (JSOC)   A group of U.S. special operations forces that conduct secret military operations around the world such as assassinations of terrorists, raids on enemy facilities, reconnaissance, and intelligence collection.

Keynesian compromise   An aspect of the *Bretton Woods* system. Nations retain the ability to intervene in their domestic economies but agree to limit interference in international economic markets.

Keynesian theory (Keynesianism)   To be Keynesian is to be in agreement with the general thrust of the political economy of John Maynard Keynes—to believe that there is a positive role for the state to play in domestic affairs (fighting unemployment and poverty, for example) and in international affairs (the kind of role conceived for the International Monetary Fund and the World Bank). Keynes's views were influenced by the catastrophe of World War I and the Great Depression of the interwar period. His ideas were reflected in the Bretton Woods institutions and policies and have gained renewed attention due to the global economic crisis.

Know-thy-customer   A principle of due diligence in banking whereby providers of financial services are expected to verify the identity and check the background of potential clients to determine if they are involved in money laundering or other criminal activities.

Kyoto Protocol   A protocol (or set of informal procedures and norms, but not a formal treaty) agreed to in Kyoto, Japan, in 1997 that established carbon emissions standard goals for all states. In order to deal with the problem of global warming, states agreed to achieve these goals within a set period of time. While many states signed the agreement and implemented the protocol, the United States did not ratify it. China, India, and other emerging economies were not required to adhere to the agreement but encouraged to do so, which created a good deal of controversy. The protocol came into effect in 2005.

La Via Campesina   Founded in 1993, the "Way of the Peasant" is an international social movement of peasants and indigenous peoples that advocates for land reform and food sovereignty and that resists industrial farming and the use of genetically modified crops.

Lacey Act   A U.S. wildlife protection law first passed in 1900 and amended in 2008. Among other things, it prohibits the import, export, or interstate trade of illegally caught wildlife or illegally harvested trees and plants.

Law of comparative advantage   According to David Ricardo, the theory of comparative advantage holds that nations should produce and export those goods they can produce at a lower cost than other nations and import those items that other nations can produce at lower cost. Often cited as the foundation of free trade policy.

Levels of analysis   The four levels of analysis are the individual, state/societal, interstate, and global levels. The levels-of-analysis approach was originally developed by political scientist Kenneth Waltz to help understand different explanations and sources of international conflict and war.

Life cycle of ideas   As part of the constructivist approach to IPE, the aim is to determine where ideas and norms originate and how they become "naturalized," that is, accepted by states and IOs as the self-evident justification of policies. Researchers often go back in history to examine individuals or movements that promoted what at the time seemed like non-mainstream ideas. Due to the global economic crisis a number of experts have explored the origins and development of economic liberal ideas and policies.

Malevolent mercantilist   A country that uses intentionally harmful policies that aim to defeat an enemy or potential enemy. Associated with Germany and Japan before World War II.

Managed float   A system in which currency exchange rates float but are affected by occasional interventions by central banks.

Managed trade system   Strong political and social interests who call for trade protection often create a political climate incompatible with completely free trade. A managed trade system often reflects a political compromise or mixture of economic liberal and mercantilist trade policies most states can adhere to.

Maquiladoras   Assembly plants in Mexico that use foreign parts and semifinished products to produce final goods for export. Structuralists are critical of maquiladoras for their use of exploited labor, hazardous working conditions, and environmental damage.

Marketization   Part of the process of economic transition from classical socialism to capitalism. When a particular commodity has been marketized, its exchange becomes governed by supply and demand rather than according to central planning.

Market socialism   A popular term in the 1990s that accounts for the effort by former Soviet bloc countries to combine their socialist economies with features of market economies. Some of the more successful were Hungary, Poland, and the Czech Republic. Many former and even still communist developing economies (e.g., China) have been or are pursuing the same objective.

Marxism   An ideology that originated in the works of the German sociologist Karl Marx (1818–1883). Many strains of Marxism have evolved from Marx's works. A critique of *capitalism* (as distinct from *economic liberalism*), Marxism holds that capitalism is subject to several distinctive flaws. Marxism tends to view economic relations from a power perspective (capital versus labor) as opposed to the cooperative relationship implicit in economic liberalism. See *Structuralism.*

Mercantilism   A seventeenth-century ideology that made accumulation of national treasure the main goal of government officials and society. Today, it is an economic philosophy and practice of government regulation of a nation's economy in ways that increase state power and security. Policies of import restriction and export promotion (to accumulate wealth at the expense of other countries) follow from this goal. See *Economic nationalism.*

Microcredit   The practice of providing very small loans to groups of people (usually women) in less developed countries who share the risk of repaying the loans. Microcredit has been heralded for its promise to directly overcome poverty by putting money into the hands of those who actually need it, thus encouraging sustainable private-sector development. It has also served as a model in some industrialized countries.

Migration   Movement of an individual or group from one place to another, often in pursuit of political or religious freedom, economic opportunity, reunification with family, or access to specific resources.

Millennium Development Goals (MDGs)   United Nations–sponsored initiatives to work on a local level to achieve the eradication of extreme hunger and poverty, universal primary education, gender equality and the empowerment of women, reduction in child mortality, improvement of maternal health, as well as efforts to combat HIV/AIDs, malaria, and other diseases, ensure environmental sustainability, and develop a global partnership for development.

Modern world system (MWS) A theory based in part on Marxist-Leninist ideologies. The MWS views economic development as conditioned by the relationship between the capitalist *core* and the less developed *periphery* nations. The historic mission of the core is to develop the periphery (often through the *semiperiphery*), but this development is exploitive in nature.

Montreal Protocol Officially called The Montreal Protocol on Substances that Deplete the Ozone Layer. An international treaty now signed by most countries that has required dramatic reductions in the production of chlorofluorocarbons and other substances that deplete the ozone layer.

Most favored nation (MFN) A trade principle under the World Trade Organization, whereby imports from a nation are granted the same degree of preference as those from the most preferred nations.

Mujahideen A term meaning Islamic freedom fighters. It originally referred to those who in the 1980s became famous for their resistance to the Soviet Union in Afghanistan, with the help of American weapons and training. This support has been blamed as a source of blowback, whereby America's former surrogates have formed terrorist organizations targeting the United States.

Multinational corporation (MNC) An international business firm that engages in production, distribution, and marketing activities that cross national boundaries (see *Foreign direct investment*). The critical factor is that the firm has a tangible productive presence in several countries. This factor distinguishes an MNC from an international firm, which produces in one country and exports to other countries. See *Transnational corporation (TNC)*.

Multipolar A security structure with more than two centers of power. Contrast with *unipolar* and *bipolar*.

Mundell Trilemma Named for Nobel laureate Robert Mundell. A property of different national monetary systems where it is impossible to achieve three objectives at once: foreign exchange stability, capital mobility, and national economic independence. Two of these goals always complement one another while contradicting the third objective. Each state decides which two objectives to pursue based on its history, national interests, and international political-economic conditions.

Mutually Assured Destruction (MAD) The Cold War strategy of the United States and the Soviet Union under which each had sufficient military power to

destroy the other, even if in doing so it destroyed itself. This supposedly ensured that neither nation could realistically "win" a nuclear war.

Name-and-shame campaigns Ways of pressuring companies and countries to change practices that are illegal or perceived to be unethical by bringing international attention to them.

National champions Key domestic companies or industries that a government deliberately nurtures for long-term development through subsidies, trade protection, and other forms of support. Although some national champions become globally competitive, they tend to reduce competition in their home economy.

National Missile Defense (NMD) A type of missile defense that states (in particular the United States and Russia) deploy so as to be able to knock down incoming ballistic missiles. The Reagan administration proposed to modernize the U.S. system by deploying a number of space-based defenses. NMD remains controversial because of its cost and how much it may incite other states to deploy such systems. See *ABM Treaty*.

National oil companies (NOCs) Large state-owned oil companies that control the majority of the world's oil reserves and produce most of the world's oil and natural gas. NOCs such as Saudi Arabia's Saudi Aramco and Iran's National Iranian Oil Company are a significant source of revenue for their nations' governments.

National treatment An important principle in the GATT, GATS, and TRIPS agreements that requires a country to treat imported products and services—once they have passed through customs—no less favorably than similar locally produced goods and services.

Neoconservatives (neocons) The term applies to those today who have a conservative economic outlook. However, the term "neocons" is also associated with officials in the George W. Bush administration who held a unilateralist outlook that included the use of force whenever the United States felt it necessary or justified. Other elements of the outlook included the idea that the United States should impose peace on the world on its own terms.

Neoimperialism An element of the structuralist interpretation of capitalism. *Core* nations exploit the periphery through financial, production, and trade structures throughout the world. While classical imperialism employs force to achieve its ends, neoimperialism emphasizes the use of nonmilitary tools to subjugate and dominate weaker states. See *Imperialism*.

Neoliberalism   A viewpoint that favors a return to the economic policies advocated by classical liberals such as Adam Smith and David Ricardo. Neoliberalism emphasizes market deregulation, privatization of government enterprises, minimal government intervention, and open international markets. Unlike classical liberalism, neoliberalism is primarily an agenda of economic policies rather than a political economy perspective.

Neomercantilism   A version of mercantilism that evolved in the post–World War II period. Rather than focusing on surplus producing trade policies, neomercantilism today includes a wide variety of protectionist trade, finance, and development policies to generate wealth and enhance national security.

Neorealism   An international relations theory that asserts that in an anarchical international system, states are compelled to behave in predictable ways as they seek to insure their own survival and security.

Nondiscrimination   A principle of the World Trade Organization system whereby products of different nations are treated equally (and equally with domestic products once imported). The products of a specific nation cannot be discriminated against under this rule. See *Most favored nation*.

Nongovernmental organizations (NGOs)   National and international voluntary organizations that have played an increasingly bigger role in the global political economy since the end of the Cold War. Many NGOs provide services that states cannot or will not. Examples of NGOs include Greenpeace, the Red Cross, and Doctors Without Borders. See *Global civil society*.

Nontariff barriers (NTBs)   Ways of limiting imports, including government health and safety standards, domestic content legislation, licensing requirements, and labeling requirements. Such measures make it difficult for imported goods to be marketed or significantly raise the price of imported goods.

North American Free Trade Agreement (NAFTA) A free-trade area among the United States, Canada, and Mexico, fully implemented in 2005. The NAFTA treaty was signed in 1992 and took effect in 1994. The treaty remains controversial to the extent that there is no agreement about how much it has benefited its members.

North Atlantic Treaty Organization (NATO)   A military alliance established in 1949 between North American and European countries to defend against potential aggression by the Soviet Union. Today the members of this collective security organization include the United States, Canada, Turkey, and most countries in the European Union.

North–South   The relationship between developed, industrialized countries (the North) and less developed countries (the South). This concept is often associated with core–periphery analysis but can also be simply a descriptive device.

Nuclear taboo   A widely shared reluctance by states since World War II to use nuclear weapons, significantly due to the moral restraint of public opinion and the efforts of a worldwide antinuclear weapons movement.

Obama doctrine   An unofficial foreign policy doctrine of the Obama administration that mixes unilateral and multilateral approaches, avoids large ground wars, and relies on selective use of drones, joint strike forces, and cyber tools. Strategically it includes a greater focus on the Asia-Pacific region and an expectation that allies will share more security burdens.

Odius debt   Foreign liabilities incurred by a former corrupt regime that leave the new government owing tremendous sums of money to banks and investors, often stifling development efforts. Many experts argue that these debts should be forgiven for the poorest of nations to better their chances of development.

Oil for Food Program   A UN program applied to Iraq after the Persian Gulf War (1990–1991) that allowed Iraq to sell some of its oil in international markets in exchange for income to buy food and emergency aid supplies. It was a controversial program to the extent that many Iraqi and some UN officials were accused of corruption related to implementing the program.

Oligarchs   A term that usually connotes a small group of people who attempt to control a government for their own benefit. In Russia, for example, wealthy media heads and oil company owners in the 1990s challenged state officials over a variety of issues.

Organization of Petroleum Exporting Countries (OPEC)   An organization of nations formed in 1960 to advance the interests of Third World oil exporters. In 1973 OPEC embargoed oil exports to the United States and the Netherlands, setting off a flurry of price hikes and notice of OPEC's new found political-economic power as a cartel.

Orthodox Economic Liberals (OELs) A group of people who rigidly adhere to economic liberal ideas, values, and policy prescriptions. Most agree that instead of the state, "open" or "free" markets should be allowed to determine socio-political outcomes whenever possible.

Outsourcing When a firm transfers part (or all) of the production process for a good or service to another country. Many economic liberals consider outsourcing to be part of the process of the globalization of international production and trade. These movements of jobs overseas displace many workers.

Ozone depletion In 1985, a hole in the ozone layer was discovered over Antarctica. It was blamed on the use of chlorofluorocarbons, a particular type of greenhouse gas used in many household products, which were later banned by the UN Montreal Protocol of 1987.

Paradox of thrift If one individual saves much more income, rationally speaking, that individual may be more secure economically. If everyone does this, however, the combined actions can cause a recession, and everyone is less secure economically. The paradox of thrift then is an example of the potential problems of an unregulated economy. Keynes supported an active role for the state in the economy to help overcome this problem.

Patents Exclusive rights that a government issues and confers to make, use, or sell an invention for a period usually of twenty years (counted from date of filing). These rights are also given to encourage research and innovation. Many companies argue that without them they would be unable to capture all of the benefits of their R&D expenditures.

Pax Americana The period of U.S. hegemony following World War II. "Pax" means "imposed peace," which implies that the period of peace after the war was imposed by the United States similar to the Pax Britannica of Great Britain during the eighteenth and nineteenth centuries. Some critics use the phrase to equate U.S. power with neoimperialism today.

UN Peacekeeping Operations (PKOs) United Nations–sponsored troops from different nations assigned to deal with conflicts in different countries. Peacekeeping was adopted in the early 1950s as an alternative to intervention by the major powers in conflicts that could involve them in war. PKO missions are located in developing regions of the world, especially in the Middle East, Africa, and parts of Asia.

Peak oil The controversial idea that the world's production of oil will reach a maximum point, after which it will gradually run out. Experts disagree when that will be, if it hasn't already occurred. Many also disagree about the effects of peak oil on the price of oil and its impact on society when global production starts to go down.

Perestroika Russian term for restructuring or economic reform, especially economic programs implemented in the Soviet Union in the mid-1980s. See *Glasnost*.

Periphery The nonindustrialized countries of the modern world system that produce mostly agricultural goods and natural resources. See *Core* and *Modern world system*. The Modern world system theory hypothesizes that peripheral states (e.g., developing countries) are usually made worse off as a result of interaction with core states.

Petrodollar recycling Since 1973, the system whereby oil exporters recirculate their oil revenues through the global financial system to provide loans to oil purchasers, fund imports by oil producers, and purchase foreign assets.

Pleasure periphery Regions in the periphery of the world system where tourists from core nations in the industrialized world seek pleasurable activities such as hiking in the rainforests in Columbia and sexual encounters in Thailand.

Positive-sum game Any interaction between actors that makes all participants simultaneously better off. See *Zero-sum game*.

Primitive accumulation A Marxist concept that is hypothesized to be at the root of capitalism's initial development. The process is one of coercive or violent seizure of assets (particularly land).

Prisoner's dilemma A term coined by Princeton mathematics professor A. W. Tucker to describe a situation in which the best interests of persons in society taken individually are opposite from those of the same individuals taken as a group. A group may benefit the most if everyone cooperates on an issue, however each individual often faces an incentive to "defect" and eschew cooperation for the sake of making the most of the situation for himself or herself.

Privatization Part of the process of economic transition from classical socialism to capitalism in which state-held property and assets are transferred into private hands. See *Market socialism*.

Problematization An process by which states and Transnational Advocacy Networks construct a problem that requires some kind of coordinated, international response. Some problems are "constructed" by political elites, powerful lobbying organizations, and social groups.

Product cycle theory (or product life-cycle theory) Terms coined by Harvard political economist Raymond Vernon to describe production and trade patterns stemming from product innovation and technological diffusion.

Profit paradox When law enforcement tries to ban an item for which there is high demand (e.g., drugs), the reduction in supply drives up prices in the short term, but this bolsters profits for those willing to illegally supply the item, thus encouraging others to enter the illegal business. Thus, the temporary reduction in supply is reversed as criminals find ways around the ban.

Proletariat In Marxian analysis, the class of workers who do not own capital and who are exploited by the bourgeoisie.

Propaganda Information and messages that are marketed and disseminated so as to promote the interests of a political elite and discredit the ideas of oppositional political forces.

Protectionism Policies that either restrict or promote trade such as import tariffs or export subsidies that benefit domestic producers. Protection also signifies an attitude whereby a state feels compelled to use a variety of measures to defend attempts by others to weaken it.

Public goods Goods or services that, once provided, cannot be denied to one person and at the same time benefit everybody simultaneously. A lighthouse or national security is a classic example of a public good.

Publicity rights The names, images, or identifying characteristics of famous people. Some countries allow celebrities to control use of them. These rights can be inherited or sold to third parties who want to use them for marketing purposes.

Qualified majority voting (QMV) rule As introduced by the 2009 Treaty of Lisbon, the QMV rule states that beginning in 2014 approval of decisions of the Council of the European Union will require the votes of at least 55 percent of EU member states (15 out of 27) representing at least 65 percent of the EU's population. In theory, QMV prevents any one state or minority of states from stopping the passage of legislation, thereby facilitating decision-making in the EU.

Quantitative easing Central banks such as the U.S. Federal Reserve or the Bank of England engage in quantitative easing (QE) by electronically creating new money which is used to buy government bonds, mortgage securities, and other assets in the hopes of lowering interest rates so that private companies make new investments and private banks make more loans. The Federal Reserve engaged in three rounds of QE between 2008 and 2012.

Reaganomics President Reagan helped make popular economic liberal ideas in the 1980s. He promoted free trade and limited state intervention in the economy, along with the idea that decreasing taxes would help grow the economy and reduce public debt.

Realism A theory of state behavior that focuses on the acquisition of power to enhance state security. The national interest is a determinant of state behavior. In the view of realists, states, like individuals, tend to act in their own self-interest.

Reciprocity A principle of the World Trade Organization system whereby trading partners mutually reduce trade barriers, providing each greater access to foreign markets.

Refugee A displaced person who cannot return to his or her country of origin because of fear of persecution or due to destruction caused by war or natural disaster. Refugees are often assisted and relocated by an international body such as the United Nations Office of the High Commissioner for Refugees.

Regime A set of rules, norms, institutions, and decision-making procedures that condition actor expectations and behavior regarding a global issue. Regime also refers to the people in power who comprise the government of any nation–state.

Regionalism A movement toward associations of nation-states in a geographic area that cooperate to achieve specific goals such as trade liberalization and political stability.

Regional trade agreements (RTAs) Agreements between different states in a geographic area to reduce trade barriers between them. RTAs are often easier to form than global trade agreements because there are fewer interests to reconcile. Some economic liberals oppose RTAs out of fear that they deter *global* free trade.

Remittances Payments made by a migrant to family or friends in their country of origin. The global economic crisis has decreased the amount of money migrant workers have been able to send back to their families in their mother countries.

Rentier state   A country that earns a large proportion of its government revenue from taxes on oil and gas exports. In the cases of Iran, Iraq, Libya, Algeria, and Gulf Cooperation Council states, the wealth generated from this income is usually concentrated in the hands of a relatively small elite.

Rent seeking   Efforts to achieve personal gain by creating an artificial scarcity rather than through efficient production. Many corrupt activities can be viewed as examples of rent-seeking.

Research and development (R&D)   An activity undertaken in states to develop new technologies and create new products and innovative processes. This activity occurs in government-funded research institutions and within private companies and is important for scientific advancement.

Reserve currency   A currency that is held by a nation's central bank in its foreign exchange reserves. The U.S. dollar is the world's most common reserve currency, and many international transactions and commodities are priced in U.S. dollars.

Resource curse   This phenomenon describes how many countries that are relatively wealthy in natural resources remain underdeveloped because of government mismanagement and corruption. Optimism based on high demand for local oil—for example, in the case of Nigeria—can easily exist alongside misery for many people.

Restriction-opportunity dilemma   A situation in which efforts to ban a material in high demand (e.g., drugs and guns) are often counterproductive because they make the black markets provision of the material more profitable.

Revenue leakages   In tourism, the loss of revenue resulting from imports of goods and services required by tourists and tourism businesses, including food, hotel fixtures, advertising costs, repatriated profits, and airport equipment.

Rogue states   States that are regarded as hostile or that refuse to cooperate with other states. Iran, Syria, and North Korea are often cited as examples. These states are also cited as supporters of terrorism.

Secrecy jurisdictions   Countries with strong banking privacy laws such as Switzerland or the Bahamas. Tax evaders and money launderers exploit these privacy guarantees to hide billions of dollars from their governments.

Securities   These are certificates traded in a market that give a purchaser the right of ownership over assets or the right to earn interest from the underlying assets. Securities are traded in a market. Bonds are a type of security whereby a government or a private company promises to repay the buyer of the bonds principal plus interest at a specified time in the future. Mortgage-backed securities are bought by investors who are promised a return from the securities' underlying mortgages. Essentially, buyers of securities are lending money to issuers who promise to repay the buyers (with interest) in the future.

Security community   Many constructivists (and realists as well) have found that sometimes seemingly hostile rivals cooperate with one another because they have a shared understanding that they are part of a "security community"—a group of people with a sense of a shared moral standards and a certain level of mutual trust. A good example is the Organization for Security and Cooperation in Europe (OSCE), which was set up in the mid-1970s as a process by which the Cold War antagonists could cooperate on security matters in Europe.

Security dilemma   According to realists, a situation wherein one state's effort to protect itself or enhance its defensive capabilities is viewed as threatening by another state.

Semiperiphery   An intermediate zone between the *core* and *periphery*. South Korea and Taiwan might be considered part of the semiperiphery today in the *modern world system* theory. See *Core*.

Sequestration   A method of storing carbon underground which, if perfected, could be particularly helpful in reducing the amount of carbon released into the atmosphere by coal energy sources.

Settler states   Countries such as the United States and Australia which allow immigrants the opportunity to become permanent residents and/or naturalized citizens.

Shadow banking system   A set of financial intermediaries such as money market mutual funds, investment banks, and hedge funds that channel flows of money between creditors and borrowers in ways that are largely unregulated by the government. Shadow banking instruments include mortgage-backed securities, special purpose vehicles, and collateralized debt obligations (CDOs). Risky and unregulated activities in the shadow banking system such as repurchase agreements made by sellers of securities and bets on credit instruments are believed to have contributed to the financial crisis.

Siloviki   The powerful political allies of Russian president Putin—called the *siloviki*—who have backgrounds in the secret police, intelligence services, and law enforcement agencies. These friends and allies have helped Putin recentralize political power, weaken the Duma, and crack down on independent media and civil society.

Single European Act (SEA)   The 1986 agreement by European Community members to advance to the next stage of integration: a union. In policy terms, this meant extensive coordination of monetary policy and investment regulations, services, migration, labor, and foreign policy.

Single Market   In 1986 the members of the European Community passed the Single European Act that created a single market with a customs union and freedom of movement of labor and capital. This act led to passage of the Treaty of Maastricht in 1993 and creation of the European Union (EU), along with other steps to further integrate the members of the European community. See *SEA* and the *Treaty of Maastricht*.

Socially responsible investing   Efforts by investors to avoid certain types of companies and countries that they perceive to be socially or environmentally unethical, such as those involved in land expropriation, oil corruption, terrorist financing, human rights abuses, or unsustainable environmental practices. These investment strategies challenge economic liberal principles by subordinating market efficiency to concerns of justice.

Soft currency   A currency of uncertain value (due, perhaps, to high inflation rates) that is not generally accepted in international transactions. Soft currency can usually be spent only within the nation that issues it, whereas a *hard currency* can be exchanged and spent in most nations.

Soft power   The power to influence international affairs through such intangible factors as culture, values, and ideals. Soft power is less direct than *hard power* but sometimes more effective.

Sovereign wealth funds (SWFs)   Large amounts of capital that have accumulated in the hands of states with large balance-of-payments surpluses. Many OELs have argued that those states should have invested a good deal of their SWFs in the United States to help offset U.S. debt and prevent the global economic crisis.

Sovereignty   The ability to exercise supreme authority in any society. For realist-mercantilists, sovereignty also refers to independence from control by an outside power.

Specialization   Adam Smith, Ricardo, and other economic liberals advocated that trading nations should concentrate their production in sectors where they possess a comparative advantage. In an age of competitive globalization, different states and regions of the world are driven to specialize in particular parts of the production process. Quite often this specialization does not reflect a natural advantage but one that is intentionally fostered by state policies, resulting in tensions over the motives behind them.

Speculation   An investment in a foreign currency based on the belief that the currency will increase in value, allowing the speculator to earn a return when the currency is sold. See *Speculative attack*.

Speculative attack   A situation where the demand for a currency quickly deteriorates, causing speculators to sell off large quantities of a currency in the hope that they will be able to buy it back later at a lower price. This often results in a dramatic devaluation of the currency, which weakens the purchasing power of those left holding the devalued currency.

Spot markets   Markets where oil is sold outside OPEC's established pricing structure. When OPEC member states decide not to cooperate with the cartel's oil production goals, they sell oil to anyone who will buy it from them (on the spot!).

State capitalism   An economic system with an important role for public enterprises that are managed independently with a focus on long-term profitability and innovation. Such a system typically has state-owned companies that make large investments in sectors such as energy, infrastructure, automobile manufacturing, and technologically sophisticated industries. China, Russia, Turkey, and Brazil are often described as being state capitalist.

Strategic resources   Resources such as oil and rubber whose supply and demand have important consequences for the national security of a nation. Most nations fear become overly dependent on others for the resources they lack.

Strategic trade policies   Efforts on the part of the state to purposefully create comparative advantages in trade by methods such as subsidizing research and development of a product or subsidizing an industry so that it can move up the "learning curve" to achieve greater production efficiency than foreign competitors. Strategic trade practices are often associated with state industrial policies—that is, intervention in the economy to promote specific patterns of industrial development.

Structural Adjustment Policies (SAPs)   Economic policies that seek to reduce state power and introduce free market reforms in less developed countries so as to establish a foundation for economic growth. The International Monetary Fund often makes the adoption of SAPs a condition for financial assistance.

Structuralism   An IPE perspective that accounts for the political–economic interconnectedness (structural relationship) between any number of entities: the *bourgeoisie* and *proletariat*, the *core* and *periphery*, and the *North* and *South*. A number of ties bind these entities to one another, including trade, foreign aid, and direct investment. Much debate exists as to whether and how structural conditions can be changed. See *Marxism*.

Subprime mortgage loans   Home loans made by banks in the United States to customers who did not have to meet the higher standards for loans as they did before the mid-1990s. Easier terms such as little evidence of the ability to pay or lower credit scores greatly increased the number of people who "qualified" for home loans. For many experts, subprime mortgages directly contributed to the global economic crisis and manifest some of the worst traits of the U.S. style of capitalism.

Super 301   An aggressive U.S. trade policy created in the 1970s and designed to open foreign markets to U.S. exports.

Sustainable development   A pattern of economic development that is consistent with the goal of nondegradation of the environment. Controversy surrounds the many problems of implementing the objective as it requires tradeoffs and choices many find unacceptable.

Tax havens   Small countries and territories that have strong banking privacy laws. These sovereign jurisdictions attract tax evaders and money launderers who wish to hide their earnings from their home government so as to avoid paying taxes on the money or provoking inquiries into the (often illicit) sources of the income.

Terms of trade   The ratio of a country's export prices to its import prices. If the ratio falls over time, it means that the country has to export more in order to import a given amount of goods.

Top currency   A currency in great demand because of its central role in international trade and financial transactions. The U.S. dollar has played the role of top currency since World War II.

Toxic securities   Packages of investments such as risky subprime mortgages that were "bundled" and sold to investors all over the world. Eventually many banks suffered huge losses on their "toxic securities," which led to the implosion of the real estate market and global financial crisis in 2008. Congress hastily passed a "rescue plan" to purchase these securities from investors (or insure them). See *TARP*.

Trade bloc   A group of nation-states united by what for the most part are regional trade agreements. See the *European Union* and the *North American Free Trade Agreement*.

Trade diversion effect   Although trade is often enhanced amongst members of a trade bloc because of lower internal barriers, this comes partly at the expense of trade diverted from more efficient non–bloc countries that are still subject to trade barriers.

Trademarks   Signs or symbols (including logos and names) registered by a company to identify its goods and services. Protection for trademarks is usually granted for ten years and is renewable. Examples of trademarks include the Nike swoosh, the brand name Kleenex, and MGM's lion's roar.

Trade-Related Aspects of Intellectual Property Rights (TRIPs)   An international agreement that is part of the WTO and that requires minimal standards of protection of copyrights, patents, trademarks, and other forms of intellectual property.

Traditional Knowledge   The accumulated knowledge of indigenous or local communities as it relates to such things as plants, plant uses, agriculture, land use, folklore, and spiritual matters. Indigenous peoples have preserved and developed a wide variety of plant diversity through harvesting and breeding practices, and in fact many of the major food crops in North America and Europe originally came from these local communities.

Tragedy of the commons   A term coined by Garrett Hardin to describe situations in which human nature, rationality, and political freedoms drive individuals to overuse communal resources. Hardin recommends strong government action to limit population growth to save the earth's resources.

Transfer pricing   A mechanism used by transnational corporations to shift their accounting measures between subsidiaries in other countries so as to avoid taxes.

Transnational advocacy networks (TANs)   International networks of activists who attempt to influence states regarding various political and social issues, including migration, refugee, and human rights policies.

Transnational agribusiness corporations (TNACs)
Also termed agribusinesses. Agribusinesses operate the world over in a variety activities such as production, processing, and marketing of commodities and food. They are often accused of exploiting labor and unduly influencing political-economic conditions in countries they invest in.

Transnational corporation (TNC) A large business that competes in regional or global markets and whose business environment therefore extends beyond any given nation-state. The key characteristic of a TNC is a high level of foreign direct investment. See *multinational corporation.*

Transnational migration The movement of an individual or group across national borders.

Transparency The public's ability to see how decisions are made. In the case of global financial institutions such as the International Monetary Fund, some argue that greater transparency would improve investors' decision making and prevent financial crises from developing.

Treaty of Lisbon Entering into force in 2009, it amends the Treaty of Rome and the Treaty of Maastricht to improve decision-making in the EU, expand the powers of the European Parliament, and introduce changes to qualified majority voting in the Council of the EU.

Treaty of Maastricht This treaty creating the *European Union* was ratified by members of the European Community in 1993. It signified agreement to a more advanced stage of integration in the economy, but also social and political institutions and policies.

Troika A group composed of representatives from the European Commission, the European Central Bank, and the International Monetary Fund that administers financial bailouts for economically troubled Euro zone countries such as Greece and Ireland. When negotiating the terms of a rescue plan with a debtor country, the group typically requires the country's government to impose austerity measures and other painful economic reforms in exchange for receiving billions of euros to help pay back creditors.

Troubled Asset Relief Program (TARP) The $700 billion recovery effort initiated by the George W. Bush administration and approved by Congress to deal with the financial crisis in October of 2008. The Obama administration continued to implement the plan, which essentially put $250 billion into U.S. big banks in the hopes of getting them to loan more to one another and to Main Street banks.

Unipolar An international security structure in which only one state has overwhelming military and economic power.

United Nations Conference on Trade and Development (UNCTAD). Created in 1964, UNCTAD is a UN institution for developing nations. Meeting every two years, it is designed to check the influence of the Organization of Economic Cooperation and Development (OECD), which reflects the political and economic interests of the developed nations.

United Nations Environment Program (UNEP) This UN agency was created to aid in the drafting of treaties, provide a forum for cooperation, and create databases and references for scientific assessments of the environment. UNEP helped create the Intergovernmental Panel on Climate Change, and the organization has made recommendations for treaties such as the Kyoto Protocol.

United Nations Framework Convention on Climate Change (UNFCCC) This environmental treaty was produced at the Earth Summit and later modified, resulting in the Kyoto Protocol.

Unmanned aerial vehicles (UAVs) The formal name for drones—small, remotely controlled aircraft that the Obama administration has used extensively in places like Afghanistan and Pakistan to target terrorists and conduct aerial surveillance.

Uruguay round Set of negotiations among the members of the General Agreement on Tariffs and Trade (1986–1994) that focused on reducing trade barriers, especially regarding services and agricultural goods. It culminated in the creation of the World Trade Organization.

Voluntary export restraint (VER) or Voluntary export agreement (VEA) An agreement that limits the quantity of an item a nation can export. Importers ask exporters to "voluntarily" set limits on the numbers of exports, backed by an implied threat of economic sanctions or some form of retaliation if the exporter does not comply with the importer's request.

Volcker rule Named after Paul Volcker, a former chairman of the Federal Reserve, it is a provision of the 2010 Dodd-Frank Act that prohibits banks with federally insured deposits from engaging in proprietary trading, i.e., making risky investments with their own money. By also limiting how much these banks can invest in hedge funds and private equity funds, the rule is designed to help prevent another financial crisis.

Washington Consensus The viewpoint, often evidenced in the policy proposals of the U.S. Treasury Department, the World Bank, the International Monetary Fund, and the World Trade Organization, that less developed countries should adopt policies to reduce inflation and fiscal deficits, privatize, deregulate, and create open markets. See *SAPs*.

Weapons of mass destruction (WMD) Technologically sophisticated weapons that have the potential to kill large numbers of people, such as nuclear, chemical, and biological weapons.

Westoxication A process in which people in the Middle East are seduced by imported Western

cultural ideas and institutions. Anti-Western leaders and some terrorists often cite it as a motive for their opposition to the United States and other industrialized states' values and institutions.

World Bank Officially called the International Bank for Reconstruction and Development (IBRD), the World Bank is an international agency with over 150 members. Created by the Bretton Woods agreements in 1944, it originally worked on the reconstruction of Europe after World War II. Today, the World Bank makes low-interest loans and grants to less developed countries to stimulate economic development.

Zero-sum game An activity whereby gains by one party create equal losses for others. The concept plays a major role in the realist-mercantilist perspective.

GLOSSARY OF ACRONYMS

APEC	Asia-Pacific Economic Cooperation
BoP	Balance of payments
BRICs	Brazil, Russia, India, and China
CAP	Common Agricultural Policy
COP	Conference of the Parties
EC	European Community
ECB	European Central Bank
EEC	European Economic Community
EFTA	European Free Trade Association
EMU	European Monetary Union
EU	European Union
FAO	Food and Agriculture Organization
FDI	Foreign direct investment
FTA	Free trade agreement
GATS	General Agreement on Trade in Services
GATT	General Agreement on Tariffs and Trade
GCC	Gulf Cooperation Council
GDP	Gross domestic product
GMO	Genetically modified organism
GNI	Gross national income
GNP	Gross national product
HIPCs	Heavily indebted poor countries
HIL	Heterodox interventionist liberal
IBRD	International Bank for Reconstruction and Development (also World Bank)
ICC	International Criminal Court
IMF	International Monetary Fund
IOs	International organizations
IPE	International political economy
IPRs	Intellectual property rights
LDC	Less developed country
MAD	Mutually Assured Destruction
MDGs	Millennium Development Goals
MENA	Middle East and North Africa
MFN	Most favored nation
MNC	Multinational corporation
MWS	Modern world system
NAFTA	North American Free Trade Agreement
NATO	North Atlantic Treaty Organization
NGO	Nongovernmental organization
NIC	Newly industrialized country
NIEO	New International Economic Order
NTB	Nontariff barrier
OECD	Organization for Economic Cooperation and Development
OEL	Orthodox economic liberal
OPEC	Organization of Petroleum Exporting Countries
OWS	Occupy Wall Street
PPP	Purchasing power parity
R&D	Research and Development
RTA	Regional trade agreement
SALT	Strategic Arms Limitation Treaty
SAP	Structural Adjustment Program
SWF	Sovereign wealth fund
TAN	Transnational advocacy network
TARP	Troubled Asset Relief Program
TNC	Transnational corporation
TPP	Trans-Pacific Partnership
TRIPS	Trade-Related Aspects of Intellectual Property Rights
UNCTAD	United Nations Conference on Trade and Development
UNEP	United Nations Environment Program
USTR	U.S. Trade Representative
VER	Voluntary export restraint
WIPO	World Intellectual Property Organization
WMD	Weapons of mass destruction
WTO	World Trade Organization

INDEX